The 14th Brooklyn Regiment in the Civil War

The 14th Brooklyn Regiment in the Civil War

A History and Roster

FRANK CALLENDA

McFarland & Company, Inc., Publishers
Jefferson, North Carolina, and London

LIBRARY OF CONGRESS CATALOGUING-IN-PUBLICATION DATA

Callenda, Frank.
 The 14th Brooklyn Regiment in the Civil War : a history and roster / Frank Callenda.
  p.   cm.
 Includes bibliographical references and index.

 ISBN 978-0-7864-4899-9
 softcover : acid free paper ∞

 1. United States. Army. New York Infantry Regiment, 84th (1861–1864) 2. United States — History — Civil War, 1861–1865 — Regimental histories.   3. New York (State) — History — Civil War, 1861–1865 — Regimental histories. 4. United States — History — Civil War, 1861–1865 — Campaigns. I. Title.
 E523.584th.C35 2013
 973.7'447 — dc23   2013005751

BRITISH LIBRARY CATALOGUING DATA ARE AVAILABLE

© 2013 Frank Callenda. All rights reserved

No part of this book may be reproduced or transmitted in any form or by any means, electronic or mechanical, including photocopying or recording, or by any information storage and retrieval system, without permission in writing from the publisher.

Front cover artwork: painting by Don Troiani, www.historicalimagebank.com

Manufactured in the United States of America

McFarland & Company, Inc., Publishers
 Box 611, Jefferson, North Carolina 28640
  www.mcfarlandpub.com

To Chrissie and Lori who are my heart

To Jessica, Danielle, Michael, Olivia, Julia, Emily & Steven
who are my heart and my future

To Esther who is my heart, my future, my —
Everything

Table of Contents

Acknowledgments	ix
Introduction	1

Part I: A History

1. The Beginning	5
2. Going South	12
3. Battle of Bull Run	23
4. The Colonel and the Private	36
5. After Bull Run	41
6. Out of Winter Quarters—1862	53
7. Gainesville, Groveton, Second Bull Run	62
8. South Mountain	78
9. Antietam	87
10. Back in Brooklyn	96
11. Battle of Fredericksburg	101
12. Chancellorsville Campaign	111
13. The Road to Gettysburg	126
14. Gettysburg: Day One	134
15. Gettysburg: Day Two	152
16. Gettysburg: Day Three	160
17. Mine Run Campaign	165
18. The Wilderness	172
19. Battle of Spotsylvania Court House	179
20. Coming Home	187

Part II: A Roster   191

Chapter Notes	299
Bibliography	310
Index	315

Acknowledgments

A book of this nature and scope could not have been written without the aid of many people around the country. Assistance from them as well as different groups and organizations helped turn this narrative from a list of dates and military reports into a more lively and interesting amalgamation that includes personal letters to home as well as reports from local newspapers that disseminated information to people back in Brooklyn. My research also included diaries and memoirs of members of the Fourteenth as well as those who fought on the opposite side of the battlefield. Added in were collections of papers in libraries as well as in private hands. Always in the back of my mind was the refrain from my daughter, "Don't make me get bored."

Because of the nature of the Fourteenth's involvement in the Eastern Theater of the Civil War (one of the most active regiments) it was necessary to visit all of the major battle sites to research their libraries and archives. At the Bull Run battlefield (covering the battles of First Bull Run, Gainesville, Groveton and Second Bull Run), I met with James Burgess, the battlefield park historian. His assistance in the library as well as his knowledge of the four battles covered by this national park were invaluable in my research.

As I roamed over Henry House Hill, I could not help but feel the excitement as the rangers pointed out the position of the Fourteenth Brooklyn in their several charges up the hill during their attacks on Jackson and his brigade.

The South Mountain Battlefield is smaller than other battle sites. However, the park historian was knowledgeable and helpful in detailing the area of operations of the First Corps during the battles.

A few minutes away from the South Mountain Battlefield is the Antietam National Battlefield Park. There I met Ted Alexander, the Antietam park historian and a Civil War author. His help in my research and our hours of conversation regarding that research as well as his suggestions for finding more background information proved both helpful and inspiring.

If you visit Antietam, walk the field, still planted with corn, that the Fourteenth walked braving the withering musket and artillery fire and view the monument to the Fourteenth Brooklyn which stands as a tribute to their courage.

Fredericksburg Battlefield Park covers the battles of Fredericksburg,

Chancellorsville, The Wilderness and Spottsylvania Court House, which are all close together. To understand the unfolding of the Battle of Fredericksburg, I suggest you climb the heights held by the Confederates and look down on the Union positions at the rivers' edge.

The park rangers and historians at Gettysburg were remarkable. They provided background information about the battle and provided pictures and anecdotes about people, both military and civilian.

In order to gather as much information as possible, I used many libraries and collections, the staffs of which gave freely of their time. The Brooklyn Public Library at Grand Army Plaza was a rich source of material on the Civil War. The Brooklyn Collection of that library was a particularly rich source of material about Brooklyn and the Fourteenth prior to the Civil War. I am grateful to Elizabeth Harvey who was always both cheerful and helpful.

Much of my research into books, maps and collections was accomplished at the 42nd Street Branch of the New York Public Library, which is one of the finest research libraries in the country. My days there, if strung together, would equal months. For the assistance in tracking down books and researching related topics and smoothing my efforts, I am grateful to the librarians of the Millstein Division of the New York Public Library.

Endless appreciation is extended to my wife Esther, who typed every word of this book along with its additions and myriad revisions. She not only allowed me the time but also gave me the encouragement to go forward with this project, and because of her input, helped shape it into something less "boring" than just dates and battles and into a story showing the personal feelings, interests, views and emotions of the soldiers of the Fourteenth Brooklyn.

Finally, I may have brought much time and energy into penning this book, but it was written by the courage, spirit and gallantry of the men of the Fourteenth Brooklyn Regiment.

Introduction

Brooklyn? The Civil War? Sounds incongruous. Most people would not think of these two in the same thought. However, Brooklyn contributed thousands of soldiers toward the effort to win the war. One group which proved its ability and bravery during that conflict was the Fourteenth Brooklyn Regiment.

The Fourteenth served courageously and strategically in most of the major battles of the Civil War in the east, including First Bull Run, Gainesville, Groveton, Second Bull Run, South Mountain, Antietam, Fredericksburg, Chancellorsville, Gettysburg, The Wilderness and Spotsylvania Court House. It was the only regiment that was engaged in all three days of the Battle of Gettysburg.

The Fourteenth saw more action than most regiments during the war and was considered to be one of the "fightingest" regiments of the war. To this point, historians have overlooked the contributions of this heroic regiment. The only material apparently ever written about the Fourteenth was a commemorative book issued to the surviving members of the regiment and their families upon the 50th anniversary in 1911 of their induction into Federal service. It was held to be an inaccurate document and was only used in this book when substantiated by other research.

Most people interested in the Civil War will recognize the name "Iron Brigade," a unit from what are now Midwestern states, so named for their tenacity and courage in battle and particularly because of their ferocity and bravery during their advance through the cornfields in the morning battle at Antietam. Yet the Fourteenth was part of a unit that was called the Iron Brigade even before that unit. The Fourteenth had the designation of First Corps, First Division, First Brigade while the Midwestern unit was designated First Corps, First Division, 2nd Brigade for most of their stint in the Army of the Potomac. It was for this reason that the two units fought side by side in many engagements. Indeed, when making that treacherous advance through the cornfield at Antietam and seeing his soldiers being decimated by the shot and shell of the enemy, Rufus Dawes, leader of the 6th Wisconsin, later wrote about his joy at seeing the red trousers of the soldiers of the Fourteenth filling in the ranks of his fallen soldiers.

Introduction

Brooklyn? The Civil War? Sounds incongruous. Most people would not think of these two in the same thought. However, Brooklyn contributed thousands of soldiers toward the effort to win the war. One group which proved its ability and bravery during that conflict was the Fourteenth Brooklyn Regiment.

The Fourteenth served courageously and strategically in most of the major battles of the Civil War in the east, including First Bull Run, Gainesville, Groveton, Second Bull Run, South Mountain, Antietam, Fredericksburg, Chancellorsville, Gettysburg, The Wilderness and Spotsylvania Court House. It was the only regiment that was engaged in all three days of the Battle of Gettysburg.

The Fourteenth saw more action than most regiments during the war and was considered to be one of the "fightingest" regiments of the war. To this point, historians have overlooked the contributions of this heroic regiment. The only material apparently ever written about the Fourteenth was a commemorative book issued to the surviving members of the regiment and their families upon the 50th anniversary in 1911 of their induction into Federal service. It was held to be an inaccurate document and was only used in this book when substantiated by other research.

Most people interested in the Civil War will recognize the name "Iron Brigade," a unit from what are now Midwestern states, so named for their tenacity and courage in battle and particularly because of their ferocity and bravery during their advance through the cornfields in the morning battle at Antietam. Yet the Fourteenth was part of a unit that was called the Iron Brigade even before that unit. The Fourteenth had the designation of First Corps, First Division, First Brigade while the Midwestern unit was designated First Corps, First Division, 2nd Brigade for most of their stint in the Army of the Potomac. It was for this reason that the two units fought side by side in many engagements. Indeed, when making that treacherous advance through the cornfield at Antietam and seeing his soldiers being decimated by the shot and shell of the enemy, Rufus Dawes, leader of the 6th Wisconsin, later wrote about his joy at seeing the red trousers of the soldiers of the Fourteenth filling in the ranks of his fallen soldiers.

It was the Midwestern brigade that received the much deserved accolades for this action, yet the Brooklyn Regiment which fought side by side with them is not acknowledged.

This same short-sightedness of history also applies to the first day of battle at Gettysburg. While blocking the Chambersburg Road approach to the town, the Fourteenth Brooklyn and the Ninety-fifth New York changed front and caught part of Davis' Confederate Brigade in a railroad cut and forced them to surrender. The Fourteenth and the Ninety-fifth were joined by the Sixth Wisconsin led by Rufus Dawes. Dawes later claimed that his unit took the railroad cut and that the Fourteenth and Ninety-fifth had very little to do with this action. A discussion of this appears later on in this book.

The book also details the symbiotic relationship between the Fourteenth Brooklyn Regiment and the people of Brooklyn. The regiment relied on the city during that period of time. Brooklyn supplied them with their distinctive uniforms and was, indeed, a city for supplies and manpower because the Fourteenth was a militia unit. In return, the people of Brooklyn took pride in the accomplishments of the regiment, which made them feel that the city was doing its part in preserving the Union and winning the war.

Those recruits from Brooklyn built a glorious tradition for the regiment. Those who joined later on in the war had this tradition of bravery to build upon. Some who joined later actually went into battle before they were fully trained because of the pride in the unit and their desire not to be left behind.

The fighting spirit of the Fourteenth was acknowledged by both its friends and enemies. Men of other Union regiments wrote in their diaries about the joy that they experienced when they saw the red pants of the Fourteenth join their lines. This book will show this respect, which was given by both Union and Confederate soldiers as well as their officers.

Gen. Abner Doubleday, who led the Fourteenth at various times as divisional commander and later as corps commander, said that he had personally seen their courage and devotion. He said the Fourteenth was a household name in the army and that they were the elite of his division.

Gen. I. McDowell, who commanded the Union forces at the First Battle of Bull Run, expressed his pride in not only mustering the Fourteenth into Federal services but also of having led them in their second charge up Henry Hill. He added that it was the most gallant, orderly and intelligent regiment in his command.

This view was also held by Confederate General Fitzhugh Lee, who, in an action report of a skirmish he was involved in while scouting with his cavalry, wrote that he had engaged units of the Fourteenth Brooklyn and that they had fought with much more bravery than the Federal troops usually exhibited.[1]

Part of the panache of the Fourteenth was their uniform. As a militia unit prior to the outbreak of the Civil War, they had adopted a chasseur-à-pied uniform, which included their distinctive red pants and kepi (cap) along with a short blue jacket. With few variations the uniform consisted of a kepi which was blue at its crown and red going down to a blue band and chin strap which were held to the kepi by a button on each side. The buttons had the New York State insignia upon it. The front of the kepi had the number "14" on it. The pants were made to look like the pantaloons of a Zouave uniform. However, they were not as baggy and were of a bright red color. The leggings at the bottom bore seven gold buttons on each, totaling fourteen, the units' designation. The coat was also blue and red and had gold buttons running down the center for the length of the coat. It was made to look like a vest was under the coat but was actually part of the front. Although during the Battle of Bull Run, many regiments had different colored uniforms and indeed many Confederate regiments wore blue and Union regiments wore gray, these were soon standardized into the Blue and the Gray. The Fourteenth Brooklyn kept their uniforms throughout the war.

I hope that this book will help uncover some shortcomings in historical research and help to establish the true place of the Fourteenth Brooklyn in the Civil War. The history of the Fourteenth Brooklyn Regiment is in great part the history of the Civil War in the East.

Part I: A History

1. The Beginning

Brooklyn was originally settled by the Dutch in the 17th century. During the 18th century, these Dutch settlers were augmented by English and Scottish settlers after the English took over New York as a colony. The village of Brooklyn expanded north towards what is now called the Navy Yard, and residential communities began to develop in the area of Brooklyn Heights, just north of where the Brooklyn Bridge is today. It was during this time that Brooklyn began to grow at an enormous rate. Between 1810 and 1860, Brooklyn increased in population from 8,303 to 279,122.

In the 1840s and the 1850s there was a great influx of Irish and German immigrants into Brooklyn. Many of the Irish settled in the area north of Fulton Street and it became known as Irishtown. The Germans settled in the newly developing area called Williamsburg. In just the decade before the Civil War the population of Brooklyn doubled from 138,000 in the 1850s to 279,122 in 1860.[1]

The Fourteenth New York State Militia originated in the militia of Kings and Richmond County. In 1844 these constituted the Second New York State Division. It was in that year that the Two Hundred Sixty-fifth Regiment was added to the Forty-fourth Brigade, which was part of that division. On May 13, 1847, the New York State Legislature passed a bill which called for the reorganization of the state militia by consolidating and reducing the number of brigades and regiments in the division. This bill provided for eight companies of light infantry, riflemen, grenadiers or infantry along with a cavalry and an artillery company. Also according to this bill, the Two Hundred Sixty-fifth Regiment was to become the Fourteenth Regiment, New York State Militia.[2]

Company "A" of the new regiment had already been organized as the Union Blues or City Grenadiers. They elected Horace Sprague as their captain. Company "B" was made up mainly from the Washington Guard, which was a volunteer group comprised principally from the No. One Fire Engine Company in Brooklyn. Sprauge, who recruited them, was elected their captain, while Edward B. Fowler, who was to be the regimental leader for most of the Civil War, was elected the first lieutenant and George Mallory was elected to the position of orderly sergeant.

No further recruiting was attempted until February 1848. At that time Company "C" was organized. It was made up of the Franklin Guard, who were recruited from No. Three Fire Engine Company. They elected David Baldwin as their captain. Company "E" was made up of the Steuben Guards and elected Capt. Schepper, as their leader. The Shields Guards became Company "F" and elected Capt. McCarthy, while Company "G" was made up of the Columbian Rifles and elected Capt. Morrison. Finally, Company "H" was made up of men recruited from nearby villages.

By 1851, the companies comprising the Fourteenth Regiment were as follows:

City Grenadiers	Capt. Burnett
Franklin Guards	Capt. Baldwin
Emmet Guards	Capt. Dodge
Shields Guards	Capt. McCarthy
Stueben Guards	Capt. Schepper
National Guards	Capt. Sprague
East New York Rifles	Capt. Beadell
Washington Guards	Capt. Mearz[3]

In June of 1854, rioting broke out in Brooklyn on several consecutive Sundays due to a street preacher who called himself the "Angel Gabriel." His real name was John Orr but he called himself the Angel Gabriel because he started each meeting by blowing a horn. Orr started as a street preacher and rabble-rouser in Boston. Several weeks before the rioting in Brooklyn, Orr created a riot when he attempted to preach against the pope in the largely Irish-Catholic section of Chelsea in Boston. Fighting between the Irish-Catholics and the followers of John Orr ensued and several people were hurt in the melee. The riot was soon suppressed by the policemen and firemen, who were called out by the ringing of firebells. Later that evening, many more followers of the Angel Gabriel arrived to join the approximately fifty followers who had arrived with him.

When John Orr again attempted to preach, another riot broke out. This time, in addition to the police and firemen, the Chelsea Light Infantry was called out to put down the riot. Before the riot was over, the followers of the Angel Gabriel had proceeded to the Catholic Church on Cottage Street, where they attempted to pull down the church. Before they could be stopped, they had partially torn down the fence around the church and the cross had been ripped from the steeple and tossed to the crowd who ripped it into pieces. At that point, the crowd, began to disperse.[4]

Several days later Orr visited the Wells School in Boston. He took a small child and said to the child, "The world is coming to end, and hell is going to open." Orr was immediately thrown out of the school by its administrators. He later went to City Hall, where he began to "abuse" the mayor and the chief of police. Still later four doctors held a consultation with regards to the sanity of John Orr. The results were inconclusive in that two physicians believed he was insane, while two others believed him to be sane. A second consultation resulted in their belief that Orr was indeed sane.[5]

Orr's philosophy of anti-catholic, anti-immigrant, anti–Church, Know-Nothing rhetoric was not new to Brooklyn. In fact, the Catholic bishop of Brooklyn issued an order through the priests of the churches in anticipation of disturbances. The Bishop requested that all people belonging to the Roman Catholic churches "avoid all places where sentiments are uttered, calculated to wound their feelings and in any event to abstain from creating disturbance." The bishop's appeal appeared to be partially successful. Later that day, a larger number of people gathered at the corner of Atlantic and Smith Street supposing to hear the discourse of a street preacher. A few stones were thrown but no one was injured. Towards the end of the sermon, a group of people arrived from New York City, headed by the secretary of the Angel Gabriel, who was playing an accordion. Although things became tense, no rioting took place and the crowd soon dispersed.[6]

During the entire week that followed rumors were rampant, that the Known Nothings from New York City, having been forced to leave Brooklyn on the previous Sunday, were going to return the next Sunday in order to obtain their revenge. It was also said that the Irish in that neighborhood were prepared to meet them and that bloody consequences were anticipated. Edward Lambert, the mayor of Brooklyn, prepared for the possibility by alerting the police and militia, which included the Fourteenth Brooklyn Regiment, under the command of Col. Jesse C. Smith.

On Sunday, June 4, 1854, the preachers again assembled at the corners of Atlantic and Smith Street, which provided a large open field for the thousands of people, including women and children, who had gathered mostly out of curiosity. Noting of great consequence occurred until the sermon was just about ended. Approximately one hundred and fifty men from New York, many of whom were there the previous week, came marching arm in arm and three abreast to the location of the gathering. From there, they continued marching up Atlantic to Boerum Street before marching back to the location of the original gathering.

By this time, Mayor Edward Lambert arrived and ordered the group from New York to cease their marching, with which they complied. However, by this time a large crowd had lined the streets that the New Yorkers had taken to arrive at the gathering and were using to return to the ferry, particularly around Main Street, where thousands of people had already gathered.

As the New Yorkers continued down this gauntlet and were reaching Main Street, they were assailed by stones and sticks thrown at them by the crowd. The New Yorkers began to fire their guns into the crowd, wounding several people. At this point, the Fourteenth — which consisted of the Franklin Guard under Captain Baldwin, the National Guard under Captain Sprague, the Grenadiers under Captain Burnett, the Steuben Guard, under Captain Schepper, the Emmet Guard under Captain Nugent and the Shield Guard under Captain McCarty — were ordered from a nearby armory, in which they were held in readiness, to Main Street, where the bulk of the bloodshed was talking place. The militia and the police were able to quiet the rioters long enough for the New Yorkers to board the ferry and return home.[7]

On June 6, 1854, Mayor Lambert, who had taken a personal part in trying to prevent the riots of June 4 by confronting the interlopers from New York and by insisting that they stop their marching and threatening them with summary action, if they breached the peace, issued a proclamation to the citizens of Brooklyn. It set forth his policies in preventing future disturbances.

PROCLAMATION
BY
EDWARD LAMBERT — MAYOR OF THE CITY OF BROOKLYN

Whereas, the public peace has on several occasions of late been disturbed by evil disposed persons, who have congregated together in the public streets with the intent of interfering with those who had quietly assembled on private grounds for religious purposes:

And Whereas, Sundry persons on several occasions, visited this city on the Sabbath, and in procession, marched through our streets causing excitement and ill feeling, and tending to a breach of the peace:

And Whereas, Many of our well dispose citizens are drawn together on such occasions out of curiosity, and their presence tend to produce and may seem to give countenance to disorder, and also by crowding the thoroughfares, retard the public authorities in quelling any disturbances which may occur.

Now, therefore, I, Edward A. Lambert, Mayor of the City of Brooklyn, do by this, my Proclamation, caution all persons from any attempt to interfere with the rights guaranteed alike to all our citizens to meet peaceably together for public worship, either within a building or on private grounds; and I also caution all persons from making a demonstration which would tend to excite ill-feeling among our citizens, by organizing and moving in procession in the public streets to such places of worship; and I do hereby request and require all citizens of Brooklyn to refrain and desist from countenancing by their presence, all such unlawful gatherings and demonstrations, and I also hereby give notice that measures have been taken to prevent any further breach of the peace in this City, and that crowds of persons found in the public streets, will be directed to dispense immediately, and for a disobedience of such order, will be promptly arrested, and that the peace and good order of this City will be maintained at all hazards.

Given under my hand and seal of office, at the City Hall, in the City of Brooklyn, this sixth day of June 1854.[8]

More rioting was anticipated for Sunday, June 11, and again special preparations were made to meet this possible occurrence. The entire military force of the Fifth Brigade under the command of Brigadier General Harmenus Duryea was called to duty. The brigade consisted of the 13th, 14th 70th and 72nd regiments. The Fourteenth regiment was to be stationed at the Catherine Street Ferry, near where most of the rioting and shooting had taken place.[9]

On Sunday, June 11, 1854, the Angel Gabriel visited Brooklyn with about one thousand of his supporters. They went to the area around Atlantic/Pacific Street near Smith Street, which was the scene of the preaching of the previous week. Between five thousand and six thousand people had assembled. At the sounding of his horn, Orr mounted a small hill and began his discourse on how he had been persecuted by the authorities in Boston and in Brooklyn. During his speech, he called the pope everything but a decent man and said they should "send the Pope to the other side of Jordan." At the conclusion of his harangue, he and his followers left the area without incident. However, as the group neared to the ferry, the crowd which had followed them began to throw stones and overwhelmed the police in the area. At this point, the Fourteenth, which had been housed in City Hall and had used the courtrooms as barracks, were called to quiet the demonstrators. This action had the desired effects, and the people began to scatter in all directions. John Orr and his followers took the ferry across the East River to New York without further molestation.[10]

The Fourteenth had shown their mettle, they had protected the Angel Gabriel and his followers, even though many of them were the targets of his preaching, being Irish Catholic and immigrants. The next day an article appeared in the newspaper focusing on the meaning of what they had done.

> The Angel preached and trumpeted, as he had a perfect right to do, when he did not block up the side-walks. As to the taste displayed in his harangues that is entirely a matter between himself and the audience; as long as any crowd of people desire to hear him they have a perfect right to do so, and to cheer and applaud until they are hoarse. Now that free speech has been vindicated to the utmost extreme we hope there will be an end to the excited crowds that block up the streets and lower the peaceable and respectable character of our city in the eyes of any stranger who might happen to visit it, desecrate the Sabbath and become a vast and intolerable nuisance in the eyes of all well disposed citizens.[11]

When the Civil War came along not all the people of Brooklyn or their neighbors in New York City favored the conflict. In the 1850s and 1860s

Brooklyn was a growing city. At this time Brooklyn was the third largest city in the United States. Its growth was because of the over-crowding in New York City as well as the massive immigration from Europe. Brooklyn was mainly middle class. However, about one-third of the people in Brooklyn were born outside of the United States. These immigrants for the most part made up the lower tier of the city's societal make-up.

In addition, Brooklyn had long been associated with the Democratic Party, in that most of the elected officials as well as the mayor of Brooklyn were Democrats. In the 1860 presidential election, Abraham Lincoln received only 44 percent of the popular vote.

Brooklyn's economic life was closely associated with nearby New York City. As it is even today, many of the people who lived in Brooklyn worked in New York City and New York City's centers of industry were shared by Brooklyn. Therefore, many people in Brooklyn were sympathetic to the Southern cause, since they needed the cotton for their industry. The lower classes of Brooklyn were also afraid that the policy of the federal government and the freeing of the slaves would cause them to lose their jobs to the migrating former slaves.[12]

Fernando Wood, the mayor of New York City, even proposed that New York should secede from New York State and from the Union, and establish it self as a "Free City" so that they might continue their commerce with the south: "With heavy investments in the South, and the textile industries, the financial and commercial interests of New York City opposed President Abraham Lincoln's war policy."[13] The *New York Times* reported that Wood, at a meeting in his office, proposed to "establish Suffolk, Queens, Kings, Westchester, and Richmond Counties along with the city of Manhattan as the State or Kingdom of Manhattan."[14]

The main newspaper in Brooklyn, the *Daily Eagle*, was anti-government and pro-secession in its publications prior to the war.

> There is no longer any reason to doubt that the authorities at Washington are bent upon dragging the country into civil war.... Brooklyn has just cast a vast majority against the men and their policy who, after having driven the South out of the Union by a fanatical crusade against its vested rights under the Constitution, have erected barriers against its return, and are now determined to render re-union hopeless by stimulating the sectional animosities they have labored so long and industriously to install into the minds of their followers, to that pitch of frenzied and brutal ferocity which can only be appeased by the shedding of human blood."[15]

However, all this changed with the firing on Fort Sumter. A wave of patriotism overran Brooklyn and there was a rebound of loyalty. Flags were flown from all public buildings as well as from private dwellings, Southern sympathizers, who would speak openly against the Union" were admonished by arguments more striking than pleasant, of the propriety of keeping their thoughts and words to themselves." Newspapers which had Southern sympathies were forced by patriotic mobs to fly the American flag. The Brooklyn *Daily Eagle* changed its editor and became a staunch supporter of the war and a favorite of the Fourteenth Regiment, which wrote often to the editorial staff.[16]

The Brooklyn Navy Yard, which was near an armory used by the Fourteenth, played a part at the beginning of the war as it did during the entire war, and the Fourteenth played a part in protecting it in the days just after the attack at Fort Sumter. In late April 1861, just after the war was declared, Capt Foote (later commodore and destined to play a larger part in the Federal navy's success against the Confederates) met with Mayor Powell of Brooklyn and committed to him his belief that Southern sympathizers from New York City would, that night, make an attempt to burn the Navy Yard and the ships that were harbored there. Foote was, therefore, requesting help from the city since he had barely 80 men to defend the government property. Mayor Powell acted quickly by placing approximately 1000 policemen near the Navy Yard and the ferries, by which the Southern sympathizers from New York were supposed to reach Brooklyn. In addition, the Fourteenth Regiment was called to arms at the armory, where they were to remain ready should the need arrive. The Southern sympathizers did not show up and the incident became known as the Navy Yard Scare. However, later evidence showed that it was only the quick action of Mayor Powell in deploying the police and the Fourteenth Regiment that prevented the Southern sympathizers from attempting their attack.[17]

The Navy Yard would have been a rich target by itself. The Brooklyn *Daily Times* reported that the USS *Wabash* was already fitted out for service, the USS *Savannah* was approaching completion, the USS *Perry* already had its armaments installed, the steam tug *Yankee* had been armed with heavy guns, the *Quaker City* was being armed with heavy cannons and the steamers *Empire City* and *Dawn* were awaiting being fitted with heavy cannon. These vessels were needed in the blockade of Southern ports.[18]

2. Going South

What the federal government needed now was volunteers, and the boys from Brooklyn did their part to meet that need. Recruiting centers were set up at every armory and park in the city. On April 24, 50,000 people gathered in Fort Greene Park to hear speakers and to adopt resolutions supporting the war. Many businesses and organizations promised to pay the wages of the soldiers to their families who were left behind and to return them to their former jobs when their service was over. Other employers paid for the uniforms and equipment of men who volunteered. Organizations were set up to raise money for the relief of the families of volunteers. The knowledge that their families would be taken care of eased the minds of the men and increased enlistments.[1]

After the start of the Civil War, the Fourteenth quickly beefed up its ranks. It was at its full complement by mid–April 1861. This was accomplished under Lincoln's[2] proclamation asking for 75,000 three-month volunteers. The regiment continued training until its commander, Col. A.M. Wood, was notified that only units volunteering for 3 years of service or the war would be accepted.

This notification came from the Union Defense Committee, which returned from Washington with orders from the president and the secretary of war to furnish 14 regiments to "serve for the war and to be sent south with all practicable speed." Nine of these regiments were to go to the Fortress Monroe and five to Washington. The Union Defense Committee consisted of the Honorable Samuel Sloan and A.A. Low. Sloan addressed the president on behalf of the 14th Brooklyn Regiment.[3]

Col. Alfred M. Wood was born on April 19, 1828, in Hempstead, Long Island. He moved to the City of Brooklyn at an early age. Wood was a clerk in the store of the respected businessman Elijah Lewis and soon became his partner. Col. Wood entered political life in 1853 as a Democratic candidate for tax collector. His good reputation helped him win this election by six hundred votes even though his party was defeated. He served faithfully for three years and was elected again with an even greater majority. In 1861 he was elected to the board of aldermen and was chosen as its presiding officer. After the outbreak of the Civil War, Wood resigned his position as the president of the board of aldermen and devoted full time to the preparation of

2. Going South

the Fourteenth, of which he had long been a member and was now its colonel.[4]

With the regiment expecting marching orders to Washington at any moment, the officers of Company C wrote to their local newspapers,

> Resolved, that we as loyal citizens and soldiers pledge our lives and fortunes and our sacred honor for the protection of that banner, promising no traitor shall pollute those stars and stripes under which our forefathers fought, bled and died. And be it further resolved that we, as a military organization, representing the City of Brooklyn in the approaching contest do further pledge ourselves to protect unsullied, untrambled, uninjured and unstained that noble banner with its beauteous constellation of "thirty four."[5]

The Fourteenth Brooklyn assembled and camped at Fort Greene. The men had been anxious for weeks and waiting to get orders to leave. They named their encampment Camp Odell for the Honorable Moses Odell, the popular congressman to whom they were indebted for the many acts of kindness to the regiment. The camp itself was on the top of a ridge, leaving the level ground for drilling.[6]

Until May 18, the regiment remained in Brooklyn drilling and equipping. When word that the U.S. government was declining to receive or order any more militia regiments to the front except organizations that enlisted for 3 years or the war. Col. Wood assembled the regiment at Fort Green, where they were bivouacked, and the terms of enlistment were proposed to them. To make sure that all members of the regiment knew to assemble at Fort Greene, Col. Wood issued the following orders in the May 18 edition of the Brooklyn *Daily Eagle*. "All members of the 14th Regiment not in camp will immediately report at their Company Headquarters, in camp, as the Regiment is under orders for immediate departure.—A.M. Wood, Col."[7] The regiment had been waiting for that order ever since April 18, 1861, when Col. Wood had telegraphed Albany the simple message, "Ready to go to the front."[8]

An adjutant general's report detailed: "The terms of enlistment were agreed to with much enthusiasm. That day the 14th Brooklyn Regiment, which at that time was made up of eight line companies and an engineer corps, a total of 825 officers and men broke camp at Fort Green and marched down Myrtle Avenue and Fulton Street to the Fulton Ferry where a ferry boat transported them to Jersey City."[9]

On 18 May, the Fourteenth Regiment left Brooklyn and headed for Washington, D.C. The *Daily Eagle* reported:

> All Brooklyn turned out with one accord to evince with heart and voice the sympathy of our noble city with the last of the three regiments raised here by the exigencies of the times namely the 28th, 13th and 14th Regiments....
> All the way down from Fort Green to Fulton Ferry was one continuous tri-

umphant ovation. From every window ladies were waving handkerchiefs and flags and clapping their hands while the sterner sex below maintained and incessant fire of cheering. There was really something sublime in the march of the men in connection with their stern mission; and as their bayonets flashed brightly in the gaslight, thoughts would obtrude as to how soon, these bayonets would be crossed in deadly strife, and with no foreign foe.[10]

As the 14th Brooklyn marched through the streets, they made a spectacular sight. The men were dressed in their chasseur-à-pied uniforms. These were reminiscent of the French Army uniforms.[11] The outfits consisted of red trousers with white leggings called gaiters which were made of canvas and buttoned up the side. The dark blue jackets had broad red chevrons and red shirts under it, although the jacket and shirt were one garment. The metal buttons on the jacket were purely decorative. The officers of the regiment wore the more traditional blue frock coat of the army but the red trousers had a gold lace stripe down the outside seam.[12]

Upon reaching the Fulton Ferry, the men filed on the awaiting steamer and were conveyed to New Jersey. While crossing the bay the band played "Auld Lang Syne," "The Girl I Left Behind Me," and "Oh, Soon Return," among other favorites. The men of the regiment occupied their time during the crossing by singing patriotic songs and cheering their regiment as well as the proud city that they had just left behind. When arriving in Jersey City they were again met with cheers from the crowd.

M.F. Odell had accompanied the Fourteenth to Jersey City and onto the railroad cars that awaited them when they disembarked from the ferry. Congressman Odell spoke to the members of the 14th Regiment reminding them of the responsibilities that they had assumed as well as of their loved ones whom they had left behind, the need for acquiescing to the difficulties that they were going to face and reminding them that the honor of the City of Brooklyn was in their hands.

The train leaving Jersey City for Philadelphia and Baltimore before reaching Washington, D.C., should have ended the control of the Military Board at Albany. However, Gov. Morgan of New York sent a letter to Gen. Duryea asking by what authority he permitted the 14th to leave[13]. This was yet another problem between the governor of New York and the 14th Brooklyn Regiment. The problems were to continue until December 1861. An editorial in the Brooklyn *Daily Eagle* stated:

> It is hoped that the misunderstanding which seems to exist between the federal authorities at Washington and the governor and the military board of this state, will be speedily terminated, so that both may act in harmony, instead of thwarting and contravening each other, as they seem lately to have done. A continuance of such a spirit would do much to distract and weaken the gov-

ernment, and fritter away in little petty jealousies the energies which ought to act in combined and harmonious operation...." The chief cause of the difficulties the action of the legislature in restricting the power of the governor, who is the commander-in-chief of the state military by virtue of his office, by appointing a military board with full power to control his action."[14]

After leaving Jersey City at approximately 11:20 P.M. the train stopped at Newark and then went onto Camden, arriving there, at approximately 4:30 A.M. At this time the men immediately left for Philadelphia. Upon their arrival the women on Washington Avenue and its vicinity welcomed the members of the regiment in fine style and invited them into their homes for breakfast. When they had finished breakfast, the regiment gave three hearty cheers to salute the ladies of Philadelphia. While marching back to their trains all kinds of items were cheerily waved at them, from handkerchiefs to nightgowns. The next stop was Wilmington, Delaware. It was here that an order was given for the members of the regiment not to leave the cars for any reason or at any place where they might stop.[15]

The regiment continued to Washington by way of Baltimore. It passed through Baltimore on Sunday, May 19. The 14th Brooklyn was the first unit to march through Baltimore since the attack on the Sixth Massachusetts Regiment, which took place on April 19, 1861.[16] Col. Edward Jones of the Sixth Massachusetts received word that his march through Baltimore might be contested by some citizens of that city. Before beginning his march he ordered that ammunition be distributed to his troops and that they load their guns. Col. Jones then went, personally, through the cars and gave the following orders:

> The regiment will march through Baltimore in column of sections, arms at will. You will undoubtedly be insulted, abused, and perhaps assaulted, to which you must pay no attention whatever, but march with your faces square to the front, and pay no attention to the mob, even if they throw stones, bricks, or other missiles; but if you are fired upon and any one of you is hit, your officers will order you to fire. Do not fire into any promiscuous crowds, but select any man whom you may see aiming at you, and be sure you drop him.

As Col. Jones' regiment marched through Baltimore, the last of the companies were attacked from behind by a shower of missiles. The regiment increased their steps to double quick, which seemed to incite the mob, leading them to believe that they dared not fire or had no ammunition. It was at this time that multiple pistol shots were fired into the ranks. As one soldier fell dead, the order to fire was given and executed. In this incident three members of the Sixth Massachusetts were killed and approximately 40 wounded.[17]

The Fourteenth Brooklyn Regiment passed through Baltimore with this on their minds. However, they passed through without incident and proceeded into Washington, D.C. After being quartered within the city for two days, the regiment was moved on May 22nd to Meridian Hill, two miles north of the city.[18] This new camp was named Camp Wood, recognizing one of New York's veteran generals: "The camp was situated on high ground very pleasantly located and much superior to Camp Odell, containing much more room too. It was almost entirely on level ground, bounded on two sides, north and south, by beautiful green woods; on the east a magnificent view of the beautiful country was to be seen and on the west a bird's eye view of the Capitol City of Washington and the Potomac River was to be had."[19]

The next day, May 23, 1861, was a monumental day in the history of the Fourteenth Brooklyn Regiment. On this day the Fourteenth was mustered into the service of the United States by General Irvin Mc Dowell.[20] The regiment was paraded before the general and then was formed on three sides with General McDowell on the forth side facing the regiment. Gen. McDowell indicated that the regiment was being mustered into service for the length of the war and proceeded to give the oath to the officers and men of the regiment. Raising their right hands the men of the regiment pledged "to bear true faith and allegiance to the United States of America, to serve them honestly and faithfully against all their enemies and opposers whatsoever."[21]

Gen. McDowell then asked the members of the regiments if there were any among them who did not take the oath or had refused to take the oath. In the five companies that were assembled to be mustered in at this time, thirty men stepped forward. McDowell stepped to these men and gave them the opportunity to ask him some questions. After being satisfied by McDowell's answers, sixteen of the thirty rejoined their companies and were mustered into service. The fourteen remaining members were taken under guard and escorted out of the camp. One soldier returned later in the day and with tears in his eyes pleading to be sworn in and allowed to join his company. Gen. McDowell consented to this and swore him in.[22]

In a letter to the editor of the Brooklyn *Daily Eagle*, a soldier from the Fourteenth wrote concerning this matter. He added that the men of the Fourteenth were living high and have everything that a man could want. He added, "You may be assured that as long as the men can carry a musket or an officer wield a sword the members of the 14th will stand to a man to the support of the Star Spangled Banner."[23]

There was much concern in the regiment and at home concerning the men who refused to be mustered into service. The soldiers wanted the people back in Brooklyn to know that they or their company were not involved in what they perceived as the disgrace of refusing service to the United States government. After this incident, letters started to arrive back in Brooklyn regarding these refusals. One letter, from Lieut. William H. Burnett of the 14th Regiment, Company C, was to set aside rumors that members of Company C did not take the oath. In the letter dated May 23, Burnett indicates that all members of Company C took the oath as put to them. This was later reiterated by T.J. Conaut of Company C.[24]

The men of the Engineer Corps were quick to defend themselves to the people back home. It had been reported in the Brooklyn newspaper that fifteen members of the Engineer Corps of the Fourteenth Regiment had refused to take the oath of allegiance. In a rebuttal to this, a member of the Engineer Corps wrote that although fifteen members of that unit did refuse to take the oath, he wanted to assure the people of Brooklyn that it was not because of cowardice. "They would not explain our position in the army; but since then everything has been explained satisfactorily and we are all together again. We came to fight, and die if needs be, with the 14th."[25]

On May 24–25, the 14th Regiment along with other troops, including the 11th New York, made the first incursion into Virginia. The Engineer Corps accompanied these soldiers to build a dock on the Virginia shore. At about midnight these soldiers crossed the Long Bridge and occupied the high ground on the other side. The Engineer Corps assigned to the Fourteenth worked for several hours both in the water and on shore to build a dock so artillery could be landed on the Virginia side. Although the engineers were praised for their efficiency, their joy was dampened when they heard that Col. Ellsworth of the 11th New York (Fire Zouaves), who was with the advance guard, had been killed when his unit had pushed into the village of Alexandria. Col. Ellsworth was well known to the men of the Fourteenth.[26]

The Fourteenth was not without casualties, although not due to enemy action. On May 20, 1861, Private Edwin Black of Company E., while trying to withdraw a bullet from his rifle, accidentally discharged his weapon. The wound, made by a Minie ball, was in his chest about one inch and a half to the right of the median line and about two inches about the right nipple, passing through and coming out at the shoulder blade. The surgeon for the Fourteenth Regiment, Dr. Homiston, indicated that the damage caused by the projectile twisting and tearing through the tissue, muscle and bone and passing through the being was devastating, and even if he survived the initial wound, he could eventually succumb in the following weeks to various complications. However, Dr. Homiston added that Private Black has "endured his suffering throughout long and weary hours without a murmur," and if he ever gets well that he is determined to take his place again in the ranks of his regiment and fight for that flag.[26] Private Edwin Black, who enlisted at Brooklyn and mustered in as a private in Company E on May 23, 1861, died of his wound on July 20, 1861. He was twenty-one years of age.[28]

To a regiment in camp, the rumor mill turns out stories as fast as a grist mill turns out flour. This was just as true of the Fourteenth Regiment as any other regiment. Stories about breaking camp and imminent battles were rife. Meanwhile, the regiment continued with its parades and drills. On June 1st, the regimental drill was reviewed by Major General Charles W. Sandford, who complimented the regiment on its perfection. In addition, the regiment attended a grand inspection by President Abraham Lincoln and General Winfield Scott; again, the men received great praise and were given the "honor of the right of the line." General Scott took Col. Wood aside and said, "Colonel, I am proud of you and your regiment, they are all intelligent looking men, and their marching is excellent."[29]

Aside from these distractions caused by the generals or by the president, life in camp was usually dull and routine. A day with the Fourteenth Regiment consisted of awaking at 5 A.M. for reveille. After awakening the soldiers had thirty minutes to wash and dress before the drum sounded for roll call. After that the regiment would drill for an hour. With this accomplished they were dismissed for breakfast. Their meals consisted of whatever the eight men in their tent could put together. This along with cleaning up their tents occupied the men until eight A.M. when they were called again to drill. Drill was continued until they received their rations and cooked dinner. In the afternoon they held a regimental parade. In the evening, at 7 P.M. and 9 P.M., the regiment was together for roll call, and at 9:30 P.M. the bugle sounded and lights out was ordered. Exceptions to this routine came in the form of guard duty. Each company provided men for this each day. This lasted for 24 hours, usually two hours on and four hours off.[30]

It was on June 9 that General Sandford ordered Col. Daniel Butterfield of the Twelfth New York State Militia and Lieut. Col. Fowler (in the absence of Col. Wood, who had left for Brooklyn on a short leave of absence) of the Fourteenth to a conference with him in Washington. At this conference the two regiments were given instructions, "that in case of an attack on the city or a tumult within it these two regiments should be a special guard for the President and his Cabinet, that without waiting for orders they should at once take position, the Fourteenth on the west and the Twelfth on the east side of the President's mansion, and be prepared to defend its occupants to the last extremity."[31]

On June 14 approximately twenty men were discharged from the regiment. These men were given certificates of disability by the U.S. Army surgeons who re-examined the members of the regiment. Almost all of those who were given the certificate wanted to stay, even though they knew that the regiment could be ordered out of camp at any moment. Two who were being discharged were Sergeant Hyer and Sergeant Kirby. These men were members of the regiment prior to the war and were highly regarded by the entire regiment.³²

On June 15, members of Company A, of which Hyer was the first sergeant, and Company H, of which Hyer was a former lieutenant, turned out to bid farewell to their comrade. Company H joined the revelry in the form of mounted cavalry of sorts. Members came mounted on the shoulders of other members of the company. Each mounted rider was fully equipped and armed according to law. They cavorted around the ballroom as if they were executing an exhibition drill. After this "drill" the members of Company H dismounted and together with others sang appropriate songs and duets. At the end of the festivities the soldiers again mounted their steeds and rode off to the barracks at double quick time, with the cheers of the regiment ringing in their ears. The next day Company H held a meeting and presented their esteemed sergeant with a set of resolutions:

> Whereas, our beloved comrade and 1st Sergeant, Jos G. Hyer, is by the visitation of Providence, deprived of the ability to continue the performance of his known and valuable duties and is compelled to leave us therefore, we the members of Company A, 14th Regiment, N.Y.S.M., expressing deep regret at this loss, knowing that he can not be replaced.
> Resolved, that, desiring to present to him some testimonial of our esteem, we do hereby elect him unanimously an honorary as well a life member of Company A from this date.
> Resolved, that we tender him our well wishes for his future success, wishing him a pleasant journey to his home, hoping that he will soon recover from the partial loss of his eyesight.
> Resolved, that a copy of the above resolutions be presented to our Comrade, J.G. Hyer.³³

That day, the members of Company A with regard and sentiment proceeded to escort Sergeant Hyer to the railroad station. They continued their cheering until the train was well out of the station.

Before those who had been discharged left the camp, each man was given thirty-one dollars and nine cents in cash, and honorable discharge from the army. In addition to these, they were given a free railroad pass back to Brooklyn.

After this, the regiment went back to its usual routine of eating, drilling and sleeping until late in June. It was at this time that some members of the regiment read a speech by Henry Ward Beecher in which he criticized the actions of Col. Wood relating to three slaves who came in the camp of the Fourteenth.

> When the Fourteenth Regiment was in Washington three dusky fugitives came into their camp, and a file of men was ordered by General Sandford to take

them — where? Not to freedom, but back to their master, and their master gladly accepted them, and departed without taking the oath of allegiance. Now, if I'd been Colonel ... I would have said: "Boys, there's the bush, and if you get there before I do you are good fellows."[34]

In reality, a picket who was guarding the camp on the evening of June 2 found and arrested three blacks who could not give any good reason for their being in the area. Since the area was under martial law the picket arrested them. The next day Col. Wood wrote to Capt. Theo. Talbot, assistant adjutant general, advising him of the arrest of three runaway slaves who were named, Dennis, age 51, Joseph Scudder, 30 years old, and Charles H. Jones, 14 years old. He advised Capt. Talbot that the slaves were the property of Mr. Webb who lived in Lisbon, Howard District, Maryland. Since the slaves had asked for the protection of the United States Government, Col. Wood asked what disposition should be made of the prisoners.[35] The same day Col. Wood received a reply from Gen. Mansfield: These slaves must be kept under guard and put at work policing, etc., till the owner comes for them, when they will be delivered up, as Maryland is a reputed loyal state."[35]

These slaves were held for a few days performing menial tasks around the camp until they were claimed by their owners and by order of Gen. Mansfield. The *Daily Eagle* stated, "Any person at all conversant with military matters cannot fail to see that Col. Wood performed his duty in the premises in a proper and soldierly manner, and no onus can be cast upon him or his officers."[37]

Another slave came into the camp of the Fourteenth while they were in Virginia at a later time. This slave, John Boston, wrote a letter to his wife, "My Dear wife It is with grate joy I take this time to let you know Where I am[.] i am now in the Safty in the 14th Regiment of Brooklyn[.] this Day i can Adress you thank good as a free man[.]"[38] The circumstances here were different. They were not in Maryland, "a reputed loyal state," but rather in Virginia.

On June 25, 1861, a detachment from the Fourteenth Brooklyn arrested a spy in Washington, D.C. When apprehended by the detachment, the spy had full details of the number of troops, positions and strength of batteries around Washington. They also found on him a sketch of a plan of attack on that city. The spy had marked the positions of all the mounted cannons in the vicinity.[39]

On July 1 the Fourteenth received the orders for which they had been waiting since leaving Brooklyn. The regiments crossed the Long Bridge and finally joined the main body of the army in Virginia. A new camp was setup just south of Arlington House about half a mile from the Potomac River. Although not as hospitable as their old camp, it had plenty of wood and water in the near vicinity and had an excellent view of the Long Bridge, the Potomac and Washington, D.C. This new camp was named "Porter" since Andrew Porter was now made the brigade commander.[40]

On July 1, 1861, while at Arlington, General Mc Dowell issued Special Order 18 as follows:

> Col. Porter, Sixth Infantry, having reported for duty in compliance from headquarters of the Army, is assigned to the command of the brigade to consist of the Eight Regiment N.Y.S.M., Col. Lyons and Fourteenth Regiment N.Y.S.M., Col. Wood. The brigade to be hereafter increased by the command of Brig. Gen McDowell.
> J.B. Fry
> Asst. Adjutant General.[41]

The brigade was shortly increased by the addition of Griffin's battery, Sykes' battalion of regular infantry, two companies of the Second United States Cavalry under Palmer and Reynolds' battalion of Marines. This made up one of the finest brigades in the army and was a direct result of Gen. McDowell's affection for the Fourteenth Regiment.[42]

The place of the Fourteenth Regiment in the scope of the United States Army was further clarified in General Order No. 13:

> Headquarters Dept. of Northwestern Virginia
> Washington, July 8, 1861
> General Order No. 13
> Until further ordered, the following will be the organization of the troops in this dept.... Second Division; Col. Hunter, 3rd Cavalry commanding 1st Brigade: Col. Andrew Porter, 16th Infantry commanding a battalion of regular infantry (2nd, 3rd, 8th Regiments) 8th Regiment N.Y. Militia, 14th Regiment N.Y. Militia, Squadron 2nd Cavalry (companies G&I) Fifth Artillery (light battery).
> James Fry
> Asst. Adjutant General.[43]

On July 12, Company H and Company C were ordered to Arlington, approximately five and one half miles from Camp Porter. Their orders were to guard the railroad, telegraph and generally do picket duty. They started at one o'clock in the afternoon and arrived at approximately 4 P.M. They were met by two companies of the Eighth New York regiment. The two companies of the Fourteenth relieved them and occupied their positions. There was a great need for this picket duty since many of the people who were living in the area were secessionists and in the past had attempted to cut the wire by throwing a rope over the wire and pulling it until it broke. The sentries received orders to shoot any one interfering with the railroad or the telegraph and not to allow anyone to pass without written orders. These two companies of the Fourteenth were now within sight of the enemy pickets.

Even with all of this, the men were in good spirits and of good appetite. One day a sentry seeing a man approaching his position challenged him "Who comes here." The stranger replied, "A friend with a chicken." Hearing this, the solider commanded. "Advance friend and drop the chicken." That evening some members of the detail had chicken for dinner.[44] On July 14, they were ordered back to camp with the understanding that during the night the brigade under Gen. McDowell was going to march on Fairfax Court House or Richmond.[45]

Later that day with the wind blowing and a cool breeze from the north, the men of the Fourteenth could see many regiments on the move, coming across the Potomac. They could see their guns and bayonets gleaming in the sun. The Fourteenth had already received orders to stand by in readiness for their march. In accordance with these orders, each man was told to take nothing but blankets, muskets and forty rounds of cartridges. All other impediments were to be brought up by wagon train in a few days.[46]

3. Battle of Bull Run

Army of Northeastern Virginia
  Brigadier General Irvin McDowell
Second Division
  Col. David Hunter
  Col. Andrew Porter
First Brigade
  Col. Andrew Porter
  14th Brooklyn
    Col. Alfred M. Wood
    Lieut. Col. Edward B. Fowler
  8th New York
    Col. George Lyons

27th New York
  Col. Henry W. Slocum
  Maj. Joseph J. Bartlett
U.S. Infantry Battalion (8 companies)
  Maj. George Sykes
U.S. Marine Corps Battalion
  Maj. John G. Reynolds
Attached Units
U.S. Cavalry Battalion (7 companies)
  Maj. Innis N. Palmer
Company D, 5th Artillery (6 guns)
  Capt. Charles Griffin

On June 2, Brigadier General P.G.T. Beauregard was given command of the Confederate troops on the "Alexandria line."

In his letter to Confederate President Jefferson Davis dated just ten days after he took command of the Confederate forces around Bull Run, Beauregard wrote of his belief that the Union forces would launch an offensive towards Harpers Ferry, thus cutting off Confederate General Joseph E. Johnston from helping Beauregard. Beauregard, therefore, requested that Johnston abandon his position and immediately concentrate with him.[1] Davis refused this request and later Johnston was able to come to his assistance by use of the railroads.

Pierre Gustave Toutant Beauregard was born in Saint Bernard Parish, Louisiana, on May 28, 1818. He graduated second in his class at West Point in 1838. He served in the Mexican War as an engineer on the staff of Gen. Winfield Scott. In January of 1861 he was assigned as the superintendent of the Military Academy at West Point but was relieved within a few days, probably because of his sympathy for the South. The next month, he resigned from the army and was appointed a brigadier general in the Provisional Army of the Confederate States of America. Beauregard was placed in command of the Confederate troops at Charleston and in April, he commanded the force that attacked Fort Sumter, which led to the start of the Civil War.[2] The main defense of the Alexandria line was at Bull Run. Beauregard had made his headquarters at Manassas Junction about twenty-six miles from Alexandria

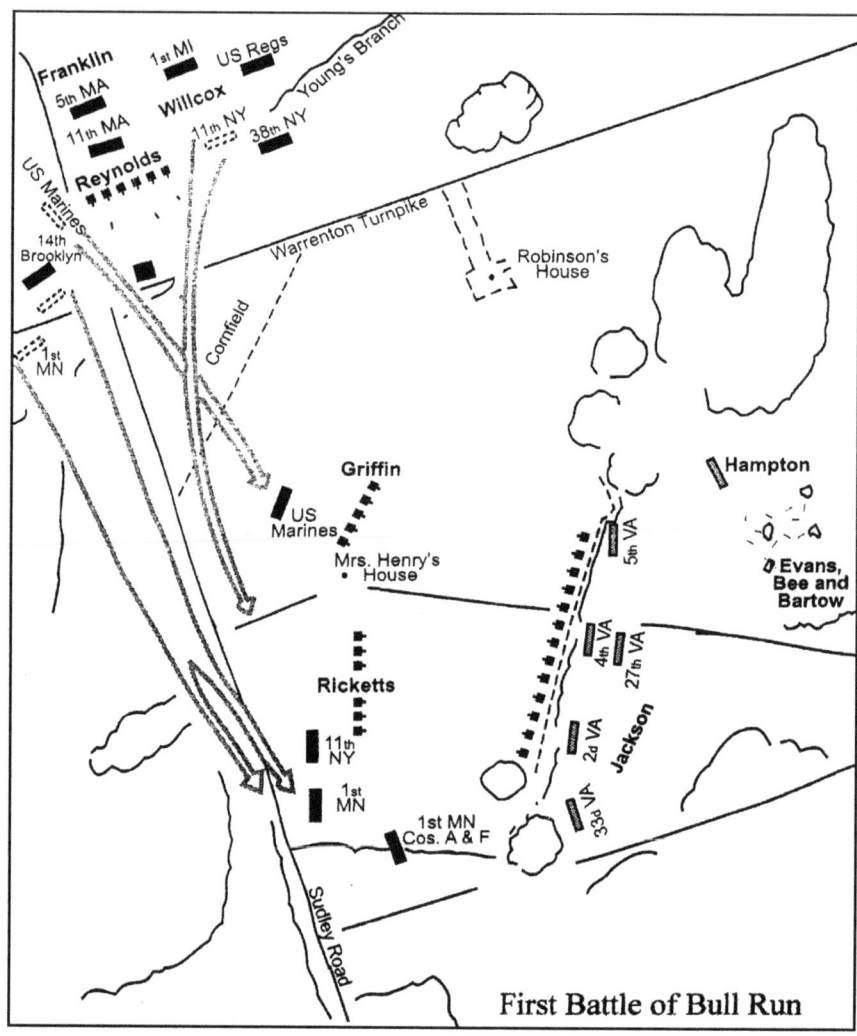

First Battle of Bull Run (from Joanna McDonald, *We Shall Meet Again: The First Battle of Manassas [Bull Run], July 18–21, 1861*, White Mane Books, 1999. Reprinted by permission of White Mane Publishing Co., Inc.).

and the Potomac River. The strategic advantage of Bull Run, was in its location. It was approximately 20 miles from the Potomac River and the movements of the Union Army could easily be observed over this stretch of land. As well, it was near the junction of the Orange and Alexandria railroad, which had connections with both Richmond and with Staunton, an important supply depot. The Orange and Alexandria railroad along with the Manassas Gap railroad gave General Joseph E. Johnson's Confederate Army a quick way of getting from the Shenandoah Valley, where they were operating, to the area around Bull Run.

In addition, there were excellent highways from Alexandria to Washington, D.C., as well as from other points to the northwest and southwest that converged at Centreville, which was about three miles east of Bull Run. The roads exiting from Centreville in almost all directions made it easy to maneuver troops to the offense on the flanks of an army which was holding the line at Bull Run. Also, there were excellent positions to the northeast side of Bull Run which could hold an army in place while flanking maneuvers could be executed to their left or the right.[3]

The Union forces were under pressure from Washington to move to the offense. To this end, McDowell ordered his troops to march. Irvin McDowell was born on October 15, 1818, in Columbus, Ohio. He received most of his education in France, but obtained an appointment to West Point and graduated in 1838 near the middle of his class. From 1841 to 1845, he taught tactics to the students of West Point. During the Mexican War he served in the office of the adjutant general of the army. On May 14, 1861, he was appointed a brigadier general in the Regular Army with the assistance of his patron, Secretary of the Treasury Salmon P. Chase. Until this time, McDowell had never commanded men in the field.[4]

McDowell's army was made up of five divisions. The First Division under Gen. Daniel Tyler was made up of four brigades of infantry and four batteries of regular United States artillery; the Second Division, commanded by Col. D.M. Hunter, consisted of two brigades of infantry, a battalion of U.S. cavalry, a battery of regular U.S. artillery and two volunteer batteries; the Third, commanded by Col. S.P. Heintzlman, was made up of three brigades of infantry and two batteries of regular United States artillery. The Fourth and Fifth Divisions were held in reserve in and around Centreville and for the most part did not take part in the battle.[5] The Fourteenth Regiment was part of Hunter's Second Division, Col. Porter's First Brigade.

The Fourteenth, along with its brigade, received orders to march on July 16. The First Brigade, of which the Fourteenth was a part, was in the lead of the advance on the first day. Due to delays from breaking camp and forming the troops into columns, it was night before the Fourteenth reached Annandale between Baileys Crossroads and Fairfax Court House. At this point the brigade left the road and established camps for the night. The next morning the men prepared their own hard tack and coffee and again formed into columns with the Fourteenth and its brigade at the head.

Approximately a mile before Fairfax Court House, the road was blocked by trees which had been cut down. This was an outpost of the South Carolina brigade that was occupying Fairfax Court House. The original plan called for Gen. Tyler's Division to be in the rear of Fairfax Court House at 8:00 A.M. with the Fourteenth and its brigade in front. If executed properly this would have left no escape for the troops of the South Carolina Brigade. However, Tyler's troops did not arrive until 3:00 P.M. and the South Carolinians departed by 11:00 A.M.[6]

On July 18, General McDowell wrote to General Tyler, "I have information which leads me to believe you will find no force at Centreville, and will meet with no resistance in getting there. Observe well the roads to Bull Run and to Warrenton. Do not bring on an engagement, but keep up the impression that we are moving on Manassas."[7]

This was the first part of McDowell's plan. This along with Major Bernard's report of finding two unprotected fords across Bull Run prompted McDowell to have Tyler's Division move towards the stone bridge of the Warrenton Turnpike to fake an attack at this point. At the same time, Hunter's Division along with Heintzelman's Division was to follow him and was to leave the Warrenton Turnpike at Cub Run. Hunter's division (of which the Fourteenth Regiment was a part) was to cross Bull Run at Sudley Springs. After crossing Bull Run, the division, "turning down to the left were to descend the stream and clear away the enemy who may be guarding the lower ford and bridge. It will then bear off to the right, to make room for the succeeding division."[8]

In order to accomplish this, the Fourteenth which was to be part of the flanking movement, was moved out of its camp at 2:00 A.M. on 21 July. Its brigade was made up of Griffin's battery along with Reynolds' Marines; the Twenty-Seventh New York Volunteers, commanded by Col. Slocum; the Eighth New York State Militia, commanded by Col. Lyons; a battalion of regulars, commanded by Major Sykes; one company Second Dragoons, two companies of the First Cavalry; and four companies all Second Cavalry, commanded by Major Palmer.[9]

This flanking column did not go totally unnoticed. Capt. Edward Porter Alexander, who at the time was an acting signal officer, sent a message to Beauregard indicating the approach of a large force of artillery and infantry crossing Bull Run approximately two miles above the Stone Bridge.[10]

Col. Ambrose Burnside commanded the Second Brigade of Hunter's Division. This unit attacked the Confederates on Matthews Hill. At his insistence, Burnside was given Sykes' battalion of regular troops.[11] While this part of the battle was taking place, the Confederates were reinforcing the hill around Henry House. The artillery of Captain John Imboden, which was part of General Bernard Bee's command, had previously been placed at that hill to support the Confederate troops on Matthews Hill. Imboden was angry that his unit had been left unsupported; however, troops were now reinforcing his position. Some were fresh troops who were just arriving from Johnston's Army, which had just joined Beauregard, and some were the remainder of brigades which had been pushed off Matthews Hill. One of these fresh units was that of General Thomas Jackson. When Jackson was approached by Imboden and told of the problem Imbodin was having, Jackson said to him simply, "I will support your battery."[12]

As the Fourteenth Brooklyn approached the battlefield, they passed a Confederate major who had been wounded. The major begged for some water and a private from the regiment gave him some. The major, thankful for this kindness, offered to give the private his gold watch in return. The private refused this offer but the major insisted and said that if he did not take it, someone else surely would.[13]

A letter written by G.H. Price to his parents explains some of the activities of the Fourteenth during the battle.

> We marched at a pretty quick time to Bull's [sic] Run ... and we could see the enemy firing from his battery.... We had our blankets, which, with two days rations, we threw away as we ran. We no sooner got there, all panting and Blowing, than we were ordered to charge up a hill and at an enemy we could not see, they being behind their masked battery. We then made a charge and fell back to reload. We were drawn into a ditch to draw the enemies fire from our artillery. We went up a road and were fired upon by some of our own men, whether the 71st, 27th or the 8th regiment I do not know. We all fell on our faces till they had done firing, when we, of course not knowing who they were, stood up and fired at them. All this took place in less time than you can read of it. We went into the ditch were [sic] we were ordered and lay there to be shot at for almost a quarter of an hour, we then made three distinct charges at the enemy who fired at us with buckshot and bullets which mowed us down like grass.

While Gen. Bee was trying to rally his forces which had just been pushed off Matthews Hill, he saw Jackson holding strong on top of Henry House Hill. He yelled to his men, "Here stands Gen. Jackson and his brigade like a stone wall, rally behind him." The troops which had been running heeded Bee's call. They ran through Jackson's brigade and reorganized themselves in his rear.[14] Jackson's position was a strong one. In addition to Imboden's artillery and Standard's artillery, he also posted Pelham's artillery. The 4th Virginia and the 27th Virginia were positioned behind these guns. The 5th Virginia was posted to the right of the artillery and the 2nd Virginia to the left of it. To the left of the 2nd Virginia was the 33rd Virginia.[15]

It was at this time that Col. Andrew Porter, who was now the divisional commander, seeing the activity on Henry House Hill, directed Capt. William Averell to order the 8th New York Militia and the Fourteenth Brooklyn to this area. The two regiments moved so rapidly that the Confederate artillery could not adjust quickly enough to find their range. Averell's instructions from Porter was to have the regiments attack Henry House Hill. However, before this could be accomplished, another officer diverted them laterally to the left along the Warrenton Turnpike so that they might engage the troops of Col. Wade Hampton's South Carolina brigade. It was here that both New York Regiments came under cannon fire from a battery near Hampton's Legion. Both New York regiments withdrew. However, they had damaged and disorganized Hampton's troops to the point to that they, too, had to withdraw.[16]

Later in the afternoon, the Fourteenth was ordered to support Griffin's battery, which had found its way though the woods and into a field. The Twenty-Seventh New York formed to the left of the battery while the Fourteenth followed the battery at double quick time. Griffin advanced his battery to within a thousand yards of the enemy and began a deadly fire on the enemy batteries. The Fourteenth rapidly helped to develop the right as well as the Marines with the cavalry in the rear of the right wing. With this, the Confederates began to retire in disorder. While the Twenty-Seventh completed the route of the enemy, the Eighth and the Fourteenth were ordered to move down the Warrenton Turnpike to cut off the Confederates, who were fleeing from Burnside and Sykes. In addition, the Fourteenth was to support the Twenty-Seventh which was routing the Confederates by charging into them.[17]

Meanwhile, Griffin's and Ricketts' batteries were ordered by McDowell to the top of Henry House Hill. They were to be supported by the Eleventh New York Fire Zouaves and the Marines. The Fourteenth entered the woods on the right in order that they might protect that flank. However, even before this was done, the Confederates opened fire on the Eleventh New York Fire Zouaves and Marines with muskets and rifles at close range. The Eleventh broke along with the Marines and the First Minnesota. Griffin's Battery was captured by these Confederate forces.[18]

One reason for Griffin's artillery being captured was the confusion of battle. As Stuart was attacking the flank of the Eleventh New York Fire Zouaves, the Thirty-Third Virginia attacked the artillery from the pines. However, the artillery did not fire on the Confederate soldiers. Major Barry, who was Griffin's superior, had ordered him not to fire, believing that the approaching soldiers were the support infantry for Griffin's artillery. This confusion gave the Confederates the time they needed to approach within seventy yards before firing, thus almost wiping out the artillerists and most of the horses.[19] Barry later testified before the Joint Committee on the Conduct of the War that he had not issued any orders to either Griffin or Ricketts.[20]

While the Eleventh New York and the Marines were retreating, the Fourteenth was running through them and up the hill. The advance was personally directed by McDowell. The Fourteenth advanced to within forty yards of the enemy. At this point, the Fourteenth opened fire on this unit, which was the Thirty-Third Virginia Regiment, part of Jackson's Brigade. One account said, "The Brooklyn soldiers quickly overlapped the left of Cummings's line, then delivered a concentrated volley of musketry into the Confederates.... A third of Cummings's regiment was killed or wounded around the guns."[21]

The Virginia Regiment suffered heavy casualties and retreated back to Jackson's Brigade.[22] The carnage inflicted by the Fourteenth upon the Thirty-Third was a result of some confusion on the part of the commander of the Thirty-Third Virginia. Before the battle the Thirty-Third had been given its own signal and password so that they might be able to tell friendly forces. This signal consisted of placing the palm of the right had out and against the forehead and giving the password, which was "Sumter." When the Fourteenth approached, the commander of the Thirty-Third, Col. A.C. Cummings, was not sure of the unit's identity since he had just come onto the battlefield and was not knowledgeable of the actions which had taken place. In order to secure the identity of the oncoming forces, Col. Cummings raised his hand to his forehead and called out the password. An officer of the Fourteenth appeared to return the proper signal and Col. Cummings ordered his regiment to hold their fire. When a few scattered shots were fired from his regiment, Cummings yelled out, "Cease fire, you are firing on friends."

Just at this moment a volley of rifle fire exploded from the ranks of the Fourteenth. "Friends hell," yelled a man in the ranks of the waiting Thirty-Third Virginia.[23] Thus, the Fourteenth got off the first volley at close range.[24] This was witnessed by John Casler of the Thirty-Third Virginia. He later wrote that during a lull in the fighting and just prior to the attack by the Fourteenth, Sgt. James Daily of his company walked to the top of the hill behind which they were hiding and proclaimed, "Boys, there is the prettiest sight from the top of the hill you ever saw, they are coming up on the other side in form ranks and all dressed in red."

Casler also witnessed Col. Cummings giving the signal and the password to the oncoming troops. "When this regiment [the 14th Brooklyn] appeared in view, Col. Cummings gave the signal, and it was returned by one of the officers; but how they got it was a mystery."[25]

The Fourteenth had recaptured Griffin's artillery. However, with fire from the front together with crossfire from the bushes and the shot and shell from Confederate artillery, the Fourteenth was compelled to withdraw. The regiment reformed at the foot of the hill and with the help of the devastated Eleventh and the First Michigan, they again attacked the hill supported by the Marines.[26]

At the top of the hill the 27th Virginia was waiting. A member of that regiment later wrote,

> Only a few moments later, a battalion of red-breeched Zouaves from Brooklyn, NY, immediately in front of the 27th Regiment, was a clear case, on their part, of self-imposed butchery. They had charged us to most uncomfortable nearness, pouring upon us their deadly fire, while their own loss was so great in actual dead it has often been said, one could walk on their dead bodies over a space of several acres without touching a foot upon the ground. That sight indeed was a dreadful one, and rendered ten-fold more conspicuous by the glittering of their bright red uniforms in the gleaming sun of that hot July.

Again cut down by the Confederate fire, the Fourteenth retreated back down the hill into the woods.[27]

Of the action around Griffin's and Rickett's batteries, Capt. Averell said,

> The 14th and the 38th held on very well ––indeed splendidly. The enemy came right over the brow of the hill, and their fire was very deadly ... their cavalry made their appearance at the same time; this 14th and 38th hung on for fifteen minutes there, while all the officers about there tried to collect these scattered troops and get them back to that position to the assistance of the 14th and 38th, and appealed to them in every way that possibly could be done. But to no avail.[28]

Major James Wadsworth of Gen. McDowell's staff (later a general who was the divisional commander of the Fourteenth) tried to rally the Federals as they retreated. In doing this, he became a target and had his horse shot out from under him. However, seeing the Fourteenth wavering in its attack, he took their colors and, "called on the boys to rally once more to the glorious old flag. Private Tyler took hold of the colors with him, and the regiment rallied to another charge, but without success."[29]

Wadsworth was not the only officer to attempt to rally the Fourteenth on that battlefield in July C.H. Beal wrote to his parents about the bravery of Major Jourdan, an officer in the Fourteenth. While leading the regiment, he tried to rally them by shouting, "recollect your uniform, Brooklyn and the flag of your country."[30]

It was during this second attack that the commander of the Fourteenth Regiment, Col. A.M. Wood, fell with a severe wound. Col. E.B. Fowler took command of the Fourteenth. The regiment organized for a third attack up Henry House Hill, but just as it was about to commence, fresh divisions from Johnson's force to the west arrived by railroad.[31]

Up until this period the result of the battle was indecisive. There is evidence that the Confederate considered the battle lost.[32] A reporter for the Richmond *Dispatch* who was at the battle wrote, "It is, however, due to truth to say that the result of this hour hung trembling in the balance.... We had lost numbers of our most distinguished officers ... your correspondent heard Gen. Johnson exclaim to Gen. Cocke just at a critical moment 'O for four regiments.'"[33]

At this time Gen. Kirby Smith came upon the field with approximately seventeen hundred Confederates. Because of their location it was thought by the Federals that these were Union troops. Because of this, Smith's men were able to move on the flank of Griffin's and Rickett's batteries and within close range. "One volley and victory was changed to defeat."[34]

Johnson was quickly sending regiments into the battle as they arrived. These fresh troops began to turn the Union right flank. It was at this time that Beauregard ordered a general attack along this entire section of the battle. This attack succeeded and the entire Union army began a retreat back to Centreville and Washington.[35] At first this was an orderly retreat. However, it soon degenerated into a rout when Capt. Delaware Kemper's Virginia battery came in range of the Cub Run Bridge. Kemper offered a civilian guest, the secessionist Edmund Ruffin, the honor of firing the first cannon shot. This well aimed shot landed in the middle of the bridge and overturned a Federal wagon, thus blocking the bridge. The Union soldiers began to panic and the rout was complete.[36]

One of the wagons trying to cross Cub Run Bridge was an ambulance carrying the wounded Col. Wood. The ambulance was being fired upon by a battery of Confederate artillery. Finally, a shell from one of these cannons took off the top of the ambulance, passed through it and proceeded to kill three men form a Rhode Island battery and dismounted their gun. The artillery fire was kept up incessantly, therefore, the ambulance crew was forced to abandon it. The ambulance became a target on which the cannon could concentrate.[37]

While the flanking column returned across Bull Run, McDowell gave orders so that he might be able to save what he could of his defeated army. McDowell gathered some regiments which were newly arrived from Alexandria along with a reserve brigade and two brigades which he had ordered up from the fords below Stone Bridge and formed a line near Centreville. McDowell was hoping that his retreating army would stabilize at this point and stop the Confederate counter attack. This did not happen. In fact, this new force joined in the retreat back to Washington. The retreating army made good time. It traveled back to Washington in one night, having taken three days of marching the prior week to cover the same ground.[38]

The evening of the battle, Gen. Beauregard and Gen. Johnston met with Jefferson Davis at Beauregard's headquarters. President Davis suggested that the army pursue the Federals back to Washington. The generals were against this for many reasons, including the very heavy rain which had started to fall, along with the exhaustion of the Confederate troops. Davis felt that since the Federal army was still a force to be reckoned with, he did not want them to rally and counterattack. Davis, who was so very well pleased with the two generals and the results of that day's battle, acceded to the advice of Beauregard and Johnston.[39]

John Vliet, a member of the Fourteenth who was at the battle and was part of the retreat, wrote to his mother about his experience:

"Dear Mother....

On Sunday morning we got on our way at 3 o'clock in the morning for Bull Run and marched until near 12 o'clock without halting scarcely any of the way, and when we arrived within a mile and a half of the battlefield they put us on the "double quick" march which exhausted the men, it being a very warm day and water scarce, so that they were unfit for the duty before them.... I was unable to move one foot before the other and I laid or dropped down under a tree which was struck three times with round shot from the enemies' batteries while I was in that condition. But that did not trouble me in the least for I thought they would call me cowardly for leaving my post, but it was impossible for me to stand up as our company had been on picket guard on Friday night and then kept on duty all Saturday then getting ready on Saturday night to march early on Sunday morning was enough to kill almost the stoutest among us. How I escaped God can only tell, for the two first rallies of our regiment the shot and shell fell like hail around us.

We fought for 5 hours in the face of their batteries and then were obliged to retreat on account of the ammunitionn [sic] from our artillery giving out. And such a retreat you never saw or heard tell of. The whole of our troops scattered in every direction and scenes I witnessed are too horrible to relate.... I walked a short distance from the field and then laid down to rest or die, then got up again walked again but could only travel a short space ... I slept until five o'clock in the morning and then started on my way, but felt very sick ... thoughts of being taken prisoner and hung kept me jogging along until I reached Centreville, where some kind ladies gave me a bowl of coffee which revived me and I was able to walk through a heavy rain until I reached our camp at Arlington, having traveled for 12 hours without scarcely eating anything except two crackers.[40]

Corporal John A. Wells of Company I, later described what he observed:

We had scarcely advanced a hundred yards, being on the double quick when a large parrott shell came crashing through the trees and wizzing [sic] over our heads struck ... it was then that a realization of a battle began to dawn. We emerged into an open field, having thrown off everything that would impede our progress. Our showey [sic] uniform was quite a mark for the enemy and they were not slow to perceive it for presently a Battery of 6 [pounders] opened on us with solid round shot. The consequence was no casualties and considerable ducking. We took position in a small ravine in an open field, lay down, and then hoisted our colors to attract the enemy's fire in order that the

69th [New York] might charge the works in front. Casualties at this time, 2 killed and 8 wounded. We had not remained long thus, when an order came to advance, which we did in line of battle over worm fences across ditches and mud, up steep declivities too, when we were brought to a halt very suddenly by the enemy bringing a battery to bear on us with an infilading [sic] fire. Our mouths were parched with the want of water and burning heat and dust, and smoke almost suffocated us. We marched by the flank up a precipitous road and rec'd our first volley of musketry, but coming from our columns by mistake, by taking us for the enemy, by which our loss was one killed and 5 wounded, making up to this time some 3 killed and 13 wounded and not having fired a shot. We were immediately ordered by Genl. [Colonel Andrew] Porter to support Rickett's [Griffin's] West Point Battery. After exchanging a number of shots the Battery changed position and we were ordered to charge the enemy's main works. On reaching the opposite summit we were met by the 1st N[ew] York Fire Zouaves in disorder, having been charged by suprize[sic] by the renowned Black Horse cavalry of the enemy. Our line of battle was arranged, some of the Zouaves joining with us when the brave [James] Wadsworth came dashing up with hat in hand, and seizing the end of our colors, led the charge to the cannon's mouth. Our Colonel Alfred Wood being wounded about this time, the 27th Vol. N.Y. came up at this time on our left. And, not being supported in our rear, [we] were forced to retire after battling for an hour in the trenches, but only to renew the charge.[41]

The regiment's return to camp was witnessed by John Jenkins, a member of the Fourteenth who had been ordered, along with others, to remain behind and protect the camp.

It was a lamentable sight, the return of our troops. The day was a gloomy one in almost every respect, for it was raining very fast a great part of that morning after the fight, and to see men, wounded and fatigued as they were ambulances, wagons, and teams filled, was indeed a sight. Everywhere along the road were scattered arms and ammunition, and though it was raining very fast, our fatigued troops could be seen in gulleys, under trees, in barns, or wherever a spot could be found where they would not be sure to be trampled upon. As I met the men from the many different regiments, they would inform me that the Red Legs were all cut to pieces. It looked much like truth when I met our men — but occasionally and few in number. We have not, however, lost as many as we at first thought, and some of those that were seen killed, in I don't know how many different ways have at last turned up as being prisoners at Richmond.[42]

The members of the Fourteenth were quick to write back to Brooklyn to explain their part in the battle. A soldier from Co. A wrote to his family, "I am very sorry to tell you we lost the battle, but I hope you and our friends won't blame us, for God knows that we did our best to win.... Brooklyn need not be ashamed of the 14th Regiment, for they did what none others dare do."

Later he told of a general who, after the repulse of their attack, asked the Fourteenth if they were tired. The men shouted, "No" He looked at them and said, "You have done your part."

As he rode up and down the lines of the other regiments, he shouted, "Give me one more rally." When they failed to rally, he shouted, "Men, can you stand and see the 14th do all the work; if you have the spunk of a louse come and rally." They failed to respond and the retreat started.[43]

There were many different reasons why the Union troops failed to take Henry House Hill. Among those reasons were the facts that McDowell waited several hours between his success on Mathews Hill and his attack on Henry House Hill. This gave the Confederates under Johnston time to arrive from the Shenandoah Valley where Union General Patterson had failed to contain them.

In addition, fifteen Union regiments attacked Henry House Hill. However, in most instances no more than two ever attacked at the same time.[44] These same tactics were to be repeated disastrously at Antietam and Fredericksburg.

For his part, Patterson did not see a failure in his not detaining Johnston's Confederates in the Shenandoah. He later testified that he had never been ordered to attack but instead, was to remain in front of Johnston until he left the area. In reply to this, Gen. Winfield Scott testified, "But, although General Patterson was never specifically ordered to attack the enemy, he was certainly told and expected, even if with inferior numbers, to hold the Rebel army in his front on the alert, and to prevent it from re-enforcing Manassas Junction, by means of threatening maneuvers and demonstrations — results often obtained in war with half the numbers."[45]

Both the Fourteenth Brooklyn Regiment and Thomas Jackson brought glory and distinction from the battlefield on that July day in 1861. Jackson's stubborn defense of Henry House Hill insured a Confederate victory and the continuation of the Confederacy and earned for him the sobriquet of "Stonewall." The equally stubborn and determined attacks of the Fourteenth upon Henry House Hill and the woods below showed a courage and tenacity which was to be their signature and the hallmark of future engagements. Their courage in charging up Henry House Hill then charging up again and again was the stuff that myths are made of. It is said that as the Fourteenth was charging up Henry House Hill, Jackson said, "Here come those red-legged devils." I could find no reference to this in any of the literature. If it is true that Jackson did not say this, then perhaps he should have. Certainly, the nickname was well earned. Their bravery, honor and distinction was noted by the commanders on both sides of the battle lines.

The next day after the battle, on July 22, Jackson wrote to his wife

Mary, "Whilst great credit is due to other parts of our gallant army, God made my brigade more instrumental than any other in repulsing the main attack."[46]

The Fourteenth was part of this main attack. As a result of the first battle of Bull Run, the Fourteenth Brooklyn Regiment lost 46 men killed and 34 men wounded.[47]

4. The Colonel and the Private

During the battle, one particular member of the Fourteenth was wounded and taken prisoner. His name was Joseph B. Darrow. After several months in a hospital in Richmond, Darrow died of his wounds on September 28, 1861. A funeral service was held for him at the Sands Street Methodist Episcopal Church in Brooklyn on October 27. Joseph had been a member of that church. The pastor, the Rev. B.H. Nadal, knew him and his family.

In his eulogy, the Reverend Nadal told of Joseph's love of country, which would not allow him to remain at home while the struggle between loyalty and treason was being fought.

Nadal spoke of how Joseph came to enter the war. Since it was not like Joseph to defy the wishes of his family, they had discussed who in the family would go off to war, Joseph or his father, and indeed whether both should go. If Joseph, who was a member of the Fourteenth, should go off to defend his country, his father felt that he would also go. He would do this not only so he would play a part in defeating this challenge to his nation, but also so he might fight side by side with his son to protect him and assist him as far as possible. Finally, it was agreed that the family could not spare both male members. Joseph's argument prevailed since he was already a member of the Fourteenth and since his going would not affect the financial stability of the family. "The brave boy lovingly and strongly argued that he might both go and die without hurt in any way."

A member of the Fourteenth related an incident which took place when the regiment went into camp at Fort Greene in Brooklyn before leaving for Washington. He told how Joseph was surprised to see so many soldiers go to sleep without saying prayers. Joseph stuck a candle in the socket of his bayonet and read from the Bible saying, "I go fought in the name of God to fight his battles, and this book shall be my guide." Still others spoke about his smiling and cheerful manner. Still another told of an incident just before the battle when he had told Joseph that he thought that his own position was a dangerous one. Joseph immediately changed positions with him. His last recollection of him was when, side by side, they began a charge and Joseph said that he put his trust in providence and that he was not afraid to die. The Reverend Nadal spoke of a letter from Richmond which told of his meekness and love of brethren as well as his courage in undergoing surgery and of a Rebel minister who wanted to take Joseph to his home and nurse him back to health.

The people of Brooklyn respected and grieved for all members of the Fourteenth who were killed in battle. Why was this soldier different? At the time of his death, Joseph G. Darrow, private, Company C, Fourteenth Regiment, New York State Militia, was age 16 years, 8 months and 14 days. He was the "Christian Boy Soldier of Brooklyn."[1]

The soldiers of the regiment wrote about their concerns relative to their commander, Col. A.M. Wood. In a letter dated July 23, and written from Camp Porter, at Arlington Heights, a soldier wrote, "I regret to inform you that our Col. (Wood) received a wound in the right leg (the ball passed through the thigh) I helped to carry him off the field. A great number of our troops were taken prisoner; I understand, and I think the Col. is among them."[2]

John P. Victory, who was the assistant corporation counsel of Brooklyn and a member of the Fourteenth, wrote of Col. Wood, "After the second rally of the 14th, his horse bcame unmanageable. He dismounted and heroically led his men on to the cannon's mount, with such soul-stirring exclamations and patriotic sentiments as 'Come on, bully 14th,' 'Rally for the honor of Brooklyn,' and 'Brooklyn expects us to do our duty.' It was then that a minnie ball entered the fleshy part of the thigh." He later added that the 14th Regiment of Brooklyn, "did more real fighting and made more charges than any other regiment and I challenge contradiction."[3]

In the Brooklyn *Daily Eagle*, Col. Wood is quoted as saying, after being wounded and lying on the ground during the battle: "Go on, boys, go on; don't mind me."

The soldiers continued their advance. However, some soldiers picked up the colonel and placed him in an ambulance going toward Centreville. The driver of the ambulance, fearing for his well being, soon cut the traces and fled off to save his life. Some members of the Fourteenth came to the aid of the colonel and brought him to a nearby wooded area. The group remained there for four days eating mostly blackberries. They were eventually captured by members of the Eighteenth Virginia Regiment in the area of Cub Run Bridge and became prisoners.[4] This was confirmed by Edward P. Dougherty of the Seventy-First Regiment, who was a prisoner of the Confederates. He says that Col. Wood was a prisoner and was sent to Richmond. Col. Wood remained in the hospital, at both Richmond and Charlottesville, for many months.[5]

In September, J.L. Cabell, a surgeon, for the Confederate States of America wrote,

At the request of Col. A.M. Wood, of the Fourteenth Regiment of New York State Militia, who was severely wounded and taken prisoner at the battle of Manassas, I certify that his wound was of such a character that though it is now healed, it will yet unfit him for active service as a soldier for many months, a minnie ball having passed through the pelvis in close proximity to the rectum and bladder. It is doubtful whether he will be able to mount a horse for a year or longer.[6]

A few days later Colonel Wood himself wrote to J.P. Benjamin, the acting secretary of war for the Confederate States of America. It was in his letter that his attitude toward the Confederacy had changed. He wrote,

I most respectfully petition to be paroled home. I have been for several years colonel of the Fourteenth Regiment New York Militia and as such was compelled to accompany it to the city of Washington or suffer in my reputation as a man of courage. I preferred the former and led the regiment not only to Washington but to the field of Manassas, where I was wounded and taken prisoner.

While in the Confederate camp and at this place I have learned what I did not believe before, that the people of the South were united and that the war will have to be a war of subjugation (if that were possible), and as such I am opposed to its continuance, and would labor for a peaceful settlement and an early recognition of the Confederate States as belligerents.[7]

The next day, October 9, 1861, J.L. Cabell, who was Wood's surgeon, wrote of his petition:

I have a strong impression that it would be a good policy to grant his petition, as I believe him to be fully satisfied that the attempt on the part of his section to subjugate the South is both unrighteous and impracticable. There is also reason to believe, as is expressly alleged by apparently competent witnesses, that Colonel Wood is a man of considerable political influence with a party already somewhat disposed to utter a protest against the continuance of the unholy war. It does not, however, become me to urge these considerations upon the attention of the authorities in the War Department. My object is simply to bear testimony to the fact that Colonel Wood, after a sojourn among us of two months, has made the most favorable impression among all who have seen him and has convinced us that he is not only sincerely grateful for the kindness shown him in the period of his bodily suffering but that he will remain in future a constant.[8]

Despite his protestations about his new feelings for the South, Wood was used as a pawn by the South in the incident involving the privateer *Savannah*. The Union had captured the Confederate privateer. The United States did not consider the crew of this ship as prisoners of war but rather as pirates. Because of this, the Union wanted to try these men, and if found guilty wanted to hang these Confederates. The Confederates said that if the Union hung the crew of the vessel, an equal number of high ranking Union soldiers would, similarly, be hung. In accordance with this decision, on November 9, 1861, J.P. Benjamin, the acting secretary of war, wrote to Brig. Gen. John Winder in Richmond:

> You will ... select thirteen other prisoners of war, the highest in rank of those captured by our forces, to be confined in the cells reserved for prisoners accused of infamous crimes, and will treat them as such as long as the enemy shall continue so to treat the like number of prisoners of war captured by them at sea, and now held for trial in New York as pirates.
>
> As these measures are intended to repress the infamous attempt now made by the enemy to commit judicial murder on prisoners of war, you will execute them strictly, as the mode best calculated to prevent the commission of heinous a crime.[9]

On November 11, General Winder answered Acting Secretary of War Benjamin, "In choosing the thirteen from the highest rank to be held to answer for a like number of prisoners of war captured by the enemy at sea, there being only ten field officers, it was necessary to draw by lot three captains.... The list of thirteen will therefore stand; Colonels Lee, Cogswell, Wilcox, Woodruff and Wood."[10]

In a letter to his friend Congressman Odell, Col. Wood described how he was informed of the notices by Secretary Benjamin. A Confederate officer came to him while he was at dinner. While apologizing profusely, the officer showed him the notice from Benjamin and took him to see General Winder. Col. Wood told Odell that all of the officers were removed to the county jail and went on to say, "You may rest assured that our fate depends upon those of the Privateersman. I trust that you will do all you can (consistent with your duty to the government) to relieve those officers that went forth to fight the battles of their country, from a position of peril and distress. See my family and give them all the consolation you can, and in the name of humanity, do all you can for your very true friend."[11]

In December, the Congress of the United States got involved in the exchange proceedings of Colonel Wood. As a result of the Trent Affair with Great Britain, two Confederate commissioners, James Mason and John Slidell were seized aboard an English ship. These commissioners were held captive in Fort Warren, Boston Harbor. The U.S. Congress adopted a resolution stating,

> Whereas Colonel Alfred M. Wood, of the Fourteenth Regiment New York State Militia, who was wounded and taken prisoner at the Battle of Bull Run, has now by Rebel authorities been ordered to confinement in a felon's prison, and by the same order is to be treated as a prisoner convicted of infamous crimes. Therefore, resolved, that the President of the United States be respect-

fully requested to order John Slidell to the same character of prison and to the same treatment until Colonel Wood shall be treated as the United States have treated all prisoners taken in battle.[12]

Through diplomatic efforts and to avoid war with England, Mason and Slidell were released. In addition, though negotiations between the North and the South, a policy for the exchange of prisoners was agreed to by both parties. Colonel Wood would be exchanged for an officer of similar rank. It was decided that Colonel Wood would be exchanged for a Virginia Colonel of infantry named George S. Patton (whose grandson was to become the illustrious general of World War II).[13]

On February 25, when General McDowell heard of Colonel Wood's release, he wrote to General Augur, who was at that time the brigade commander of the Fourteenth Regiment. Colonel Wood was on his way to his regiment. "To do honor to a brave and excellent officer I have ordered an escort of cavalry to go with him. He will probably arrive at 3:30 P.M. Will you give orders to his regiment to be prepared to receive him. If I were not detained here I would go myself to assist at his reception."[14]

Colonel Wood arrived back in Brooklyn on March 3, 1862, amid tumultuous applause and great celebration. To the throngs of people and public officials who had waited to welcome him, he said, "This more than repays me for my sufferings and the captivity I have endured. He later added that he was willing again to lead the regiment when duty called him, and when his health permitted. This was in direct opposition[15] to his letter to Secretary of War (CSA) Benjamin.

Wood settled down and continued his political career. He had been elected tax collector in 1851 and president of the board of aldermen in 1861. In 1864, Wood was elected as the mayor of the City of Brooklyn.[16]

5. After Bull Run

The regiment returned to its old camp at Arlington on July 22. Among the last to arrive were Lieutenant Colonel Fowler, Captain Mallory, Lieutenant Uffendill and Captain Jordan. They had met the regimental wagon at Annandale on the afternoon of July 22 and were taken into camp.[1] The soldiers of the Fourteenth lost no time in relating their actions during the battle back to family and friends in Brooklyn. Almost daily beginning on July 23, letters arrived at the office of the Brooklyn *Daily Eagle* attesting to the actions of the regiment and the individual efforts of the soldiers of the Fourteenth Regiment. Many of the members of the Fourteenth were upset about reports that their battle flag had been captured by the enemy during the Battle of Bull Run. Corporal Alex Barrie, Co. H, Francis Doyle, Co. A, and George Hudson, Co. C, jointly wrote a letter saying,

> We saw a few remarks purporting to emanate from a member of the 14th regiment in regard to the colors of our regiment stating that our colors were taken from us by the Rebels. This we assert is untrue in every respect, and if not corrected might cast a stigma upon our regiment. We are happy to say that no Rebel hand polluted our flag with his unholy touch. After our brave Ensign (F.T. Head) was wounded one of the color guard, Baldwin Cano, of Company B (Captain George Mallory) caught it up and carried it safely and triumphantly from the field.

Another member of Co. B wrote a description of the battle and ended his letter by saying, "Our flag still waves."[2]

William Collins of the Fourteenth wrote to his parents assuring them of his safety and the bravery of his regiment,

> Dear Parents:
> I take the pleasure to write you a few lines, to let you know I am well, and hope this will find you the same. I hope you will not be worried about me. I was in the battle, and was the only drummer on the field. At the time of fighting, a cannon ball hit my drum and sent it up in the air. Then I left the field at once, and started for the White House, where we put our dead and wounded. Our colonel is wounded. I have not seen him since. We expect he is dead or taken prisoner. I think we shall come home, for we have not many men left, as there were most of them shot. Capt. Jordan, of our company, was shot, and a great many more of our officers. Our major was the bravest man

in the regiment; also our ensign bearer he was a brave young man. He took our flag and went right through with it, and was shot in the thigh. Then "Old General": took hold of our colors, and said, "Come gallant 14th fellows" and rode to his post. Our regiment did more duty than any other out here. We marched one day and night without a bit to eat, but one cracker and drink of water. We arrived safe at Camp Porter. This is all I have to say at present, as the mail is about leaving. So good-bye until next time.

From your affectionate son,
William T. Collins.

P.S.—We expect to be home by the 23rd of next month. My love to all friends. Tell them I am not wounded, but my feet are full of blisters."[3]

In addition, a correspondent of the New York *Tribune* who was at the battle wrote: "The Brooklyn Fourteenth deserves no second place for conduct on the field."[4] Still another letter written to the Brooklyn *Daily Times* also defends the bravery of the regiment:

> It has been well known that the officers of the Regular service have looked with distrust upon Militia and Militia officers. In the late Mexican war, this feeling was at first shared by both Generals Scott and Taylor, but at one of Taylor's battles, he remarked that the difference between the Regulars and the Volunteers was that the latter did not know when they were whipped, but would continue charging, while the Regulars never charged over twice after being repulsed. The same holds good in this battle, the 14th having charged batteries three times, and would have continued charging had they received the least support while the marines, when ordered to support them, broke without firing a gun. It is to be hoped that the citizens of Brooklyn will remember the gallant 14th not only when they return home, but now, when the men, weary and worn from their late exertions and excitement, naturally feel that justice has not been done them, they having made three distinct charges, twice on covered batteries, thus drawing the fire of the Rebels upon themselves, and made several gallant rallies.... I would here say to your readers, that if any of them wish to join a regiment that has been tried and tested, both in officers and men, (and that in the most exposed position) let them join the 14th, which has proved itself the banner regiment.... The men of the Regiment consider it an outrageous blunder to say the least that they should have been placed in the position they were, being surrounded by masked batteries and exposed to the crossfire of muskets—every position so guarded that the first shot from the battery shut in their ranks. The Rebels regarded them as completely hemmed in, and directed all their efforts to cut them off, and in one of the charges they shouted now we have got you, you red legged rascals, or words to that effect. They did not have them however, but had a great deal more then they wished.[5]

At about the beginning of August, rumors started in the camp that the regiment would be going home at the end of their thirty-day enlistment period. This resulted from the fact that the regiment left New York without authority or the consent of the governor. The Fourteenth was part of the regular state militia and therefore under the control of the governor of New York. These rumors were supported by Brooklyn lawyers who believed that under New York state law a regiment could not be removed from New York for more than ninety days without the consent of the governor. Believing this to be the case and with the horror of battle fresh in their minds some members of the Fourteenth left for home on their own.[6] The problems between the governor of New York and the federal government over the Fourteenth Regiment were to continue for many months to come.

Life in camp soon returned to its monotonous regularity. Drills, parades, meals and picket duty took place without much comment. The members of the Fourteenth took every opportunity to end the boredom of camp life. Sergeant Michael McCarty of Company F often told the story of the sutler who came down from Washington to sell cider to soldiers of the regiment. The sutler set up his barrel against the side of a tent and began to sell his refreshment. However, the Brooklynites, always looking for amusement and a method of outsmarting the next guy, surreptitiously entered the tent and bored a hole in the barrel and placed a spigot on the opposite end of the barrel. Thus, while the sutler sold the cider from the front of the barrel almost every member of the regiment received a free drink from the rear of it.

Again, during the cold winter months the members of the Fourteenth would keep warm by staying close to or sleeping near a tin stove which was in each of the huts that the members occupied. At times some members of the regiment would take cartridges, remove the bullet and throw them down the chimney of the stove. The resulting explosions would create a giant rush for the exits to the huts and thereby redistribute their contents in a most disorderly manner.[7]

On August 12, 1861, the surgeons who had remained with Colonel Wood or were captured at Bull Run were returned to their units. Each had to sign a parole of honor that they would not "unless released or exchanged, by arms, information or otherwise, during the existing hostilities between the United States and the Confederate States of America, aid or abet the enemies, of the said Confederate States, or any of them, in any form or manner whatever."[8]

On August 27, the Fourteenth's brigade and another brigade were to undergo an inspection with the judges being Abraham Lincoln, William Seward and Generals McClellan and McDowell. That day the regiment put on their new red caps, new jackets and fronts and blue pants. Lieutenant Colonel Fowler later told the regiment the judges said they were the best drilled and finest looking set of men on the parade ground and that they were very proud of them.[9]

The problem of the blue pants was one that bothered many members of the Fourteenth. As Prince Napoleon of France was visiting General McDowell after Bull Run, he saw a group of soldiers and asked what regiment they were from. He was informed that they belonged to the Fourteenth. The prince was surprised, since he had heard of the Fourteenth and knew that they wore red pants. It was explained to him that the Fourteenth had red pants for dress and blue pants for picket duty or rough work. The prince then told General McDowell that General Beauregard told him that his forces had sustained more casualties from the fire of the Fourteenth Regiment than from any other regiment in the Union Army. This information was also included in a letter written by a member of the Fourteenth: "Gen. [Fitz John] Porter seems to think our boys did well, and from what conversation the prince Napoleon had with Gen. McDowell, it seems to be verified, for it is reported here that Napoleon informed McDowell that the Red Legs did more harm and were the greatest source of trouble to the secessionists (and this information was given by [Gen. P.G.T] Beauregard to Napoleon) than all the rest, and that they lost 900 killed and wounded from one regiment, by the Red Legs."[10]

Since the Fourteenth was a favorite of General McDowell, he promptly notified Lieutenant Colonel Fowler of the remarks of the prince. Later the general came to the camp of the Fourteenth and made the remarks known to the entire regiment.[11]

The fact that the Fourteenth inflicted much damage upon the Confederate soldiers was affirmed in a dispatch from Washington on September 3, 1861. These statements were made to M.F. Odell, congressman from Brooklyn, by captured members of the Eighth Georgia Regiment. They also said that it was for this reason that the dead of the Fourteenth Regiment were left to the last before they were buried.[12] Although these reports were not new, they remained unsettling to the soldiers of the Fourteenth. These reports were originally stated by Edward P. Dougherty of the Seventy-First Regiment, who had been a prisoner of the Confederates at Sudley's Church. He reported that the Confederates buried all of the dead on the battlefield except those with red shirts (Zoaves) and red breeches (14th Brooklyn). He also reported that the stench was so great that no living person could remain on the field.[13]

Atrocities committed by the Rebels were documented by the U.S. Congress at hearings the following April. Dr. J.M. Homistan, who was the surgeon for the Fourteenth Brooklyn Regiment, testified that the Rebels refused to allow him to remain on the battlefield and administer to the wounded. While in captivity, he received no food or drink for twenty-four hours and he and his companions were forced to stand in the streets of Manassas surrounded by a boisterous and threatening mob. In addition, he was not allowed to operate on any of his wounded comrades. Instead, the Rebel surgeon allowed his young assistants to perform these operations. Homistan noted that some of them had "no more knowledge of what they were doing than an apothecary's clerk."

Homistan told the story of Corporal Prescott of the Fourteenth who needed to have his leg amputated to prevent his death. After being promised that he could perform the operation, it was instead performed by the assistants. Upon hearing this, Homistan went to the area where the operation was being performed and found that the leg had already been amputated and that it had been performed incorrectly.

> The assistants were pulling on the flesh at each side, trying to get flap enough to cover the bone. They had sawed off the bone without leaving any of the flesh to form the flaps to cover it; and with all the force they could use they could not get flap enough to cover the bone They were then obliged to saw off about an inch more of the bone, and even then, when they came to put in the sutures they could not approximate the edges within less than an inch and a half; of course as soon as there was any swelling, the stitches tore out and the bone stuck through again.

Because of his weakened condition, Corporal Prescott did not survive.[14]

Another and notable witness concerning the atrocities at the battle was Gen. James Ricketts. Gen. Ricketts confirmed the mistreatment of the Union soldiers and told of Confederate guards who shot two Union prisoners, killing one and wounding the other. He went on to describe how the Rebel had rested his gun on the sill of the window in order to get a more accurate shot. The general also referred to Private Louis Francis of the Fourteenth Brooklyn Regiment.[15] Private Francis testified that he was bayoneted by a Rebel in the leg and while he was on the ground two Rebels began to bayonet him again and again. He had been bayoneted fourteen times before one Rebel left and the other was shot in the chest. Private Francis was left on the battlefield for twenty-four hours before being removed to a building where his wounds were only partially treated.

It was a week before he was removed to Manassas and finally to a hospital in Richmond. However, by this time his leg had mortified and had to be removed. Before allowing the operation, Francis insisted that Dr. William Swain, assistant surgeon of the Fourteenth, who was also captured at the battle, be present at the operation. Again because of neglect, the sutures in the leg broke and the band around the leg slipped, causing the bone to protrude. Another operation was performed in which another section of the thigh was sawed off. Pvt. Francis survived. After being released, Francis underwent two more operations. The final one was performed at the Brooklyn Navy Yard.[16]

In a letter to his aunt, George Macy of Co. K told his aunt that the Rebels who were holding Munson's Hill had started to fire at the troops and that the Fourteenth had received orders not to fire at enemy pickets unless they were fired upon or unless the Confederates started to advance. He told how the regiment had, for weeks, expected to move out or even that the Confederates might attack. To add to the expectation of a battle, the trees had been cut down for several miles so as to deny cover to the Confederates.[17]

The Fourteenth remained in camp until September 28, 1861. The Confederates, who had taken possession of the Munson's Hill, pushed their lines close to the Federals. From this point, Washington could be seen by the Confederates. This move was of no military value but it gave the Confederates the distinction of being able to fly the Stars and Bars in view of the capital of the Union. They then began to erect artillery at the different sites on the Virginia side of the Potomac and thereby obstructed the navigation of the river.[18] The regiment under the command of Lieutenant Colonel Fowler participated in the movement of the army up Munson's, Hall's, and Upton's Hills. These hills were occupied after only a small show of resistance on the part of the Confederates. The Fourteenth moved with its brigade to Upton's Hill.[19]

This operation was described by a member of the Fourteenth:

> Last Saturday afternoon [Sept. 28], an order came to the old camp for marching directly after our return from parade and inspection by Gen. McDowell and staff. Our time was so brief that we had not sufficient to pack all our knapsacks in, but slinging our blankets over our shoulders, and with accoutrements, etc., we marched forth. As soon as we arrived at the crossroads we made a halt, and got our position, and then proceeded. The night was very dark and as regiment after regiment, cavalry and artillery, were passing to and fro, or rattling over the rough roads — with the views of signal lights and fires — it really was a soul stirring theme to contemplate. Several halts had to be made in consequence of having to cut away trees and logs that were thrown across the roads by the retreating enemy. We arrived on this hill at about half-past nine o'clock and our pieces being stacked prepared for bivouacking. We soon had our camp-fire burning in honor of our new position. Early on the following morning (Sunday), our boys were to be seen, with their red caps, on each surrounding hill. After I had swallowed my piece of bread and cup of tea — an article that I happened to stow away — I also took a stroll, and visited the different places where secesh were but a few days since quartered with then cavalry and infantry."[20]

General McClellan had been keeping check on the Confederate movement by the use of observation balloons. These balloons, which were developed and used by Prof. T.S.C. Lowe, were at the disposal of General McClellan and his generals in the immediate area of Washington after Lowe finished building one on August 28, 1861. His main areas of observation were around Munson's Hill, Upton's Hill, Falls Church and Clark's Hill. On September 22, 1861, Lowe reported to General Porter that he observed a heavy picket force on Upton's Hill. In addition, be observed what appeared to be a full regiment on the west slope of Munson's Hill.[21] These balloons were used again just a few days later to the benefit of the Fourteenth. On October 5 the Confederates advanced toward Fairfax Court House, which was near Falls Court House. In addition to infantry, the Confederates had a battery of cannons. From this point they began shelling the Fourteenth, and its entire brigade soon responded with its own artillery. The Confederates withdrew. It was at this time that the observation balloons were sent up. However, they could not see the enemy, who had already retired from the field.[22]

After taking Upton's Hill, the regiment settled into winter quarters. The men of the Fourteenth proved to be of little value at cutting the logs necessary to build the winter quarters, since they were city boys from Brooklyn. Col. Fowler brought this to the attention of General McDowell. The General replied "This is so, but I know what they can do. They can be depended on to fight. I will relieve them from duty on the working parties and detail them to picket."[23]

The general was true to his word. The Fourteenth was assigned to picket duty. "This assignment brought the Fourteenth into much closer contact with the Confederates both in actuality an perception. A member of the Fourteenth wrote of his adventures in picket duty,

> The company I belong to was stationed so that we had very good opportunities of seeing the Rebel scouts — one of which came within fifteen feet of the tree behind which I stood watching him; but as soon as he saw our men, he retreated behind the barn-sheds, into the woods, and vanished. I felt a strong inclination to fire — which could not have been resisted, had the individual approached closer — for I already felt it unsafe to allow such proceedings from strangers to go on unheeded — but our orders were strict, and to the effect that we must not fire unless advanced upon, after a challenge.
>
> We imagined we saw any quantity of scouts, but I feel liberal enough, after what I felt positive of having witnessed, to let some of them go for mere freaks of imagination, caused by the presence of a cow or two, a horse, and a young colt, which were innocently going their rounds in quest of fodder around about the out-houses of the farm-house at which I, with six men, were posted. If said animals only know what excitement they were making during that dark and quiet night, and the dangers they were laying themselves liable to of being shot, through such influences, they would certainly be more careful, and perhaps get the countersign — or, at least be more considerate of their safety than the old sow, who on one occasion, being challenged, and told to halt, heeded not the request, but walked along, apparently well assured of being quite safe: and to the inquiry. "Who comes there?" only answered with a gruff grunt and a whiff. As our gallant guardsmen, the challenger, felt satisfied that Mrs. Pork was not one of the enemy, and attributing that peculiar kind of an answer to the ignorance of said sow, thought, no doubt, that where ignorance is bliss, 'twas folly to be wise.[24]

It was while on picket duty that some members of the Fourteenth saw their next action. On November 18, 1861, Company H was on picket duty on the road leading from Falls Church to Fairfax Court House. At approximately 3:00 P.M. a body of about three hundred Confederate cavalry troops attacked Company H. They drove the pickets into the nearby woods and captured some of them. Col. Fowler, who was at a nearby village and heard the shooting, was informed of the nature of the attack. He immediately ordered three companies of infantry to advance down the road so that he might check the Confederate advance should they continue down the road. After advancing about a mile, Lieut. Col. Fowler deployed a company as skirmishers on the right flank and also placed skirmishers on both sides of the road. Fowler notified the headquarters of General Porter about the attack and advanced a unit under Major Jourdan to the outpost that had just been attacked. Fowler then advanced with the main body of his forces. When Fowler arrived at the outpost he found that the Confederates had fled after taking a cart from a nearby house to carry away dead, wounded and prisoners. Two members of the Fourteenth were listed as killed in this engagement.[25]

The unit that attacked Company H was the First Virginia Cavalry under the command of Lieut. Col. Fitzhugh Lee, who was the nephew of Robert E. Lee. The purpose of his mission was to obtain information about the vicinity around Falls Church. Lieut. Col. Lee indicated that because his way was blocked and because the enemy fought with bravery and desperation, it became too late in the day to carry out his mission. Therefore, he returned to camp with his wounded and prisoners. In his report Lieut. Col. Lee added that the soldiers he had engaged were part of the Fourteenth New York State Militia of Brooklyn and that they had fought with much more bravery than the Federal troops usually exhibited. He also added, as if by reminder, that the Fourteenth was the same regiment that "so thickly dotted the field of Manassas upon the 21st with red."[26]

On November 20, 1861, the report of Lieut. Col. Lee was forwarded by his commander along with this note:

> Respectfully forwarded for the information of the Commanding General, Army of the Potomac
>   This gallant and successful affair of Lieutenant Col. Lee and his detachment of First Virginia Cavalry against the enemies best troops in chosen positions receives my unqualified praise and commendation.
>   J.E.B. Stuart
>   Brig.—Gen. Commanding[27]

The two members of the Fourteenth who were killed during the engagement were Privates James Seymour and Walter Taylor, and among those taken prisoner was Sgt. John McNeill. The prisoners were taken to the rear to be questioned. During this time Sgt. McNeill's watch was taken from him. When he reached Centreville, he was questioned by Col. Lee in the presence of Gen. J.E.B. Stuart concerning the amount and position of Federal troops. Stuart, who was impressed by McNeill, along with the fact that McNeill would give them no intelligence, returned McNeill's watch to him. Stuart also offered McNeill a position in his cavalry, saying that McNeill was just the kind of man that he was looking for to serve as his orderly, which would offer McNeill the opportunity for rapid promotion. McNeill's reply was, "You can offer me no inducement to make me fight against the old flag." McNeill and the other prisoners were taken to Richmond until the following summer, at which time they were paroled and exchanged.[28]

The events which took place on November 18, 1862, were documented by Josiah Grumman, who was a sergeant in Co. H of the Fourteenth.

> While on picket with Company H under my command we were attacked by a body of cavalry under the command of Lieut. Col. Lee, and after a short skirmish myself and nine men were taken prisoners and one man Wm. H.H. Stryker of Gravesend was left on the road mortally wounded. Sergeant John McNeil, was severely wounded in the leg no bones broken. Theodore Rich was wounded in the arm. The rest, Daniel McCamley, Wm. Ludden, Nathaniel Lyon, Wm. Campbell, Eskine Rich and George Roller were uninjured. We were taken to the Head Quarters of Brig. Genl. Stuart and from there to the Guard House at Centreville.[29]

William Stryker recovered from his wounds but was discharged because of them on January 15, 1862.[30]

In December, Gov. Morgan of New York again tried to assert his control over the Fourteenth. The problems between the governor and the Fourteenth and then between the governor and the federal government over the Fourteenth had been going on since the Fourteenth left Brooklyn in May without the permission of the governor but under the authority of the federal government. The Fourteenth was a militia unit and it had been mustered into the U.S. Army as a militia unit. Gov. Morgan tried to reorganize the militia units as volunteer units. On December 7, 1861, the Adjutant General's Office of the State of New York issued Special Order 544, which said: "The following regiments heretofore a portion of the militia forces of the state and now in the service of the United States as volunteers are hereby organized into regiments and will hereafter be known and designated by the following numbers viz.:

> 2nd Reg. NY State Militia to be the 82nd NYS Volunteer
> 9th Reg. NY State Militia to be the 83rd Reg. NYS Volunteer
> 14th Reg. NY State Militia to be the 84th Reg. NYS Volunteer
> 20th Reg. NY State Militia to be the 80th Reg. NYS Volunteer
> 55th Reg. NY State Militia to be the 55th Reg. NYS Volunteer
> 79th Reg NY State Militia to be the 79th Reg. NYS Volunteer

The commissions for officers in the above regiments will be issued whenever a list of the Field, Staff and company officers certified to by the Colonel of the Regiment shall have been filed with the Adjutant General of the State."[31]

The members of the Fourteenth were disturbed by the planned change in the designation of their unit. At home in Brooklyn, it was felt that as the Fourteenth Regiment had earned a place in military history and that little was done by the state on behalf of the Fourteenth since they had left without the permission or authority of the government. The state only recognized the regiment after their display of bravery at Bull Run. The members of the Fourteenth and their supporters felt that by changing the Fourteenth Regiment New York State Militia into the Eighty-Fourth New York State Volunteers, the state with a swipe of a pen was about to do what the bullets of the Jackson's Brigade and the entire Confederate Army could not do. That is, to wipe out the Fourteenth. The people back home were also wondering, "May we be permitted to ask whether it is meant as a punishment for marching to the defense of the old flag without direct order, or in violation of the orders of Gov. Morgan? It looks like it."[32]

A letter written by a member of the Fourteenth described the revelry in Camp Marion on New Year's Day but added that their enjoyment was subdued by the fact that the colonel had received word from Gov. Morgan that he had given away number fourteen to another regiment and had changed their regimental number to Eighty-Four: "We fought at Bull Run as the Fourteenth. The battle field was strewn with our brave boys, and we have thus dearly earned a place in history. We are known as fighters in Rebeldom as well as at home. Our men are prisoners of war as the 14th and we feel to not yield our honors and name by which we were baptized by fire and blood at Bull Run to any other.... We have the confidence of our brigadier general; also of Gen. McDowell, who led us at Bull Run, and he strongly objects to the action of Gov. Morgan."[33]

The governor of New York insisted that he had not heard any reason why the number of the Fourteenth Regiment should not be changed to the Eighty-Fourth. This was a battle the regiment knew would have to be fought by friends of the regiments and the people back home in Brooklyn. Thus, back in Brooklyn, the local newspaper — which had supported the Fourteenth through its articles and by printing many letters written by members of the Fourteenth — wrote an article which countered the attempts by the governor and judge advocate general of New York. The arguments that carried any weight were based on misapprehension or ignorance of the facts. The supporters of the regiment then went on to list the arguments in favor of the Fourteenth. The regiment was never received into service as a volunteer regiment; that the authorities of the state refused to recognize it as a volunteer regiment, and withheld from it the rights and privileges to which a volunteer regiment should have been entitled. In addition, they reiterated that the Fourteenth Regiment left Brooklyn under the direct orders of the president of the United States and the Department of War and through the Union Safety Committee of the city.

It proceeded to Washington as the Fourteenth Regiment, New York State Militia. They were mustered into the U.S. Army as militia and when Lieutenant Col. Fowler recruited two extra companies to fulfill the legal requirements of a regiment. The two companies were raised and the muster rolls were sent to Albany as militia companies. Also, the men of the volunteer regiments are entitled to certain uniforms from the state. No uniforms were furnished to the Fourteenth, they were instead uniformed by their city. This was shown when Lieut. Col. Fowler applied to the state quartermaster for uniforms and was informed by him that the Fourteenth was not a state volunteer unit and therefore not entitled to uniforms. The quartermaster suggested that he communicate with the governor. The governor returned a verbal answer by way of Lieut. Booth indicating that the Fourteenth Regiment was not volunteers and therefore not entitled to uniforms and that the regiment should look to the same parties that sent it to Washington.[34]

On March 27, 1862, Governor Morgan wrote to Secretary of War Edwin M. Stanton, informing him that the commanding officers of certain regiments from New York State were refusing to acknowledge the authority of the governor of New York regarding the commissioning of officers and the filling of vacancies or to recognize the appointment made by the governor in accordance with the laws of Congress and orders of the War Department. Morgan further stated the Eightieth (formerly the 20th Militia), the Eighty-Third (formerly the 9th Militia) the Eighty-Fourth (formerly the 14th Militia) all claim to still be militia units; they claim militia instead of volunteer commissions, and elect their officers in accordance with the militia law of the state.[35]

The Fourteenth Regiment, acting as a militia unit, had elected its officers as they had always done. On January 2, 1862, Major James Jourdan resigned from the regiment to accept a promotion as lieutenant colonel of the Fifty-Sixth New York Volunteers. Immediately after his resignation, the regiment held an election to fill his vacancy. This was in compliance with the militia laws of New York State and the acceptable method for choosing an officer for the regiment. Pursuant to the results of the election, Capt. William H. DeBevoise of Company H, who was the senior captain, was elevated to the rank of major. This caused a vacancy for the rank of captain in Company H. Lieut. George Davy of Company H was elevated to the rank of captain. Just prior to this, on December 11, 1861, Capt. William Stears resigned. His place was filled by the election of Lieut. George Elcock to the vacancy.[36]

Things really came to a head when Lieut. Hampden Waldron of the Eighty-Fourth New York Volunteers, who had previously been assigned to the regiment, was refused his position. Now, Waldron was sent with orders from the secretary of war to install him as an officer in the regiment. General C.C. Auger, who was at that time the commander of the Fourteenth's Brigade, sent Waldron along with the brigade assistant adjutant, Major George Halstead, to the camp of the Fourteenth Regiment. General Auger knew that this was going to be unpopular. When they arrived at the camp the Major told Col. Fowler of Lieut. Waldron's assignment. Major Halstead thought that Col. Fowler would be forced to adhere to the orders. Instead, on the back of the order, Col. Fowler wrote a note to the secretary of war indicating that it would be impracticable to comply with the order in that the position claimed by Lieut. Waldron had been filled prior to his appearance. Col. Fowler indicated that the position had been filled by the election of Lieut. Ramon Cardona, who was mustered in to service with the Fourteenth and also was in battle with the Fourteenth. Lieut. Cardona had indeed even received pay in that position.

Lieut. Waldron was returned along with his orders and the note written by Col. Fowler through military channels until it reached the office of General McDowell, who was ever a friend of the Fourteenth Regiment. The general sent his inspector general, General Van Rennselear, to the camp of the Fourteenth so that he could find the details of the situation from the colonel. General McDowell used his influence in the War Department to have an order issued from the adjutant general's office stating that militia units from New York State which were under the authority of General Mc Dowell were to retain their organization and designation.[37]

General McDowell sent a note to Col. Fowler and the members of the Fourteenth Regiment saying, "You were mustered by me into the service of the United States as part of the Militia of the State of New York known as the Fourteenth. You have been baptized by fire under that Number and such you shall be recognized by the United States Government and by no other number."[38] From that point and for the remainder of the service of the regiment whether reports, payroll or correspondence, all communications were headed "Fourteenth New York State Militia."

6. Out of Winter Quarters — 1862

Christopher Columbus Auger was born on July 10, 1821, in Kendall, New York. Shortly after his birth his widowed mother moved to Michigan. He received an appointment to the Military Academy and graduated sixteenth of the thirty-nine members in the class of 1843. After graduating, he spent several years on garrison duty and fought well in the Mexican War after which he saw service on the frontier. He was promoted through grades and on May 14, 1861, was given the rank of major in the Regular Army. At the beginning of the war he was the commandant of cadets at West Point, after which he was assigned to the defense of Washington, where in November of 1861 he was appointed as a brigadier general of volunteers.[1]

On March 10, 1862, the Fourteenth Regiment left the winter quarters at Camp Marion and moved toward Centreville. The Rebels had been reported as occupying the area in strength, and were entrenched around the town. The brigade commander, Gen. C.C. Auger, expected a fight.

All unnecessary equipment was sent to the rear and each member of the regiment carried his Springfield rifle, forty rounds of ammunition, a blanket, shoes and tenting equipment. Stripped for battle and carrying only this equipment, the Fourteenth led the brigade, which included the Twenty-Second, the Twenty-Fourth and the Thirteenth New York State Volunteers.

The brigade marched across the field to Bailey's Crossroads, then by turnpike through Falls Church. After this march it was discovered that the Rebels had evacuated Centreville. However, before leaving they had erected logs in such a way that from a distance they resembled artillery. In the popular usage of the day, these were referred to as "Quaker Cannons."

While the brigade camped on the side of the road for the night, Gen. Auger and several officers from the regiment rode through Centreville and across Bull Run to the battlefield of the previous July, where so many members of the Fourteenth had fallen. Here the officers of the Fourteenth were horrified by what they encountered. Scattered around the field could be seen the bones and remains of soldiers from the Fourteenth Regiment. Fragments of the clothing and red pants could be seen still clinging to their bodies which had never been buried or in some cases, washed out of their shallow graves by rain or still yet, uprooted by animals in the fields.[2]

Frederick Scholes of Brooklyn, who was the brother of a member of the Fourteenth who had fallen at First Bull Run, visited the battlefield to try to determine the location of his brothers grave. While there he met a freed former slave named Simon or Simons who told him that it was a common practice for Rebel soldiers to dig up and exhibit the bones of Union soldiers. Scholes then met another freed former slave named Hampton who lived in the area; he told Scholes how the Rebels had exhumed the bodies just two or three days after they had been interred. Hampton told Scholes that originally they just wanted the buttons off the uniforms but that later they started to collect the bones. Hampton told Scholes that the Rebels disinterred the Union dead by pushing rails into the ground on each side of the middle of the grave and prying them up. Scholes also spoke to the slaves of Benjamin Franklin Lewis, who confirmed Hampton's account. Lewis himself confirmed the statements of these witnesses and added that this conduct was mainly performed by the Louisiana Tigers of Gen. Wheat's division. Scholes later found several Union soldiers who had been disinterred in this manner.[3]

In a letter written to the people back in Brooklyn, a soldier of the Fourteenth wrote about his feelings toward returning to the area of Centreville and Bull Run, from which the regiment had fled leaving their dead and wounded friends behind,

> Our tramp to the battle ground was marked with interest in so far as the frequent recognition of old landmarks by the "red legs" called forth forgotten incidents of the retreat after the fight.... A great desire to tread again the ground which was so hotly contested between the men of the 14th and the Alabama and Louisiana and other Southern regiments, inspired the men upon this occasion to extend their tramp for a mile or more beyond the ruins of the Stone Bridge.... At the field the men scattered in all directions, as their curiosity led them, to points where one and another could identify some objects familiar in their recollection of Bull Run.[4]

The brigade, including the Fourteenth, remained in camp here in what was christened "Camp Auger" for about four days. It was during this time that Capt. Mallory and groups from the Fourteenth were dispatched from the regiment to the July 21 battlefield. The purpose of this detachment was to re-inter the bodies of fallen members of the Fourteenth.[5]

On March 16, 1862, the Fourteenth left this camp and marched approximately 21 miles to Alexandria, Virginia. The march was a treacherous one since heavy rain had swelled the streams to dangerous proportions. In some instances the men barely escaped drowning in the violent currents. Indeed, it was later learned that several men from a regiment which crossed just after

6. Out of Winter Quarters—1862

the Fourteenth were swept away and drowned. The regiment finally reached Alexandria after dark and the members began to look for shelter. Most of the regiment spent the night in warehouses where bat dung had been stored. However, the regiment was happy to find dry shelter even if the smell was highly objectionable.

Everyone in the regiment believed that they were going to embark from Alexandria and sail down the Virginia Peninsula to take part in McClellan's campaign against Richmond. However, the next morning the regiment boarded railroad cars and were taken to Camp Marion. They made themselves as comfortable as they could in their old camp. The next day, on March 18, 1862, the entire brigade along with the Fourteenth moved back toward Alexandria. The brigade spent about ten days camped in a plowed field before they received orders from the president that Gen. McDowell and his entire division were not to embark for McClellan's Peninsula Campaign but were to remain behind to defend Washington.

It was in late March that John C. Brown, a member of the Fourteenth, wrote to his sister about the events of that time period.

> I rested a few minutes and as I gazed upon the ... earth works erected by the Rebels. I thought, Did they think the Army of the Potomac would halt before that? They could not have thought that it was but a feint to keep us back to allow them to have more time. Well we pressed on an halted three miles this side of Centreville.... Well after being there the third day we all donned our red pants and marched to Centreville. There we stacked arms and the Gen. gave us leave to visit the old Battle ground. It was a long walk, eight miles, but as we want to see the old field where we fought and some of us fell, it did not seem so far. Well we arrived there about one o'clock, and a tear would come as I would notice one, two, yes ten of (?) our boys unburied, not even allowed the common rites of man. We could tell them by the red pants and above all not one had a head on, oh the Rebels will feel the effect of our sorrow when we meet them again. How soon that meeting will take place I do not know but we hope (?) the sooner the better. The next day we sent a squad of men to bury them and mark the spot also where they lay.
>
> We left Centreville Saturday morning and returned to Alexandria in a drenching rain. I never seen such storm on shore before, if it ever rained, it rained that day. Well as regard to myself, I was sick, worn out, tired and hungry, my feet were all blistered and much swollen. Well we arrived in Alexandria at eight o'clock in the evening and worse than all, my knapsack was in the wagon and the wagon was many miles from me.... The cars came along and rode singing to our old encampment (Upton Hill) where we arrived Sunday afternoon at three o'clock having been away just a week. Tuesday we received orders to get ready for marching again and left there and proceeded back to Alexandria. We are encamped four miles this side of Alexandria.... We are waiting our turn to embark on the same steamer that you and I have so often seen in the East River. They are on the Potomac. I can stand on this hill and

see it in the distance, where they are bound I do not know. The divisions are all embarking as fast as they can be taken, some eighty-thousand soldiers.[6]

The regiment remained in the area of Upton Hill until April 4. On this date, the Fourteenth, along with other units, were dispatched to the area of Fairfax Court House. The men of the regiment, being from the city, were businessmen, clerks, and bookkeepers, and as with any groups of soldiers they would think of ingenious methods to ease their workload. As they neared Centreville, they captured a young bull from a nearby field. After much thought and industry, the soldiers of the Fourteenth succeeded in harnessing the bull to a wagon. They then proceeded to pile their heavy knapsacks onto the wagon. The bull, showing some reluctance to cooperate with the soldiers, was poked with a bayonet so that it might walk along with the soldiers. The young bull, terrified beyond any comprehension, suddenly bolted down the road. The other regiments marching down the same turnpike were unaware of the danger which was galloping down the road toward them. Suddenly, yells of "Clear the track!" were heard from behind and men and horses began to leave the road into field, and crowded against fencing. The bull, still in terror, came raging down the turnpike which had been cleared of every living thing. As it ran, knapsacks were being thrown in every direction of the compass. The bull, who succeeded in kicking off his harness and wagon, also succeeded in routing the several brigades who were using the turnpike. While the bull was still rampaging down the turnpike, "red legs" could be seen searching for knapsacks.[7]

On April 5, 1862, the regiment resumed its march. After covering approximately fifteen miles by way of Fairfax, Centreville and Blackburn's Ford, the regiment occupied a camp formerly belonging to the Fifth North Carolina Volunteers. They immediately christened it "Camp Brooklyn." They remained in this camp just one night before again resuming their march.[8]

On April 6, 1862, the regiment marched to the area of Bristow Station by way of Manassas Junction and Broad River. While there they camped in a swampy wood. It was during their stay in this area that mother nature took a hand in the well-being of the regiment. The weather was horrendous in that they had rain and snow storms for five days. The troops, whose only protection from the inclement weather was small canvas tents, which did not protect them from the mud and water in which they had to sleep, suffered greatly. Fevers and illness that were to register at a later date could be traced to their day at what the regiment called "Camp Misery."[9]

On April 15, the regiment left this camp and began a march to Catlett's Station. It was as a result of this march and the march of the following day that the First Corps, First Division, First Brigade, which included the Second United States Sharpshooters, the Twenty-Second Regiment, the Twenty-

Fourth Regiment, the Thirtieth Regiment and the Fourteenth Regiment, earned the title of the "Iron Brigade."[10]

John Bryson, a member of the Thirtieth New York Volunteers, wrote a poem regarding this famous march:

> **"The March of the Iron Brigade"**
> See, where the morning's beam
> Purples the Cedar stream,
> Long lines of bayonets gleam,
>
> Fiercely and bright arrayed.
> Tramp, tramp, with step so true,
> As if on grand review
> It is the march, I know,
>
> Of the Iron Brigade.
> Bristoe and Catlett's glen
> All are alive with men,
> Cheery and blithe as when
>
> Forming on dress parade:
> Onward, thro' wood and field,
> Hearts all with courage steel'd
> Ne'er to the foe shall yield
>
> The Iron Brigade.
> Tramp, tramp, with weary feet,
> Thro' rivers wide and deep,
> O'ver pathways rough and steep,
>
> Breastwork and barricade:
> Covering ten leagues and more,
> To Rappahannock's shore,
> Men never marched before
>
> Like the Iron Brigade.[11]

This title is usually used to refer to Gibbon's Brigade, including the Second Wisconsin, Sixth Wisconsin, Seventh Wisconsin, Nineteenth Indiana and Twenty-Fourth Michigan which were also in the same division as the brigade of the Fourteenth. However, the Twenty-Second, Twenty-Fourth and Thirteenth New York were two year regiments and were mustered out in May, 1863, thus this brigade was broken up.

> The Eighty-Fourth New York (14th Brooklyn) was an exceptionally fine regiment, while the other regiments in the brigade made a reputation, also as efficient commands. It seems strange that two brigades in the same division should adopt like synonyms; but in justice to Hatch's Brigade, it should be stated that it was the original Iron Brigade and that Gibbon's Brigade was not known by that title until [later] at which time it was so designated by

a war correspondent, who was apparently unaware of his lack of originality"[12]

To further serve the cause of justice, it must be stated that Gibbon's Brigade earned the title beginning at Gainesville (Brawner Farm) in August of 1862. During its tour in the war, the five regiments making up the brigade lost 1,131 men killed or who died of their wounds.[13] Perhaps we should leave it as history does by referring to them as the Iron Brigade of the East and Iron Brigade of the West.

The next morning, on the 16 April, General McDowell received information from a slave named Alfred about the Confederates in the area of Fredericksburg. McDowell decided to send Auger's Brigade, of which the Fourteenth was part, along with Gibbon's Battery B of the Fourth U.S. Artillery and Harris' Light Cavalry to repel the Confederates and take possession of the town. The units moved out with the Fourteenth behind the cavalry and leading the rest of the brigade and the artillery. After marching for about twenty miles in heat and heavy marching order, the troops were scarcely able to step any further. After meeting with Col. Fowler, General Auger decided to rest the infantry with the exception of the Fourteenth. This was done because Auger was anxious to march on to the enemy's camp some five miles ahead. Each member of the regiment was ordered to throw off his backpack to the side of the road. They were then ordered to pair themselves with a cavalry trooper who would carry their rifle and whose stirrup they could hold onto. These orders were carried out, although within a short time the cavalrymen were walking and carrying rifles while red legs could be seen straddling the horses.

The Fourteenth proceeded in this manner for several miles. At about this time, the head of the column hit the Confederate pickets. Quickly, the regular order of marching was resumed with the cavalry in front followed by the Fourteenth. As darkness fell the cavalry charged the Confederate camp, followed by the Fourteenth as rapidly as their tired legs could carry them. The enemy, a company of cavalry, quickly retreated before the Union force.[14]

During that night the commanding general tried to gain possession of the bridges across the Rappahannock River. The cavalry was ordered to make a wide sweeping maneuver around the Confederates and to meet the road in their rear. The purpose of this maneuver was to reach the river in time to save the bridges from being set afire and to cut off the retreat of the Confederates. When the Union cavalry reached the bridges, the Fourteenth was to attack the Rebels. However, either suspecting the plan or being informed in advance, the Rebels had withdrawn earlier in the night and had prepared an ambush, with the help of additional infantry from Fredericksburg. The Union cavalry, being unaware of these developments, fell into this trap and suffered severely.

6. Out of Winter Quarters—1862

The remainder of the brigade, two miles to the rear, heard the noise of the fighting, began to beat the long roll and marched to the aid of the Union forces. The Confederates, hearing this, were made aware of the approaching Union reinforcement. They in turn fell back across the river and set fire to the bridges as they were retreating. The Union reinforcements arrived just as the last of the Confederates were leaving the area. Artillery was set up and a few parting shots were fired at the retreating foe. However, the only damage done was to unhorse a few of the Confederates who had lingered in the area a little too long.

The departure of the Confederates was so rapid that they could not evacuate their supplies. The Fourteenth witnessed the burning of large amounts of ammunition, quartermaster and commissary stores. Soon afterward a detachment under Capt. Mallory of the Fourteenth captured about three hundred barrels of flour that were hidden on an island in the Rappahannock River just above Falmouth. Fredericksburg soon fell into the hands of the Union forces and Company C of the Fourteenth Regiment was detailed to occupy the city. Soon after this a pontoon bridge constructed of lumber and canal boats was built across the Rappahannock River.[15]

The regiment remained in this location until May 25, 1862. The camp was christened "Camp Prospect."[16] During this encampment the regiment got a chance to refit both emotionally and physically. It required new uniforms since their old uniforms were ravaged by battle and poor weather. As usual, with encampment, the regiment underwent many drills to perfect their skills at battlefield maneuvering. General McDowell, as always proud of the Fourteenth in appearance and their military skills, held an exhibition drill for the benefit of some visiting English noblemen.[17]

Col. Fowler wanted to keep the new uniforms as parade fresh as possible. Therefore, one Sunday afternoon when the enemy was reported advancing on the Fourteenth, Col. Fowler ordered that the regiment change their red trousers to their blue fatigue trousers before beginning their march. This caused much dissatisfaction on the part of the members of the Fourteenth. The feelings of the soldiers was that if they were to die they wanted to be wearing their red trousers. From that point the colonel decided that he would never take the regiment into battle unless they were wearing the distinctive red uniform.[18]

The regiment remained in Camp Prospect until May 25. Gen. McDowell had spent the time concentrating his forces at that location in order that he might join McClellan, who was returning his forces to the area after his Peninsula Campaign. On this day the troops broke camp and crossed the river and stopped at Massaponax Creek, which was eight miles south of Fredericksburg. The troops were stopped at this location because word had been received that

Jackson had moved his regiments up the valley. Upon hearing this, McDowell countered by sending Shields' Division into the valley. On May 29, the Fourteenth and the remainder of its brigade followed the same route after leaving a small contingent at Fredericksburg. The next day, the regiment resumed its march towards Catlett Station. They had marched approximately twenty miles on that day and camped four miles from their destination.[19]

On May 31 they reached Catlett Station at about eleven o'clock and boarded trains for Front Royal. Gen. Rufus King, told Gen. McDowell that Gen. Augur and two regiments of the infantry (the 2nd U.S. Sharpshooters and the Fourteenth Brooklyn) were on board cars and ready to start on their mission.[20]

On June 1, 1862, the regiment bivouacked on the side of the road. The next day they boarded a train again. When they reached the bridge across the Shenandoah River, the engineer refused to cross until daylight (they had boarded the train at approximately 3:00 A.M.). When daylight arrived, they examined the underpinning of the bridge before attempting to cross. This examination led to the discovery that the timbers supporting the bridge had been partially cut. Thus, the precaution of the engineer saved the regiment from disaster.[21]

It was also at this time, that Jackson started his retreat back down the Shenandoah Valley. Gen. Shields was still in pursuit of Jackson, and Gen. McDowell again started his troops towards Fredericksburg to join Gen. McClellan. The Fourteenth proceeded as far as Haymarket, Virginia, where they waited for the remainder of the division to catch up to them. On June 6, they marched to Warrenton, a distance of twelve miles, before making camp at Camp Jefferson. The next day they left Warrenton and marched to Warrenton Station, which was an additional eleven miles. On June 9 they marched to within five miles of Catlett Station, on the road to Falmouth. That night and for the next few nights they made their encampment at Camp Jackson. The brigade was held at this location because McDowell had heard of Shields' reversal in the Shenandoah Valley. On June 14, the regiment left Camp Jackson and marched twenty-six miles, arriving at Falmouth across from Fredericksburg on the morning of June 15 and immediately re-occupied their old encampment at Camp Prospect.

On July 21, 1862, the Third Indiana Cavalry skirmished with the Confederates a few miles from Fredericksburg on the Richmond Telegraph Road. As a result, two companies of the Fourteenth Brooklyn and a squadron of the Harris Light Cavalry went in pursuit of the enemy.[22]

This expedition led by Lieut. Col. Judson Kilpatrick of the Harris Light Cavalry left Fredericksburg at approximately 4:00 P.M. on 22 July. It consisted of 390 men in the combined command. The expedition crossed the Massaponax River at 8:00 in the evening and bivouacked four miles on the other side of the river. The Fourteenth Regiment and thirty cavalry troopers were left to guard the ford and the roads leading from Bowling Green and New Market. At two o'clock in the morning Kilpatrick started his march to the Rebel camp, which was supposed to be at Carmel Church. Two skirmishes with the enemy ensued and the entire force returned to Fredericksburg at eleven o'clock in the evening of July 23. Kilpatrick reported the capture of 24 horses along with saddles and other arms. He did not know the number of killed and wounded on the Confederate side but reported that no men were lost in his command. He also added, "During the long march and the two skirmishes in the morning the whole command, officers and men, conducted themselves most nobly."[23]

This report was made to General King, the divisional commander. He in turn informed the chief of staff at Warrenton,

> The cavalry I sent out on the Telegraph Road Tuesday afternoon (22nd) returned at 11 o'clock last night, having successfully accomplished their work. They attacked and defeated two bodies of Confederate cavalry, 200 or 300 strong, burned one camp and a quantity of corn, medicines, and other stores; broke up the telegraph line; chased the enemy to within a short distance of Hanover Junction, an brought in 3 prisoners, a number of horses, and sundry arms. We did not loose a man. The loss of the enemy was 31 killed and a dozen or more wounded. Our people behaved admirably.[24]

Between that date and August 5, the regiment remained in camp with the exception of some detachments which occasionally were part of a scouting party to the other side of the Rappahannock. On the morning of August 5, the entire division went on a reconnaissance mission to the area of Spotsylvania Court House approximately seventeen miles from camp. The division was divided into two columns and proceeded along different roads. The column of which the Fourteenth was a part did not meet any Confederate troops. However, the second column met with Confederate cavalry and a brisk encounter ensued without loss to either side. The regiment returned to camp by another route on August 8th and accomplished their mission.[25]

7. Gainesville, Groveton, Second Bull Run

Army of Virginia	14th Brooklyn
Maj. Gen. John Pope	Lieut. Col. Edward B. Fowler
3rd Corps	22nd New York
Maj. Gen. Mc Dowell	Col Walter Phelps
1st Division	24th New York
Brig. Gen. Rufus King	Col. Timothy Sullivan
Brig. Gen. John Hatch	30th New York
Brig. Gen. Abner Doubleday	Col. Edward Frisby
First Brigade	2nd U.S. Sharpshooters
Brig. Gen. John Hatch	Lieut. Col. Henry Post
Col. Timothy Sullivan	

In late July and early August of 1862, General Pope, having been given command of the Army of Virginia, began to gather his army in the area of Culpeper, Virginia. John Pope was born on March 22, 1822, in Louisville, Kentucky. Pope was a descendent of George Washington. His father was active in politics and his uncle was a U.S. senator from Kentucky. He was related by marriage to the family of Mary Todd Lincoln, the wife of the president. Pope graduated from West Point in 1842. After four years of survey duty, he served with honor in the Mexican War, after which he was assigned to the Corps of Topographical Engineers. After the start of the Civil War, he was appointed as a brigadier general. Pope opened the upper Mississippi River almost to Memphis, Tennessee, with his capture of Madrid, Illinois, and Island No. 10 in March and April of 1862. During the Union advance on Corinth, Mississippi, his forces made up the left wing of the army under Gen. Henry Halleck.[1]

Pope was now facing Robert E. Lee. Robert Edward Lee was born in Westmoreland County, Virginia, on January 19, 1807, to the wife of Light Horse Harry Lee, who was a general in the Revolutionary War. He entered West Point in 1825 and graduated second in his class in 1829, after which he was commissioned a brevet second lieutenant of engineers. Between his graduation and the Mexican War, he was stationed at various posts throughout

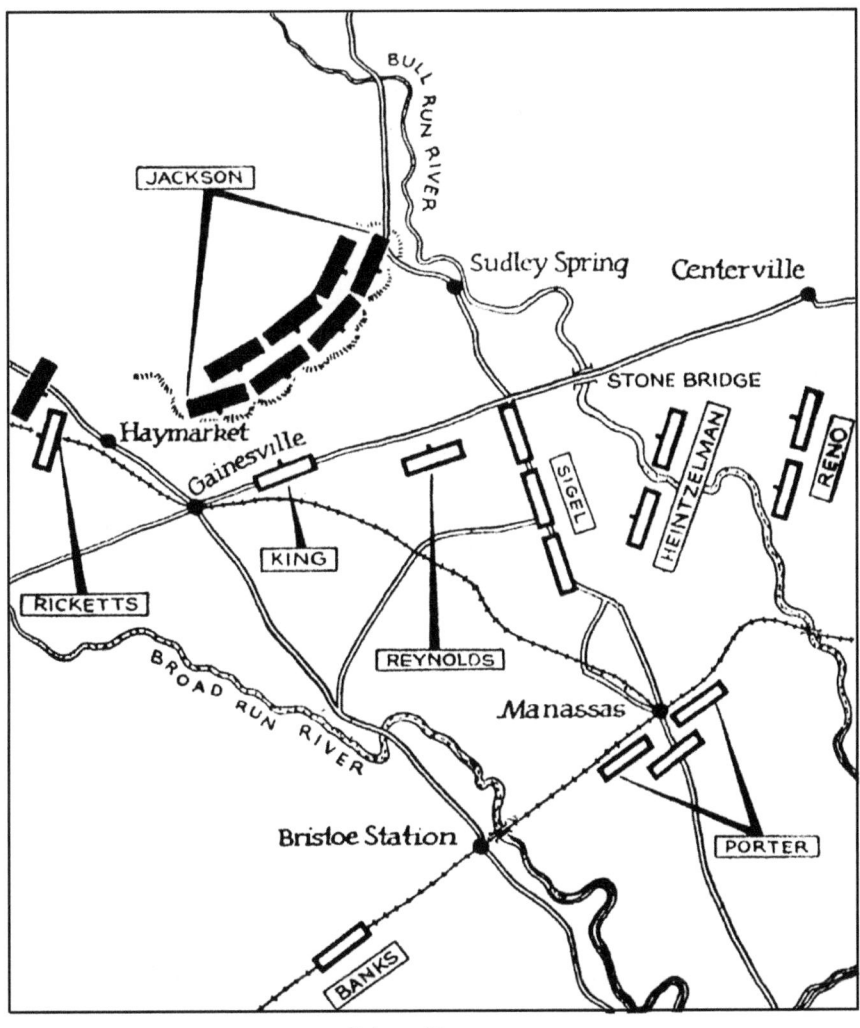

Gainesville

Battle of Gainesville (from Fletcher Pratt, *A Short History of the Civil War: Ordeal by Fire*, Dover Publications, 1997. Reprinted by permission of Dover Publications).

the United States. At the outbreak of the Mexican War, he was assigned to the staff of Gen. Winfield Scott as a captain of engineers in the Vera Cruz expedition. During the march to Mexico City, he won the confidence and esteem of Gen. Scott and was breveted three times to the rank of colonel. In 1852, he was appointed as superintendent of West Point. In 1861, while on

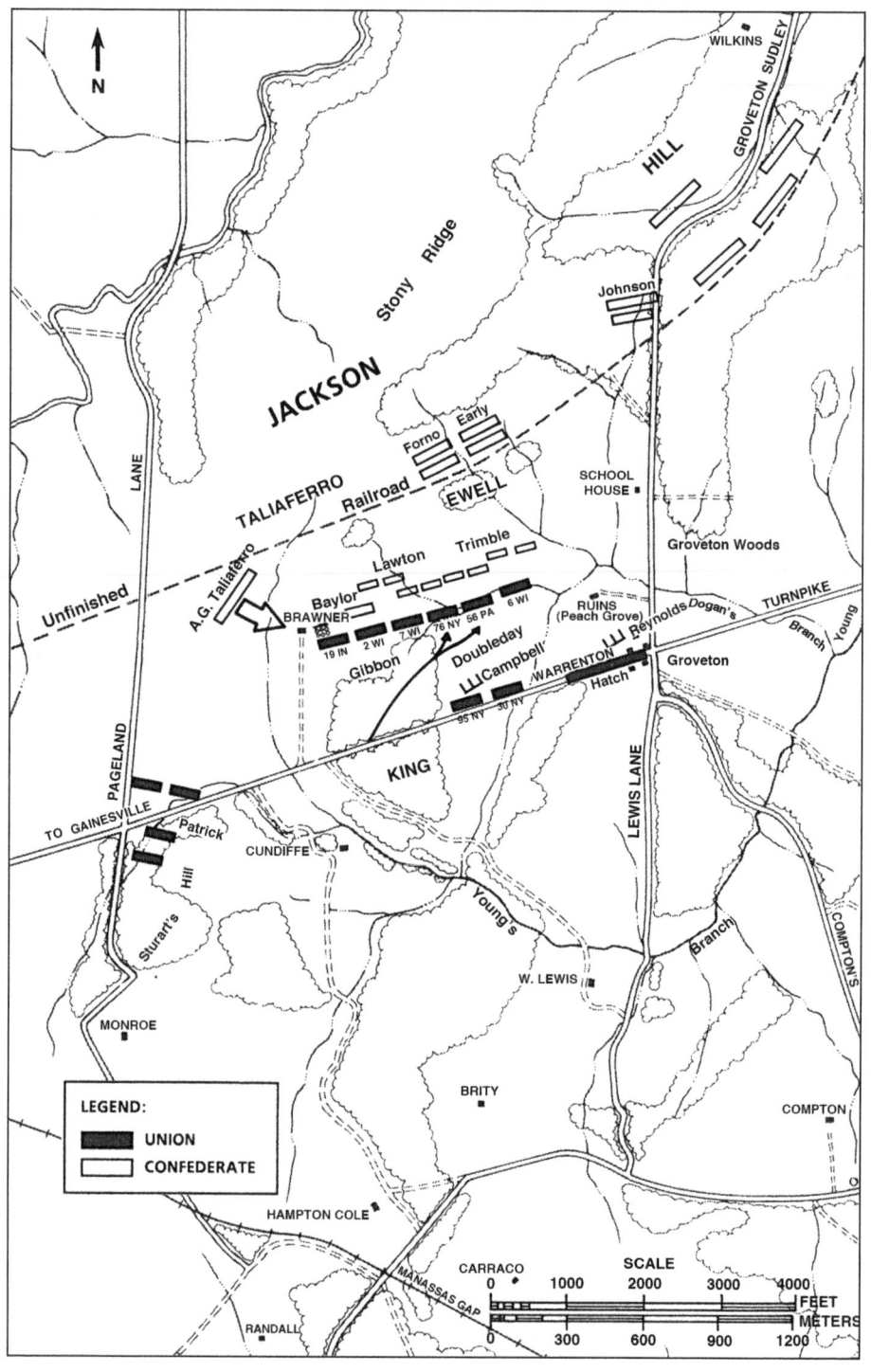

7. Gainesville, Groveton, Second Bull Run 65

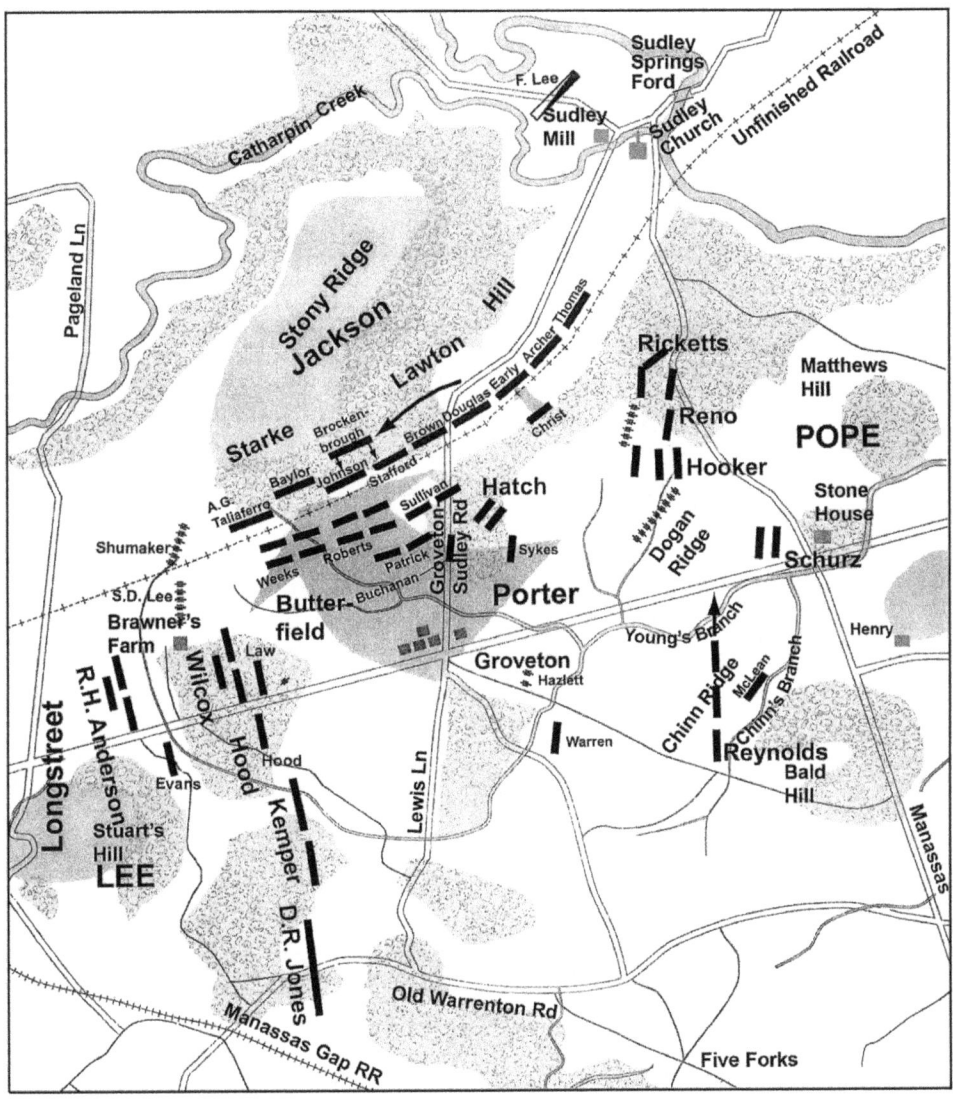

Above: Second Battle of Bull Run, actions 3 P.M., August 30, 1862 (Map by Hal Jespersen, www.cwmaps.com).

Opposite: Battle of Groveton (from John J. Hennessey, *Return to Bull Run: The Campaign and Battle of Second Manassas*, Simon & Schuster, 1993, courtesy John J. Hennessey).

leave in Virginia, Lee was placed in command of the men who were being sent to Harpers Ferry to arrest John Brown, who had seized the arsenal there.

After the start of the Civil War, President Lincoln, at the insistence of Gen. Scott, offered the command of Union forces to Lee. Lee refused, insisting that he could not fight against his native state of Virginia. Lee returned to Virginia, and was placed in charge of the military forces in that state. When Virginia joined the Confederacy, he was appointed as a brigadier general in the Regular Confederate States Army. In March of 1862, he was appointed as the military advisor to Jefferson Davis, and after Gen. Johnston was wounded, Lee was put in command of the Army of Northern Virginia.[2]

By the end of July 1862, the Union Army was spread out in the area of northern Virginia. The First Corps of the Union Army was near Sperryville east of the Blue Ridge Mountains. Gen. Banks was in a town named Little Washington, which was four miles north of Sperryville and McDowell and his corps was in the area of Fredericksburg.[3]

On August 2, Lee ordered Jackson to send a detachment of his cavalry to the area around Orange Court House, where they met a Union cavalry unit and a skirmish resulted. On August 8, Jackson's entire corps followed.

The Union Army had placed an advance outpost at Cedar Run. This outpost was held by cavalry and Crawford's Brigade of infantry. With Jackson's approach, Cedar Run was reinforced by the Second Corps under Banks, with Ricketts' Division in supporting positions of the advanced post. On August 9, Jackson found these forces in strong positions around Cedar Run. The clash that followed found both sides deeply involved until almost midnight.[4]

Hatch's Brigade of King's Division, of which the Fourteenth Brooklyn was a part, was dispatched at daylight of Sunday, August 10. The regiment traveled along the northern bank of the Rappahannock River until it reached Eli's Ford. The men waded across the river, which was waist deep, holding their cartridge boxes above their heads to prevent damage to the ammunition. Once on the opposite shore, they camped for the night. The next day, August 11, the regiment continued its march towards Culpeper. The sun was particularly hot that day and the troops marched under the heavy weight of their backpacks and muskets. The dry dust which was kicked up by the marching regiment filled their ears, noses and mouths choking the soldiers as they made their way. The springs were far apart and inadequate to the needs of the entire regiment. However, they pushed forward. They believed that the needs of their fellow Union soldiers at Cedar Run required this massive effort. Finally, the regiment reached within two miles of Culpeper, where the entire brigade bivouacked in line of battle. Shortly afterward, they learned that the Confederates had withdrawn across the Rapidan River. That day they had marched twenty-eight miles.[5]

On August 16, the regiment left what they had called Camp King and marched six miles to Camp Halstead at Cedar Mountain. The next day at about 5:00 P.M. the Fourteenth marched to the Rapidan River to support the Harris Light Cavalry, which was guarding Mitchell Ford. The purpose of this march was to cover the withdrawal of the Union Army to the north bank of the Rappahannock River. On the night of August 18, the brigade withdrew and became the rear guard of the army. On August 20, the Fourteenth re-crossed the Rappahannock River and was closely followed by the Confederates.

Once Lee reached the Rappahannock, he found the terrain favorable to the Union. The flow of the river was from north to south. Gen. Pope had placed artillery on the bluffs above the river. These guns dominated the approaches to the fords of the river. If Lee tried to force a crossing downstream to the east of Pope's position, it could become very costly for him. Again, moving upstream could result in his moving too far away from Richmond, should the need arise for him to defend the city. Therefore, Lee tried to find an adequate crossing. Beginning on August 21, the Confederate batteries began a constant cannonading all along the Rappahannock. At the same time, Lee ordered Jackson to move up the western bank of the Rappahannock to the north until he found a crossing beyond the Union flank.[6]

During this time, the First Corps, of which the Fourteenth was a part, was given the assignment of protecting the area of the railroad bridge at Rappahannock Station.[7] The cannonading continued for several days while the regiment was moved from one place to another to support the Union artillery or wherever the Confederates seemed to be building a force in order to cross the river.[8]

In a letter to the *Sunday Mercury*, a soldier from the Fourteenth described this period of time:

> Passing through Falmouth some of the villagers showed their sorrow at our departure by many a tear filled eye. It has been scorching, supporting batteries, hunting for and retreating from the enemy ever since. On our way we had to ford the Rappahannock, marching about twenty-four miles and then sleep in our wet clothes on the wet ground. So on reaching near the battle-field of Culpeper (Slaughter's Cedar Mountain), and tired lay by our arms expecting a brisk time the following day, but the enemy had skedaddled as seems to have been their secret and successful forte. A "rest" of a day or two after changing camp was allowed us and gratefully appreciated — then were marched in front of the mountain of the battle-field, in which locality we were camped only one day; and it appears just as the whole army was moving backward our regiment was sent for some purpose to the front on the Rapidan and near where we were bivouacking, the Harris Cavalry had a skirmish....
>
> We returned to where our camp had been ... to be ready to march at 1 o'clock, morning and at that hour were off again. Since that we have passed

through Culpeper, crossed the Rappahannock again, where we had three or four days of supporting batteries to do and afterward through Warrenton, toward the Sulpher Springs....[9]

Another soldier described the cannonading in the following manner,

> The battle opened by the enemy commencing to shell our camps on this side of the Rappahannock (they were on the south side) and such a scampering, you never saw or heard of. We were immediately ordered under arms and marched up the river a short distance where we lay on our faces in the hot boiling sun till dark when we moved about a mile further up the river. All day Thursday, all Friday, and all the afternoon of Saturday, we lay exposed to the most deafening charges of Artillery I ever conceived of. I cannot describe it.[10]

With Jackson continuing to move north, Pope decided to give up his defense of the Rappahannock. General Pope had already written to General Halleck. "Our true position, as it seems to me, should the enemy advance with his whole force, would be considerably in the rear of the Rappahannock, until we are strong enough to advance.... The line of the Rappahannock offers no advantage for defense, but you may rely upon our making a very hard fight in case the enemy advances on us."[11]

With McDowell's entire corps ordered back toward Warrenton, the bridge at Rappahannock Station was burned.[12] The Confederates again continued to move to the right, and Stuart's cavalry, having made a raid in the Union depot at Catlett Station, the brigade, including the Fourteenth, was also moved toward Warrenton. They arrived there on August 23, just after General Stuart had passed through the town.[13]

The next day, August 24, the regiment marched thirteen miles toward Sulphur Springs and camped for the night. On August 26, the regiment marched again in the direction of Sulphur Springs. It was here that another artillery duel occurred. Skirmishing developed all along the banks of the river. The Confederates continued to move to the right along the Rappahannock and succeeded in passing around to the rear of the Union Army.[14]

This was accomplished by Jackson, who had been ordered on August 25, to break away from Lee's main force with his left wing and march by way of the crossing of the upper tributaries through Thoroughfare Gap and strike at the Union supply depot in the Union rear at Manassas Junction. Jackson accomplished this and bivouacked that night near Salem. On the 26th, he passed through Thoroughfare Gap to Gainesville.[15]

The men of the Fourteenth Regiment along with the other regiments and brigades of King's Division discussed the many rumors which were passed from group to group. They had heard through the grapevine that Jackson had outflanked Pope and was in danger of cutting communication with Washington, D.C.[16] Also, considering the amount of miles which the Fourteenth and the brigade had marched and countermarched in the last few days, it was well that they did not know that their division was in effect leaderless. General King had suffered an epileptic seizure and was not fit to carry out his duties as a divisional commander.[17]

On the morning of August 27, Pope ordered McDowell's Corps, which included the Fourteenth, to Gainesville. This was done so that he might concentrate his army in this area. The following day August 28, Pope ordered McDowell's corps to Manassas.[18] When Jackson left Manassas Junction, McDowell was ordered to the area of Centreville, where it was believed that Jackson was heading.[19]

Centreville was a small town on a hill about twenty miles west of Alexandria. The distance between Centreville and Manassas Junction to the south was six miles, and from Centreville to Gainesville, a stop on the Manassas Gap railroad, was nine miles. In traveling this road, the first object of any consequence is the old stone bridge across Bull Run. This is three miles from Centreville. Still another mile down the road you cross Sudley Road and still another mile down the same road brings you to still another crossroad with three or four houses grouped together. This area is called Groveton. About a mile west of Groveton, the Warrenton Turnpike passes through some woods for about a quarter of a mile. Except for this area, the road is well exposed to view from the numerous hills on both sides of the road from the stone bridge to Gainesville.

Another important feature of the area was a line of about a mile of isolated railway grade lying about three thousand feet north from the turnpike at Groveton. The grade consisted of a cut through a considerable distance of high ground and as well as the excavation from the cut which had been used to continue the level of the proposed railroad across the low land at each end of the line. This railroad cut and excavation presented a formidable defensive position, as the Fourteenth was about to see.[20]

General Hatch's Brigade, which consisted of the Twenty-Second New York, the Twenty-Fourth New York, the Thirtieth New York, the Second U.S. Sharpshooters and the Fourteenth Brooklyn, led King's Division in the advance toward Centreville. Hatch's Brigade was followed by Gibbon's Brigade, then Doubleday's and finally the Brigade of Marsena Patrick. McDowell accompanied the Fourteenth Brooklyn, which was at the head of Hatch's Brigade, and was the lead element of King's Division. Nearing the farm of John Brawner, McDowell ordered Hatch to reconnoiter the area north of the road since there was Confederate activity in that area earlier in the day. Hatch ordered the red-legged Fourteenth Brooklyn Regiment to the location as flankers.[21]

While the Fourteenth was crossing the field of the Brawner Farm, General

Hatch had his batteries shell the wooded hills north and east of the brigade line of march. The members of the Fourteenth turned up several Confederate cavalrymen. However, they withdrew when fired upon and no great weight was associated with this encounter.[22] Col. Rufus Dawes of the Sixth Wisconsin remembers "seeing the line of their red legs on the green slopes" as the Fourteenth was reconnoitering in the area of the Brawner Farm.[23]

The movement of the Union forces toward Centreville did not go unnoticed by Jackson and his Confederate troops, who were hidden from view by a large wooded area and on the far side of the unfinished railroad. Jackson had twenty four thousand men stretched across a front that was more than a mile long. General A.P. Hill was on the left between the Manassas Sudley Road and the Groveton Sudley Road, Ewell in the center, just above the railroad cut and Taliaferro on the right just north of the Brawner Farm.[24] The men were resting and eating. Although they were not allowed to light fires which would give away their position, they had plenty of cooked food from their raid at Catlett Station. One account detailed, "The men were packed like herring in a barrel in the woods behind the old railroad: there was scarce room enough to ride between the rows of stacked arms, with the men stretched out on the ground between them, laughing and playing cards."[25]

Jackson was also enjoying a quiet moment when that was ended by the appearance of some of his mounted scouts, who reported the approach of a large force of Union soldiers who were passing eastward along the Warrenton Turnpike and only a few hundred yards from the Confederate position. Jackson immediately mounted his horse and rode off to observe the Federal column.[26] After a short time he returned to his command, where the officers had gathered and were waiting. He rode up to the group "as calm as a May morning and touching his hat in a military salute said in a soft voice as if he had been talking to a friend in ordinary conversation, 'Bring up your men, gentlemen.'"

The officers quickly ran back into the woods to their individual commands and in rapid fashion issued orders to form into brigades which were quickly deployed into line of battle. "Then all advanced in as perfect order as if they had been on parade, their bayonets sparkling in the light of the setting sun and their red battle flags dancing gayly in the breeze."[27]

The Union soldiers who were approaching Jackson's position were King's Division with Hatch's Brigade in the lead. This brigade was what Jackson had seen. By the time Jackson's Confederates had gotten into position they had passed and Gibbon's and Doubleday's brigades were passing in front of his position.[28]

It is also possible that Jackson let Hatch's Brigade pass so that he might judge the size of the total force in front of him since the other brigades of King's Division were strung out for four miles along the Warrenton Turnpike.

Jackson attacked these brigades with both artillery and infantry. The resulting battle, which became known as the Battle of Brawner Farm (Gainesville) fell mostly on the brigade of John Gibbon, which was made up of Midwesterners, including the Nineteenth Indiana, Second Wisconsin, Sixth Wisconsin and Seventh Wisconsin Regiments. Hatch's Brigade was skirmishing to their front and Patrick's Brigade had not come up.[29]

Gibbon's Brigade and two regiments of Doubleday's Brigade were hotly engaged with two regiments of Taliaferro's Division and two regiments of Ewell's Division, both of Jackson's Corps. The Fourteenth along with Hatch's Brigade could only stay under cover and listen until daylight ended. If they were to withdraw, it would have uncovered the flank of the Union line.[30]

Hatch's Brigade, including the Fourteenth, but with the exception of the Thirtieth New York, supported Reynolds' battery during the battle.[31] Afterwards, the brigades remained on the battlefield assisting and caring for the wounded and the dead. One witness described: "Few will ever forget the horrors of that awful night as we stood among the dead and the dying. It was pitiful to hear the Rebels carrying off their wounded comrades and more sad to listen to the groans and crys of our own boys whose suffering we were powerless to relieve."[32]

The brigade commander of the Fourteenth, General Hatch, has been much criticized for not doing more to aid Gibbon's Brigade, however, Bryson writes that the "brigade not only began but ended the fight, and held possession of the field after all others had been restored. It was not until after midnight that we withdrew to Manassas Junction."[33] Most of the criticism for the lack of support for Gibbon's Brigade fell upon Gen. King, who did not commit his brigades to assist Gibbon.[34]

When Gen. Reynolds arrived at the battlefield, he asked Gen. Doubleday what troops had been engaged. Doubleday told him that it was Gibbon's Brigade of King's Division. Reynolds asked why the remainder of the division had not been brought up to assist Gibbon. Many historians have asked the same question.[35]

The entire division of Rufus King withdrew toward Manassas Junction in the early morning hours of August 29. While at this location, the Fourteenth rested and King finally gave up the command of his division to General Hatch. Col. Sullivan of the Twenty-Fourth New York was given command of the brigade. It was at this time that General Porter's Corps was ordered to advance on Gainesville along with King's Division (now under Hatch).[36] General Porter's Corps was fresh from Bristoe Station and King's Division joined them on the march to the old Bull Run battlefield and Gainesville. McDowell joined King's Division on the march. At the juncture of the Warrenton Turnpike and Sudley Springs Road, Porter advanced along Dawkins Branch while McDowell took King's Division farther to the right. His intention was to bring Porter's Corps and King's Division on Jackson's extreme right flank.[37] King's Division halted at the stone house on the Warrenton Road. The records of the Fourteenth indicate that the entire division remained in reserve there until late in the afternoon.[38] Sullivan's Brigade, which was leading the division, was deployed on the left just west of the Sudley Springs Road. The right of the brigade was resting near the road. The Fourteenth was the second regiment behind the Second U.S. Sharpshooters and posted near the Sudley Springs Road.[39]

Later in the day, under the mistaken belief that the Confederates were in retreat, Pope sent orders to McDowell to send a division west on the Warrenton Turnpike. McDowell selected Hatch's Division, who sent Doubleday's Brigade and Sullivan's Brigade, including the Fourteenth, in pursuit.[40] As the brigade neared Young's Run near the old stone house, they passed Gen. McDowell, who told them that the Confederates were in retreat. "Cheered however, by the thought that our efforts were at last crowned with success, we sprang forward with alacrity but it was not long before we were brought to a very sudden and unexpected halt."[41] The brigades proceeded down the turnpike, but they almost immediately became engaged north of the road. Thus, Hatch realized that the Confederates were not retreating and that he was facing a large enemy force.[42]

Just short of the Groveton Crossing, Sullivan's Brigade turned toward the left into a valley which formed the hypotenuse of a triangle, the other two sides of the triangle being the turnpike and Groveton lane. The head of the force was a few hundred feet from the turnpike and a few yards from the lane. Now Sullivan's Brigade, which had followed Doubleday's, was under heavy fire. Soldiers were falling on all sides. The line formation for the brigade was lost but the soldiers continued to shoot at the fire flashes to their front.[43] However, this confusion affected the Confederates as much as the Federals and the Union forces in front of the Confederates seemed formidable. Therefore, Hatch was able to drive the Confederates back beyond Groveton.[44] During this time, troops were seen moving toward the brigade from the trees toward the left. Neither the officers nor the men of the brigade could tell if they were Federals or Confederates. As they approached the brigade, they could hear them yell, "Don't fire at us boys, were coming to help you." Some members of the brigade felt reassured for the assistance of these soldiers. Still others did not believe them and thought they were Confederates. It was not until the approaching soldiers fired their muskets that the gun flashes revealed their gray uniforms.[45]

When the Confederates were within a few yards of the regiment, they opened an enfilading fire which mowed down the front of the regiment, killing and wounding dozens of men. This attack by the Confederates changed the entire complex of the battle and Sullivan's Brigade had to fall back. Col. Fowler was severely wounded. At the time of his injury, Col. Fowler was leading his regiment and urging them forward. A later report praised Col. Fowler for his courage and bravery: "The bullets rained like hail about him as he rode in front of his own men cheering them on, and ... the Rebel artillery was not more than twenty yards off, pouring in its deadly vollies. At first, the Colonel thought he was hit by a piece of shell, and kept his saddle, but the loss of blood soon taught him the real fact, and he gave the command to Major De Bevoise."[46]

Captains Davy and Mallory were mortally wounded. The wounded who were unable to walk were left on the battlefield. The command of the regiment now passed to Lieutenant Col. De Bevoise.[47] Col. Fowler was taken from the battlefield to Washington, D.C. Even in his weakened condition Col. Fowler was able to give important information to Gen. J.D. Cox, who reported on August 30:

> Col. Fowler, Fourteenth Brooklyn, has just passed my headquarters in an ambulance, wounded.... The fighting now going on he reports to be north of the Little River Turnpike and between it and Thoroughfare Gap.... Longstreet passed through the Gap, which was partially obstructed afterwards by our forces by prying off heavy rocks from above. He thinks artillery cannot well get though it, and that the enemy will hardly be able to make use of it as a direct line of retreat.[48]

Years later a soldier of the Fourteenth Regiment wrote his wife about what transpired in August of 1862, he wrote;

> I may say that all through that month of August, day and night with little sleep, sometimes without our Commissary train and scarcity of food for some two weeks disputing his fording of the Rappahannock by giving him determined resistance and spoiling all their attempts, thereby delaying him and looking anxiously to the support promised which was very slow in coming, and which finally brought us in very critical engagements with forces outnumbering us till we (our Division) finally got engaged with Jackson's command on the 28th.of August 1862 commencing the battle of what is known as Second Bull Run, although fought several miles from that of the first, and nearer to and what we call the Battle of Gainesville.
>
> Our General after driving back the enemy with the Division of his command fell back on supports at Manasses, for we had encountered a force largely superior in numbers. Both sides had suffered severely and at Manasses we were very much encouraged at seeing Fitz John Porter's command arrive, and after reconnaissance and getting rations badly needed, for we were without any food, and worn out by the hard service, we were assigned to positions to attack the enemy on different points with results as history tells. It was an attack by our Division which, when we opened the attack, was to be assisted by that of the large force that had so encouraged us seeing them arrive in the morning, only to disappoint and instead of their guns supporting us, we were met my the enemy's guns, now largely reinforced, and those we had counted on for support, withdrawing without firing a gun or making any attempt at

diverting the enemy, throwing all the weight of its force on us already worn out. Notwithstanding, it is known we put up a strong fight only to fall back when outflanked and having to meet the force in front as well as on our flank, the latter where we had to expect friends, and which for a time puzzled us as we thought it was our friends' fire mistaking us for the enemy.
History tells how the General was court martial, and expelled from the army.
Your affectionate Husband
[James Edie][49]
Private, Co. K, 14th. Brooklyn Regiment, New York State Militia.

As a result of the Battle of Groveton, twenty boys from Brooklyn died and sixty were wounded.[50] James Edie was one of those who were wounded.[51] Josiah Grumman, who had been captured by Fitzhugh Lee on November 18, 1961, at Falls Church and had returned to his regiment after his release, was one of those killed as a result of this battle.[52]

Also wounded at the Battle of Groveton was Capt. Charles Baldwin. While he was lying on the battlefield, having been left for dead, a Confederate soldier took his sword, pistol, haversack and canteen. The next day, Capt. Baldwin was recovered by the Confederates and taken to a hospital, where he was treated by a surgeon of the Nineteenth Virginia Infantry. After approximately two weeks, Capt. Baldwin was paroled and taken to Emory Hospital in Washington, D.C. He was discharged as disabled on December 24, 1862.

In 1895, Major John Gould wrote to Col. Fowler, informing him that a former Confederate soldier, John C. Cox of Texas, published a notice in the *Confederate Veteran* that he was in the possession of a pistol taken from the battlefield at Groveton. He further indicated that the pistol was inscribed, "Chas. F. Baldwin, Co. "D." 14th Regt, N.Y.S.M" and that he was prepared to return the gun to whoever was the rightful owner. Fowler then informed Baldwin.

Baldwin and Cox then wrote letters to each other in which they both conveyed their remembrances from that battle over thirty years before. Cox wrote to Baldwin on April 1, 1896.

Well your letter of February 13th came in due course by mail. I cannot describe my feelings on reading your letter and looking at the pistol. My mind reverted to August, 1862, trying to picture the scenes just as I saw them. Well my brother, you know it is often said that no two persons or witnesses saw and related the same circumstance just alike. Your letter was truly interesting to me, yet I could not take in the situation and circumstances just as you related them in your letter. In your description of the pistol I discover that you are a little mistaken. It is a six chambered revolver, instead of a five, and the word presented is not on it. I never took the haversack from a wounded soldier in my life, and as for water, I always gave it when in my power to do so freely. Texan soldiers as a general thing were kind hearted and treated prisoners and wounded soldiers in a kind hearted way. I am not sure whether it was August 29 or 30, 1862, that I obtained the pistol. I know that it was late in the evening and the man from whom I got it was, I thought, shot to pieces, a ball through right breast or shoulder and wounded in hip or leg, and I have no recollections of any words passing between us. I obtained sword belt, sword and pistol, and my recollection is that I did not know of the engraving on the pistol until the next day.

Cox also wrote that he had given the gun to his sister, who had the butt end engraved, "Captured August 30, 1862, by J.C. Cox." When his sister visited him in 1895, the subject of the gun came up and he decided to advertise in the *Confederate Veteran* for its owner.[53]

The decision on the part of Pope to remain on the battlefield and continue the fight was unjudicious. Instead, he should have withdrawn his army across Bull Run and back toward Centreville or even the fortified positions around Washington. In this way he could have joined up with the corps of Sumner and Franklin, who were at that time between Centreville and Washington. Pope's army had suffered many casualties during the previous two days' fighting, thousands of soldiers had been separated from their units, they had little to eat during those two days, the troops had been on the march for ten days and horses of the cavalry and artillery had been harnessed and saddled for ten days.[54]

"The morning of the 30th was clear and beautiful as if smiling on the harvest of death." The division of Hatch was scattered across the battlefield of the previous day and it took most of the morning to gather them together. However, by noon this was accomplished and Sullivan's brigade was formed at the Stone House.[55] As a result of reports on the morning of August 30, Pope believed that the Confederates were retreating. He (issued orders for pursuit Gen. McDowell was named commander of this force, which included most of Pope's command. Porter's Corps was to lead the advance down the Warrenton Turnpike. He would be assisted by Hatch's Division and Reynolds' Division. Ricketts' Division would travel the road leading from Sudley, west to Haymarket and Heintzelman's Corps would follow Ricketts.[56]

Porter and Ricketts soon ran into the Confederates and the amount of artillery fire and musketry proved to them that the enemy was not in retreat, but were instead in force to their front.[57] When Porter received Pope's order to march down the Warrenton Turnpike, he had already commenced on action at Groveton Woods north of the turnpike. Now, with Hatch's Division attached to him, he ordered Hatch's Division to join the right of his corps, which had already engaged the enemy.[58]

Once Gen. Hatch had brought his four brigades to their position on the far right of Porter's Corps, he arranged four brigades in six lines and put the

Second U.S. Sharpshooters, out as skirmishers. Just behind the skirmishers and on the western edge of the woods was Sullivan's Brigade. The brigade was arranged in two lines. The front line was made up of the Twenty-Fourth New York and the Thirtieth New York. Just to the rear of them were the Twenty-Second New York and the Fourteenth Brooklyn. Behind Sullivan would be two lines of Marcena Patrick's Brigade. Behind Patrick would be the brigades of Gibbon and Doubleday, both of whom had suffered heavy losses in the previous two days. They would be formed in a single battle line.[59]

The Twenty-Fourth and the Thirtieth began their march toward the Confederates. The reminder of the brigade, the Twenty-Second and the Fourteenth were watching their progress. As the Twenty-Fourth and the Thirteenth emerged from the woods, they were less than a thousand feet from Stafford's Louisiana Brigade. Before them was a rail fence and beyond that an open field and then the railroad embankment, which was approximately fifteen feet high. The embankment, which was made of broken stones and gravel, had been altered by the Confederates so that a ledge was constructed about five feet below its top. This allowed a man standing on the ledge to expose only his rifle and head to the enemy. The gleam of musket barrels could be seen across the top of the railroad embankment.

As the Federal regiments crossed the field the Confederates opened fire. Many from each regiment fell. Others, seeing the intense fire as well as the fortifications, retreated to their own lines. Theron Haight, a member of the Twenty-Fourth, wrote that less than a dozen men of his regiment, including himself, made it to the embankment. Those few who had made it could not even attempt to drive out the Confederates and therefore hugged the ground. The only thing they could do was look to their rear for assistance.[60]

Within minutes Sullivan's remaining two regiments, the Twenty-Second and the Fourteenth Brooklyn, moved out from the woods and rushed across the field to aid the other two regiments of the brigade. As they crossed the field the Confederates fired into their ranks. Members of the Fourteenth and Twenty-Second could be seen with their arms across their faces, as if to ward off the hail of a storm. At about this time, artillery fire from Longstreet's Batteries, which had newly arrived on the left and about a mile away, began to shell the advancing troops. The Confederates were using solid shot shells and foot long sections of railroad iron, which meant death to anyone in its path.[61] Longstreet later wrote, "It was evident that they could not stand fifteen minutes under the fire of batteries planted at that point."[62] According to Haight, the artillery ripped the lines of the Twenty-Second and the Fourteenth. This fire was more than the New Yorkers could tolerate and their ranks quickly degenerated into confused, frightened men. The artillery which proved so effective was under the command of S.D. Lee.[63]

One of Stafford's regiments, the First Louisiana, was commanded by Col. E.D. Willets who later wrote: "When the smoke arose the line of the Federals was almost swept away with the exception of a gallant band who advance and secured protection on the opposite side of the embankment."[64]

Col. Stafford, who commanded the Louisiana Brigade, describing the action on this day, reported,

> The enemy commenced throwing forward large bodies of skirmishers in the woods on our left, who quickly formed themselves into regiments ... massing a large body of troops at this point with the evident design of forcing us from our position. They made repeated charges upon us while in this position, but were compelled to retire in confusion, sustaining heavy loss and gaining nothing. It was at this point that the ammunition of the brigade gave out. The men procured some from the dead bodies of their comrades, but the supply was not sufficient, and in the absence of ammunition the men fought with rocks and held their position. The enemy retreated.[65]

Sullivan's Brigade retreated to an area north of the Warrenton Turnpike and east of the Manassas Sudley Road, above the Stone House.[66] Later, the brigade joined the remainder of the division and Pope's entire army in the retreat down the Warrenton Turnpike to Centreville.[67]

During the Second Battle of Bull Run, Gen Reynolds dispatched several Pennsylvania regiments to assist Meade, whose troops had run into resistance from Hood's men near Groveton, in the area where the Fourteenth had fought the previous day. As the Pennsylvanians crawled through the field, they came across the dead bodies of members of the Fourteenth Brooklyn. At first, just seeing the red trousers and blue jackets, one of them thought it to be colorful display. However, as he got closer he remembered: "It was sad to gaze upon their cold pale faces."[68]

The Fourteenth had suffered badly during the Battle of Groveton on August 29, and therefore their losses on August 30, at the Second Battle of Bull Run, were severe in relation to the amount of men available for service. On that day five boys from Brooklyn lost their lives and twenty were wounded.[69]

8. South Mountain

Army of the Potomac	**First Brigade**
Major General George B. McClellan	Col. Walter Phelps, Jr.
First Corps	**14th Militia Regiment**
Major Gen. Joseph Hooker	Maj. William H. DeBevoise
Brig. Gen. George G. Meade	**22nd New York, Regiment**
First Division	Lieut. Col. John McKie, Jr.
Brig. Gen. Rufus King	**24th New York**
Brig. Gen. John P. Hatch	Capt. John D. O'Brian
Brig. Gen. Abner Doubleday	**30th New York**
	Col. William M. Searing

On August 31, McDowell's Corps regrouped and was ordered to deploy behind Centreville and to act as a rear guard. As part of this deployment the Fourteenth was ordered to an area near Fairfax Courthouse and arrived there at about 5:00 P.M. on September 1. They bivouacked here for the night. McDowell had been ordered to intercept the Confederates who were moving down the Little River Turnpike toward the area of Fairfax Courthouse. On September 2, McDowell and his corps were ordered to retreat to Hall's Hill and Upton Hill, to again defend Washington. The Fourteenth had left Fairfax Courthouse at about 2 P.M. and encamped at Camp Marion on Upton Hill at about 7:00 P.M.[1] on September 3.

General Halleck, who was the general-in-chief of the Union Armies, sent a letter to General McClellan indicating his belief that because the Confederates were stymied in their attempt to capture Washington, he thought they might invade Pennsylvania or Maryland. Halleck ordered McClellan, who was newly installed as the commander of the Army of the Potomac, to organize a force to meet this threat.[2]

George Brinton McClellan was born in Philadelphia, Pennsylvania, on December 3, 1826. He graduated from West Point in 1846 and ranked second in his class of fifty-nine. He served in the Corps of Engineers until the outbreak of the Mexican War, when he was attached to the army of General Winfield Scott. McClellan received praise for his gallantry, zeal and ability in the construction of bridges and roads. After the Mexican War he wrote manuals for the army and served on engineering duty and explored for the source

8. South Mountain

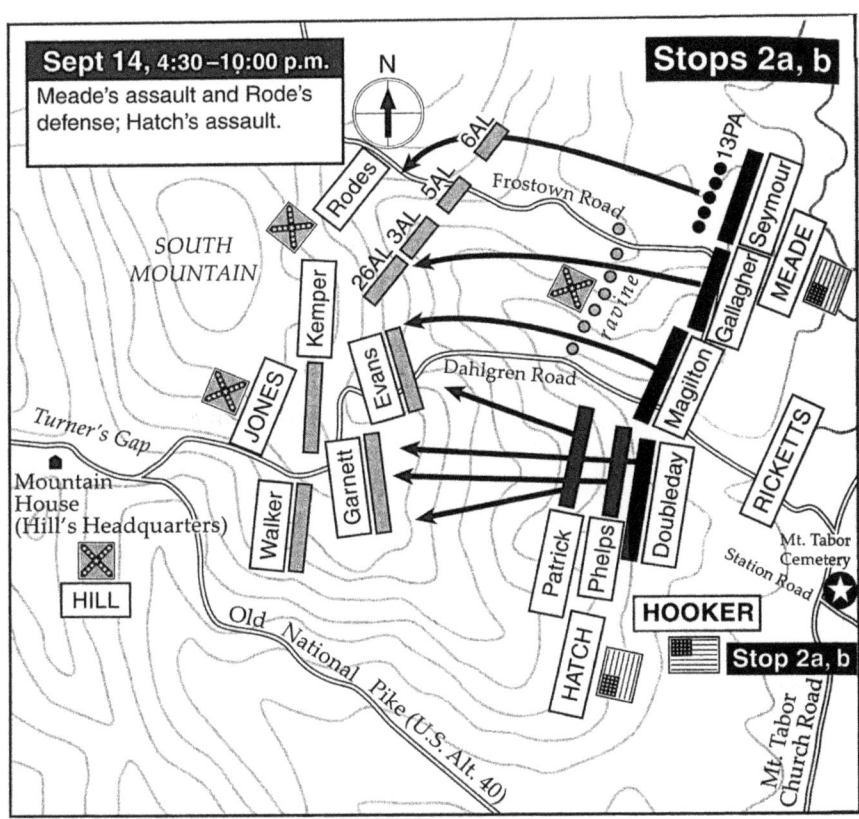

Battle of South Mountain (from Ethan S. Rafuse, *Antietam, South Mountain and Harpers Ferry: A Battlefield Guide*, University of Nebraska Press, 2008. Reprinted by permission of the University of Nebraska Press).

of the Red River. McClellan also surveyed several possible routes for the transcontinental railroad. He was sent abroad to study the armies of Europe and the Crimean War. As an outcome to this trip, he invented the "McClellan saddle" which became the standard for the army until mechanization put an end to the use of horses. In 1857, he resigned his commission to become chief engineer for the Illinois Central Railroad. When the Civil War broke out, McClellan was the president of the Ohio and Mississippi Railroad and became a major general of Ohio volunteers. Because of his reputation for efficiency, capability and organization, President Lincoln appointed him major general in the Regular Army.[3]

McClellan, whose army had been trying to capture Richmond in what came to be known as the Peninsula Campaign, could not arrive in time to help Pope at Second Bull Run. Many historians believe that McClellan delayed his arrival so that Pope, if defeated, would lose favor in Washington.

In fact, McClellan received orders to reinforce Pope on August 3; however, his troops did not begin to leave to reinforce Pope until August 14, and his last units did not leave until September 3, a full month after he received his orders. McClellan wrote to his wife, "I don't see how I can remain in the service if placed under Pope — It would be too great a disgrace." Another time he wrote, if "Pope is beaten in which case they may want me to save Washn again ... I know that with God's help I can save them."[4]

General Halleck was correct in his analysis. General Lee was indeed planning an invasion of Maryland. His reasons for attempting this were many. Lee hoped to inflict upon the demoralized Union Army a horrendous defeat as he had just accomplished at Second Bull Run. Also, he hoped that the people of Maryland would rise against the federal government, causing the government to tie up tens of thousands of troops in the Rebellious state.[5] Between September 4 and 7, the Confederates crossed the Potomac east of the Blue Ridge Mountains at the fords near Leesburg, Virginia. This was done so that the Federals would have to withdraw from the south bank of the Potomac to defend against a possible threat to Washington and Baltimore. This withdrawal also preserved for the Confederates their communications with, as well as the safety of, those who were engaged in the removal of the wounded and the captured supplies of the Second Bull Run battlefield. After this was accomplished, Lee proposed to move his army into western Maryland so that he might establish communications with Richmond through the Valley of the Shenandoah and threaten an invasion of Pennsylvania, thereby cajoling the Federals farther from their base of supplies.[6]

In order for Lee to open a line of communication with Richmond, he had to open the Shenandoah Valley by capturing Harpers Ferry. In order to do this Lee ordered General Jackson down the south side of the Potomac River to Harpers Ferry. General McLaws' Division along with Gen. R.A. Anderson's Division were ordered to capture Maryland Heights north of Harpers Ferry above the Potomac and opposite it. General Walker was to seize Loudoun Heights east of Shenandoah River where it unites with the Potomac. Gen. D.H. Hill was given the assignment of protecting the passes through South Mountain so that the Union Army could not attack the Confederates at Maryland Heights from the rear and relieve Harpers Ferry. Lee directed that all elements were to rejoin at Boonesboro or Hagerstown west of South Mountain as soon as Harpers Ferry was captured.[7]

Meanwhile, on September 6, the Fourteenth Regiment left Camp Marion at about 10:00 P.M. and crossed the Aqueduct Bridge across the Potomac River, marched through Georgetown and Washington, and made camp near Leesburg on September 7th. The Fourteenth remained here until September 9, when it left about 3:00 P.M. and marched to Rockville, Maryland. The regiment continued their march on the next day and arrived at Lisbon at about 4:00 P.M. They remained here until September 12, when the regiment marched to New Market, arriving at about 8:00 P.M. and bivouacked here for the night. On September 13, the regiment marched to within a mile of Frederick City and again bivouacked for the night.[8]

The stage was being set for an encounter between the Union Army of McClellan and the Army of Northern Virginia. Originally Lee was not going to contest the passes through South Mountain. However, Jackson failed to promptly subdue the Union forces at Harpers Ferry and therefore delayed the reuniting of Lee's army at Boonesboro or Hagerstown. This along with McClellan's rapid movement of his army to South Mountain forced Lee to defend the three passes through South Mountain so that he might obtain the needed time for his army to reunite.[9]

South Mountain is part of the Blue Ridge Mountains. The topography of the mountain is irregular and marked by many ravines, hollows and hills which gently crest toward the top. The sides of these hills contain forests and thick ground cover. Near the top of the hill the forests had to be cut in part so that farm houses, pastures and fields could be put in places. These were bordered by rail fences and rock walls that would play a large part in the coming battle.[10]

There were four main roads that passed through South Mountain from the Middletown Valley. The National Turnpike was the main highway that passed through Frederick, Maryland, and across South Mountain at Turner's Gap (sometimes called Curry's Gap). The Sharpsburg road crosses South Mountain less than a mile south at Fox's Gap, the Burkittsville road crossed the mountain a few miles farther south at Crampton Gap, and the road to Hagerstown was parallel to the National Road.[11]

At this time, the Fourteenth was part of Hooker's Corps (First), Hatch's division (First) and Phelps brigade (First) and was commanded by Col. DeBevoise, who had been in command since Col. Fowler was wounded at the Battle of Groveton. Besides the Fourteenth, Phelps brigade included the Twenty-Second New York, Twenty-Fourth New York, Thirtieth New York and the Second U.S. Sharpshooters. These were the same units which fought together during the battles of Gainesville, Groveton and Second Bull Run. These units were again destined to play a part in this battle at South Mountain and in particular the battle at Turner's Gap. The entire division had suffered greatly during these battles. The Fourteenth Regiment was reduced to about one hundred men by the time the battle at Turner's Gap took place.[12]

General Lee had ordered D.H. Hill's Division to Boonesboro with the main intent of preventing the Union forces at Harpers Ferry from escaping through Pleasant Valley.[13] However, with Hooker advancing so rapidly, Lee ordered D.H. Hill to defend the passes using part of his five brigades consisting of about 5,000 men.[14] Hill thought he would be facing a small force of about two brigades of Union troops. However, from the top of the mountain Hill described what he saw.

> I had seen from the lookout station near the Mountain House the vast army of McClellan spread out before me. The marching columns as far as the eye could see in the distance ... many of the troops had already arrived and were in double lines of battle and those advancing were taking up positions as fast as they arrived. It was a grand and glorious spectacle, and it was impossible to look at it without admiration. I had never seen so tremendous an army before, and I did not see one like it afterward.[15]

Turner's Gap, which was west of Middletown and on the road to Boonesboro, was the main site for the Battle of South Mountain and where the Fourteenth Regiment was destined to fight. On September 13 and in the early morning hours of September 14, few Confederates occupied this particular gap through the mountain. McClellan, had he moved quicker, could have secured this pass without much opposition. However, his delay allowed the Confederates to move more of Hill's brigade from Boonesboro and even allowed Longstreet to move in troops from Hagerstown.[16]

On September 14, the Fourteenth left its bivouac near Frederick City as part of Hookers Corps, which was being roused from its camps near the Monocacy River. The division was now under the command of Gen. Hatch, Gen. King having just been relieved of command. The division passed through the town of Middleton and arrived at Catochin Creek at the base of South Mountain.[17]

The Confederates had installed themselves at the top of the mountain and began to open fire from their batteries which occupied the crest of the hill. In order to avoid this artillery fire, the brigade and division were ordered to leave the main road and march to the right, which brought them to the base of South Mountain and to a stone church at the foot of the mountain. At this point, Col. Phelps, brigade commander of the Fourteenth regiment, received orders from Gen. Hatch. The brigade was to advance up the mountain, "in column of division at half distance, preserving the intervals of deployment."[18]

At the top of the hill, D.H. Hill described the advance of Hatch's division as being in three lines, a brigade in each: "Hatch's general and field officers were on horseback, his colors were all flying and the alignment of his men seemed to be perfectly preserved."[19]

As Gen. Hatch's Division, including the Fourteenth, was advancing up the mountain, there were no Confederate troops to oppose them. Gen. D.H. Hill was able to get some artillery from Col. Cutts to bring fire down upon the Union forces. However, this fire was ineffective due to the inexperience of the gunners, the great angles of depression which had to be used on the cannons themselves and the general terrain.[20] At about 5:00 P.M., Gen. Longstreet sent Gen. James Kemper's brigade, consisting of the 1st, 7th, 11th, 17th, and 24th Virginia regiments, and Gen. Richard Garnett's brigade, consisting of the 8th, 18th, 19th, 28th, and 56th Virginia regiments, to oppose the advance of General Hatch's Division.[21] The division marched up the mountain headed by two regiments of Patrick's brigade, who served as skirmishers, and the remaining two regiments serving as their support. These regiments were to be followed by Phelps' brigade, which included the Fourteenth. They were to advance at about 200 paces behind Patrick's regiment. Phelps' brigade was to be followed by Doubleday's brigade again at about 200 paces behind Phelps.[22]

Phelps advanced his brigade — consisting of the 22nd, 24th and 30th New York regiments as well as the Fourteenth Brooklyn regiment — in battle formation. Phelps, in his haste, inadvertently pushed his brigade through a gap in the line of Patrick's skirmishers who were, as a result, on his left and right. Phelps halted his brigade and sent word to Gen. Hatch in order to get instructions regarding his overrunning the skirmishers. Hatch responded by riding to the front. He personally ordered the skirmishers to continue their advance and ordered Phelps' brigade to continue their advance at a distance of 30 paces to their rear. While waiting for Patrick's skirmishers to clear the interval, Phelps rode his horse to the edge of the woods. When he saw that the Rebels could not see his approach, he rode back to his regiments and ordered them forward.

The Fourteenth Brooklyn was on the right and extended beyond the Confederate lines as the brigade moved toward the crest of the mountain. The 8th.and 18th Virginia regiments fired wildly at the oncoming brigade. As Phelps' brigade returned their fire, Gen. Hatch urged them forward and the brigade charged the crest of the mountain. Skirmish lines disappeared as the brigades of Patrick and Phelps merged together.[23]

Ezra Carman who was at this battle, describes this advance as follows:

> At the edge of the woods is a fence, and beyond, a cornfield on the left and a large open field on the right. The skirmishers of the enemy hold the cornfield and the fences ... across the open field a large force of the enemy is rapidly approaching the fence in our front, an important position which we are just in time to secure.
>
> Our skirmishers are already up to the fence ... Hatch's brigade, on the left, reaches it at about the same time, and in another moment a fierce volley wel-

comes our friends in gray, and they are driven back with terrible loss to the fence on the other side, where they rally and return the fire. Rapid and continuous is the fusillade that follows; the mountain top reeks with sulfurous veil, out of which rises a horrid turmoil, and the echoes fly to hide in every nook and valley, so peacefully slumbering an hour ago, while beneath its deadly shadow a mortal struggle piles its earth with victims.[24]

Bryson, in his writings about the Thirtieth Regiment, indicated that the advancing Union and Confederate lines were racing to obtain possession of the fence which was between them.[25] Each side visited devastation upon the other. The brigade of the Fourteenth Brooklyn lost thirty-five percent of their effective force in just fifteen minutes.[26]

As would be true at the Battle of Antietam, which would take place in just three days, the Fourteenth had with them recruits who were not yet familiar with or trained in the different aspects of soldiering. In many instances, out of loyalty to the regiment, these recruits wanted to take part in upcoming battles.

Capt. Cardona told about a "rookie" who joined the regiment just before the Battle of South Mountain. Capt. Cardona described him as "handsome and over six feet in height." Since he had been with the regiment only five days, Cardona asked him if he understood how to load and fire his rifle and "that if he did not feel familiar enough with a soldier's duties to go into battle, I would leave him behind. The young man insisted upon going in with us."

As the battle began the Fourteenth was ordered to charge up the mountain. When the order was given the recruit rushed to the front of the line. Before fifty feet had been covered he was struck by a bullet to the neck and fell dying. His rifle contained three full loads stacked one on top of the other, never having been discharged.[27]

After ordering an attack on the Confederate positions, Gen. Hatch was wounded in the leg and command of the division was given to Brig. Gen. Abner Doubleday.[28]

The Fourteenth proceeded up the side of the mountain at a slow pace due to the fallen trees and boulders which were scattered along their path. They were following close behind the skirmish line and could come upon the enemy at any time lurking behind these natural fortifications. As the line was approaching the summit, the sound of shots could be heard up and down the line. The order to charge was given and the Fourteenth quickly moved up to the crest of the mountain. They reached the Confederate skirmishers before they could retreat to the safety of their main force. The skirmishers were captured and the crest taken. For a brief time the Fourteenth had outdistanced the remainder of the brigade, and the Confederates counterattacked to drive the Fourteenth from the crest. However, the Fourteenth held them off with fatal volleys of rifle fire. The Fourteenth continued its charge and the Confederates continued to retreat.[29]

After some of the hardest fighting of the day, Garnett's Brigade—consisting of the 8th, 18th, 19th, and 28th Virginia regiments—finally broke. Col. Phelps ordered the Fourteenth Regiment northeast along the wood line to deliver enfilade fire on the cornfield to their front, "which did great execution."[30]

The Fourteenth Brooklyn, which remained on the right of the line, was relieved by the Twenty-Sixth New York[31] of Rickett's Division. Ezra Carman of Doubleday's Division described the relief of Hatch's unit;

> Another minute and the edge of the woods is gained, and there at the fence which skirts it at Hatch's brigade, standing, falling, desperately fighting at this bloodily contested boundary. Cheer upon cheer from our men goes up to Heaven, and now, in admirable order, they rush into their places, Hatch's brigade falling back to rest awhile after their fence encounter.[32]

In a letter, Joseph Pettiner, who had joined the Fourteenth Brooklyn in August 1862, described his experience at South Mountain:

> In the afternoon our lieutenant came and gave us 40 rounds of cartridges apiece. We were then marched until we came to the bottom of a hill covered with woods. Here we discovered parties of men taking aim from behind trees, etc. and firing at the "Rebs." Just ahead we could hear the batteries playing upon each other. We would advance a few steps, then lay down, rise up go a few steps further, then lay down. Then we all advanced and fired, driving the Rebels into a corn field in front of us and on top of the mount.
>
> I fired off nearly all my ammunition, then we were relieved by Doubleday's Brigade.... I came off "without a scratch," only in getting from the woods I tore all one side of my red pants, from the knee down.[33]

As night came Phelps ordered the Fourteenth and the other regiments in his brigade to fall back in order after being relieved. Phelps formed his brigade into a third line of battle behind Ricketts and Doubleday. These three lines occupied the field that night.[34]

During the night of September 14, Gen. McClellan notified General in Chief Halleck of his victory at South Mountain and indicated that he did not know whether the Confederates would retreat during the night or would contest the field again in the morning with even greater forces.[35] As day broke over the mountains on September 15, the intensity of the carnage of the previous day's battle became evident. The Twenty-Sixth Regiment, which had relieved the Fourteenth and had spent the night with their guns loaded and their bayonets fixed, saw the dead and wounded of their Virginia opponents lying in piles of three and four just 30 yards to their front.[36]

Lee decided not to continue the engagement at South Mountain and therefore withdrew both Longstreet and D.H. Hill across Pleasant Valley and Elk Ridge toward the town of Sharpsburg and the creek called Antietam.[37]

In his battle report Gen. Doubleday commended Col. Phelps for his "gallantry and good conduct" which contributed to the victory.[38] General Hatch reported that Col. Phelps "displayed the most distinguished courage, bringing up and handling his brigade in a most gallant manner." Hatch also commended Major DeBevoise, who commanded the Fourteenth New York State Militia by stating that "he gallantly led a gallant regiment, which this day added fresh laurels to those already won.[39] Col. Phelps, in his report, states: "I cannot allow the conduct of Lieut. Cranford, Fourteenth New York State Militia and Lieut. Schenek, Twenty-Second New York volunteers, aides to myself, to pass unnoticed. I was often obliged to send them, through a galling fire, to different parts of the field with orders. There conduct on this occasion was most gallant, and all that I could have desired."[40]

In a letter to his wife, Eliza, dated September 16, 1862, Col. Phelps wrote: "The 14th did finely, in fact all the regiments behaved as well as I could have wished."[41]

At the battle of South Mountain, the Fourteenth Regiment again gained glory but lost seven men killed and thirteen wounded.[42]

9. Antietam

Army of the Potomac
  Major General George B. McClellan
First Corps
  Major Gen. Joseph Hooker
  Brig. Gen. George G. Meade
First Division
  Brig. Gen. Rufus King
  Brig. Gen. John P. Hatch
  Brig. Gen. Abner Doubleday
First Brigade
  Col. Walter Phelps, Jr.

14th Brooklyn Militia
  Col. DeBevoise
22nd New York Regiment
  Lieut. Col. John McKie, Jr.
24th New York Regiment
  Capt. John D. O'Brian
30th New York Regiment
  Col. William M. Searing
2nd U.S. Sharpshooters
  Col. Henry Post

    When Lee withdrew from South Mountain, he retreated toward Keedysville. With him was D.H. Hill and the brigades of McRae, Ripley and Anderson along with the brigades of Kemper, Garnett, Drayton and Walker. He intended to make a defensive stand here. However, Lee received information that the area around Keedysville was not suitable for this purpose. The high ground around Keedysville was bare of any area which could be used to anchor this section of his line. Lee, therefore, decided to withdraw from Keedysville and cross Antietam Creek toward Sharpsburg.[1]

    Ezra Carmen, who was at the Battle of Antietam, reported that Sharpsburg "occupies a saucer shaped depression in the Antietam Valley about two miles from its junction with the Potomac." The importance of the town lies in the fact that four major roads passed through or near it. The Hagerstown Turnpike began at Sharpsburg and ran north. The Boonesboro Turnpike ran east and slightly north of Sharpsburg and crossed Antietam Creek about a mile east of the town. The Harpers Ferry road started in Sharpsburg and went due south. Finally, the Shepherdstown Road, which started in Sharpsburg, and ran slightly south of west. This road reached the Potomac River at the Shepherdstown Ford approximately two and a half miles away.[2]

    The topography of the area dictated the scope and intensity of the battle. Sharpsburg sits almost at the confluence of Potomac River and Antietam Creek, which forms an irregularly shaped triangle. A low ridge runs north-south and the Hagerstown Turnpike ran parallel to this ridgeline and there

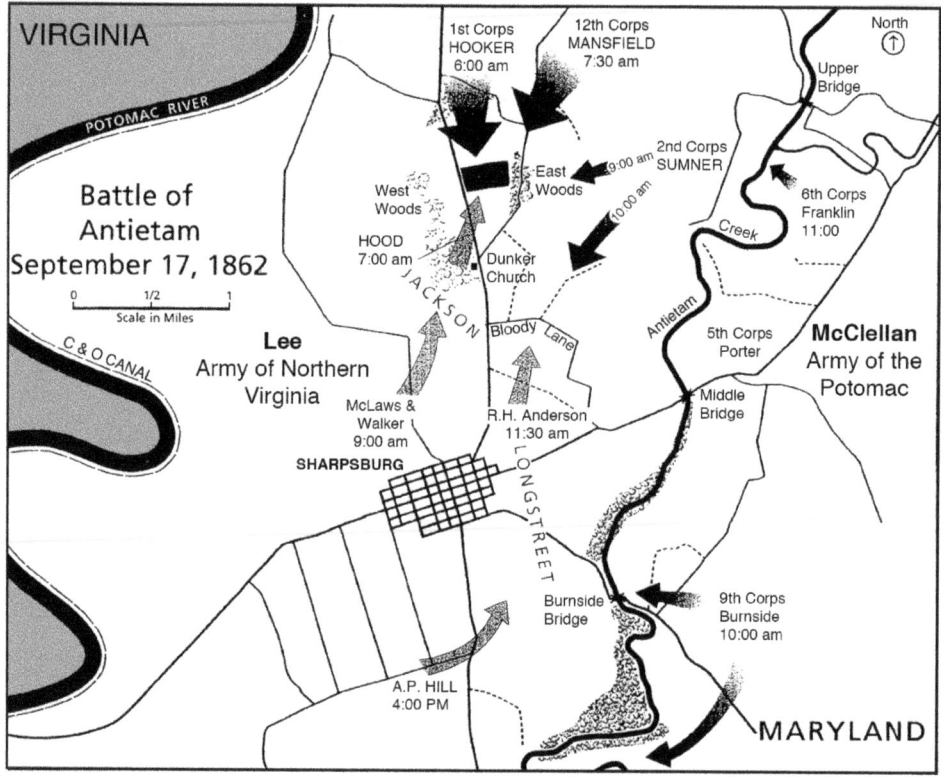

Battle of Antietam (courtesy National Parks Service).

were low rolling hills between the two bodies of water.³ A mile to the north of Sharpsburg was the Dunkard Church. This church stood where the Hagerstown Turnpike met the Smoketown Road. In addition, there were three stands of trees in the area. The north woods was situated on both sides of the Hagerstown Turnpike and about two miles from Sharpsburg and just above the cornfield which was to play such a significant part in the coming battle, particularly for the Fourteenth Brooklyn. Approximately half a mile north of the Dunkard Church and on both sides of the Smoketown Road was East Woods. The West Woods was located on the western side of the Hagerstown Turnpike and surrounded the Dunkard Church on three sides. Because of the numerous turnpikes, roads and farm lanes that crisscrossed the area as well as the strategic location of the wooded areas, there were very few impediments to the movement of large numbers of troops.⁴

The only obstacle in the area of battle was Antietam Creek itself. The creek was not particularly wide or deep. However, it was just wide enough and just deep enough to require a bridge for a large force to use in order to cross. Three bridges crossed the Antietam in the area of the battle. The landscape around the Southern Bridge was difficult and provided a limited area for the movement of troops. The Middle Bridge was heavily defended. The only crossing that met the requirements was the Upper Bridge.[5]

Gen. Lee placed his army on a line approximately four miles long in front of the town of Sharpsburg. It extended north along the Hagerstown Turnpike and south to about a mile below the Lower Bridge across the Antietam. Lee found this area to be good defensive ground and had a clear field of fire for the approximately 200 cannons that he had available for this battle. He also understood that the Hagerstown Turnpike, the country roads and farm lanes in the area provided excellent mobility for the movement of troops.[6]

At about daylight on the morning of the fifteenth of September, D.H. Hill was the first of Lee's army to reach the area of Antietam Creek. He took up position between the main Sharpsburg ridge and the west bank of the Antietam. D.R. Jones' division took up position on Hill's left. From this position he was overlooking the Hagerstown Turnpike in the area of the Dunkard Church and the West Woods.[7]

McClellan's plan of battle was to attack the Confederate left and then attack the right. If one or the other attacks would be successful, he would then attack the center of the Confederate line. On the afternoon of the 16th of September, McClellan ordered Hooker's Corps to cross Antietam Creek by way of the Upper Bridge near Keedysville, which was left undefended by the Confederates.[8]

In the early evening of September 16, the Fourteenth Regiment, leading the brigade, crossed the Antietam. While using two companies of the regiment as skirmishers, Col. DeBevoise moved forward towards a wooded area to his front. The skirmishers soon encountered the sentries of the Confederate force. After a brief firefight the enemy remained quiet except for the occasional shot from a picket. Since it was rapidly growing dark, the soldiers of the Fourteenth could see the flash from the guns on both sides.

At about 8 o'clock on that evening, the Fourteenth finally got into the position it was going to occupy for that night. Orders were issued to the regiment that no fires were to be lighted since this would draw Confederate fire. "To be deprived of our coffee was to withhold from us the panacea of nearly all a soldiers ills and discomforts, but under the circumstances the order 'No fires' was imperative, and submitted to without much grumbling." The Fourteenth bivouacked there for the night. They slept in line of battle with or near their arms.[9]

Hooker's objective was to gain the high ground between the Potomac and Antietam and then to follow that high ground toward the left of Lee's army. Within a short time, Hooker's skirmishers met Hood's advanced positions. The shooting became constant and Hood eventually retreated during the darkness.[10]

The Fourteenth was part of the division of Abner Doubleday. Abner Doubleday was born at Ballston Spa, New York, on June 26, 1819. He graduated from West Point in 1842 and served in the Mexican War. In April of 1861, he was garrisoned at Fort Sumter in Charleston Harbor and was captured after its surrender. Following his release by the Confederates, Doubleday served in the Shenandoah Valley and was promoted to brigadier general of volunteers.[11]

As part of Doubleday's division, the Fourteenth was posted along Hagerstown Turnpike facing west. The line of Doubleday's Division connected with Mead's Division and was perpendicular to it. Mead's division was positioned north of the North Woods and faced to the south. Hooker's entire corps, including the Fourteenth, rested on their arms that night with occasional harassment by skirmish fire throughout the night from the Confederates.[12]

In the early hours of September 17, Gen. Hooker surveyed the landscape to his front. From this vantage point, he could see that from the area of his corps by the North Woods and the Joseph Poffenberger farm, the Hagerstown Turnpike went south past the farm of David Miller and past his corn field, which stood tall and ripe between the turnpike and East Woods and finally to the high ground around Dunkard Church. Hooker had decided to attack due south along the Smoketown Road and the Hagerstown Turnpike, through the Miller Cornfield, and then take the high ground around the Dunkard Church.[13]

The high plateau around the church was the key to the Battle of Antietam. The ground in front of the church fell off sharply and led to the Sunken Road. This in turn was the lynch pin to the brigades covering the Middle Bridge.[14] If Hooker could take the plateau, then he would have outflanked D.H. Hill's brigades of Colquitt, Garland, Rodes and Anderson, who occupied the Sunken Road to the east of the Hagerstown Turnpike. However, in order for Hooker to reach the plateau, his brigade and divisions had to pass Stuart's artillery positioned on Nicodemus Hill, which was west of the Hagerstown Turnpike, Poagues' artillery in the West Woods and S.D. Lee's artillery atop the plateau near the Dunkard Church. In addition to the artillery, he had to surmount the brigades of Lawton, and Jones in the West Woods about four hundred yards north of the Dunkard Church. Lawton had another brigade in a pasture south of the cornfield and still another still farther east on the farm of Samuel Mumma. Hood's division had been relieved the previous night after their engagement and they were in reserve around the Dunkard Church, and Early's Brigade was on the Confederates' left protecting Stuart's artillery on Nicodemus Hill. Winder's Brigade along with that of Stark and Taliaferro were situated west of the Hagerstown Turnpike in the area of the West Woods.[15]

Unaware of all that stood in his path, Hooker started his corps at about dawn, just after the Union and Confederate artillery began to exchange shots. As Hooker started he placed Ricketts Division on the left with Meads' Division in reserve and Doubleday's division on the right. Gibbon's brigade was placed in front followed by the Fourteenth and the remainder of Phelps' Brigade.[16] After a short time, Hooker realized that the Confederates had occupied the Miller cornfield to his front.[17]

As Gibbon's brigade moved southward, the artillery on Nicodemus Hill began to rip into his brigade, which was led by the Sixth Wisconsin. The brigade of Gibbon, followed by Phelps, finally pushed the Confederates out of the area around the Miller farm house. Ahead lay the cornfield. Phelps followed Gibbon into the cornfield and deployed his brigade in line of battle about 50 paces behind Gibbon.[18] When Gibbon's Brigade was emerging from the Southern part of the cornfield, the Confederates who were behind a fence and sheltered by woods arose in front of them and both sides fired simultaneously. The effect on each side was devastating. "Men, I can not say fell; they were knocked out of their ranks by dozens. But we jumped over the fence and pushed on. Loading, firing and shouting as we advanced."

The Fourteenth moved forward to the assistance of the Sixth Wisconsin and filled in the gaps in their line that was caused by Confederate fire. "Men and officers of New York and Wisconsin are fused into a common mass, in the frantic struggle to shoot fast. Everybody tears cartridges, loads, and passes guns or shoots…. The soldier who is shooting is furious in his energy. The soldier who is shot looks around for help with an imploring agony of death on his face."[19]

The Wisconsin troops of Rufus Dawes and Fourteenth Brooklyn continued relentlessly south and into the pasture of D.R. Miller just below the cornfield. By 6:45 A.M., these troops had covered several hundred yards of open space and were about one third of the distance from the Miller cornfield and the high ground around the Dunkard Church. Under this severe pressure, the three regiments of Lawton's Georgia brigade began to retreat. As they were running, a new threat to the advance appeared on the field. From the West Woods and through the pasture west of the Hagerstown Turnpike, Gen. Starke, who had replaced Gen. Jones as division commander, brought up his two remaining Confederate brigades. The advance of Gibbon and Phelps was finally stopped.

However, Starke's men were caught in a murderous crossfire of rifles and artillery. After Starke was wounded (he later died) and about fifteen minutes into the attack, the Confederates were ordered to retreat.[20] Starke's men "left a grim tableau of wounded and dead heaped up on the ground and spread-eagled on the fence."[21] Dawes later wrote, "The men are loading and firing with demoniacal fury.... The whole battlefield before us is covered with Rebels fleeing for life, into the woods. Great numbers of them are shot while climbing over the high post and rail fences along the turnpike."[22]

The troops of Gibbon and Phelps again began to advance, cheering as they went.[23] Lawton's brigades began to disappear, as did his battle lines. The Union troops had crushed two of Jackson's divisions and were about to turn Lee's left flank, and were in sight of the Dunkard Church. It was 7:00 A.M.[24]

The Fourteenth, along with the remainder of Phelps' and Gibbon's brigades resumed the advance only to hit head on into the division of Gen. John Bell Hood, consisting of his old brigade now commanded by Col. William Wofford and the brigade of Col. Evander Law, totaling approximately 2,300 men. Hood's division had engaged these same troops of Doubleday as well as those of Meade the previous night. Hood's division was enjoying their first hot meal in several days when they were called upon to stem the advance of Phelps' and Gibbon's troops. Hood placed his division across the battlefield from the Hagerstown Turnpike across to the East Woods and started his advance, thus countering all the divisions Hooker had placed in the field.[25]

Hood's Division consisted in part of the Texas Brigade. This was made up of the First, Fourth and Fifth Texas, the Eighteenth Georgia and Hampton's Legion. A member of this unit, after being pulled away from the only food his unit had had in days, described what it was like to be placed under arms again and wait while under fire:

> This is the time that tries the souls of men standing inactive, [conscious] of unseen danger, with bullets whistling over and around them, the increasing rattle of musketry in front, with now and then the ominous shriek of a shell as it tears through the ranks, taking out perhaps a file of men.... The strain upon the men is terrible. It takes more than brute courage to make him stand. There must be some higher, nobler feeling to prompt him or he will run in this moment of his great trial.[26]

The Fourteenth, the rest of its division, and the divisions of Meade and Rickets had been fighting in the woods, pastures and cornfields for an hour and a half without support, while Lee and Jackson brought fresh divisions from different parts of the battlefield to oppose them. If McClellan had reinforced Hooker with two divisions from Mansfield's corps, then Hooker might have succeeded in turning Lee's left flank, as was his orders from McClellan and was his intention in attacking the area of the Dunkard Church and attaining the high ground. However, Mansfield did not commit his corps to the battle until after Hooker's corps was tired and low in supplies.[27]

With Hood's Division advancing and the brigades of Phelps and Gibbon exhausted and out of ammunition, the Fourteenth, which had been in line of battle with other regiments in the brigade, were ordered to fall back "slowly and in good order."[28]

Joseph Pettiner, a member of the Fourteenth, wrote of his experience during the Battle of Antietam:

> Where we were engaged was just at the edge of a cornfield. As we advanced over a ploughed field we were obliged to lay down to escape the round shot and bomb shells, and when in the corn had to lay down every few steps, and you may try to imagine us laying there the balls going whiz, whiz, whiz within a step of us and over our heads and seeing the round shot tear up everything around a few steps off.
>
> At last we were ordered to rise, advance and relieve another regiment who were firing into the Rebels. I had fired about 12 rounds when the Rebels came up to the brow of the hill, about 50 feet from where I was firing. A number of men said, "Don't fire, they are friends." But as soon as I saw them raise their pieces and fire I fired my piece in that direction. When I discovered my brigade on the "schedaddle" through the corn, I thought it was time for me to leave.
>
> As I was running I tried to help a wounded man off but he was so heavy and helpless we were forced to leave him. I had just let go his arm when a bullet struck him in the side. I tell you it was rough running through that corn the way those bullets were firing, perfectly careless whether they put an end to your present life or not. The battle continued to rage all day, although we did not have to go in again. This was the 17th or 18th. The Rebels sent a flag of truce to bury their dead.
>
> On the 19th we marched from near the battlefield to where we are now. They do say the battle extended 5 miles around. As we were on the march we passed numbers of dead bodies in every conceivable shape and form. Some appeared as though they had fallen asleep, but most of them appeared as though in extreme agony. There they lay, some as black as a nigger, and others in all kinds of postures of pain. But I will not dwell upon the horrors of the battle field. It is perfectly awful.[29]

By 7:30 A.M. about an hour and a half from the start of the battle, Hooker and Jackson had devastated each other's forces and had committed almost every soldier in their commands. Dead and wounded littered the cornfield and the area of the Hagerstown Turnpike where battle lines at some points were only a hundred feet apart.[30] Hooker, who could see the entire battle unfolding before him, later wrote, "In the time I am writing every stalk of corn in the northern and greater part of the field was cut as closely as could have been done with a knife, and the slain lay in rows precisely as they had stood in their ranks a few moments before. It was never my fortune to witness a more bloody, dismal battle field."[31]

Hood called the fighting the "most terrific clash of arms, by far, that has occurred during the war."[32] Hood's Division paid a large price for its counterattack in the cornfield. His Fourth Texas regiment lost half of their number, while the First Texas regiment lost over three-quarters of its force to killed or wounded.[33]

The battle would rage on for the remainder of the day. As Hooker took his corps off the field at about 7:30 A.M., Mansfield brought his corps onto the field. They succeeded in driving the Rebels from the East Woods and the bloody cornfield up to the Dunkard Church where they were stopped. At about 9:00 A.M., Gen. Sumner, who had waited several hours for his orders, finally launched an attack. His corps moved past the East Woods and advanced down to the Sunken Road. However, again, McClellan failed to follow up this advantage. At about 10:00 A.M., Burnside started his corps in its advance across the lower bridge of the Antietam. Burnside tried to cross the bridge several times but each time the assault was repulsed. After finding fords above the bridge and below the bridge, a final assault at all three locations resulted in the Federals gaining control of the lower Antietam by 1:00 P.M. However, it took Burnside until 3:00 P.M. before his entire corps crossed the bridge. Burnside's men began to advance toward Sharpsburg when, at approximately 4:00 P.M., the 2,000 man division of A.P. Hill arrived from Harpers Ferry to push back the advance that Burnside had made.[34]

This advance was again not followed up by McClellan. Because McClellan's failed to follow up Hooker's advantage in the north or Sumner's advantage in the middle of Lee's line or Burnside's advantage at the lower bridge, and because he committed his troops in a piecemeal fashion, he lost the opportunity to destroy Lee's entire army. As it was, McClellan's army lost 12,410 killed, wounded or missing, while Lee's army lost 13,724.[35]

The casualties of the First Corps amounted to almost one-third of the nine thousand men in Hooker's command. Of the 425 officers and men in his brigade, Col. Phelps reported over forty-three percent as casualties. The Confederates, who defended the farm of D.R. Miller against the first attack of Gibbon and Phelps, lost fifty percent of their force. Hood's Division as well as the three brigades of D.H. Hill were devastated.[36]

As night fell and the bloody Battle of Antietam came to a close, the Fourteenth was ordered to lay on their arms for the night.[37] In his report, Phelps commended Major DeBevoise, commander of the Fourteenth, who "had his horse shot, and was considerably injured by his fall, but remained on the field to the end, acquitting himself with great credit."[38]

Lee and McClellan had to decide what they were going to do on the next day. Lee called a meeting of his lieutenants. All were of the opinion that the battle should not be renewed on the 18th. Lee still was not convinced and kept his army in place. However, beginning at about 2:00 A.M. on the 19th, Lee's troops began to cross the Potomac at the ford near Shepherdstown. By 10:00 A.M. the entire army of Northern Virginia had crossed into Virginia without molestation by any Union forces.[39] Lee informed President Davis of the conditions of his army and the danger of a renewed attack.[40]

McClellan, the ever cautious commander, did not want to renew the battle on the 18th.[41] His preference was to wait until reinforcements arrived. "This army is not now in condition to under take another campaign nor to bring on another battle, unless great advantages are offered by some mistake of the enemy or pressing military exigencies render it necessary."[42]

While the commanders were trying to determine their next step, the Fourteenth lay on arms for the entire day. The work of burying the dead was started since some of the bodies had been lying in the sun for two days and the process of decomposition had already started. The stench was becoming sickening. The next day, September 19, after the Confederates had withdrawn back across the Potomac River into Virginia, the Fourteenth advanced toward Sharpsburg and encamped about a half mile from there. On their way they passed through the battlefield of two days previous. Before them were the blue or gray clad bodies of soldiers that were so confined in some areas that the members of the Fourteenth had to go over the bodies since they could not go around them. As they traveled through the wooded areas, the denuded trees whose bark had been shot away by bullets and cannon fire, the huge limbs which had been separated from their trees, gave silent testimony to the intensity and ferocity of the battle.[43]

As a result of the Battle of Antietam, twelve boys from Brooklyn would never return and 15 were wounded.[44]

10. Back in Brooklyn

The Fourteenth remained encamped near Sharpsburg for the next month. They changed camp several times for sanitary reasons but did not venture far from Sharpsburg. While in camp, the regiment concentrated on refitting and the training of new recruits. The available members of the regiment were severely depleted. This was not only due to killed and wounded of the previous battles but also due to fatigue and illness. A correspondent from the Brooklyn *Eagle* wrote that after the Second Battle of Bull Run, many of the survivors of the Fourteenth had to be sent to hospitals because of over exertion from their "continued skirmishing for a week before the fight." Before the battle, the regiment had 275 men."[1] On September 18, an article appeared about the Fourteenth that said:[2] "A large number of the old members, about 75 are at Hospital, Meridian Hill, having been sent back after their recent march toward Frederick, by Surgeon Farley."[3]

Another article written about the Fourteenth on September 7, indicated that while the regiment was marching through Washington on its way to Maryland, several members were left on the side of the road "beat out." The regiment was at this time mustering about 216 men.[4] Again, due to the same reasons of killed, wounded, fatigue, and illness, after the Battle of South Mountain, the Fourteenth had been reduced to about 100 men.[5]

Recruiting for the Fourteenth was an ongoing occurrence, although sometimes with greater emphasis than at others. The records indicate that at both the Battle of South Mountain and the Battle of Antietam, recruits who had not finished their training joined the regular members of the Fourteenth in the battles.[6] This was no doubt due to the feelings they had for the Fourteenth as well as the need for every man available.

An article in the Brooklyn newspaper on September 4 indicated that "new recruits that left Brooklyn on Saturday [August 31] have today gone forward in fine spirits at the prospect of immediate work." It concluded, "The new recruits for the 14th should come forward without delay — hurry them on."[7]

After the Battle of Antietam, on September 17, an entry was made in the regimental records of the Fourteenth. It said, "It would be well to note here, that previous to the battle of the 14th, a number of recruits joined the regiment, but being neither armed nor drilled were not put into our ranks. In some few instances they got possession of arms and entered our ranks, and their records at both battles was full as commendable as the record of the older members of the regiment."[8]

The recruits did their share but many more were needed. After a month of sustained combat and movement the regiment was depleted. In October 1862, Col. Rufus Dawes of the Sixth Wisconsin was ordered to assist Capt. McClellan of Gen. George B. McClellan's staff for the purpose of inspecting the regiments of Gen. Doubleday's Division. The Twenty-Fourth New York and the Fourteenth Brooklyn were assigned to Col. Dawes.

Dawes considered this a disagreeable task in that the deficiencies of regiments had to be reported back to the headquarters of the army. His inspection of the Fourteenth showed that the regiment had no field officers present and that the regiment, had as a result of the lack of soldiers, been consolidated into a battalion of four companies. One company of the regiment had 74 men present but for various reasons 43 were listed as non-effective. The main reason was that they did not have weapons. Dawes also reported that the men were accounted for and that the guns he inspected were in good condition.[9]

The people back in Brooklyn were also concerned about the conditions of the regiment. They were afraid it would be disbanded. The *Daily Eagle* said, "It will be a lasting disgrace to Brooklyn if a regiment which, from the first battle of Bull Run, has covered itself and Brooklyn with glory, should be allowed to lose its glorious renown, and its members be divided up among other regiments whose deeds will not cast a ray of honor upon Brooklyn."[10]

The people of Brooklyn responded. All over Brooklyn meetings were held with the purpose of recruiting for the Fourteenth Regiment and raising money to pay a bounty to those who needed an extra incentive to join. In addition, the people of Brooklyn raised money for the families of members, who were already serving so that they would not have any wants or needs while their men were fighting for the Union. One such meeting was held at the Plymouth Church of the Reverend Henry Ward Beecher. The call to the meeting started, "Let the city in mass respond to the call, and by their presence tonight and deed show to the brave men in arms that they have the confidence of the people. They must have two hundred new recruits at once. No consolidation must take place with this organization. It has made its record as the 14th, and honored themselves and the city."[11]

Henry Ward Beecher was one of the most famous clergymen in the United States. He was a steadfast abolitionist and took every opportunity to preach against slavery from his pulpit in Brooklyn. He became famous during the 1850s when he, along with others, began to send guns into Kansas so that the anti-slavery forces could defeat the pro-slavery forces in a struggle which came to be called "Bleeding Kansas." This would allow Kansas to come into the Union as a free state. These guns, which were paid for by funds donated to Beecher, came to be known as "Beecher's Bibles."[12] As an ardent abolitionist, Henry Ward Beecher supported the war, and the Fourteenth regiment often used his church as a meeting point for rallies to raise money and men for the regiment.

Another such meeting was held at the Washington Street M.E. Church. The meeting started off with a plea on behalf of the Fourteenth: "Unless the regiment be speedily recruited up to its minimum compliment at least, its amalgamation with some other regiment is inevitable. Our citizens are very much opposed to the idea of the brave Brooklyn 14th losing their regimental identity."[13]

Captain Jordan and other members of the Fourteenth were on hand as guests. During the meeting William H. Burleigh reviewed the "career of the brave 14th boys throughout the campaign, which has so sadly thinned their ranks." Burleigh concluded by reading a verse of his own composition which has come down through history as a homage to the Fourteenth.

"The Gallant Fourteenth"
By William H. Burleigh

Forget them not — our gallant boys —
Who for the Nation's Life, have stood
Amid the Battles grime and noise,
Baptized into its flame and blood!

The Brave Fourteenth! — how well they wrought
For Freedom, let our annals tell —
A cheer for those who stoutly fought;
A tear for those who nobly fell!

Where first our broken squadrons reel
On sad Manassas, slaughter — dyed,
To Antietam's glorious field,
Their faith and courage have been tried;

And as pure gold from furnace heats,
So come they from the fiery tests,
True Heroes! — When their country greets
Among her bravest and her best!

But more than praise and more than thanks
To valor such as theirs, is due —
Then fill again their shattered ranks,
With men as loyal, brave and true!

No craven hearts with them may mate
Whose deeds are titles of renown;
No traitorous soul, that deprecate
The blow that dashes Treason down.

> No!—send them Men! for such are they—
> Of courage tried, of faith sublime,
> Who know the work, they do today
> Is wrought for all the Coming Time—
>
> Who swear,—whatever be the costs,
> The heritage our Fathers gave,
> Shall never by their sons be lost,
> Nor Freedom's home become her grave.[14]

The appeal for volunteers to enlist in the Fourteenth Regiment, the appeal for money for bounties to be paid to others to encourage their enlistment, as well as money to be paid to former members of the Fourteenth who had been invalided out of service and money to be given to the families of serving members was met with great enthusiasm and generosity by the people of Brooklyn. Money for the beloved Brooklyn Regiment came from all classes of society. In many instances, contributions from all strata of society came to Congressman Odell for the Fourteenth.

> Hon. Moses Odell
> Dear Sir,—In response to your application in behalf of the Brooklyn 14th, I am authorized to say that the Grocers War Committee of this city will appropriate One Thousand Dollars of their fund, to be expended under the direction of yourself and Mr. John D. McKenzie, for the benefit of said regiment.
> Very respectfully yours,
> Charles E. Beebe, Secretary.
> New York, Sept. 29, 1862
>
> MERCHANTS' BANK, NEW YORK
> September 29, 1862.
> Hon. Moses Odell;
> Dear Sir,—I understand that a meeting is to be held this evening to promote the enlistments to our Brooklyn Fourteenth. As a citizen of Brooklyn feeling great pride in this noble Regiment, will you allow me to ask the favor of application of the enclosed One Hundred dollars to its use.
> Yours very truly,
> A.E. Silliman
>
> Hon. Moses Odell
> Sir—Enclosed is a small amount which you will please present to the first two volunteers to the Fourteenth Regiment, from a *workwoman*, who wishes to contribute her nite to aid those who go forth in defense of her *adopted* country—would she could say her *native*—but she loves it none the less, and prays God to bless its armies and protect and shield its soldiers in the day of battle.[15]

Because of the efforts of Congressmen Moses Odell, who worked long and hard chairing meetings and collecting money from his constituents, as well as the deep feeling that the people of Brooklyn had for their regiment, over three hundred new recruits had been sent to the Fourteenth by the end of September.[16]

Towards the end of October, the women of Brooklyn, with the assistance Representative Moses Odell, met in the Tabernacle on Fulton Avenue to procure a new battle flag for the gallant Fourteenth Regiment. The old flag, which had been in the possession of the regiment since its inception fourteen years earlier, was now returned to Brooklyn tattered, ripped and full of bullet holes, which bore witness to the battles and bravery through which it was carried, giving honor to the Fourteenth and the people of Brooklyn. The flag was hung over the speakers table and the meeting was called to order. Soon after brief prayers, women adopted and passed the following resolution:

> Whereas, The surviving members of the Brooklyn 14th Regiment having sent home their torn, weather worn, and battle scarred standard, to bear witness of the many conflicts through which it has been bravely borne, and whereas the regiment is now without a standard or ensign, therefore
>
> Resolved, "That the Brooklyn 14th" has covered itself with glory, and is entitled to the gratitude of all the loyal, and especially the sympathy of the wives, mothers, daughters and sisters in this community, that we hold ourselves indebted to their bravery — their self sacrifice, their patient devotion to the flag; and that the many noble men who have fallen in battle and wasted away with sickness, shall ever be enshrined in our memory and cherished in our heats.
>
> Resolved that we the ladies of Brooklyn claim the privilege of replacing the regimental standard, and thus unfurl our love for our country and exhibit our gratitude to its defenders, confident that the new banner will never be dishonored by those who shall bear it.

At the end of the meeting, because of his interest in the wellbeing of the regiment, Moses Odell was recognized as the "Father of the Fourteenth Regiment."[17]

11. Battle of Fredericksburg

Army of the Potomac	**14th Brooklyn Regiment**
Major Gen. Ambrose E. Burnside	Lieut. Col. William H. DeBevoise
Left Grand Division	**22nd New York Regiment**
Major Gen. William B. Franklin	Lieut. Col. John McKie, Jr.
First Army Corps	**24th New York Regiment**
Major Gen. John F. Reynolds	Lieut. Col. Samuel Beardsley
First Division	**30th New York Regiment**
Brigadier Gen. Abner Doubleday	Lieut. Col. Morgan H. Chrysler
First Brigade	**2nd U.S. Sharpshooters**
Col. Walter Phelps, Jr.	Major Homer Stoughton[1]

By early October, President Lincoln had become annoyed at McClellan's lack of movement against Lee's Army. He therefore issued an order directing McClellan to cross the Potomac and engage Lee's army or, at the least, to drive him farther south. Lincoln wanted McClellan to cross the Potomac between Lee's army and Washington, thereby affording protection to that city. The order ended, "He [Lincoln] is very desirous that your army move as soon as possible."[2] However, McClellan continued his dalliance until Oct. 26, at which time he began to bring his army across the Potomac at Harpers Ferry and Berlin. This operation took six days to complete, after which McClellan moved his army to the area around Warrenton, Virginia. The Army of the Potomac was now east of the Blue Ridge Mountains while Lee was west of the Mountains. This put McClellan in a position to make a dash for Richmond. Again, McClellan became afflicted with his inability to act, thus giving Lee the chance to cross the Blue Ridge Mountains and march to Culpeper, Virginia. At this location Lee had placed his army between McClellan and Richmond.[3]

Meanwhile, the Fourteenth, which had spent its time on the outskirts of Sharpsburg since the Battle of Antietam, used this time to drill and train its new recruits. Every day the Fourteenth anticipated being called to a new battle. However, it was not until October 20 that the Fourteenth left its camp and marched six miles to Fairplay, Maryland. On October 26, when McClellan moved his army across the Potomac, the Fourteenth marched ten miles over terrible roads and during a rainstorm to Buena Vista. The next day, October

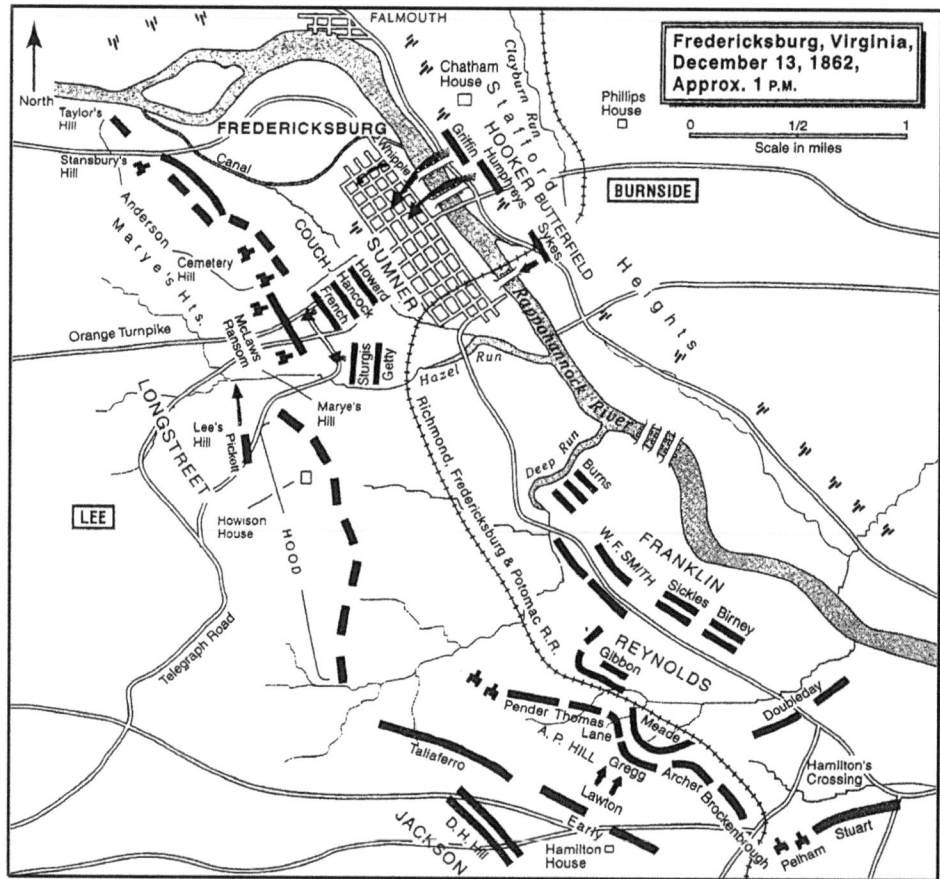

Battle of Fredericksburg (from William Marvel and Donald Pfanz, *The Battle of Fredericksburg* Eastern National Park and Monument Association, 1993. Map by George Skoch, courtesy Eastern National Publishers).

27, the Fourteenth arrived at Crampton's Gap. The next day they marched through Burkittsville, Maryland, and stopped at Camp Davey near Petersville, Maryland. On October 29, the Fourteenth crossed the Potomac River via a pontoon bridge and halted at Camp Meyers near Lovettsville, Virginia. Over the next few days the Fourteenth marched through Purcellville and Union Bloomfield, and on November 6, they were assigned to picket the Waterloo Road near Warrenton, Virginia. After being relieved on November 7, the Fourteenth bivouacked at Camp Baldwin on the Sulfur Springs Road.[4]

Meanwhile, Lincoln had already grown tired of McClellan's lack of aggressiveness and decided to replace him. On November 5, Lincoln issued a directive to Gen. Halleck, the general-in-chief of all Union armies, to replace General McClellan. This was followed up by General Order 182: "By the direction of the President of the United States, it is ordered that Major General McClellan be relieved from the command of the Army of the Potomac, and that Major General Burnside take the command of that army."[5]

Ambrose Burnside was born on May 23, 1824, at Liberty Union County, Indiana. His father was born in South Carolina and had been a slave owner. The family freed the slaves when they moved to Indiana. He received an elementary education and was apprenticed to a tailor and subsequently opened a shop with a partner in Liberty. However, through his father's political connections, he was able to secure an appointment to West Point. He served on garrison duty during the Mexican War, then resigned his commission in 1853. In the years before the Civil War, he manufactured a breech-loading rifle of his own design, was appointed as a major general of the Rhode Island Militia, was nominated to Congress and held a job with the Illinois Central Railroad under his friend George B. McClellan. With the outbreak of the Civil War, Burnside organized the 1st Rhode Island Infantry and fought at the First Battle of Bull Run, after which he was promoted to brigadier general of volunteers. As a favorite of President Lincoln, he was given command of an expedition to the coast of North Carolina. This successful effort earned him the rank of major general of volunteers. In July of 1862, his troops joined the Army of the Potomac and he served as a corps commander during the Battle of Antietam.[6]

General Burnside did not want command of the Army of the Potomac. In fact, it had been offered to him twice before and he had refused it. Burnside felt that he did not have the ability to lead the army. However, he was convinced by his staff to accept.[7] Considering the dire results of the Battle of Fredericksburg, it could be said that Burnside knew the limits of his own abilities and resisted the urge to take command. However, Burnside immediately set about reorganizing the Army of the Potomac. He consolidated the army's six corps to three Grand Divisions, each one consisting of two corps. The Right Grand Division was to be comprised of the Second and Ninth Corps under the command of Major Gen. Edwin V. Sumner. The Center Grand Division, made up of the Third and Fifth Corps, were placed under the command of "Fightin'" Joe Hooker, while Major Gen. William B. Franklin commanded the Left Grand Division.[8] The Fourteenth Regiment was in Franklin's Left Grand Division, Major Gen. John F. Reynold's First Corps and Abner Doubleday's First Division.

It was already November and the Army of the Potomac should have established its winter quarters. However, Burnside knew that this prospect would not sit well with Lincoln. After all, Lincoln's purpose in removing

McClellan was to get the Union army moving. Therefore, on November 9, the day Burnside took over command of the army, he sent Washington his plan of action. Burnside's plan consisted of a series of feints towards Culpeper and Gordonsville in Virginia while rapidly moving his entire army toward Fredericksburg and then advancing toward Richmond. Using this line of march Burnside would shield Washington from a possible attack by Lee while proceeding toward his ultimate goal. Along with his plan, Burnside requested that pontoons be sent to him for use in bridging the Rappahannock River.[9]

On November 16, the Left Grand Division of Major General Franklin began to move out of Warrington. The following day, November 17, the Fourteenth left its camp at about 9:30 A.M. and acted as the rear guard for the Left Grand Division. After marching approximately thirty miles in two days and passing through or near Elk Run, White Ridge and Garrisonville, the Fourteenth arrived in the area of Stafford Court House along with the rest of Franklin's Left Grand Division.

If Burnside could have attacked at this time (his three Grand Divisions were in place) he could have crossed the Rappahannock, taken Fredericksburg and the hills beyond it without much opposition. Only a part of Longstreet's First corps was at Fredericksburg. Lee did not order the remainder of his Corps to Fredericksburg until the morning of November 19, and Jackson's Corps in the Shannondoah Valley was not ordered to Fredericksburg until November 26. Thus the entire Confederate army was not in place at Fredericksburg until December 5. However, because of inclement weather and poor organization, the pontoon bridges that Burnside had ordered from Washington did not arrive until November 25. Because of this, Burnside decided to reevaluate his plan for crossing the Rappahannock.[10]

Burnside considered crossing the Rappahannock at Skinker's Neck, fourteen miles down river from Fredericksburg, and at Port Royal even farther down river. However, quick action by Lee in both instances thwarted these possibilities. Burnside then believed that with Lee's army spread out to oppose his crossing down river, he might be successful by crossing at Fredericksburg, which was his original plan. He decided upon five bridges across the Rappahannock so that he might bring his divisions and artillery across as rapidly as possible. At the upper end of the town of Fredericksburg two bridges were built across the river opposite Hawke Street and a third was built near a burned out railroad bridge at the lower end of town. The first two bridges were to be known as the upper bridges and the one at the lower end of the town was to be called the middle bridge. Farther south and approximately two miles below the upper bridges near the mouth of Deep Run, two more pontoon bridges were built. The lower bridges were built by Major James Magruder of the Fifteenth New York Engineers. Gen. Franklin, who commanded the Left Grand Division in the area of the lower bridges, realized that he had enough material left over for another bridge. Therefore, on December 12, he ordered the building of a third pontoon bridge across the Rappahannock alongside the first two lower bridges. It was at the lower bridges that the Fourteenth would eventually cross.[11]

On December 11, while the pontoon bridges were being built across the Rappahannock, Col. (later General) Edward Porter Alexander of the Confederate Army was on the heights overlooking Fredericksburg. He later recalled:

> Then I think I was presented the most impressive exhibition of military force, by all odds, which I ever witnessed. The whole Federal Army had broken up their camps, packed their wagons and moved out on the hills, ready to cross the river as soon as the bridges were completed. Over 100,000 infantry were visible, standing apparently in great solid squares upon the hilltops, for a space of three miles, scattered all over the slopes were endless parks of ambulances, ordnance, commissary, quartermaster and regimental white-topped wagons, also parked in close squares and rectangle, and very impressive in the sense of order and system which they conveyed, and still more impressive to military eyes though less conspicuous and showy were the dark colored parks of batteries of artillery scattered here and there among them . Then, in front, was the three mile line of angry blazing guns firing through white clouds of smoke and almost shaking the earth with their roar. Over and in the town the white winkings of the bursting shells reminded one of the countless swarm of fire-flies. Several buildings were set on fire, and their black smoke rose in remarkably slender, straight and tall columns for two hundred feet, perhaps before they began to spread horizontally and unite in a great black canopy. And over the whole scene there hung, high in the air, above the rear of the Federal lines, two immense black, captive balloons, like two great spirits of the air attendant on the coming struggle.[12]

Fredericksburg is located on the southwesterly side of the Rappahannock River. The river itself runs in a southerly direction at this point. Falmouth is on the north side of the Rappahannock and was in front of the Federal positions. Behind Falmouth was a plain leading up to the high ground called Stafford Heights. Beyond Fredericksburg was a plain leading up to a series of heights called Taylor's Hill, Stansbury Hill, Marye's Hill, Telegraph Hill, Howison Hill, and Prospect Hill, ending in the area of the Massaponax River. The plain behind Fredericksburg varied in size from between three-quarters of a mile behind Fredericksburg to a width of approximately two and one-half miles at the extreme left of the battlefield which was to be occupied by the First Corps and therefore the Fourteenth Regiment.

Lee, the engineer, had himself a formidable position. His army was situated on high ground above a plain and was bounded by the Rappahannock to the east, a series of hills to the north and west and the Massaponax River to the south. In addition, because of Burnside's long delay in assaulting the Rappahannock, Lee had plenty of time to dig rifle pits and to afford his soldiers maximum protection. Because of these advantages and because he knew that the large amount of Union artillery on the top of Stafford Heights could decimate his army should they attempt to cross the plain toward Fredericksburg, Lee decided to fight a defensive battle and let Burnside come to him.[13]

Lee had posted Longstreet's First Corps from Taylor's Hill to Deep Run. He had four of his five divisions in line of battle. They consisted of Major Gen. R. Anderson in the area of Taylor's Hill in the north, then McLaws, Pickett and ending with John Bell Hood's division along the Military Road west of its juncture with Deep Run. The Fifth Division under Brigadier Gen. Robert Ransom was held in reserve. Jackson's Second Corps was situated on the tree covered hills around Hamilton's Crossing that made up the Confederate right. To the front of Jackson's Corps was Ambrose Powell Hill's division with the brigade of Archer, Lane and Pender up front and the brigades of Thomas, Gregg and Brockenhough on the second line. Behind them were the divisions of Taliaferro and Jubal A. Early. D.H. Hill's division was posted on the right to the rear. Stuart's cavalry and horse artillery were on the extreme right in the Massaponax Valley to protect that area and support Jackson's Second Corps.

Jackson's section of the battle line did not have as many high hills as did Longstreet's area. Therefore, Jackson's section was harder to defend. Lee had given Longstreet approximately five miles to defend while Jackson was given only about two miles of the line to defend with his thirty thousand men. This meant that Jackson had about ten men to every yard of front and therefore could align his brigades in great depth.[14]

Just as they had at the battles of First Bull Run, Gainesville, Groveton, Second Bull Run and Antietam, the Fourteenth was, again, going to face Jackson and his corps.

On December 11, Burnside started the building of his pontoon bridges across the Rappahannock. Lee had positioned Gen. William Barksdale's brigade of McLaws' division, consisting of the 13th, 17th, and 21st Mississippi regiments and a Florida regiment into Fredericksburg to harass the bridge builders. After the Seventh Michigan, the Nineteenth and Twentieth Massachusetts Regiments of Howard's division volunteered to cross the river by boat and began to take possession of the buildings along the waterfront. Franklin's Grand Division was already crossing at the lower bridges after clearing away light resistance (there were no buildings in which the Confederates could obtain a vantage point). Barksdale withdrew his brigade but not until over a hundred of his soldiers were captured. While these bridges were being built, the Fourteenth left Muddy Creek at abut 7:30 A.M. and marched about four miles to the area of the Rappahannock River.

On December 12, the Fourteenth marched to the river and crossed on the upper of the two lower bridges. The regiment along with the remainder of the brigade took positions to the front and right of the Bernard House. The brigade deployed in four lines of battle and bivouacked for the night, sleeping on their arms and without making fires. Campfires were not permitted since this would give the Confederate artillerists fine targets or at the least allow the Rebels the opportunity to harass them during the night.[15]

Burnside's plan of battle was to have Sumner's Right Grand Division cross the Rappahannock using the upper bridges and Franklins Left Grand Division to cross using the lower bridges. Hooker and his Center Grand Division were to cross after Sumner. Hooker was not given a specific role in the coming battle other than to give support to either Sumner or Franklin depending upon who made the best progress against the Confederates.[16] Sumner was to cross through the town of Fredericksburg, cross the plain beyond it and carry Marye's Hill and the heights around it. Franklin and his two corps commanders, Reynolds of the First Corps and William F. Smith of the Sixth Corps, urged Burnside to let their Left Grand Division attack the extreme right of the Confederate line with at least 30,000 men then using the Military Road built by Lee to connect his forces on the five mile line of battle, to roll up the Confederate forces. They were of the opinion that they had convinced Burnside of the value of this plan. However, when Franklin received his orders on the morning of December 13, they were completely different from those that he anticipated. Instead, Franklin was ordered to send a division to seize the high ground near Hamilton Crossing, while holding the remainder of his Left Grand Division in position to move down the old Richmond Road.[17]

Atop Telegraph Hill (later called Lee's Hill), Longstreet surveyed the spectacle before him.

> Secure on our hills we grimly awaited the onslaught. The valley, the mountain tops, everything was enveloped in the thickest fog, and the preparations for the fight were made so if under cover of night. The mist brought the preparation for battle, but we were blind to the movement of the Federals. Suddenly ... the warmth of the sun brushed the mist away and revealed the mighty panorama in the valley below. Franklin's 40,000 men, reinforced by two divisions of Hooker's grand division, were in front of Jackson's 30,000. The flags of the Federals fluttered gaily, the polished arms shone brightly in the sunlight, and the beautiful uniforms of the buoyant troops gave to the scene the air of a holiday occasion rather than the spectacle of a great army about to be thrown into the tumult of battle. From my place ... I could see almost every soldier Franklin had, and a splendid array it was. But off in the distance was Jackson's ragged infantry, and beyond was Stuarts battered cavalry with their

soiled hats and yellow butternut suits, as striking contrast to the handsomely equipped troops of the Federals.[18]

Burnside chose Reynolds' First Corps to make the attack. John Fulton Reynolds was born in Lancaster, Pennsylvania on September 20, 1820. After attending school in Pennsylvania and Maryland, he was admitted to West Point in 1837, graduating in 1841. During the Mexican War he served on the Texas frontier and was cited for meritorious conduct and bravery. In 1860, he was appointed commandant of cadets and instructor of tactics at West Point. He held this position until war broke out the following spring. He was then appointed to lieutenant colonel of the 14th U.S. Infantry in May of 1861 and a brigadier general of volunteers in August of that year. After being captured by the Confederates during McClellan's Peninsula Campaign, he rejoined the army and was assigned to the 3rd Division, Pennsylvania Reserves, which was temporarily assigned to McDowell's Third Corps during the Battle of Second Manassas. After being promoted to the rank of major general, Reynolds was given the command of the First Corps.[19]

After choosing Reynolds for the attack, Reynolds in turn chose the division of Major Gen. George G. Meade. Meade began his movement at approximately 8:30 A.M. After advancing about 750 yards, it turned and crossed the Bowling Green Road (also called the Old Richmond Stage Road). The Fourteenth was moving parallel to the Bowling Green Road for about a mile when they and the brigade were ordered to the Bowling Green Road to take up positions there. As soon as they arrived, the Fourteenth, Twenty-Second and Thirteenth Regiments were ordered to change direction and move at the double quick to the left in order to support artillery, which was being positioned personally by Gen. Reynolds. This artillery was coming under fire from Major John Pelham of Stuart's horse artillery and from Confederate skirmishers sent out by Stuart. Col. Phelps then advanced his three battle lines parallel to the Bowling Green road and about 200 yards to its left. The records of the Fourteenth Regiment indicate: "After getting in position, we opened with our batteries, but were annoyed by the Rebel sharpshooters, who picked off our artillerists. Four companies of the regiment were advanced to a road on our front, some-what sunken, and from this cover were enabled to silence the sharpshooters and a battery which got into position soon after the companies were detached."[20]

After pushing the Confederate sharpshooters back for approximately half a mile, Doubleday's Division, which included the Fourteenth, seized a band of woods which was on the bank of the Rappahannock. This placed them below the end of the Confederate high ground. Doubleday immediately placed three brigades facing the high ground and moved toward the Bowling Green Road. The Fourth's Brigade was situated on the left flank of the division. The

Fourteenth along with its brigade were now situated along with Doubleday's Division at the extreme left of Franklin's Grand Division. Their task was to prevent an attack on Mead's flank while he was unsuccessfully trying to attack Jackson in the area of Prospect Hill. Thereafter, they were to protect the left flank of First Corps from and attack by Stuart or D.H. Hill. Hill had been moved into position to assist Stuart by Jackson, who was afraid that Doubleday's movements were a prelude to an attempt to turn his right flank.[21]

At about 5:00 P.M., the Fourteenth moved to the left and rear of their position so that they would give support to Battery B of the Fourth U.S. Artillery, commanded by Lieut. James Stewart. Lieut. Stewart reported that his position was under such intense cannon and musket fire that he had already lost several men and a number of horses in addition to harnesses which were so cut up by shell fragments as to be useless. From the time that the Fourteenth arrived to support the artillery until about 9:00 P.M., the Confederates continued to intermittently shell the area from masked batteries in different locations, sometimes using canister. The Fourteenth was out of range of some of the canister shot; however, the Confederates had calculated the correct elevation for the Union artillery and the golf ball size pellets came down from the skies like giant hailstones, but with a much more dire effect.[22]

There can be little doubt that the very presence of Stuart on the flank kept Doubleday from aiding Meade in his attack on the Confederates, and also prevented him from attempting a move on Jackson's right. If the left bank of the Massaponax Creek could have been swept of Confederates, then a combined attack by Meade, Gibbon and Doubleday might very well have succeeded in breaking Jackson's lines.[23]

As night fell, Burnside came to realize that his entire plan of battle was a complete and utter failure. Franklin, on the Union left, almost met success with Meade's limited attack, but in the end it was a failure because it was not reinforced with enough strength so that they could push through the Confederate defenses. Sumner on the right was so far from success that the Union soldiers who so bravely crossed the plain below Marye's Heights never even seriously approached a Confederate position.

On Sunday, December 14, the Fourteenth remained in its position protecting the artillery, which occasionally fired their cannon but did not receive return fire from the Confederates. However, at about 3:00 P.M., the Confederate long range artillery opened fire from the left and was enfilading the entire brigade. Col. Phelps moved the Fourteenth along with the reminder of his brigade to the rear and out of range of the artillery. The Fourteenth remained in this position until 8:00 P.M. on the evening of December 14, when it received orders to prepare to fall back and cross the Rappahannock with the rest of the division.[24]

Late in the afternoon of December 15, Burnside informed his generals that he intended to move his entire army back across the Rappahannock later that evening. In order to prevent the Confederates from realizing his plan, the Union soldiers built camp fires, barricaded streets and erected Quaker guns from logs so that the Confederates would believe that the Union cannons were still in place. Burnside's army then began to re-cross the Rappahannock using the same pontoon bridges that they had used just a few days before. The Fourteenth crossed at about 1:00 A.M. on December 16. By 2:00 P.M. the entire army had crossed undetected by the Confederates and were marching toward their assigned bivouacs. That night the Fourteenth rested. "Sleep never came to more grateful eyelids. For three days we had been continually under fire. Our nights were almost sleepless ... we were continually under arms, moving hither and thither.... To lie down without the ring of musketry and the roar of artillery in one's ears, and to close one's eyes in pure forgetfulness, is a boon no one can appreciate who was not passed through such scenes."[25]

Burnside's re-crossing of the Rappahannock after the disaster at Fredericksburg was probably the most successful part of his operation during the entire campaign. At 4:00 A.M. on December 16, Gen. Burnside notified General-in-Chief Henry Halleck that he was withdrawing his army from the field and crossing the Rappahannock. Within a short time Halleck replied that the president wanted to know the reasons for his withdrawal. By 5:30 P.M., Burnside wrote that in his opinion the enemy's positions to his front could not be carried and that an attempt to do this could have disastrous effects. Since he could not attack successfully, he decided to withdraw. On December 17, Burnside made a more complete report to Gen. Halleck, in which he detailed his activities and reasonings beginning with his crossing the Rappahannock at Fredericksburg on December 12. Included in his reports was a thank you to his army:

> To the brave officers and soldiers who accomplished the feat of this recrossing in the face of the enemy I owe everything. For the failure in the attack, I am responsible, as the extreme gallantry, courage and endurance shown by them was never excelled and would have carried the points, had it been possible.
>
> To the families and friends of the dead, I can only offer my heartfelt sympathy, but for the wounded I can offer my earnest prayer for their comfort and final recovery.[26]

At the Battle of Fredericksburg three Brooklynites lost their lives and three were wounded.[27]

12. Chancellorsville Campaign

Port Royal — April 23; Fitzhugh Crossing; April 29 to May 2;
Battle of Chancellorsville May 2–3

Army of the Potomac	14th Brooklyn Regiment
Major Gen. Joseph Hooker	Col. Edward Fowler
First Corps	22nd New York Regiment
Major Gen. John F. Reynolds	Major Thomas Strong
First Division	24th New York Regiment
Brigadier Gen. James S. Wadsworth	Col. Samuel Beardsley
First Brigade	30th New York Regiment
Col. Walter Phelps, Jr.	Col. William Searing[1]

After the Battle of Fredericksburg, the Confederates settled into the hills and ridgelines which they had defended during the battle. The Union forces settled on their side of the Rappahannock in the approximate positions that they had occupied prior to December 13. Each side waited for some activity on the part of the other. The Union soldiers again participated in drills, but during the remainder of the day they were engaged in time killing pursuits such as card playing, letter writing and waiting. The Fourteenth was no different than the remainder of the Union Army after marching to Camp Reynolds outside of Belle Plain, Virginia, near the Potomac River on December 23. Here the Fourteenth engaged in company and regimental drills with a frequency of inspection which indicated, along with orders to remain in readiness, that a move might be made with very short notice.[2]

On January 20, Burnside issued orders for his army to move. His plan was to cross the Rappahannock upstream at Bank's Ford and attack Fredericksburg from the west. On that day, the Fourteenth marched to Stoneman Station about twelve miles distant. During that night, the rain that was to seal Burnside's fate as the commander of the Army of the Potomac began to fall. The winter nor'easter with its high wind, cold and driving rain would continue for two days. On January 21, the Fourteenth continued its march through the heavy rain and camped a short distance away from Falmouth on the Rappahannock River. They had marched that day through mud which was several inches deep, due to the ground thaw which had taken place.

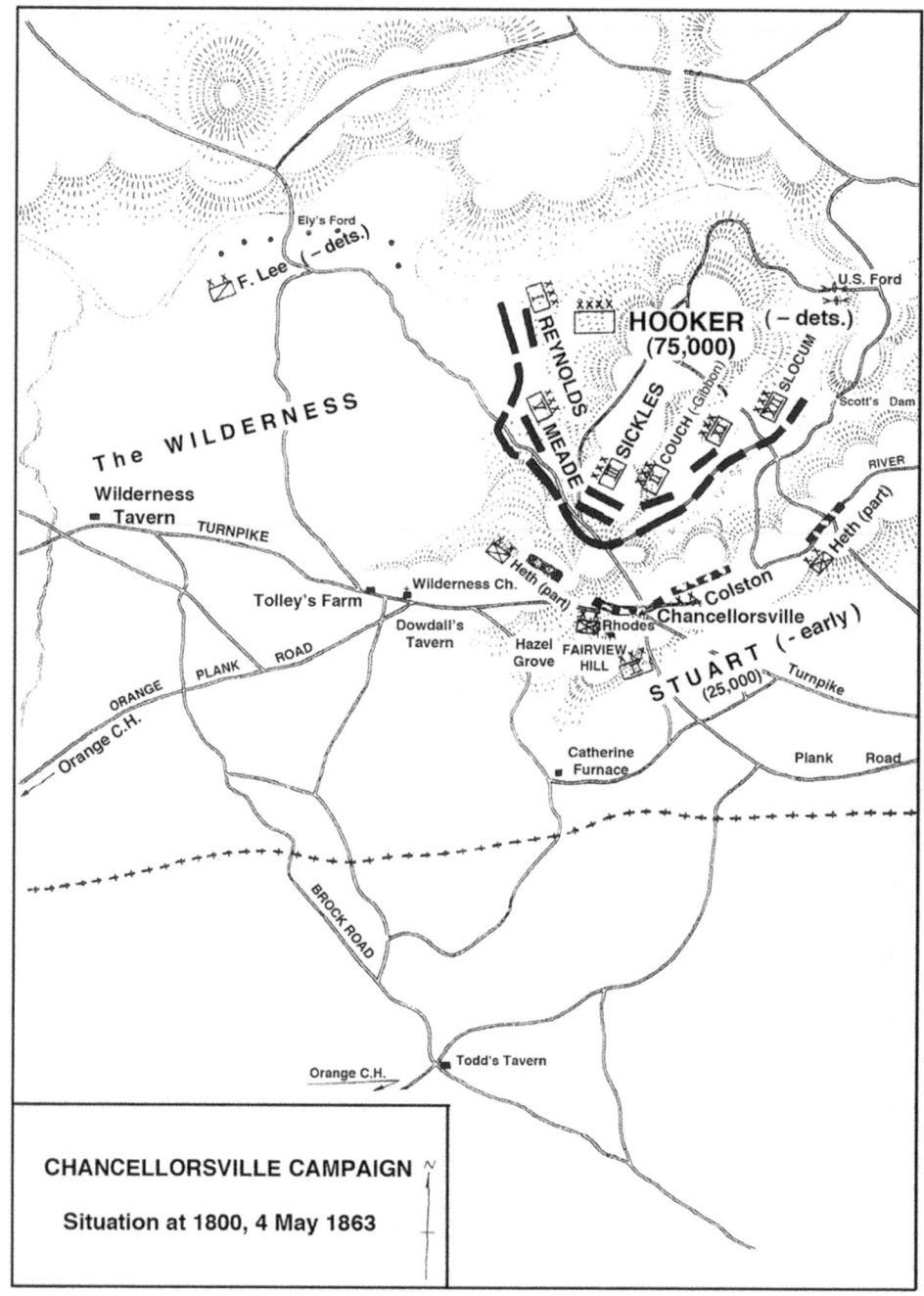

Battle of Chancellorsville (Department of History, U.S. Military Academy).

Artillery, wagons, horses, pontoon bridges, and mules became mired in the mud and had to be temporarily abandoned. The next day the Fourteenth remained in camp. The roads were even in worse condition than the day before. The only good note sounded during this entire "Mud March," as far as the Fourteenth was concerned, was that on January 20. Col. Fowler, who had been wounded at the Battle of Groveton, returned to the regiment.[3]

On January 22, Burnside cancelled his plan and the soldiers of the Union Army limped back to their camps covered in mud and taunted by the Confederates who were watching them.[4] On January 25, Lincoln replaced Burnside as the commander of the Army of the Potomac and in his stead installed Major General Joseph Hooker to this post.[5] The last official act on the part of Burnside was to issue General Order 9, in which he transferred command of the Union Army to Hooker and paid tribute to his troops in a statement issued by Assistant Adjutant General Lewis Richmond: "The short time that he has directed your movements has not been fruitfull of victory, or any considerable advancements of our lines, but it has again demonstrated an amount of courage, patience and endurance that under more favorable circumstances would have accomplished great results. Continue to exercise these virtues; be true to your country and principals you have sworn to maintain." Hooker responded with his own general order in which he accepted the command and said to his men, "In equipment, intelligence, and valor the enemy is our inferior; let us never hesitate to give him battle wherever we can find him."[6]

Joseph Hooker was born in Hadley, Massachusetts, on November 13, 1814. He attended West Point and graduated in the class of 1837 in the middle of his class. Even before his service in the Mexican War, he demonstrated leadership qualities. His executive abilities were shown during the Mexican War as a staff officer under General P.F. Smith, Benjamin Butler, and Gideon J. Pillow. He took part in the campaigns of Zachary Taylor and Winfield Scott, showing gallantry and meritorious service. He resigned his commission in February of 1853 and became a farmer in Sonoma, California. This not proving successful, he requested reinstatement in 1858. Nothing happened until the start of the Civil War. In August of 1862, he was commissioned a brigadier general of volunteers and served with McClellen in the Peninsula Campaign, before his service at Second Manassas, South Mountain, Antietam, and Fredericksburg.[7]

Soon after taking command Hooker began a reorganization of the Army of the Potomac. Hooker abolished the grand divisions which he considered unwieldy and "impeding rather than facilitating." In addition, because of reorganization, losses in battle, voluntary and involuntary transfers, resignations, etc., over seventy-five generals from brigade level or higher had to be replaced.[8] The Fourteenth was not untouched by this military shake-up.

Although they remained in the First Corps under Reynolds, their First Division commander, General Abner Doubleday, was moved to command the Third Division while General James S. Wadsworth, who had been the military governor in Washington, was placed in charge of the First Division.[9]

James Samuel Wadsworth was born in October 30, 1807, in Genesco, New York. He attended Harvard for two years, after which he was admitted to the bar. In 1861, he was a member of the Washington peace conference, which was a group of Northern and Southern men whose aim was to prevent a war. When war broke out he offered himself as a volunteer aide to Gen. Irwin McDowell at First Manassas. Afterward, McDowell recommended that he be appointed a brigadier general. Although Wadsworth had no military training, he had a lifetime of experience upon which to draw. He allowed his supporters to run him as the Republican candidate for the gubernatorial election in New York. After the Battle of Fredericksburg, he was assigned to command the First Division of the First Corps.[10]

The wholesale shuffling of senior officers along with the devastating defeat at Fredericksburg, coupled with the disastrous and humiliating "Mud March," made for very low morale in the Union Army and low morale inevitably leads to desertions. This was causing a serious problem to Hooker after he took over command of the army. In mid February, Hooker informed Washington that at the time that he took command, 85,123, officers and men were absent from his army. The Fourteenth's First Corps averaged just under eleven percent of their total.[11]

Hooker later testified that also at the time of his taking command of the Union Army, it was losing approximately 200 men a day to desertion.[12] In order to combat the desertions, straggling and misconduct in the ranks, Hooker issued the following orders on March 21.

> For the purpose of ready recognition of corps and divisions in this army, and to prevent injustice by reports of straggling and misconduct through mistake as to its organization, the chief quartermaster will furnish without delay the following badges to be worn by the officers and enlisted men of all the regiments of the various corps mentioned. They will be securely fastened upon the center of the top of the cap.
>
> | | |
> |---|---|
> | First Corps, a Sphere | First Division, red; Second, white; Third, blue; |
> | Second Corps, Trefoil | First Division, red; Second, white; Third, blue; |
> | Third Corps, Lozenge | First Division, red; Second, white; Third, blue; |

Fifth Corps, Maltese Cross	First Division, red; Second, white, Third, blue; (Light Division, green)
Sixth Corps, Cross	First Division, red; Second, white; Third, blue.
Eleventh Corps, Crescent	First Division, red; Second, white; Third, blue;
Twelfth Corps, Star	First Division, red; Second, white; Third, blue.[13]

Therefore, the insignia for the Fourteenth Brooklyn was a red sphere with the number "14" in its center. These would indicate the First Corps, First Division, Fourteenth Regiment.

While Hooker was reorganizing his army, the Fourteenth encamped at Belle Plain, Virginia, where they had there camp life interrupted on March 3. On this date, a detachment of soldiers consisting of approximately seventy-five men from the Fourteenth under the command of Capt. Gill, along with other units from the First Brigade, in addition to a cavalry unit under the command of Capt. Craig Wadsworth, left camp. All units were under overall command of Col. Phelps. They left Belle Plain Landing and proceeded down-stream until the next day when they reached Cowes Point, where they disembarked and marched to Heaths Point. From here foraging parties were sent in all points of the compass. They returned that evening with corn, cattle, horses and mules. As night fell, pickets were ordered out and precautions taken in case the Confederates were aware of their activities. The next day foragers were again sent forward. Throughout the day, groups returned with the results of their quest. That night, all the Union soldiers along with approximately twenty head of cattle, sixty horses and mules and about one thousand bushels of corn along with a large number of men, women and children who had taken this opportunity to leave their slave holders, were taken onto the awaiting barges.

On the morning of March 6, the barges left for their return trip to Belle Plain. However, a severe gale blew up soon after their departure and the entire force had to be put in at St. Georges Harbor. While there, the unit replenished their supply of fresh water which was running low because of the addition of the former slaves. The unit remained in this safe haven until the morning of March 7th, when the strong winds had abated. They arrived back at Belle Plain at about noon of that day.[14]

After this assignment, the regiment again settled back in to the routine of drills and inspections. This monotony was interrupted only when units of the Fourteenth were dispatched from Camp Reynolds at Belle Plain to outpost duty. Each time on March 4, 10, 22 and April 3, three officers and eighty-nine enlisted men left camp and returned three days later, their tour being completed.[15]

In a letter dated April 6, 1863, a member of the Fourteenth described a review of the division by Gen. Hooker, in which every available member of the regiment was put on parade.

> In heavy marching order, with overcoats rolled for said coats had seen a whole winter's service — was certainly the best manner in which the regiment could appear to advantage in point of dress: but I think the addition of white gloves was quite unnecessary, and only served to mark a more glaring discrepancy when we were in position of about face from the front, for the Quartermaster, or somebody, has been very remiss in his duty, as our pants, when we are in the above mentioned position, will sadly attest. Altogether, we acquitted ourselves in a very creditable manner.[16]

By the third week of April, Hooker had formulated his plan for crossing the Rappahannock and attacking Lee's Confederate forces. Hooker would take three corps up the Rappahannock to Kelly's Ford, which was approximately twenty-five miles to the northwest of the town of Fredericksburg. At that place, he would cross both the Rappahannock and Rapidan River, thereby positioning himself both on the left flank and the rear of the Confederate Army.[17] The Second Corps under Gen. Couch was to take up position opposite Banks Ford, but leave a division behind to deceive the Confederates into believing that no movement had been made.[18] Hooker then ordered that the Sixth Corps under Gen. Sedgwick, the First Corps under Gen. Reynolds, and the Third Corps under Gen. Sickles position themselves so that they could cross the river at Franklin's Crossing (Sixth Corps) and below Pollock's Mill Creek (First Corps) and the Third Corps, acting as support, would cross at either.[19]

As can be seen by Hooker's orders to Couch, deception was a major part of Hooker's plan. He had to keep Lee from knowing this plan. To accomplish this Hooker ordered several diversions and feints during March and April.[20] On, April 21, Hooker wrote to Washington, "As I can only cross the river by stratagem, without great loss, which I wish to avoid, it may be a few days before I make it. I must threaten several points, and be in readiness to spring when a suitable opportunity presents itself."[21]

The Fourteenth's part in this deception took place on April 22. Early on this day, the Fourteenth received orders to march. They were issued three days' rations and were told to leave their knapsacks behind. They left their camp by 1:00 P.M. What the soldiers of the Fourteenth did not know was that Gen. Reynolds had ordered Gen. Wadsworth to, "detail two picked regiments to march to Port Conway, at once, with the pontoon train, so as to arrive there tonight, keeping out of sight of the opposite shore of the river. You will direct the officers in command to throw a regiment, or a part of one, over in the boats and sweep through the town of Port Royal capturing all the enemy he can pick up and then return."

The other regiment picked for this assignment was the Twenty-Fourth Michigan, commanded by Col. Henry A. Morrow of Gen. Meredith's Fourth Brigade. In addition, the expedition contained one gun from Battery "B," under the command of Lieutenant Stewart, and sixteen unassembled wood and canvas pontoons. The arrival of the pontoons led the members of the Fourteenth to believe that part of their mission was the crossing of the Rappahannock River.

About three hours into the mission, the Fourteenth was ordered to stop and orders were received to supply six officers and one hundred and twenty men. Captains Elcock and McNeill, along with Lieutenants Cardona, Henderson, Manderville and one hundred and twenty enlisted men volunteered for this detachment. The Fourteenth then continued its march, arriving at Port Conway across from Port Royal between 10:00 and 11:00 P.M. It was at this time that the purpose of the expedition was partially revealed. The Twenty-Fourth Michigan and the volunteers from the Fourteenth were to cross the Rappahannock at first light under the command of Col. Morrow, who was the senior officer.[22]

After hearing their mission, some members of the Fourteenth were beginning to feel some trepidation. They knew that just a few days before an entire division had attempted this same crossing and were repulsed by a strong force of Confederates who occupied rifle pits all along the embankments they were about to assail. What they did know was that this crossing had to be accomplished no matter the cost.[23]

Before dawn on April 23 the volunteers form the Fourteenth, along with two hundred volunteers from the Twenty-Fourth Michigan, began to assemble the pontoon boats which consisted of pine frames over which waterproof canvas had been stretched. It had been raining all night and was still raining when the volunteers pushed off for the opposing shore approximately 350 yards away. As the rifle pits came into view, the Michigan soldiers who had seen some action at Fredericksburg, but were relatively new, were happy to have the Brooklyn soldiers with them on this mission: "The Fourteenth Brooklyn ... was a hard nosed old militia outfit which had joined at the beginning of the conflict and had been in the division since 1862. They had seen rough going but still wore their zoaves [sic] uniforms with red breeches, which made them a conspicuous target for the enemy. The Twenty fourth was in good company"[24]

Both regiments expected strong resistance. Each man in the crowded boats waited for the report of the first shot, the signal for a blistering fuselage of shots and shelling which would cost the regiments many brave soldiers, since the Confederate defenders would have a distinct advantage.[25] The Federals knew that the shots could rip into their canvas boats sinking them and putting them into the water at the mercy of the Confederates.[26] As the pontoon boats reached the opposite shore, not a shot had been fired. The assaulting force of Michigan and Brooklyn soldiers leaped from their boats and ran up the embankment to the rifle pits which had occupied so much of their thoughts on the trip across the Rappahannock. To their surprise and relief, the rifle pits were unoccupied. Without wasting time, the assaulting force entered the town of Port Royal. In doing so, a group of Confederate cavalrymen numbering about seventy-five fled the town without firing a shot. The wagon train which they were guarding tried to flee, but the sight of Union riflemen made a decided change in their plans. The wagon train filled with grain and meal was quickly set on fire by the Federals.

After searching the town and obtaining whatever information they could, the Federal force reassembled at the pontoon boats. Their search of the town produced six Confederate prisoners, fifteen horses and mules, a bag of Confederate mail and two women who claimed loyalty to the Union and who had been detained in the town. All embarked for the opposite shore while the horses and mules swam alongside the boats. As they reached the safety of the reminder of the Twenty-Fourth Michigan and the Fourteenth Brooklyn on the opposite shore, the Confederates, who were about six miles from the town and had been alerted by the Confederate cavalry, began to arrive at the river. They could do little except fire a few shots as the last of the boats reached the shore. The men from the assault group each rejoined their respective regiments. The Fourteenth marched back to their camp through the continued rain, arriving there at about 8:00 P.M., after marching approximately thirty-six miles in twenty-four hours.[27]

The effectiveness of these feints is questionable. Doubleday, who participated in one of these demonstrations, also at Port Royal, indicates that they caused Jackson "to strengthen his force in that quarter."[28] However, Joseph Cullen writes that Lee was not disturbed by these diversions at the extreme right of his line. Lee believed that the real attempt to cross the Rappahannock would be made above Fredericksburg. Lee did not intend to move his troops until he could see a large scale movement on the part of the Federals.[29]

The next day, there was much jubilation in the camp of the Fourteenth. During their celebration of this successful and bloodless expedition against the Confederates, a communiqué arrived from General Reynolds. "The general commanding takes occasion to thank the Twenty Fourth Michigan and the

Fourteenth Brooklyn for the prompt manner in which they accomplished the object of the expedition to Port Royal. The endurance shown by their march of nearly thirty-six miles in twenty-four hours, during the very inclement weather of yesterday, proves their valor as tried and experienced soldiers, and entitles them to the highest admiration and praise."[30] Their happiness was multiplied by the ration of whiskey which was issued to them because of the successful mission.[31]

On April 27, Hooker was ready to implement his plan. Lee, who controlled all the crossings of the Rappahannock, as well as the heights between Skinker's Creek and the United States Ford, which was a distance of approximately twenty-five miles, had men and artillery strategically placed so that he could sweep the slope of the hills as well as the bottomlands upon which an attacking force had to march. Lee was secure in his positioning of his troops on his left flank and felt that an assault on his right flank would draw Hooker too far away from his base and require too many pontoon bridges, too many artillery trains and too many supply trains over too long a distance to be practical for Hooker. However, this is exactly what Hooker proposed to do.

The success of this movement was due in large part not only to the fifty thousand soldiers of the Army of the Potomac, who marched with great speed the 37 miles in two days, each carrying approximately sixty pounds of equipment and burdened with artillery and supplies and who crossed the Rappahannock River and the Rapidan River, which was closely guarded by the Confederates, without any appreciable loss of men or supply but also to the forces of Gen. Sedgwick, who were left at Fredericksburg with the First, Third and Sixth Corps to hide the movement of Hooker's force.[32]

The Fourteenth, which was part of the force left at Fredericksburg, had received its orders on the 27th of April. They were directed to leave camp on April 28, with eight days' rations. They halted for the night at about 10:00 P.M., just a short distance form the river and near the Fitzhugh House.[33] The crossing at this point is variously called Fitzhugh Crossing, Pollock's Mill Creek Crossing and Reynolds Crossing. This crossing point on the Rappahannock River is located one and three quarter miles below the lower pontoon crossing used by part of Gen. Franklin's Left Grand Division during the Battle of Fredericksburg the previous December. Fitzhugh Crossing is also located just a short distance downstream from where Pollock's Mill Creek joins the Rappahannock.[34]

One man who witnessed the events in late April was James Rich. He was a member of the Fourteenth and a Quaker. James enlisted in the Fourteenth at Brooklyn on September 15, 1862, and was described as being born in Philadelphia, age 24, 5 feet 10 inches tall, light complexion, blue eyes and brown hair. To his friend Sue Sheppard he wrote,

> On the 23rd of last month ... our regiment marched 20 miles through the pouring rain, and crossed the river at Port Royal in boats. Captured several prisoners and returned again to Camp. Marched 41 miles through wind and rain, and accomplished our errand in 20 hours. What does thee think of that Sue. Broke Camp again on the 27th. Rained as usual [sic]. Marched within one mile of the Rappanhock and halted till 10 o'clock at night. Then marched to the River under cover of Darkness, and succeeded in crossing 8 o'clock in the morning of 28th under a heavy fire from the enemy. 24th Michigan crossed first in Boats, charged on the Rebs and drove them at point of the Baynot. Our Regt were deployed as skirmishers in the River bank. Had 25 wounded none killed. The Balls flew very thick around thy humble servent [sic] but haven't had a scrach as yet, and I feel as though I was going to get through safe. Last night part of our Regt were the advance picket had some heavy artillery fighting yesterday afternoon. Dident do much damage. Killed some few. I fergot to state that we took about 100 prisoners, several wounded. They are coming in all the time.[35]

A member of the Twenty Fourth Michigan who made the Fitzhugh Crossing wrote to his family describing his activities:

> We commenced moving down to the river. We moved so slow that we did not get down to the bank of the river until nearly daylight, and we had got about half the pontoons in the water when it began to get light and the Rebels opened a sharp fire upon us from their intrenchments [sic] on the opposite side of the river.... They opened fire upon our engineers laying the pontoons and sent them flying to the rear ... cross over and drive the Rebels out of their intrenchments — and if successful we could then lay the bridges. The 24th Michigan. and 6th Wisconsin were the ones ordered to do this. So we formed battalion front, came down to the river with yells like demons or something else, rushed into the boats and went over, bullets flying like hail stones. The 7th Wis. and 14th Brooklyn were to cover us with their fire, but after we got across and were going up the bank, their bullets flew into and around us about as fast as the Rebels. But the most of us got up the hill and made the rebs skedaddle out of that double quick.[36]

Across from these Union forces which had been left at Fredericksburg, Gen. Jubal Early of Jackson's Corps had already posted his four brigades along the Richmond, Fredericksburg and Potomac Railroad, between Deep Run on the left and Hamilton's Crossing on the extreme right. At this point the railroad was about a mile from the Rappahannock and was parallel to it. In addition, Early had positioned three regiments forward of this area, towards the Richmond Stage Road approximately a half mile from the river. These three regiments were to be used as skirmishers.[37] Jackson then assigned Gen. Robert Rodes' Division to assist Early on his right at Hamilton's Crossing. The division under A.P. Hill was brought into line behind Early and Gen. Raleigh Colston was positioned behind Rodes and held in reserve.[38]

12. Chancellorsville Campaign

The crossing of the Rappahannock below Fredericksburg began in the early hours of April 29 while Hooker's flanking force crossed the river some thirty miles above Fredericksburg. Hooker's orders were that the First Corps was to cross at or before 3:00 A.M. at Fitzhugh's Crossing, the Sixth Corps was to cross at or before 3:30 A.M. at Franklin's Crossing and the Third Corps was to cross at or before 4:30 A.M. using either crossing. Brig. Gen. Henry Benham, of the Engineers, was to be in charge of constructing the pontoon bridges. However, due to delays and arguments as to who was in command of the soldiers crossing the pontoon bridges, both bridges were delayed in their construction and the First Corps did not get into their boats until 9:00 A.M.[39]

Gen. Reynolds had picked Wadsworth's Division as the spearhead to crossing the river. Wadsworth, in turn, picked the Iron Brigade to make the initial assault. The Sixth Wisconsin and the Twenty-Fourth Michigan boarded their boats and rowed toward the Confederate side. The Thirteenth Georgia, and the Sixth Louisiana, who were on the opposite shore, opened up with rifle fire. To support the troops who were crossing, the remainder of the Iron Brigade, consisting of the Nineteenth Indiana, Second Wisconsin and Seventh Wisconsin, were assigned to cover their advance. The Fourteenth Brooklyn was also assigned to this task only after they had finished carrying the pontoon boats to the shoreline at the behest of Gen. Wadsworth. This was supposed to be accomplished by the pontooniers, but they were repelled by the severe Confederate fire. After the Sixth Wisconsin and the Twenty-Fourth Michigan got to the opposite shore, they jumped into the water and waded ashore, pulling themselves along by grasping onto bushes. Once ashore, they assaulted the rifle pits and drove off the Confederate defenders, capturing approximately 120 prisoners. In the excitement of the moment, some members of the Fourteenth crossed with the troops, and although unarmed, offered moral support to the troops by their cheering. After the successful assault and the completion of the pontoon bridges, the Fourteenth, along with the remainder of the division, crossed the river. The Fourteenth formed a line of battle along with the brigade on the brow of the hill formerly occupied by the Confederates.[40]

On April 30, Stewart's Battery was positioned in the area of the Fourteenth and Phelps was then ordered to position his brigade to the left, so that they might link up with the Fourth Brigade, which was instrumental in the previous night's assault. During that day, the Confederates began to fire artillery into their positions. Neither side attacked that day and no advances were made by either side. However, that night Gen. Wadsworth ordered that rifle pits and entrenchments be constructed all along the front. This raised the expectations of the regiment that the next day would see some kind of operation commence. However, May 1 brought neither cannon nor rifle fire, and to the relief of the regiment, nothing unusual happened.[41]

By this date, Lee became convinced that Hooker's main thrust would be somewhere else rather than at Fredericksburg. He had received reports of the movement of Union Troops and had decided that Hooker's attack would come west of Fredericksburg. He, therefore, withdrew many of his troops from the area around Fredericksburg, and redistributed them west of the town along the turnpike between Salem Church and Chancellorsville. To Jubal Early went the job of defending Fredericksburg and holding up the left wing of the Union Army. To do this, Lee left Early approximately 9,000 men and 45 cannons. This consisted of Hays' Louisiana Regiments, Gordon's five Georgia Regiments, four regiments and one battalion of Hokes North Carolinians, four Virginia Regiments of William Smith, and four batteries of artillery under Col. R. Snowden Andrews. In addition, 1,500 Mississippians from Barksdale's four regiments were detached from McLaws' Division, along with the artillery reserve of Brig. Gen. William Pendleton. With these insufficient forces, Early was to defend Fredericksburg and the pontoon bridges below the town against the approximately 30,000 troops of three corps which were arrayed against him.[42]

On May 2, Early ordered Pendleton to open fire on the Union force with his long range artillery. His purpose in doing this was to see the type of action with which the Union forces would respond. These were replied to by the Union artillerists. Soon afterwards Early saw large amounts of infantry marching toward Fredericksburg and thought that a large scale attack was about to take place in that area. In reality, these troops, the Fourteenth among them, had been ordered to re-cross the Rappahannock River. The Fourteenth received these orders at approximately 9:00 A.M. By 10:30 A.M., the entire division was marching on the north side of the river towards United States Ford. After marching about twenty miles, the Fourteenth bivouacked for the night approximately two miles from United States Ford.

The next day, Sunday, May 3, the Fourteenth crossed the Rappahannock again at United States Ford and at 4:30 A.M. Gen. Wadsworth, who met the brigade after their crossing, personally designated the position which the brigade was to occupy. This position was to the right of the general line. At this point the Fourteenth prepared rifle pits and put up whatever defenses they could gather.[43]

Originally, Reynolds' First Corps was to have moved away from Fredericksburg on May 2. However, a communication error and a slow courier delayed Hooker's order. It was Hooker's intent to move the First Corps to the right of Howard in the area of Chancellorsville. Hooker knew that Howard's end was not anchored and was subject to attack from the west.[44] This was exactly what occurred on May 2 when Jackson brought his forces along the Federal front, concealed by the woods, and emerged on Howard's right to roll up the Union defenses. However, because of the attack, Hooker placed Gen. Meade's Fifth Corps as well as Reynolds' First Corps along Hunting Run, near the Ely's Ford Road. Their purpose was to protect the Rappahannock crossings from attack by the Rebel forces and so that it could be used by the Federals as a path of retreat. This position also put Meade and Reynolds on Jackson's flank. Meade offered a plan to attack Jackson. However, Hooker thought the plan was risky and decided against it. Hooker's sole purpose now was to save the army and this he set about accomplishing.[45]

General G. Warren, who was Hooker's engineer, had set up a defensive line that was a large salient. The western arm of this salient was anchored by the Rapidan River and the eastern arm by the Rappahannock River, thus protecting the pontoon bridges at the United States Ford. The salient was about three and a half miles deep and approximately three miles at its base. The First Corps held the westernmost portion of the line and it was in this area that Gen. Wadsworth had personally placed the Fourteenth and its brigade.[46]

The Fourteenth spent May 4 in line of battle ready for advance or defense. In the afternoon, the Confederates attacked their line, but were repulsed with the loss of many Confederate lives. The next day, May 5, there was heavy fighting to the left and center of the line of the Fourteenth but none to their front.[47]

On May 5, at midnight all of the corps commanders, with the exception of Sedgwick and Slocum, met with Hooker to discuss the options left to the Army of the Potomac. Hooker's purpose was to find out the opinions of his commanders as to whether the army should advance or withdraw beyond the Rappahannock. Hooker left the meeting so that they might discuss the issues. When he returned to the meeting Reynolds, Meade, and Howard reported in favor of attacking, while Sickles and Couch voted to retreat. Hooker, who had already made up his mind to retreat, no doubt, was hoping to get a vote in favor of this action so that his explanation to Washington would seem like a consensus. However, Hooker took the responsibility for the decision and ordered his army to retreat across the Rappahannock at United States Ford.[48]

The Fourteenth received its orders to retreat at approximately 2:00 A.M. on May 5. It had been raining for several days and the roads were almost impossible to negotiate because of the mud. As they neared the bridge across United States Ford, Gen. Wadsworth found Col. Fowler and asked him to form his regiment in line at the approach to the bridge. Gen. Wadsworth was afraid that the so far orderly retreat of the Union Army might degenerate into a rout and that the sight of the regiment would restore confidence in the soldiers crossing the bridge. Col. Fowler complied with the directions of Gen. Wadsworth and formed the Fourteenth in line of battle at the entrance to the bridge and remained in form until the entire corps had passed. The general praised the Fourteenth for this action and the regiment crossed the river at 8:00 A.M. and bivouacked about four miles from Falmouth near Brears Church, after marching thirteen miles to camp.

Between May 7 and May 10, the regiment camped near the Fitzhugh farm at about the same place that it had rested on the evening of April 28 and finally at Camp Wadsworth.[49]

The Chancellorsville Campaign was over. It had started out with great expectations and achievements. Hooker had successfully led the major part of his army away from Fredericksburg, crossed the Rappahannock and the Rapidan and came up on Lee's flank and rear, before he even knew that they were gone from Fredericksburg. Having accomplished this, Hooker failed to attack but instead delayed, thus giving Lee almost two days to concentrate his forces in the area of Chancellorsville. On Saturday, May 2, Jackson was allowed to execute his flanking march across the Federal front, while the Union Army was held in check by Anderson's Division and a part of McLaws' Division, totaling about twelve thousand men. In addition, Hooker became defensive and remained in his salient awaiting the arrival of Sedgwick from Fredericksburg; nor did Hooker make no attempts to reach Sedgwick. Finally, Hooker had been out generaled by Lee. At the time that Hooker broke off the engagement and withdrew across the Rappahannock, he still had almost three times as many troops as Lee, many of whom had not been engaged in combat in the prior days.[50]

E. Porter Alexander, who was one of Lee's ablest artillerists and was present at Chancellorsville and Fredericksburg in April–May of 1863, wrote, "On the whole I think this plan was decidedly the best strategy conceived in any of the campaigns ever set on foot against us."[51]

During this campaign an old enemy was lost. On the evening of May 2, Jackson along with several of his staff, was reconnoitering the ground over which he expected the next day's battle to transpire and was beyond the pickets of his own lines when volleys of musket fire broke the silence of the night. Confederate soldiers had fired on the group. Jackson had been hit three times. "Three .57 caliber bullets struck him at the same time. One splintered bone and tendons three inches below the left shoulder before passing out the arm. Another entered the left forearm an inch below the elbow and exited on the other side just above the wrist. A third ball passed through his right palm, broke two fingers, and lodged against the skin on the back of the hand."[52] Jackson's arm was amputated, but on May 10 he succumbed to pneumonia.[53]

Jackson was beloved by his own soldiers and respected by his enemies. The Brooklyn *Daily Eagle* reported, "There is now apparently no reason to doubt the death of the most valiant and the most successful of the Rebel leaders, Stonewall Jackson.... His command seldom had exceeded twenty thousand men, but every man was brought into action.... Had he died in the nation's service his memory would have been kept green for ages. As it is, his death removes one of the ablest enemies the national forces had to contend against."[54]

The Fourteenth Brooklyn had faced him at First Manassas, Gainesville, Groveton, Second Manassas, South Mountain, Antietam, and Fredericksburg. They would face him no more.

During the Chancellorsville campaign, the Fourteenth Regiment suffered the death of four men and the wounding of nineteen, all during the fighting at Fitzhugh Crossing.[55]

13. The Road to Gettysburg

After the Chancellorsville campaign, the Army of the Potomac retreated across the Rappahannock to its former location opposite Fredericksburg. However, neither side wanted to remain encamped for a long period of time. Hooker still had his army intact and even after his recent defeat, his army contained more troops than Lee had in his entire command. Lee for his part had defeated Pope at Second Bull Run, McClellan at Antietam, Burnside at Fredericksburg and Hooker at Chancellorsville. Now, he decided, it was the time to attempt a second invasion of the north. Lee knew that his army grew weaker with each battle and supplies were harder and harder to come by. Therefore, the South needed a large scale battle that would conclude the war in its favor. His movement north would also break up any plans the Union Army might have by way of an offensive in the area of northern Virginia. In addition, by crossing the Potomac in the area of Pennsylvania, he hoped that the Federals might draw troops from other areas, in particular Vicksburg, to protect Washington.[1]

With the death of Jackson, Lee reorganized his army into three corps. Longstreet would retain his First Corps while Richard Ewell and Ambrose P. Hill were elevated to the rank of lieutenant general and given command of the Second and Third Corps respectively. Longstreet's Corps consisted of the divisions of Generals McLaws, Pickett and Hood. Gen. Ewell's Corps consisted of the divisions of Generals Early, Johnson and Rodes, while General A.P. Hill's Corps consisted of the divisions of Generals Anderson, Heth, and Pender.

On June 3, 1863, Lee began the campaign which was to result in the bloodiest clash on American soil and lead to the downfall of the Confederacy. On that day Lee ordered Gen. McLaws to lead his troops along the south bank of the Rappahannock to Culpeper, Virginia, to join Hood and Pickett, who had stopped there after coming from Suffolk. Richard Rodes was dispatched to Culpeper on June 4; Gen. Early and Gen. Johnson followed the next day. Gen. A.P. Hill and his three divisions were to remain at Fredericksburg.[2] After leaving Culpeper, Lee's army used the Valley of the Shenandoah to good advantage. The valley contained good roads for their travel north and their movements would be shielded from the Federals by the Blue Ridge and

South Mountains. Longstreet's Corps was to reach Pennsylvania by traveling along the base of the Blue Ridge Mountains. They were to cross the Potomac at Williamsport. Ewell's Corps was to march through the Shenandoah Valley and cross the Potomac River at Williamsport and Shepherdstown. The troops marching through Williamsport were to continue past Hagerstown and Chambersburg, into the area of Harrisburg. His troops passing through Shepherdstown were to go through Sharpsburg, Emmitsburg and Gettysburg until they reached the bridge over the Susquehanna River, at Wrightsville. A.P. Hill's Corps was to travel behind the Blue Ridge Mountains, cross the Potomac River at Shepherdstown and follow Ewell's troops by way of Sharpsburg, Emmitsburg and Gettysburg to the Susquehanna. The passage of Lee's army into Maryland and Pennsylvania took several weeks to accomplish but for the most part was accomplished by June 23rd.[3]

While Lee was making his preparations for the invasion of the North, Hooker was trying to come up with a plan of his own. With Lee's forces stretched out along a 100 mile line between Hill's Corps at Fredericksburg on the right and Longstreet situated at Culpeper, while Ewell's Corps was at the Shenandoah Valley on the left, Hooker wanted to cross the Rappahannock and strike Hill at Fredericksburg. These plans were rejected by President Lincoln and Gen. Halleck.[4] Hooker also wanted to abandon the Union fortifications at Harpers Ferry and use those ten thousand troops in his campaign against Lee.[5] Gen. Halleck refused to allow the abandonment of Harpers Ferry or Maryland Heights because he believed that they were strategic locations and had been fortified at much expense.[6] Hooker, feeling that he no longer had the confidence of the administration in Washington, offered his resignation, in essence stating that with the troops under his present command he could not fulfill his original instructions to protect both Harpers Ferry and Washington.[7] Hooker's resignation was accepted and on June 28 command of the Army of the Potomac was given to Maj. Gen. George G. Meade.[8] Meade accepted and became the new commander of the army.[9]

George Gordon Meade was born on December 31, 1815, in Cadiz, Spain. His father was a wealthy American businessman who lost his fortune because of his association with Spain during the Napoleonic Wars. Meade graduated from West Point in 1834, ranking nineteenth in a class of fifty-six. He resigned his commission in 1836 and began a career as a civil engineer. In 1842, he joined the army again and was appointed to the Corps of Topographical Engineers, where he constructed lighthouses and breakwaters along with coastal and geodetic survey work. Soon after the Civil War started Meade was promoted to brigadier general of volunteers by Pennsylvania Governor Andrew Curtin and given command of a brigade of Pennsylvania volunteers.[10]

Hooker and Lee were moving their armies, the Fourteenth Regiment returned to the area of Fitz Hugh House, Virginia, and settled into Camp Wadsworth on May 8. On the 13th, Lieut. Col. DeBevoise, who had commanded the regiment since the wounding of Col. Fowler at the Battle of Groveton in August of 1862, and whose resignation after the return of Col. Fowler was accepted by Washington, left for Washington. He was considered a brave and able officer and his loss was regretted by every member of the regiment regardless of his rank.

Life in the camp continued as usual until May 21. On this date 13 officers and 275 enlisted men left camp to picket the Rappahannock. They returned two days later without having incurred any incidents.

May 31, was an important date in the history of the Fourteenth. On that day the two year enlistments of the Twenty-Second, Twenty-Fourth and Thirteenth Regiments of New York Volunteers expired. The Fourteenth had been brigaded with these units since they arrived in Virginia. The Fourteenth, having enlisted for three years, was now reassigned into the Second Brigade of the First Division, which consisted of Seventy-Sixth, Ninety-Fifth and One Hundred Forty-Seventh New York along with the Fifty-Sixth Pennsylvania and the Seventh Indiana. The Second Brigade was commanded by Gen. Lysander Cutler.[11]

Before the Civil War broke out Cutler had a varied career which included school master, selectman, railroad director, college trustee, state senator and militia colonel. He saw military service as the commander of the Maine militia in the Aroostook Indian Wars. He began his Civil War experience as the colonel of the Sixth Wisconsin Regiment. He was severely wounded in the leg at the Second Battle of Manassas and was appointed as a brigadier general later that year.[12]

John Vliet, of the 14th Regiment, wrote home about being placed in the Second Brigade under Cutler: "Genl. Cutler appears a very good officer & visits our Camp almost daily & looks after us more than any General we have been under yet."[13]

Since deserting was a continuing problem in the Army of the Potomac, Hooker had taken several initiatives to alleviate it. Among them was the establishment of an orderly and fair system for granting leaves and furloughs which afforded the soldiers relief from homesickness. In addition, Hooker established roving patrols of soldiers in Washington and Baltimore as well as the major arteries leading north. The purpose of these patrols was the capture and return of deserting soldiers. Hooker also issued commands restricting packages which contained civilian clothing and punished the civilian population who sold such clothing to soldiers.[14]

In the early hours of June 12, the Fourteenth Regiment was ordered to leave Camp Wadsworth. They ended the day near Deep Run at about 6:00 P.M. after traveling about twenty-five miles. However, the regiment had made a disturbing stop at Hartwood Church at approximately midday. The entire First Division had been drawn up in a hollow square to witness the execution of Pvt. Wood of the Nineteenth Indiana. Private Wood had been convicted of desertion when, after the Battle of Chancellorsville, he stole a Confederate uniform and traveled to Washington, where he pretended to be a deserter from Lee's Army. Woods' firing squad consisted of one man from each of the regiments of the First Division. A soldier from Company C was chosen from the Fourteenth for this morbid duty. "The deliberate and ghastly preparation for his execution affected scores of men throughout the division more than any fight which they had ever participated in had been able to do."

Wood's grave had already been dug and his coffin had been placed next to it. He was blindfolded and his arms tied. An officer had been given the assignment of dropping his handkerchief as a signal for the squad to fire. When they did, Wood fell across his own coffin. He was buried and the division continued their march. However, it was many miles before many of then could recover from the experience.[15] For those who knew of it, the grief and sorrow felt by all those who witnessed the execution was compounded by the fact that within an hour of the event, his father appeared at division headquarters with a pardon signed by Abraham Lincoln.[16] A letter to the *Sunday Mercury* stated, "From this sad scene, we were marched on our journey and instead of the joke, the song, or the merry laugh as we wended our way, all eyes were cast down, and not a word seemed to be spoken. It really was the stillness of death, and showed that each heart was touched."[17]

When Lee moved his army into the Shenandoah Valley, Hooker broke up his camps along the Rappahannock and moved his entire army toward Washington. The route that he followed was along the Orange and Alexandria Railroad. His army first reached Bealton, Warrenton and Catlett's Station on June 13 and 14. The Fourteenth arrived at Bealton on June 13, after a warm and dusty march of fifteen miles via the Warrenton Road. Hooker then moved his army to Fairfax Station and Manassas on the 15th and 16th of June. He remained here for several days, until he found out more about Lee's intentions. Meanwhile, The Fourteenth resumed its march on June 14 passing Warrenton Junction, Kettle Run, Broad Run and Bristow Station. On the 15th the regiment crossed the Manassas Plains and crossed Bull Run at Blackburn's Ford, then traversed the battlefield which marked Bull Run.

As the battlefield was crossed the veterans began to tell the newer troops about the battle and the locations and movements of different units during the fighting, testimony of which was all around them. The skeletons of Northern and Southern soldiers lay all about the field uncovered from their hastily made graves by the weather of the previous two years. "To the newer men in the division the sight of those bare bones sticking out of the earth ... was an eloquent reminder that there is more of the pitiful and terrible than of the grand and spectacular in the game of war."[18]

That night the regiment camped at Centerville Heights and remained there until about 4:00 A.M. on the 17th, when the regiment began its march toward Leesburg. During these days the men of the regiment recovered their strength from their long marches and had enough time to wash their clothes and eat substantial and properly cooked food.[19] At about midday on the 17th, the regiment was on the countermarch until it reached Hundon. The members assumed that the officers had misdirected the regiment, thereby necessitating the countermarch. The distance they traveled that day was approximately twenty miles and it was reported to be the hottest day of the season. Consequently, many men suffered the effects of the sun, including Capt. Gill. The next day the regiment rested but on the 19th they marched the short distance to Guilford Station.[20]

A letter written near Guilford Station by James Rich to Sue Sheppard was typical of a soldier Union or Confederate. He writes about coming battles, life in camp and things at home. Although this letter was about nothing in particular, writing or receiving letters provided a welcomed break in the misery of their condition and the deprivation of war, and gives some insight into what the soldiers were contemplating and for what they were longing.

> Dear Friend Sue
>
> Thy very welcome letter of the 8th is before me. I received it a little over a week since while on the march, and was indeed very much pleased to hear from thee. I was so unwell when it was handed to me, I could not read it till next morning. It was our second days' march out the 19th the weather was very warm, and water scarce. We had a very severe trial of it I tell thee. It proved almost too much for me. Our marches were long from 19 to 24 miles a day. Sunday the 14th we marched all day and all night. I don't think I ever felt so near dead, before, it was too much. A great many fell on the road side. Quite a number were sun struck. It was forced march to get to Manassas plains before the Rebs did and we accomplished it, and by so doing I think, got clear of a Battle there. We Biyvauacked at Manassas one day, and got tolerabely well rested and had the pleasure of getting some good water. Sue I drank water that your Hogs woldent scarcely wallow in and glad to get it. How often I thought of Bogg's sweet pump water, and longed for just one drink. Our hurried marched is over now, I hope. We have laid here three days and have gone into Camp count again. We had rain a day or two ago and the weather is quite cool and pleasant. My health isn't very good. I'm under the Dr care but I guess I will be all right again in a day or two. I'm very much reduced down Sue. I don't suppose I would weigh now over 140 lbs. I doubt if thee would know me.
>
> Well Sue, did thee get much frightened last week when thee herd Lee was going to visit you. I expect you must have had quite an exciting time. I'm glad

13. The Road to Gettysburg

something has happened to arouse the creeping north. It was high time something took place to drive them to arms. I have some hopes of the war being settled now, perhaps between this and New Year. I don't think it possible for it to last much longer, but there is not telling though....

Sue thee does Indeed seem to be very fortunate in getting to weddings. I presume the next one thee attends will be thy own, or has thee concluded to wait till the soldiers come home. I think that would be a sensible conclusion because thee knows, Sue, they will want something pretty nice and I recommend thee as being a good eater Laugher & talker.... Thee is very kind to offer thy services so cheep, Sue. If I hadn't already come to the conclusion to be an Old Back I would engage thy little self to assist me. But Sue lets live Single. I know I shall have to any how, for the Girles all merry fool me. Cant believe a word they say and more, about the time a fellow thinks he is all right, some body else comes along and cuts him out. Thee knows Sue I speak from experience Ahem! Yes Sue.

I bought about a pint of splendid strawberries the other day, bought them of a colord Lady. When thee is helping thyself to a right nice dish just think of thy humble servent, and take some extray in my behalf, and every time thee takes a mouthful think of Jim....

Well Sue when thee writes till me al the news—who had spunk enough to go to war, and who hadent. How is Buck Jones getting along, any one gowing there is perticular, and how is George flourishing. I expect he will marry soon. When did thee here from Mary R. I suppose thee has heard they are rebuilding their house. It really looks like something don't it.

Perhaps thee will have another wedding to attend soon. I very seldom here from her any more. Her mind I presume is too much engaged. Wish well thee knows who. I must now close hopingto hear from thee very soon.

Thy true Friend, J.B. Rich
B Co. 14 Regt. N.Y.S.M. Washington D.C, or Elsewhere[21]

The Fourteenth remained at Guilford Station for several days during which time it rained heavily. Many of the regiments who had discarded their blankets and overcoats during the very hot days of the prior week soon regretted their short-sightedness. Some members of the regiment went to the top of a railroad embankment where the drainage was better in order to avoid sleeping on the wet sloppy ground.[22]

On June 25, Hooker began to move his army across the Potomac River into Maryland by using Edwards Ferry. By June 28, his entire army was in the area of Frederick, Maryland. The Fourteenth crossed on June 25, also using Edwards Ferry. They immediately marched through Poolsville to Barnesville, where they camped for the night. The next day the Fourteenth continued its march, crossing the Monocacy River at Greenfield and stopping at Jefferson after traveling fifteen miles during the day. In the next two days, they completed their march, and on the 28th of June, arrived near the area of Frederick. It was at Frederick that Meade took command of the Army of the Potomac.[23]

The following day, June 29, Meade continued his march north. He sent Gen. Reynolds' First Corps along with Howard's Eleventh Corps to join Brig. General Buford's Cavalry Division at Emmitsburg, Maryland. These made up the army's left wing. That same day, the Fourteenth was assigned to guard a supply train. The members of the regiment found this to be very tiresome work. It rained almost the entire day and the regiment was required to march at the double quick in order to keep up with the fast moving wagon train. After traveling about twenty-five miles that day, the Fourteenth reached Emmitsburg at about 9:00 P.M. The next day, June 30, Gen. Meade ordered Gen. Reynolds to take command of the First Corps and Eleventh Corps, which were at Emmitsburg, and the Third Corps, which was on its way from Taneytown to Emmitsburg.

Gen. Reynolds now commanded the entire left wing of the Army of the Potomac. One of the first orders he gave was for the First Corp, now under the command of Maj. Gen. Abner Doubleday, to march towards Gettysburg and camp for the night along Marsh Creek.[24] The Fourteenth, along with the remainder of the Second Brigade, camped on the south side of the creek in a plowed field. The officers occupied themselves with writing out payrolls and muster rolls as well as other reports required since that day was the end of the fiscal year. The enlisted men refreshed themselves at an adjacent dam, rested and foraged for food.[25] A chicken farmer from a nearby farm house approached Col. Fowler and asked that he remove his regiment. When Fowler told him that it would be impossible, the farmer told Fowler that he would hold the Colonel personally responsible for all items taken from his farm. It is not known how seriously Fowler tried to keep his men in check. What is known is that almost every man in the regiment had chicken for dinner that night.[26]

This was not the only incident of this type that took place on the way to Gettysburg. John Vliet, who was now an officer in the Fourteenth, wrote several letters to his boss, Charles Collins. On July 2 during the Battle of Gettysburg, Vliet wrote of the regiment's activities in the prior two weeks and their march through Maryland, "Our men did not behave as well as might be expected as pigs, sheep, chickens etc. suffered at first considerably until a guard was detailed each day before marching who kept the men within a certain distance when bivouacking for the night."[27]

Gettysburg was a strategic location even though neither side was anticipating a battle there. It was the hub of ten different roads and a railroad. These roads led to passes through the mountains as well as the Potomac and Susquehanna Rivers, in addition to the cities of Baltimore and Washington. From the northwest the Mummersburg Road entered the town. From the north came the road from Carlisle and from the northeast was the road from Harrisburg, the capital of Pennsylvania, while the Hanover Road, the York

Pike and the Gettysburg and Hanover Railroad came from the east. To the south was Taneytown Road, while the Baltimore Pike approached the town from the southeast and Emmitsburg Road from the southwest. The Chambersburg Road and the Hagerstown Road each crossed Willoughby Run and approached Gettysburg from the west after crossing a ridge near a Lutheran Seminary. This ridge later became known as Seminary Ridge. About two miles north of the town, the ridge divides. This second ridge is McPherson's Ridge and is approximately fifteen hundred feet from Seminary Ridge. Along the Chambersburg Pike and just north of it was an unfinished railroad cut. South of the town was another ridge, the highest of which is Cemetery Hill. East of this is Culp's Hill. This hill is well wooded with a very steep eastern slope. East of this, Rock Creek flows toward the south. From Cemetery Hill the ridge runs south for approximately three miles, culminating at a hill called Round Top, after passing rock elevations known as Little Round Top and Devil's Den.[28]

On June 30, Gen. Henry Heth of A.P. Hills' Corps, having been notified about a possible supply of shoes warehoused in Gettysburg, sent Gen. Pettigrew and his brigade to investigate. As Pettigrew was about to enter the town, Gen. Buford and two brigades of Union cavalry were observed coming toward Gettysburg along the Eimmitsburg Road. Pettigrew withdrew and reported back to Gen. Heth. Gen. A.P. Hill was at Heth's headquarters when Pettigrew reported his findings. After discussion, they concluded that the force in Gettysburg was only for the purpose of observation. Heth asked and was given permission to bring his entire division to Gettysburg and obtain the much needed supply of shoes.[29]

None of the enlisted men in the Fourteenth knew what was in store for them. That evening, eating their chicken, they did not know that they were about to take part in the largest and bloodiest battle ever to take place on American soil. For many of them, that chicken was going to be their final meal. The next day, they were going to Gettysburg.

14. Battle of Gettysburg: Day One

Army of the Potomac
  Major General George G. Meade
First Corps
  Major General John F. Reynolds
  Major General Abner Doubleday
  Major General John Newton
First Division
  Brigadier General James S. Wadsworth
Second Brigade
  Brigadier General Lysander Cutler
14th Brooklyn Regiment
  Col. Edward B. Fowler
7th Indiana Regiment
  Col. Ira Grover

76th New York Regiment
  Major Andrew Grover
  Capt. John E. Cook
95th New York Regiment
  Col. George B. Biddle
  Major Edward Pye
147th New York Regiment
  Lieut. Col. Francis Miller
  Major George Harvey
56th Pennsylvania Regiment
  Col. J. W. Hofmann

As dawn broke on July 1, Meade's Army of the Potomac, which was spread throughout the area around Gettysburg, was issued the orders which he had drafted the night before. The right wing of his army, the Fifth Corps, was to march from Union Mills to Hanover and was to be supported by the Sixth Corps, which was to proceed through Westminster to Manchester, Pennsylvania, 10 miles to the south of Hanover. The Twelfth Corps, which was at Littletown, was to proceed to Two Taverns. The Second Corps would serve as the reserve at Taneytown, where Meade would maintain his headquarters. Gen. Reynolds, on the left, would advance his First Corps from the area around Marsh Creek toward Gettysburg. Following the First Corps would be the Eleventh Corps. The Third Corps was to proceed to Emmitsburg, from which it was in a position to support the First and Eleventh Corps. To the cavalry was given the responsibility of guarding the front and flanks at a sufficient distance as to give Meade "timely notice" of the direction and movement of the Confederates.[1]

At 5:00 A.M. on July 1, Confederate Gen. Heth started his division—consisting of the brigades of General's Davis, Pettigrew, Archer and Col.

14. *Gettysburg: Day One* 135

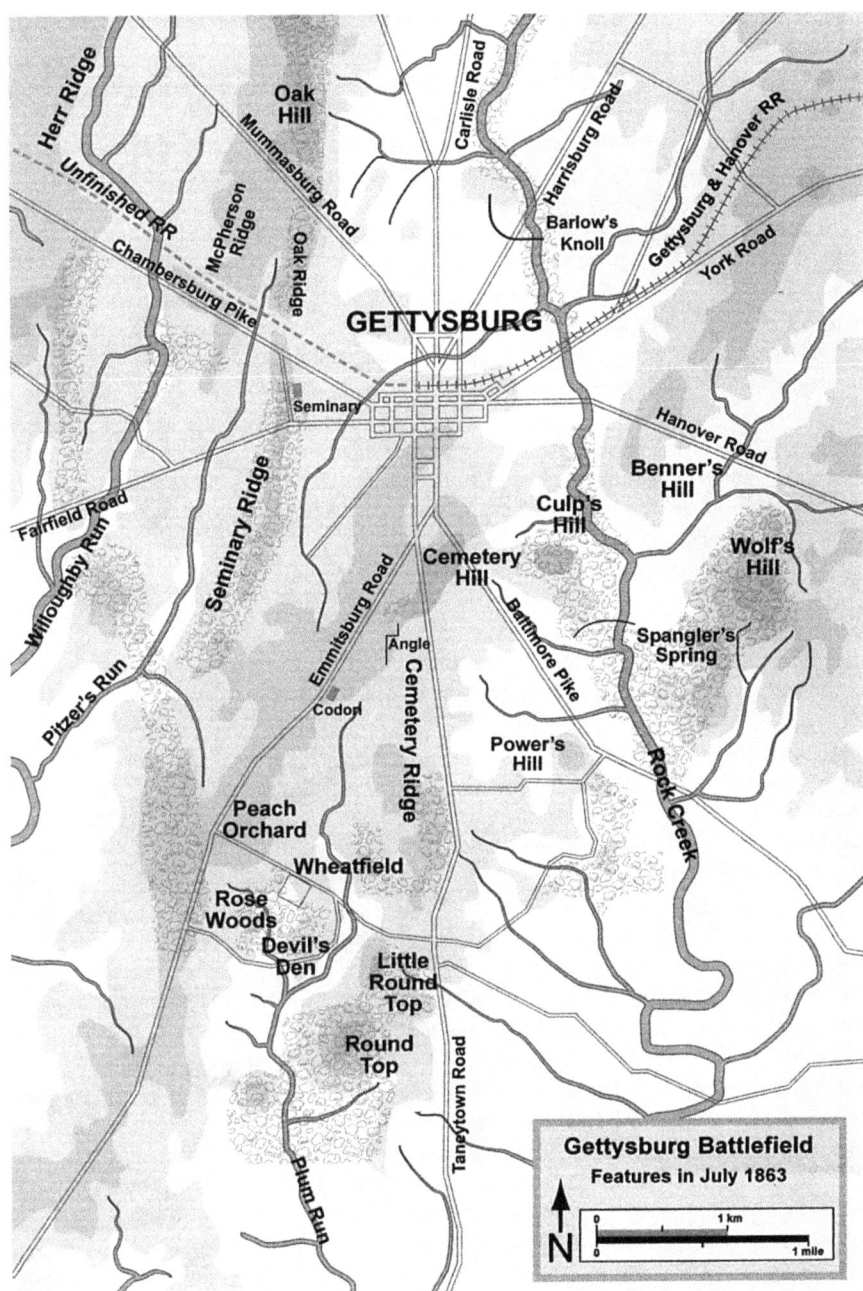

Overview of Gettysburg (map by Hal Jespersen, www.cwmaps.com).

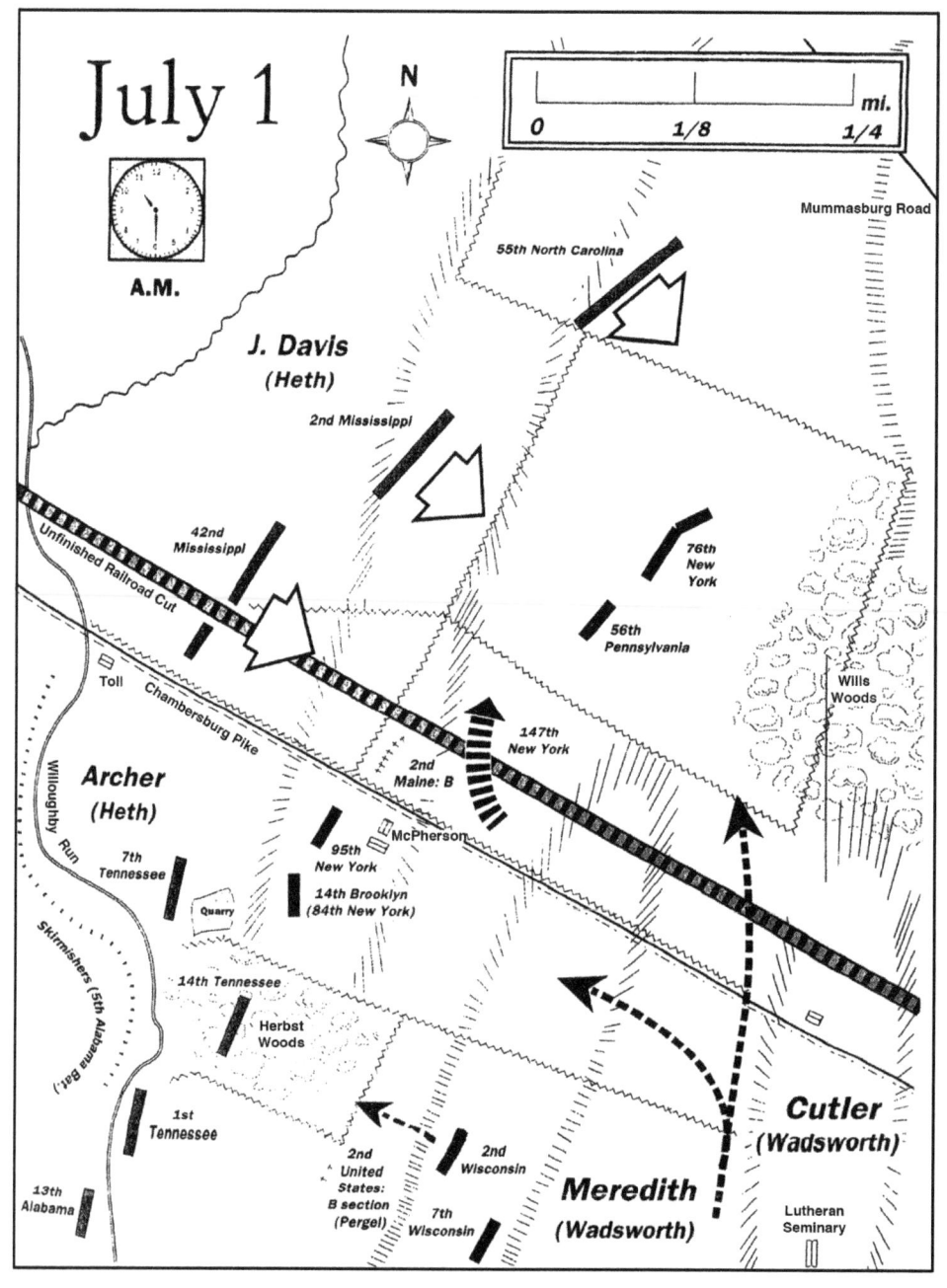

Position of the 14th, Day One, 10:30 A.M. (from Noah Andre Trudeau, *Gettysburg: A Testing of Courage*, HarperCollins, 2002. Reprinted by permission of Harper-Collins Publishers).

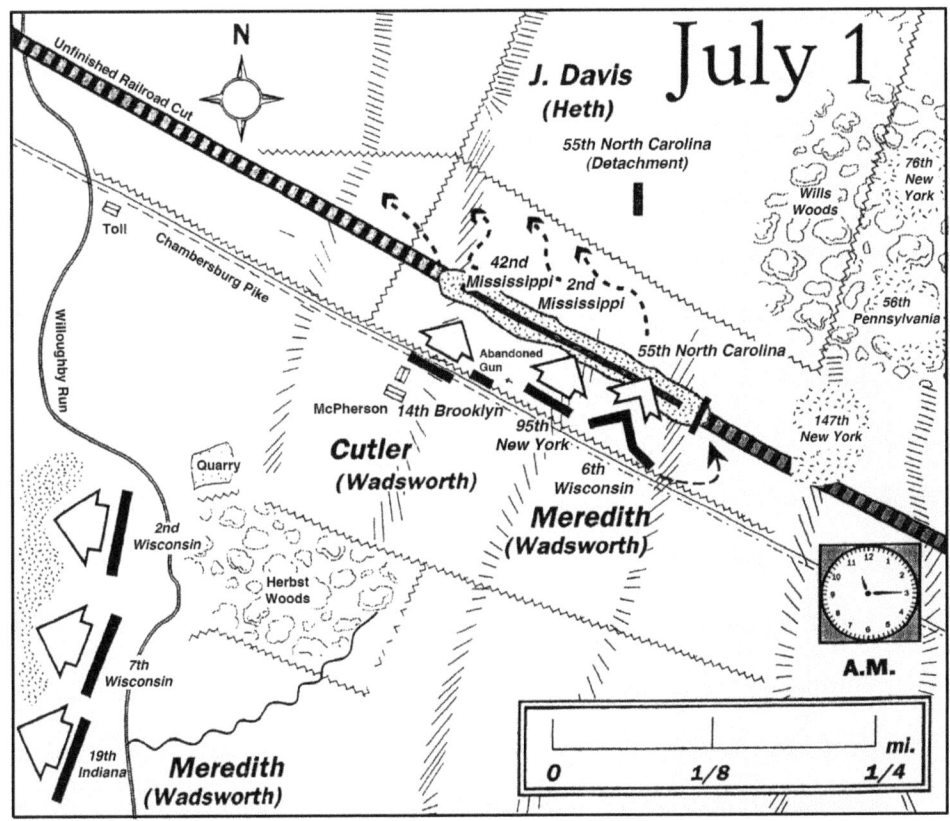

Fowler pivots to attack Davis (from Noah Andre Trudeau, *Gettysburg: A Testing of Courage*, HarperCollins, 2002. Reprinted by permission of HarperCollins Publishers).

Brockenbrough — toward Gettysburg. He expected little opposition from a force which he believed was small and inadequate to his numbers. However, as he neared the town it became evident that he was facing a large force consisting of infantry, artillery and cavalry. Archer's Brigade was to the right of the Chambersburg Turnpike and Davis's Brigade was to the left of the turnpike. Both were in line of battle. Gen. Pettigrew's and Col. Brockenbrough's Brigades were held in reserve.

Heth directed Archer and Davis to advance so that they might judge the strength of the Union forces before them. They soon encountered Union Gen. Buford's dismounted cavalry in the form of Col. William Gamble's First Brigade consisting of about 1,600 men. Davis engaged in heavy fighting with these Union troopers and advanced, eventually capturing the Union cannon,

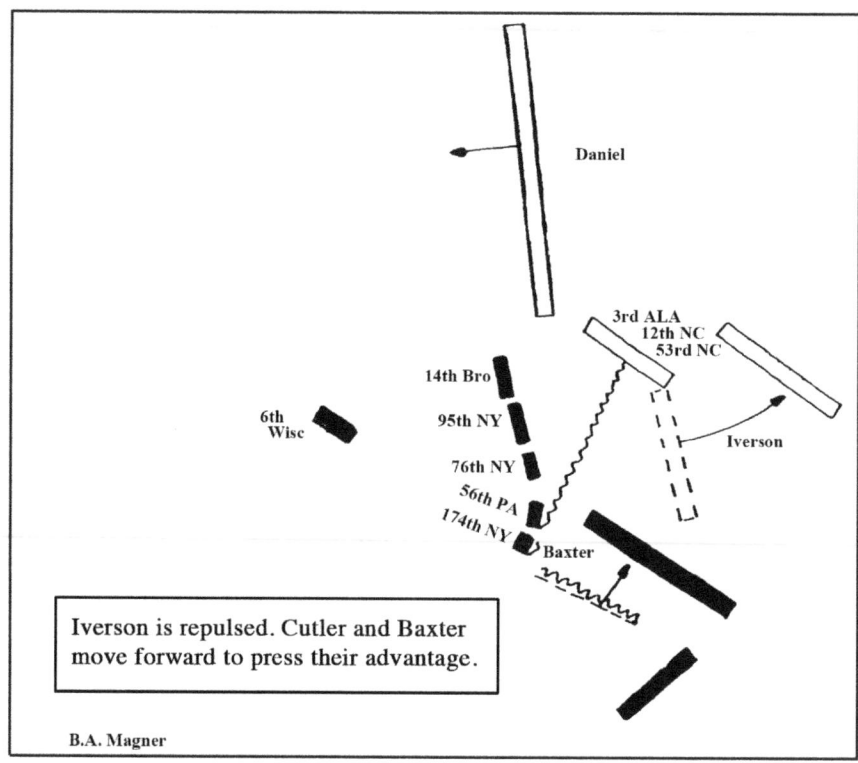

Cutler deploys against Daniel, Iverson, and O'Neil (from James L. McLean, *Cutler's Brigade at Gettysburg*, Butternut and Blue, 1994. Courtesy Butternut and Blue Publishers).

but after suffering the loss of many of his men, including all but two of his field officers. He was forced to retreat. Archer became almost surrounded by the Union troopers and was forced to retreat.[2]

The Fourteenth Regiment rose early on that muggy morning. Gen. Reynolds had ordered his First Corps now under the leadership of Gen. Doubleday to Gettysburg. Reports had come to Reynolds about Buford's engagement of the Confederates west of town. The Third Division was supposed to take the lead that morning but Reynolds had stopped to speak with Gen. Wadsworth, and since his division was closer to Gettysburg, Reynolds ordered Wadsworth's Division to the head of the corps. Since Cutler's Brigade was ready they took the lead.[3]

General Reynolds then galloped out to meet with Gen. Buford west of Gettysburg. After meeting with Buford and analyzing the positions on McPherson Ridge, Reynolds ordered Buford to hold the position since it covered the western approaches to Gettysburg. Reynolds knew that Wadsworth's Division was only 30 minutes away.[4] Meanwhile, Wadsworth sent word to his regiments to prepare to march. Col. Fowler received his orders from a rider sent by Wadsworth and within minutes bugles sounded signaling the breakup of the camp. The entire brigade was readied by 8:00 A.M. They marched out of their encampment and crossed Marsh Creek by using the main bridge on the Emmitsburg-Gettysburg Road. Cutler's Brigade led Wadsworth's Division on that day and Wadsworth's Division led the corps. Gen. Cutler led his brigade on that July morning and was accompanied by Gen. Wadsworth. Leading the brigade was the Seventy-Sixth New York, followed by the Fifty-Sixth Pennsylvania, the One Hundred Forty-Seventh New York, the Ninety-Fifth New York, and the Fourteenth Brooklyn. At the rear of the infantry were six 3 inch cannons of Capt. James Hall's Second Maine Artillery.[5]

After meeting with Buford, Gen. Reynolds rode south along Seminary Ridge so that he might hurry Cutler's Brigade. At the Codori Farm, Cutler's Brigade met Gen. Reynolds, who was waiting for them. The brigade and the Fourteenth had been moving at double quick time, since the men had seen puffs of white smoke and heard the sounds of artillery fire along the ridges west of Gettysburg. The Fourteenth knew that there was serious work to be done on that day and the veins of every man swelled with the thought of what was ahead of them. Reynolds directed the brigade to leave the road at the Codori farm and cross the field to the north toward the Seminary. When the Fourteenth reached the area near the Seminary, they were ordered to load their rifles.[6]

General Reynolds had by this time returned to the front, where Buford's dismounted troopers were finding it hard to hold back the Confederates. Reynolds knew that he would need fresh artillery to hold the Confederates while Wadsworth's Division was getting into position to relieve Buford. Knowing that Hall's Second Maine artillery was with Wadsworth's command, he ordered them forward immediately. Hall met with Reynolds, who told him where he wanted his artillery placed and to fire at the Confederates' artillery until Wadsworth's Division had been placed and Buford's troopers could be relieved.[7] Reynolds placed Hall's artillery between the Chambersburg Pike and the unfinished railroad cut. Since Hall's guns were in an exposed position, he ordered Wadsworth to deploy Cutler's Brigade in such a way as to protect Hall's guns.

When Cutler's Brigade arrived, the Seventy-Sixth and One Hundred Forty-Seventh, New York along with the Fifty-Sixth Pennsylvania were ordered to cross the railroad cut and to the right of Hall's Battery. The Fourteenth Brooklyn and the Ninety-Fifth New York were directed personally by

Reynolds south of the Chambersburg Pike, near McPherson's Farm, so that they might protect the left of Hall's Battery. Since Fowler's Fourteenth Brooklyn and Biddle's Ninety-Fifth New York had been detached from Cutler's Brigade by Gen. Reynolds, Fowler was given command of this demi-brigade below the Chambersburg Pike. Fowler placed the Fourteenth on the western edge of the McPherson orchard with the left next to Herbst (McPherson) Woods. He then placed the Ninety-Fifth New York near the McPherson house and its garden. Fowler had placed these regiments on a direct line with Hall's artillery and battery.[8] Reynolds then left to hurry the First Brigade, consisting of the Second, Sixth, Seventh Wisconsin, Twenty-Fourth Michigan and Nineteenth Indiana. As these regiments were entering the low area west of the Seminary, they were ordered up the eastern slope of the hill to counter Archer's advance up the western slope. At this point one of the great questions of the Civil War occurs. Cutler indicates that the Fifty-Sixth Pennsylvania fired the first infantry shots of the Battle of Gettysburg while others from Wisconsin claim that distinction.[9]

As the Second Wisconsin went up the slope and reached its summit, a volley from the Confederates brought down many from the regiment as well as Gen. Reynolds, who had been struck in the back of the neck with a shot from the Confederates.[10] Some controversy exists as to whether Reynolds was hit by a sharpshooter or during a volley by the Confederates. E.T. Boland and his friend John Hendrix, both of Company F of the Thirteenth Alabama, were on the field that day. Boland later wrote that while under attack by a Wisconsin unit, a group of Union officers appeared 80 to 100 yards in front of them and at the same location as Reynolds' monument now stands. Hendrix fired and an officer fell from his saddle. Years later, while visiting the battlefield, Boland affirmed that John Hendrix had shot an officer off his horse at the spot which indicates where Gen. Reynolds was shot.[11] The fact that Reynolds was killed by a volley was also confirmed by Thomas Hopkins of the Sixteenth Maine.[12]

Davis's Brigade — consisting of the Second, Eleventh and Forty-Second Mississippi and the Fifty Fifth North Carolina — was attacking the three regiments of Cutler's Brigade north of the Chambersburg Pike while Archer's Brigade — the Thirteenth Alabama and the Fifth Alabama Battalion along with the First, Seventh and Fourteenth Tennessee — was attacking the Fourteenth Brooklyn and the Ninety-Fifth New York south of the Chambersburg Pike.[13] Davis's Brigade continued eastward. The Forty-Second Mississippi was on the right and had its right beginning on the Chambersburg Pike, the Second Mississippi occupied the center of the lines and the Fifty-Fifth North Carolina anchored the left of the brigade. At about 10:30 A.M., Davis formed his three brigades into a line of battle. His fourth brigade, the Eleventh, had been detached to guard the division wagon train. Davis, like Doubleday and

Reynolds, understood the importance of the terrain to his front. "Between us and the town, and very near it, was a commanding hill in wood, the intervening space being enclosed fields of grass and gain, and was very broken. On our right was a turnpike and a railroad with deep cuts and heavy embankments, diverging from the turnpike as it approached the town. On the high hill the enemy had artillery, with infantry supports."[14]

The Forty-Second Mississippi was attacking the One Hundred Forty-Seventh New York. The Forty-Second's left extended beyond that of the One Hundred Forty-Seventh. The Second Mississippi was in front of the Fifty-Sixth Pennsylvania and the Seventy-Sixth New York, while the Fifty-Fifth North Carolina was well beyond their flanks.

Col. John Connally, the commander of the Fifty-Fifth North Carolina, urged his regiment forward, then wheeled his regiment to the right. The maneuver out flanked the Fifty-Sixth Pennsylvania and the Seventy-Sixth New York and brought the North Carolina Regiment perpendicular to the flank of the Seventy-Sixth New York. This caught the two New York regiments in a withering crossfire and casualties rose sharply.[15] Capt. J.V. Pierce of the 147th later said of this, "A regiment — the Fifty-Fifth North Carolina was pressing far to our right and rear, and came over to the south side of the rail fence. The colors dropped to the front. An officer in front of the center corrected the alignment as if passing in review. It was the finest exhibition of discipline and drill I ever saw."[16]

Wadsworth realizing that these regiments were about to be annihilated, ordered their retreat so that they might reform and continue the fight. The Fifty-Sixth Pennsylvania and the Seventy-Sixth New York withdrew to the woods around Seminary Ridge. However, the One Hundred Forty-Seventh New York did not receive the order and therefore did not withdraw.[17]

Meanwhile, south of the Chambersburg Pike, Archer's Brigade was attacking the Fourteenth Brooklyn and the Ninety-Fifth New York. This demi-brigade was commanded by Col. Fowler. Archer's skirmishers could be seen in the wooded area in front and to the left of Fowler's men. As the Confederates were crossing Willoughby Run, both sides began firing. The firing on both sides was intense. Col. Biddle of the Ninety-Fifth New York was wounded and replaced by Major Pye. Col. Fowler's horse was struck several times in his head as was that of his adjutant. In addition, Col. Fowler was struck in his thigh by a spent Minie ball, which passed through his clothes and caused a severe contusion.[18] The fire from Fowlers' demi-brigade was so effective that the Confederates angled their advance so that they might use McPherson's Woods as protection during their advance.

McPherson's Woods was the main point of contention in the fighting south of the Chambersburg Pike and commanded the entry way into the town of Gettysburg. The north side of the woods stretched east from Willoughby Run, approximately 1,800 feet across the western arm of McPherson's Ridge. The woods were shaped like a truncated triangle with its 1,200 feet base along Willoughby Run. The trees in the woods were widely spaced. The area had been used for grazing and picnicking and had very little undergrowth, thereby allowing good vision and very little impediment to movement.[19]

However, Wadsworth's First Brigade — the Second and Seventh Wisconsin, the Nineteenth Indiana and the Twenty Fourth Michigan — was placed in line to the left of the Fourteenth and entered the woods from the opposite direction. The Sixth Wisconsin was held in reserve. After severe fighting the Confederates were driven from the woods. Gen. Archer himself was captured and several hundred of his men were killed or captured.[20]

During this defense of the Chambersburg Pike, one member of the Fourteenth saw what he described as an old man who appeared to be over seventy years of age and others "loading and firing gallantly defending their homes and their county's honor." The person was probably John Burns, a cobbler and at times a constable who was a veteran of the War of 1812 and the Mexican War. He had tried several times to enlist, but was turned down each time.

On the morning of July 1, when he heard the thunderous noise of the cannon fire, put on his best clothes, consisting of a swallow-tailed blue coat with gold colored buttons and a tall bell-crowned hat and, ignoring the pleas of his wife, left his home and headed for the battle along with the One Hundred Fiftieth Pennsylvania. After arriving at the battlefield Burns was sent to join the Iron Brigade in the area of McPherson's Woods. John gave good service to his country that day and was cheered by members of the Seventh Wisconsin for shooting a Confederate officer from his horse. During the battle Burns was hit by a bullet to his belt buckle which doubled him over. He also received a painful cut on his ankle.[21]

At about this same time, Col. Fowler, who was south of the Chambersburg Pike along with the Fourteenth Brooklyn and the Ninety-Fifth New York, noticed that the Confederates north of the Pike were passing his flank in their pursuit of Hall's Artillery, which was being withdrawn along with the Fifty-Sixth Pennsylvania and the Seventy-Sixth New York. While Hall's battery was being overrun, Col. Fowler saw the last of the artillerists fire his cannon before running off. In another instance of bravery, another artillerist, who had hitched some horses to a cannon and was preparing to carry it to safety, was approached by a Rebel lieutenant who demanded that the gunner surrender the cannon. The artillerist instead took up the reins of the horse so that he might make a dash to the rear. The Rebel officer saw that the artillerist was not heeding his warning. He cocked his gun and placed it at the Union solder's head while he repeated his demand. The Union soldier ignored the request and began to gallop off when the Confederate officer discharged his pistol, hitting the cannoneer in the back. The Union artilleryman managed to remain on the horse until he reached the Union lines and had brought his cannon to safety before he fell from his horse and died.[22]

Realizing that his regiments, along with the Iron Brigade, who were attacking Archer, were now in peril of being out flanked should Davis's Brigade cross the Chambersburg Pike, Fowler ordered his men to face to the rear. He marched them until they were aligned with the Confederates at which time he changed their front to the right. Both regiments then advanced toward the fence along the Chambersburg Pike with the Ninety-Fifth New York to the right of the Fourteenth Brooklyn.[23]

Major Blair of the Second Mississippi wrote that after the Union line which he was attacking began to retreat, he decided to pursue them into Gettysburg and capture the town.[24] His intentions were quickly stymied when they began to receive flanking fire from the Fourteenth and Ninety-Fifth from across the Chambersburg Pike.

Since Cutler's men north of the Pike needed help, Gen. Doubleday ordered the Sixth Wisconsin to their aid. On their way to the Pike, they joined Fowlers' demi-brigade along the Pike and to the right of the Ninety-Fifth New York. Together, the three regiments attacked Davis's Brigade north of the turnpike.[25]

As Col. Fowler gave the order to charge, the Fourteenth advanced with a cheer. They mounted the fence along the Chambersburg Pike and up to the roadway. During this time, all three regiments were under intense musketry from the Mississippians who where opposing them. After crossing the Pike, the Fourteenth recovered the cannons which had been lost by Hall during his retreat. Again the Fourteenth met heavy fire: "The balls came as thick and fast that the whirring noise they made sounded like the steady rhythm of machinery. For just an instant, as the full force of this terrible fire broke along their front, the line wavered. But it was only for an instant, and then, with another cheer louder and more determined, the men rushed on."[26]

The Second and Forty-Second Mississippi Regiments were surprised by the fire coming from their flanks. In their pursuit of the One Hundred Forty-Seventh Regiment, as well as Cutler's other two regiments north of the Pike, they had lost all cohesion as a force. To avoid the fire from the Federals south of the Pike, the Mississippians ran into an unfinished railroad cut that ran parallel to the Chambersburg Pike. The railroad cut had sides that were between 10 and 15 feet high and therefore they could not fire above the rim and effectively took themselves out of the battle. Davis, therefore, ordered their retreat and also ordered the Fifty-Fifth North Carolina to cover them.[27]

Upon seeing this, Col. Fowler ordered his troops to charge the railroad cut.[28] After severe fighting, some of it hand to hand, the Confederates surrendered. Col. Fowler, whose demi-brigade had attacked the center and right of the railroad cut, and Col. Dawes of the Sixth Wisconsin, whose regiment had attacked the left of the railroad cut, had captured most of Davis's Second and Forty-Second Mississippi Regiments, as well as Hall's Battery, which had been over-run earlier in the day.[29]

John Jenkins of the Fourteenth described the charge in a letter, "Then came the order to advance the line and 'charge' them. The boys rushed forward with a will, the enemy fell back to a railroad cut in which they took cover, showering their bullets on us, our brave boys dropping at every step. On, on they advanced and retook the lost gun.... With a tremendous cheer the boys advanced to the cut. The enemy rose up, threw down their arms and surrendered."[30]

One of the men involved in the charge was Private Edward Riker. When Riker, of Company D, enlisted in the Fourteenth Regiment, he purchased a diary in which he could put all of his activities during the war. Throughout his years of service, he would write his activities in camp or campaigning or marching to battle and how he missed being home.

On the first days battle at Gettysburg, Riker participated in the charge of the Fourteenth which resulted in the capture of Davis' entire brigade of Mississippi soldiers. During this time, Riker lost his diary. After the battle Riker thought that he would never be able to find the diary and resolved himself to its loss.

Several weeks later, a young girl from Gettysburg was walking through the area when she came across the diary. Thinking that the owner, whose name and company were on the inside flyleaf, had been killed, she kept the diary. Periodically, she would visit the National Cemetery and look for the name that appeared in the diary.

In October of 1887, twenty-four years after the battle, a monument was dedicated to the Fourteenth Regiment. A member of the town, Mr. Weaver, attended the dedication and asked several members of the Fourteenth who were in attendance if they knew of a private Riker. To his amazement, Private Riker was pointed out to him. Weaver asked Riker to follow him so that he could introduce his wife. Mrs. Weaver then told him about her visit to the railroad cut after the battle 24 years earlier and finding a diary. She then gave the book which she had been holding for all those years to its rightful owner.[31]

A dispute regarding Fowler and the Fourteenth, and Dawes and the Sixth Wisconsin, has been raging continuously since that morning of July 1. The Dawes faction contends that the charge capturing the railroad cut was made by the Sixth alone and that the Fourteenth along with the Ninety-Fifth did not come up until after the capture of the Mississippians. Fowler contends that he ordered the charge and had sent his aide to notify Dawes.[32]

After the capture of the railroad cut the Fourteenth was ordered to join Cutler's other regiments which were reforming north of the Pike in the same area that the Fifty-Sixth Pennsylvania and the Seventy-Sixth New York had fought just a short time before.[33] In addition, in order to strengthen the position, Gen. Wadsworth ordered Calef's Battery to the location that Hall's Battery had occupied prior to the morning's battle. This position was between the Chambersburg Pike and the railroad cut. The battery immediately began to fire and received fire from the Confederates.[34]

It was about this time that the wounded were being retrieved from the field. Several members of the Fourteenth had fallen that morning. Four had volunteered to find Corporal George W. Forrester of Company C, who was wounded in the earlier fighting. They made their way through an intense bombardment of rifle and cannon fire to reach him. They rolled him onto a piece of canvas, which they had brought with them. With each rescuer holding a corner of the canvas, they lifted him up. Just as they did this, a shell from a Confederate cannon exploded in their midst. Forrester and three of his four comrades were killed outright. The fourth man had his leg blown off. His cries of pain and suffering could be heard even above the deafening noise of battle. He later died from the loss of blood while he was being taken to the hospital.[35]

While all this was happening, the Fourteenth was detached from Cutler's Brigade by Gen. Wadsworth. They and the Sixth Wisconsin were ordered to support Calef's Battery.[36] Soon after the Fourteenth was detached, Cutler saw artillery and infantry emerging from the hills and woods to the north. Cutler changed front to meet the new challenge. In addition, because the Fourteenth and Sixth were so far advanced, he ordered the Fourteenth along with the Sixth and Calef's artillery to retreat since they were now under pressure from the north and west. They fell into line with Cutler's other regiments.[37]

This new threat from the north was Gen. Rodes' Division from Gen. Ewell's Corps. He decided to attack Cutler, who had been reinforced by Baxter's Brigade from Robinson's Division. Rodes attacked this position by sending O'Neal's Brigade to the left, Iverson's Brigade in the middle and Daniel's Brigade on the right with Ramseur's Brigade to be held in reserve. O'Neal's Brigade was beaten back by Baxter. Iverson's Brigade had targeted the Federal line which was held by Cutler. Iverson's Brigade consisted of the Fifth, Twelfth, and Twenty-Third North Carolina regiments. As the North Carolinians approached Cutler's position, Baxter's Brigade, which was hidden, opened fire along with Cutler's men when the Confederates were less than 300 feet away. At this point the Fourteenth along with the remainder of Cutler's Brigade pushed forward to Iverson's flank. Iverson's Brigade was devastated, losing approximately five hundred men in killed and wounded.

Cutler again changed his front to meet Daniel's Brigade, which was approaching Cutler's left flank. This caught Daniel's Brigade in a crossfire between Cutler and Stone's Pennsylvania Brigade. Cutler's men soon had to retire from the field since they were running out of ammunition. They were replaced by parts of Robinson's Division. The Fourteenth along with the remainder of the brigade were finally able to get some rest. It was about 4:00 P.M. The Fourteenth had been up since 4:00 A.M., on the march since about 7:00 A.M., and in combat since 10:00 A.M.[38]

The Fourteenth did not rest for long. Shortly after arriving at the rest area, Cutler was ordered to send three regiments to support Steward's Battery B of the Fourth U.S. Artillery, which was called up from its reserve position near the Seminary. Steward had placed three of his guns to the right of the railroad cut and three more to the left of it.[39] For this task, Cutler selected the Fourteenth Brooklyn along with the One Hundred Forty-Seventh and Seventy-Sixth New York Regiments.[40] While in this position, these soldiers and artillerists, assisted by the Sixth Wisconsin, which had also been assigned to protect the battery, repulsed several charges made by Scales' Brigade of Pender's Confederate Division.[41]

North of this area of the battlefield, Col. Fowler had observed that Gen. Howard's Eleventh Corps was retreating before the attacking Confederate soldiers of Gen. Richard Ewell. This information was sent to both Cutler and Wadsworth. The retreating Eleventh Corps left the flank of the First Corps exposed as well as threatening its line of retreat.[42] Finally, Cutler was ordered to fall back. While withdrawing, the Fourteenth helped to retrieve one of Stewart's cannon and dragged it with them. The defense of Stewart's artillery allowed hundreds of Union soldiers from other brigades to retreat without being captured.[43]

As the Union forces were retreating through Gettysburg, many members of the community who had a commitment to the Union cause stood in their doorways and windows giving food or refreshing drink to the soldiers as they passed.[44] In a letter a member of the Fourteenth wrote, "In passing through the town, bullets whizzing rather fast and promiscuously, I remarked to a young lady, who handed me a drink of water, that I thought it unsafe for her to expose herself outside of the door while so many bullets were striking about her. She said she did not care; she was going to help all she could to a drink, and was not afraid of the Rebels."[45]

As the Fourteenth retreated through Gettysburg, a cannon shot struck a building causing brick and mortar to be showered down on Col. Fowler and his adjutant, nearly crushing them. When the Confederates entered the town the shelling stopped and the fire of musketry could be heard.[46] The hospital for the Fourteenth and the One Hundred Forty-Seventh was located in the hotel as well as in nearby buildings in Gettysburg. The more severely wounded were under the care of the doctors, but the less wounded had the run of the hotel and soon found the hotel's supply of liquor, of which they imbibed liberally. At about 3:00 P.M. the surgeon for the One Hundred and Forty-Seventh, A.S. Coe, was called away to treat several officers and soldiers at a nearby location. As he was returning to the hotel, he found that the Confederates were in the process of driving the Union forces through the town and taking possession of it. He was able to avoid the advancing Rebels, and as he approached the hotel, he saw about a dozen members of the Fourteenth Brooklyn in position at the front of the hotel defending it against about 20 Confederates who were about to open fire. Surgeon Coe called to them not to fire and informed them that the soldiers were wounded. The Southern officer who was in charge of the Rebels ordered them not to shoot and ordered Coe to disarm the Union soldiers or he would order them shot. Coe ordered the men to give up their weapons and return to the hospital. Most of the members of the Fourteenth complied with the instructions, but a few were so drunk that they had little regard for their own well being. However, Coe was able to get them to lay down their arms as well. In the incident, one member of the Fourteenth was killed.

After this, Coe saw a mounted Confederate officer avowing that he was going to raze the hospital because his soldiers had received rifle fire from an upstairs window. After approaching Coe, the Confederate officer satisfied himself with bragging to Coe about the trophies he had taken that day and left without fulfilling his threat to raze the hospital. After entering the hospital, Coe found the cause of the Rebel officer's ire. It seems that several Fourteenth men who had occupied an upstairs window, seeing the Confederate enter the town, began to fire at them. After the Confederates returned the fire the men of the Fourteenth proceeded down the stairs and placed themselves across the entrance to the hospital. This was where Coe had found them upon his return.

Subsequent to this tense episode, Coe found these same Union and Confederate soldiers sitting with each other laughing and joking as if they were longtime friends. Indeed, these soldiers had often met on the picket line and had many times engaged in a game of cards or traded Union coffee for Confederate tobacco. Coe later wrote of this incident,

> I was greatly indebted to the Brooklyn boys for their ingenuity and enterprise in obtaining food for our wounded in hospital during the three days we were within Rebel lines. We were in no way molested by the enemy, save by a guard placed in the hall of the hotel; but we were cut off from our own supplies and were dependent upon the enemy. In the confusion of the battles of the 2nd and 3rd of July I was unable to get the attention of the proper Rebel officers to supply us, but the fertility of resources of the 14th Brooklyn was equal to the occasion, and the wounded did not want for anything.[47]

These soldiers along with many more from the Fourteenth were taken prisoner on that day. Some members of the Fourteenth who had been captured were marched to the Confederate camp. On the way they passed a Rebel general who called out, "Hallo, 14th, where are you bound for?" It was obvious that he knew of the Fourteenth, and not just because of their distinctive chasseur dress. After a short while they arrived at the headquarters of Gen. A.P. Hill. He was described as a man of middle age and medium size who was dressed in a suit of gray clothes and not very noticeable among the others in the room.

The men of the Fourteenth had been captured by troops from a Georgia regiment. It was reported that troops from this state treated Union prisoners fairly in contrast to Louisiana or Mississippi regiments. Two Fourteenth members who had been captured went on to relate a story about Pvt. David Wilson of Company G, who also had been captured on that day. It seems that a soldier from Mississippi walked up to Pvt. Wilson and said that he wanted to trade with him. The Mississippian immediately took Wilson's kepi and substituted his own worn Rebel cap. He then made Wilson take off his shoes, which were confiscated by the Rebel for his own use.

They went on to tell how the Fourteenth is a respected regiment among its foe. They related about how when on the Rappahannock, the pickets of the Fourteenth would trade frequently with the Confederate pickets. The Confederate pickets always wanted to know when the "14th boys would be down."

The captured Union soldiers were divided into groups according to the regiment to which they belonged. The Confederate officer took their names and explained that they could be paroled back to the Union lines if they agreed not to bear arms against the Confederates until they were released from the agreement they were about to make. A great many refused these terms and were marched even farther to the rear. Approximately eleven of the Fourteenth agreed and were paroled.[48]

With his regiment taking fire at each cross street, Fowler momentarily considered taking down his colors and dispersing his men. He immediately reconsidered this, and next thought about halting his retreat and forming a battle line to engage and slow down the advancing Confederates. However, Fowler feared that his entire regiment might be cut off and forced to surrender. Therefore, Fowler continued his retreat until he reached the foot of Culp's Hill.[49]

Cemetery Hill had been fortified earlier in the day by a part of Gen. Howard's Eleventh Corps just in case the Union forces west of the town were forced to retreat. Gen. Howard had placed von Steinwehr's Division on Cemetery Hill. One brigade of his division remained on the hill while the balance fought west of the town. The brigade of Col. Orlando Smith was placed around the bottom of the hill, positioned around walls and fences. He also placed skirmishers in the houses that approached the town. In addition to them, he placed Wiedrich's artillery, consisting of six three inch rifles, on top of the hill across from the cemetery. The tired retreating Union soldiers were heartened to see Smith's Brigade and the cannon ready to repel any Confederate attack.[50]

Howard's Eleventh Corps was not very popular with the members of the First Corps who had been engaged that morning. It was the Eleventh Corps that had buckled before Jackson's Corps two months earlier at Chancellorsville, and it was the Eleventh Corps whose retreat that morning forced the First Corps to retreat to Cemetery Hill. A member of the Fourteenth expressed his feelings,

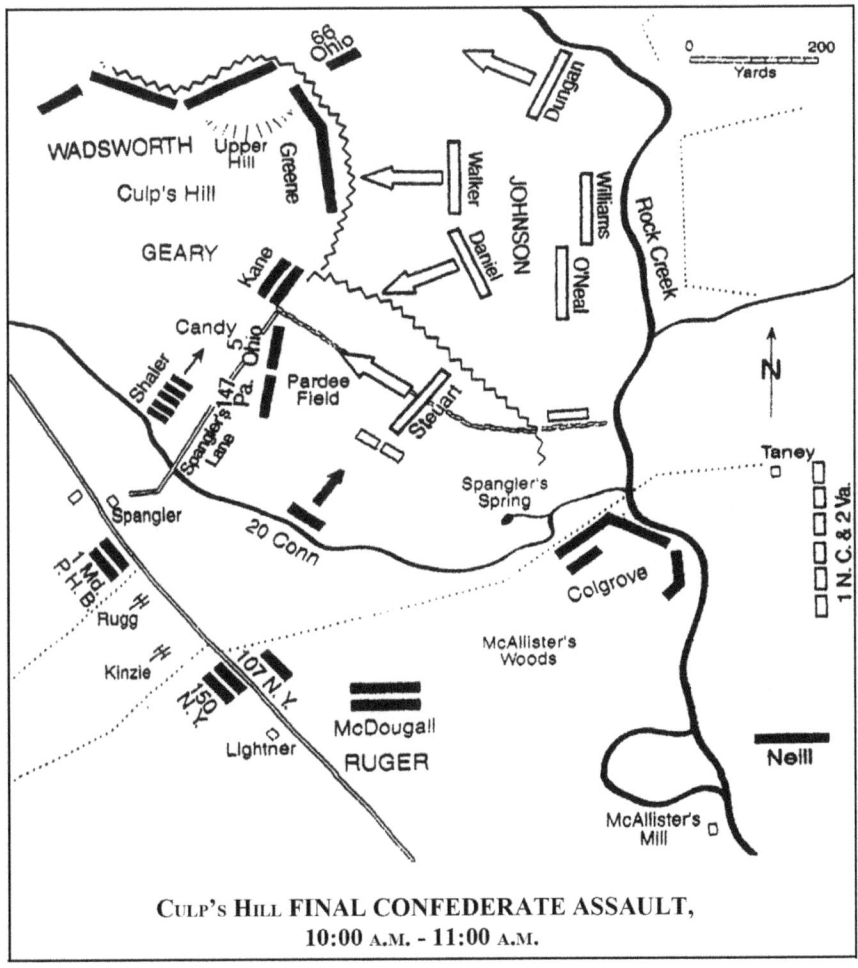

Culp's Hill, Day Three, morning (map by Hal Jespersen, www.cwmaps.com).

I never have felt disposed to say a word against the Eleventh Corps but when reading in the newspaper that it fought well, and that the First Corps ran, it makes me feel it my duty to state that the facts are just vice versa. The little remnant that is left of the First Corps stood the brunt, which their losses in killed and wounded on the first day prove, and the Eleventh — the flying Eleventh — flew. The propensity shown by the gallant Eleventh in this case was proverbial with the Rebels, and some that we took prisoners in the following fights are that they were told that they had the Eleventh Corps only to fight; and that made them feel secure of success.[51]

The men of the Fourteenth would have been even more annoyed at the Eleventh Corps had they known that Brig. Gen. Alexander Schimmelfennig of the Eleventh Corps had saved himself from capture after his brigade had been routed on the field by hiding in Gettysburg. Schimmelfennig was a veteran of the Prussian Army and a political appointment of Abraham Lincoln, who had made him a general in order to gain support for the war among the German-American population. Schimmelfennig, who was hiding between a woodshed and a pigsty, behind a house on Baltimore Street, stayed there for the entire three days of the battle, having his food brought to him by the women of the house.[52] Because of their activities at Chancellorsville and that morning at Gettysburg, a popular saying if anyone screwed up was, "Put them in the 11th Corps."[53]

At about the time that the troops were retreating, Gen. Winfield Hancock arrived and took command of all Union forces. He ordered Doubleday to send Wadsworth's Division to occupy Culp's Hill. Cutler's weary brigade with the addition of its remaining regiment, the Seventh Indiana, which had been assigned guard duty for the entire day, was sent to occupy the hill.[54] That night the Fourteenth set up camp in a meadow outside the entrance to Gettysburg Cemetery. On the cemetery gate at Gettysburg was a sign which read, "All persons found using firearms on these grounds will be prosecuted with the utmost rigor of the law."[55]

Col. Fowler rested on the grass with his gloved hands on his head. While in this position a bullet struck a fence near him. The bullet ricocheted off the nearby fence and the spent bullet hit the hand holding his head. The colonel was stunned and saw stars, but suffered no more than a headache for the remainder of the night.[56]

The Fourteenth's Division was ordered to occupy Culp's Hill on the extreme right of the Federal position. If the Union defense is described as a fish hook shaped line of battle, then the position of Wadsworth's Division must be called the barb of the fish hook. The Eleventh Corps was positioned to the left of Wadsworth, and Ewell's Confederate Corps was opposed to them.[57]

14. Gettysburg: Day One

A member of the Fourteenth described his participation during the first day battle:

> Yesterday we left our bivouac at 7:30 and marched outside of Gettysburg at 10:30 & engaged the enemy. Our regiment was on the field until 3:30 P.M. when the whole line fell back on the rear of the town where we are strongly entrenched — a portion of the 11th Corps as usual instead of retreating in good order fell back in confusion & nearly created a panic among the whole troops — as it was the Reb. skirmishers followed us through the town & their batteries shelled us & their was a right smart time for a half hour — we finally got on the hills nearby & opened our batteries again which gave us time to reform and today we feel full of hope and confidence again although I must say that I did not like the idea of being driven from our own ground but think if Gen. Reynolds had not been killed at the opening of the engagement we might have told a different tale although we were outnumbered — our regiment never fought better & Col Fowler highly complimented us the boys stood right up to their work as on going into the fight we had something over 300 men & today we only number 100 — we cannot tell how many were killed but the greater portion are wounded — our division suffered severely although we captured many prisoners.[58]

That day the Fourteenth made history. It was part of the first infantry brigade to engage the Confederates. It met Archer's Brigade, and the fire of the Fourteenth caused his brigade to seek the shelter of McPherson's Woods, where the unseen Iron Brigade engaged them with such disastrous results for the Confederates. Afterward, because of the Fourteenth's excellent discipline, they engaged Davis' Brigade, resulting in the loss of Davis's effectiveness for the remainder of the battle. Also, while the remainder of Cutler's Brigade was fighting Iverson's and Daniel's Brigade, the Fourteenth was holding off Scales' Brigade and protecting Calef's Artillery.

Reynolds and Doubleday had correctly observed that the Chambersburg Pike, McPherson's Woods and McPherson's Ridge were the key positions to the western approaches to Gettysburg. While the Fourteenth and the other regiments were bloodied on the ridges and in the woods, they stopped the Confederates long enough for Gen. Meade to bring the remainder of the Army of the Potomac into position.

15. Gettysburg: Day Two

As daylight broke on July 2, the Federals were positioned from the heights of Cemetery Hill, sloping to the southwest for about two and a half miles to a rocky height called Little Round Top, and then proceeded farther south approximately half a mile to a higher elevation called Round Top. This was the main front presented to Lee on this second day of battle. At Cemetery Hill, the Union line turned to the east and then the southeast and ended at Culp's Hill.[1]

Culp's Hill lay approximately 800 yards east of Cemetery Hill.[2] It is, in reality, made up of two hills which are separated by a small valley. Both hills are composed of heavily wooded areas and large boulders. The larger of the two hills stands at a height of approximately 180 feet and the smaller of the two at about 80 feet. The summits of the two heights of Culp's Hill are about 1,200 feet apart. This area is encompassed by Rock Creek on the east and the Baltimore Pike on the Southwest. The slope from the larger hill to the smaller one creates a ridge.[3]

In addition to the trees, which could be cut to form barricades, there was a stone wall which ran in a westerly direction from Rock Creek to the smaller of the two hills, then turned to the northwest, thereby forming an angle. This rock wall then went up the smaller hill, and then into the valley between the two hills after passing through an open field which was bordered by trees. In the area to the south of the smaller hill, the land contained less wooded areas at the end of which was a meadow. This area was called Spangler's Meadow, and is marshy in some areas and approximately 300 feet wide. Spangler Spring is at the Southern base of the smaller of the two hills. The spring and meadow drains into Rock Creek, which flows in a southerly direction until it begins to curve in a easterly direction approximately 1,000 feet to the northeast of the larger hill. This change in direction proceeds for approximately 600 feet before it turns to the west.

These areas were named after Henry Spangler, who had a farm on the easterly side of the Baltimore Pike. It was a little less than a quarter mile from the summit of Culp's Hill. In the rear of Spangler's Farm was an access road which leads to the valley between the two peaks of Culp's Hill.[4]

General Meade established the "fishhook" line of defense by following the natural topography of the land. He placed the Eleventh Corps of Gen. Howard on Cemetery Hill. Here it was supported by Robinson's and Doubleday's Division of Newton's (formerly Reynolds') First Corps. To the right of this was placed Wadsworth's Division, including the Fourteenth Brooklyn, and the Twelfth Corps of Gen. Slocum on Culp's Hill. Culp's Hill formed the right of the Army of the Potomac. The Second Corps of Gen. Hancock connected to the left of the Eleventh Corps along Cemetery Ridge, and the Third Corps of Gen. Sickles connected to the left of Hancock's Second Corps. The Fifth Corps of Gen. Sykes was held in reserve in the area to the right of the Twelfth Corps and the left of the Second Corps.[5]

General Lee placed his forces to oppose Meade's positions. Seminary Ridge was approximately one mile from Cemetery Ridge. Lee's lines were also

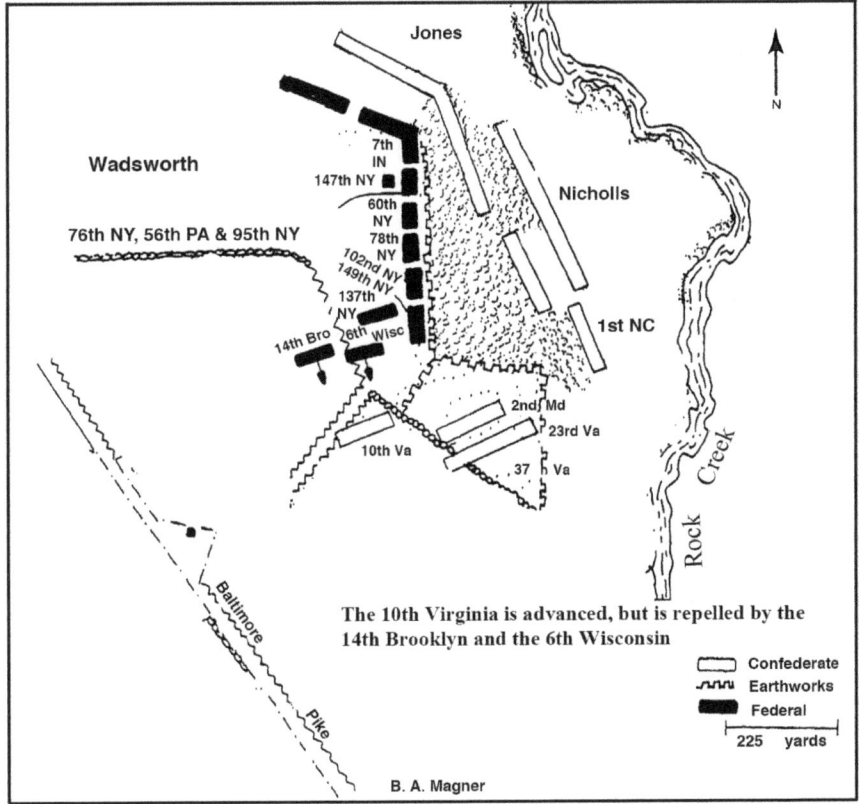

Battle of Gettysburg, Day Two, 14th Brooklyn beats back the 10th Virginia (from James L. McLean, *Cutler's Brigade at Gettysburg,* Butternut and Blue, 1994. Courtesy Butternut and Blue Publishers).

exterior to Meade's lines. Longstreet held the right of Lee's line with the divisions of Hood and McLaws opposite the Round Tops and part of Cemetery Hill, which were occupied by the troops of Sickles and Hancock. The divisions of Gen. A.P. Hill occupied Seminary Ridge from the left of Longstreet, and were opposed to Hancock's troops along Cemetery Ridge. Gen. Ewell's Corps connected to the left of Gen. Hill's troops and continued through the town of Gettysburg, then went around Cemetery Hill and ended the Confederate line facing Culp's Hill, opposing the remainder of the First Corps and Slocum's Twelfth Corps.

The entire Confederate line was well concealed by forests along Seminary Ridge and was about five miles long.[6] Because Lee's line was exterior to Meade's, it was much longer and this caused problems for the Confederates. Because of the greater distances between different locations on the Confederate line, it took much longer for Lee's orders to reach his corps commanders and therefore, longer for his commanders to relay messages to Lee. It also took longer to move troops into different locations on the battlefield in preparation for an attack.[7]

Lee's plan of attack for the second day involved daybreak attacks by both Longstreet, on the left of the Union line, and an attack by Ewell on the right of the Union line at Culp's Hill. Longstreet's attack was to be the major effort of the Confederate Plan.[8] Hill, in turn, was to threaten the Union center so that they could not reinforce either wing of the Union Army.[9]

However, Longstreet delayed the start of his offensive. He asked permission to wait until the brigade of Gen. Laws reached the battlefield. When Laws arrived the commencement of battle was delayed even further by the difficulty in positioning the division of Gen. Hood and Gen. McLaws.[10] Longstreet finally was able to launch his attack, which took place at four o'clock in the afternoon rather than in the early hours of the morning.[11]

Gen. Ewell, who was supposed to attack the opposite end of the Union line upon hearing the artillery announcing the start of Longstreet's attack, failed to initiate his attack, thereby allowing Gen. Meade to strip the Twelfth Corps from Culp's Hill and use it to help defend against Longstreet's attack on the Union left. Lee's sole purpose in planning Ewell's attack was to prevent this.[12]

While Longstreet was delaying his attack and Ewell was waiting for Longstreet's attack to start, Wadsworth's Division as well as the Twelfth Corps occupied Culp's Hill. The Twelfth Corps was used to extend the line of the First Corps on Culp's Hill. This was the general condition of affairs at Gettysburg on the second day of battle. However, for our purposes we shall limit our research to the occurrences on Culp's Hill.

As already mentioned, the Seventh Indiana Regiment, had been sent by Wadsworth to occupy Culp's Hill on the evening of July 1, as the retreating

First and Eleventh Corps reached Cemetery Hill. It took possession of the west crest and summit of the hill by extending the right of Wadsworth's line. As it did so, the commander of the Seventh Indiana, Col. Ira Glover, sent Company B of his command to the right so that they might establish a picket force at an angle to the remainder of the regiment.

At about this time, a reconnaissance force sent by Gen. Johnson of Ewell's Corps to see if Culp's Hill had been occupied approached the summit of the hill. At about 10:00 P.M., the reconnaissance force, which was from the Forty-Second Virginia Regiment, was fired on by the Union soldiers and was quickly aided by the remainder of Company B of that Union regiment by surprising the Confederates, who fled and reported back to Gen. Johnson that the hill was being held in force.

Gen. Ewell, who thought that the key to the entire Union defense was Cemetery Hill, also thought that the key to Cemetery Hill was Culp's Hill. Therefore, when he asked Gen. Johnson about the practicability of Johnson attacking Culp's Hill, he was told that Culp's Hill was heavily fortified. In reality, at this point in time, there were only a few hundred Union soldiers occupying Culp's Hill.[13]

Early on July 2, the Second Division of the Twelfth Corps was ordered to Culp's Hill. The left of the corps was placed at a right angle to the right of Gen. Wadsworth's Division. The remainder of the Fourteenth's Brigade was brought to Culp's Hill that morning. Cutler extended the line of the Seventh Indiana by placing the Seventy-Sixth New York, the Fifty-Sixth Pennsylvania and the Ninety-Fifth New York to the right of the Seventh Indiana, facing east. This in turn connected to Gen. Greene's Brigade of the Twelfth Corps. The Fourteenth Brooklyn and the One Hundred Forty-Seventh were held behind their brigade in reserve. Throughout the skirmishing of July 2, the Fourteenth was moved from location to location to wherever the skirmishing was the most intensive and was held in reserve in those areas.[14]

The Third Brigade of the Second Division was commanded by Brig. Gen. George Greene, who positioned his troops, all of whom came from New York State, to the left of the Seventh Indiana. The brigade stretched for a quarter mile, beginning at the top of the larger hill and descending to the valley between the larger and smaller hill. The remainder of the division extended from the crest of the larger hill, then down the valley between the two peaks, then up to the crest of the smaller hill, then along Rock Creek to the Baltimore Pike.[15]

George Sears Greene was born on May 6, 1801, in Apponaug, Rhode Island. He moved to New York and in 1819 was appointed to West Point, from which he graduated in 1823. Until his resignation from the army he taught engineering for the most part at West Point. In 1836, he began working as a civil engineer on various projects including the building of the Croton Reservoir in Central Park, New York. He re-entered the army in 1862 with a rank of colonel and served in the area of Washington until promotion to brigadier general of volunteers in April of 1862. One of the oldest field commanders in the army, Greene, led his brigade and at times his division at Cedar Mountain and the Carolina campaign as well as Antietam and Chancellorsville.[16]

Both the First Corps and the Twelfth Corps, using the abundance of trees in the area, began to build breastworks. At times Greene, who was a civil engineer, supervised the construction of these breastworks as well as the trenches which were being built. In addition, the soldiers placed logs across the top of the earthworks. This served to protect the heads of the soldiers in the trenches and provided slits between the earthworks and the logs from which the soldiers could fire their rifles in complete protection.[17]

With Longstreet's attack on the Union left gaining momentum, Gen. Meade moved the divisions of Ruger and Geary from Slocum's Twelfth Corps to assist Sickles along Cemetery Ridge. Only Greene's Brigade of 1,424 officers and men from Geary's Division were left behind to man the trenches on Culp's Hill.[18] As soon as the five of the six brigades left Greene's Brigade to defend Culp's Hill, Greene started to move and extend regiments of his command to fill in the vacant trenches, which were just abandoned by the Twelfth Corps to the right of his command. The 1,424 men of Greene's brigade would have to face three of Johnson's brigades, totaling approximately 4,700 men. The numerical advantage of Johnson should have been enough to determine the outcome of the battle on Culp's Hill except for the trenches and breastworks.[19]

At about this time, Ewell began his assault on Cemetery Hill and Culp's Hill. He ordered Gen. Johnson's division, which included the brigades of Gen. Steuart, Gen. Jones and Col. Williams, to attack. Before Johnson could cross Rock Creek and force the Union skirmishers to retreat, it was approaching darkness. Gen. Greene's brigade was now trying to defend an area which was previously defended by two divisions.[20]

Jones' Brigade — which was made up of the Twenty-First, Twenty-Fifth, Forty-Second, Forty-Fourth, Forty-Eighth, and Fiftieth Virginia Regiments — attacked Cutler's brigade, with the Fourteenth being kept in reserve, in the second line of defense.[21]

Jones' Brigade was on the right of the Confederate advance and his men were gaining ground in their attack against Cutler's Brigade. However, they were under heavy fire from the Union forces who where entrenched behind the breastworks. The fighting was intense. One of Jones' regiments, the Forty-Second Virginia, advanced until it was approximately 10 paces from the Union works when, because of their numbers killed and wounded, together with the fortifications of the Union soldiers, they were forced to retreat.[22]

Col. Williams, who commanded the brigade of Gen. Nicholls, which consisted of the First, Second, Tenth, Fourteenth, and Fifteenth Louisiana Regiments, attacked Gen. Greene's Brigade in the center of the line. Finally, Gen. Steuart's Brigade, consisting of the First Maryland Battalion, the First and Third North Carolina and the Tenth, Twenty-Third and Thirty-Seventh Virginia Regiments, attacked and overlapped the One Hundred Thirty-Seventh Regiment of Greene's brigade at the Southern end of the line of battle.[23]

Gen. Greene was hard pressed to defend against this onslaught by Gen. Johnson's Division. He asked Gen. Howard and Gen. Wadsworth for reinforcements. Wadsworth sent the Sixth Wisconsin, the One Hundred and Forty-Seventh New York and the Fourteenth Brooklyn.[24]

Col. Fowler immediately marched the Fourteenth down to the base of Culp's Hill, where he met Capt. Cantine of Gen. Greene's brigade. Greene had sent him to guide Fowler's Regiment to where Gen. Greene wanted the regiments to be posted. Col. Fowler halted the Fourteenth, and followed Capt. Cantine, who was moving parallel to the Union lines. After moving a short distance, a soldier jumped out from the wooded area to the right and demanded that Cantine surrender. As Cantine dismounted, he and Fowler were immediately fired upon. Fowler drew his pistol. They had received a volley of between twenty and thirty shots from the woods. Fowler returned to the Fourteenth and formed the regiment facing the wooded area. Since Fowler and Cantine had been traveling behind the Union lines when attacked, Fowler did not know if they had been attacked by Union or Confederate soldiers. Fowler ordered his men to hold their fire so that he could send out scouts to identify the forces to his front. As Fowler called for volunteers, two men from Company I, musician John Cox and Sergeant James McGuire, came forward. The Fourteenth was under continuous heavy fire as the two volunteers slipped out of the protection of their trenches and made their way toward the unknown force.

During the entire time the Fourteenth received fire from the woods, but did not receive orders to return fire. When Cox returned, he reported that McGuire had been wounded and that the force to their front was the Tenth Virginia. Upon receiving this intelligence, Fowler ordered the Fourteenth to return the Confederate fire. He then ordered a charge into the woods, which dislodged the Rebels, who fled.[25] From here the Fourteenth was ordered to relieve the One Hundred Thirty-Seventh New York, which was at the extreme end of the Union line. The One Hundred Thirty-Seventh, under the command of Col. David Ireland, had been fighting off attacks by Gen. Steuart's Regiments, who had occupied the vacant trenches of the Twelfth Corps. It was at this time that the Tenth Virginia of Steuart's Brigade, while attempting to out flank Col. Ireland's Regiment, ran into the Fourteenth Brooklyn.[26]

The Tenth Virginia Regiment in its attempt to outflank the One Hundred Thirty-Seventh New York, had found the Federals in its rear, "compelling the regiment to charge front and beat off a bayonet charge made by an enemy regiment (probably the 84th New York Infantry) trying to regain the captured lines."

The darkness made it impossible for both sides to continue the fight. Years later, Joseph Dunivin of the Tenth Virginia wrote, "The enemy in the darkness, searching for the Confederates, came upon them unexpectedly. After the usual challenge, the Federal officers deliberately gave the regulation order; 'Ready-aim-fire!' But Capt. Yancy impetuously shouted; 'Shoot, boys, shoot.'"[27]

The Army of the Potomac had barely survived this attempt to turn its flank. Had the darkness of the hour and the encounter with the "Red Legs" from Brooklyn not curtailed the Confederate attack, the Rebels could have captured Culp's Hill and the Baltimore Turnpike, which was just yards away from the point at which they encountered the Fourteenth. If this had happened, the outcome of the battle would have been entirely different.[28]

The Fourteenth defended the position of the One Hundred Thirty-Seventh New York for the remainder of the evening and into the early hours of July 3. It was relieved by the returning regiments of the Twelfth Corps. At this time, Gen. Geary's Division, which consisted of the brigades of Col. Kane and Col. Candy, formed to the right of Gen. Greene's Brigade. The Fourteenth returned to its brigade location.[29] One account noted, "The greatest service of the evening was performed by the 14th Brooklyn. Had the 10th Virginia been able to route the outflanked 137th New York, the entire Union position on Culp's Hill could have been taken in reverse. A successful attack by the 10th Virginia would have given Steuart the opportunity to march up the hill and force each entrenched regiment out of its position. This chance was thwarted by the gallant charge of the 14th Brooklyn."[30]

The One Hundred Thirty-Seventh New York had held the hottest position on Greene's entire line since it was at the extreme right of his line. Beyond their line, Steuart's Confederates had occupied the abandoned breastworks of the Twelfth Corps. The One Hundred Thirty-Seventh lost 137 men, which was more then the remainder of Greene's Brigade combined.[31]

The battle at Culp's Hill was unusual for combat in the Civil War for many reasons. Armies usually did not fight at night. In darkness, it was too easy to mistake friend for foe. Indeed, the occurrence of friendly fire was more frequent at Culp's Hill than at any other place during the entire Battle of Gettysburg. Also, it was very easy to get lost at night, as did Gen. Geary's Division of the Twelfth Corps, who were ordered to the left wing of the Army during Longstreet's assault. In addition, the First Corps and the Twelfth Corps had prepared breastworks as well as trenches, not generally used until the siege at Petersburg the following year.[32]

The defense of Culp's Hill, in which the Fourteenth played a major part, kept the Confederates from seizing the hill and secured Cemetery Hill and the Baltimore Pike, as well as the ammunition trains and artillery reserves, which were in the area. If Culp's Hill had fallen, the Confederates could have rolled up the Union forces on Cemetery Hill and down Cemetery Ridge to the Round Tops.[33]

16. Gettysburg: Day Three

On the morning of July 3, Lee surveyed his position after the attacks of Longstreet and Ewell at each end of the Union lines on the previous day. Small success had been achieved with Longstreet's First Corps holding ground at the Devil's Den, the Peach Orchard and the Wheatfield, and Ewell's men holding ground at the base of Cemetery hill and Culp's Hill with Steuarts Brigade of Johnson's Division holding the breastworks which had been abandoned by the Twelfth Corps. Therefore, Lee continued his plans to attack both flanks of the Union Army in concert.[1] However, Longstreet insisted that he never got any orders from Lee regarding a battle[2] plan for the morning of July 3.

This delay caused Lee to re-evaluate his plans for that day. His second plan called for a change in location of his attack. He ordered Gen. Pickett from Longstreet's Corps along with troops from the Third Corps of Gen. A.P. Hill, to attack the center of Cemetery Ridge from the front instead of attacking the left of the Union line, as Hood and McLaws had done the previous day.[3] Again, this was to be coordinated with an attack by Gen. Ewell on the Union right. However, Longstreet could not complete the disposition of his troops in a timely fashion and before Ewell received notice of Longstreet's tardiness, Johnson had already committed his troops to a renewed battle at Culp's Hill.[4]

The Twelfth Corps had returned to Culp's Hill in the early hours of the morning. If the Confederates wanted to exploit the small advantage gained the night before, they needed to reinforce Johnson's Division for its renewed attack on Culp's Hill. To that end, Ewell ordered the brigades of Brigadier Gen. Junius Daniel and Col. Edward O'Neal of Gen. Rodes' Division and Brig. Gen. William Smith's Brigade from Early's Division while Johnson recalled Brig. Gen. James Walker's Stonewall Brigade for the assault on Culp's Hill. Altogether, the Confederates had committed more than nine thousand men, consisting of thirty-three regiments from seven brigades, to this assault.[5]

The battle for Culp's Hill on July 3 began at about 4:30 in the morning with a cannonading by the Union artillerists. After approximately fifteen minutes, Geary's Division was supposed to attack the Confederates in the area of the breastwork, which had been occupied by the Confederates on the previous evening. However, before he could do this, the Confederates launched their own attack.[6]

The Union defense consisted of Greene's Brigade of Geary's Division, which held the hill, while Candy's and Kane's Brigades of Geary's Division connected Greene's right with the Baltimore Pike. This line ran from the area between the larger and smaller hills along Spangler's Lane to the Spangler Farm.[7] Opposed to these forces, Col. Nicholl's Confederate Brigade faced the right and center of Greene's Brigade and stayed approximately three hundred feet to the front of his works. His Louisiana regiments were so close to the Union line that his men had to whisper so that they would not be discovered.[8] Steuart's Brigade opposed the area between the two hills, which made up Culp's Hill and the lower hill. Walker's Stonewall Brigade was used to support Steuart's Brigade and was placed to the rear of it. Jones' Brigade was placed opposite Greene's line on the upper part of Culp's Hill. The brigade of Brig. Gen. Daniel was placed behind Jones to support him. Col. O'Neal's Brigade was placed behind Nicholl's Brigade in support.[9]

Shortly after the battle started, Greene again asked Gen. Wadsworth for assistance and again Wadsworth sent the Fourteenth and the One Hundred Forty-Seventh to his aid. The Fourteenth had been back with Cutler's Brigade on the north slope of Culp's Hill barely long enough to eat breakfast when they returned to assist Greene. When the Fourteenth arrived, they were placed alongside the One Hundred Forty-Ninth New York at the right of Greene's line. As the Fourteenth entered the trenches, they gave a shout and began firing at the Confederates, continuing until their ammunition had been expended. Col. Fowler ordered his sergeant major to retrieve more ammunition for his troops. He returned with a supply which was also being exhausted by his regiment. As Fowler saw his relief approaching, he ordered his men to retain a load in their rifles to be used in covering the troops approaching their trench, and while the Fourteenth was exiting the trench, the relieving regiment covered Fowler's regiment. In this manner no members of the Fourteenth were lost in the transfer of troops.[10]

Most of the members along the battle line received wounds to the upper part of their body since this was the only part exposed to the enemy fire because of the entrenchments and breastworks. Those who received wounds to the lower parts of their body resulted from the relief of regiments climbing in and out of these defenses. Most companies would loose a minimum of one soldier killed or wounded each time the unit came into or out of the entrenchment.[11] Fowler was able to avoid this.

The fighting had been so intense that the state flag of the Fourteenth, in addition to being riddled with bullet holes, had its staff shot in two by a bullet. Capt. Cardona, while under fire from the Confederates, spliced the two pieces of the staff together and again raised the flag over the position of the Fourteenth. The Fourteenth flew the same tattered flag on the spliced pole for the remainder of the war.[12] It was at this time, that the Fourteenth was relieved on the line so they could rest and clean their weapons before going back to the trenches to relieve another unit.[13] "Again it was to the front, when the regiment there had exhausted its ammunition; again relieved; again in the pits. Back and forth, back and forth, staggering through the heat and smoke of battle, red eyed, gasping, but indomitable, presenting its seared ranks to the flame almost of the enemy's fire to pour volley after volley into their ranks."[14]

The men of the One Hundred Forty-Ninth New York looked with admiration at the men of the Fourteenth, whom they knew to be a fighting regiment. It was written of the Fourteenth:

> This same regiment was ordered to the front and it was interesting to watch the conduct of men said to be brave. They were nearly all young boys, and as they took their places in line and waited the direction of their commander, their pale faces and ashy lips told how great was the conflict within. Most of them trembled like an aspen leaf from head to foot, and as they looked at each other and tried to laugh(,) the very smile they gave had impressed upon it the inward agony they endured. It was feared, so great was their trepidation, they would be unable to go forward, but when the word of command came the lips tightened, the eyes flashed, every nerve was strained, and they moved forward with almost mechanical ease and firmness. As they advanced, a thousand men, observing their heroic conduct in sympathy and admiration, rose in their places and cheered, while their prayers ascended to God that he would spare those young men possessed of so much courage and manliness.[15]

After three attacks by Johnson's Division failed, he decided to withdraw his troops and give up his attempts at conquering Culp's Hill.[16] The captured works of the Twelfth Corps were back in the control of the Union and the right wing of the Army of the Potomac was again secure. The trenches and breastworks of the Union defenders, supervised by the former engineer Gen. George Greene, were too much for the sustained efforts of the Confederates to overcome. More than any other unit, Greene's Brigade, to which the Fourteenth had been assigned on July 2 and 3, beat back successive attacks, thereby holding its ground and preventing the collapse of the entire Union position at Gettysburg. Although Greene's Brigade and those regiments sent to assist him numbered a little over three thousand men, only approximately thirteen hundred were on the line at any one time.

After the battle, four hundred fifty Confederates lay dead in front of his defenses and across Rock Creek and one hundred and thirty prisoners were taken.[17] "Gradually the smoke cleared and the slopes and fields and woods in the front of the Yankee lines were found to be empty of Rebels, except for the dead and the helpless wounded. By 11:00 A.M. Culp's Hill fell silent.... Pop Greene's Brigade broke the silence with three rousing cheers."[18] Gen. Steuart, who commanded a brigade in Johnson's division, later wrote, "The enemy's position was impregnable, attacked by our small force, and any further effort to storm it would have been futile, and attended with great disaster, if not total annihilation."[19]

The Fourteenth remained with Greene's Brigade for the rest of the day.[20] The battle for Culp's Hill was over. "When time came for a withdrawal, Johnson's men were not pursued. The firing seemed to stop by mutual agreement. Both armies were exhausted. It was 11:00 A.M. Johnson retired slowly to the foot of the hill, then formed a new line along the west bank of Rock Creek, which he held for the remainder of the day.... When the results were reviewed, it was recognized that Culp's Hill had been the scene of some of the most determined sanguinary fighting of the war."[21]

A former citizen of Gettysburg was fighting in the Second Virginia Regiment at Culp's Hill. Although born in Gettysburg, he moved to Virginia when the carriage maker he worked for moved his business for whatever reason. When the war came along, he enlisted in the Confederate Army on April 20, 1861, at Harpers Ferry and was assigned to Company B of the Second Virginia Infantry.

A friend of his, Jack Skelly, had enlisted in the Eighty-Seventh Pennsylvania regiment and had been wounded at the battle of Carter's Woods on June 15, 1863. He was able to visit with Jack before the Second Virginia moved north towards Gettysburg. During the meeting, Jack gave him a message to give to his sweetheart, Mary Virginia Wade, if he ever got to Gettysburg. The Second Virginia, which was part of the Stonewall Brigade, arrived at Gettysburg on the evening of July 1 and this son of Gettysburg met with his family and told them that he had a message from Jack Skelly to Jennie (Mary Virginia Wade was called Jennie by her family and friends). He did not give the message to them but wanted to deliver it in person.

On the morning of July 3, the Second Virginia was attacking the wooded slopes of Culp's Hill near Rock Creek and he was killed. His name was Wesley Culp. He died on the hill named for his great-grandfather and in sight of his uncle's farm.

Jennie Wade was staying with her sister, Mrs. McClellan, who had just given birth. Mrs. McClellan's home was on Baltimore Street and was within the Union lines between East Cemetery Hill and the Confederate occupied town. On July 1, Jennie had provided bread and biscuits to the Union soldiers as they retreated toward Cemetery Hill. On July 2, Jennie baked more bread and again supplied it to any Union soldier who asked for it.

The home of Mrs. McClellan, Jennie's sister, had at times been peppered with shots from Confederate sharpshooters due to its proximity to Union sharpshooters and the Union lines. On this day Jennie Wade made breakfast for her mother and sister consisting of bread, butter, applesauce and coffee.

She then said her morning prayers consisting of Psalms xxvii to xxx, commenting on the different passages as she read them. At about eight o'clock she began to make the bread and biscuits that her family would need and that had been promised to the Union soldiers who had come to her door earlier. She had just about finished kneading the dough when a bullet from a Confederate sharpshooter pierced the front door and the kitchen door and struck Jennie in her heart, killing her instantly. Jennie was buried the next day not knowing that her sweetheart Jack Skelly had sent her a note nor that he had died of his wounds shortly after his visit with Wesley Culp. Jennie Wade was the only civilian killed during the three day engagement at Gettysburg.[22]

The battle for Culp's Hill was one of the truly defining events of the Battle of Gettysburg. Greene and his brigade, along with the regiments sent to assist him on the second and third day of the battle, prevented Meade's mistake of moving the Twelfth Corps from unraveling the right wing of the Union defense. The men on the hill also secured the safety of Cemetery Hill and the Baltimore Turnpike, which would have been the main avenue for retreat of the Union Army and would have laid open the road to Washington and would have lost the Union Army's entire reserve of artillery as well as all of their ammunition supply.

The Adjutant General's Report on the Fourteenth Brooklyn's service at Gettysburg states: "On every portion of our line our success was perfect, the enemy repulsed at every point with great slaughter. So ends this memorable battle."[23]

At the Battle of Gettysburg, the Fourteenth regiment lost 13 men killed and 105 wounded. Their total losses with missing amounted to 217, or 68.2 percent of the 318 men engaged.[24]

17. Mine Run Campaign

Army of the Potomac	**14th Brooklyn**
Major General George Meade	Col. Edward Fowler
First Corps	**76th New York**
Major General John Newton	Lieut. Col. John Cook
First Division	**95th New York**
Brig. General Solomon Meredith	Major Edward Pye
Second Brigade	**147th New York**
Brig. General James C. Rice	Major George Harney
7th Indiana	**56th Penn.**
Col. Ira Glover	Col. J. William Hofmann

After their defeat at Gettysburg, Lee began to withdraw his troops back toward Virginia. On the evening of July 3, he issued orders for his troops to take defensive positions and prepare for the retreat.[1] Johnson's Division was ordered to retreat from its positions to the west of Rock Creek at about 10:00 P.M. on July 3 and to take up new positions on Seminary Ridge. By midday of July 5, the Confederates had left Gettysburg.[2]

Gen. Meade was purposely slow in following them. In fact, the Fourteenth remained on the field during the 4th and 5th of July during heavy rain storms and did not leave Gettysburg until July 6th, when most of the Army of the Potomac marched towards Emmittsburg.[3]

During these days the men of the Fourteenth got a chance to visit the battlefield around their position. Lieut. William C. Rae of Co. B, Fourteenth Regiment, wrote to this sister Carrie: "I went over a portion of the field and saw a great many men of the Rebel army who were killed and also a few wounded ones. July 5th we marched about 1 mile & looked at the men burying the dead, they dug a large hole & tumbled them in one by one."[4]

Between July 6 and the middle of August, the Fourteenth was almost continually on the march. They left Emmitsburg on July 7 and crossed the Catoctin Mountains to near Beltsville. On July 8 they marched to near Middletown and stopped at Boonsboro. On July 9, the regiment was issued new shoes and stockings. Many of the Fourteenth had worn out their shoes and were walking shoeless. Since leaving Gettysburg, the Fourteenth was traveling ahead of the supply train but on this day, the train caught up with them.

When the Fourteenth left Boonsboro, they marched through Beaverdam and Funkstown. On July 13, the Rebels crossed the Potomac. On July 18, the Fourteenth crossed the Potomac by the use of pontoon bridges and entered the town of Waterford. The Adjutant General's Report said, "The inhabitants of this town or village met us literally with open arms, they threw open their doors, and hospitably welcomed every one, officer or private, who crossed their threshold. On the following morning at our departure, the stars and stripes appeared as if by magic, fluttering from every window. Bouquets were showered upon the column as it passed through the main street and hearty blessings fell from every lip."[5]

On July 23, the Fourteenth marched with the First Corps as its advance guard and entered Warrenton after putting out skirmishers to reconnoiter the town. However, the Rebels were not in Warrenton and the Fourteenth was detailed as the provost guard for the town with Lieut. Col. Jordan in charge.

On August 1, the Fourteenth approached within two miles of the Rappahannock, along with the First Corps. During the evening, the Rebels began to fire on the Union troops; however, the Fourteenth did not take part in the skirmishing. The next day the Fourteenth crossed the Rappahannock and put up entrenchments a short distance from the bank of the river and pitched their tents between the entrenchments and the river bank. Early on August 3, the Rebels were reported to be approaching the camp. The regiment quickly took down the tents and manned the entrenchments to await the arrival of the Confederate force. However, they did not appear and in the evening the regiment was again ordered to pitch their tents. That night they slept on their arms as a precaution against a surprise attack.[6]

On August 8, the Fourteenth was withdrawn from this position and recrossed the Rappahannock. Here they performed picket duty until August 19. On this date, reports of the approach of the Rebels caused the Fourteenth to cross the Rappahannock again and take up positions in the entrenchments which they had previously prepared. When no Rebels approached, the Fourteenth returned again to their previous camp, where they remained until September 14.

On that day, Gen. Pleasanton's advance toward Culpeper was met by Confederate Cavalry. The resulting engagement allowed the Second Corps to enter Culpeper and the Fourteenth was expected to join in that advance. On September 16, the Fourteenth left Camp Newton near Rappahannock Station, where they had been performing picket duty since August 8, and marched to Pony Mountain near Culpeper Court House.

On October 10, the regiment crossed Morton's Ford and camped near Culpeper, Virginia. However, within twenty-four hours of their arrival, the Fourteenth was assigned as the rear guard to the division supply train. The

Fourteenth again crossed the Rappahannock. This time, as rear guard to the wagon train, they were followed by Confederate Cavalry and occasionally skirmished with them before they bivouacked near Kelly's Ford that night. Three days later, the Fourteenth was relieved and rejoined its brigade.

After leaving Bristoe Station, where they had been bivouacked since October 13, some advance units of Confederates opened fire and the entire First Corps was ordered to march toward the high ground around Centreville, while the Second Corps repulsed the attack.[7]

On October 19, the Fourteenth left Centreville and marched to Haymarket, Virginia, by way of Gainesville, which was a distance of approximately ten miles. That afternoon the pickets which had been put out by the Fourteenth were attacked by Confederates and had to be reinforced before the Rebels were driven off.

As a result of the engagement, Lieut. Col. Robert Jordan was charged with misconduct in the face of the enemy. A court-martial had been initiated by Gen. Newton, who commanded the First Corps. Gen. Rice, who commanded the Second Brigade, to which the Fourteenth belonged, acted as president of the court, while Col. Rufus Dawes of the Sixth Wisconsin acted as the judge advocate. Major Edward Pye, who commanded the Ninety-Fifth New York and was a judge in the New York courts, acted as Lieut. Col. Jordan's defense.

The specific charges against Lieut. Col. Jordan were cowardice and disobedience of orders. These stemmed from his actions upon the approach of a small Confederate force on that day. Jordan had been placed in charge of the pickets for the First Division of the First Corps in a line connecting to the pickets of Third Division of the First Corps. The charge further stipulated that at the approach of a small enemy force and without giving any resistance, Jordan pulled his pickets off the line, thus endangering the pickets of the Third Division and leaving his command in the hands of a subordinate officer, left the field to report to Gen. Cutler, the division commander, that a large force of the enemy were approaching in line of battle. In addition, he had left his command without proper authority.

The trial lasted only a few days and on October 29, 1863, the court ruled that Jordan was not guilty of the charge of cowardice but rather guilty of misbehavior before the enemy. Of all other charges and specifications, Jordan was found guilty and sentenced to be dismissed from the service.[8] However, the president of the United States interceded on his behalf and he was reinstated to his rank. The entire court-martial board, including the judge advocate, agreed with this recommendation because of Jordan's good service and fine character prior to this incident.[9] A good part of this leniency was due to Col. Fowler's testimony. As a witness for the defense, Fowler testified that

Jordan's conduct as a officer at the First Battle of Bull Run, where he was wounded, at Fitz Hugh Crossing and at Gettysburg was that of "a good and brave officer."[10]

Between late October and early November, Lee and Meade played a chess game of maneuvers, each trying to outflank the other. On November 9, the Fourteenth bivouacked near Bealton, which was approximately seven miles from Bristoe Station. There they built an encampment and remained until November 27. Their time was spent mainly in building the railroad and doing fatigue duty.[11]

In late November, Meade saw an opportunity to attack the Confederates. Lee had positioned his army with its right wing anchored on the Rapidan River in the proximity of Morton's Ford but left its other wing at the lower fords almost unprotected except for a line of entrenchments along the river and along the left bank of Mine Run, which was a small branch of the Rapidan. Gen. Richard Ewell's Corps held the responsibility of securing the area from Morton's Ford to Orange Courthouse. Gen. Hill had positioned his corps below Ewell and along the railroad toward Charlottesville. However, Lee had left an opening of several miles between the corps of Ewell and Hill.

With this gap in the Confederate lines, Meade saw an opportunity to cross the Rapidan at the lower fords and turn the flank of Lee's Army. It was Meade's intention to march toward Orange Courthouse, split the two corps and destroy each in turn.

On November 26, Meade started his army across the Rapidan River. The Fifth Corps crossed at Culpeper Mine Ford followed by the First Corps. The Fourteenth left Bealton and marched to Richardsville, which was about fifteen miles from Bealton.[12] Lee, realizing what Meade was about, extended his lines.

> The Confederate line was drawn along a prominent ridge or series of heights, extending north and south for six or eight miles. This series of hills formed all the angles of a complete fortification, and comprised the essential elements of a fortress. The centre of the line presented four or five well-defined facings of unequal length, occupying a space of more than three thousand yards, with such angles of defense that the fire of the enemy was able to enfilade every avenue of approach, while his right and left flanks were not less strongly protected. Stretching immediately in the rear and on the flanks of this position was a dense forest of heavy timber while some twelve hundred yards in front was Mine Run.[13]

The next day, November 27, the Fourteenth got an early start on this day, reveille having sounded at 2:30 A.M. By 4:00 A.M. the regiment crossed the Rapidan River at Gold Mine Ford on pontoon bridges which had been constructed. They proceeded to Germanna Ford, the Fredericksburg Plank

Road, and the Fredericksburg Orange Plank Road to Parker's store where they halted for dinner. After their dinner, they proceeded to Robertson's Tavern, where they bivouacked at 7:45 P.M.

On November 28, the Fourteenth again awoke at about 2:30 A.M. and were on the road by 4:00 A.M. By 5:30 A.M. the regiment had formed a line of battle perpendicular and to the left of the road leading to Orange Court House. At about 9:00 A.M., Cutler moved his brigade forward in two lines to find the pickets of the Confederates. Col. Fowler was in command of the second line, which consisted of the Fourteenth Brooklyn and the Seventy-Sixth and Ninety-Fifth New York. As they advanced during a heavy rain storm, they drove the Confederates from their defenses through swamps and dense woods to Mine Run, where the Rebels were found to be in force and in a fortified position. The advance was stopped at this point. The next day was quiet with no major fighting taking place.[14]

About this time, General James Rice was placed in command of the Fourteenth's brigade. James Clay Rice was born on December 27, 1829, in Worthington, Mass. He did not have very much formal education, but entered Yale University and graduated in 1854. He moved to New York in 1855 after studying law and was admitted to the practice of law the following year. Between May 1861 and September 1862, he rose from the rank of lieutenant to that of colonel and briefly commanded a brigade at Second Manassas. He was at the Battle of Chancellorsville and later Gettysburg, where he served heroically at Little Round Top and received a promotion to brigadier general of volunteers.[15]

On November 30, Gen. Meade sent a message to the commanders of the First, Third, Fifth and Sixth Corps asking their opinion as to whether the entrenchments directly to their front could be carried if they were to be attacked.[16] Early that morning, Gen. Rice ordered Col. Fowler and his troops to reconnoiter Mine Run in the area to his front. The purpose was to determine whether it would be possible to cross artillery in that area without the use of bridges. Col. Fowler sent the right wing of his regiment out as skirmishers while they were being supported by the left wing, which was kept in reserve. At Col. Fowler's command, the Fourteenth moved forward across Mine Run and drove the pickets from their entrenchments. Col. Fowler also indicated in his report that because the stream was only ten to fifteen feet across and heavy oak timbers in the area were plentiful, the stream could easily be crossed.

After holding the area for about thirty minutes, the Confederates began to advance on his flanks and he was ordered to withdraw. Col. Fowler ordered his reserves to the banks of the stream so that the skirmishers could be protected as they re-crossed Mine Run. Having been successful in his mission, Col. Fowler and the Fourteenth returned to their brigade.[17]

Gen. Newton responded to Gen. Meade's inquiry regarding the forces to his front in the following manner: "The papers enclosed are the answers of my division commanders, to an inquiry as the nature of the ground in their respective fronts. I regard any attempt to storm as hopeless, unless the troops can be massed near the point of attack without the knowledge of the enemy, and unless strongly supported on both right and left. The works of the enemy in my immediate front appear to be heavy, and their attention seems to have been drawn to the possibility of an attack."[18] Gen. Cutler, who was newly appointed as the division commander, had reported: "I think that the works can be carried at or near the first angle of the pike to the left provided that the enemy is first dislodged from the pines in front of the works by an attack from the left. This is the only practical way I see, and that at a great sacrifice."[19] This report was included in Newton's message to Meade. Gen. French of the Third Corps and Gen. Sykes of the Fifth Corps also submitted favorable reports to Gen. Meade.[20] Meade also received a favorable report from Gen. Warren of the Second Corps. Therefore, Meade decided to attack the Confederates. The next day, after Gen. Warren reassessed the Confederate forces to his front, Meade cancelled the attack.[21]

The Fourteenth had their own method of determining that they were going to be withdrawing, as told by John Jenkins in a letter: "On the morning of 1st December the rifle cannon were displaced by our favorite Battery B. Fourth Regulars. When we saw them we suspected what was in the wind, and that we were going to fall back; for Battery B is always used for close quarters, and on a retreat many a hundred Secessionists have been made to bite the dust from those brass howitzers. At about 4 o'clock, orders came to fall back, and soon we were on the return march."[22]

The Fourteenth, who were preparing to march on the Confederate breastworks, could hear the artillery fire all along the Union line. Suddenly the firing stopped and rumors were spreading that the offensive at Mine Run had been cancelled. Shortly, the regiment received orders to move back toward Germanna Ford. When they got there, the Fourteenth was used to cover the Fifth and Sixth Corps, who crossed in the afternoon. The next day, the regiment traversed the river and covered the crossing of the remainder of the Army of the Potomac.

After this, nothing of importance took place outside of preparing quarters for what was anticipated to be a long stay. However, on December 18 the regiment was again called out to witness the execution of a soldier who had deserted several times. This time the soldier was from the Seventy-Sixth New York Volunteers.

> This perhaps, is the saddest scene in a soldier's life, to be called upon to witness a strong man, under a bright sun, pay the penalty of his crime. In the

heat of battle one sees a comrade struck down, hardly noticing the event, unless it be a very dear friend or brother but, as in this instance, one had time to reflect, and thoughts go back to the time when the poor mortal who stands before us, his face blanched with the awful certainty of a disgraceful death, induced by the most exalted motive, love of country, left home and friends, a gay dream, ambitious dream, to be realized and the strength of contending armies, to return home laden with honors, and with the consciousness of having performed the first of earthly duties. A volley from the muskets of his comrades shatters the dream, and the curtain drops over the scene.[23]

During the Mine Run campaign, one soldier from Brooklyn was wounded.[24]

18. The Wilderness

The Union Army	**14th Brooklyn**
Lieut. General Ulysses S. Grant	Col. Edward B. Fowler
The Army of the Potomac	**76th New York**
Major General George G. Meade	Lieut. Col. John E. Cook
Fifth Army Corps	**95th New York**
Major General Gouverneur K. Warren	Col. Edward Pye
Fourth Division	**147th New York**
Brig. General James S. Wadsworth	Col. Francis C. Miller
Brig. General Lysander Cutler	**56th Pennsylvania**
Second Brigade	Col. J. William Hofmann
Brig. General James C. Rice	

The Fourteenth had spent winter quarters building its ranks with recruits, drilling and acting as provost guard in Culpeper as well as presenting the "Fourteenth Regiment Opera Troupe." While acting as provost guard for the town, the members of the Fourteenth availed themselves of the many hotels in Culpeper, which indeed was a change from the small cabins that they had built for the previous winter quarters.

By way of entertainment, some members had procured musical instruments and permission from Corps Headquarters to organize a band of minstrels for the enjoyment of the regiment and members of other regiments. On the evening of February 5, 1864, the "Fourteenth Regiment Opera Troupe" gave its first performance. The concert was a great success and a series of performances were organized. These concerts were attended by almost every general officer as well as members of nearby camps and the local citizenry.[1]

On February 9th John Jenkins again wrote to the *Sunday Mercury* from Culpeper.

> The Fourteenth Regiment's Troupe of Minstrels gave their first entertainment last Friday night, and the performances were a perfect success. Stars were in the ascendant on more ways than one, and with them were their ladies and families. A grand galaxy of the fair sex were in attendance, lending, as they always do, a charm to the entertainments, as well as viewing in this case with the beautiful scenery and sketches from the brush of our "veteran" young artist, Freytag. The performances were rapturously received — particularly the

originalities and peculiarities adapted by the troupe to the Fourteenth Regiment. Evan's "Billy Barlow," a Fourteenth song, and Richardson's "Essence of Old Virginny," Desmond's Plantation Jig, and our friend De Vere's Banjo Solos (the inst. by the by, is from our glorious fellow-militiamen, the gallant Ninth) brought down the house in raptures. Last night, the second concert was given, and was as complete and successful as any I ever attended in Gotham. The quartet, by McDowell, Warburton, Day, and Baker, beside the duet of "Larboard Watch" by Baker and Bowen, was good. Stevens and Coleman keeping all in good humor by their witty sayings and actions. Cole's "Marsilles Hymn" and Brett's song were both well done, and as well received.[2]

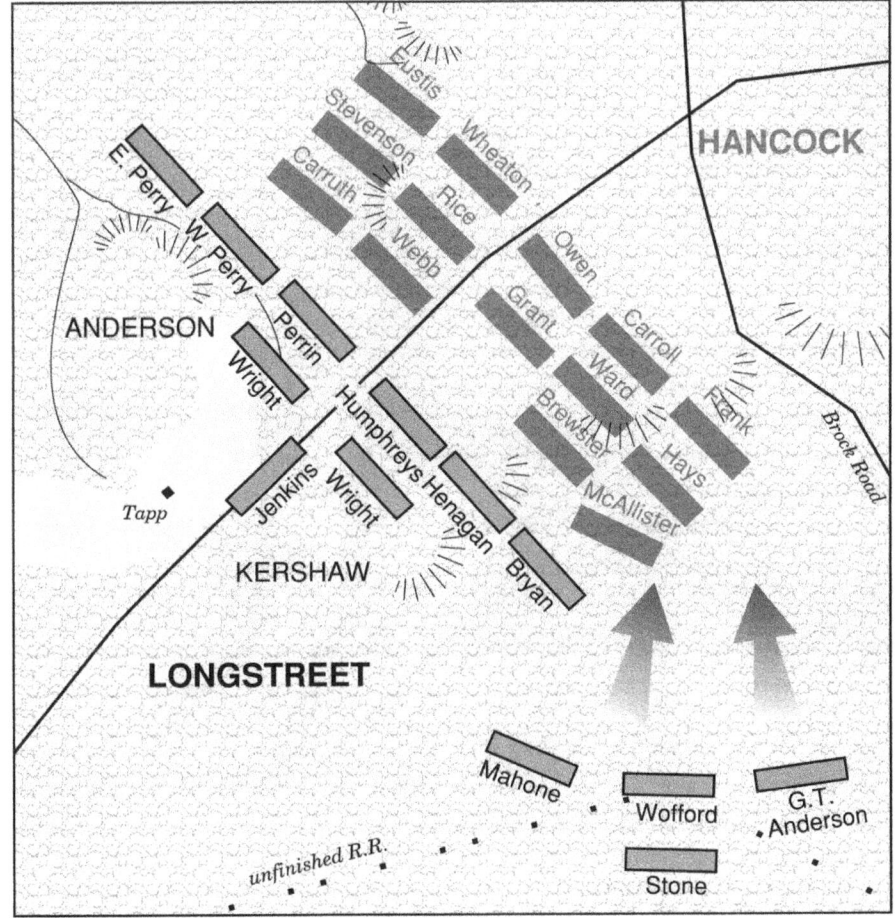

Battle of the Wilderness (from Gordon C. Rhea, *The Battles of Wilderness and Spotsylvania*, Eastern National Park and Monument Association, 1995. Map by George F. Skoch, courtesy Eastern National Publishers).

By April, the Fourteenth's troupe of minstrels were performing on a regular basis, as Jenkins later relays,

> The concerts by the "minstrels" of the Second Brigade still continue a success, and concerts are still given at the Fourteenth Regiment's Concert Hall. A grand serenade was given last night to Generals Rice. [James] Wadsworth and [Lysander] Cutler at this [Gen. Rice's] headquarters. The music was really splendid and without doubt was a great treat to our much loved commanders. The arrival of Gen. Wadsworth among us is hailed with joy for he had endeared himself in the affections and memory of all under his command. The same affection and respect exist for our late Corps General [Newton], and our present Brigadier-General [Rice], not forgetting Gen. Cutler. At these headquarters we have had a very gentlemanly set of officers — from the General to his Aids. They all invariably make it a point to look to the interest and comfort of the men under their command — and the result is the love and respect of subordinates in return.[3]

On March 23, 1864, the War Department issued orders reorganizing the Army of the Potomac. Under this order, the five corps were reduced to three. This was due to the severe losses at the Battle of Gettysburg. The new organization called for the elimination of the First and Third Corps and the soldiers from those corps to be absorbed into the remaining three corps of the army. The First Corps was shifted to the Fifth Corps. Therefore, the Fourteenth Brooklyn Regiment was now part of the Fifth Corps under the command of Maj. Gen. Warren; the Fourth Division was assigned to Gen. Wadsworth who was given his command on March 27, and Second Brigade with Gen. Rice, retaining his command. However, each unit was allowed to keep its old corps and division insignia.[4]

As 1864 began, Lincoln was again looking for strong movement by the Army of the Potomac. High on his list to replace Halleck as general in chief was Ulysses S. Grant, a major general from the West. This feeling was shared by many people in government. In fact, Elihu Washburne, a member of Congress from Illinois and a friend of Grant, had said that he would introduce into Congress a bill authorizing the revival of the rank of lieutenant general.[5] No one had held this rank on a permanent basis since George Washington and the only other man to hold the rank was Winfield Scott, who held it by brevet (temporary).[6] This measure was passed by the Congress of the United States and signed by the president on February 29, 1864. Gen. Grant was assigned this position on March 2. Grant was asked to come to Washington to accept his new position.[7]

On March 9, after speaking to the assembled audience, Lincoln presented Grant, who said, "Mr. President, I accept this commission with gratitude for the high honor conferred. With the aid of the noble armies that have fought on so many fields for our common country, it will be my earnest endeavor not to disappoint your expectations."[8] In his new position Grant outranked Gen. Halleck and replaced him as general in chief of all the armies, not just the Army of the Potomac. However, it was Grant's intention to keep Gen. Meade as the commander of the Army of the Potomac and travel with Meade instead of remaining in Washington, as did Halleck.[9]

As the new general in chief Grant went about visiting the different commands and organizing a grand strategy for winning the war. This involved all of the armies east of the Mississippi. However, we will deal only with Meade's Army of the Potomac and Lee's Army of Northern Virginia.[10]

Lee had stretched his army along the south side of the Rapidan River and along the bluffs that line the area. This gave him a very strong defensive position against a direct attack. His earthworks had only improved since the Mine Run Campaign, which forced Meade to withdraw without a battle. In addition, the area gave Lee room to maneuver. However, Lee did not know where Grant might choose to attack. He therefore had Gen. Hill and Gen. Ewell continue at their present location across from Gen. Meade's Army. Lee had Gen. Longstreet remain at Gordonville where he could support Hill or Ewell as the situation developed.[11]

Gen. Grant had positioned the Army of the Potomac with Warren's Fifth Corps at and around Culpeper Court House, the Second Corps under Hancock was positioned south of Brandy Station and the Sixth Corps, under Gen. Sedgwick, was positioned north of Brandy Station. Burnside's Ninth Corps, which was not part of the Army of the Potomac, but answered directly to Grant, ran from just north of Rappahannock Station to the area of Manassas Junction. Ninth Corps was kept in reserve in case Lee attacked Meade's right flank after they crossed the Rapidan.[12]

Gen. Grant did not want to face Lee's formidable fortifications. Therefore, he adopted a plan which would draw Lee out from his position. Grant chose to try to turn Lee's right flank by moving toward the left. This was a disturbing decision to many. It brought his army into an area of Virginia known as the Wilderness, because of its thickets and heavy undergrowth and woodlands. These would render his superior cavalry and artillery useless in battle as well as reduce the maneuverability of his infantry.[13]

The best description of the wilderness was written by Morris Schaff, who was a Union officer during the battle:

> It is made up chiefly of scrubby, stubborn oaks, and low-limbed, disordered, haggard pines,—for the soil is cold and thin,—with here and there scattering clumps of alien cedars. Some of the oaks are large enough to cut two railroad ties, and every once in while you come across an acre or two of pines some ten to twelve inches in diameter, tall and tapering, true to the soaring propensities of their kind. But generally, the trees are noticeably stunted, and so close

together, and their lower limbs so intermingled with a thick underbrush, that it is very difficult indeed to make one's way through them.

The Southern half of this lonely region may be designated as low or gently rolling; but the northern half, along the rivers, is marked by irregularly swelling ridges. Where the battle was fought, which is at about the heart of the Wilderness, and especially on Warren's front, the surface of the ground resembles a choppy sea more than anything else. There, like waves, it will heave, sometimes gradually and sometimes briskly, into ridges that all at once will drop and break in several directions. Soon recovering itself, off it will go again, smoothly ascending or descending for a while, then suddenly pile up and repeat what it did before, namely, fall into narrow swells and shallow swamps where willows and alders of one kind and another congregate, all tied together more or less irrevocably by a round, bright-green, bamboo-like vine.

There is something about the scrawny, moss-tagged pines, the garroted alders, and hoary willows, that gives a very sad look to these wet thickets; and yet, for a few weeks in May and June, from them a swamp honeysuckle, and now and then a wild rose, will greet you joyously. As might be expected where the trees stand so thickly as they do in the wilderness a large number are dead. There and there a good-sized oak has been thrown down by a storm, smashing everything in its way and pulling up with its roots a shock of reddish-gray earth, making a bowl-shaped pool on whose banks the little tree-frogs pipe the solitude. Others in falling have been caught in the arms of their living competitors and rest there with their limbs bleaching and now and then is one standing upright, alone, with lighting-scored trunk and bare, pronged limbs, dead, dead among the living green. The woods everywhere abound in tall huckleberry bushes, from whose depending limbs hang racemes of modest, white, bell-shaped flowers.

As in all the woods of Virginia, there are many dogwoods scattered about. Both they and the huckleberries were in full bloom when the battle was going on, the dogwoods, with outspread, shelving branches, appearing at times through the billowing smoke like shrouded figures.[14]

The prize for Grant was that beyond the Wilderness and a continued movement to the left, brought the advantage of having his supplies brought by water routes along the Chesapeake Bay rather than overland with its greater cost in men and the possibility of Confederate raids interrupting his supply line.[15]

On May 2, Gen. Grant issued orders for the entire Army of the Potomac to begin its advance in two days, on May 4.[16] Gen. Warren's Fifth Corps, began its advance at midnight on May 3 and crossed the Rapidan River at Germanna Ford and then proceeded to the area of the Wilderness Tavern. On the following day, May 4, they were to proceed past Catharpin Run and cross the Orange Court House Plank Road at Parker's Store.[17]

However, the Fourteenth had a different assignment on May 4. On that morning the Fourteenth left Culpeper. Their responsibility was the protection of the large wagon train and supplies of the army. Since they were the provost guard of that town during winter quarters, they also brought the seventy-two prisoners who had been confined in the local jail. The right wing of the regiment crossed the Rapidan that evening. The remainder crossed during that night.[18]

As stated before, Grant did not want to fight in the Wilderness, but instead wanted to compel Lee to abandon his strong position and fight him in the open country beyond the Wilderness. However, Lee chose the Wilderness as his battlefield. By doing so, Lee knew that he could negate Grant's two-to-one advantage in soldiers. Lee did not want to defend the different crossings of the Rapidan or to attack the Union forces during their crossing of the Rapidan. Instead, Lee intended to attack when Grant's entire force, including the wagon trains, were across the river. When Grants large wagon train was meshed in the tangle of the thickets which was the Wilderness, he would attack their right flank and roll it up with the possibility of destroying the entire army.[19]

The men of the Fourteenth could hear the heavy fighting that was taking place as they waited for word as to what was happening to their front. As reports of Warren's losses came in, they heard that Lieut. Mitchell of Co. C, who had been temporarily assigned to Gen. Wadsworth, and Capt. Gill, Co. I, who was assigned to Brig. Gen. Rice, both had been captured by the Confederates.[20]

In the afternoon of May 5, Gen. Wadsworth had his three brigades, consisting of Cutler's, Stone's and Rice's, head from Saunders Farm southward. Cutler's brigade was able to advance against the Sixth Virginia Brigade of Gen. John Jones. Gen. Stone and Cutler found the Confederates and the terrain harder to negotiate. The assault having failed, Wadsworth withdrew his division to the Lacy House, which was the headquarters for the Fifth Corps.[21]

Later, on the evening of May 5, Gen. Warren ordered Gen. Wadsworth to attack the northern end of A.P. Hill's line. Since his troops were already at the Lacy House, Wadsworth organized his men. They moved south along Wilderness Run, then through a densely wooded area for approximately one mile. Wadsworth was supposed to hit the Confederates on their left flank and rear. However, the march of Wadsworth's force had been noticed and reported to Lee, who notified Hill. Wadsworth withdrew again not so much because of the Rebel force to his front, but rather because of the woods and thickets in which they were fighting.[22]

The next day, on May 6, while fighting near the Orange Plank Road, the Confederates began to break through the Union lines and Gen. Rice's 56th Pennsylvania and Seventy-Sixth New York retreated. Gen. Wadsworth, while trying to inspire the Twentieth Massachusetts to charge the Confederates, lost control of his horse, who ran toward the Rebel lines. Almost immediately, a volley from the Eighth Alabama rang out, hitting Wadsworth in the head. He fell into Confederate hands and later died of his wounds.[23]

Just a few days before, Wadsworth had written to his wife, " We have just received marching orders ... and all is bustle and confusion.... [I] feel sure of a victory. — I wish I could tell you how much I love you, and our dear children, how anxious I am that all should go well with you, that you all live in affection and kindness, and that none of our dear children will ever do anything to tarnish the good name which we who are here hope to maintain on the battlefield.... [With] all the love and affection I can express ... believe me, my dear wife, fondly and truly yours."[24]

The Fourteenth had received orders on the morning of May 6, to immediately march to the front. Col. Fowler brought his regiment, consisting of 383 men, to Gen. Warren, who was at the Lacy house. The regiment was posted in the second line of battle and acted in a supporting capacity until two in the afternoon. At this time the entire division was ordered to reinforce Burnside. Here, the Fourteenth and its brigade formed part of the third line of battle. For the remainder of the day the Fourteenth underwent the most severe fighting it had experienced in the entire war.

As Longstreet tried to turn the right flank of the Union line, the two battle lines in the front of the Fourteenth failed to hold the attack and those Union soldiers ran through the ranks of the Fourteenth. This caused some confusion among the newest recruits of the regiment. However, the veterans soon rallied the recruits and the entire regiment made a stand which turned back Longstreet's attack.

Later the Fourteenth moved up to the first line of battle and remained there until morning. The next day, Saturday, both sides were relatively quiet and Grant decided to make a flanking movement by way of Spotsylvania Court House.[25]

At the Battle of the Wilderness, the Fourteenth Brooklyn Regiment lost two men killed and one wounded.[26]

19. Battle of Spotsyvania Court House

Army of the Potomac	**14th Brooklyn**
Major General George G. Meade	Col. Edward B. Fowler
Fifth Corps	**76th New York**
Major General Gouverneur K. Warren	Lieut. Col. John Cook
Fourth Division	**95th New York**
Brig. General Lysander Cutler	Col. Edward Pye
Second Brigade	**147th New York**
Brig. General James C. Rice (k)	Col. Francis Miller
Col. Edward B. Fowler	**56th Pennsylvania**
	Col. J. William Hofmann

Grant's purpose in moving southeast from the Wilderness was to try and place the Army of the Potomac between Lee and Richmond in order to cut off Lee's supplies from the Confederate capital. It was approximately fifteen miles from the area of the Wilderness to Spotsylvania Court House. The most direct route to this area is by way of the Brock Road to Todd's Tavern. This was the route taken by Warren's Fifth Corps. The Fourteenth arrived at Todd's Tavern at approximately 4 o'clock on the morning of May 8.[1]

Warren's Corps was to make a rapid march to seize Spotsylvania's Court House, while Sedgewick and Burnside were to move using other routes by way of Chancellorsville. Hancock would follow Warren's route. However, Warren's advance was delayed and the Confederates reached Spotsylvania before the Federals.[2]

As Gen. Robinson, who had been placed in command of the Second Division of Warren's Corps and Gen. Griffin approached Spotsylvania Court House, Humphrey's Mississippian's attacked from the trees to the east of Brock Road and forced the Union soldiers to retreat.[3] The Fourth Division came to Griffin's aid as it arrived about one half mile north of their fellow soldiers in an area called Laurel Hill.[4] There the division was allowed to fall out and prepare coffee. Near the Fourteenth, a band was playing "Hail Columbia" when a Rebel artillery shell exploded over their heads. The musicians and their instruments hastily departed (in later years Col. Fowler often spoke of how cannon fire affected music).

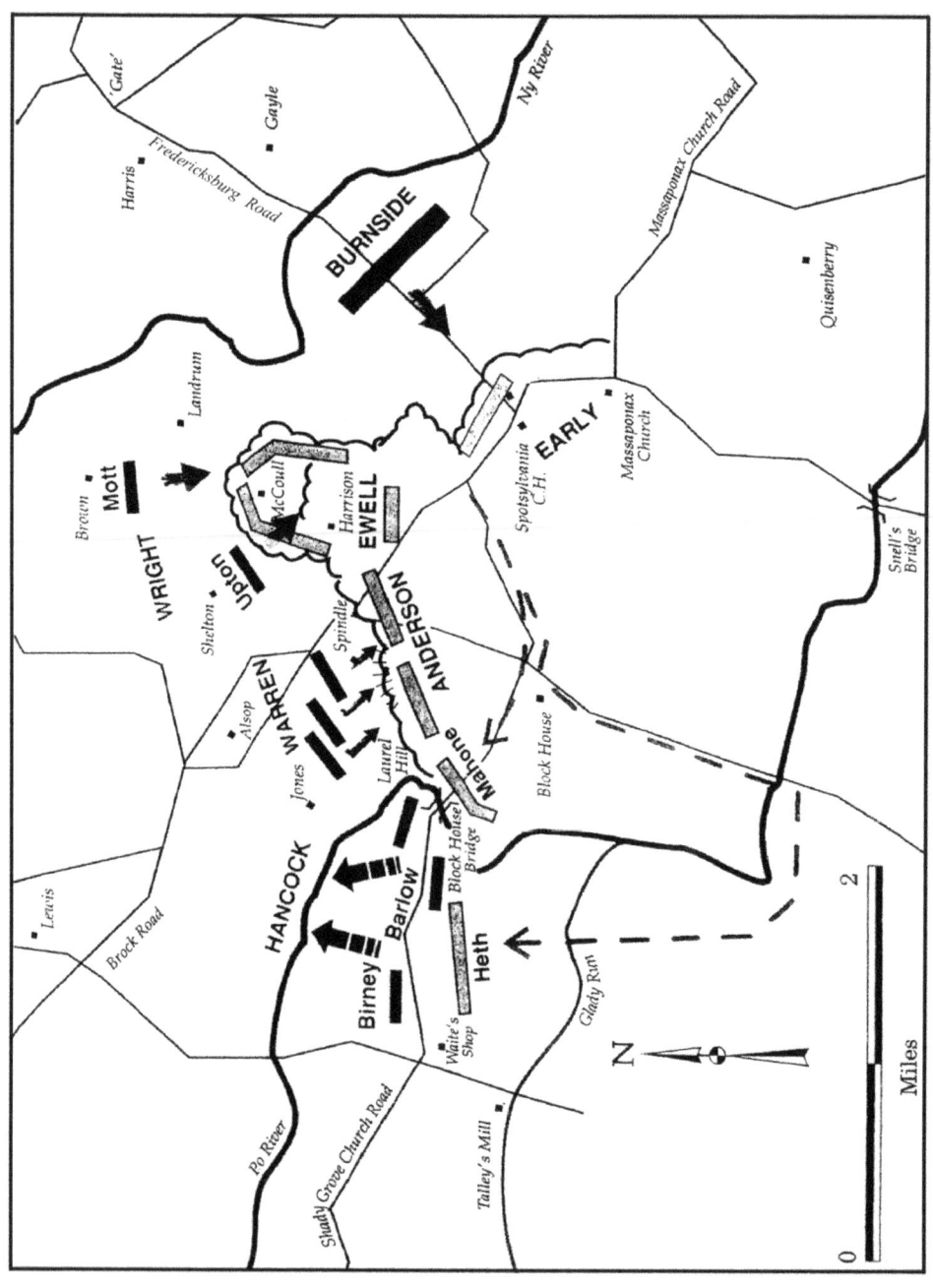

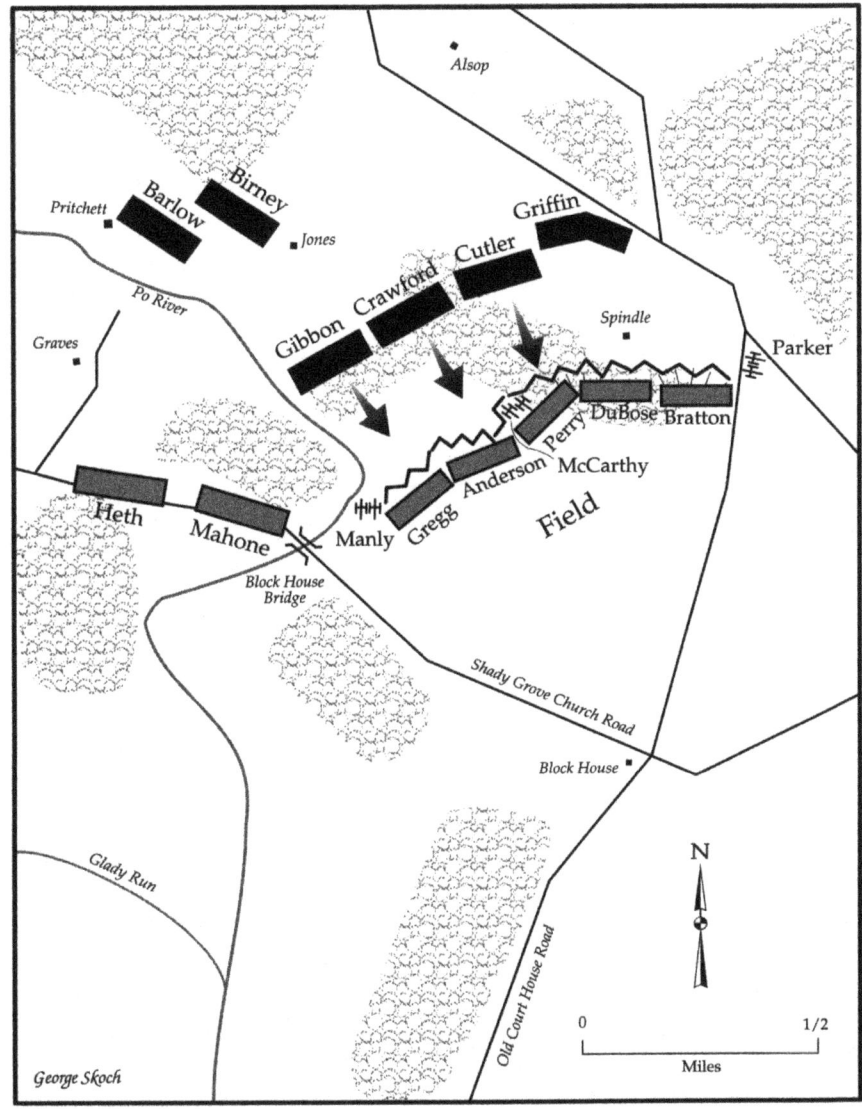

Above: Battle of Spotsylvania Court House, May 12 (from Gordon C. Rhea, *The Battles of Wilderness and Spotsylvania*, Eastern National Park and Monument Association, 1995. Map by George F. Skoch, courtesy Eastern National Publishers).

Opposite: Battle of Spotsylvania Court House, May 10 (from Gordon C. Rhea, *The Battles of Wilderness and Spotsylvania*, Eastern National Park and Monument Association, 1995. Map by George F. Skoch, courtesy Eastern National Publishers).

The entire division was soon ordered into battle. Gen. Rice ordered the Fifty-Sixth Pennsylvania and the Ninety-Fifth New York to chase the Confederate skirmishers from an orchard near a farm house.[5] The farm house was the home of Sarah Spindle, who lived there with her five children, at least one of whom was in the Confederate Army. On the morning of May 8, while Sarah was eating her breakfast, Union troops occupied her home and property as well as the nearby buildings from which sharpshooters began to pick off the soldiers from South Carolina, who were across the way. To stop the sharpshooters, the Confederate artillery set the building on fire using incendiary shells.[6]

The Fifty-Sixth Pennsylvania and Ninety-Fifth New York were successful in clearing the Rebels from the orchard but could not hold the ground. Therefore, Gen. Rice ordered his remaining three regiments, the Seventy-Sixth, One Hundred Forty-Seventh New York and Fourteenth Brooklyn to assist in holding the orchard.[7] As the Fourteenth advanced, they came under heavy fire from the Confederates, who were located in the woods, and the regiment returned their fire with brisk volleys. The only cover for the members of the Fourteenth was a rail fence which ran along the side of a road. The left wing of the regiment did not even have this minimal cover. In order to obtain better cover from the incessant Confederate fire, the regiment found some nearby woods not occupied by the Rebels and continued the fight from their new position.

It was then that the Fourteenth was joined by a regiment of regulars who formed on their right. However, the losses to that regiment and to the Fourteenth were so severe that they fell back for a short distance to regroup before they again went on the assault. The two regiments again attacked, but then the regulars began to retreat. The Fourteenth was also forced to withdraw, even though they tried to hold the position. The Fourteenth had suffered casualties not only from the Confederates but also from the heat of the day, combined with the heat of the burning building. "After the regiment reached the partial shelter of the trees, the old men gave three cheers for the '63 recruits, who had bravely demonstrated their mettle, and this compliment was returned. The boys also gave three cheers for Col. Fowler."[8]

The Fourteenth, along with its entire brigade, was moved to the rear of a nearby ridge, where they remained until approximately 5:00 P.M., when they advanced to the right of the orchard, where they began to build breastworks and occupied them until 2:00 P.M. on May 10. At that time, the brigade was ordered to attack the Confederate breastworks, which was about 600 yards to their front. The same assignment was given to Cutler's brigade.[9] The division was at the left of the Fifth Corps and the brigade of Gen. Rice was leading.

As the orders to attack were given, the men who were organized with precision, began to march. Soon they began to traverse ravines filled with undergrowth and endure artillery and musket fire, all of which destroyed the orderly attack.[10] The artillery and musket fire came from the Confederate soldiers of Gen. Law's Alabama Brigade, who were delivering both the front and enfilading fire. The Fourteenth, after about two hundred yards, sought the cover of some trees to their right. From this position, the Fourteenth returned the Confederate fire until their ammunition ran out. "The artillery and infantry fire of the enemy was most disastrous. The solid shot and the shells hurtled through the woods tearing off limbs of trees and ploughing deep furrows in the ground."[11] Subsequently, the Fourteenth was relieved and the entire brigade was moved to the rear in the area of the breastworks which they had occupied.[12]

During the attack, Gen. Rice, who was attempting to hurry his other troops into battle, was wounded in the leg. The wound was severe and the leg had to be amputated at the field hospital. Afterwards, the Union surgeon asked Rice in which direction he wanted to face. He replied, "Turn me with my face to the enemy." "These were his last words and indicated the true character of the man, the soldier and the patriot."[13]

Later, after being re-supplied with ammunition, the Fourteenth again was returned to the line. Soon the regiment would again charge the Confederate breastworks. "Each face was like stone; none could read the thoughts of the men — but in five minutes they were to face almost certain death. Not a man flinched; each seemed as cool as if waiting for the evening parade. It is in such moments as these that a man's hair turns gray. Everything was made ready for the charge."[14]

When the signal was given, the Fourteenth began, but you could hardly call it a charge. Because of the woods, the undergrowth and the darkness, the regiment found the going very difficult. Still they pushed forward down a ravine and up the other side with the Confederates in their breastworks ahead of them. The artillery and musket fire were severe and the first line of Federal troops seemed to "melt" away then all the troops began to retreat. However, the left wing of the regiment along with the colors of the regiment remained at the point at which the charge had been halted. For some unexplained reason they had not received the order to retreat. Those members of the Fourteenth in the left wing who had stood their ground were now in danger of being killed or captured by the Rebels. Col. Fowler, seeing the plight of the left wing, which was being led by Col. Jordan, ordered a patrol to reach Jordan and advise him of the retreat. However, Col. Jordan after some discussion, realized his situation and ordered his troops to retreat. On the way back to the Federal lines, Jordan's group met the party sent by Col. Fowler.[15]

On the morning of May 12, Gen. Hancock's Second Corps started an attack on the Confederate lines. The members of the Fourteenth could hear the artillery fire far to their left, beginning at about 5:00 A.M. At 7:00 A.M. the Fourteenth was notified of the attack and that Hancock's charge of the Confederate breastworks had succeeded in carrying the enemy position and capturing several Confederate units along with Generals Johnston and Steuart.[16]

While Hancock was attacking what became known as the "Bloody Angle," Warren and his corps were to remain in their trenches and to occupy the trenches of Gen. Hancock, who was to make the main assault on the Confederates. This made the Fifth Corps responsible for the right wing of the Federal Army.[17] With Hancock attacking, Meade felt sure that Lee had to have weakened his flanks. He therefore ordered Warren's Corps to attack. Warren, however, could not ascertain that the Confederates to his front had diminished to any degree. "The order struck Warren as ludicrous. The previous four days had convincingly established that Laurel Hill could not be taken by direct assault."[18] Warren finally gave in to Meade's orders and ordered an attack.

Cutler's Division advanced in the center of Warren's Corps. Col. Bragg's Pennsylvanian Brigade and Robinson's Iron Brigade made up the first line of the advance, followed by the second line consisting of the brigades of Col. Peter Lyle and Col. Fowler, who had been placed in command of the brigade after the death of General Rice. Both lines met in a ravine, beyond which was a stretch of open land, sharpened abatis and earthworks and finally the Georgia Brigade of Col. Dudley DuBose. Again, the artillery and musket fire were decimating the Union forces. The ravine was filling with the dead and wounded. Again, the Union troops had to retreat.

Warren had tried several times to overrun the Confederates on Laurel Hill. Yet, the division of Confederate Major Gen. Charles Field, protected by its breastworks and artillery, had resisted Warren's entire corps. Nor did Warren succeed in drawing Confederate troops away from the salient that Hancock had attacked.[19]

Both Grant and Meade were now dissatisfied with Warren's performance.[20] It was decided that Warren would defend his breastworks with one division, while his other two divisions could be used to reinforce Hancock and Wright (who had replaced Gen. Sedgewick, who had been killed).[21] This gave Warren a very small role in the remainder of the battle. Indeed, Grant was on the verge of dismissing Warren.[22]

At about midday the Fourteenth began a march to its left. They were, as was Cutler's Division, on their way to assist Gen. Wright's Sixth Corps in a major assault of the Confederate lines, as Grant had ordered.[23] They arrived at about 3:00 P.M. However, rather than joining the Sixth Corps in an assault, the division was used to relieve some of Wright's troops.[24]

Fowler's men were placed in the west angle to relieve part of the first line just outside the Confederate fortifications. The Fourteenth was ordered to fire at the second line of the Confederates. It had started to rain. The Fourteenth kept up their constant firing while lying in the mud, until 3:00 A.M. While the Fourteenth was fighting in the west angle, Wright became disillusioned with the idea of an attack and communicated this to Grant, who cancelled it.[25]

The next morning the Fourteenth and the remainder of Cutler's Division rejoined Warren's Fifth Corps. When they arrived they formed the second line of battle and again began to build breastworks. They were under artillery fire for the remainder of the day.[26]

Grant determined that Lee's position was too strong. Again, he decided to try to maneuver him out of his fortifications. The Fifth and Sixth Corps moved behind the Second and Ninth Corps, to the area of the Fredericksburg Road. To accomplish this, the Fourteenth had to march on muddy roads for about seven miles moving behind Burnside's (Ninth) Corps and cross the Ni River and Madison Creek. They ended their march at dawn, approximately three-quarters of a mile from Spotsylvania Court House.[27]

The remainder of Grant's plan called for Warren's Corps to attack down the Fredericksburg Road towards Spotsylvania Court House. Wright's (Sixth) Corps was to march down the Massaponax Church Road to the left of Warren and join the attack.[28] Muddy roads, night marches and tired soldiers all played a part in delaying the planned attack. At approximately 9:00 A.M. Gen. Meade notified Gen Warren that his and Gen. Wright's combined attack on Spotsylvania Court House had been cancelled. Due to the hardship of that march, only eighty-seven men out of the entire brigade arrived at the destination. The Fourteenth rested for the remainder of the day and waited for its members who had dropped out of the march.[29]

On the May 16, the Fifth Corps prepared to charge the entrenched Confederates to their front. The Fourteenth was drawn up and three lines of battle were formed. At this point, very little land separated the Federals from the Confederate breastworks. The Fifth Corps was to attack only if Burnside's Ninth Corps were to be attacked by the Confederates. However, this did not occur, and no advance took place on either side.[30] The next day Gen. Meade instructed Hancock to move his corps to the left in preparation for still another attack. Gen. Burnside was also informed and was instructed to move his corps to the left behind Warren. With all of these troops moving to the left of Warren and Wright, Warren's Corps became the right wing of the Union Army. He, therefore, spent the remainder of the day fortifying his position.

To accomplish this, Cutler's Division was extended to the Ni River. The Fourteenth was moved to the right of the brigade and began to fortify their position by building breastworks and traverses.[31]

The attack by Hancock and Wright went badly and in the afternoon of May 18, Grant decided to again move his Army southward.[32] On the 19th, all Union Troops in the right wing were withdrawn, but skirmishing continued until darkness.[33]

Finally, the May 21 arrived. It had been exactly three years since Gen. McDowell had inducted the Fourteenth into Federal service. At noon the Fourteenth evacuated its position in the line and were replaced by the Third and Fourth Delaware and the One Hundred Fifty-Seventh Pennsylvania.[34] They marched with Warren's Corps to Massaponex Church, where the Fourteenth left the Second Brigade and reported to the wagon train. They accompanied the wagon train to Guinea Station, which was also the destination of Warren's Corps. At this point the Fourteenth Regiment separated itself from the Army of the Potomac and prepared to come home.[35]

Several months earlier there had been reports that the Fourteenth was going home. In a letter to his sister, Lieut. William C. Rae wrote about this misunderstanding, "The rumor of our regiment was to return to Brooklyn was an error in a telegraphic dispatch, which was this, that the 14th was still in the front, and none fit for duty would be allowed to go home. The telegraph operator put a comma in between the words duty and would, which made it read as if the regiment would be sent home." Later in the letter, he wrote in response to a question asked by her in a previous letter: "Why do you ask such a question in regard to Henry Granger? I do not know as I should have objections to him as a brother in law if such an affair should take place."[36]

Lieut. William C. Rae, who thought his regiment was going home early and who had been questioned by his sister regarding a possible brother-in-law, would not return to Brooklyn. He was one of the thirteen men from Brooklyn who died at the Battle of Spotsylvania Court House.[37]

20. Coming Home

On May 22, the Fourteenth was waiting for the arrival of the railroad cars that would take them home to Brooklyn. They had waited for this time since they left their home city. Three years earlier they had marched down the streets of Brooklyn in their bright clean uniforms. Now they were returning. Although the soldiers were unkempt, bearded, bloodied and the uniforms were worn and ripped by weather, time and battles, they all knew why they were at that place and at that time.

The well disciplined regiment waited patiently for the official word that would send them home. Finally, Col. Fowler appeared and had one of his officers read the order. Before he could finish reading the order, the regiment broke, cheered, threw their caps into the air and hugged each other.[1] However, for some, there was sadness. The order referred to only members of the Fourteenth who were sworn into Federal service in May of 1861. Those who joined after that time, the so-called '62 recruits, had to finish their length of service and were assigned to the Fifth New York Veteran Volunteers.[2]

After the order was read, Col. Fowler spoke to his regiment. In addressing his '62 recruits, he spoke of his sorrow for having to leave then behind and told them of his willingness to aid them in any way he could. The '62 men raised a cheer because they knew of his sincerity and because they knew that he would no longer be their commander. The veterans who were going home then raised a cheer to honor their comrades who were staying behind. Finally, the '62 recruits, forgetting their own sorrow and disappointment, raised a cheer for those who were going home.

After the colonel finished his speech, the regiment divided itself into two groups. Lining up on the right were the members of the Fourteenth who had left from Brooklyn to the cheers of their fellow Brooklynites in May of 1861. They were to march toward Fredericksburg on the first leg of their trip home. To the left were lined up those who had not yet completed their enlistment and were heading back to the front to join the Fifth New York Volunteers.

On the evening of May 22, the regiment reached Fredericksburg, and on the following day, departed for Washington from Aquia Creek. While in Washington the soldiers began to clean their uniforms of the years of battle, weather and grime. They shaved, shined their shoes and became again what they had not been in a long time.

On May 24, they boarded trains which had been provided for their trip home. They barely had a day to rest and refit, but none were complaining. They expected to reach Brooklyn the following morning and had no knowledge of the great reception that the city was planning for them.[3] All the newspapers in Brooklyn were publishing articles about the 14th Regiment and their accomplishments during the war and expressed the feelings of all Brooklynites about their return.

> The city has been on the qui vive today to welcome home its pet regiment, the noble Fourteenth. Brooklyn takes a particular pride in this gallant organization, which was one of the first to volunteer for the war, and which has covered itself with glory in almost every battle of the Army of the Potomac. It now returns with but a handful of braves, but not a tithe of the love and honor which Brooklyn bears for it has been lost, and we now aim to pour upon the few that are left to us the honor we once felt for all.[4]

Meanwhile, the city fathers made preparations for the return of the Fourteenth. They were expected to arrive at Jersey City, New Jersey, at approximately 7:00 A.M., at which time they would be fitted with breakfast at one of the local hotels. A parade route was laid out and city buildings were festooned with Union flags and ribbons. The parade route was to start at the Fulton Ferry, then proceed up Fulton Street to Court Street, through Court Street to Atlantic Avenue, then down Atlantic Avenue to Smith Street, then down Fulton Avenue and from there to Clinton Avenue, Myrtle Avenue and Fort Greene Park, where they had bivouacked in May of 1861 while waiting to leave for the war.[5]

The people of Brooklyn flew flags and strung up signs all along the parade route, from one side of the street to the other. All over it could be seen, signs proclaiming, "All Hail Gallant Fourteenth," "Our Flag Was There," "Welcome Home, Gallant Fourteenth."[6]

The Fourteenth was expected to arrive in Brooklyn at about 10:00 A.M. and thousands of people as well as the military and firemen had been waiting for their arrival. To entertain the people during this long period of waiting, the military put on a display of marching and the firemen showed off their fire fighting equipment. Finally, Gen. Crooke, who was in charge of the military, received a dispatch indicating that the Fourteenth had been delayed along its route and would not arrive until later that evening.[7]

When the train reached Elizabethtown, New Jersey, the Common Council Committee, consisting of prominent Brooklyn citizens, got on board and accompanied the Fourteenth to Jersey City. When the regiment disembarked they were marched to the Taylor Hotel, where dinner had been prepared for them. Along the route the men of the regiment were greeted by friends and loved ones who had made the trip to Jersey City. Tears and hugs were rampant as they greeted one another.

With dinner over, the Fourteenth boarded the ferryboat *Hamilton* for the final leg of its journey.[8] Aboard the ferryboat, which had signaled its approach with cannon fire, roman candles, and other fireworks, were the Seventh regiment band, the Fourteenth Veterans Association band, and representatives of the board of aldermen and members of the Thirteenth Regiment.[9]

At about 9:50 P.M. the ferryboat arrived at the Fulton Ferry Pier. As it approached the pier, the ferryboat fired cannon and roman candles to announce its approach. The pyrotechnic demonstrations made a beautiful display to those waiting on shore. This was answered by a salute of artillery and cheers from the shore. A large crowd of Brooklynites awaited the soldiers' arrival, and the large detachment of police officers who were there to control the crowd were hard pressed to keep a passage open for those on the ferryboat to disembark.

Once off the ferryboat the regiment and its escorts organized themselves into formations for the parade. The parade stepped off as follows:

A detachment of police
Thirteenth Regiment as escorts
Veterans of the Fourteenth Regiment
The Fourteenth Regiment
The mayor and heads of city departments (in carriages)
Committee of the board of aldermen (in carriages)
Fire department.

Although the streets were filled with the people of Brooklyn earlier in the day when the regiment was expected to arrive in the morning, they had thinned out after long hours of waiting and announcements that the regiment would not be arriving until later. However, when they heard that the regiment was arriving, they again filled the streets along the parade route. "Cheer after cheer went up as the veterans made their appearance. It was, in fact, a grand ovation, such as was never before witnessed in the city, and as creditable to the citizens as it was deserved by the recipients of these honors."[10]

At the end of the parade route they had reached Fort Greene Park. The time was approximately 1:00 A.M. It was here that Mayor A.M. Wood, who had been their commander when they left from that same location three years earlier, greeted them and welcomed them home on behalf of the people of Brooklyn.

> Officers and soldiers of the Fourteenth Regiment, veterans of the Army of the Potomac! It is with feelings of profound emotion that I greet you, not only in

behalf of the citizens of Brooklyn, whom I represent on this occasion, but personally as your former comrade and commander. Your deeds of valor and of heroism on many a hard fought battlefields entitles you to honor everywhere, but nowhere so much as here, in you native city, whose battle flag you have borne from the plains of Manassas, on a three years' willing march to the gory fields of Spotsylvania, without one blot or stain of dishonor. Welcome! Thrice welcome home! Your names are emblazoned imperishably high on the scroll of fame; your deeds have passed into history; and your children's children shall read of them and be proud that they are descended from such noble men."[11]

Of the 1,751 men who served in the Fourteenth Brooklyn Regiment between April 1861 and May 1864, only 140 officers and men returned to Brooklyn on that day. It was one of only 198 regiments whose losses during the war exceeded 10 percent (11.8). Of the regiments who lost the greatest number of men at any one battle, the Fourteenth is listed as one of the thirty-four at the Battle of Spotsylvania. It is also listed as one of forty-five regiments which sustained the greatest loss at the Battle of Gettysburg with 68.2 percent.[12]

The Fourteenth had heard its country's call. They had climbed Henry House Hill to meet Jackson at Bull Run. They had defended the Rappahannock and faced Jackson and Hood's onslaught at Second Bull Run. They had climbed the hills and walked the valley at South Mountain. They had marched the bloody cornfields at Antietam. They had protected the army's flank at Fredericksburg and deceived Lee at Chancellorsville. They had helped to save the day at Gettysburg. They had served at Mine Run and the Wilderness. They had tirelessly fought at Spotsylvania where many Red Legs had fallen.

They had heard their country's call and answered with a hurrah! Now, the Fourteenth regiment, the "Red Legged Devils," the boys were finally home — in Brooklyn.

Part II : A Roster

Abbott, Thomas — Age, 22 years. Enlisted, April 18, 1861, at Brooklyn, to serve three years; mustered in as private, Co. B, May 23, 1861; wounded in action, September 17, 1862, at Antietam, Md.; promoted sergeant, January 1, 1863; wounded in action, May 8, 1864, at Spotsylvania, VA; mustered out of company, June 6, 1864, at New York City; also borne as Abbotts.

Abrams, Joseph — Age, 41 years. Enlisted at Brooklyn, to serve three years, and mustered in as private, Co. C, September 27, 1861; transferred to Co. H, Fifth Veteran Infantry, June 2, 1864.

Ackerman, William H. — Age, 41 years. Enlisted at Brooklyn, to serve three years, and mustered in as private, Co. E, August 25, 1862; wounded in action, September 17, 1862, at Antietam, Md.; died of his wounds, October 17, 1862.

Ackley, Andrew F. — Age, 19 years. Enrolled, April 18, 1861, at Brooklyn, to serve three years; mustered in as private Co. H, May 23, 1861; promoted corporal, July 1, 1861; sergeant, March 1, 1862; mustered in as second lieutenant, October 24, 1862; transferred to Co. G, May 29, 1863; re-transferred to Co. H, January 9, 1864; mustered out with company, June 6, 1864, at New York City. Commissioned second lieutenant, October 24, 1862, with rank from August 29, 1862, vice J. McNiel, promoted.

Adams, John — Age, 21 years. Enlisted, December 21, 1863, at Brooklyn, to serve three years; mustered in as private, Co. A, December 30, 1863; transferred to Co. A Fifth Veteran Infantry, June 2, 1864.

Adams, Robert — Age, 19 years. Enlisted, April 18, 1861, at Brooklyn, to serve three years; mustered in as private, Co. F, May 23, 1861; captured in action, at Bull Run, Va.; paroled, June 2, 1862, at Washington, D.C.; mustered out with company, June 6, 1864, at New York City.

Adams, Thomas — Age, 25 years. Enlisted at Brooklyn, to serve three years; mustered in as private; unassigned, August 18, 1862; no further record.

Adamson, John — Age, 19 years. Enlisted, April 18, 1861, at Brooklyn, to serve three years; mustered in as private, Co. A, May 23, 1861; discharged, August 10, 1862.

Adatte, Joseph — Age, 21 years. Enlisted, September 29, 1861, at Brooklyn to serve three years; mustered in as private, Co. F, September 30, 1861; transferred to Veteran Reserve Corps, July 1, 1863.

Addison, Mathew — Age, 19 years. Enlisted, April 18, 1861, at Brooklyn, to serve; three years; mustered in as private, Co. C, May 23, 1861; discharged for disability, October 17, 1862, at Washington, D.C.

Alger, Charles — Age, 36 years. Enlisted, December 7, 1863, at Brooklyn, to serve three years; mustered in as private, Co. F, December 13, 1863; transferred to Co. G, Fifth Veteran Infantry, June 2, 1864.

Allen, Alexander — Age, 26 years, Enlisted August 19, 1861, at Brooklyn, to serve three years; mustered in as private, Co. K, August 21, 1861; wounded, April 28, 1861, while on skirmish line at Rappahannock Crossing, Va.; died of his wounds May 9, 1863.

Allen, Edward T. — Age, 35, years. Enlisted,

August 25, 1862, at Brooklyn, to serve three years; mustered in as private, Co. D, August 26, 1862; transferred to Co. H, Fifth Veteran infantry, June 2, 1864.

Allen Hamilton — Age, 21 years. Enlisted, at Brooklyn, to serve three years; mustered in as private, Co. G, December 15, 1863, killed in action, May 8, 1864, at Piney Church, Va.

Allen, Joseph S. — Age, 16 years. Enlisted, August 16, 1862, at Brooklyn, to serve three years; mustered in as private, Co. H, August 18, 1862, transferred to Co. K, Fifth Veteran Infantry, June 2, 1864.

Allen, Mettioyn — Age, 22 years. Enlisted, September 22, 1862, at Brooklyn, to serve three years; mustered in as private; unassigned, September 23, 1862; no further record.

Allen, William C. — Age, 20 years. Enlisted, April 18, 1861, at Brooklyn, to serve three years; mustered in as private, Co. C, May 23, 1861; appointed wagoner, November 25, 1861; mustered out with company at New York City, June 14, 1864.

Alling, Isaac H. — Age, 19 years. Enlisted, May 18, 1861, at Brooklyn to serve three years; mustered in as private, Co. B, May 23, 1861; deserted, August 11, 1861, at Arlington, Va.

Ames, Henry — Age, 24 years. Enlisted April 18, 1861, at Brooklyn, to serve three years; mustered in as private, Co. C, May 23, 1861, deserted, September 30, 1861, at Arlington, Va.

Anderson, Carman — Age, 20 years. Enlisted, April 18, 1861, at Brooklyn, to serve three years; mustered in as private, Co. E, May 23, 1861; discharged for disability, June 19, 1861, at Washington, D.C.

Anderson, Louis — Age, 37 years. Enlisted, December 4, 1863, at Brooklyn, to serve three years; mustered in as private, Co. I, December 8, 1863; transferred to Co. G, Fifth Veteran Infantry, June 2, 1864; also borne as Lewis D., and Louis D. Anderson.

Anderson Peter — Age, 31 years. Enlisted, September 22, 1861, at Brooklyn, to serve three years; mustered in as private; Co. C, September 24, 1862; transferred to Co. H, Fifth Veteran Infantry, June 2, 1864.

Anderson, Peter — Age, 29 years. Enlisted, September 22, 1861, at Brooklyn, to serve three years; mustered in as private, Co. G, May 23, 1861; deserted, January 1, 1863, at Belle Plains, Va.

Andrea, Charles H. — Age, 19 years. Enlisted, January 6, 1863, at Brooklyn, to serve three years; mustered in as private, Co. A, January 7, 1863; transferred to Co. H, Fifth Veteran Infantry, June 2, 1864; also borne as Andre.

Anthony, Edward — Age, 18 years. Enlisted April 18, 1861, at Brooklyn, to serve three years; mustered in as private, Co. D, May 23, 1861, wounded to action, May 10, 1864, at Laurel Hill, Va.; mustered out with company, June 6, 1864, at New York City.

Apel, Alexander — Age, 42 years. Enlisted, April 18, 1861, at Brooklyn, to serve three years; mustered in as private, Co. H, May 23, 1861; promoted to corporal and returned to ranks, no dates; discharged for disease, June 18, 1862.

Archer, Henry — Age, 28 years. Enlisted, January 25, 1864, at Brooklyn, to serve three years; mustered in as private, Co. H, January 27, 1864; wounded in action, May 10, 1864, at Laurel Hill Va.; transferred to Co. H, Fifth Veteran Infantry, June 2, 1864.

Ardeis, Thomas A. — Age, 26 years. Enlisted, August 28, 1862, at Brooklyn, to serve three years; mustered in as private, Co. K, August 29, 2862; wounded, April 28, 1863, while on skirmish line at Rappahannock Crossing, Va.; discharged for disability September 12, 1863, from Convalescent Camp, Alexandria, Va.

Armitage, Lewis — Age, 30 years. Enlisted at Brooklyn, to serve three years; mustered in as private, Co. C, March 17,

1864, transferred to Co. H, Fifth Veteran Infantry, June 2, 184.

Armstrong, Morrison — Age, 20 years. Enlisted April 25, 1861, at Brooklyn, to serve three years; mustered in as private, Co. G, May 23, 1861; promoted corporal, no date; killed in action, August 29, 1862, Bull Run, Va.

Atkins, Francis C.— Age, 23 years. Enlisted at Brooklyn, to serve three years; mustered in as private, Co. D, August 30, 1862; deserted, September 16, 1863, from hospital, Annapolis, Md.; also borne as Atkin and Frank C. Atkins.

Atkins, George H.— Age, 21 years. Enlisted at Brooklyn to serve three years; mustered in as private, Co. D, August 29, 1862; killed in action, July 1, 1863, at Gettysburg, Pa.

Austin, Thomas — Age, 35 years, Enlisted, October 1, 1861, at Brooklyn, to serve three years; mustered in as musician in hand, October 24, 1861; discharged with rank, August 17, 1862, at Camp Halstead, Va.

Autrop, Swan — Age, 35 years. Enlisted, June 1, 1861, at Brooklyn, to serve three years; mustered in as private, Co. I, August 1, 1861; wounded in action, August 29, 1862, at Bull Run, Va.; transferred to Veteran Reserve Corps, July 1863. Also borne as Autroph Swan.

Avila, Edward C.— Age, 18 years. Enlisted, August 29, 1862, at Brooklyn to serve three years; mustered in as private, Co. D, August 30, 1862; discharged for disability, February 26, 1863, at New York City.

Avis, Isaac T.— Age, 32 years. Enlisted, April 18, 1861, at Brooklyn, to serve three years; mustered in as private, Co. C, May 23, 1861, died of disease, May 29, 1862, at Washington, D.C.

Axteli, Enos A.— Age, 18 years. Enlisted, April 1861, at Brooklyn, to serve three years; mustered in as private, Co. D, May 23, 1861, promoted corporal, November 1, 1862, captured in action, July 1, 1863, at Gettysburg, Pa; paroled, no date; mustered out with company, June 6, 1864, at New York City.

Ayre, William — Age, 23 years. Enlisted, April 18, 1861, at Brooklyn, to serve three years; mustered in as private, Co. I, December 6, 1863; transferred to Co. A, Fifth Veteran Infantry, June 2, 1864.

Bagley, George W.— Age, 19 years. Enlisted, September 6, 1862, at Brooklyn, to serve three years; mustered in as private, Co. D, September 8, 1862, discharged for disability, January 18, 1863, at Patent Office Hospital, Washington, D.C.

Bagley, Lawrence — Age, 26 years. Enlisted, august 21, 1862, at Brooklyn, to serve three years; mustered in as private, Co. B, August 22, 1862; transferred to Co. I, Fifth Veteran Infantry, June 2, 1864; also borne as Bayles.

Baird, John — Age, 31 years. Enlisted, December 28, 1863, at Brooklyn, to serve three years; mustered in as private, Co. G, December 30, 1863; transferred to Co. K, Fifth Veteran Infantry, June 2, 1864; also borne as Beard.

Baker, Henry — Age, 42 years. Enlisted, December 14, 1863, at Brooklyn, to serve three years; mustered in as private, Co. G, December 21, 1863, discharged for disability, January 5, 1865, at hospital, David's Island, New York Harbor.

Baker, Horace G.— Age, 32 years, Enlisted, October 23, 1862, at Brooklyn, to serve three years; mustered in as private, Co. F, October 245, 1862; transferred to Co. H, Fifth Veteran Infantry, June 2, 1864.

Baker, John C.— Age, 30 years. Enlisted August 27, 1862, at Brooklyn, to serve three years; mustered in as private, Co. D, August 29, 1862, transferred to Co. H, Fifth Veteran Infantry, June 2, 1864.

Baker, Karl — Age, 28 years. Enlisted at New York City, to serve three years; mustered in as private, Co. C; unassigned, March 8, 1864, no further record.

Ballantine, William — Age, 18 years. Enlisted, April 18, 1861, at Brooklyn, to serve three years; mustered in as private, Co. C, May 23, 1861; killed in action, august 29, 1862, at Groveton, Va.

Baldwin, Charles F.—Age, 25 years. Enrolled, May 18, 1861, at Brooklyn, to serve three years; mustered in as captain, Co. D, May 23, 1861; wounded in action August 29, 1862, at Groveton Va.; mustered in as major, October 24, 1862, with rank from October 1, 1862, vice W.H. De Bevoise, promoted.

Baldwin, George E.—Age, 19 years. Enlisted, April 18, 1861, at Brooklyn, to serve three years; mustered in as private, Co. B, May 23, 1861; promoted corporal, no date; returned to ranks, August 24, 1863; wounded in action, May 8, 1864, at Piney Church Va.; mustered out with company, June 6, 1864, at New York City.

Baldwin, James H.—Age, 20 years. Enlisted, May 18, 1861, at Brooklyn, to serve three years; mustered in as private, Co. B, May 23, 1861; deserted, August 10, 1862, at Fairmouth, Va.

Baldwin, William H.—Age, 25 years. Enlisted, April 18, 1861, at Brooklyn to serve three years; mustered in as private, Co. F, May 23, 1861; wounded and captured in action, July 21, 1861, at Bull Run, Va.; paroled, no date; mustered out, May 23, 1864, at Washington, D.C.

Baldwin, William M.—Age, 29 years. Enlisted, April 18, 1861, at Brooklyn, to serve three years; mustered in as second lieutenant, Co. D, May 23, 1861; as first lieutenant, October 11, 1861; as captain, October 1, 1862; wounded in action, May 10, 1864, at Laurel Hill, Va.; mustered out with company, June 6, 1864, at New York City Commissioned second lieutenant to 14th Militia, June 29, 1861, with rank from May 15, 1861; not commissioned first lieutenant; commissioned captain, October 24, 1862, with rank from October 1, 1862, vice C.F. Baldwin promoted.

Ball, James M.—Age, 24 years. Enlisted at Brooklyn, to serve three years; mustered in as private, Co. K, July 26, 1861; deserted, December 24, 1861, from guard house; also borne as George W. Ball.

Ball, James M.—Age, 19 years. Enlisted at Brooklyn, to serve three years; mustered in as private, Co. F, September 29, 1862; promoted corporal no date; transferred to Co. K, Fifth Veteran Infantry, June 2, 1864.

Ball, William A.—Age, 24 years. Enrolled, April 18, 1861, at Brooklyn, to serve three years; mustered in first sergeant, Co. F, May 23, 1861; as second lieutenant August 3, 1861; as captain, January 11, 1863; wounded in action, July 1, 1863, at Gettysburg, Pa.; mustered out, June 14, 1864; commissioned second lieutenant in 14th Militia, August 12, 1861, with rank from August 3, 1861, vice James H. Jourdan, resigned; captain, February 10, 1863, with rank from January 13, 1863, vice James H. Jourdan, resigned.

Balmer, James L.—Age, 36 years. Enlisted, April 18, 1861, at Brooklyn, to serve three years; mustered in as private, Co. H, May 23, 1861; discharged for disability, October 14, 1862, at Philadelphia, Pa.

Banham, Samuel, P.—Age, 26, years. Enlisted, April 18, 1861, at Brooklyn, to serve three years; mustered in as private, Co. H, May 23, 1861, promoted corporal, March 1, 1862; mustered out with company, June 6, 1864, at New York City.

Barbetta, Forunato—Age, 33 years. Enlisted, April 18, 1861, at Brooklyn, to serve three years; mustered in as private, Co. H, May 23, 1861, discharged for disability, April 4, 1862, at Upton Hill Va.

Barnard, John T.—Age, 26 years. Enlisted, August 25, 1862, at Brooklyn, to serve three years; mustered in as private, Co. F, May 23, 1862; wounded in action, December 13, 1862, at Fredericksburg, Va.; transferred to Veteran Reserve Corps. July 1, 1863.

Barnard, Robert G.—Age, 22 years. Enlisted, April 18, 1861, at Brooklyn to serve three years; mustered in as private, Engineers, May 23, 1861; mustered out, August 28, 1861, at Arlington, Va.

Barnard, Warren — Age, 30 years. Enlisted, September 5, 1862, at Brooklyn, to serve three years; mustered in as private, Co. D, September 6, 1862; transferred to Co. C, November 14, 1862; discharged for disability, March 30, 1863, at Philadelphia, Pa.

Barnes, James — Age, 23 years. Enlisted, April 18, 1861, at Brooklyn to serve three years; mustered in as private, Co. A, May 23, 1861; discharged for disability, August 2, 1861, at Arlington, Va.; also borne as James A. Barnes.

Barnes, John — Age, 23 years. Enlisted, August 30, 1862, at Brooklyn, to serve three years; mustered in as private, Co. F, August 30, 1862; transferred to Co. I, Fifth Veteran Infantry, June 2, 1864.

Barnes, William H. — Age, 23 years. Enlisted, April 18, 1861, at Brooklyn, to serve three years; mustered in as private, Co. H, May 23, 1861; discharged, September 3, 1861, for promotion.

Barnie, Alexander, Jr. — Age, 23 years. Enlisted, April 18, 1861, at Brooklyn, to serve three years; mustered in as corporal, Co. H, May 23, 1861; promoted quarter-master-sergeant, September 1, 1861; mustered out with regiment, June 2, 1864, at New York City.

Barr, James P. — Age, 28 years. Enlisted at Brooklyn, to serve three years; mustered in as private, Co. B, August 28, 1862; transferred to Co. I, Fifth Veteran Infantry, June 2, 1864.

Barrett, Anthony — Age, 19 years. Enlisted, May 18, 1861, at Brooklyn, to serve three years; mustered in as private, Co. B, May 23, 1861; discharged February 2, 1862.

Barrokell, Warren — Age, 18 years. Enlisted, May 1861, at Brooklyn, to serve three years; mustered in as private, Co. I, August 4, 1861; no further record.

Barto, Charles — Age, 18 years. Enlisted, April 18, 1861, at Brooklyn, to serve three years; mustered in as private, Co. E, May 23, 1861; wounded in action, May 1, 1863, at Gettysburg, Pa.; promoted corporal, December 1, 1863; mustered out with company, June 6, 1864, at New York City, as Charles A. Barto

Barton, Stephen B. — Age, 17, years. Enlisted, September 11, 1862, at Brooklyn, to serve three years; mustered in as musician, Co. E, September 12, 1862; transferred to Co. H, Fifth Veteran Infantry, June 2, 1864.

Battell, William H. — Age, 18 years. Enlisted, April 18, 1861, at Brooklyn, to serve three years; mustered in a private, Co. H, May 23, 1861; deserted, November 29, 1862, from Soldiers Rest, at Washington, D.C.; also borne as Battelle.

Bayard, Auguste — Age, 27 years. Enlisted at Brooklyn, to serve three years; mustered in as private; unassigned, October 15, 1862; no further record.

Beal, Caleb H. — Age, 28 years. Enlisted, April 18, 1861, at Brooklyn, to serve three years; mustered in as private Co. H, May 23, 1861; discharged April 6, 1863; for promotion as second lieutenant 147th Infantry.

Beals, Joseph — Age, 32 years. Enlisted, April 18, 1861, at Brooklyn, to serve three years; mustered in as private, Co. H, May 23, 1861; discharged for disability, July 11, 1862, at Alexandria, Va.

Beard, James — Age, 28 years. Enlisted, April 18, 1861, at Brooklyn, to serve three years; mustered in as private, Engineers, May 23, 1861; mustered out, August 28, 1861, at Arlington, Va.

Beardsley, Charles — Age, 18 years. Enlisted, August 26, 1862, at Brooklyn, to serve three years; mustered in as private, Co. B, August 27, 1862; transferred to Veteran Reserve Corps, March 14, 1864; also borne as Beardslee.

Bearns, Fred J. — Age, 24 years. Enlisted, May 18, 1861, at Brooklyn, to serve three years; mustered in as private, Co. D, May 23, 1861; deserted, February 5, 1862, at Upton Hill Va.

Beatty, William W.—Age, 20 years. Enlisted, April 18, 1861, at Brooklyn, to serve three years; mustered in as private, Co. E, May 23, 1861; deserted, February 5, 1862, at Upon Hill, Va.

Beck, Augustus W.—Age, 32 years. Enlisted at Brooklyn, to serve three years; mustered in as private, Co. B, September 30, 1862; wounded. no date; deserted on expiration of furlough, August 15, 1864.

Beckett, Henry—Age, 21 years. Enlisted, august 27, 1862, at Brooklyn, to serve three years; mustered in a private, Co. D, August 28, 1862; wounded in action, July 1, 1863, at Gettysburg, Pa.; transferred to Co. I, Fifth Veteran Infantry, June 1, 1864.

Bedell, Charles E.—Age, 27 years. Enlisted at Brooklyn, to serve three years; mustered in as private, Co. F, August 22, 1862; captured in action, July 1, 1863, at Gettysburg, Pa.; paroled, August 25, 1863, at City Point, Va.; transferred to Co. G, Fifth Veteran Infantry, June 2, 1864.

Beers, Andrew J.—Age, 33 years. Enlisted, June 1861, at Brooklyn, to serve three years; mustered in as sergeant, Co. I, August 1, 1861; deserted January 22, 1862, at Upon Hill, Va.

Begbie, George L.—Age, 30 years. Enlisted, April 1861, at Brooklyn; mustered in as corporal, Co. H, to serve three years, May 23, 1861; returned to ranks and promoted sergeant, no dates; discharged, August 24, 1863, for promotion as first lieutenant, 33rd New Jersey Infantry.

Bell, George—Age, 34 years. Enlisted at Brooklyn, to serve three years; mustered in as private, Co. A, January 7, 1864; deserted, March 30, 1864.

Bell, James—Age, 23, years. Enlisted, July 1, 1861, at Brooklyn, to serve three years; mustered in as private, Co. I, August 4, 1861, deserted, January 31, 1862, at Upton Hill, Va.

Bell, Robert—Age, 31 years. Enlisted, August 21, 1861, at Brooklyn, to serve three years; mustered in as private, Co. C, August 22, 1862; transferred to Veteran Reserve Corps, December 1, 1863.

Bene, John—Age, 23 years. Enlisted at Brooklyn, to serve three years; mustered in as private, Co. E, August 25, 1862; wounded in action, April 29, 1863, at Reynolds Crossing, Va.; transferred to Co. A, Fifth Veteran Infantry, June 2, 1864.

Bennet, John—Age, 27 years. Enlisted at Brooklyn, to serve three years; mustered in as private; unassigned, January 4, 1864; no further record.

Bennett, George W.—Age, 22 years. Enlisted, May 18, 1861, at Brooklyn, to serve three years; mustered in as private, Co. D, May 31, 1861; discharged for disability, January 31, 1863, at Camp Banks, Va.

Bennett, Henry—Age, 30 years. Enlisted, April 1861, at Brooklyn, to serve three years; mustered in as private, Co. H, May 23, 1861; promoted sergeant, January 1, 1863; missing in action July 1, 1863, at Gettysburg, Pa.; returned, December 25, 1863; mustered out with company, June 6, 1864, at New York City, as Henry W. Bennett.

Bennett, John—Age, 19 years. Enlisted, April 18, 1861, at Brooklyn, to serve three years; mustered in as private, Co. E, May 23, 1861; discharged for disability, September 2, 1864, at Big Falls, Md. Also borne as John F. Bennett.

Bennett, John—Age, 27 years. Enlisted at Brooklyn, to serve three years; mustered in as private, Co. E, January 4, 1864; transferred to Co. H, Fifth Veteran Infantry, June 2, 1864.

Bennett, John R.—Age, 20 years. Enrolled, April 25, 1861, at Brooklyn, to serve three years; mustered in as corporal, Co. G, May 23, 1861; promoted sergeant, no date; mustered in as second lieutenant, January 8, 1864; mustered out with company, June 6, 1864, at New York City. Commissioned second lieutenant, August 18, 1863, with rank from March 25, 1863, vice H. Waldron, promoted.

Bannit, Charles N.—Age, 19 years. Enlisted, October 17, 1861, at Brooklyn, to serve three years; mustered in as private, Co. H, October 29, 1861; wounded in action, August 30, 1862, at Bull Run, Va.; discharged for wounds, October 8, 1862, at Fairfax Seminary, Va.; also borne as Charles Bennet and Bennitt.

Benton, Lawrence—Age, 35 years. Enlisted, September 18, 1861, at Brooklyn, to serve three years; mustered in as private, Co. C., September 24, 1861; wounded, May 12, 1864; transferred to Co. H. Fifth Veteran Infantry, June 2, 1864.

Berlew, James G.—Age, 29 years. Enlisted, April 18, 1861, at Brooklyn, to serve three years; mustered in as private, Co. C, May 23, 1861; promoted corporal, January 1, 1864; mustered out June 14, 1864, at New York City; also borne as Beolin.

Berry, George P.—Age, 21 years. Enlisted, April 18, 1861, at Brooklyn, to serve three years; mustered in as private, co. C, May 23, 1861; deserted, January 11, 1863, at Belle Plains, Va.

Berry, Jacob—Age, 27 years. Enlisted, April 18, 1861, at Brooklyn, to serve three years; mustered in as private, Engineers, May 23, 1861; mustered out, August 28, 1864, at Arlington, Va.

Berry, John M.—Age, 18 years. Enlisted, April 1861, at Brooklyn, to serve three years; mustered in as private, Co. C, May 23, 1861; promoted corporal, March 1, 1863; sergeant, June 1, 1863; wounded in action, July 1, 1863, at Gettysburg, Pa.; discharged, December 2, 1863, for promotion as second lieutenant, 147th Infantry.

Birdsall, George E.—Age, 23 years. Enlisted, April 18, 1861, at Brooklyn, to serve three years; mustered in as private, Co. F, May 23, 1861; deserted, August 10, 1862, at Falmouth, Va.

Bishop, John H.—Age, 24 years. Enlisted at Brooklyn, to serve three years; mustered in as private, Co. A, September 6, 1862; transferred to Co. H, Fifth Veteran Infantry, June 2, 1864.

Bissett, Thomas M.—Age, 22 years. Enrolled, April 18, 1861, at Brooklyn, to serve three years; mustered in as corporal, Co. C, May 23, 1861; as second lieutenant, July 1, 1861; discharged, August 2, 1861; commissioned second lieutenant in 14th Militia, July 8, 1861, with rank from July 1, 1861, vice Wm. H. Burnett, promoted.

Bitter, Fred S.—Age, 19 years. Enlisted, April 18, 1861, at Brooklyn, to serve three years; mustered in a private, Co. F, May 23, 1861; missing, August 24, 1862, near Warrenton, Va.; no further record.

Black, Edwin J.P.—Age, 21 years. Enlisted, April 18, 1861, at Brooklyn, to serve Three years; mustered in as private, Co. E, May 23, 1861; accidentally wounded, May 20, 1861; died of his wounds, July 20, 1861.

Blackburn, George—Age, 23 years. Enlisted, in Brooklyn, to serve three years; mustered in as private, Co. G, December 7, 1863, transferred to Co. A, Fifth Veteran Infantry, June 2, 1864.

Blackwood, Clinton R.—Age, 20 years. Enlisted, April 18, 1861, at Brooklyn to serve three years; mustered in as private, Co. E, May 23, 1861; captured in action, August 28, 1862, at Gainesville, Va.; paroled, no date; discharged for disability, June 8, 1863, at Annapolis, Md.

Blake, George—Age, 21 years. Enlisted, May 18, 1861, at Brooklyn, to serve three years; mustered in as private, Co. B, May 23, 1861; killed in action, July 21, 1861, at Bull Run, Va.; also borne as George W. Blake.

Blake, William—Age, 27 years. Enlisted April 18, 1861, at Brooklyn, to serve three years; mustered in as private, Co. E, May 18, 1861; discharged for disability, May 6, 1862, at Upton Hill, Va.

Blanchard, N.L.—Age, 24 years. Enlisted, May 18, 1861, at Brooklyn, to serve three years; mustered in a private, Co. B, May 23, 1861; discharged, June 28, 1861; also borne as Nathaniel L. Blanchard.

Bliss, George W.—Age, 20 years. Enlisted, April 18, 1861, at Brooklyn, to serve three years; mustered in as private, Co. H, May 23, 1861; captured in action, July 21, 1861, at Manassas, Va.; paroled, June 2, 1862, at Washington, N.C.; deserted, September 28, 1862, near Camp Parole, Md.

Bloomfield, James—Age, 23 years. Enrolled, April 18, 1861, at Brooklyn, to serve three years; mustered in as corporal, Co. E, May 23, 1861; as second lieutenant, February 23, 1862, at Reynolds Crossing, Va.; died of his wounds, May 24, 1863; also borne as James H. Bloomfield; not commissioned second lieutenant.

Blydenburg, William—Age, 24 years. Enlisted, May 18, 1861, at Brooklyn, to serve three years; mustered in as private, Co. B, May 23, 1861; captured in action July 21, 1861, at Bull Run, Va.; paroled, June 2, 1862; transferred to Co. G, Fifth Veteran Infantry, June 2, 1864.

Bodger, Thomas—Age, 24 years. Enlisted, June 30, 1861, at Brooklyn, to serve three years; mustered in as private, Co. I, August 1, 1861; transferred to Co. G, Fifth Veteran Infantry, June 2, 1864.

Bogart, Harris—Age, 18 years. Enlisted, July 1, 1861, at Brooklyn, to serve three years; mustered in as private, Co. A, august 1, 1861; appointed wagoner, and returned to company, no dates; transferred to Co. I, Fifth Veteran Infantry, June 2, 1864. Also borne as Bogert.

Bogert, Adrian—Age, 25 years. Enlisted, April 18, 1861, at Brooklyn, to serve three years; mustered in as private, Co. A, May 23, 1861; deserted, September 19, 1861, at Arlington, Va.

Bold, Robert—Age, 42 years. Enlisted, April 18, 1861, at Brooklyn, to serve three years; mustered in as private, Co. B, May 23, 1861; deserted from hospital, December 13, 1862, at Washington, D.C.

Bond, John L.—Age, 17 years, Enlisted, March 4, 1862, at Brooklyn, to serve three years; mustered in as private, Co. A, March 7, 1862; discharged, for disability, August 12, 1862, at Washington, D.C.

Bond, William W.—Age, 18 years. Enlisted, August 20, 1862, at Brooklyn, to serve three years; mustered in as private, Co. B, August 30, 1862; transferred to Co. I, Fifth Veteran Infantry, June 2, 1864.

Bonner, Charles—Age, 22 years. Enlisted at Brooklyn, to serve three years; mustered in as private, Co. E, September 25, 1861; deserted October 28, 1862, from hospital, at Washington, D.C.

Bonner, Titus—Age, 25 years. Enlisted at Brooklyn, to serve three years; mustered in as private, Co. E, October 12, 1861; transferred to Fifth Veteran Infantry, June 2, 1864.

Boorman, Fred—Age, 21 years. Enlisted at Brooklyn, to serve three years; mustered in as private, Co. K, July 26, 1861; deserted, September 23, 1861, from guard house, Camp Wood, Va.

Boughton, Joseph W.—Age, 20 years. Enlisted April 18, 1861, at Brooklyn, to serve three years; mustered in as private, Co. H, May 23, 1861; wounded in action July 21, 1861, at Bull Run, Va.; discharged for disability; April 18, 1862, at Upton Hill Hospital, Va.

Bowen, John R.—Age, 23 years. Enlisted, August 25, 1862, at Brooklyn, to serve three years; mustered in as private, Co. D, August 26, 1862; transferred to Co. H, Fifth Veteran Infantry, June 2, 1864.

Bowers, David A.—Age, 21 years. Enlisted, May 18, 1861, at Brooklyn, to serve three years; mustered in as corporal, Co. B, May 23, 1861; promoted sergeant, no date; discharged for disability, January 10, 1863, at Providence, R.I.

Bowers, Isaac—Age, 19 years. Enlisted, April 18, 1861, at Brooklyn, to serve three years; mustered in as private, Co. A, May 23, 1861; mustered out with company, June 6, 1864, at New York City.

Bowers, Lawrence M.—Age, 19 years. Enlisted, May 18, 1861, at Brooklyn, to serve three years; mustered in as private, Co. D, May 23, 1861; discharged for disability, February 9, 1863, at hospital, Washington, D.C.

Bowers, Robert—Age, 19 years. Enlisted, June 30, 1861, at Brooklyn, to serve three years; mustered in as private, Co. I, August 1, 1861; promoted corporal, no date; wounded in action, July 1, 1863, at Gettysburg, Pa.; deserted, July 23, 1863, at Germantown Pa.; also borne as Robert W. Bowers.

Bowman, George—Age, 33 years. Enlisted at Brooklyn, to serve three years; mustered in as private, Co. K, December 10, 1863; transferred to Co. K, Fifth Veteran Infantry, June 2, 1864; also borne as Bauman.

Bowman, Louis—Age, 28 years. Enlisted at Brooklyn, to serve three years; mustered in as private, Co. G, February 5, 1864; no further record.

Boyce, Edward—Age, 23 years. Enlisted, October 1, 1861, at Brooklyn, to serve three years; mustered in as musician in bank, October 24, 1861; discharged, August 17, 1862, at Camp Halstead, Va.

Boyce, Frederick—Age, 21 years. Enlisted, August 15, 1862, at Brooklyn, to serve three years; mustered in as private, Co. E, August 16, 1862; captured, May 14, 1864; transferred to Co. H, Fifth Veteran Infantry, June 2, 1864.

Boyce, John—Age, 19 years. Enlisted, August 16, 1862, at Brooklyn, to serve three years; mustered in as private, Co. E, August 19, 1862; captured, May 14, 1864, at Spotsylvania, Va.; paroled, February 28, 1865, at Wilmington, N.C.; mustered out, July 3, 1865, at Annapolis, Md.

Boyce, John—Age, 24 years. Enlisted at Brooklyn, to serve three years; mustered in as private, Co. G, December 7, 1863; transferred to Co. D, Fifth Veteran Infantry, June 2, 1864.

Boyd, Frederick—Age, 31 years. Enlisted at Brooklyn, to serve three years mustered in as private, Co. G, December 17, 1863; transferred to Co. K, Fifth Veteran Infantry, June 2, 1864.

Boylan, Thomas, F.—Age, 25 years. Enlisted, April 18, 1861, at Brooklyn, to serve three years; mustered in as private, Co. F, May 23, 1861; wounded in action, August 30, 1862, at Manassas, Va.; mustered out, May 23, 1864, at New York City; also borne as Boyland.

Boyle, Edward—Age, 21 years. Enlisted, April 25, 1861, at Brooklyn, to serve three years; mustered in as private, Co. G, May 23, 1861; discharged for disability, August 30, 1862, at Fort Columbus, New York Harbor.

Boyle, John—Age, 27 years. Enlisted, May 1, 1861, at Brooklyn, to serve three years; mustered in as private, Co. G, May 23, 1861; deserted, January 22, 1862, at Upton Hill, Va.

Boyle, John T.—Age, 20 years. Enlisted, April 18, 1861, at Brooklyn, to serve three years; mustered in a private, Co. A, May 23, 1861; mustered out with company, June 6, 1864, at New York City.

Bradford, John H.—Age, 20 years. Enlisted, August 26, 1862, at Brooklyn, to serve three years; mustered in as private, Co. B, August 27, 1862; wounded in action, July 1, 1863, at Gettysburg, Pa.; discharged for wounds, March 8, 1864, at Satterlee Hospital, West Philadelphia, Pa.

Bradley, John—Age, 18 years. Enlisted may 18, 1861, at Brooklyn, to serve three years; mustered in as private, Co. B, May 23, 1861; wounded and captured in action, July 21, 1861, at Bull Run, Va.; died of his wounds, August 8, 1861, at Richmond, Va.

Bradley, John H.—Age, 23 years. Enlisted at Brooklyn, to serve three years; mustered in as private, Co. A, March 7, 1862; promoted corporal, June 23, 1863; re-enlisted as a veteran, March 23, 1864; transferred to Co. I, Fifth Veteran Infantry, June 2, 1864; also borne as Bradly.

Bradshaw, John J.—Age, 31 years. Enlisted, May 18, 1861, at Brooklyn, to serve three years; mustered in a sergeant, Co. B, May 23, 1861; returned to ranks, no date; deserted, January 30, 1862, at Upton Hill, Va.

Brady, Charles—Age, 23 years. Enlisted, June 30, 1861, at Brooklyn, to serve three years; mustered in as private, Co. K, August 1, 1861; promoted corporal, no date; sergeant, April 11, 1863l; transferred to Co. K, Fifth Veteran Infantry, June 2, 1864; also borne as Charles P. Brady.

Brady, James—Age, 18 years. Enlisted at Brooklyn, to serve three years; mustered in as private, Co. G, December 13, 1863; appointed musician, no date; transferred to Co. K, Fifth Veteran Infantry, June 2, 1864.

Brady, Thomas—Age, 20 years. Enlisted, May 18, 1861, at Brooklyn, to serve three years; mustered in as private, Co. B, May 23, 1861; deserted, October 23, 1861, at Upon Hill, Va.

Brainerd, Charles—Age, 18 years. Enlisted, September 15, 1862, at Brooklyn, to serve three years; mustered in a private; unassigned, September 16, 1862; no further record.

Brannerly, Martin—Age, 26 years. Enlisted, April 18, 1861, at Brooklyn, to serve three years; mustered in a private, Co. B, May 23, 1861; mustered out with company, June 6, 1864, at New York City as Brannelly.

Brazneli, William—Age, 18 years. Enlisted at Brooklyn, to serve three years; mustered in as private, Co. G, December 14, 1861; transferred to Co. B, Fifth Veteran Infantry, June 2, 1864; also borne as Branell, and Bruzmain.

Brennan, John—Age, 22 years. Enlisted, May 18, 1861, at Brooklyn, to serve three years; mustered in as private, Co. B, May 12, 1861; deserted, August 11, 1861, at Arlington, Va.

Brennan, Phillip F.—Age, 19 years. Enlisted, April 18, 1861, at Brooklyn, to serve three years; mustered in as private, Co. C, May 23, 1861; wounded in action, August 19, 1862, at Groveton, Va.; promoted corporal, no date; wounded in action, July 1, 1863, at Gettysburg, Pa; promoted sergeant, April 1, 1864; mustered out, June 14, 1864, at New York City.

Brill, Jacob—Age, 38 years. Enlisted at Brooklyn, to serve three years; mustered in as private, Co. F, December 2, 1863; transferred to Co. K, Fifth Veteran Infantry, June 2, 1864.

Brinnan, David—Age, 35 years. Enlisted at New York City, to serve three years; mustered in as private; unassigned, March 8, 1864; no further record.

Bristol, Herman W.—Age, 21 years. Enlisted, April 18, 1861, at Brooklyn, to serve three years; mustered in as private, Co. H., May 23, 1861; missing in action, July 21, 1861, at Manassas, Va.; no further record.

Britt, John—Age, 21 years. Enlisted, August 23, 1861, at Brooklyn, to serve three years; mustered in as private, Co. F, August 25, 1861; promoted corporal, no date; transferred to Co. K, Fifth Veteran Infantry, June 2, 1864.

Britt, Michael—Age, 26 years. Enlisted April 18, 1861, at Brooklyn, to serve three years; mustered in as private, Co. E, May 23, 1861; deserted, September 22, 1861, at Arlington, Va.

Broach, James A.—Age, 18 years. Enlisted April 18, 1861, at Brooklyn, to serve three years; mustered in as private, Co. G; discharged for refusing to take the oath, August 1, 1861, at Camp Wood, Arlington, Va.

Brockett, Warren—Age, 18 years. Enlisted, August 4, 1861, at Brooklyn, to serve three years; mustered in as private, Co. D, August 5, 1861; deserted, February 8, 1862, from Camp Marion, Upton Hill, Va.

Brockett, William H—Age, 28 years. Enlisted, September 5, 1861, at Brooklyn, to serve three years; mustered in as private, Co. D, September 6, 1861; transferred to Co. H, Fifth Veteran Infantry, June 2, 1864.

Brockway, Charles — Age, 18 years. Enlisted, September 16, 1861, at New York City, to serve three years; mustered in as private, Co. A, September 19, 1861; transferred to Co. I, Fifth Veteran Infantry, June 2, 1864.

Brogle, Joseph — Age, 31 years. Enlisted, at Brooklyn, to serve three years; mustered in as private; unassigned, October 4, 1862; no further record.

Brokaw Theodore — Age, 22 years. Enlisted, at Brooklyn, to serve three years; mustered in as private, Co. D, September 9, 1861; wounded in action, August 29, 1862, at Bull run, Va.; promoted corporal, November 1, 1862; wounded in action, July 1, 1863, at Gettysburg, Pa.; transferred to Veteran Reserve Corps, December 27, 1863.

Bromberger, John — Age, 21 years. Enlisted, December 14, 1863, at Brooklyn, to serve three years; mustered in as private, Co. G, December 23, 1863; killed in action May 8, 1864, at the Wilderness, Va.; also borne as Brumberger.

Broughton, George — Age, 21 years. Enlisted, at Brooklyn, to serve three years; mustered in as private, Co. H, October 1, 1862; transferred to Co. I, Fifth Veteran Infantry, June 2, 1864.

Brower, Charles — Age, 31 years. Enlisted, June 30, 1861, at Brooklyn, to serve three years; mustered in as private, Co. K, July 1, 1861; appointed wagoner, no date; returned to company as private, June 29, 1863; wounded in action, July 1, 1863, at Gettysburg, Pa.; mustered out, June 30, 1864, at New York City.

Brower, John — Age, 21 years. Enlisted, April 18, 1861, at Brooklyn, to serve three years; mustered in as private, Co. E, May 23, 1861; discharged for disability, June 3, 1862, at Arlington, Va.

Brown, Alexander — Age, 30 years. Enlisted, April 18, 1861, at Brooklyn, to serve three years; mustered in as private, Co. B, May 23, 1861; wounded, no date; died of his wounds, May 8, 1864, at Alexandria, Va.

Brown, Augustus T. — Age, 22 years. Enlisted, at Brooklyn, to serve three years; mustered in as private, Co. C, July 1, 1861; killed in action, July 21, 1861, at Bull Run, Va.

Brown, Charles L. — Age, 24 years. Enlisted, May 18, 1861; discharged October 1, 1863; also borne as Browne.

Brown, David — Age, 19 years. Enlisted at Brooklyn, to serve three years; mustered in as private, Co. G, December 15, 1863; discharged for disability, March 6, 1864, at Culpeper Court House, Va.

Brown, George — Age, 19 years. Enlisted at Brooklyn, to serve three years; mustered in as private, Co. A, December 23, 1863; transferred to Co. H, Fifth Veteran Infantry, June 2, 1864.

Brown, Henry — Age, 37 years. Enlisted, at Brooklyn, to serve three years; mustered in as private, Co. F, December 5, 1863; deserted, February 21, 1864, from guard at New York.

Brown, Henry, Jr. — Age, 36 years. Enrolled, June 1, 1861, at Brooklyn, to serve three years; mustered in as private, Co. I, August 1, 1861; promoted first sergeant, December 3, 1862; mustered in as second lieutenant, Co. A, December 20, 1862; transferred to Co. F, March 1, 1863; mustered in as first lieutenant, March 23, 1863; mustered out, June 14, 1864, at New York City. Commissioned second lieutenant, January 16, 1863, with rank form December 20, 1862, vice D.S. Unckles, resigned; first lieutenant, August 1863, with rank from March 2, 1863, vice W. H. Tigney, promoted quartermaster.

Brown, John — Age, 26 years. Enlisted, May 18, 1861, at Brooklyn, to serve three years; mustered in as private, Co. B, May 23, 1861; discharged for disability, November 28, 1862, at Governors Island, New York.

Brown, John A. — Age, 20 years. Enlisted,

May 18, 1861, at Brooklyn, to serve three years; mustered in as private, Co. D, May 23, 1861; deserted from Camp Marion, Upon Hill, Va.

Brown, John C.—Age, 20 years. Enlisted, April 18, 1861, at Brooklyn, to serve three years; mustered in as private, Co. D. May 23, 1861; promoted corporal, July 14, 1862, sergeant, July 1, 1863; re-enlisted as a veteran, February 12, 1864; transferred to Co. A, Fifth Veteran Infantry, June 2, 1864.

Brown, William C.—Age, 15 years. Enlisted, April 18, 1861, at Brooklyn, to serve three years; mustered in as musician, Co. C, May 23, 1861; appointed principal musician, July 1, 1863; mustered out with regiment, June 6, 1864, at New York City.

Brownell, Charles A.—Age, 26 years. Enlisted, August 29, 1862, at Brooklyn, to serve three years; mustered in as private; unassigned, August 30, 1862; discharged, November 5, 1862, for promotion as second lieutenant 173rd Infantry.

Browning, Henry—Age, 34 years. Enlisted, at Brooklyn, to serve three years; mustered in as private, Co. F, December 7, 1863; transferred to Navy, April 26, 1864.

Bryant, Charles—Age, 22 years. Enlisted, May 18, 1861, at Brooklyn, to serve three years; mustered in as private. Co. D, May 23, 1861; discharged for disability, September 25, 1862, at Hospital, Washington, D.C.

Bryant, Henry—Age, 20 years. Enlisted at New York City, to serve three years; mustered in as private; unassigned, March 7, 1864; no further record.

Bryant, James M.—Age, 19 years. Enlisted at Brooklyn, to serve three years; mustered in as private, Co. A, December 26, 1861; deserted, January 12, 1864, at Culpeper, Va.; also borne as Jervis M. Bryant.

Bryson, Joseph D.—Age, 21 years. Enlisted, August 19, 1862, at Brooklyn, to serve three years; mustered in as private, Co. H, August 20, 1862; killed in action, September 14, 1862; at South Mountain, Va.

Buckley, John J.—Age, 20 years. Enlisted, October 7, 1861, at Brooklyn, to serve three years; mustered in as private, Co. G, October 9, 1861; transferred to Co. K, Fifth Veteran Infantry, June 2, 1864.

Buckmaster, William K.—Age, 44 years. Enlisted at Brooklyn, to serve three years; mustered in as private; unassigned, January 11, 1864; no further record.

Buckstone, Samuel—Age, 32 years. Enlisted, April 18, 1861, at Brooklyn, to serve three years; mustered in as private, Co. C, May 23, 1861; discharged for disability, June 16, 1861; also borne as Samuel Buxton and Sonal Buckstone.

Buggy, Richard—Age, 44 years. Enlisted, August 21, 1862, at Brooklyn, to serve three years; mustered in as private, Co. G, August 23, 1862; discharged for disability, no date; also borne as Biggy and Buggard.

Burglund, Peter—Age, 28 years, Enlisted, May 18, 1861, at Brooklyn, to serve three years; mustered in as private, Co. D, May 23, 1861; deserted, September 25, 1861, from Camp Wood, Arlington, Va.

Burke, John N.—Age, 27 years. Enlisted, at Brooklyn, to serve three years; mustered in as private, Co. G, December 15, 1863; transferred to Co. G, 14th Artillery; April 14, 1864; also borne as John M. Burke.

Burnes, Samuel—Age, 21 years. Enlisted, April 18, 1861, at Brooklyn, to serve three years; mustered in as private, Co. A, May 23, 1861; deserted, October 16, 1862; also borne as Burns.

Burnett, Joseph M. E.—Age, 25 years. Enlisted, April 18, 1861, at Brooklyn, to serve three years; mustered in as private, Co. F, May 23, 1861; discharged for disability, September 9, 1861.

Burnett, Levi F.—Age, 23 years. Enlisted August 8, 1862, at Brooklyn, to serve three years; mustered in as private, Co.

A, August 16, 1862; transferred to Veteran Reserve Corps, September 1, 1863.

Burnett, Thomas A.—Age, 20 years. Enrolled, April 18, 1861, at Brooklyn, to serve three years; mustered in as sergeant, Co. C, May 23, 1861; as second lieutenant, October 28, 1861; as first lieutenant, September 21, 1862; as captain, February 1, 1863; mustered out June 14, 1864; also borne as Thomas M. Burnett; not commissioned second lieutenant; commissioned first lieutenant, October 24, 1862, with ran from September 21, 1862, vice C.F. Toby, promoted; captain, February 10, 1863, with rank from January 29, 1863, vice C.F., Toby, discharged.

Burnett, William M.—Age, 52 years. Enrolled, at Brooklyn, to serve three years; appointed captain, Co. C, April 18, 1861; discharged June 30, 1861; not commissioned captain.

Burns, Albert M.—Age, 19 years. Enrolled, April 18, 1861, at Brooklyn, to serve three years; mustered in as private, Co. C, May 23, 1861; promoted sergeant, January 1, 1863; sergeant-major, March 13, 1863; mustered in as second lieutenant, Co. F, January 9, 1864; mustered out, June 14, 1864, at New York City; also borne as H.M. Berns; commissioned second lieutenant, August 15, 1863, rank from March 2, 1863, vice H. Brown Jr., promoted.

Burns, George—Age, 22 years. Enlisted, April 18, 1861, at Brooklyn, to serve three years; mustered in as private, Co. B, May 23, 1861; deserted, December 13, 1862, from hospital, Washington, D.C.

Burns, John C.—Age, 21 years. Enlisted, September 15, 1862, at Brooklyn, to serve three years; mustered in as private; unassigned, September 16, 1862; no further record.

Burns, Thomas—Age, 19 years. Enlisted, May 18, 1861, at Brooklyn, to serve three years; mustered in as private, Co. B, May 23, 1861; discharged for disability, January 10, 1863, at Providence, R.I.

Burns Thomas J.—Age, 21 years. Enlisted, August 21, 1862, at Brooklyn, to serve three years; mustered in as private, Co. D, August 22, 1862; wounded in action, July 1, 1863, at Gettysburg, Pa.; deserted, August 25, 1863, from hospital at Annapolis, Md.; also borne as Byrns and Barnes.

Burns, William—Age, 21 years. Enlisted, April 18, 1861, at Brooklyn, to serve three years; mustered in as private, Co. A, May 23, 1861; transferred to Co. C, First U.S. Cavalry, December 2, 1862.

Burnton, Thomas—Age, 20 years. Enlisted, August 14, 1862, at Brooklyn, to serve three years; mustered in as private, Co. H, August 16, 1862; wounded in action, September 17, 1862, at Antietam, Md.; deserted, October 1, 1862, from hospital, Washington, D.C.; also borne as Banton, and Bunton.

Burr, Sidney—Enlisted at Brooklyn, to serve three years; mustered in as private, Co. K, July 1, 1861; killed in action, July 21, 1861, at Bull Run, Va.

Burtis, James—Age, 42 years. Enlisted, April 1861, at Brooklyn, to serve three years; mustered in as private, Engineers, May 23, 1861; mustered out August 28, 1861, at Arlington Va. Also borne as John Burtis.

Burtis, Sylvanus A.—Age, 21 years. Enlisted, April 18, 1861, at Brooklyn, to serve three years; mustered in as private, Co. E, May 23, 1861; deserted, July 10, 1861, at Washington, D.C.

Busher, Louis L.—Age, 26 years. Enlisted, April 18, 1861, at Brooklyn, to serve three years; mustered in as private, Co. H, May 23, 1861; promoted corporal, March 1, 1862; died of disease, May 23, 1862, at hospital, Falmouth, Va. Also borne as Buhrer.

Butt, Frank R.—Age, 18 years. Enrolled, April 18, 1861, at Brooklyn, to serve three years; mustered in as private, Engineers, May 23, 1861; mustered out August 28, 1861, at Arlington, Va. Also borne as R. Frank But.

Butt, Richard—Age, 42 years. Enrolled, April 18, 1861, at Brooklyn, to serve three years; mustered in as captain, Engineers, May 23, 1861; mustered out, August 28, 1861, at Arlington, Va.; commissioned captain in 14th Militia, July 1, 1858, rank from May 14, 1858.

Byers, Samuel—Age, 22 years. Enlisted, August 20, 1862, at Brooklyn, to serve three years; mustered in as private, Co. A, August 21, 1861; wounded in action, July 1, 1863, at Gettysburg. Pa.; transferred to Co. I, Fifth Veteran Infantry, June 2, 1864.

Byram John J.—Age, 34 years. Enlisted, April 18, 1861, at Brooklyn, to serve three years; mustered in as private Co. C, May 23, 1861; transferred to Co. G, 51st Infantry, October 31, 1861; also borne as John S. Byroun.

Byrne, Martin—Age, 28 years. Enlisted at Brooklyn, to serve three years; mustered in as private, Co. G, December 2, 1863; transferred to Co. K, Fifth Veteran Infantry, June 2, 1864.

Cadwell, Robert A.—Age, 19 years. Enlisted at Brooklyn, to serve three years; mustered in as a private, Co. E, March 25, 1862; killed in action, September 17, 1862, at Antietam, Md.

Caffery, George—Age, 24 years. Enlisted April 18, 1861, at Brooklyn to serve three years; mustered in as a private, Co. A, May 23, 1861; discharged for disability, December 13, 1862, at Washington, D.C., also born as Cafferey.

Cairns, Henry—Age, 19 years. Enlisted, April 18, 1861, at Brooklyn, to serve three years; mustered in as private, Co. F, May 23, 1861; deserted, June 29, 1862, at —, Va.

Callahan, John—Age, 19 years. Enlisted April 18, 1861, at Brooklyn, to serve three years; mustered in as a musician, Co. A, May 23, 1861; deserted, November 16, 1861.

Callis, Jacob—Age, 20 years. Enlisted, April 18, 1861, at Brooklyn, to serve three years; mustered in as private, Co. E, May 23, 1861; mustered out with company June 6, 1864, at New York City.

Cameron, John F.—Age, 18 years. Enlisted at Brooklyn, to serve three years; mustered in as private, Co. H, January 27, 1864; wounded in action, May 12, 1864, at Laurel Hill, Va.; transferred to Co. K, Fifth Veteran Infantry, June 2, 1864; also borne as Cameron.

Campbell, Archibald—Age, 23 years. Enlisted, August 21, 1862, at Brooklyn, to serve three years; mustered in as private Co. C, August 22, 1862; transferred to Co. I, Fifth Veteran Infantry, June 2, 1864.

Campbell, Bernard J.—Age, 21 years. Enlisted September 6, 1862, at Brooklyn to serve three years; mustered in as private, Co. C, September 6, 1862; transferred to Co. H, Fifth Veteran Infantry, June 2, 1864.

Campbell, John—Age, 20 years. Enlisted April 18, 1861, at Brooklyn, to serve three years; mustered in as private, Co. C, May 23, 1861; mustered out June 14, 1864, at New York City.

Campbell, Joseph A.—Age, 23 years. Enlisted April 18, 1861, at Brooklyn to serve three years; mustered in as private, Co. C, May 23, 1861; wounded and captured, July 21, 1861, at Bull Run, Va.; died of his wounds August 20, 1861, at Richmond.

Campbell, Samuel—Age, 18 years. Enlisted October 1, 1862, at Brooklyn to serve three years; mustered in as musician October 1, 1863. Co. C, October 4, 1862; transferred to Co. D, March 1, 1863; to Co. H, Fifth Veteran Infantry, June 2, 1864.

Campbell, Thomas J.—Age, 19 years. Enlisted at Brooklyn to serve three years; mustered in as private Co. G May 1, 1861; Deserted in the face of the enemy, December 11, 1862, at Fredericksburg, Va.

Campbell, William—Age, 18, years. Enlisted in New York City to serve three years; mustered in as private Co. H, October 29, 1861; promoted corporal, January 1, 1863; wounded in action, July 3, 1863, at Gettysburg, Pa.; transferred to Veterans Reserve Corp, March 6, 1864; mustered out October 28, 1864, as sergeant, Co. G, Sixth Regiment Reserve Corp; also borne as William M. Campbell.

Cann, Baldwin — Age, 23 years. Enlisted April 18, 1861, at Brooklyn, to serve three years; mustered in as private, Co. B, May 21, 1861; promoted sergeant, and returned to the ranks, no dates; re-enlisted as a veteran, December 29, 1863; discharged for promotion to first lieutenant, Co. H, Fourth Cavalry, February 13, 1864.

Cannavan, Thomas — Age, 18 years. Enlisted December 4, 1863, at Brooklyn to serve three years; mustered in as private; unassigned, December 8, 1863; deserted, February 1, 1864, at New York City; also borne as Cavanagh and Conovan.

Canning, Cornelius — Age, 28 years. Enlisted August 26, 1862, at Brooklyn to serve three years; mustered in as private Co. C, August 27, 1862; wounded in action, July 1, 1863, at Gettysburg, Pa.; transferred to Co. H, Fifth Veteran Infantry, June 2, 1864.

Canning, John — Age, 19 years. Enlisted April 25, 1861, at Brooklyn to serve three years; mustered in as private, Co. G, May 23, 1861; deserted July 23, 1861, at Arlington, Va.

Carberry, Peter — Age, 30 years. Enlisted at Brooklyn to serve three years; mustered in as private, Co. A, November 12, 1861; promoted corporal, no date; sergeant, February 28, 1863; wounded in action, July 1, 1863, at Gettysburg, Pa.; transferred to Co. I, Fifth Veteran Infantry, June 2, 1864; also borne as Carbery and Carbey.

Cardona, Ramon — Age, 21 years. Enlisted April 18, 1861, at Brooklyn to serve three years; mustered in May 23, 1861, as sergeant, Co. H; second lieutenant, Co. I, February 26, 1862; first lieutenant, August 29, 1862.

Carll, George W — Age, 29 years. Enlisted April 18, 1861, at Brooklyn to serve three years; mustered in as private, Co. A, May 23, 1861; missing in action, July 1, 1863, at Gettysburg, Pa.; returned to company, October 8, 1863; mustered out with company, June 6, 1864, at New York City.

Carlton, Nathaniel E. — Age, 22 years. Enlisted April 18, 1861, at Brooklyn to serve three years; mustered in as private, Co. E, May 23, 1861; promoted to sergeant, no date; wounded in action July 1, 1863, at Gettysburg; died of his wounds, July 18, 1863.

Carney, Bernard — Age, 34 years. Enlisted April 18, 1861, at Brooklyn to serve three years, mustered in as private, May 23, 1861; mustered out with company, June 6, 1864, at New York City; also borne as Cearney.

Carroll, John — Age, 34 years. Enlisted at Brooklyn to serve three years; mustered in as private, Co. F, December 8, 1863; transferred to Co. G, Fifth Veteran Infantry, June 2, 1864.

Carroll, Peter — Age, 26 years. Enlisted August 19, 1862, at Brooklyn to serve three years; mustered in as private Co. H, transferred to Co. K, Fifth Veteran Infantry, June 2, 1864.

Carshaw, Nathaniel C. — Enlisted at Brooklyn to serve three years; mustered in as private, Co. K, March 19, 1862; killed in action September 14, 1862, at South Mountain, Md.

Carshaw, William L. — Age, 21 years. Enlisted March 9, 1862, at Brooklyn to serve three years; mustered in as private, March 10, 1862; wounded in action, no date; discharged for disability, December 10, 1862, at Providence, R.I.

Case, Edward — Age, 31 years. Enlisted at Brooklyn to serve three years; mustered in as private, Co. A, August 10, 1862, deserted November 16, 1862.

Casey, John — Age, 28 years. Enlisted May

18, 1861, at Brooklyn to serve three years; mustered in as private, Co. D, May 21, 1861; deserted January 23, 1862, from Camp Marion, Upton Hill, Va.

Casey, Lawrence — Age, 22 years. Enlisted September 6, 1862, at Brooklyn to serve three years; mustered in as private; unassigned, September 8, 1862; no further record.

Casler, Adam — Age, 20 years. Enlisted April 25, 1861, at Brooklyn to serve three years; mustered in as private, Co. G, May 23, 1861; wounded in action August 30, 1862, at Bull Run, Va.; no further record subsequent to November 3, 1862; also borne as Caslur.

Cassidy, Ambrose L. — Age, 40 years. Enlisted April 18, 1861, at Brooklyn to serve three years; mustered in as first lieutenant and quartermaster, May 23, 1861; discharged January 27, 1862, for promotion to major, 93rd Infantry.

Cassidy, Andrew — Age, 22 years. Enlisted July 31, 1861, at Brooklyn to serve three years; mustered in as private, Co. I, August 4, 1861; promoted to corporal and sergeant, no dates; transferred to Co. G, Fifth Veteran Infantry, June 2, 1864.

Cassidy James — Age, 21 years Enlisted April 18, 1861, at Brooklyn to serve three years; mustered in as private, Co. A, May 23, 1861; missing in action, July 1, 1863, at Gettysburg, Pa.; returned to company, October 8, 1863; mustered out with company, June 6, 1864, at New York City.

Castle, William — Age, 20 years. Enlisted September 17, 1862, at Brooklyn to serve three years; mustered in as private, Co. F, September 18, 1862; transferred to Co. G, Fifth Veteran Infantry, June 2, 1864; also borne as Castles.

Chambers, William H. — Age, 41 years. Enlisted at Brooklyn to serve three years; mustered in as private, Co. C, September 30, 1862; discharged for disability, May 21, 1863, at Washington, D.C.

Chapple, Augustus F. — Age, 26 years. Enlisted in Brooklyn, April 18, 1861, to serve three years; mustered in as private, Co. F, May 23, 1861; promoted to corporal, no date; discharged, April 1, 1863, for promotion.

Chapin, Albert M. — Age, 19 years. Enlisted April 5, 1862, at Brooklyn to serve three years; mustered in as private, Co. C, September 6, 1862; killed in action July 1, 1863, at Gettysburg, Pa.

Chester, William — Age, 44. Enlisted at Brooklyn to serve three years; mustered in as private, Co. F, December 8, 1863; discharged for disability, March 7, 1864, at Culpeper, Va.

Chisom, Jesse R. — Age, 30 years. Enlisted September 15, 1862, at Brooklyn to serve three years; mustered in as private, Co. F, September 16, 1862; transferred to Co. K, Fifth Veteran Infantry, June 2, 1864.

Christmas, Frederick — Age, 28 years. Enlisted August 29, 1862, at Brooklyn to serve three years; mustered in as private, Co. D, August 30, 1862; transferred to Co. I, Fifth Veteran Infantry, June 2, 1864.

Claggett, Charles C. — Age, 26 years. Enlisted in Brooklyn to serve three years; mustered in as private, Co. D, September 18, 1862; wounded in action, December 12, 1862, at Fredericksburg, Va.; transferred to Veterans Reserve Corp, November 1, 1863; re-transferred from Forty-Sixth Co., Second Battalion, Veterans Reserve Corp, no date; no further record.

Clark, Albert H. — Age, 29 years. Enlisted September 22, 1862, in Brooklyn to serve three years; mustered in as private, Co. D, September 23, 1862; transferred to Co. E, November 14, 1862, transferred to Veterans Reserve Corp, July 1, 1863.

Clark, Edwin R. — Age, 31 years. Enlisted August 27, 1862, at Brooklyn to serve three years; mustered in as private, Co. B, August 28, 1862; promoted corporal, no date; transferred to Co. I, Fifth Veteran Infantry, June 2, 1864.

Clark, John C. — Age, 19 years. Enlisted April 25, 1861, at Brooklyn to serve three years; mustered in as private, Co. G, May 23, 1861; mustered out with company, June 6, 1864, at New York City.

Clarke, Francis J.—Age, 20 years. Enlisted June 30, 1861, at Arlington, Va., to serve three years; mustered in as a private, Co. C, September 18, 1861; transferred to Co. H, Fifth Veteran Infantry, June 2, 1864.

Clarke, John—Age, 20 years. Enlisted at Washington, D.C., to serve three years; mustered in as private, Co. G, January 5, 1862; discharged at Emory Hospital, Washington, D.C., December 11, 1862.

Cleary, James—Age, 21 years. Enlisted July 1, 1861, at Brooklyn to serve three years; mustered in as private, Co. I, August 1, 1861; transferred to Co. G, Fifth Veteran Infantry, June 2, 1864.

Cleary, Michael—Age, 20 years. Enlisted December 8, 1863, at Brooklyn to serve three years; mustered in as private; unassigned, December 13, 1863; no further record.

Clucas, Richard H.—Age, 18 years. Enlisted at Brooklyn to serve three years; mustered in as musician, Co. G, September 15, 1862; transferred to Co. K, Fifth Veteran Infantry, June 2, 1864.

Cockle, Thomas B.—Age, 21 years. Enlisted May 18, 1861, in Brooklyn to serve three years; mustered in as private, Co. D, May 28, 1861; transferred to Illinois Artillery Regiment, August 2, 1861.

Coddington, William H.—Age, 40 years. Enlisted August 22, 1862, at Brooklyn to serve three years; mustered in as private, Co. D, August 23, 1862; wounded in action, September 14, 1862, at South Mountain, Md.; died of his wounds September 19, 1862, in hospital at Middleton, Md.

Coe, James—Age, 35 years. Enlisted April 25, 1861, at Brooklyn to serve three years; mustered in as private, Co. G, May 23, 1861; promoted sergeant, no date; deserted January 28, 1863, at Falmouth, Va.

Coggins, Patrick—Age, 25. Enlisted at Brooklyn to serve three years; mustered in as private, Co. G, December 17, 1863; transferred to Co. C, Fifth Veteran Infantry, June 2, 1864.

Coine, James—Age, 29. Enlisted April 25, 1861, at Brooklyn to serve three years; mustered in as private, Co. G, May 23, 1861; deserted December 12, 1861, at Upton Hill, Va. Also borne as James Coyne.

Coit, Mason B.—Age, 34. Enlisted April 18, 1861, at Brooklyn to serve three years; mustered in as corporal of engineers, May 21, 1861, mustered out August 28, 1861, at Arlington, Va.

Cole, Jeremiah—Age, 31. Enlisted April 18, 1861, at Brooklyn to serve three years; mustered in as private, Co. H, May 23, 1861, mustered out with company June 6, 1864, at New York City.

Cole, Richard F.—Age, 31. Enlisted in Brooklyn to serve three years; mustered in as private, Co. C, May 23, 1861; wounded in action, July 21, 1861, at Bull Run, Va. Discharged May 23, 1864, at Washington, D.C.

Cole, William—Age, 27 years. Enlisted September 29, 1861, at Brooklyn to serve three years; mustered in as private; unassigned, September 30, 1861; no further record.

Coleman, Jr., John—Age, 24. Enlisted April 18, 1841, at Brooklyn to serve three years; mustered in as private, Co. E, May 23, 1861; captured in action August 28, 1862, at Gainesville, Va.; paroled, no date; mustered out with company June 6, 1864, at New York City.

Colgan, Dominick—Age, 20 years. Enlisted at Brooklyn to serve three years; mustered in as private, Co. B, May 23, 1861; mustered out with company June 6, 1864, at New York City.

Colgan, Patrick—Age, 19 years. Mustered in as private, Co. K, August 1, 1861; died of disease, October 29, 1862, at Washington, D.C.

Colgan, Patrick H.—Age, 17 years. Enlisted

April 18, 1861, at Brooklyn to serve three years; mustered in as musician, Co. F, May 23, 1861; mustered out June 14, 1864, at New York City.

Collier, John G.—Age, 18 years. Enlisted at New York City to serve three years; mustered in as private; unassigned, January 27, 1864; no further record.

Collins, Richard T.—Age, 27 years. Enlisted May 18, 1861, at Brooklyn to serve three years; mustered in as private Co. D, May 23, 1861; deserted November 11, 1861, from Camp Marion, Upton Hill, Va.

Collins, William—Age, 20 years. Enlisted, April 18, 1861, at Brooklyn to serve three years; mustered in as musician, Co. A, May 23, 1861; deserted August 1, 1861, at Arlington, Va.

Colton, Thomas—Age, 22 years. Enlisted April 25, 1861, at Brooklyn to serve three years; mustered in as private, Co. G, May 23, 1861; deserted September 20, 1861, at Arlington, Va.

Compston, David B.—Age, 38 years. Enlisted April 18, 1861, at Brooklyn to serve three years; mustered in as private, company of engineers, May 23, 1861; mustered out August 28, 1861, at Arlington, Va.

Conant, Roger—Age, 26 years. Enlisted April 18, 1861, at Brooklyn to serve three years; mustered in as private, Co. C, May 23, 1861; discharged for disability, July 29, 1861.

Condon, Michael—Age, 19 years. Enlisted on April 18, 1861, at Brooklyn to serve three years; mustered in as private on May 23, 1861; discharged for disability August 25, 1861, at Arlington, Va.

Coney, Franklin—Enlisted December 23, 1863, at Brooklyn to serve three years; mustered in as private, Co. G, December 30, 1863; deserted May 4, 1864; also borne as Franklin Cooney.

Congor, John M.—Age, 21. Enlisted May 18, 1861, at Brooklyn to serve three years; mustered in as private, Co. D, May 23, 1861; discharged for disability, April 5, 1862, at Upton Hill Va.

Conklin, Charles—Age, 25 years. Enlisted September 18, 1861, at Brooklyn to serve three years; mustered in as private, Co. K, September 24, 1861; promoted corporal March 10, 1862; sergeant April 1, 1863; killed in action July 1, 1863, at Gettysburg, Pa.; also borne as Charles E. Conklin.

Conklin, James W.—Age, 24 years. Enlisted in New York City to serve three years; mustered in as private; unassigned, March 12, 1864; no further record.

Connelly, James—Age, 41 years. Enlisted December 19, 1863, at Brooklyn to serve three years; mustered in as private, Co. A, December 21, 1863; discharged for disability March 8, 1864, at Culpeper, Va.

Connelly, Mathew—Age, 21 years. Enlisted at Brooklyn to serve three years; mustered in as private, Co. A; missing in action July 1, 1863, at Gettysburg, Pa.

Connoly, John H.—Age, 30 years. Enlisted August 22, 1862, at Brooklyn to serve three years; mustered in as private, Co. F, August 23, 1862; wounded in action July 1, 1863, at Gettysburg, Pa.; discharged for disability March 19, 1864, at New York City.

Connolly, Michael—Age, 25. Enlisted April 28, 1861, at Brooklyn to serve three years; mustered in as private, Co. F, May 23, 1861; wounded in action September 14, 1862, at South Mountain, Md.; deserted October 14, 1862, from City Hospital, Brooklyn.

Connor, Christopher—Age, 16. Enlisted April 18, 1861, at Brooklyn to serve three years; mustered in as private, company of engineers; May 23, 1861; mustered out, August 28, 1861, at Arlington, Va.

Connor, George A.—Age, 36. Enlisted October 1, 1861, at Brooklyn to serve three years; mustered in as bandmaster, October 24, 1861; discharged August 17, 1862, at Camp Halstead, Va.

Connor, Paul S.—Age, 21. Enlisted October 1, 1861, at Brooklyn to serve three years; mustered in as musician in band October 24, 1861; discharged August 17, 1862, at Camp Halstead, Va.

Connor, William E.—Age, 14 years. Enlisted October 1, 1861, in Brooklyn to serve three years; mustered in as musician in band October 24, 1861; discharged August 17, 1862, at Camp Halstead, Va.

Conway, Patrick—Age, 19 years. Enlisted at New York City to serve three years; mustered in as private; unassigned, March 12, 1864; no further record.

Cook, Andrew—Age, 28 years. Enlisted at Brooklyn to serve three years; mustered in as private; unassigned, February 1, 1864; mustered out May 8, 1865, at Hart's Island, New York Harbor; also borne as Andrew J. Cook.

Cook, Anthony—Age, 22 years. Enlisted April 18, 1861, at Brooklyn to serve three years; mustered in as private, Co. C, May 23, 1861; missing in action July 21, 1861, at Bull Run, Va.; no further record.

Cook, Charles S.—Age, 21 years. Enlisted August 21, 1862, at Brooklyn to serve three years; mustered in as private, Co. B, August 22, 1862; deserted June 24, 1863, at Smoketown, Md.

Cook, George—Age, 21 years. Enlisted April 18, 1861, at Brooklyn to serve three years; mustered in as private, Co. G, May 23, 1861; discharged at Camp Wood, Washington, D.C., June 24, 1861.

Cook, Henry C.—Age, 22 years. Enlisted August 27, 1862, at Brooklyn to serve three years; mustered in as private, Co. C, August 28, 1862; transferred to Co. H, Fifth Veteran Infantry, June 2, 1864.

Cook, John—Age, 26 years. Enlisted May 18, 1861, at Brooklyn to serve three years; mustered in as private, Co. B, May 23, 1861; discharged for disease February 9, 1863, at Convalescent Camp, Alexandria, Va.

Cook, John E.—Age, 34 years. Enlisted August 27, 1862, at Brooklyn to serve three years; mustered in as private, Co. H, August 28, 1862; transferred to Co. K, Fifth Veteran Infantry.

Cookson, Henry J.—Age, 26 years. Enlisted at Brooklyn to serve three years; mustered in as private, May 23, 1861; promoted to sergeant, March 11, 1863; first sergeant, June 1, 1863; wounded in action November 30, 1863, at Mine Run, Va. Discharged May 23, 1864.

Cooley, Rivhard—Age, 26 years. Enlisted at Brooklyn to serve three years; mustered in as private, unassigned, October 21, 1862; no further record.

Cooney, John—Age, 44 years. Enlisted at Brooklyn to serve three years; mustered in as private, Co. E, November 30, 1863; transferred to Fifth Veteran Infantry, June 2, 1864.

Cooper, Frederick—Age, 26 years. Enlisted at Brooklyn September 26, 1862, to serve three years; mustered in as private; unassigned, September 27, 1862; no further record.

Copeley, Alfred J.—Age, 20 years. Enlisted April 18, 1861, at Brooklyn to serve three years; mustered in as private, Co. E, May 23, 1861; killed in action, May 10, 1864, at Laurel Hill, Va; also borne as Copley.

Corbett, Alexander B.—Age, 23 years. Enlisted April 18, 1861, at Brooklyn to serve three years; mustered in as private Co. E, May 23, 1861; promoted corporal, no date; discharged for disability, September 3, 1862, at Washington, D.C.; also borne as Corbitt.

Cordona, Ramon—Age, 21 years. Enrolled April 18, 1861, at Brooklyn to serve three years; mustered in as corporal, Co. H, May 23, 1861; promoted sergeant, July, 1861; mustered in as second lieutenant, Co. I, February 26, 1862; promoted first lieutenant, August 29, 1862; mustered out June 13, 1864, at New York City; also borne as Raymon Cordovia.

Corlies, Joseph—Age, 24 years. Enlisted May 18, 1861, at Brooklyn to serve three years; mustered in as private, Co. B, May

23, 1861; wounded in action, August 29, 1862, at Bull Run, Va.; discharged for wounds, February 12, 1863, at Washington, D.C., as Joseph H. Corliss.

Cornwell, Sylvester — Age, 22 years. Enlisted April 18, 1861, at Brooklyn to serve three years; mustered in as private, Co. A, May 23, 1861; wounded in action August 29, 1862, at Bull Run, Va.; transferred to Veterans Reserve Corp, July 1, 1863.

Corr, Edward L. — Age, 23 years. Enlisted at Brooklyn to serve three years; mustered in as private, Co, H, August 14, 1862; wounded in action, September 17, 1862, at Antietam, Md.; discharged for wounds January 13, 1863, at New York City; also borne as Conn.

Cosgrove, Harry — Age, 22 years. Enlisted September 25, 1862, at Brooklyn to serve three years; mustered in as private; unassigned, no further record.

Cottier, John C. — Age, 18 years. Enlisted at Brooklyn to serve three years; mustered in as private, Co. I, January 27, 1864; discharged May 14, 1864.

Cotty, Edward — Age, 38 years. Enlisted April 18, 1861, at Brooklyn to serve three years; mustered in as private, Co. H, May 23, 1861; discharged for disease, May 25, 1863, at Washington, D.C.

Coughran, James — Age, 22 years. Enlisted at Brooklyn to serve three years; mustered in as private; unassigned, December 21, 1863; no further record.

Cox, Bernard D. — Age, 22 years. Enlisted May 18, 1861, at Brooklyn to serve three years; mustered in as private, Co. D, May 28, 1861; deserted October 17, 1862, at Washington, D.C.

Cox, James P. — Age, 21 years. Enlisted April 18, 1861, at Brooklyn to serve three years; mustered in as private, Co. H, May 23, 1861; deserted February 4, 1862, at Upton Hill, Va.

Cox, John — Age, 18 years. Enlisted April 18, 1861, at Brooklyn to serve three years; mustered in as private May 23, 1861; promoted drum-major, June 21, 1861; returned to ranks and transferred to Co. I, August 18, 1861; appointed musician, no date; wounded in action, July 2, 1863, at Gettysburg, Pa.; discharged for disability, May 19, 1864, at Philadelphia, Pa.

Cox, Michael — Age, 19 years. Enlisted April 18, 1861, at Brooklyn to serve three years; mustered in as private, Co. F, May 23, 1861; re-enlisted as a veteran, December 31, 1863; transferred to Co. B, Fifth Veteran Infantry, June 2, 1864.

Crammer, William — Age, 19 years. Enlisted April 18, 1861, at Brooklyn to serve three years; mustered in as private, Co. A, May 23, 1861; deserted, November 29, 1861, at Upton Hill, Va.

Crane, George L. — Age, 24 years. Enlisted April 18, 1861, at Brooklyn to serve three years; mustered in as private, Co. C, May 23, 1861; discharged August 21, 1863.

Crane, Patrick — Age, 19 years. Enlisted May 18, 1861, at Brooklyn to serve three years; mustered in as private, Co. B, May 23, 1861; transferred June 2, 1864, to the Fifth Veteran Infantry.

Cranford, Henry L. — Age, 28 years. Enrolled April 18, 1861, at Brooklyn to serve three years; mustered in as commissary sergeant, May 23, 1861; as first lieutenant, Co. G, July 1, 1861; promoted quartermaster, February 20, 1862; mustered out at Pratt's Landing, Va., March 23, 1863, for promotion to captain, and Commissary of Subsistance, U.S. Volunteers; also borne as Crawford.

Cranor, Jacob — Age, 18 years. Enlisted December 19, 1863, at Brooklyn to serve three years; mustered in as private; unassigned, December 21, 1863; no further record.

Cranston, Alfred — Age, 21 years. Enrolled June 30, 1861, at Brooklyn to serve three years; mustered in as private, Co. I, August 1, 1861; promoted sergeant, September 1, 1862; mustered in as second lieutenant, September 17, 1862; mustered out June 13, 1864, at New York City; also borne as Cranson.

Crask, William — Age, 42 years. Enlisted August 27, 1862, at Brooklyn to serve three years; mustered in as private, Co. D, August 28, 1862; transferred to Co. E, November 14, 1862; to Co. H, Fifth Veteran Infantry, June 2, 1864.

Crawford, Michael — Age, 35 years. Enlisted at Brooklyn to serve three years; mustered in as private, Co. A, December 19, 1863; transferred to Co. H, Fifth Veteran Infantry, June 2, 1864.

Creagan, James — Age, 21 years. Enlisted April 18, 1861, at Brooklyn to serve three years; mustered in as private, Co. D, May 23, 1861; discharged June 15, 1861.

Creighton, Robert — Age, 23 years. Enlisted May 3, 1861, at Brooklyn to serve three years; mustered in as private, Co. G, May 23, 1861; deserted August 1, 1861, at Arlington, Va.

Crocker, Peleg B. — Age, 21 years. Enlisted April 18, 1861, at Brooklyn to serve three years; mustered in as private, Co. F, May 23, 1861; promoted first sergeant, August 3, 1861; wounded in action August 29, 1862, at Bull Run, Va.; discharged for disability January 15, 1863, at Washington, D.C.

Crofford, Michael — Age, 35 years. Enlisted December 19, 1863, at Brooklyn to serve three years; mustered in as private; unassigned, December 23, 1863; no further record.

Cronan, John — Age, 19 years. Enlisted April 18, 1861, at Brooklyn to serve three years; mustered in as private, Co. A, May 23, 1861; deserted September 19, 1861, at Arlington, Va.; also borne as Cronin.

Cronin, Timothy — Age, 20 years. Enlisted April 18, 1861, at Brooklyn to serve three years; mustered in as private, Co. E, May 23, 1861; promoted corporal April 4, 1862; discharged for disability April 8, 1863, at Baltimore, Md.

Cronlies, George B. — Age, 29 years. Enlisted September 16, 1861, at New York City, to serve three years; mustered in as private, Co. B, September 19, 1861; deserted December 6, 1861, at Upton Hill, Va.; also borne as Curless and Curlis.

Crook, James — Age, 22 years. Enlisted August 20, 1862, at Brooklyn to serve three years; mustered in as private August 21, 1862; no further record.

Cross, James F. — Age, 28 years. Enlisted April 12, 1864, at Brooklyn to serve three years; mustered in as private Co. C, April 19, 1864, transferred to Co. H, Fifth Veteran Infantry, June 2, 1864.

Cullen, Andrew — Age, 28 years. Enlisted April 18, 1861, at Brooklyn to serve three years; mustered in as private, Co. H, May 23, 1861, promoted sergeant August 1, 1862; wounded in action August 29, 1862, at Bull Run, Va.; discharged for wounds December 22, 1862, at Washington D.C.

Cullen, Jeremiah — Age, 18 years. Enlisted at Brooklyn to serve three years; mustered in as private, Co. F, December 8, 1863; transferred to Fifth Veteran Infantry, June 2, 1864.

Cully, James — Age, 27 years. Enlisted April 18, 1861, at Brooklyn to serve three years; mustered in as sergeant, Co. A, May 23, 1861; promoted first sergeant, no date; deserted at New York City, no date.

Cummings, Edward — Age, 21 years. Enlisted September 18, 1862, at Brooklyn to serve three years; mustered in as private; unassigned; September 19, 1862; no further record.

Cunningham, John — Age, 43 years. Enlisted August 26, 1862, at Brooklyn to serve three years; mustered in as private, Co. B, August 27, 1862; wounded in action September 14, 1862, at South Mountain, Md.; discharged for wounds January 10, 1863, at Baltimore, Md.

Cunningham, Robert — Age, 24 years. Enlisted September 2, 1862, at Brooklyn to serve three years; mustered in as private, Co. H, September 3, 1862; transferred to Co. G, December 1, 1862; captured in action July 1, 1863, at Gettysburg, Pa.; returned to company October 10, 1863, from Annapolis, Md.; promoted corporal and returned to ranks, no date; transferred to Co. A, Fifth Veteran Infantry, June 2, 1864.

Cunningham, Thomas—Age, 33 years. Enlisted at Brooklyn to serve three years; mustered in as private, Co. B, September 9, 1861; transferred to Fifth Veteran Infantry, June 2, 1864.

Curley, John—Age, 23 years. Enlisted April 18, 1861, at Brooklyn to serve three years; mustered in as private, Co. H, May 23, 1861; deserted February 6, 1862, at Upton Hill, Va.

Curry, John E.—Age, 23 years. Enlisted April, 18, 1861, at Brooklyn to serve three years; mustered in as private, Co. D, May 23, 1861; wounded in action September 17, 1862, at Antietam, Md.; transferred to Veterans Reserve Corp July 1, 1863, as James E. Currey.

Curtis, William—Age, 23 years. Enlisted April 18, 1861, at Brooklyn to serve three years; mustered in as private, Co. D, May 23, 1861; discharged April 2, 1864, for promotion to hospital steward, U.S. army.

Cuscadden, Felix—Age, 30 years. Enlisted June 1861, at Brooklyn to serve three years; mustered in as private Co. I, August 1, 1861; wounded in action July 21, 1861, at Bull Run, Va. Died of his wounds September 14, 1861.

Cuscaden, George—Age, 36 years. Enlisted April 25, 1861, at Brooklyn to serve three years; mustered in as private, Co. G, May 23, 1861; promoted corporal, no date; sergeant January 8, 1864; mustered out with company June 6, 1864, at New York City.

Cutts, John—Age, 21 years. Enlisted April 18, 1861, at Brooklyn to serve three years; mustered in as private, Co. H, May 23, 1861; discharged, May 23, 1864, at Washington, D.C.

Daclon, William—Age, 44 years. Enlisted at New York City to serve three years; mustered in as private; unassigned, March 11, 1864; no further record.

Dagnall, Philip M.—Age, 21 years. Enlisted April 18, 1861, at Brooklyn to serve three years; mustered in as private, Co. C, May 23, 1861; transferred to Co. H, Fifth Veteran Infantry, June 2, 1864; also borne as Philip F. Dagnall.

Dakin, William—Age, 27 years. Enlisted May 18, 1861, at Brooklyn to serve three years; mustered in as private, Co. B, May 23, 1861; captured in action July 21, 1861, Bull Run, Va.; paroled June 2, 1862, at Washington, N.C.; no record subsequent to September 28, 1862.

Daly, Michael—Age, 29 years. Enlisted April 18, 1861, at Brooklyn to serve three years; mustered in as private, Co. F, May 23, 1861; killed in action September 17, 1862, at Antietam, Md.

Daly, William—Age, 21 years. Enlisted at Brooklyn to serve three years; mustered in as private, Co. B, March 10, 1862; discharged for disability July 6, 1862, at Washington, D.C.

Danager, William—Age, 19 years. Enlisted December 29, 1863, at Brooklyn to serve three years; mustered in as private Co. E, December 30, 1863; transferred to Co. H, Fifth Veteran Infantry, June 2, 1864; also borne as Dunigan and Dunnigan.

Daniels, Frank—Age, 42 years. Enlisted September 22, 1862, at Brooklyn to serve three years; mustered in as private, Co. H, September 23, 1862; transferred to Co. G, Seventh Regiment Veterans Reserve Corp, December 17, 1864, from which mustered out June 28, 1865, at Washington, D.C.; also borne as Franz Daniels.

Danielson, John—Age, 33 years. Enlisted April 18, 1861, at Brooklyn to serve three years; mustered in as private, company engineers, May 23, 1861; discharged for disability July 31, 1861, at Arlington, Va.

Darrow, Joseph E.—Age, 17 years. Enlisted April 18, 1861, at Brooklyn to serve three years; mustered in as private, Co. C, May 23, 1861; wounded and captured July 21, 1861, at Manassas, Va.; died of his wounds September 28, 1861, at Richmond, Va.

Darvey, John—Age, 33 years. Enlisted at New York City to serve three years; mustered in as private; unassigned, March 11, 1864; no further record.

Dauch, Anthony—Age, 28 years. Enlisted April 18, 1861, at Brooklyn to serve three years; mustered in as private, Co. A, May 23, 1861; deserted December 2, 1861, at Arlington, Va.; also borne as Dausch and Dusch.

Daum, Leonard—Age, 33 years. Enlisted at Brooklyn to serve three years; mustered in as private, Co. I, December 4, 1863; transferred to Co. G, Fifth Veteran Infantry, June 2, 1864.

Dauncey, Edward N.—Age, 19 years. Enlisted May 18, 1861, at Brooklyn to serve three years; mustered in as private, Co. B, May 23, 1861; transferred to Co. I, Fifth Veteran Infantry, June 2, 1864; also borne as Edward W. Dauncey.

Davenport, Abraham C—Age, 24 years. Enlisted September 6, 1862, at Brooklyn to serve three years; mustered in as private, Co. E, September 8, 1862; transferred to Co. H, Fifth Veteran Infantry, June 2, 1864; also borne as Abram C. Davenport.

Davenport, Charles E.—Age, 19 years. Enlisted, April 18, 1861, at Brooklyn, to serve three years; mustered in as private, Co. E, May 23, 1861; captured in action, July 21, 1861, at Bull Run, Va.; paroled, no date; discharged, February 25, 1864, at Washington, D.C.

Davenport, John R.—Age, 19 years. Enlisted, April 18, 1861, at Brooklyn, to serve three years; mustered in as private, Co. H, May 23, 1861; promoted sergeant, January 1, 1863; wounded in action July 1, 1863, at Gettysburg; mustered out with company June 6, 1864, at New York City.

Davey, George R.—Age, 33 years. Enrolled, April 18, 1861, at Brooklyn, to serve three years; mustered in as first lieutenant, Co. H, May 23, 1861; promoted captain, February 26, 1862; killed in action, August 29, 1862, at Bull Run, Va.; commissioned first lieutenant, in 14th Militia, March 25, 1868, with rank from same date; not commissioned captain.

Davey, Thomas L. R.—Age, 19 years. Enlisted, April 18, 1861, at Brooklyn, to serve three years; mustered in as private, Co. H, May 23, 1861; discharged, September 3, 1863, at Washington, D.C.; also borne as Davy.

Davis, Alfred W.—Age, 18 years. Enlisted, May 1861, at Brooklyn, to serve three years; mustered in as private, Co. B, May 23, 1861; discharged, August 2, 1861; refused to swear in.

Davis, Evan—Age, 20 years. Enlisted, May 18, 1861, at Brooklyn, to serve three years; mustered in as private, Co. E, May 23, 1861; mustered out with company, June 6, 1864, at New York City.

Davis, Henry W.—Age, 20 years. Enlisted, April 18, 1861, at Brooklyn, to serve three years; mustered in as private, Co. B, May 23, 1861; deserted October 23, 1861, at Upton Hill, Va.

Davis, Richard—Age, 34 years. Enlisted at Brooklyn, to serve three years; mustered in as private, Co. I, January 14, 1864; transferred to. Co. G, Fifth Veteran Infantry, June 2, 1864.

Davis, Theodore C.—Age, 21 years. Enlisted, August 26, 1862, at Brooklyn, to serve three years; mustered in as private, Co. C, August 27, 1862; transferred to Co. H, Fifth Veteran Infantry, June 2, 1864.

Davis, William—Age, 32 years. Enlisted, April 18, 1861, at Brooklyn, to serve three years; mustered in as private, company of engineers, May 23, 1861; mustered out August 28, 1861, at Arlington, Va.

Davis, William W.—Age, 20 years. Enlisted, April 18, 1861, at Brooklyn, to serve three years; mustered in as private, Co. H, May 23, 1861; promoted corporal, May 25, 1862; wounded in action, August 29, 1862, at Bull Run, Va.; transferred to Veteran Reserve Corps, July 16, 1863.

Dawsen, Thomas H.—Age, 27 years. Enlisted, May 18, 1861, at Brooklyn, to serve three years; mustered in as private, Co. D, May 23, 1861; promoted commissary sergeant, November 1, 1862; mustered out with regiment, June 6, 1864, at New York City.

Day, James—Age, 19 years. Enlisted, July 1, 1861, at Brooklyn, to serve three years; mustered in as private, Co. K, August 1, 1861; promoted sergeant, January 1, 1864; transferred to Co. I, Fifth Veteran Infantry, June 2, 1864.

Dayton, John W.—Age, 27 years. Enlisted at Brooklyn, to serve three years; mustered in as private, Co. E, August 1, 1861; deserted, November 13, 1861, at Upton Hill, Va.

Deacon, Alfred—Age, 18 years. Enlisted, April 18, 1861, at Brooklyn, to serve three years; mustered in as private, Co. C, May 23, 1861; promoted corporal, no date; sergeant, January 1, 1864; mustered out, June 14, 1864, at New York City.

Dean, Charles N.—Age, 30 years. Enlisted, April 18, 1861, at Brooklyn, to serve three years; mustered in as private, Co. H, May 23, 1861; promoted corporal, March 1, 1862; killed in action, May 10, 1864, at Laurel Hill, Va.

Deasy, John J.—Age, 32 years. Enlisted at Brooklyn, to serve three years; mustered in as private, Co. C, September 10, 1862; wounded in action, July 1, 1863, at Gettysburg, Pa.; transferred to Co. H, Fifth Veteran Infantry, June 2, 1864; also borne as Dasey.

De Bevoise, George B.—Age, 26 years. Enlisted, April 18, 1861, at Brooklyn, to serve three years; mustered in as corporal, Co. H, May 23, 1961; promoted sergeant, July 1, 1861; died June 14, 1862, in hospital, Washington, D.C.

De Bevoise, William H.—Age, 35 years. Enrolled, April 18, 1861, at Brooklyn, to serve three years; mustered in as captain, Co. H, May 23, 1861; as major, February 20, 1862; as lieutenant-colonel, October 1, 1862; discharged for disability, May 11, 1863; commissioned captain in 14th Militia, May 12, 1860, with rank from February 4, 1859; not commissioned major; commissioned lieutenant-colonel, October 24, 1862, with rank from October 1, 1862, vice E.B. Fowler, promoted.

Decker, George—Age, 20 years. Enlisted December 23, 1863, at Brooklyn, to serve three years; mustered in as private, Co. A, December 30, 1863; transferred to Co. B, Fifth Veteran Infantry, June 2, 1864.

Decker, Robert—Age, 36 years. Enlisted at New York City, to serve three years; mustered in as private; unassigned, March 7, 1864; no further record.

Decker, Robert A.—Age, 33 years. Enlisted, April 25, 1861, at Brooklyn, to serve three years; mustered in as private, Co. G, May 23, 1861; discharged for disability, January 2, 1864, at Convalescent Camp, Va.

Deering, George R.—Age, 34 years. Enlisted, April 18, 1861, at Brooklyn, to serve three years; mustered in as hospital steward, May 23, 1861; mustered out, April 1, 1862, at Washington, D.C., for promotion to assistant surgeon, 30th Infantry; also borne as Rodger M. Deeing, and George R. Drewny.

Degan, Edward—Age, 21 years. Enlisted, April 25, 1861, at Brooklyn, to serve three years; mustered in as private, Co. G, May 23, 1861; killed in action, July 21, 1861, at Bull Run, Va.

De Graff, Isaac H.—Age, 26 years. Enlisted April 18, 1861, at Brooklyn to serve three years; mustered in as private, Co. D, May 23, 1861; missing in action, July 21, 1861, at Bull Run, Va.; returned April 9, 1863; mustered out with company June 6, 1864, at New York City.

Delaney, George W.—Age, 23 years. Enlisted August 27, 1862, at Brooklyn to serve three years, mustered in as private, Co. F, August 28, 1862; transferred to Co. K, Fifth Veteran Infantry, June 2, 1864.

Demarest, Alfred M.—Age, 21 years. Enlisted at Brooklyn to serve three years; mustered in as private; unassigned, September 24, 1862; no further record.

Dempsey, John—Age, 26 years. Enlisted at Brooklyn to serve three years; mustered in as private, Co. A, December 28, 1863; transferred to Fifth Veteran Infantry, on June 2, 1864.

Denham, Francis—Age, 26 years. Enlisted August 14, 1862, at Brooklyn to serve three years; mustered in as private, Co. A, September 21, 1862; transferred to Co. A, Fifth Veteran Infantry, in June 1864; also borne as Demham.

Dennin, William H.—Age, 27 years. Enlisted April 18, 1861, at Brooklyn to serve three years; mustered in as private, Co. A, May 23, 1861; promoted corporal, no date; returned to ranks June 23, 1863; mustered out with company on July 6, 1864, at New York City; also borne as Denin.

De Orsay, James—Age, 26 years. Enlisted at Brooklyn to serve three years; mustered in as private, Co. F, December 9, 1863; died of disease on January 25, 1864, at Culpeper, Va.

De Shonneas, Thomas—Age, 18 years. Enlisted December 28, 1863, at Brooklyn to serve three years; mustered in as private, Co. A, on December 29, 1863; deserted on April 15, 1864; also borne as Delouris and DeThonnear.

Desmond, Dennis—Age, 26 years. Enlisted April 18, 1861, at Brooklyn to serve three years, mustered in as private, Co. D, May 23, 1861; mustered out with company on June 6, 1864, at New York City.

De Touhey, John—Age, 22 years. Enlisted May 18, 1861, at Brooklyn to serve three years; mustered in as private, Co. B, May 23, 1861; promoted corporal, February 15, 1862; wounded in action on August 29, 1862, at Gainsville, Va.; died of his wounds on October 13, 1862, at Georgetown, D.C.

Devlin, Bartholomew—Age, 21 years. Enlisted at Brooklyn to serve three years; mustered in as private, Co. B, September 8, 1862; deserted on May 2, 1863, on the march to Chancellorsville, Va.; also borne as Develin.

Devlin, James—Age, 25 years. Enlisted April 18, 1861, at Brooklyn to serve three years; mustered in as private, Co. E on May 23, 1861; discharged for disability, June 9, 1861.

Dewey, Alfred E.—Age, 19 years. Enlisted at Brooklyn to serve three years; mustered in as private, Co. H, November 8, 1861; deserted August 9, 1862, from hospital at Washington, D.C.

Dewey, David B.—Age, 30 years. Enlisted at Arlington, Va., to serve three years; mustered in as assistant surgeon on January 1, 1862; discharged for disability, April 29, 1863; commissioned assistant surgeon on June 23, 1862, with rank from December 29, 1861.

De Witt, William W.—Age, 33 years. Enlisted on April 18, 1861, at Brooklyn to serve three years; mustered in as private, Co. C, May 23, 1861; discharged for disability, October 20, 1862, at Washington, D.C.

De Wolfe, Stephen—Age, 19 years. Enlisted April 25, 1861, at Brooklyn to serve three years; mustered in as private, Co. G, on May 23, 1861; promoted corporal, March 1, 1862; killed in action, August 30, 1862, at Bull Run, Va.

Dey, Samuel—Age, 28 years. Enlisted at Brooklyn to serve three years; mustered in as private, Co. A, January 20, 1864; transferred to Fifth Veteran Infantry, on June 2, 1864; also borne as Dye.

Dick, Robert—Age, 43 years. Enlisted August 27, 1862, at Brooklyn to serve three years; mustered in as private, Co. D, August 28, 1862; transferred to Co. H, Fifth Veteran Infantry, on June 2, 1864.

Dickenson, Amos — Age, 25 years. Enlisted on April 18, 1861, at Brooklyn to serve three years; mustered in as private, Co. L, engineers, May 23, 1861; mustered out August 28, 1861, at Arlington Va.; also borne as David Dickenson.

Dietz, Jacob — Age, 21 years. Enlisted on April 18, 1861, at Brooklyn to serve three years; mustered in as private, Co. F, May 23, 1861; wounded and captured on July 21, 1861, at Bull Run, Va.; died on October 27, 1861, at Richmond, Va.

Dilks, Henry — Age, 16 years. Enlisted April 25, 1861, at Brooklyn to serve three years; mustered in as musician, Co. G, May 23, 1861; deserted July 23, 1861, at Arlington, Va.; also borne as Henry M. Dilks, subsequent service in Co. C, Thirty-Seventh Militia.

Dillon, Michael — Age, 24 years. Enlisted April 18, 1861, at Brooklyn to serve three years; mustered in as private, Co. A, May 23, 1861; discharged for disability, August 2, 1861, at Arlington, Va.

Dinely, William — Age, 28 years. Enlisted on August 21, 1862, at Brooklyn to serve three years; mustered in as private, Co. B, August 22, 1862; deserted on November 10, 1863, from Central Park Hospital, New York City.

Ditmas, Henry C. — Age, 19 years. Enlisted on April 18, 1861, at Brooklyn to serve three years; mustered in as private, Co. E, May 23, 1861; discharged for disability, July 27, 1861, at Arlington, Va.

Dixon, William — Age, 22 years. Enlisted May 18, 1861, at Brooklyn to serve three years; mustered in musician, Co. B on May 23, 1861; captured in action on August 29, 1862, at Manassas, Va.; paroled and deserted, no date.

Doan, Spencer K. — Age, 33 years. Enlisted August 25, 1862, at Brooklyn to serve three years; mustered in as private, Co. D, August 26, 1862; transferred to Co. H, Fifth Veteran Infantry, on June 2, 1864.

Dobson David — Age, 27 years. Enlisted on April 18, 1861, at Brooklyn to serve three years; mustered in as private, Co. of Engineers, May 23, 1861; mustered out August 28, 1861, at Arlington, Va.

Dobson, Frederick — Age, 20 years. Enlisted at Brooklyn to serve three years; mustered in as private, Co. I, January 5, 1864; transferred to Co. G, Fifth Veteran Infantry, on June 8, 1864.

Doepper, John — Age, 25 years. Enlisted at Brooklyn to serve three years; mustered in as private, Co. H, September 9, 1862; captured in action July 1, 1863, at Gettysburg, Pa.; paroled on August 25, 1863, at City Point Va.; transferred to Co. K, Fifth Veteran Infantry, on June 2, 1864; also borne as Doepher.

Doherty, Hugh — Age, 21 years. Enlisted on April 18, 1861, at Brooklyn to serve three years; mustered in as private, Co. B, on May 23, 1861; mustered out with company, June 6, 1864, at New York City as Dougherty.

Doherty, James H. — Age, 21 years. Enlisted July 21, 1861, at Brooklyn to serve three years; mustered in as private, Co. G, July 5, 1861; deserted July 22, 1861, at Arlington, Heights, Va.; also borne as Dougherty.

Doherty, William — Age, 19 years. Enlisted May 18, 1861, at Brooklyn to serve three years; mustered in as private, Co. B, May 23, 1861; deserted August 11, 1861, at Upton Hill, Va.; also borne as Dougherty.

Dolan, John — Age, 22 years. Enlisted at Brooklyn to serve three years; mustered in as private, unassigned, October 13, 1862; no further record.

Donaghue, John — Age, 30 years. Enlisted at Brooklyn to serve three years; mustered in as private, Co. G, December 2, 1863; deserted May 12, 1864; also borne as Donohue.

Donahue, James — Age, 29 years. Enlisted April 18, 1861, at Brooklyn to serve three years; mustered in as private, Co. A, May

23, 1861; promoted sergeant, no date; first sergeant April 1, 1863; missing in action July 1, 1863, at Gettysburg, Pa.; returned October 8, 1863; mustered out with companion June 6, 1864, at New York City, as James C. Donahue; also borne as Donohue.

Donahue, James F.—Age, 20 years. Enlisted at Brooklyn to serve three years; mustered in as private, Co. F, February 1, 1862; deserted June 2, 1863.

Donahue James T.—Age, 20 years. Enlisted May 18, 1861, at Brooklyn to serve three years; mustered in as private, Co. B, May 23, 1861; deserted July 30, 1861.

Donahue, Matthew—Age, 28 years. Enlisted August 19, 1862, at Brooklyn to serve three years; mustered in as private, Co. A, September 20, 1862; wounded in action and died on May 8, 1864, at Laurel Hill, Va.; also borne as Donohue.

Donahue, Patrick—Age, 29 years. Enlisted at Brooklyn to serve three years; mustered in as private, Co. A, December 3, 1861; transferred to Co. I, Fifth Veteran Infantry, on July 2, 1864; also borne as Donohue.

Donelly, Patrick—Age, 30 years. Enlisted August 28, 1862, at Brooklyn to serve three years; mustered in as private, Co. C, August 29, 1862; transferred to Co. H, Fifth Veteran Infantry, on June 2, 1864.

Donnelly, James—Age, 20 years. Enlisted April 18, 1861, at Brooklyn to serve three years; mustered in as private on May 23, 1861, Co. A, deserted on November 14, 1861, at Upton Hill, Va.

Donoghue, John—Age, 24 years. Enlisted at Brooklyn to serve three years; mustered in as private, unassigned, October 2, 1862; no further record.

Donohue, James—Age, 21 years. Enlisted April 18, 1861, at Brooklyn to serve three years; mustered in as private, Co. F, on May 23, 1861; missing in action July 1, 1863, at Gettysburg, Pa.; returned on October 9, 1863; mustered out on June 14, 1864, at New York City.

Donohue, James P.—Age, 21 years. Enlisted October 7, 1861, at Brooklyn to serve three years; mustered in as private; unassigned, October 9, 1861; no further record.

Donovan, Patrick H.—Age, 21 years. Enlisted August 26, 1862, at Brooklyn to serve three years; mustered in as private, Co. G, August 28, 1862; discharged on September 20, 1864.

Dorph, Charles—Age, 41 years. Enlisted October 1, 1861, at Brooklyn to serve three years; mustered in as musician in band, October 24, 1861; discharged August 17, 1862, at Camp Halstead, Va.

Dougherty, Dominick—Age, 22 years. Enlisted April 18, 1861, at Brooklyn to serve three years; mustered in as private, Co. A, on May 23, 1861; discharged for disability on July 29, 1861, at Arlington, Va. also borne as Dominick G. Dougherty.

Dougherty, James—Age, 20 years. Enlisted on June 30, 1861, at Brooklyn to serve three years; mustered in as private, Co. K, on August 1, 1861; wounded in action on August 29, 1862, at Manassas, Va.; deserted, no date, at Washington D.C.

Dougherty, Patrick—Age, 18 years. Enlisted April 18, 1861, at Brooklyn to serve three years; mustered in as private, Co. H, on May 23, 1861; deserted on July 14, 1861, at Arlington, Va.; also borne as Daugherty.

Douglass, George—Age, 18 years. Enlisted April 18, 1861, at Brooklyn to serve three years; mustered in as private, Co. F, May 23, 1861; wounded in action on July 1, 1863, at Gettysburg, Pa.; died of his wounds on July 31, 1863.

Douglass, William B.—Age, 20 years. Enlisted April 18, 1861, at Brooklyn to serve three years; mustered in as private, Co. C, on May 23, 1861; mustered out on March 30, 1864.

Dowd, John—Age, 19 years. Enlisted May 18, 1861, at Brooklyn to serve three years; mustered in as private, Co. D, on May 23, 1861; killed in action July 21, 1861, at Bull Run, Va.

Dowdell, Andrew—Age, 19 years. Enlisted

August 26, 1862, at Brooklyn to serve three years; mustered in as private, Co. G, on August 28, 1862, deserted December 16, 1862; also borne as Dowden.

Dower, Charles — Age, 21 years. Enlisted at Brooklyn to serve three years; mustered in as private, Co. B, on January 11, 1864; transferred to Co. B, Fifth Veteran Infantry, on June 2, 1864.

Downey, Patrick — Age, 36 years. Enlisted at Brooklyn to serve three years; mustered in as private, Co. F, on June 1, 1861; promoted sergeant on August 17, 1861; discharge for disability on December 16, 1862, at Washington, D.C.

Doxeey, William — Age, 26 years. Enlisted on April 18, 1861, at Brooklyn to serve three years; mustered in as private, Co. D, on May 23, 1861; wounded in action on July 1, 1863, at Gettysburg, Pa.; mustered out with company on June 6, 1864, at New York City; also borne as Doxey.

Doyle, Francis — Age, 22 years. Enlisted on April 18, 1861, at Brooklyn to serve three years; mustered in as private, Co. A, on May 23, 1861; promoted corporal on September 13, 1861; wounded in action on August 29, 1862, at Bull Run, Va.; discharged for wounds on October 14, 1862, at Alexandria, Va.

Drain, William L. — Age, 18 years. Enlisted on August 18, 1861, at Brooklyn to serve three years; mustered in as private, Co. D, August 18, 1861; transferred to Co. I, Fifth Veteran Infantry, on June 2, 1864.

Drake, William H. — Age, 18 years. Enlisted on August 18, 1862, at Brooklyn to serve three years; mustered in as private, Co. D, August 19, 1862; died of disease on July 9, 1863, at Washington, D.C.

Drew, John T. — Age, 22 years. Enlisted on August 26, 1862, at Brooklyn to serve three years; mustered in as private, Co. G, August 28, 1862; wounded in action on September 17, 1862, at Antietam, Md.; died of his wounds on October 18, 1862, at Smoketown, Md.; also borne as John F. Drew.

Drummond, Morris D. — Age, 20 years. Enlisted on May 18, 1861, at Brooklyn to serve three years; mustered in as private, Co. B, on May 23, 1861; discharged for disability on August 4, 1861, at Arlington, Va.

Dubois, Robert K. — Age, 26 years. Enlisted April 18, 1861, at Brooklyn to serve three years; mustered in as private, Co. C, on May 23, 1861; deserted January 28, 1862, at Upton Hill, Va.

Duck, Frederick G. — Age, 19 years. Enlisted April 18, 1861, at Brooklyn to serve three years; mustered in as private, Co. E, May 23, 1861; deserted October 11, 1861, at Arlington, Va.

Duel, John — Age, 28 years. Enlisted August 21, 1862, at Brooklyn to serve three years; mustered in as private, Co. G, August 22, 1862; discharged for disability on January 13, 1863, at New York City.

Duffy, James — Age, 21 years. Enlisted on May 18, 1861, at Brooklyn to serve three years; mustered in as private on May 23, 1861; mustered out on May 23, 1864, at Washington, D.C.

Eagan, Dennis — Age, 19 years. Enlisted May 18, 1861, at Brooklyn to serve three years; mustered in as private, Co. B, May 23, 1861; deserted August 11, 1861, at Arlington, Va.

Eagan, John — Age, 22 years. Enlisted April 18, 1861, at Brooklyn to serve three years; mustered in as private, Co. G, May 23, 1861; discharged for disability on July 29, 1861, at Arlington, Va.

Eagan, Stephen — Age, 19 years. Enlisted on September 9, 1861, at New York City to serve three years; mustered in as private, Co. H, September 13, 1861; discharged for disease on July 19, 1863, at Alexandria, Va.

Earle, George A. — Age, 22 years. Enrolled on April 18, 1861, at Brooklyn to serve three years; mustered in as corporal, Co. C, on May 23, 1861; wounded in action on August 29, 1862, at Groveton, Va.; promoted second lieutenant on September 21, 1862; mustered in as first lieutenant on February11, 1863; discharged for wounds on April 4, 1863; commissioned second lieutenant on October 24, 1862, with rank from September 21, 1862.

Early Thomas — Age, 28 years. Enlisted November 29, 1862, at Brooklyn to serve three years; mustered in as private, Co. B, December 1, 1862; transferred to Co. I, Fifth Veteran Infantry, on June 2, 1864.

Eason, John W.— Age, 18 years. enlisted April 25, 1861, at Brooklyn to serve three years; mustered in as private, Co. G, May 23, 1861; promoted corporal, no date; sergeant on January 8, 1864; mustered out with company on June 6, 1864, at New York City; also borne as Easton.

Eastburn, William S.— Enlisted on September 2, 1861, at Brooklyn to serve three years; mustered in as private, Co. K, September 3, 1861; discharged on February 20, 1864.

Edie, James — Age, 22 years. Enlisted on June 30, 1861, at Brooklyn to serve three years; mustered in as private, Co. K, August 1, 1861; wounded in action on August 29, 1862, at Bull Run, Va.; discharged for wounds on December 15, 1862, at New York City.

Edwards, James — Age, 38 years. Enlisted at Brooklyn to serve three years. mustered in as private, Co. A, February 24, 1864; transferred to navy on March 23, 1864.

Edwards, James — Age, 24 years. Enlisted on May 18, 1861, at Brooklyn to serve three years; mustered in as private, Co. B, on May 23, 1861; deserted August 11, 1861, at Arlington, Va.

Edwards, John — Age, 28 years. Enlisted at Brooklyn to serve three years; mustered in as private; unassigned, November 24, 1862; no further record.

Edwards, John S.— Age, 28 years. Enlisted at Brooklyn to serve three years; mustered in as private, Co. E, September 25, 1862; wounded in action on July 1, 1863, at Gettysburg, Pa.; transferred to Veterans Reserve Corp on January 16, 1864; re-transferred to this company on March 31, 1864, and transferred to Co. H, Fifth Veteran Infantry, on June 2, 1864.

Edwards, William H.— Age, 18 years. Enlisted on April 18, 1861, at Brooklyn to serve three years; mustered in as private, Co. F, May 23, 1861; discharged for disability on July 3, 1863, at Baltimore, Md.

Egolf, John — Age, 21 years. Enrolled April 18, 1861, at Brooklyn to serve three years; mustered in as private on May 23, 1861; promoted corporal, no date; wounded in action on July 1, 1863, at Gettysburg, Pa.; mustered in as second lieutenant on January 18, 1864; mustered out with company on June 6, 1864, at New York City; also borne as John A. Egolff.

Egolf, Thomas — Age, 20 years. Enlisted at Brooklyn to serve three years; mustered in as private, Co. E, on June 9, 1862; died of disease on January 24, 1863, at Convalescent Camp, Alexandria, Va.

Egolf, William — Age, 23 years. Enlisted September 27, 1861, at Brooklyn to serve three years; mustered in as private, Co. E, on September 28, 1861; promoted corporal, no date; wounded in action on July 1, 1863, at Gettysburg, Pa.; died of his wounds July 18, 1863, at Gettysburg, Pa.; also borne as Egolff.

Eichholz, Joseph — Age, 28 years. Enlisted August 28, 1862, at Brooklyn to serve three years; mustered in as private, Co. B, on August 27, 1862; transferred to 121st Company, Second Battalion, Veterans Reserve Corps, on September 22, 1862; also borne as Eicholz.

Elcock, George S.— Age, 21 years. Enrolled April 18, 1861, at Brooklyn to serve three years; mustered in as second lieutenant, Co. E, on May 23, 1861; first lieutenant on August 4, 1861; as captain on February 22, 1862; mustered out with company on June 6, 1864, at New York City; commissioned second lieutenant in Fourteenth Militia on May 6, 1861, with rank from April 29, 1861; first lieutenant in militia, August 12, 1861, with rank from

August 4, 1861; not commissioned captain.

Eldard, James—Age, 35 years. Enlisted April 18, 1861, at Brooklyn to serve three years; mustered in as private, Co. H on May 23, 1861; appointed wagoner, no date; returned to company as private on November 19, 1863; mustered out with company on June 6, 1864, at New York City.

Eldard, James E.—Age, 19 years. Enlisted at Brooklyn to serve three years; mustered in as private, Co. D, on August 21, 1861; discharged for disability on December 19, 1862, at hospital in Philadelphia, Pa.

Elks, John—Age, 37 years. Enlisted December 28, 1863, at Brooklyn to serve three years; mustered in as private, Co. G, on December 30, 1863; transferred to Co. G, Fifth Veteran Infantry, on June 2, 1864.

Ellis, Charles W.—Age, 18 years. Enlisted April 18, 1861, at Brooklyn to serve three years; mustered in as private Co. G, on May 23, 1861; discharged August 1, 1861, at Camp Wood, Arlington, Va.; refused to take oath; also borne as Charles B. Ellis.

Ellis, George—Age, 20 years. Enlisted January 29, 1864, at Brooklyn to serve three years; mustered in as private, Co. E, on January 30, 1864; mustered out on May 8, 1865, at Hart's Island, New York Harbor.

Elwood, Leroy—Age, 31 years. Enlisted at Brooklyn to serve three years; mustered in as private, Co. G, on August 20, 1862; deserted on September 10, 1862, at Antietam, Md., while in the face of the enemy.

Ennis, Edward—Age, 20 years. Enlisted on May 10, 1861, at Brooklyn to serve three years; mustered in as private, Co. G, on May 23, 1861; wounded and captured in action on July 21, 1861, at Bull Run, Va.; died of his wounds on August 12, 1861, at Richmond, Va.

Eranamann, Johannes—Age, 25 years. Enlisted December 4, 1863, at Brooklyn to serve three years; mustered in as private, Co. I on December 8, 1863; transferred to Co. G, Fifth Veteran Infantry, June 2, 1864; also borne as Johennes Ernamana.

Erkenbrack, Joseph—Age, 20 years. Enlisted on April 18, 1861, at Brooklyn to serve three years; mustered in as private, Co. B, on May 23, 1861; captured in action on July 1, 1863, at Gettysburg, Pa.; returned to company, no date; promoted sergeant on January 4, 1864; mustered out with company on July 6, 1864, at New York City; also borne as Joseph R. Erkenbrack.

Erkenbrack, Thomas—Age, 19 years. Enlisted on August 26, 1862, at Brooklyn to serve three years; mustered in as private, Co. B, on August 27, 1862; captured in action on July 1, 1863, at Gettysburg, Pa.; returned to company, no date; transferred to Co. B, Fifth Veteran Infantry, on June 6, 1864.

Eustice, Daniel—Age, 19 years. Enlisted at New York City to serve three years; mustered in as private; unassigned, March 12, 1864; no further record.

Evans, Eleazer—Age, 22 years. Enlisted June 30, 1861, at Brooklyn to serve three years; mustered in as private, Co. K, on August 1, 1861; promoted corporal on April 1, 1863; captured in action on July 1, 1863, at Gettysburg, Pa.; returned to company on October 9, 1863; promoted sergeant on January 1, 1864; transferred to Co. K, Fifth Veteran Infantry, on June 2, 1864.

Evans, Frederick—Age, 19 years. Enlisted June 30, 1861, at Brooklyn to serve three years; mustered in as private, Co. I, August 1, 1861; promoted corporal on January 1, 1864; transferred to Co. G, Fifth Veteran Infantry, on June 2, 1864; also borne as Evers.

Evens, George—Age, 22 years, Enlisted April 18, 1861, at Brooklyn to serve three years; mustered in as private, Co. C, on May 23, 1861; discharged for disability, November 3, 1862, at Washington, D.C.; also borne as Everus.

Everding, Henry — Age, 30 years. Enlisted April 25, 1861, at Brooklyn to serve three years; mustered in as sergeant, Co. G, on May 23, 1861; discharged for disability on July 7, 1862, at Eckington Hospital, Washington, D.C.

Everite, William D. — Age, 22 years. Enlisted April 18, 1861, at Brooklyn to serve three years; mustered in as private, Co. C, on May 23, 1861; discharged for disability on February 12, 1863, at Washington, D.C.; also borne as William R. Everett.

Evers, William T. — Age, 34 years. Enlisted on September 15, 1862, at Brooklyn to serve three years; mustered in as private, Co. D, on September 16, 1862; dishonorably discharged on May 25, 1864.

Eyre, Charles — Age, 30 years. Enlisted on April 18, 1861, at Brooklyn to serve three years; mustered in as private, Co. C, on May 23, 1861; discharged for disability on September 22, 1862, at Washington, D.C.

Eyre, George — Age, 37 years. Enlisted on April 18, 1861, at Brooklyn to serve three years; mustered in as private, Co. C, on May 23, 1861; discharged for disability on September 22, 1862, at Washington, D.C.

Fagan, Thomas J. — Age, 19 years. Enlisted on May 18, 1861, at Brooklyn to serve three years; mustered in as corporal, Co. B, on May 23, 1861; wounded in action on July 21, 1861, at Bull Run, Va.; discharged for wounds on November 17, 1861, at Upton Hill, Va.

Fales, Eugene H. — Age, 21 years. Enlisted April 18, 1861, at Brooklyn to serve three years; mustered in as private, Co. E, on May 23, 1861; mustered out on April 5, 1862, for promotion to first lieutenant, 131st Infantry.

Fallon Patrick — Age, 25 years. Enlisted at Brooklyn to serve three years; mustered in as private, Co. G, December 14, 1863; discharged for disability on March 6, 1864, at Culpeper, Va.

Farley, Charles — Age, 21 years. Enlisted April 18, 1861, at Brooklyn to serve three years; mustered in as sergeant, Co. F, on May 23, 1861; mustered out on June 14, 1864, at New York City.

Farley, James L. — Age, 26 years. Enrolled April 18, 1861, at Brooklyn to serve three years; mustered in as assistant surgeon, May 23, 1861; as surgeon on January 24, 1862, discharged for disability on June 10, 1863; commissioned assistant surgeon in Fourteenth Militia on May 13, 1861, with rank from April 24, 1861; as surgeon, June 23, 1862, with rank from January 24, 1862.

Farrell John — Age, 21 years. Enlisted on May 18, 1861, at Brooklyn to serve three years; mustered in as private, Co. D, on May 23, 1861; deserted on October 6, 1861, from Camp Wood, Arlington, Va.

Farrell, Patrick — Age, 28 years. Enlisted on September 2, 1862, at Brooklyn to serve three years; mustered in as private, Co. D, on September 3, 1862; transferred to Co. H, Fifth Veteran Infantry, on June 2, 1864.

Farrell, Thomas — Age, 28 years. Enlisted August 22, 1862, at Brooklyn to serve three years; mustered in as private, Co. B, August 26, 1862; killed in action on July 1, 1863, at Gettysburg, Pa.

Farrell, William — Age, 21 years. Enlisted August 25, 1862, at Brooklyn to serve three years; mustered in as private, Co. H on August 26, 1862; wounded in action on July 3, 1863, at Gettysburg, Pa.; transferred to Veterans Reserve Corps on February 15, 1864; mustered out July 14, 1864, as of Co. K, First Regiment, Veterans Reserve Corps, at Elmira, New York.

Farrell, William M. — Age, 24 years. Enlisted April 18, 1861, at Brooklyn to serve three years; mustered in as private, Co. A, on May 23, 1861; deserted on September 21, 1861, at Arlington, Va.

Farris, John — Age, 19 years. Enlisted at Brooklyn to serve three years; mustered in as private, Co. C, February 23, 1864; transferred to Co. H, Fifth Veteran Infantry, June 2, 1864.

Faskett, William — Age, 25 years. Enlisted April 18, 1861, at Brooklyn to serve three years; mustered in as private, Co. D, on May 23, 1861; mustered out with company on June 6, 1864, at New York City; also borne as Foskett.

Fay, John — Age, 26 years. Enlisted April 18, 1861, at Brooklyn to serve three years; mustered in as private, Co. F, on May 23, 1861; killed in action on July 21, 1861, at Bull Run, Va.

Fearous, John — Age, 25 years. Enlisted April 18, 1861, at Brooklyn to serve three years; mustered in as private, Co. F, on May 23, 1861; deserted September 22, 1861, at Upton Hill, Va.

Ferry, Daniel — Age, 23 years. Enlisted August 20, 1862, at Brooklyn to serve three years; mustered in as private, Co. G, on August 28, 1862; deserted December 29, 1862, at Cockpit Point, Va.

Files, Levi M. — Age, 18 years. Enlisted at New York City to serve three years; mustered in as private, Co. I, on March 1, 1862; discharged for disability on December 28, 1862, at Baltimore, Md.

Finley, William H. — Age, 43 years. Enlisted at New York City to serve three years; mustered in as private; unassigned, March 10, 1864; no further record.

Fenn, Peter — Age, 21 years. Enlisted April 18, 1861, at Brooklyn to serve three years; mustered in as private, Co. F, on May 23, 1861; wounded on October 5, 1861, at Upton Hill, Va.; discharged for disability on January 30, 1863, at Washington D.C.

Fish, Henry — Age, 42 years. Enlisted August 29, 1862, at Brooklyn to serve three years; mustered in as private, Co. C, on August 30, 1862; discharged for disability on September 3, 1863, at Alexandria, Va.

Fisher George — Age, 31 years. Enlisted October 1, 1861, at Brooklyn to serve three years; mustered in as musician in band on October 24, 1861; discharged on August 17, 1862, at Camp Halstead, Va.

Fisher, John H. — Age, 23 years. Enlisted April 18, 1861, at Brooklyn to serve three years; mustered in as private, Co. G, on May 23, 1861; promoted hospital steward on April 20, 1862; mustered out with regiment on June 6, 1864, at New York City.

Fitting, Jacob — Age, 24 years. Enlisted at Brooklyn to serve three years; mustered in as private, Co. G, on December 14, 1863; transferred to Co. G, Fifth Veteran Infantry, on June 2, 1864.

Fitzgerald, Edward — Age, 21 years. Enlisted at Brooklyn to serve three years; mustered in as private, Co. G, on December 16, 1863; transferred to Co. K, Fifth Veteran Infantry, on June 2, 1864.

Fitzgerald, Michael — Age, 21 years. Enlisted at Brooklyn to serve three years; mustered in as private; unassigned, December 12, 1863; deserted, no date, from Hart's Island, New York Harbor.

Fitzgerald, Michael — Age, 40 years. Enlisted at Ninth Congressional District to serve three years; mustered in as private; unassigned, March 9, 1864; no further record.

Fitzpatrick, Arthur — Age, 30 years. Enlisted April 18, 1861, at Brooklyn to serve three years; mustered in as private, Co. A, on May 23, 1861; deserted on August 18, 1861, at Arlington, Va.

Fitzpatrick, Patrick — Age, 22 years. Enlisted at Brooklyn to serve three years; mustered in as private, Co. B, on March 4, 1862; deserted on April 18, 1862, at Catlett's Station, Va.

Fitzsimmons, Edward — Age, 28 years. Enlisted August 26, 1862, at Brooklyn to serve three years; mustered in as private, Co. G, on August 28, 1862; deserted on December 16, 1862, at Rappahannock, Va.

Flaherty, Patrick — Age, 40 years. Enlisted on June 30, 1861, at Brooklyn to serve three years; mustered in as private Co.

K, on August 1, 1861; wounded on the skirmish on August 29, 1863, at Reynolds Crossing, Va.; re-enlisted as a veteran on January 4, 1864; died of disease on July 26, 1864, at Washington, D.C.

Flint, James — Age, 16 years. Enlisted April 18, 1861, at Brooklyn to serve three years; mustered in as musician, Co. E, on May 23, 1861; discharged on July 24, 1862, at Falmouth, Va.

Flavin, Edward — Age, 22 years. Enrolled April 18, 1861, at Brooklyn to serve three years; mustered in as corporal, Co. A, on May 23, 1861; promoted sergeant on September 13, 1861; mustered in as second lieutenant, Co. F, on February 26, 1863; transferred to Co. A on March 1, 1863; mustered in as first lieutenant, to date January 7, 1863; mustered out with company on June 6, 1864, at New York City.

Flood, Thomas — Age, 21 years. Enlisted at Brooklyn to serve three years; mustered in as private, Co. F, on November 28, 1863; transferred to Co. G, Fifth Veteran Infantry, on June 2, 1864.

Flynn, Edward — Age, 19 years. Enlisted August 28, 1862, at Brooklyn to serve 3 years; mustered in as private, Co. F, on August 28, 1862; unassigned, August 30, 1862; no further record.

Flynn, James — Age, 18 years. Enlisted at Brooklyn to serve three years; mustered in as private, Co. F, on December 8, 1863; transferred to Co. G, Fifth Veteran Infantry, on June 2, 1864.

Flynn, Patrick — Age, 21 years. Enlisted April 18, 1861, at Brooklyn to serve three years; mustered in as private, Co. B, on May 23, 1861; promoted sergeant on February 1, 1863; wounded April 29, 1863, at Pollock's Creek, Va.; mustered out with company on June 6, 1864, at New York City.

Foe, Edward — Age, 21 years. Enlisted April 18, 1861, at Brooklyn to serve three years; mustered in as private, Co. B, on May 23, 1861; deserted on July 16, 1863, from near Elkton Station, Md.

Fohs, Joseph — Age, 18 years. Enlisted October 1, 1861, at Brooklyn to serve three years; mustered in as musician in band, October 24, 1861; discharged on August 17, 1862, at Camp Halstead, Va.; again enlisted September 27, 1862, as musician in Co. C; transferred to Co. A on May 1, 1863; to Co. I, Fifth Veteran Infantry, on June 2, 1864.

Fohs, Prter — Age, 43 years. Enlisted on October 1, 1861, at Brooklyn to serve three years; mustered in as musician in band on October 24, 1861; discharged on August 17, 1862, at Camp Halstead, Va.

Foller, Peter — Age, 19 years. Enlisted on May 18, 1861, at Brooklyn to serve three years; mustered in as private, Co. B, on May 23, 1861; discharged for disability on September 19, 1861, as Peter Faller.

Forder, William — Age, 20 years. Enlisted on April 18, 1861, at Brooklyn to serve three years; mustered in as private, Co. H, on May 23, 1861; died of disease on August 31, 1861, in hospital at Washington, D.C.; also borne as William F. Forder.

Forman, John L. — Age, 22 years. Enlisted on April 18, 1861, at Brooklyn to serve three years; mustered in as private, Co. H, on May 23, 1861; deserted on September 25, 1861, at Arlington, Va.

Forrester, George W. — Age, 18 years. Enlisted on April 18, 1861, at Brooklyn to serve three years; mustered in as private, Co. C, on May 23, 1861; promoted corporal on November 1, 1862; wounded in action on July 1, 1863, and died of his wounds on July 2, 1863, at Gettysburg, Pa.

Forrester, Henry — Age, 34 years. Enlisted on September 8, 1862, at Brooklyn to serve three years; mustered in as private; unassigned, September 9, 1862; no further record.

Foster, Andrew — Age, 21 years. Enlisted on April 18, 1861, at Brooklyn to serve three years; mustered in as private, Co. E, on May 23, 1861; deserted November 1, 1861, at Upton Hill, Va.

Fowler, Edward B.—Age, 35 years. Enrolled on April 18, 1861, at Brooklyn to serve three years; mustered in as lieutenant colonel on April 19, 1861; as colonel on October 24, 1862; mustered out with regiment on June 6, 1864, at New York City; commissioned lieutenant colonel in Fourteenth Militia on April 27, 1861, with rank from April 19, 1861; colonel on October 24, 1862, with rank from October 1, 1862.

Fowler, John C.—Age, 23 years. Enlisted at Brooklyn to serve three years; mustered in as private; unassigned, September 25, 1862; no further record.

Fox, George—Age, 29 years. Enlisted December 16, 1863, at Brooklyn to serve three years; mustered in as private, Co. G, on December 21, 1863; transferred to Fifth Veteran Infantry, on June 2, 1864.

Fox, James—Age, 21 years. Enlisted at Brooklyn to serve three years; mustered in as private, Co. G, on December 16, 1863; transferred to Co. K, Fifth Veteran Infantry, on June 2, 1864.

Fox, Joseph—Age, 29 years. Enlisted at Brooklyn to serve three years; mustered in as private, Co. G, on December 16, 1863; transferred to Co. K, Fifth Veteran Infantry, on June 2, 1864.

Fox, Philip—Age, 21 years. Enlisted September 17, 1862, at Brooklyn to serve three years; mustered in as private, Co. C, on September 18, 1862; transferred to Veterans Reserve Corps on September 8, 1863.

Francis, Louis—Age, 40 years. Enlisted on July 1, 1861, at Brooklyn to serve three years; mustered in as private, Co. I, on August 1, 1861; discharged for disability on July 12, 1864, at New York City.

Frank, Martin—Age, 21 years. Enlisted April 18, 1861, at Brooklyn to serve three years; mustered in as private, Co. A, on May 23, 1861; killed in action on July 21, 1861, at Bull Run, Va.; also borne as Martin Franks and Frank Marten.

Franklin, Lucien—Age, 23 years. Enlisted April 18, 1861, at Brooklyn to serve three years; mustered in as private, Co. E, on May 23, 1861; discharged for disability on July 24, 1861, at Arlington, Va.

Franson, Emile—Age, 30 years. Enlisted at Brooklyn to serve three years; mustered in as private, Co. G, on December 21, 1863; transferred to Co. C, Fifth Veteran Infantry, on June 2, 1864; also borne as Eimel and Eimil Fransen.

Frazier, Robert—Age, 31 years. Enlisted April 18, 1861, at Brooklyn to serve three years; mustered in as private, Co. D, on May 23, 1861; mustered out with company on June 6, 1864, at New York City.

Frear, George B.—Age, 27 years. Enlisted August 25, 1862, at Brooklyn to serve three years; mustered in as private, Co. D, on August 26, 1862; died of disease on March 16, 1863, in regimental hospital at Belle Plain, Va.

Freitag, Conrad—Age, 19 years. Enlisted September 10, 1862, at Brooklyn to serve three years; mustered in as private, Co. B, on September 11, 1862; promoted corporal on September —, 1863; wounded in action on May 8, 1864, at Laurel Hill, Va.; mustered out May 22, 1865, at Ladies Home Hospital, New York City; also borne as Frietag.

French, John—Age, 18 years. Enlisted July 28, 1861, at Brooklyn to serve three years; mustered in as private, Co. B, on August 4, 1861; promoted corporal, no date; sergeant on January 1, 1864; transferred to Co. H, Fifth Veteran Infantry, on June 2, 1864.

French, William—Age, 21 years. Enlisted April 18, 1861, at Brooklyn to serve three years; mustered in as private, Co. H, on May 23, 1861; deserted on September 6, 1862.

Fritchler, Charles L.R.—Age, 23 years. Enlisted September 10, 1861, at Brooklyn to serve three years; mustered in as private, Co. C, on September 11, 1861; transferred to Co. H, Fifth Veteran Infantry, on June 2, 1864; also borne as Frits —.

Frow, John — Age, 25 years. Enlisted at Brooklyn to serve three years; mustered in as private, Co. C, on September 30, 1861; promoted corporal on April 10, 1864; killed in action on May 10, 1864, at Laurel Hill, Va.; also borne as Frew.

Fuller, Charles — Age, 25 years. Enlisted at Brooklyn to serve three years; mustered in as private, Co. G, on December 14, 1863; transferred to Co. K, Fifth Veteran Infantry, on June 2, 1864.

Fuller, Lora M. — Private, Co. C, Twenty-First Infantry; transferred to Co. G, this regiment, no date; to Co. G, Fifth Veteran Infantry, on June 2, 1864.

Fulton, John — Age, 35 years. Enlisted April 18, 1861, at Brooklyn to serve three years; mustered in as corporal, Co. L, engineers on May 23, 1861; mustered out on August 28, 1861, at Arlington, Va.

Funk, James R. — Age, 19 years. Enlisted on December 16, 1861, at Brooklyn to serve three years; mustered in as private, Co. D, on December 18, 1861; discharged on November 16, 1863.

Furey, John V. — Age, 30 years. Enlisted, April 1861, at Brooklyn, to serve three years; mustered in as private, Co. C, May 23, 1861; discharged September 28, 1862, for promotion to quartermaster, U.S. Volunteers; also borne as John W. Fevery and John N. Ferry.

Furey, Jr. Robert — Age, 30 years. Enlisted, July 1, 1861, at Brooklyn, to serve three years; mustered in as private, Co. H, May 23, 1861; discharged for hernia, December 12, 1862, at Washington, D.C.

Gallager, Michael — Age, 23 years. Enlisted, July 1, 1861, at Brooklyn, to serve three years; mustered in as private, Co. I, August 1, 1861; deserted January 23, 1862, at Upton Hill, Va.; also borne as Gallagher.

Gallagher, George — Age, 23 years. Enlisted, May 18, 1861, at Brooklyn to serve three years; mustered in as private, Co. B, May 23, 1861, deserted October 23, 1861, at Upton Hill Va.

Gannon, John — Age, 28 years. Enlisted at Brooklyn, to serve three years; mustered in as private, Co. F, October 29, 1861; deserted, January 24, 1862, at Upton Hill Va.

Garcia, Manuel — Age, 19 years. Enlisted, April 18, 1861, at Brooklyn, to serve three years; mustered in as private, Co. F, May 23, 1861; discharged for disability, May 23, 1862.

Gardener, Robert — Age, 22 years. Enlisted, December 3, 1863, at Brooklyn, to serve three years; mustered in as private, Co. G, December 8, 1863, killed May 8, 1864, at the Wilderness, Va.

Gardner, George, B — Age, 24 years. Enlisted, April 18, 1861, at Brooklyn, to serve three years; mustered in as private, Co. H; deserted August 9, 1863; also borne as Gardiner.

Garman, Francis — Age, 20 years. Enlisted, April 1861, at Brooklyn, to serve three years; mustered in as private, Co. B, May 23, 1861; promoted corporal, February 1, 1863; wounded in action, July 1, 1863, at Gettysburg, Pa.; mustered out with company, June 6, 1864, at New York City.

Garvin, Oliver C. — Age, 21 years. Enlisted, April 1861, at Brooklyn, to serve three years; mustered in as private, Co. C, May 23, 1861; discharged September 7, 1861, for promotion to captain, Co. G, Fifty-Second Infantry.

Gasider, Isaac L. — Age, 19 years. Enlisted, September 25, 1862, at Brooklyn, to serve three years; mustered in as private; unassigned, September 25, 1862; no further record.

Gaston, Albert G — Age, 28 years. Enrolled, April 18, 1861, at Brooklyn, to serve three years; mustered in as paymaster, May 23, 1861; discharged, July 28, 1864; commissioned paymaster in Fourteenth Militia, February 17, 1860, with rank from January 2, 1860.

Gaufrau, Marcelin — Age, 20 years. Enlisted, April 18, 1861, at Brooklyn, to serve three years; mustered in as private,

Co. H, May 23, 1861; deserted, August 9, 1862, from hospital; also borne as Fauffeau and Marcelin Gauffreau.

Gault, Robert — Age, 33 years. Enlisted, April 18, 1861, at Brooklyn, to serve three years; mustered in as private, Co. E, May 23, 1861; discharged for disability, September 13, 1861, at Arlington, Va.

Geary, Manus — Age, 18 years. Enlisted, April 18, 1861, at Brooklyn, to serve three years; mustered in as private, Co. A, May 23, 1861; wounded in action, July 1, 1863, Gettysburg, Pa; returned to company, October 8, 1863; mustered out with company, June 6, 1864, at New York City, as Manny J. Geary; also borne as Manus J. Gearney.

Geissellman, Francis H. — Enlisted, April 25, 1861, at Brooklyn to serve three years; mustered in as private, Co. G, May 23, 1861; discharged for disability, January 13, 1863, at New York city; also borne as Dayton Geissellman, Giesleman, Girsekman.

Geoghagan, Thomas — Age, 21 years. Enlisted at Brooklyn, to serve three years; mustered in as private, Co. D, August 26, 1862; wounded in action July 1, 1863, at Gettysburg, Pa.; deserted, April 11, 1864, from hospital, Germantown, Pa.; also borne as Geaghan.

George, Charles E. — Age, 26 years. Enlisted, December 26, 1861, at Brooklyn, to serve three years; mustered in as private, Co. D, December 30, 1861; discharged for disability, October 25, 1862, at hospital, Philadelphia, Pa.

George, Thomas C. — Age, 38 years. Enlisted August 21, 1862, at Brooklyn, to serve three years; mustered in as private, Co. C, August 23, 1862; wounded in action, July 1, 1863, at Gettysburg, Pa.; transferred to Co. H, Fifth Veteran Infantry, June 2, 1864.

Gerow, Alexander D. — Age, 22 years. Enlisted, April 18, 1861, at Brooklyn, to serve three years; mustered in as private, Co. C, May 23, 1861; wounded, July 21, 1861, at Bull Run, Va.; died of his wounds, August 21, 1861.

Gibbs, James — Age, 28 years. Enlisted, September 3, 1862, at Brooklyn, to serve three years; mustered in as private, Co. A, September 10, 1862; wounded in action, July 1, 1863, at Gettysburg, Pa.; transferred to Co. G, Sixth Regiment; Veteran Reserve Corps., March 16, 1864, from which mustered out, July 14, 1865, at Cleveland, Ohio.

Gibbs, John — Age, 21 years. Enlisted at Brooklyn, to serve three years; mustered in as private, Co. K, February 25, 1864; transferred to Co. K, Fifth Veteran Infantry, June 2, 1864.

Gibney, Thomas F. — Age, 21 years. Enlisted April 18, 1861, at Brooklyn, to serve three years; mustered in as private, Co. E, May 23, 1861; promoted corporal, no date; wounded in action, August 29, 1862, at Bull Run, Va.; returned to ranks, December 1, 1863; mustered out with company, June 6, 1864, at New York City.

Gilbertson, James G. — Age, 21 years. Enlisted, April 18, 1861, at Brooklyn, to serve three years; mustered in as private, Co. D, May 23, 1861; transferred to Veteran Reserve Corps, January 18, 1864.

Gildersleeve, Alonzo — Age, 18 years. Enlisted, September 12, 1862, at Brooklyn, to serve three years; mustered in as musician, Co. G, September 15, 1862; deserted, May 31, 1863, at expiration of furlough.

Gill, Adolphus W. H. — Age, 31 years. Enrolled, April 18, 1861, at Brooklyn, to serve three years; mustered in as first lieutenant and adjutant, May 23, 1861; as captain, Co. I, August 1, 1861; captured and paroled, no date; discharged, March 11, 1865; commissioned first lieutenant and adjutant, Fourteenth Militia, May 6, 1861, with rank from April 20, 1861; not commissioned captain.

Gillen, Daniel J. — Age, 19 years. Enlisted at Brooklyn, to serve three years; mustered in as private, Co. H, November 27,

1861; transferred to Co. K, Fifth Veteran Infantry, June 2, 1864.

Gillespie, Charles H — Age, 20 years. Enlisted, May 18, 1861, at Brooklyn, to serve three years; mustered in as private, Co. B, May 23, 1861; discharged for disability, July 2, 1861, at Arlington, Va., as Charles A. Gellespie.

Gillin, John — Age, 23 years. Enlisted, April 25, 1861, at Brooklyn, to serve three years; mustered in as private, Co. G, May 23, 1861; discharged for disability, November 18, 1862, at Annapolis, Md.; again enlisted and mustered in as private, December 14, 1863; transferred to Co. C, Fifth Veteran Infantry, June 2, 1864; also borne as Gillon.

Gilmour, George — Age, 22 years. Enlisted, August 21, 1862, at Brooklyn to serve three years; mustered in as private, Co. A, August 22, 1862; transferred to Veteran Reserve Corps, August 1, 1863, from which discharged as sergeant, July 3, 1865, at Harrisburg, Pa.

Glanville, Henry E. — Age, 21 years. Enlisted, December 17, 1863, at Brooklyn to serve three years; mustered in as private, Co. I, December 21, 1963; transferred to Co. C, Fifth Veteran Infantry, June 6, 1864; also borne as Glenvill.

Glasson, Robert — Age, 44 years. Enlisted, August 27, 1862, at Brooklyn, to serve three years; mustered in as private, Co. D, August 28, 1862; discharged for disability, November 25, 1862, at New York City.

Glinnan, John — Age, 20 years. Enlisted April 18, 1861, at Brooklyn to serve three years; mustered in as private, Co. H, on May 23, 1861; deserted on July 24, 1861, at Arlington, Va.; also borne as Glennan.

Glover, Edward — Age, 22 years. Enlisted August 28, 1862, at Brooklyn to serve three years; mustered in as private, Co. D, on August 29, 1862; transferred to Co. I, Fifth Veteran Infantry, on June 2, 1864.

Glover, Robert — Age, 18 years. Enlisted April 18, 1861, at Brooklyn to serve three years; mustered in as private, Co. H, on May 23, 1861; discharged for disability on April 18, 1862, at Upton Hill, Va.

Goetz, Jacob — Age, 22 years. Enlisted at Brooklyn to serve three years; mustered in as private, Co. G, on December 15, 1863; transferred to Co. K, Fifth Veteran Infantry, on June 2, 1864; also borne as Gratz.

Goldy, Joseph — Age, 25 years. Enlisted April 28, 1861, at Brooklyn to serve three years; mustered in as private, Co. A, on May 23, 1861; transferred to Co. A, Fifth Veteran Infantry, on June 2, 1864; also borne as Joseph H. Goldy, Goldie and Goldey.

Goldsmith, William F. — Age, 35 years. Enlisted August 21, 1862, at Brooklyn to serve three years; mustered in as private, Co. C, on August 27, 1862; transferred to Co. B on November 15, 1862; discharged for disability on March 10, 1864, at De Camp Hospital, David's Island, New York Harbor; also borne as William H. Goldsmith.

Goodenough, Rollin H., Jr. — Age, 21 years. Enrolled April 25, 1861, at Brooklyn to serve three years; mustered in as second lieutenant, Co. G, on May 23, 1861; dismissed on August 31, 1863, for desertion; commissioned second lieutenant in Fourteenth on April 28, 1861, with rank from same day.

Goodison, William — Age, 31 years. Enlisted at Brooklyn to serve three years; mustered in as private, Co. C, on February 24, 1864; transferred to Co. H, Fifth Veteran Infantry, on June 2, 1864.

Gorman, Charles P. — Age, 27 years. Enlisted August 22, 1862, at Brooklyn to serve three years; mustered in as private, Co. G, on August 23, 1862; deserted on March 1, 1863, from hospital, Rappahannock, Va.

Gost, George F. — Age, 34 years. Enlisted June 30, 1861, at Brooklyn to serve three years; mustered in as private, Co. K, on

August 1, 1861; transferred to Co. G, Fifth Veteran Infantry, on June 2, 1864, as Geist.

Gottfried, Thomas — Age, 37 years. Enlisted at New York City to serve three years; mustered in as private; unassigned, March 8, 1864; no further record.

Gotthiener, Edward — Age, 38 years. Enlisted September 16, 1862, at Brooklyn to serve three years; mustered in as private; unassigned, September 18, 1862; no further record.

Gould, William — Age, 42 years. Enlisted on May 18, 1861, at Brooklyn to serve three years; mustered in as private, Co. D, on May 23, 1861; discharged for disability on April 13, 1862, at Upton Hill, Va.

Gouldrick, Thomas — Age, 22 years. Enlisted at Brooklyn to serve three years; mustered in as private, Co. G, on December 12, 1863; deserted on January 17, 1864, at Culpeper, Va.; also borne as Goldrick and McGoldrick.

Gowan, James — Age, 20 years. Enlisted at New York City to serve three years; mustered in as private; unassigned, March 11, 1864; no further record.

Graef, Francis — Age, 26 years. Enlisted April 18, 1861, at Brooklyn to serve three years; mustered in as private, Co. F, on May 23, 1861; deserted on September 24, 1861, at Upton Hill, Va.

Graen, Charles A. — Age, 18 years. Enlisted April 18, 1861, at Brooklyn to serve three years; mustered in as private, Co. C, on May 23, 1861; discharged for disability on June 16, 1861; also borne as Charles H. Gruen.

Graham, John — Age, 18 years. Enlisted at Brooklyn to serve three years; mustered in as private, Co. A, on August 20, 1862; deserted November 12, 1862.

Graham, John — Age, 25 years. Enlisted December 29, 1863, at Brooklyn to serve three years; mustered in as private, Co. G, on December 30, 1863; transferred to Co. G, Fifth Veteran Infantry, on June 2, 1864.

Graham, Thomas — Age, 23 years. Enlisted April 25, 1861, at Brooklyn to serve three years; mustered in as private, Co. G, on May 23, 1861; deserted April 25, 1863, at Rappahannock, Va.

Granville, Henry C. — Age, 21 years. Enlisted December 17, 1863, at Brooklyn to serve three years; mustered in as private; unassigned, December 23, 1863; no further record.

Gray Cyrus — Age, 34 years. Enlisted at Brooklyn to serve three years; mustered in as private, Co. F, on December 7, 1863; died of disease on January 4, 1864, at Alexandria, Va.

Greely, Samuel — Age, 38 years. Enlisted, September 23, 1861, at Brooklyn, to serve three years; mustered in as private, Co. I, September 30, 1861; deserted, August 28, 1862, at Warrenton, Va.

Green, Benjamin T. — Age, 34 years. Enlisted, June 30, 1861, at Brooklyn, to serve three years; mustered in as sergeant, Co. I, August 1, 1861; wounded in action, August 29, 1862, at Bull Run, Va.; died of his wounds, September 17, 1862, at Fairfax Seminary, Alexandria, Va.

Green, Henry S. — Age, 25 years. Enlisted, April 18, 1861, at Brooklyn, to serve three years; mustered in as private, Co. E, May 23, 1861; deserted January 29, 1862, at Upton Hill, Va.

Greenough, Charles H. — Age, 19 years. Enlisted, August 22, 1862, at Brooklyn, to serve three years; mustered in as private, Co. H, August 23, 1862; transferred to Co. I, June 1, 1863; captured in action, July 1, 1863, at Gettysburg, Pa.; paroled, no date; deserted, January 15, 1864, at Parole Camp, Annapolis, Md.

Greenslade, George D. — Age, 18 years. Enlisted, August 20, 1862, at Brooklyn, to serve three years; mustered in as private, Co. K, August 21, 1862; transferred to Co. G, Fifth Veteran Infantry, June 2, 1864, as George C. Greenlake.

Gregg, Joseph — Age, 27 years. Enlisted, April 1861, at Brooklyn, to serve three years; mustered in as private, Co. I, engineers, May 23, 1861; mustered out, August 28, 1861, at Arlington, Va.; again enlisted August 27, 1862, and mustered in as private, Co. D, August 28, 1862; transferred to Co. I, Fifth Veteran Infantry, June 2, 1864; also borne as Joseph W. Gregg.

Gregson, Joseph — Age, 22 years. Enlisted, May 18, 1861, at Brooklyn, to serve three years; mustered in as private, Co. B, May 23, 1861; deserted January 13, 1862, at Upton Hill, Va.

Gribbin, Thomas — Age, 22 years, Enlisted, May 2, 1861, at Brooklyn, to serve three years; mustered in as private, Co. G, May 23, 1861; deserted September 21, 1864, at Arlington, Va.

Griffin, William H. — Age, 19 years. Enlisted, April 18, 1861, at Brooklyn to serve three years; mustered in as private, Co. H, May 23, 1861; promoted sergeant, January 1, 1863; discharged May 8, 1863; promotion to second lieutenant, 102nd Infantry.

Griffing, James F. — Age, 23 years. Enlisted April 18, 1861, at Brooklyn, to serve three years; mustered in as private, Co. E, May 23, 1861; mustered out with company, June 6, 1864, at New York City, as James T. Griffing.

Griffith, William S. — Age, 21 years. Enlisted, April 18, 1861, at Brooklyn, to serve three years; mustered in as private, Co. A, May 23, 1861; deserted, July 21, 1863, at Washington, D.C.

Griffiths, Charles W. — Age, 20 years. Enlisted, at Brooklyn, to serve three years; mustered in as private, Co. E, October 25, 1862; transferred to Co. H, Fifth Veteran Infantry, June 2, 1864.

Griffiths, Frederick H. — Age, 23 years. Enlisted at Brooklyn, to serve three years; mustered in as private, Co. K, July 1, 1861; transferred to Co. A, July 9, 1861; promoted corporal, no date; killed July 1, 1863, at Gettysburg, Pa.

Grindell, John — Age, 32 years. Enlisted August 27, 1862, at Brooklyn to serve three years; mustered in as private, Co. D, on August 28, 1862; transferred to Co. F on November 11, 1862, to Co. K, Fifth Veteran Infantry, on June 2, 1864; prior service in Co. D, 25th Infantry.

Grogan, Philip H. — Age, 32 years. Enlisted April 18, 1861, at Brooklyn to serve three years; mustered in as first sergeant, Co. L, engineers on May 23, 1861; discharged on August 28, 1861, at New York City.

Groves, John — Age, 29 years. Enlisted at Brooklyn to serve three years; mustered in as private; unassigned, September 6, 1862; no further record.

Guinand, Peter W. — Age, 25 years. Enlisted April 18, 1861, at Brooklyn to serve three years; mustered in as private, Co. D, on May 23, 1861; appointed wagoner on July 1, 1862; mustered out with company on June 6, 1864.

Grumman, Josiah M — Age, 28 years. Enrolled April 18, 1861, at Brooklyn to serve three years; mustered in as first sergeant, Co. H, on May 23, 1861; as second lieutenant on August 5, 1861; captured while on picket, November 18, 1861, at Falls Church, Va.; paroled on February 22, 1862; mustered in as first lieutenant on February 26, 1862; wounded in action on August 29, 1862, at Manassas, Va.; died of his wounds September 9, 1862, at Washington, D.C.; commissioned second lieutenant, 14th Militia on August 12, 1861, with rank from August 5, 1861, not commissioned first lieutenant.

Gummerson, Dayton — Age, 32 years. Enlisted on May 4, 1861, at Brooklyn to serve three years; mustered in as private, Co. G, on May 23, 1861; deserted October 10, 1861, at Upton Hill, Va.

Gunson, John J. — Age, 28, years. Enlisted September 19, 1862, at Brooklyn to serve three years; mustered in as private, Co. B, on September 20, 1862; transferred to Co. I, Fifth Veteran Infantry, on June 2, 1864.

Guy, Robert W. — Age, 29 years. Enlisted

at Brooklyn to serve three years; mustered in as private, Co. F, on August 25, 1862; wounded in action on July 1, 1863, at Gettysburg, Pa.; discharged for wounds on March 30, 1864, at New York City.

Haard, Franz — Age, 20 years. Enlisted at New York City to serve three years; mustered in as private; unassigned, March 3, 1864; no further record.

Haberman, John H. — Age, 30 years. Enlisted August 20, 1862, at Brooklyn to serve three years; mustered in as private; unassigned, August 21, 1862; no further record.

Hackett, George W. — Age, 27 years. Enlisted April 18, 1861, at Brooklyn to serve three years; mustered in as private, Co. L, engineers on May 23, 1861; mustered out on August 28, 1861, at Arlington, Va.

Hagan, Peter. Age, 23 years. Enlisted April 18, 1861, at Brooklyn to serve three years; mustered in as private, Co. E on May 23, 1861; discharged for disability on July 7, 1862, at Alexandria, Va.

Hagemann, Ernst — Age, 38 years. Enlisted at Brooklyn to serve three years; mustered in as private, Co. F, on December 9, 1863; transferred to Co. K, Fifth Veteran Infantry, on June 2, 1864, also born as Hagarman and Erast Hagerman.

Hagerty, John — Age, 32 years. Enlisted May 18, 1861, at Brooklyn to serve three years; mustered in as private, Co. B, on May 23, 1861; deserted on September 23, 1861, at Arlington, Va.; also borne as Hagherty.

Haigh, Edwin D. — Age, 22 years. Enlisted April 18, 1861, at Brooklyn to serve three years; mustered in as private, Co. E, on May 23, 1861; discharged for disability on December 13, 1861, at Upton Hill, Va.

Hall, George S. — Age, 23 years. Enlisted August 20, 1861, at Brooklyn to serve three years; mustered in as private, Co. H, on August 21, 1861; wounded, no date; transferred to Co. K, Fifth Veteran Infantry, on June 2, 1864.

Hall, Joseph — Age, 19 years. Enlisted April 18, 1861, at Brooklyn to serve three years; mustered in as private, Co. C, on May 23, 1861; discharged September 11, 1861, for promotion.

Hall, Samuel — Age, 31 years. Enlisted on May 18, 1861, at Brooklyn to serve three years; mustered in as private, Co. B, on May 23, 1861; deserted August 11, 1861, at Arlington, Va.

Hallenbeck, Jacob A. — Age, 24 years. Enlisted at Hudson to serve three years; mustered in as private, Co. G, on November 30, 1861; wounded in action on July 1, 1863, at Gettysburg, Pa.; transferred to Co. A, Fifth Veteran Infantry, on June 2, 1864.

Hallorin, Patrick — Age, 18 years. Enlisted April 18, 1861, at Brooklyn to serve three years; mustered in as private, Co. A, on May 23, 1861; transferred to Co. C, Fifth Veteran Infantry, on June 2, 1864; also borne as Halloran.

Haly, Thomas — Age, 21 years. Enlisted April 18, 1861, at Brooklyn to serve three years; mustered in as private, Co. F, on May 23, 1861; promoted corporal, no date; wounded in action July 3, 1863, at Gettysburg, Pa; reenlisted as a veteran on December 31, 1863; transferred to Co. G, Fifth Veteran Infantry, on June 2, 1864.

Ham, Morris — Age, 24 years. Enlisted at Hudson to serve three years; mustered in as private, Co. G, on December 1, 1861; discharged for disability on May 23, 1862, at Falls Church Hospital, Va.; also borne as Hann.

Hamilton, George — Age, 19 years. Enlisted on May 18, 1861, at Brooklyn to serve three years; mustered in as private, Co. D, on May 23, 1861; deserted on July 26, 1861, from Camp Wood, Arlington, Va.

Hamilton, John — Age, 21 years. Enlisted on May 18, 1861, at Brooklyn to serve three years; mustered in as private, Co. B, on May 23, 1861; deserted January 30, 1862, at Upton Hill, Va.

Hamilton, John — Age, 18 years. Enlisted

April 18, 1861, at Brooklyn to serve three years; mustered in as private, Co. A, on May 23, 1861; wounded in action on August 30, 1862, at Bull Run, Va.; discharged for wounds on April 16, 1863, at Fairfax Seminary, Va.; also borne as John F. Hamilton.

Hammerer, Henry — Age, 18 years. Enlisted at Brooklyn to serve three years; mustered in as private; unassigned, December 23, 1863; no further record.

Hampton Robert J.— Age, 21 years. Enlisted at Brooklyn to serve three years; mustered in as private, Co. H, on August 21, 1862; promoted corporal, no date; transferred to Co. B, Fifth Veteran Infantry, on June 2, 1864.

Hampton, Zachias — Age, 21 years. Enlisted April 18, 1861, at Brooklyn to serve three years; mustered in as private, Co. H on May 23, 1861; promoted first sergeant on January 1, 1863; mustered out with company on June 6, 1864, at New York City, as Zaccheus Hampton.

Hancock, John — Age, 25 years. Enlisted August 27, 1862, at Brooklyn to serve three years; mustered in as private, Co. D, on August 29, 1862; transferred to Co. E on November 11, 1862; no further record.

Hancock, Samuel — Age, 18 years. Enlisted September 1, 1862, at Brooklyn to serve three years; mustered in as private, Co. E, on September 3, 1862; promoted corporal on December 1, 1863; transferred to Co. H, Fifth Veteran Infantry, on June 2, 1864.

Hanly, Larry — Age, 27 years. Enlisted April 18, 1861, at Brooklyn to serve three years; mustered in as private, Co. L, engineers on May 23, 1861; mustered out August 28, 1861, at Arlington, Va.; also borne as Lawrence Hanley.

Hannemy, Edward — Age, 40 years. Enlisted April 18, 1861, at Brooklyn to serve three years; mustered in as private, Co. F, on May 23, 1861; died of disease on April 27, 1862, at Brooklyn.

Hardiman, Francis — Age, 25 years. Enlisted April 18, 1861, at Brooklyn to serve three years; mustered in as private, Co. E, on May 23, 1861; killed in action on July 21, 1861, at Bull Run, Va.

Harley, Bernard — Age, 21 years. Enlisted December 8, 1863, at Brooklyn to serve three years; mustered in as private, Co. F, on December 14, 1863; transferred to navy on April 26, 1864; also borne as Hailey.

Harnickell, Albert G. A.— Age, 24 years. Enrolled April 18, 1861, at Brooklyn to serve three years; mustered in as captain, Co. F, May 23, 1861; discharged on September 29, 1862; commissioned captain, Fourteenth Militia, on May 4, 1861, with rank from May 2, 1861.

Harraday, Charles E.— Age, 22 years. Enlisted April 18, 1861, at Brooklyn to serve three years; mustered in as sergeant, Co. D, on May 23, 1861; promoted first sergeant on October 11, 1861; mustered out with company on June 6, 1864, at New York City.

Harraday, John — Age, 32 years. Enlisted May 18, 1861, at Brooklyn to serve three years; mustered in as corporal, Co. D, on May 23, 1861; killed in action on July 21, 1861, at Bull Run, Va.

Harris, Francis — Age, 28 years. Enlisted December 1, 1863, at Brooklyn to serve three years; mustered in as private, Co. I, on December 23, 1863; deserted on March 31, 1864, at Culpeper, Va.

Harris, Harry H.— Age, 25 years. Enlisted August 25, 1862, at Brooklyn to serve three years; mustered in as private, Co. D, on August 26, 1862; deserted on March 2, 1864, from hospital at Germantown, Pa.

Harrison, George — Age, 22 years. Enlisted December 18, 1863, at Brooklyn to serve three years; mustered in as private, Co. I, on December 21, 1863; transferred to Fifth Veteran Infantry, on June 2, 1864.

Hart, George W.— Age, 19 years, Enlisted August 23, 1862, at Brooklyn to serve three years; mustered in as private, Co. H, on August 25, 1862; transferred to Co. C, Fifth Veteran Infantry, on June 2, 1864.

Hart, John J.—Age, 25 years. Enlisted on May 18, 1861, at Brooklyn to serve three years; mustered in as corporal, Co. B, on May 23, 1861; returned to ranks, no date; deserted on February 6, 1862, at Upton Hill, Va.

Hart, Michael J.—Age, 19 years. Enlisted May 18, 1861, at Brooklyn to serve three years; mustered in as private, Co. B, on May 23, 1861; deserted on August 11, 1861, at Arlington, Va.; also borne as Michael M. Hart.

Harte, Daniel J.—Age, 18 years. Enlisted June 30, 1861, at Arlington, Va., to serve three years; mustered in as private, Co. C, on September 18, 1861; wounded in action on July 1, 1863, at Gettysburg, Pa.; discharged for disability on March 29, 1864, at Washington, D.C.

Hartney, Arthur—Age, 18 years. Enlisted at Brooklyn to serve three years; mustered in as private, Co. A, on December 6, 1864; transferred to Co. H, Fifth Veteran Infantry, on June 2, 1864.

Harty, James—Age, 19 years. Enlisted at Brooklyn to serve three years; mustered in as private, unassigned, September 29, 1862; no further record.

Harvey, Bernard—Age, 35 years. Enlisted at Brooklyn to serve three years; mustered in as private, Co. I, on December 16, 1863; transferred to Co. G, Fifth Veteran Infantry, on June 2, 1864.

Harvey, John—Age, 39 years. Enlisted at Brooklyn to serve three years; mustered in as private, Co. F, on December 9, 1863; transferred to Co. K, Fifth Veteran Infantry, on June 2, 1864.

Harway, George W.—Age, 36 years. Enlisted at Brooklyn to serve three years; mustered in as private, Co. I, on December 1, 1863; transferred to Co. G, Fifth Veteran Infantry, on June 2, 1864; also borne as George Hasway.

Haskell, Thomas F.—Age, 18 years. Enlisted April 18, 1861, at Brooklyn to serve three years; mustered in as private, Co. C, on May 23, 1861; discharged on August 14, 1861, for promotion.

Hastings, Stephen—Age, 19 years. Enlisted May 18, 1861, at Brooklyn to serve three years; mustered in as private, Co. B, on May 23, 1861; killed in action on July 21, 1861, at Bull Run, Va.

Hawkins, Joseph—Age, 28 years. Enlisted April 18, 1861, at Brooklyn to serve three years; mustered in as private, Co. A, on May 23, 1861; discharged for disability on September 19, 1861, at Arlington, Va.

Hawkins William—Age, 21 years. Enlisted at Brooklyn to serve three years; mustered in as private, Co. I, on December 18, 1863; discharged for disability on September 24, 1864, at Willets Point, New York Harbor.

Hawks, Thomas—Age, 27 years. Enlisted April 18, 1861, at Brooklyn to serve three years; mustered in as private, Co. A, on May 23, 1861; mustered out with company on June 6, 1864, at New York City.

Hawsey, Abram G.—Age, 23 years. Enlisted April 18, 1861, at Brooklyn to serve three years; mustered in as private, Co. E, on May 23, 1861; mustered out with company on June 6, 1864, at New York City as Hawney; also borne as Hawvey.

Hawthorne, Mathew—Age, 35 years. Enlisted August 29, 1862, at Brooklyn to serve three years; mustered in as private on August 30, 1862; transferred to Veterans Reserve Corps on September 30, 1863.

Hawthorne, Samuel—Age, 18 years. Enlisted August 29, 1862, at Brooklyn to serve three years; mustered in as private, Co. K, on August 30, 1862; wounded in action on July 1, 1863, at Gettysburg, Pa.; promoted corporal, no date; transferred to Co. G, Fifth Veteran Infantry, on June 2, 1864.

Hayes, John J.—Age, 37 years. Enlisted at Brooklyn to serve three years; mustered in as private; unassigned, September 4, 1862; no further record.

Hays, John—Age, 42 years. Enlisted at Brooklyn to serve three years; mustered in as private, Co. I, on December 12, 1863; transferred to Co. G, Fifth Veteran Infantry, on June 2, 1864; also borne as Hayes and Heyes.

Head Frank F.—Age, 22 years. Enlisted April 18, 1861, at Brooklyn to serve three years; mustered in as sergeant, Co. C, on May 23, 1861; wounded in action on July 21, 1861, at Bull Run, Va.; died of his wounds on July 22, 1861.

Head, Henry T.—Age, 24 years. Enrolled April 13, 1861, at Brooklyn to serve three years; mustered in as sergeant-major on May 23, 1861; promoted Adjutant on August 3, 1861; mustered in as major on July 12, 1863; mustered out with regiment on June 6, 1864, New York City; commissioned adjutant in 14th Militia on August 12, 1861, with rank from August 1, 1861.

Heald, Joseph—Age, 20 years. Enlisted at Brooklyn to serve three years; mustered in as private, Co. D, on August 25, 1862; transferred to Co. E on November 11, 1862; transferred to Veterans Reserve Corps on September 30, 1863; mustered out November 17, 1865, as of Co. B, Ninth Regiment Veterans Reserve Corps; also borne as James Heald.

Healy, Jeremiah—Age, 19 years. Enlisted at Brooklyn to serve three years; mustered in as private, Co. I, on December 16, 1863; transferred to Co. G, Fifth Veteran Infantry, on June 2, 1864; also borne as Healey and Haley.

Healy, John—Age, 20 years. Enlisted at Brooklyn to serve three years; mustered in as private unassigned, December 23, 1863; no further record.

Healy Thomas—Age, 21 years. Enlisted at Brooklyn to serve three years; mustered in as private, Co. D, August 26, 1862; wounded in action on July 1, 1863, at Gettysburg, Pa.; discharged for disability on April 9, 1864, at New York City.

Hecker, Jacob—Age, 24 years. Enlisted December 9, 1863, at Brooklyn to serve three years; mustered in as private, Co. I, on December 21, 1863; transferred to Co. G, Fifth Veteran Infantry, on June 2, 1864.

Heedless, Manuel—Age, 39 years. Enlisted at Brooklyn to serve three years; mustered in as private, Co. E, November 1, 1861; captured in action, August 29, 1862, at Groveton, Va.; paroled, no date; transferred to Co. B, Fifth Veteran Infantry, on June 2, 1864.

Hefferman, James—Age, 28 years. Enlisted July 1, 1861, at Brooklyn to serve three years; mustered in as private, Co. K, on August 1, 1861; discharged for disability on August 16, 1861, At Arlington, Va.

Hegerman, _____—Age, 21 years. Enlisted on June 30, 1861, at Brooklyn to serve three years; mustered in as private, Co. I, on August 1, 1861; promoted corporal, no date, mustered out on June 30, 1864, at New York City.

Heller, Herman—Age, 24 years. Enlisted December 16, 1863, at Brooklyn to serve three years; mustered in as private; unassigned, December 23, 1863; deserted, no date, from Hart's Island, New York Harbor.

Henderson, James—Age, 25 years. Enlisted at Brooklyn to serve three years; mustered in as private, Co. B, on January 13, 1864; transferred to Co. D, Fifth Veteran Infantry, on June 2, 1864.

Henderson, Robert—Age, 28 years. Enlisted April 18, 1861, at Brooklyn to serve three years; mustered in as private, Co. A, on May 23, 1861; promoted first sergeant on January 1, 1863; mustered in as second lieutenant on April 5, 1863; mustered out with company on June 6, 1864, at New York City as Robert D Henderson. Commissioned second lieutenant on March 17, 1863, with rank from December 24, 1862.

Henderson, Samuel—Age, 21 years. Enlisted April 18, 1861, at Brooklyn to serve three years; mustered in as private, Co. B, on May 23, 1861; mustered out with company on June 6, 1864, at New York City.

Hennigar, Charles F.—Age, 21 years. Enlisted August 26, 1862, at Brooklyn to serve three years; mustered in as private, Co. K, Fifth Veteran Infantry, on June 6, 1864.

Henson, Joseph—Age, 49 years. Enrolled on April 5, 1864, at New York City to serve three years; mustered in as chaplain on April 28, 1864; mustered out with regiment on June 6, 1864, at New York City; commissioned chaplain on April 13, 1864, with rank from April 5, 1864.

Herbert, John—Age, 27 years. Enlisted April 18, 1861, at Brooklyn to serve three years; mustered in as private, Co. F, on May 23, 1861; transferred to Co. G, on June 1, 1861; discharged for disability on June 17, 1861.

Hergunother, Michael—Age, 34 years. Enlisted at Brooklyn to serve three years; mustered in as private, Co. E, on December 30, 1863; transferred to Co. H, Fifth Veteran Infantry, on June 2, 1864; also borne as Hergenroether.

Hermance, Charles—Age, 18 years. Enlisted April 25, 1861, at Brooklyn to serve three years; mustered in as private, Co. G, on May 23, 1861; discharged September 22, 1862, at Washington, D.C., for promotion to second lieutenant, 158th Infantry.

Hermance, Fraser A.—Age, 30 years. Enlisted April 25, 1861, at Brooklyn to serve three years. mustered in as corporal, Co. G, on May 23, 1861; promoted sergeant, no date; first sergeant, March 1, 1862; mustered out with company on June 2, 1864, at New York City.

Hess, Frederick—Age, 41 years. Enlisted at Brooklyn to serve three years; mustered in as private, Co. A, on December 19, 1863; discharged for disability on April 3, 1864, at Culpeper Court House, Va.

Hewstler, Joseph—Age, 20 years. Enlisted at Brooklyn to serve three years; mustered in as private, Co. I, on January 11, 1864; transferred to Fifth Veteran Infantry, on June 2, 1864; also borne as Hewiller.

Hickman, George W.—Age, 37 years. Enlisted July 1, 1861, at Brooklyn to serve three years; mustered in as private, Co. I, on August 4, 1861; wounded in action on September 17, 1862, at Antietam, Md.; died of his wounds on September 18, 1862.

Hicks, Edward F.—Age, 21 years. Enlisted May 18, 1861, at Brooklyn to serve three years; mustered in as private, Co. D, on May 23, 1861; deserted February 4, 1862, from Camp Marion, Upton Hill, Va.

Hicks, Joseph H.—Age, 21 years. Enlisted September 6, 1862, at Brooklyn to serve three years; mustered in as private, Co. H, on September 8, 1862, transferred to Co. I, on June 1, 1863; wounded in action on July 1, 1863, at Gettysburg, Pa.; transferred to Co. G, Fifth Veteran Infantry, on June 2, 1864.

Higginbothom, Richard, D.—Age, 23 years. Enlisted June 30, 1861, at Brooklyn to serve three years; mustered in as private, Co. I, July 1, 1861; killed in action on July 21, 1861, at Bull Run, Va.; also borne as Richmond D. Higginbotham.

Higginbotham, Samuel—Age, 19 years. Enlisted April 18, 1861, at Brooklyn to serve three years; mustered in as private, Co. D, on May 23, , 1861; promoted corporal on March 1, 1862; sergeant on November 1, 1862; re-enlisted as a veteran on February 12, 1864; transferred to Fifth Veteran Infantry, on June 2, 1864.

Higgins, Patrick—Age, 44 years. Enlisted at Brooklyn to serve three years; mustered in as private, Co. I, on December 28, 1863; transferred to Co. G, Fifth Veteran Infantry, on June 2, 1864; prior service in Co. K, Thirty-First New Jersey Infantry.

Higgins, Richard—Age, 18 years. Enlisted at Brooklyn to serve three years; mustered in as private, Co. B, on January 23, 1864; transferred to Co. I, Fifth Veteran Infantry, June 2, 1864.

Hilbert, George — Age, 26 years. Enlisted at Brooklyn to serve three years; mustered in as private, Co. B, on January 11, 1864; transferred to Co. I, Fifth Veteran Infantry, on June 2, 1864.

Hill William H. — Age, 21 years. Enlisted April 18, 1861, at Brooklyn to serve three years; mustered in as sergeant, Co. E, May 23, 1861; discharged August 18, 1861, for promotion to second lieutenant, Co. C, Fifth New Jersey Infantry.

Hilton George — Age, 25 years. Enlisted April 25, 1861, at Brooklyn to serve three years; mustered in as private, Co. G, on May 23, 1861; deserted on January 22, 1862, at Upton Hill, Va.

Hines, Charles — Age, 18 years, Enlisted April, 18, 1861, at Brooklyn to serve three years; mustered in as private, Co. H, on May 23, 1861; wounded in action on July 21, 1861, at Bull Run, Va.; discharged for wounds on August 3, 1861, at Arlington, Va.; also borne as Hines.

Hines, Francis — Age, 28 years. Enlisted at Brooklyn to serve three years; mustered in as private; unassigned, March 21, 1864; no further record.

Hingle, Henry W. — Age, 21 years. Enlisted April 18, 1861, at Brooklyn to serve three years; mustered in as private, Co. E, on May 23, 1861; transferred to Veterans Reserve Corps on July 1, 1863.

Hingle, Louis L. — Age, 23 years. Enlisted April 18, 1861, at Brooklyn to serve three years; mustered in as private, Co. E, on May 23, 1861; deserted January 10, 1863, from hospital, Washington, D.C.

Hingston, Richard — Age, 36 years. Enlisted September 9, 1862, at Brooklyn to serve three years; mustered in as private; unassigned, September 10, 1862; no further record.

Hingston, William — Age, 23 years. Enlisted September 4, 1862, at Brooklyn to serve three years; mustered in as private; unassigned, September 5, 1862; no further record.

Hinkley, George H. — Age, 26 years. Enlisted September 9, 1862, at Brooklyn to serve three years; mustered in as private; unassigned, September 10, 1862; no further record.

Hoagland, Edward — Age, 25 years. Enlisted April 18, 1861, at Brooklyn to serve three years; mustered in as private, Co. C, on May 23, 1861; mustered out on June 14, 1864, at New York City.

Hodges, William A. — Age, 24 years. Enlisted June 30, 1861, at Brooklyn to serve three years; mustered in as private, Co. I, on August 1, 1861; transferred to Co. G, Fifth Veteran Infantry, on June 2, 1864; also borne as Hodge.

Hoey, George W. — Age, 25 years. Enlisted April 18, 1861, at Brooklyn to serve three years; mustered in as private, Co. H, on May 23, 1861; deserted on January 25, 1862, at Upton Hill, Va.

Hoge, Moses — Age, 25 years. Enlisted at New York City to serve three years; mustered in as private, Co. I, on March 1, 1862; discharged for disability on June 13, 1862, at Washington, D.C.; also borne as Hogue.

Holbrook, Asa — Age, 20 years. Enlisted April 18, 1861, at Brooklyn to serve three years; mustered in as private, Co. F, on May 23, 1861; promoted corporal on September 14, 1862; sergeant on February 1, 1863; wounded in action on April 29, 1863, at Reynold's Crossing, Va.; mustered out on June 14, 1864, at New York City; also borne as Asa A. Holbrook.

Holmes, Henry — Age, 28 years. Enlisted May 18, 1861, at Brooklyn to serve three years; mustered in as sergeant, Co. D, on May 23, 1861; wounded and captured on July 21, 1861, at Bull Run, Va., escaped from Richmond, Va., no date, no further record.

Holmes, Reuben — Age, 25 years. Enlisted July 1, 1861, at Brooklyn to serve three years; mustered in as corporal, Co. K, on August 1, 1861; deserted April 14, 1862, near Bristoe Station, Va.

Holzapfel, John—Age, 27 years. Enlisted August 26, 1862, at Brooklyn to serve three years; mustered in as private, Co. E, on August 27, 1862; transferred to Co. H, Fifth Veteran Infantry, in June 2, 1864.

Homan, Selah H.—Age, 40 years. Enlisted at Brooklyn to serve three years; mustered in as private, Co. F, December 7, 1863; transferred to navy on March 1, 1864; also borne as Silah H. Herman.

Homeston, Joseph M.—Age, 30 years. Enrolled April 18, 1861, at Brooklyn to serve three years; mustered in as surgeon on May 23, 1861; discharged on October 13, 1862; commission surgeon, 14th Militia, on February 26, 1861, with rank from February 1, 1861.

Hooper, William H.—Age, 27 years. Enlisted September 16, 1862, at Brooklyn to serve three years; mustered in as private, Co. D, on Sept, 17, 1862; transferred to Veteran Reserve Corps on September 30, 1863.

Horan, John H.—Age, 24 years. Enlisted April 18, 1861, at Brooklyn to serve three years; mustered in as private, Co. F, on May 23, 1861; promoted corporal on September 14, 1862; missing in action on July 1, 1863, at Gettysburg, Pa.; returned October 8, 1863; promoted sergeant on January 12, 1864; mustered out on June 14, 1864, at New York City; also borne as Horne.

Horning, Gotlieb—Age, 28 years. Enlisted December 12, 1863, at Brooklyn to serve three years; mustered in as private, Co. I, on December 23, 1863; transferred to Veterans Reserve Corps on February 15, 1864; mustered out August 23, 1865, at Washington, D.C., as of Eight Company, Second Battalion, Veteran Reserve Corps; also borne as Harming.

Horton, Alburtis A.—Age, 29 years. Enlisted September 3, 1862, at Brooklyn to serve three years; mustered in as private, Co. H, on September 3, 1862; wounded in action on July 2, 1863, at Gettysburg, Pa.; mustered out on May 26, 1865, at Satterlee Hospital, Philadelphia, Pa.; also borne as Alburtis F. Horton.

Horton, Michael—Age, 21 years. Enlisted April 25, 1861, at Brooklyn to serve three years; mustered in as private, Co. G, on May 23, 1861; mustered out with company on June 6, 1864, at New York City; also borne as Holton.

Hotte, Charles—Age, 25 years, Enlisted April 18, 1861, at Brooklyn to serve three years; mustered in as private, Co. L, engineers on May 23, 1861; mustered out on August 28, 1861, Arlington Va.; also borne as Charles J. Holt.

House, Alfred—Age, 28 years. Enrolled at Washington, D.C., to serve three years; mustered in as assistant surgeon on December 31, 1862; discharged for disability on August 7, 1863; commissioned assistant surgeon on December 5, 1862, with rank from October 28, 1862.

Hovey, Hanford A.—Age, 26 years. Enlisted at Brooklyn to serve three years; mustered in as private, Co. B, on January 21, 1862; promoted corporal no date; transferred to Co. H, Fifth Veteran Infantry, on June 2, 1864.

Howard, Henry—Age, 21 years. Enlisted September 13, 1862, at Brooklyn to serve three years; mustered in as private; unassigned, September 15, 1862; no further record.

Howard, John B.—Age, 30 years. Enlisted April 18, 1861, at Brooklyn to serve three years; mustered in as first lieutenant, Co. K, on May 23, 1861, discharged June 30, 1862, for promotion to captain, and assistant quartermaster, U.S. Volunteers; not commissioned first lieutenant.

Howell, William G.—Age, 21 years. Enlisted December 10, 1963, at Brooklyn to serve three years; mustered in as private, Co. I, on December 13, 1863; transferred to Co. G, Fifth Veteran Infantry, on June 2, 1864.

Howick, James—Age, 21 years. Enlisted July 1, 1861, at Brooklyn to serve three years; mustered in as private, Co. I, on August 1, 1861; deserted on April 7, 1863, at Belle Plains, Va.

Howland, Frank A.—Age, 20 years. Enlisted April 18, 1861, at Brooklyn to serve three years; mustered in as private, Co. C, on May 23, 1861; discharged September 2, 1862, for promotion to second lieutenant, Co. K, Forty-Eighth Infantry; also borne as Albert F. Howland.

Hubbard, Ashbil—Age, 28 years. Enlisted December 15, 1863, at Brooklyn to serve three years; mustered in as private, Co. I, on December 21, 1863; transferred to Co. G, Fifth Veteran Infantry, on June 2, 1864.

Hubbleman, John—Age, 30 years. Enlisted at Brooklyn to serve three years; mustered in as private, Co. G, on August 18, 1862; discharged December 22, 1862, at Patent Office Hospital, Washington, D.C., also born as Haveman, and Haverman.

Hudson, George—Age, 23 years. Enlisted April 18, 1861, at Brooklyn to serve three years; mustered in as private, Co. C, on May 23, 1861; discharged November 27, 1861.

Huestler, Joseph—Age, 20 years. Enlisted December 11, 1863, at Brooklyn to serve three years; mustered in as private; unassigned, December 23, 1863; no further record.

Hughes, George G.—Age, 28 years. Enlisted at Brooklyn to serve three years; mustered in as private; unassigned, September 5, 1862; no further record.

Hull, Andrew—Age, 36 years. Enlisted April 18, 1861, at Brooklyn to serve three years; mustered in as private, Company of Engineers, on May 23, 1861; mustered out on August 28, 1861, at Arlington Va.; also borne as Addison Hall.

Hulse, Charles L.—Age, 22 years. Enlisted, May 18, 1861, at Brooklyn, to serve three years; discharged, February 27, 1864, at Washington, D.C.

Hunnegan, Jacob—Age, 37 years. Enlisted, December 12, 1863, at Brooklyn to serve three years; mustered in as private. Co. I, December 21, 1863; transferred to Co. G, Fifth Veteran Infantry, June 2, 1864; also borne as Hannegan, Honneger and Honnegger.

Hunter, Thomas H.—Age, 22 years. Enlisted, April 18, 1861, at Brooklyn, to serve three years; mustered in as private, Co. A, May 23, 1861; deserted, October 1, 1861, at Upton Hill, Va.

Hussey, Richard—Age, 20 years. Enlisted, August 20, 1862, at Brooklyn, to serve three years; mustered in as private, Co. G, August 21, 1862; transferred to Veteran Reserve Corps, November 6, 1863.

Huttimier, Frederick—Age, 35 years. Enlisted, April 18, 1861, at Brooklyn, to serve three years; mustered in as private, Co. G, May 23, 1861; transferred to Veteran Reserve Corps, July 1, 1863; also borne as Huttamier and Huttemier.

Hyde, Gordian K., Jr.—Age, 19 years. Enlisted, September 3, 1862, at Brooklyn, to serve three years; mustered in as private, Co. D, September 4, 1862; transferred to Co. H, Fifth Veteran Infantry, June 2, 1864.

Hyde, Henry M.—Age, 27 years. Enlisted, April 18, 1861, at Brooklyn, to serve three years; mustered in as private, Co. C, May 23, 1861; promoted corporal, no date; discharged, November 12, 1861.

Heyer, Joseph G.—Age, 32 years. Enlisted, April 18, 1861, at Brooklyn, to serve three years; mustered in as first sergeant, Co. A, May 23, 1861; discharged for disability, June 18, 1861; also borne as Hyler.

Hyson, Edward—Age, 30 years. Enlisted August 30, 1862, at Brooklyn to serve three years; mustered in as private, Co. G, August 21, 1862; missing in action on July 2, 1863, at Gettysburg, Pa; returned October 7, 1863; transferred to Co. K, Fifth Veteran Infantry, on June 2, 1864.

Ilsley, Silas A.—Age, 21 years. Enrolled April 18, 1861, at Brooklyn, to serve three years; mustered in as corporal, Co. E, on May 23, 1861; as second lieutenant, Co.

I, on August 1, 1861; discharged on February 17, 1862, for promotion to first lieutenant, Co. I, Fifty-Sixth Infantry; not commissioned second lieutenant.

Inskip, Joseph S.—Age, 44 years. Enrolled, April 18, 1861, at Brooklyn to serve three years; mustered in as chaplain, May 23, 1861; discharged on July 21, 1862; commissioned chaplain in Fourteenth Militia on June 29, 1861, with rank from May 10, 1861.

Inyard, Nicholas, Jr.—Age, 21 years. Enlisted, May 18, 1861, at Brooklyn, to serve three years; mustered in as private, Co. D, on May 23, 1861; deserted November 21, 1861, from Camp Marion, Upton Hill, Va.

Ireland, Patrick—Age, 22 years. Enlisted April 18, 1861, at Brooklyn, to serve three years; mustered in as private, Co. A, on May 23, 1861; missing in action on July 1, 1863; returned to company on October 8, 1863; mustered out with company on June 6, 1864, at New York City.

Irving, William—Age, 30 years. Enlisted at Brooklyn, to serve three years; mustered in as private, Co. E, December 31, 1863; transferred to Co. B, Fifth Veteran Infantry, on June 2, 1864.

Isler, Ludwig—Age, 19 years. Enlisted at New York City, to serve three years; mustered in as private, Co. K, July 26, 1861; killed in action on July 1, 1863, at Gettysburg, Pa.; also borne as Ludwig Yzler.

Ivers, James—Age, 22 years. Enlisted April 18, 1861, at Brooklyn, to serve three years; mustered in as private, Co. A, on May 23, 1861; killed in action on July 1, 1863, at Gettysburg, Pa.; also borne as Ireno.

Jackson, John—Age, 22 years. Enlisted, May 18, 1861, at Brooklyn, to serve three years; mustered in as private, Co. D, on May 23, 1861; discharged for disability on August 12, 1862, at hospital, Washington, D.C.

Jacob, Louis—Age, 26 years. Enlisted, April 18, 1861, at Brooklyn, to serve three years; mustered in as private, Co. H, May 23, 1861; discharged April 23, 1864, at Fort Wood, New York Harbor.

Jacobowski, Herman—Age, 26 years. Enlisted at Brooklyn, to serve three years; mustered in as private, Co. F, on December 1, 1863; wounded in action on May 8–14, 1864, at Spotsylvania, Va.; died of his wounds on May 22, 1864, at Emory Hospital, Washington, D.C.

Jacobs, Nathaniel—Age, 44 years. Enlisted at Brooklyn to serve three years; mustered in as private, Co. D, October 1, 1862; wounded in action on May 10, 1864, at Laurel Hill, Va.; transferred to Co. I, Fifth Veteran Infantry, on June 2, 1864; also borne as Nathaniel Jacobs and Jacobus.

Jacobus, Thomas H.—Age, 25 years. Enlisted, August 19, 1862, at Brooklyn, to serve three years; mustered in as private, Co. D, on August 20, 1862; discharged for disability on January 5, 1863, at New York City.

Jacoby, Gotthardt—Age, 24 years. Enlisted, May 10, 1861, at Brooklyn, to serve three years; mustered in as private, Co. G, May 23, 1861; discharged for disability on July 27, 1861, at Arlington, Va.

Jauncey, Frederick—Age, 19 years. Enlisted on September 5, 1862, at Brooklyn, to serve three years; mustered in as private, Co. C, on September 6, 1862; died of disease on February 5, 1863, at Baltimore, Md.

Jauncey, James—Age, 23 years. Enlisted on September 5, 1862, at Brooklyn, to serve three years, mustered in as private, Co. B, on September 6, 1862; wounded in action on July 1, 1863, at Gettysburg, Pa.; discharged for wounds on April 12, 1864, at hospital, David's Island, New York Harbor.

Jelly, James—Age, 21 years. Enlisted, April 18, 1861, at Brooklyn, to serve three years; mustered in as private, Co. A, on May 23, 1861; deserted July 25, 1861, at Arlington, Va.

Jelly, John—Age, 19 years. Enlisted April

18, 1861, at Brooklyn to serve three years; mustered in as private, Co. H, on May 23, 1861; promoted corporal on July 1, 1863; mustered out on March 13, 1865, at Ladies Home Hospital, New York City, as John H. Jelly.

Jenkins, John — Age, 27 years. Enlisted June 30, 1861, at Brooklyn to serve three years; mustered in as sergeant, Co. I, on August 1, 1861; returned to the ranks on February 7, 1862; mustered out on July 13, 1864, at New York City.

Jennings, William P. — Age, 41 years. Enlisted August 22, 1862, at Brooklyn to serve three years; mustered in as private, Co. D, on August 23, 1862; discharged for disability on March 28, 1863, at hospital, West Philadelphia, Pa.

Jochum, John — Age, 25 years. Enlisted August 20, 1862, at Brooklyn to serve three years; mustered in as private, Co. B, on August 21, 1862; wounded in action on July 1, 1863, at Gettysburg, Pa.; transferred to Co. I, Fifth Veteran Infantry, on June 2, 1864.

Johnson, Albert — Age, 19 years. Enlisted on May 18, 1861, at Brooklyn to serve three years; mustered in as private, Co. D, on May 23, 1861; deserted November 10, 1861, from Camp Marion, Upton Hill, Va.; also borne as Alfred Johnson.

Johnson, George — Age, 23 years. Enlisted at Brooklyn to serve three years; mustered in as private; unassigned, November 24, 1862, no further record.

Johnson, John P. — Age, 42 years. Enlisted October 1, 1861, at Brooklyn to serve three years; mustered in as musician in band, October 24, 1861; discharged on August 17, 1862, at Camp Halstead, Va.

Johnson, Richard — Age, 20 years. Enlisted May 18, 1861, at Brooklyn to serve three years; mustered in as private, Co. B, on May 23, 1861; deserted on August 10, 1862, at Falmouth, Va.

Johnson, Robert H. — Age, 22 years. Enlisted at Brooklyn to serve three years; mustered in as private, Co. H, September 29, 1862; mustered out on May 23, 1865, at Frederick, Md.

Johnston, Hugh — Age, 31 years. Enlisted at Brooklyn to serve three years; mustered in as private, Co. D, on September 12, 1862; deserted on September 10, 1863, from Camp Parole, Westchester, Pa.

Jones, George B. — Age, 34 years. Enlisted April 18, 1861, at Brooklyn to serve three years; mustered in as sergeant, Co. A, on May 23, 1861; promoted quartermaster-sergeant the same date; discharged for disability on August 24, 1861, at Arlington, Va.

Jones, George C. — Age, 35 years. Enlisted September 25, 1862, at Brooklyn to serve three years; mustered in as private, Co. E, on September 26, 1862; deserted on March 24, 1863, from hospital, Windmill Point, Va.

Jones, H. Sergent — Age, 19 years. Enlisted April, 18, 1861, at Brooklyn to serve three years; mustered in as private, Co. F, on May 23, 1861; promoted sergeant-major on January 11, 1864; mustered out with regiment on June 6, 1864, at New York City; also borne as Henry S.

Jones, Jeptha A. — Age, 36 years. Enrolled on May 18, 1861, at Brooklyn to serve three years; mustered in as first lieutenant, Co. D, on May 23, 1861; wounded in action on July 21, 1861, at Bull Run, Va.; discharged September 7, 1861; commissioned first lieutenant, 14th Militia on June 29, 1861, with rank from May 15, 1861.

Jones, Josiah — Age, 16 years. Enlisted on May 18, 1861, at Brooklyn to serve three years; mustered in as musician, Co. B, on May 23, 1861; deserted on January 31, 1862, at Upton Hill, Va.

Jones, Philip W. — Age, 27 years. Enlisted at Brooklyn to serve three years; mustered in as private, Co. B, on December 11, 1861; killed in action on August 30, 1862, at Gainesville, Va.

Jones William — Age, 25 years. Enlisted at Brooklyn to serve three years; mustered in as private; unassigned, October 18, 1862; no further record.

Jones, William — Age, 19 years. Enlisted at Brooklyn to serve three years; mustered in as private; unassigned, December 12, 1863; deserted, no date, from Hart's Island, New York Harbor.

Jones William H. — Age, 20 years. Enlisted August 29, 1862, at Brooklyn to serve three years; mustered in as private, Co. C, on September 3, 1862; discharged for disability on May 26, 1863, at Philadelphia, Pa.

Jordan, Frederick — Age, 30 years. Enlisted August 13, 1862, at Brooklyn to serve three years; mustered in as private, Co. F, on August 14, 1862; died of disease on September 17, 1863, at Brooklyn.

Jordan, James H. — Age, 23 years. Enrolled April 18, 1861, at Brooklyn to serve three years; mustered in as second lieutenant, Co. I on May 23, 1861; discharged on August 2, 1861; enrolled and mustered in as captain on September 29, 1862; discharged January 13, 1863; commissioned second lieutenant, 14th Militia on May 4, 1861, with rank from May 2, 1861; original captain, October 24, 1862, with rank from September 29, 1862.

Jordan, Robert B. — Age, 34 years. Enrolled April 18, 1861, at Brooklyn to serve three years; mustered in as captain, Co. A, on May 23, 1861; as on December 25, 1862; as lieutenant-colonel on May 12, 1863; dismissed September 2, 1863; reappointed and mustered in as lieutenant-colonel on March 6, 1864; mustered out with regiment on June 6, 1864, at New York City; commissioned captain in 14th Militia on February 26, 1861, with rank from October 24, 1860; major on March 17, 1863, with rank from December 24, 1862; lieutenant-colonel on June 23, 1863, with rank from May 12, 1863.

Jordan, Thomas — Age, 36 years. Enlisted April 18, 1861, at Brooklyn to serve three years; mustered in as private, Co. L, engineers on May 23, 1861; mustered out August 28, 1861, Arlington, Va.

Joslin, Chauncy C. — Age, 49 years. Enrolled July 13, 1863, at Frankstown, Md., to serve three years; mustered in as assistant surgeon on August 7, 1863; discharged for disability on January 7, 1864; commissioned assistant surgeon on July 23, 1863, with rank from July 6, 1863.

Jourdan, James — Age, 30 years. Enrolled April 18, 1861, at Brooklyn to serve three years; mustered in as major on May 23, 1861; discharged on January 2, 1862, for promotion to lieutenant-colonel 56th Infantry; commissioned major, 14th militia, on April 27, 1861, with rank from April 19, 1861.

Jourdan William H. — Age, 19 years. Enlisted at Brooklyn to serve three years; mustered in as private, Co. E, on July 19, 1861; discharged for disability on August 27, 1861.

Judd, Charles D. — Age, 19 years. Enlisted April 18, 1861, at Brooklyn to serve three years; mustered in as private, Co. C, on May 23, 1861; discharged on February 27, 1862, for promotion to second lieutenant, Co. F, Second Artillery; also borne as Charles P. Judd.

Judge, Nicholas — Age, 26 years. Enlisted at Brooklyn to serve three years; mustered in as private, Co. F, on February 22, 1862; discharged for disability on April 24, 1862.

Jukes, Henry — Age, 23 years. Enlisted April 18, 1861, at Brooklyn to serve three years; mustered in as private, Co. B, on May 23, 1861; wounded in action on July 21, 1861, at Bull Run, Va.; discharged for wounds on December 13, 1861, at Upton Hill, Va.

Kalt, Hyron — Age, 25 years. Enrolled April 18, 1861, at Brooklyn to serve three years; mustered in as second lieutenant, engineers, on May 23, 1861; mustered out on August 28, 1861, at Arlington, Va., not commissioned second lieutenant.

Kammorar, Henry—Age, 18 years. Enlisted December 14, 1863, at Brooklyn to serve three years; mustered in as private, Co. I, on December 21, 1863; transferred to Co. G, Fifth Veteran Infantry, on June 2, 1864; also borne as Kamerer and Keemmerer.

Kane, Thomas—Age, 21 years. Enlisted August 25, 1862, at Brooklyn to serve three years; mustered in as private, Co. A, on August 26, 1862; missing in action on July 1, 1863, at Gettysburg, Pa.; returned October 8, 1863; transferred to Co. A, Fifth Veteran Infantry, on June 2, 1864.

Kanzer, Christian—Age, 38 years. Enlisted on July 31, 1861, at Brooklyn to serve three years; mustered in as private, Co. I, on August 4, 1861; transferred to Co. K, Fifth Veteran Infantry, on June 2, 1864; also borne as Kenzer and Kerger.

Kaufman, Adam—Age, 23 years. Enlisted August 29, 1862, at Brooklyn to serve three years; mustered in as private, Co. G, August 30, 1862; discharged for disability on October 15, 1862, near Sharpsburg, Md.

Kaufman, Peter—Age, 22 years. Enlisted August 29, 1862, at Brooklyn to serve three years; mustered in as private, Co. G, on August 30, 1862; transferred to Co. K, Fifth Veteran Infantry, on June 2, 1864.

Kearsing, Ambrose W.—Age, 19 years. Enlisted at Brooklyn to serve three years; mustered in as private, Co. K, on August 23, 1862; discharged for disability on February 18, 1863, at Washington, D.C.

Kearsing, Edward F.—Age, 27 years. Enlisted August 29, 1862, at Brooklyn to serve three years; mustered in as private, Co. K, on August 30, 1862; discharged for disability December 1862, at Washington D.C.

Keating, David—Age, 23 years. Enlisted on May 18, 1861, at Brooklyn to serve three years; mustered in as private, Co. B, on May 23, 1861; discharged for disability on May 20, 1862, from hospital, Washington D.C.

Keating, James—Age, 27 years. Enlisted April 18, 1861, at Brooklyn to serve three years; mustered in as private, Co. A, on May 23, 1861; promoted corporal on May 1, 1863; mustered out with company on June 6, 1864, at New York City; also borne as Keaton.

Keck, August—Age, 19 years. Enlisted June 30, 1861, at Brooklyn to serve three years; mustered in as private, Co. K, on July 1, 1861; promoted corporal on April, 1863; returned to ranks, no date; re-enlisted as a veteran on January 4, 1864; transferred to Co. H, Fifth Veteran Infantry, on June 2, 1864; also borne as Kick and Kuck.

Keenan, Andrew—Age, 20 years. Enlisted April 18, 1861, at Brooklyn to serve three years; mustered in as private, Co. F, on May 23, 1861; discharged for disability on January 25, 1863, at Convalescent Camp, Va.

Keenan, James—Age, 21 years. Enlisted August 23, 1862, at Brooklyn to serve three years; mustered in as private, Co. D, on August 25, 1862; transferred to Co. H, Fifth Veteran Infantry, on June 2, 1864.

Keenan, John F.—Age, 19 years. Enlisted April 18, 1861, at Brooklyn to serve three years; mustered in as private, Co. F, on May 23, 1861; deserted on September 1, 1861, at Upton Hill, Va.

Keenan, William J.—Age, 19 years. Enlisted July 1, 1861, at Brooklyn to serve three years; mustered in as private, Co. G, on July 5, 1861; deserted November 9, 1861, at Upton Hill, Va.

Kehoe, Daniel—Age, 24 years. Enlisted June 30, 1861, at Brooklyn to serve three years; mustered in as private, Co. K, on August 1, 1861; deserted on February 23, 1863, on expiration of furlough.

Kehoe, Joseph—Age, 29 years. Enlisted July 1, 1861, at Brooklyn to serve three years; mustered in as private, Co. K, on

August 1, 1861; promoted corporal on April 1, 1863; re-enlisted as a veteran on January 4, 1864; transferred to Co. G, Fifth Veteran Infantry, on June 2, 1864.

Kellogg, Lewis M.—Age, 28 years. Enlisted August 21, 1862, at Brooklyn to serve three years; mustered in as private, Co. B, on August 22, 1862; transferred to Co. I Fifth Veteran Infantry, on June 2, 1864; also borne as Louis M. Kellogg.

Kells, Francis—Age, 20 years. Enlisted August 23, 1862, at Brooklyn to serve three years; mustered in as private, Co. E, on August 25, 1862; discharged on October 31, 1863.

Kelly, Charles—Age, 19 years. Enlisted April 18, 1861, at Brooklyn to serve three years; mustered in as private, Co. F on May 23, 1861; killed in action on July 21, 1861, at Bull Run, Va.

Kelly George W.—Age, 28 years. Enlisted June 30, 1861, at Brooklyn to serve three years; mustered in as private, Co. I, on August 1, 1861; deserted August 26, 1862, from hospital in Brooklyn.

Kelly, Michael, Age, 21 years. Enlisted April 18, 1861, at Brooklyn to serve three years; mustered in as private, Co. A, on May 23, 1861; wounded in action on July 21, 1861, at Bull Run, Va.; discharged for wounds on January 11, 1863, at Alexandria, Va.

Kelly, Robert—Age, 22 years. Enlisted April 18, 1861, at Brooklyn to serve three years; mustered in as private, Co. A, on May 23, 1861; discharged for disability on July 27, 1861, at Arlington, Va.

Kelly Thomas—Age, 45 years. Enlisted at Troy to serve three years; mustered in as private, Co. C, on February 24, 1864; died of disease on March 21, 1864, at Albany, N.Y.

Kelly, William—Age, 27 years. Enlisted August 22, 1862, at Brooklyn to serve three years; mustered in as private, Co. F, on August 23, 1862; deserted on December 12, 1862, at Brooks Station, Va.

Kelsey, William H.—Age, 19 years. Enlisted August 23, 1862, at Brooklyn to serve three years; mustered in as private, Co. H, on August 25, 1862; wounded in action on September 17, 1862, at Antietam, Md.; discharged for wounds on October 7, 1862, at Frederick City, Md.

Kelty, Simon—Age, 23 years. Enlisted May 18, 1861, at Brooklyn to serve three years; mustered in as private, Co. B, on May 23, 1861; discharged for disability on January 10, 1863, at Providence, R.I.

Kennedy, George H.—Age, 21 years. Enlisted at Brooklyn to serve three years; mustered in as private, Co. A, on August 14, 1862; deserted on November 10, 1862.

Kent, Edward B.—Age, 24 years. Enlisted October 9, 1861, at Brooklyn to serve three years; mustered in as private, Co. D, on October 10, 1861; transferred to Co. H, Fifth Veteran Infantry, on June 2, 1864.

Kerby, Charles—Age, 32 years. Enlisted April 18, 1861, at Brooklyn to serve three years; mustered in as first sergeant, Co. E, on May 23, 1861; discharged for disability on June 18, 1861.

Kerchieffer, Ernest—Age, 31 years. Enlisted April 18, 1861, at Brooklyn to serve three years; mustered in as private Co. E on May 23, 1861; killed in action on July 21, 1861, at Bull Run, Va.; also borne as Kerschoffer.

Kernan, Barnard—Age, 31 years. Enlisted at Brooklyn to serve three years; mustered in as private, Co. G, on August 21, 1862; wounded in action on July 2, 1863, at Gettysburg, Pa.; transferred to Co. G, Fifth Veteran Infantry, on June 2, 1864; also borne as Barney and Bernard Keenan.

Kerr, Peter—Age, 34 years. Enlisted at Brooklyn to serve three years; mustered in as private, Co. B, on January 28, 1864; transferred to Fifth Veteran Infantry, on June 2, 1864.

Kershaw, William E.—Age, 19 years. Enlisted April 18, 1861, at Brooklyn to serve three years; mustered in as private, Co. E, on May 23, 1861; wounded in action on July 1, 1863, at Gettysburg, Pa.; discharged for disability on December 10, 1863, at Providence, R.I., also born as William A. and E. Carshaw.

Kiaser, Charles — Age, 19 years. Enlisted August 26, 1862, at Brooklyn to serve three years; mustered in as private, Co. D, on August 27, 1862; wounded in action on July 1, 1863, at Gettysburg, Pa.; transferred to Co. K, Fifth Veteran Infantry, on June 2, 1864; also borne as Kaiser.

Kiernan, Patrick — Age, 18 years. Enlisted at Brooklyn to serve three years; mustered in as private, Co. I, on December 17, 1863; transferred to Co. G, Fifth Veteran Infantry, on June 2, 1864.

Kimmey, Jacob — Age, 45 years. Enlisted July 1, 1861, at Brooklyn to serve three years; mustered in as private, Co. K, on August 1, 1861; died of disease on December 19, 1861, at Upton Hill, Va.

Kinchlow, Thomas — Age, 21 years. Enlisted at Brooklyn to serve three years; mustered in as private; unassigned, December 23, 1863; no further record.

King, James M. — Age, 21 years. Enlisted April 18, 1861, at Brooklyn to serve three years; mustered in as private, Co. E, on May 23, 1861; deserted on January 30, 1862, at Upton Hill, Va.

King, Joseph — Age, 27 years. Enlisted April 18, 1861, at Brooklyn to serve three years; mustered in as private, Co. C, on May 23, 1861; transferred to Co. K, Fifth Veteran Infantry, on June 2, 1864.

Kirchner, Heinrich — Age, 19 years. Enlisted at Brooklyn to serve three years; mustered in as private, Co. F, on December 8, 1863; transferred to Co. A, Fifth Veteran Infantry, on June 2, 1864; also borne as Kierchmed and Kirchmea.

Kissell, John — Age, 22 years. Enlisted at Brooklyn to serve three years; mustered in as private, Co. F, on November 30, 1863; deserted October 30, 1864, from De Camp Hospital, David's Island, New York Harbor.

Klassman, George — Age, 40 years. Enlisted September 8, 1862, at Brooklyn to serve three years; mustered in as private, Co. H, on September 13, 1862; wounded in action on July 1, 1863, at Gettysburg, Pa.; transferred to Co. K, Fifth Veteran Infantry, on June 2, 1864; also borne as Klassiman.

Knower, Charles A. — Age, 22 years. Enlisted September 5, 1861, at Brooklyn to serve three years; mustered in as private, Co. D, on September 13, 1861; promoted corporal on November 1, 1862; discharged for disability on February 6, 1863, from hospital, Washington, D.C.

Knowles, Henry B. — Age, 38 years. Enlisted April 18, 1861, at Brooklyn to serve three years; mustered in as private, Co. H, on May 23, 1861; killed in action on August 29, 1861, at Bull Run, Va.; also borne as Knowls.

Knowlton, John M. — Age, 34 years. Enlisted April 18, 1861, at Brooklyn to serve three years; mustered in as private, Co. C, on May 23, 1861; deserted on April 10, 1864, at Washington D.C.

Koester, Charles — Age, 23 years. Enlisted April 18, 1861, at Brooklyn to serve three years; mustered in as private, Co. F, on May 23, 1861; deserted on November 1, 1861, from near Upton Hill, Va.

Kollnyer, James H. — Age, 22 years. Enlisted April 18, 1861, at Brooklyn to serve three years; mustered in as private, Co. E, on May 23, 1861; transferred to Fifth Veteran Infantry, on June 2, 1864; also borne as Kellinger.

Kolmeyer, Joseph — Age, 30 years. Enlisted at Brooklyn to serve three years; mustered in as private, Co. F, on December 7, 1863; transferred to Veterans Reserve Corps on March 17, 1864.

Konnegar, Joseph — Age, 37 years. Enlisted December 12, 1863, at Brooklyn to serve three years; mustered in as private; unassigned, December 23, 1863; no further record.

Krack, Henry — Age, 30 years. Enlisted

December 8, 1863, at Brooklyn to serve three years; mustered in as private, Co. F, on December 23, 1863; transferred to Co. K, Fifth Veteran Infantry.

Kranor, Jacob—Age, 18 years. Enlisted at Brooklyn to serve three years; mustered in as private Co. A, on December 19, 1863; transferred to Co. I, Fifth Veteran Infantry, on June 2, 1864; also borne as Kramer, Kraner, and Kreener.

Krogere, Benjamin—Age, 28 years. Enlisted at Brooklyn to serve three years; mustered in as private, Co. C, on February 18, 1864; transferred to Co. C, Fifth Veteran Infantry, on June 2, 1864.

Kruser, Frederick B.—Age, 21 years. Enlisted April 18, 1861, at Brooklyn to serve three years; mustered in as private, Co. H, on May 23, 1861; captured in action on August 30, 1862; released and exchanged October 1862; returned to company on October 17, 1863; mustered out with company on June 6, 1864, at New York City, as Frederick P. Kruser; also borne as Kreuser or Krusser.

La Combe, Gardieu, Age, 21 years. Enlisted April 18, 1861, at Brooklyn to serve three years; mustered in as private, Co. F, on May 23, 1861; discharged for disability on March 2, 1862.

Laidlaw, Leffert L.—Age, 25 years. Enrolled April 18, 186X, at Brooklyn to serve three years; mustered in as first lieutenant, Co. G, on May 23, 1861; promoted adjutant on July 1, 1861; discharged August 2, 1861; commissioned first lieutenant, 14th Militia, on April 28, 1861, with rank from same date.

Lake, Robert—Age, 21 years. Enlisted May 18, 1861, at Brooklyn to serve three years; mustered in as private, Co. D, on May 23, 1861; deserted November 18, 1861, from Camp Marion, Upton Hill, Va.

Laley, Michael—Age, 18 years. Enlisted July 1, 1861, at Brooklyn to serve three years; mustered in as private, Co. G; discharged on September 25, 1861, refused to take the oath.

Landon, Samuel—Age, 29 years. Enlisted August 27, 1862, at Brooklyn to serve three years; mustered in as private, Co. D, on August 28, 1862; discharged for disability on March 31, 1863, at Belle Plains, Va.

Lane, Daniel—Age, 22 years. Enlisted June 30, 1861, at Brooklyn to serve three years; mustered in as private, Co. I, on August 1, 1861; promoted sergeant, no date; wounded in action on July 1, 1863, at Gettysburg, Pa.; transferred to Veterans Reserve Corps, no date; also borne as Lain.

Lane, George E.—Age, 24 years. Enlisted August 25, 1862, at Brooklyn to serve three years; mustered in as private, Co. D, on August 26, 1862; deserted on November 22, 1862, at Stafford Court House, Va.

Lang, John—Age, 20 years. Enlisted October 14, 1861, at Brooklyn to serve three years; mustered in as private, Co. I, on October 24, 1861; deserted on January 23, 1862, at Upton Hill, Va.

Langdon, William A.—Age, 23 years. Enlisted April 18, 1861, at Brooklyn to serve three years; mustered in as corporal, Co. D, on May 23, 1861; promoted sergeant on March 1, 1862; re-enlisted as a veteran on February 12, 1864; wounded in action on May 8, 1864, at Laurel Hill, Va.; transferred to Co. I, Fifth Veteran Infantry, on June 2, 1864.

Lange, Ludwig A.—Age 27 years. Enlisted December 8, 1863, at Brooklyn to serve three years; mustered in as private, Co. F, on December 23, 1863; transferred to Veterans Reserve Corps on March 17, 1864; discharged on December 19, 1865, as of Thirty-Second Company, Second Battalion, at Washington D.C.; also borne as Louis A. Lainge.

Langley, Willuian A.—Age, 24 years. Enlisted, September 4, 1862; at Brooklyn, to serve three years, mustered in as private, Co. E, September 4, 1862; transferred to Co. I, Fifth Veteran Infantry, June 2, 1864.

Lapine, Isaac M.—Age, 20 years. Enlisted, May 18, 1861, at Brooklyn, to serve three years; mustered in as private, Co. D, May 23, 1861; deserted July 26, 1861, at Arlington, Va.

Larkin, Washington—Age, 18 years. Enlisted, August 29, 1862, at Brooklyn, to serve three years; mustered in as private, Co. B, August 30, 1862; killed in action, July 1, 1863, at Gettysburg, Pa.

Larkins, James—Age, 24 years. Enlisted, May 10, 1861, at Brooklyn, to serve three years; mustered in as private, Co. G, May 23, 1861; deserted, July 22, 1861, at Arlington, Va.

Larrabee, David—Assistant surgeon, Eighty-Sixth Infantry; mustered in as surgeon of this regiment, July 29, 1863; discharged March 16, 1864; commissioned surgeon July 23, 1863, with rank from June 25, 1863, vice J. L. Farley, discharged.

Lathrop, Christopher—Age, 44 years. Enlisted at Brooklyn, to serve three years; mustered in as private, Co. I, December 3, 1863; transferred to Co. G, Fifth Veteran Infantry, June 2, 1864.

Latimer, John—Age, 19 years. Enlisted, April 18, 1861, at Brooklyn, to serve three years; mustered in as private, Co. H, May 23, 1861; deserted, September 26, 1861, at Arlington, Va.

Latta, Alfred C.—Age, 25 years. Enlisted, December 8, 1863, at Brooklyn, to serve three years; mustered in as private, Co. I, December 8, 1863; transferred to Co. G, Fifth Veteran Infantry, June 2, 1864.

Laughlin, James—Age, 22 years. Enlisted at Brooklyn, to serve three years; mustered in as private, Co. F, December 21, 1863; transferred to Co. K, Fifth Veteran Infantry, June 2, 1864.

Lavery, Daniel—Age, 42 years. Enlisted at Brooklyn, to serve three years; mustered in as private, Co. F, December 8, 1863; transferred to Co. K, Fifth Veteran Infantry, June 2, 1864.

Lawrence, Smith B.—Age, 19 years. Enlisted, April 18, 1861, at Brooklyn, to serve three years; mustered in as private, Co. H, May 23, 1861; deserted, January 28, 1862, at Upton Hill, Va.; also borne as Laurence.

Lawrence Thomas, H.—Age, 26 years. Enlisted, April 18, 1861, at Brooklyn, to serve three years; mustered in as corporal, company of engineers, May 23, 1861; mustered out, August 28, 1861, at Arlington, Va.

Lawson, William—Age, 22 years. Enlisted, April 18, 1861, at Brooklyn, to serve three years; mustered in as private, Co. A, May 23, 1861; mustered out with company, June 6, 1864, at New York City; also borne as William B. Lawson.

Layton, John W.—Age, 27 years. Enlisted, August 21, 1862, at Brooklyn, to serve three years; mustered in as private, Co. B, August 22, 1862; transferred to Co. I, Fifth Veteran Infantry, June 2, 1864.

Leary, Robert T.—Age, 18 years. Enlisted, April 18, 1861, at Brooklyn, to serve three years; mustered in as private, Co. D, May 23, 1861; deserted December 23, 1862, from hospital, Portsmouth Grove, R.I.; also borne as Robert D. Leary.

Leckey, John—Age, 28 years. Enlisted, September 9, 1862, at Brooklyn, to serve three years; mustered in as private, Co. C, September 10, 1862, discharged for disability, February 4, 1863, at Washington, D.C.; also borne as Lackey and Seckey.

LeClerce, Alfred—Age, 20 years. Enlisted, April 18, 1861, at Brooklyn, to serve three years; mustered in as private, Co. F, May 23, 1861; discharged for disability, July 28, 1861, at Arlington, Va.

Lee, John—Age, 28 years, Enlisted, October 1, 1861, at Brooklyn, to serve three years; mustered in as musician in band, October 21, 1861; discharged August 17, 1862, at Camp Halstead, Va.

Lee, John W.—Age, 24 years. Enlisted as corporal, June 30, 1861, at Brooklyn, to serve three years; not mustered in Co. I; killed in action, July 21, 1861, at Bull Run, Va.

Lee, Patrick — Age, 25 years. Enlisted, August 2, 1862, at Brooklyn, to serve three years; mustered in as private, Co. D, September 3, 1862; wounded in action, July 1, 1863, at Gettysburg, Pa.; deserted April 1, 1864, from hospital, Germantown, Pa.

Leggett, Charles E. — Age, 23 years. Enlisted at Hudson, to serve three years; mustered in as private, Co. G, December 1, 1864; mustered out, June 27, 1864, at New York City.

Lencioni, Pietro — Age, 23 years. Enlisted, April 18, 1861, at Brooklyn, to serve three years; mustered in as private, Co. F, May 23, 1861; discharged for disability, July 20, 1861, at Arlington, Va.

Leng, Ludwig — Age, 27 years. Enlisted at Brooklyn, to serve three years; mustered in as private; unassigned, December 8, 1863; no further record.

Lennon, Thomas — Age, 19 years. Enlisted, August 20, 1862, at Brooklyn, to serve three years; mustered in as private; unassigned, August 21, 1862; no further record.

Leonard, John V. — Age, 21 years. Enlisted at Brooklyn, to serve three years; mustered in as private, Co. G, December 5, 1863; discharged for disability, March 6, 1864, at Culpeper, Va.; also borne as John W. Leonard.

Leslie, Richard — Age, 30 years. Enlisted April 18, 1861, at Brooklyn to serve three years; mustered in as private, Co. H, on May 23, 1861; appointed wagoner and returned to company as private, no date; discharged for disease on February 17, 1864, at Camp Distribution, Alexandria, Va.

Lester, Francis W. — Age, 20 years. Enlisted at Brooklyn to serve three years; mustered in as private, Co. I, on January 4, 1864; transferred to Co. G, Fifth Veteran Infantry, on June 2, 1864.

Levert, Mack — Age, 22 years. Enlisted September 17, 1862, at Brooklyn to serve three years; mustered in as private; unassigned, September 19, 1862; no further record.

Lewis, James — Age, 22 years. Enlisted at Brooklyn to serve three years; mustered in as private; unassigned, October 21, 1862; no further record.

Lewis, John — Age, 22 years. Enlisted June 30, 1861, at Arlington, Va., to serve three years; mustered in as private, Co. C, on September 18, 1861; promoted corporal on March 1, 1863; wounded in action on July 1, 1863, at Gettysburg, Pa.; promoted sergeant on January 1, 1864; discharged for disability on April 7, 1864, at Washington, D.C.

Lewis, William T. — Age, 22 years. Enlisted August 29, 1862, at Brooklyn to serve three years; mustered in as private; unassigned, August 30, 1862; no further record.

Libby, Henry — Age, 22 years. Enlisted April 18, 1861, at Brooklyn to serve three years; mustered in as private, Co. C, on May 23, 1861; discharged for disability on October 16, 1862, at Washington, D.C.; also borne as Henry A. Libbey.

Liming, Isaac — Age, 32 years. Enlisted August 28, 1862, at Brooklyn to serve three years; mustered in as private, Co. B, on August 29, 1862; transferred to Co. I, Fifth Veteran Infantry, on June 2, 1864.

Lindsay, William — Age, 21 years. Enlisted April 18, 1861, at Brooklyn to serve three years; mustered in as private, Co. E, on May 23, 1861; killed in action on May 10, 1864, at Laurel Hill, Va.; also borne as Lindsey.

Lindsay, Thomas — Age, 39 years. Enlisted at Brooklyn to serve three years; mustered in as private, Co. C, on August 22, 1862; promoted corporal, no date; discharged on January 4, 1864, for promotion; also borne as Thomas W. Lindsay.

Linnane, Peter F. — Age, 19 years. Enlisted April 18, 1861, at Brooklyn to serve three years; mustered in as private, Co. H, on May 23, 1861; captured on July 22, 1861, and paroled at Manassas, Va., no date; discharge on May 21, 1862, at Washington, D.C.

Livingston, John — Age, 30 years. Enlisted

April 18, 1861, at Brooklyn to serve three years; mustered in as private, Co. F, on May 23, 1861; deserted on January 28, 1862, at Upton Hill, Va.

Lize, Alexander A.—Age, 30 years. Enlisted at Brooklyn to serve three years; mustered in as private, Co. D, on January 15, 1862; discharged for disability on January 21, 1863, at Washington, D.C.

Lloyd, Edward—Age, 23 years. Enlisted on May 18, 1861, at Brooklyn to serve three years; mustered in as private, Co. B, on May 23, 1861; deserted on January 30, 1862, at Upton Hill, Va.

Lloyd, Joseph—Age, 19 years. Enlisted at Brooklyn to serve three years; mustered in as private, Co. B, on September 18, 1861; deserted on February 4, 1862, at Upton Hill, Va.

Long, James—Age, 18 years. Enlisted on May 18, 1861, at Brooklyn to serve three years; mustered in as private, Co. G, on May 23, 1861; promoted corporal, no date; sergeant, January 8, 1864; transferred to Co. K, Fifth Veteran Infantry, on June 2, 1864.

Long, Ludwig—Age, 37 years. Enlisted December 8, 1863, at Brooklyn to serve three years; mustered in as private; unassigned, December 13, 1863; no further record.

Loughhead, ____—Age, 23 years. Enlisted May 18, 1861, at Brooklyn to serve three years; mustered in as private, Co. B, on May 23, 1861; deserted on August 10, 1861, at Arlington, Va., as Lonehead.

Lourteback, David—Age, 42 years. Enlisted at Brooklyn to serve three years; mustered in as private, Co. I, on December 9, 1863; transferred to Co. G, Fifth Veteran Infantry, on June 2, 1864; also borne as Loniteback and Loutiback.

Loutringer, Martin—Age, 32 years. Enlisted April 18, 1861, at Brooklyn to serve three years; mustered in as private, Co. F, on May 23, 1861; deserted February 12, 1863, at McDougall Hospital, Fort Schuyler, New York Harbor.

Lowen, Charles—Age, 25 years. Enlisted May 18, 1861, at Brooklyn, to serve three years; mustered in as private, Co. D, May 23, 1861; deserted January 23, 1862, at Camp Marion, Upton, Hill, Va.

Loyd, Alfred—Age, 36 years. Enlisted, May 18, 1861, at Brooklyn, to serve three years; mustered in as private, Co. H, Fifth Veteran Infantry, June 2, 1864.

Luckey, Cornelius B.—Age, 19 years. Enlisted at Brooklyn, to serve three years; mustered in as private, Co. H, Fifth Veteran Infantry, June 2, 1864.

Luckey, George—Age, 21 years. Enlisted at Brooklyn, to serve three years; mustered in as private, Co. H, August 21, 1862; transferred to Co. K, Fifth Veteran Infantry, June 2, 1864.

Ludden, William A—Age, 19 years. Enlisted, April 18, 1861, at Brooklyn, to serve three years; mustered in as private, Co. H, May 23, 1861; captured while on picket, November 18, 1861, at Falls Church, Va.; paroled, February 22, 1862; discharged for disease, April 10, 1863, at New York City.

Ludwig, August—Age, 39 years. Enlisted, December 17, 1863, at Brooklyn, to serve three years; mustered in as private, Co. I, December 21, 1863; transferred to Co. G, Fifth Veteran Infantry, June 2, 1864; also borne as Ludwing.

Lundy, William—Age, 19 years. Enlisted, July 1, 1861, at Brooklyn, to serve three years; mustered in as private, Co. I, August 4, 1861; discharged, October 4, 1863.

Lush, Jr. Thomas R.—Age, 18 years. Enlisted, April 18, 1861, at Brooklyn, to serve three years; mustered in as private, Co. H, May 23, 1861; deserted on expiration of furlough, December 9, 1861.

Lusk, Samuel—Age, 19 years. Enlisted, August 28, 1862, at Brooklyn, to serve three years; mustered in as private, Co. D, August 30, 1862; transferred to Co. H, Fifth Veteran Infantry, June 2, 1862.

Lynch, Edward—Age, 21 years. Enlisted, May 10, 1861, at Brooklyn, to serve three years; mustered in as private, Co. G, May 23, 1861; promoted corporal, no date; deserted January 25, 1862, at Upton Hill, Va. also borne as Edward F. Lynch.

Lynch, John — Age, 22 years. Enlisted at Brooklyn, to serve three years; mustered in as private, Co. G, May 23, 1861; deserted September 20, 1861, at Arlington, Va.

Lynch, Michael — Age, 21 years. Enlisted at Jamaica, to serve three years; mustered in as private, Co. F, December 23, 1863; transferred to Co. K, Fifth Veteran Infantry, June 2, 1864.

Lynch, William — Age, 20 years. Enlisted at Brooklyn, to serve three years; mustered in as private, Co. C, January 28, 1864; transferred to Co. H, Fifth Veteran Infantry, June 2, 1864.

Lynn, James — Age, 35 years. Enlisted, December 15, 1863, at Brooklyn, to serve three years; mustered in as private, Co. K, December 23, 1863; discharged September 3, 1864, at Insane Asylum, Washington, D.C.

Lyon, Nathaniel — Age, 24 years. Enlisted, September 9, 1861, at New York City, to serve three years; mustered in as private, Co. H, September 13, 1861; captured, November 18, 1861, while on picket at Falls Church, Va.; paroled, February 22, 1862, discharged, April 7, 1862.

Lyon, Timothy — age, 35 years. Enlisted, December 15, 1863, at Brooklyn, to serve three years; mustered in a private, Co. K, December 23, 1863; killed in action, May 11, 1864, at Spotsylvania, Va.

Maas, William B. — Age, 26 years. Enlisted April 18, 1861, at Brooklyn to serve three years; mustered in as private, Co. D, on May 23, 1861; promoted corporal on July 1, 1863; mustered out with company on June 6, 1864, at New York City.

Mack, John — Age, 20 years. Enlisted April 18, 1861, at Brooklyn to serve three years; mustered in as private, Co. A, on May 23, 1861; promoted corporal on June 12, 1863; missing in action on July 1, 1863, at Gettysburg, Pa.; returned October 8, 1863; mustered out with company on June 6, 1864, at New York City.

MacKay, Donald — Age, 21 years. Enlisted April 18, 1861, at Brooklyn to serve three years; mustered in as private, Co. C, on May 23, 1861; discharged for disability on August 23, 1861, at Arlington, Va.; also borne as McKay.

Mackey, John H. — Age, 25 years. Enlisted at Brooklyn to serve three years; mustered in as private, Co. D, on October 14, 1862; missing in action on July 1, 1863, at Gettysburg, Pa.; returned December 25, 1863; transferred to Co. I, Fifth Veteran Infantry, on June 2, 1864.

Madden, Christopher — Age, 25 years. Enlisted at Brooklyn to serve three years; mustered in as private, Co. B, on March 10, 1862; wounded in action on August 29, 1862, at Bull Run, Va.; discharged for wounds on October 27, 1863, at Portsmouth Grove, R.I.

Madden, John — Age, 28 years. Enlisted at Brooklyn to serve three years; mustered in as private, Co. A, on May 23, 1861; missing in action on July 1, 1863, at Gettysburg, Pa.; returned October 1863; mustered out with company on June 6, 1864, at New York City.

Madden, John V. — Age, 22 years. Enlisted at New York City to serve three years; mustered in as private; unassigned, March 9, 1864; no further record.

Madden, William — Age, 22 years. Enlisted May 18, 1861, at Brooklyn to serve three years; mustered in as private, Co. B, on May 23, 1861; wounded in action on September 14, 1862, at South Mountain, Md.; discharged for wounds on January 13, 1863, at New York City.

Madden, William — Age, 33 years. Enlisted at Brooklyn to serve three years; mustered in as private, Co. F, on December 21, 1863; transferred to Co. K, Fifth Veteran Infantry, on June 2, 1864.

Madrick, John — Age, 34 years. Enlisted at Brooklyn to serve three years; mustered in as private; unassigned, October 22, 1862; no further record.

Mager, James — Age, 32 years. Enlisted at Brooklyn to serve three years; mustered in as private, Co. A, on December 2, 1863; transferred to navy on march 23, 1864; also borne as Major.

Magonigle, William B. — Age, 35 years. Enlisted August 25, 1862, at Brooklyn to serve three years; mustered in as private, Co. D, on August 26, 1862; transferred to Co. C, on November 14, 1862; wounded in action on July 1, 1863, at Gettysburg, Pa.; transferred to Co. H, Fifth Veteran Infantry, on June 2, 1864; also borne as McGonigle.

MacGrath, Peter — Age, 24 years. Enlisted December 9, 1863, at Brooklyn to serve three years; mustered in as private, Co. G, on December 23, 1863; discharged for disability on December 12, 1864, at McDougall Hospital, New York Harbor; also borne as McGrath.

Mahon, Patrick — Age, 25 years. Enlisted June 30, 1861, at Brooklyn to serve three years; mustered in as private, Co. K on August 1, 1861; discharged for disability on March 11, 1863, at Baltimore, Md.; also borne as Mahan.

Mahoney, Cornelius J. — Age, 19 years. Enlisted April 25, 1861, at Brooklyn to serve three years; mustered in as private, Co. G, on May 23, 1861; mustered out with company on June 6, 1864, at New York City; also borne as McHoney.

Mahoney, David — Age, 23 years. Enlisted on May 10, 1861, at Brooklyn to serve three years; mustered in as private, Co. G, on May 23, 1861; deserted on September 29, 1861, at Arlington Heights, Va.

Main William A — Age, 18 years. Enlisted August 18, 1862, at Brooklyn to serve three years; mustered in as private, Co. D, on August 29, 1862; transferred to Co. E, on November 14, 1862; wounded in action on July 1, 1863, at Gettysburg, Pa.; transferred to Veterans Reserve Corps on February 15, 1864, from which discharged on June 25, 1865, as of Co. B, 24th Regiment, at Washington, D.C.

Maitland, William H. — Age, 31 years. Enlisted December 9, 1863, at Brooklyn to serve three years; mustered in as private, Co. G, on December 23, 1863; transferred to Co. K, Fifth Veteran Infantry, on June 2, 1864.

Maley, Thomas W. — Age, 23 years. Enlisted April 18, 1861, at Brooklyn to serve three years; mustered in as private, Co. H, on May 23, 1861; discharged on May 23, 1864, at Washington D.C.; also borne as Marley.

Mallory, George — Age, 34 years. Enrolled on May 18, 1861, at Brooklyn to serve three years; mustered in as captain, Co. B, on May 23, 1861; killed in action on August 29, 1862, at Gainsville, Va.; also borne as Mallery; commissioned captain, 14th Militia, on May 4, 1861, with rank from May 2, 1861.

Maloy, John — Age, 18 years. Enlisted at Brooklyn to serve three years; mustered in as private, Co. E, on February 24, 1862; deserted on June 5, 1862, at Catletts Station, Va.

Manderville, Stephen O. — Age, 23 years. Enrolled April 18, 1861, at Brooklyn to serve three years; mustered in as sergeant, Co. E, on May 23, 1861; as second lieutenant on August 4, 1861; as first lieutenant on February 23, 1862; as captain Co. G, on November 24, 1863; mustered out with company on June 6, 1864, at New York City; commissioned second lieutenant, 14th Militia, on August 12, 1861, with rank from August 4, 1861; not commissioned first lieutenant; commissioned captain on November 13, 1863, with rank from October 10, 1863.

Manee, George — Age, 21 years. Enlisted April 18, 1861, at Brooklyn to serve three years; mustered in as private, Co. C, on May 23, 1861; promoted corporal on July 1, 1863; sergeant on April 1, 1864; missing in action on May 8, 1864, at the Wilderness, Va.; also borne as George Mann; no further record.

Manesca, Lewis—Age, 44 years. Enlisted April 18, 1861, at Brooklyn to serve three years; mustered in as private, Co. D, on May 23, 1861; promoted corporal on November 1, 1862; mustered out with company on June 6, 1864, at New York City; also borne as Louis Manesca.

Manning, James—Age, 42 years. Enlisted at Brooklyn to serve three years; mustered in as private, Co. K, on December 16, 1863; discharged for disability on March 31, 1864, at Culpeper, Va.

Mansfield, William—Age, 28 years. Enrolled May 18, 1861, at Brooklyn to serve three years; mustered in as private, Co. D, on May 23, 1861; discharged for disability on July 10, 1862, at Philadelphia, Pa.

Marfing, Joseph—Age, 22, years. Enlisted April 18, 1861, at Brooklyn to serve three years; mustered in as private, Co. E, on May 2, 1861; transferred to Veteran Reserve Corps on February 15, 1864.

Markey, Andrew—Age, 22 years. Enlisted April 18, 1861, at Brooklyn to serve three years; mustered in as private, Co. A, on May 23, 1861; deserted on expiration of furlough on Aug, 7, 1861.

Mars, Henry—Age, 23 years. Enlisted at Brooklyn to serve three years; mustered in as private, Co. K, on February 3, 1864; transferred to Co. G, Fifth Veteran Infantry, on June 2, 1864; also borne as Marsh.

Marshall, Frank M.—Age, 27 years. Enlisted April 18, 1861, at Brooklyn to serve three years; mustered in as private, Co. C, on May 23, 1861; discharged on March 13, 1863.

Marshall, George E.—Age, 18 years. Enlisted April 18, 1861, at Brooklyn to serve three years; mustered in as private, Co. A, on May 23, 1861; wounded in action on July 1, 1863, at Gettysburg, Pa.; mustered out with company on June 6, 1864, at New York City.

Marshall, Joseph—Age, 22 years. Enlisted May 18, 1861, at Brooklyn to serve three years; mustered in as private, Co. B, on May 23, 1861; deserted on July 15, 1862, at Alexandria, Va.

Martin, Addison D.—Age, 20 years. Enrolled, April 18, 1861, at Brooklyn, to serve three years; mustered in as private, Co. E, May 23, 1861; promoted sergeant, no date; mustered in as first lieutenant, November 2, 1963; mustered out with company, June 6, 1864, at New York City; also borne as Anderson D. Martin; commissioned, not mustered, second lieutenant, August 18, 1863, with rank from October 10, 1863, vice J. Manderville, promoted.

Martin, Frank see Martin Frank

Martin, George M.—Age, 22 years. Enrolled, April 18, 1861, at Brooklyn, to serve three years; mustered in as private, Co. C, May 23, 1861; promoted first sergeant, March 1, 1863; mustered in as second lieutenant, May 27, 1863; mustered out, June 14, 1864, at New York City; also borne as J.M. Martin.

Martin, George W.—Age, 24 years. Enlisted, May 18, 1861, at Brooklyn, to serve three years; mustered in as private, Co. D, May 23, 1861; died of disease, June 15, 1862, in hospital, Washington, D.C.

Martin, Michael—Age, 21 years. Enlisted, April 18, 1861, at Brooklyn, to serve three years; mustered in as private, Co. E, May 23, 1861; deserted, July 24, 1861, at Arlington, Va.

Martindale, Joseph B.—Age, 27 years. Enlisted, August 26, 1862, at Brooklyn, to serve three years; mustered in as private, Co. B, August 27, 1862; wounded in action, July 3, 1863, at Gettysburg, Pa.; transferred to Co. I, Fifth Veteran Infantry, June 2, 1864.

Mason, Jr., Nehemiah—Age, 26 years. Enlisted, August 28, 1862, to serve three years; mustered in as private, Co. D, August 29, 1862; transferred to Co. E, November 14, 1862; died of disease December 18, 1862, at Fredericksburg, Va.

Mathews, James — Age, 19 years. Enlisted, September 9, 1861, at New York City, to serve three years; mustered in as private, Co. B, September 13, 1861; wounded in action, August 29, 1862, at Bull Run, Va.; transferred to Veteran Reserve Corps, July 1, 1863; mustered out, September 14, 1864, as of Co. F, Thirteenth Regiment, Veteran Reserve Corps.

Mathews, Philip — Age, 30 years. Enlisted September 8, 1862, at Brooklyn to serve three years; mustered in as private, Co. D, on September 9, 1862; missing in action on July 1, 1863, at Gettysburg, Pa.; returned January 15, 1864; transferred to Co. I, Fifth Veteran Infantry, on June 2, 1864; also borne as Matthews.

Mathews, Samuel — Age, 21 years. Enlisted August 19, 1862, at Brooklyn to serve three years; mustered in as private, Co. K, on August 21, 1862; promoted corporal, no date; transferred to Co. K, Fifth Veteran Infantry, on June 2, 1864.

Matthews, James — Age, 30 years. Enlisted at Brooklyn to serve three years; mustered in as private, Co. G, on December 8, 1863; transferred to Co. G, Fifth Veteran Infantry, on June 2, 1864.

Matthews, John T.— Age, 21 years. Enlisted August 22, 1862, at Brooklyn to serve three years, mustered in as private, Co. H, on August 23, 1862; discharged for disability on February 26, 1863, at Mount Pleasant Hospital, Washington, D.C.

Mauser, S. John — Age, 51 years. Enlisted on July 1, 1861, at Brooklyn to serve three years; mustered in as private, Co. K, on August 1, 1861; no record subsequent to June 22, 1862; also borne as Mausser and Mouser.

Maxwell, Joseph — Age, 26 years. Enlisted August 28, 1862, at Brooklyn to serve three years; mustered in as private, Co. E, on August 29, 1862; transferred to Co. E, on August 29, 1862; transferred to Co. H, Fifth Veteran Infantry, on June 2, 1864.

Maxwell, William — Age, 26 years. Enlisted April 18, 1861, at Brooklyn to serve three years; mustered in as private, Co. H, on May 23, 1861; wounded in action on August 29, 1862, at Bull Run, Va.; discharged for disability on July 13, 1863, at New York City.

McCluskey, Thomas — Age, 21 years. Enlisted April 25, 1861, at Brooklyn to serve three years; mustered in as private, Co. G, on May 23, 1861; deserted on May 1, 1862, at Falmouth, Va.

McClusky, Hugh — Age, 40 years. Enlisted December 17, 1863, at Brooklyn to serve three years; mustered in as private, Co. K, on December 23, 1863; discharged for disability on March 31, 1863, at Culpeper, Va.; also borne as McClaskey.

McConnalogue, William — Age, 19 years. Enlisted August 25, 1862, at Brooklyn to serve three years; mustered in as private, Co. F, on August 27, 1862; missing in action on July 1, 1863, Gettysburg, Pa.; returned October *, 1863; transferred to Co. K, Fifth Veteran Infantry, on June 2, 1864; also borne as McCoulong.

McConnell, George — Age, 19 years. Enlisted July 31, 1861, at Brooklyn to serve three years; mustered in as private, Co. I, on August 4, 1861; wounded in action on July 1, 1863, at Gettysburg, Pa.; died of his wounds on July 8, 1863.

McConnochie, Alfred — Age, 20 years. Enlisted at Brooklyn to serve three years; mustered in as private, Co. E, on December 30, 1863; transferred to Co. H, Fifth Veteran Infantry, on June 2, 1864; also borne as McConnichie.

McConnochie, William J.— Age, 23 years. Enlisted August 27, 1862, at Brooklyn to serve three years; mustered in as private, Co. C, on August 28, 1862; mustered out on June 12, 1865, at Judiciary Square Hospital, Washington, D.C.

McCormack, Bernard — Age, 28 years. Enlisted at Brooklyn to serve three years; mustered in as private, Co. D, on August 25, 1862; transferred to Co. G, on November 14, 1862; wounded in action on July 1, 1863, at Gettysburg, Pa.; transferred to Co. D, Fifth Veteran Infantry, on June 2, 1864.

McCormick, James — Private, Co. H, Thirtieth Infantry; transferred to this regiment on February 29, 1864; no further record.

McCue, Charles — Age, 24 years. Enlisted September 19, 1862, at Brooklyn to serve three years; mustered in as private, Co. F, on September 20, 1862; missing in action on July 1, 1863, at Gettysburg, Pa.; deserted on October 25, 1863, from Camp Parole, Annapolis, Md.

McCurry, John — Age, 21 years. Enlisted April 18, 1861, at Brooklyn to serve three years; mustered in as private, Co. E, on May 23, 1861; discharged for disability on June 6, 1862, at Washington, D.C., as John McClure.

McDermott, Timothy — Age, 39 years. Enlisted at Brooklyn to serve three years; mustered in as private, Co. E, on December 29, 1863; transferred to Co. H, Fifth Veteran Infantry, on June 2, 1864; also borne as Lawrence McDermot.

McDonald, James — Age, 44 years. Enlisted December 28, 1863, at Brooklyn to serve three years; mustered in as private, Co. I, on December 30, 1863; discharged for disability on April 3, 1864, at Culpeper, Va.

McDonald, James — Age, 20 years. Enlisted April 18, 1861, at Brooklyn to serve three years; mustered in as sergeant, Co. A, on May 23, 1861; discharged on September 14, 1861, at Arlington, Va., for promotion to lieutenant, Sixth Heavy Artillery.

McDonald, John — Age, 25 years. Enlisted at Brooklyn to serve three years; mustered in as private, Co. B, on February 5, 1864; transferred to Co. I, Fifth Veteran Infantry, on June 2, 1864.

McDonald, Michael — Age, 30 years. Enlisted November 21, 1863, at Brooklyn to serve three years; mustered in as private; unassigned, December 13, 1863; no further record.

McDonnough, Michael — Age, 21 years. Enlisted on August 28, 1862, at Brooklyn to serve three years; mustered in as private, Co. C, on August 29, 1862; transferred to Co. I, Fifth Veteran Infantry, on June 2, 1864.

McDowell, Robert C. — Age, 21 years. Enlisted on August 27, 1862, at Brooklyn to serve three years; mustered in as private, Co. C, on August 28, 1862; transferred to Co. H, Fifth Veteran Infantry, on June 2, 1864.

McFael, Thomas p. — Age, 29 years. Enlisted on April 18, 1861, at Brooklyn to serve three years; mustered in as private, Co. E, on May 23, 1861; discharged for disability on April 5, 1862, at Upton Hill, Va.

McFail, Thomas — Age, 20 years. Enlisted at Brooklyn to serve three years; mustered in as private, Co. K, February 10, 1864; transferred to Co. B, Fifth Veteran Infantry, on June 2, 1864.

McGahey, John — Age, 20 years. Enlisted April 18, 1861, at Brooklyn to serve three years; mustered in as private, Co. F, on May 23, 1861, deserted on January 29, 1862, at Upton Hill, Va.

McGee, James — Age, 32 years. Enlisted at Brooklyn to serve three years; mustered in as private, Co. F, on December 2, 1863; transferred to Co. K, Fifth Veteran Infantry, on June 2, 1864; also borne as McGee.

McGeehan, James — Age, 25 years. Enlisted July 1, 1861, at Brooklyn to serve three years; mustered in as private, Co. I, on August 1, 1861; wounded in action on July 21, 1861, at Bull Run, Va.; discharged for disability on November 1, 1862, at Washington, D.C.; subsequent service in Co. A, Sixteenth Artillery.

McGeehin, Richard — Age, 18 years. Enlisted September 20, 1862, at Brooklyn to serve three years; mustered in as musician, Co. B, on September 30, 1862; transferred to Co. I, Fifth Veteran Infantry, on June 2, 1864.

McGlinchy, John D. — Age, 21 years. Enlisted August 23, 1862, at Brooklyn to serve three years; mustered in as private, Co. B, on August 25, 1862; transferred to Co. I, Fifth Veteran Infantry, on June 2, 1864; also borne as McGlinchey.

McGlom, James — Age, 26 years. Enlisted April 18, 1861, at Brooklyn to serve three years; mustered in as private, Co. E, on May 23, 1861; discharged for disability on June 19, 1861; also borne as McGlone.

McGovrin, John — Age, 18 years. Enlisted at Brooklyn to serve three years; mustered in as private, Co. I, on December 11, 1863; transferred to Co. G, Fifth Veteran Infantry, on June 2, 1864; also borne as McGovern.

McGowan, John H. — Age, 29 years. Enlisted April 18, 1861, at Brooklyn to serve three years; mustered in as private, Co. D, on May 23, 1861; mustered out with company on June 6, 1864, at New York City.

McGrath, Michael — Age, 22 years. Enlisted at Brooklyn to serve three years; mustered in as private, Co. G, on October 27, 1862; absent in arrest at Fort Columbus, New York Harbor, February and April, 1864; no further record.

McGrotty, James — Age, 22 years. Enlisted May 18, 1861, at Brooklyn to serve three years; mustered in as private, Co. B, on May 23, 1861; died of disease on September 23, 1861, at Arlington, Va.; also borne as McGroarty and McGroatty.

McGuire, Francis — Age, 18 years. Enlisted at Brooklyn to serve three years; mustered in as private; unassigned, December 21, 1863; deserted, no date, at Hart's Island, New York Harbor.

McGuire, James — Age, 18 years. Enlisted April 18, 1861, at Brooklyn to serve three years; mustered in as private, Co. A, on May 23, 1861; promoted sergeant on April 5, 1863; mustered out with company on June 6, 1864, at New York City.

McGuire, Patrick — Age, 28 years. Enlisted September 11, 1862, at Brooklyn to serve three years; mustered in as private; unassigned, September 12, 1862; no further record.

McGuire, Thomas — Age, 21 years. Enlisted July 1, 1861, at Brooklyn to serve three years; mustered in as private, Co. K, on August 1, 1861; discharged for disability on February 6, 1863, at Washington, D.C.

McGuirk, Samuel — Age, 20 years. Enlisted at Brooklyn to serve three years; mustered in as private, Co. E, on March 8, 1862; deserted on July 28, 1862, at Falmouth, Va.

McGunigle, John — Age, 29 years. Enlisted on May 18, 1861, at Brooklyn to serve three years; mustered in as private, Co. G, on May 23, 1861; wounded in action on July 21, 1861, at Bull Run, Va.; died of his wounds, no date, at Centreville, Va.; also borne as Miaggonigle and McCunicle.

McHenry, James — Age, 22 years. Enlisted April 18, 1861, at Brooklyn to serve three years; mustered in as private, Co. C, on May 23, 1861; discharged for disability on November 15, 1861, at Arlington, Va.

McHenru, Michael — Age, 43 years. Enlisted at Brooklyn to serve three years; mustered in as private, Co. G, on December 9, 1863; transferred to Co. K, Fifth Veteran Infantry, on June 2, 1864.

McIntire, George — Age, 21 years. Enlisted April 18, 1861, at Brooklyn to serve three years; mustered in as private, Co. B, on May 23, 1861; promoted corporal on January 1, 1864; wounded May 8, 1864; mustered out with company on June 6, 1864, at New York City, as George F. McIntire, also born as McIntyre.

McIntyre, John — Age, 24 years. Enlisted April 18, 1861, at Brooklyn to serve three years; mustered in as private, Co. A, on May 23, 1861; discharged for disability on February 14, 1863, at Convalescent Camp, Va.

McKane, William — Age, 34 years. Enlisted on May 18, 1861, at Brooklyn to serve three years; mustered in as private, Co. B, on May 23, 1861; discharged for disability on June 8, 1862, at Upton Hill, Va.

McKee, Robert — Age, 20 years. Enlisted at Brooklyn to serve three years; mustered in as private; unassigned, May 11, 1864; no further record.

McKinney, Allan — Age, 43 years. Enlisted December 21, 1863, at Jamaica, to serve three years; mustered in as private; unassigned, December 24, 1863; no further record.

McLeer, James — Age, 22 years. Enlisted April 18, 1861, at Brooklyn to serve three years; mustered in as private, Co. C, on May 23, 1861; promoted corporal on November 1, 1861; wounded in action on July 21, 1861, at Bull Run, Va., and August 29, 1862, at Groveton, Va.; discharged as sergeant for physical disability on July 27, 1863.

McMillan, Robert — Age, 28 years. Enlisted September 29, 1862, at Brooklyn to serve three years; mustered in as private, Co. D, on September 30, 1862; transferred to Co. G on November 1, 1862; promoted corporal, no date; transferred to Co. G, Fifth Veteran Infantry, on June 2, 1864; also borne as McMillen.

McNamara, James — Age, 19 years. Enlisted April 18, 1861, at Brooklyn to serve three years; mustered in as private, Co. H, on May 23, 1861; discharged on December 10, 1862; also borne as McMamara.

Mcnamee, John — Age, 29 years. Enlisted on May 18, 1861, at Brooklyn to serve three years; mustered in as private, Co. B, on May 23, 1861; transferred to Co. I, Fifth Veteran Infantry, on June 2, 1864.

McNeely, Cornelius J. — Age, 18 years. Enlisted at Brooklyn to serve three years; mustered in as private; unassigned, October 17, 1862; no further record.

McNeil, John — Age, 27 years. Enrolled on April 18, 1861, at Brooklyn to serve three years; mustered in as sergeant, Co. H, on May 23, 1861; promoted first sergeant on August 5, 1861; mustered in as second lieutenant on March 2, 1862, captured, no date; paroled on December 6, 1862; mustered in as captain on January 17, 1863; mustered out with company on June 6, 1864, at New York City; not commissioned second lieutenant; commissioned captain on October 24, 1862, with rank from August 29, 1862.

McPhail, Alexander — Age, 18 years. Enlisted at Brooklyn to serve three years; mustered in as private, Co. K, on December 14, 1863; transferred to Co. A, Fifth Veteran Infantry, on June 2, 1864.

Mc Quillen, John — Age, 31 years. Enlisted on May 18, 1861, at Brooklyn to serve three years; mustered in as first sergeant, Co. B, on May 23, 1861; returned to ranks, no date; died of his wounds on May 10, 1864.

McTasney, Daniel — Age, 22 years. Enlisted on May 18, 1861, at Brooklyn to serve three years; mustered in as private, Co. B, on May 23, 1861; deserted on February 1, 1862, at Upton Hill, Va.; also borne as McTassney.

Meadrick, John — Age, 34 years. Enlisted at Brooklyn to serve three years; mustered in as private, Co. H, on October 22, 1862; wounded in action on April 29, 1863, at Reynold's Crossing, Va.; transferred to Co. Seventy-Second Company, Second Battalion, Veteran Reserve Corps, on March 1, 1864; also borne as Maedrick.

Mears, George W. — Age, 26 years. Enlisted April 18, 1861, at Brooklyn to serve three years; mustered in as private, Co. C, on May 23, 1861; discharged on December 28, 1861, for promotion to first lieutenant, Co. E, Fourth Artillery; also borne as J. W. Morris.

Meehan, Patrick — Age, 18 years. Enlisted January 19, 1864, at Brooklyn to serve three years; mustered in as private, Co. H, on January 27, 1864; transferred to Co. I, Fifth Veteran Infantry, on June 2, 1864; also borne as Mehan.

Meeker, George H. — Age, 37 years. Enlisted on May 4, 1861, at Brooklyn to serve three years; mustered in as private, Co. G, on May 23, 1861; promoted sergeant, no date; killed in action on December 13, 1862, at Fredericksburg, Va.

Melio, Michael — Age, 23 years. Enlisted on April 18, 1861, at Brooklyn to serve three years; mustered in as private, Co. B, on May 23, 1861; Mustered out with company on June 6, 1864, at New York City; also borne as Melia.

Menken, Joseph — Age, 39 years. Enlisted at Brooklyn to serve three years; mustered in as private, Co. G, on December 7, 1863; discharged on August 23, 1864, at New York City, as Joseph Mangdill.

Merritt, Mordecai — Age, 19 years. Enlisted on April 18, 1861, at Brooklyn to serve three years; mustered in as private, Co. C, on May 23, 1861; mustered out on June 14, 1864, at New York City.

Metzler, Augustus — Age, 32 years, Enlisted on April 18, 1861, at Brooklyn to serve three years; mustered in as private, Co. E, on May 23, 1861; promoted corporal, no date; transferred to 65th Company, Second Battalion, Veteran Reserve Corps, on October 9, 1863.

Metzler, Charles Z. — Age, 29 years. Enlisted on August 28, 1862, at Brooklyn to serve three years; mustered in as private, Co. F, on August 29, 1862; transferred to Co. K, Fifth Veteran Infantry, on June 6, 1864.

Meyer, Henry — Age, 23 years. Enlisted August 28, 1862, at Brooklyn to serve three years; mustered in as private; unassigned, September 19, 1862; no further record.

Michaelis, Augustus — Age, 44 years. Enlisted at Brooklyn to serve three years; mustered in as private; unassigned, October 2, 1862; no further record.

Michell, Harry W. — Age, 24 years. Enrolled on April 18, 1861, at Brooklyn to serve three years; mustered in as private, Co. C, on May 23, 1861; promoted corporal on August 1, 1861; sergeant, November 1, 1861; first sergeant, November 1, 1862; mustered in as second lieutenant, on February 1, 1863; wounded in action on July 1–2, 1863, at Gettysburg, Pa.; mustered in as first lieutenant on April 5, 1863; captured in action on May 5, 1864, at the Wilderness, Va.; paroled on March 10, 1865; mustered out on March 12, 1865; commissioned February 12, 1863, with rank from January 29, 1863.

Middleton, Benjamin F. — Age, 19 years. Enlisted on April 18, 1861, at Brooklyn to serve three years; mustered in as corporal, Co. E, on May 23, 1861; promoted sergeant, no date; wounded in action on July 21, 1861, at Bull Run, Va.; deserted on February 4, 1862, at Upton Hill, Va.

Middleton, Stiles — Age, 17 years. Enlisted at Brooklyn to serve three years; mustered in as private, Co. E, on July 1, 1861; captured and paroled, no dates; discharged on April 15, 1862, at Washington, D.C.

Middleton, William H. — Age, 33 years. Enrolled on April 18, 1861, at Brooklyn to serve three years; mustered in as first lieutenant, Co. E, on May 23, 1861; discharged on July 29, 1862; commissioned first lieutenant in 14th Militia on May 6, 1861, with rank from April 29, 1861.

Millard, William S. — Age, 19 years. Enlisted on June 30, 1861, to serve three years; mustered in as private, Co. I, on August 1, 1861; killed in action on July 1, 1863, at Gettysburg, Pa.

Miller, Andrew — Age, 35 years. Enlisted, April 18, 1861, at Brooklyn, to serve three years; mustered in as private, company of engineers, May 23, 1861; mustered out on August 28, 1861, at Arlington, Va.

Miller, Charles — Age, 25 years. Enlisted, April 18, 1861, at Brooklyn, to serve three years; mustered in as sergeant, Co. A, May 23, 1861; discharged for disability, August 24, 1861, at Arlington, Va.

Miller, Joseph J. — Age, 23 years. Enlisted at Brooklyn to serve three years; mustered in as private; unassigned, September 4, 1862; no further record.

Miller, Robert—Age, 29 years. Enlisted, August 29, 1862, at Brooklyn, to serve three years; mustered in as private; unassigned, August 30, 1862; no further record.

Miller, Valentin—Age, 18 years. Enlisted, September 8, 1862, at Brooklyn, to serve three years; mustered in as private, Co. B, September 9, 1862; missing in action, July 1, 1863, at Gettysburg, Pa.; returned, January 13, 1864; transferred to Veteran Reserve Corps, March 16, 1864; also borne as Mistor.

Miller, William—Age, 21 years. Enlisted at Brooklyn, to serve three years; mustered in as private, Co. F, December 21, 1863; transferred to Co. K, Fifth Veteran Infantry, June 2, 1864.

Miller, William G.—Age, 20 years. Enlisted, August 12, 1862, at Brooklyn, to serve three years; mustered in as private, Co. A, August 14, 1862; killed in action, September 14, 1862, at South Mountain, Md.

Milligan, Robert—Age, 21 years. Enlisted, May 18, 1861, at Brooklyn, to serve three years; mustered in as private, Co. D, May 23, 1861; discharged for disability, October 24, 1862, at Philadelphia, Pa.

Mills, John—Age, 32 years. Enlisted, August 25, 1862, at Brooklyn, to serve three years; mustered in as private; unassigned, August 26, 1862; no further record.

Millspaugh, Virgil—Age, 42 years. Enlisted at Brooklyn, to serve three years; mustered in as private, Co. K, December 7, 1863; transferred to Co. G, Fifth Veteran Infantry, June 2, 1864.

Minchen, John—Age, 22 years. Enlisted, April 18, 1861, at Brooklyn, to serve three years; mustered in as private, Co. D, May 23, 1861; mustered out with company, June 2, 1864, at New York City.

Mimew, John—Age, 25 years. Enlisted, May 18, 1861, at Brooklyn, to serve three years; mustered in as private, Co. D, May 23, 1861; killed in action, July 21, 1861, at Bull Run, Va.

Minew, Joseph—Age, 22 years. Enlisted, May 10, 1861, at Brooklyn, to serve three years; mustered in as private, Co. G, May 23, 1861; discharged for disability on June 17, 1861.

Mitchell, David—Age, 22 years. Enlisted at Brooklyn, to serve three years; mustered in as private; unassigned, March 10, 1864; no further record.

Moffatt, James—Age, 45 years. Enlisted, June 30, 1861, at Brooklyn, to serve three years; mustered in as private, Co. K, August 1, 1861; discharged for disability, February 13, 1863, at Convalescent Camp, Va.

Moffatt, James—Age, 40 years. Enlisted at Brooklyn, to serve three years; mustered in as private; unassigned, March 11, 1864; no further record.

Mokler, Edward—Age, 24 years. Enlisted, April 18, 1861, at Brooklyn, to serve three years; mustered in as private., Co. A, May 23, 1861; wounded in action on July 1, 1863, at Gettysburg, Pa.; mustered out with company, June 6, 1864, at New York City, as Edward Moakler.

Molony, James—Age, 22 years. Enlisted. October 20, 1862, at Brooklyn, to serve three years; mustered in as private; unassigned, October 21, 1862; no further record.

Monger, George—Age, 38 years. Enlisted, December 9, 1863, at Brooklyn, to serve three years; mustered in as private, Co. G, December 23, 1863; transferred to Co. K, Fifth Veteran Infantry, June 2, 1864.

Monks, Samuel—Age, 39 years. Enlisted, July 1, 1861, at Brooklyn, to serve three years; mustered in as private, Co. K, August 1, 1861; transferred to Veteran Reserve Corps, September 30, 1863, from which discharged as of Co. D, Thirteenth Regiment, at Portland, Me.

Monroe, John—Age, 23 years. Enlisted at Brooklyn, to serve three years; mustered in as private; unassigned, November 8, 1862; no further record.

Montanus, Henry — Age, 18 years. Enlisted at Brooklyn to serve three years; mustered in as private, Co. F, July 1, 1861; deserted on March 10, 1862, at Upton Hill, Va.

Montanus, John — Age, 19 years. Enlisted, April 18, 1861, at Brooklyn, to serve three years; mustered in as private, Co. A, May 23, 1861; discharged for disability, February 21, 1863; also borne as Montenus, and Mantarnis.

Moody, John — Age, 28 years. Enlisted at Brooklyn, to serve three years; mustered in as private, Co. A, August 20, 1862; transferred to Co. K, Fifth Veteran Infantry, June 2, 1864.

Moore, Alfred — Age, 24 years. Enlisted, April 18, 1861, at Brooklyn, to serve three years; mustered in as private, Co. H, May 23, 1861; captured in action, August 29, 1862, at Groveton, Va.; exchanged October, 1862; mustered out with company, June 6, 1864.

Moore, Elias H. — Age, 19 years. Enlisted at Brooklyn, to serve three years; mustered in as private, Co. I, January 11, 1864; transferred to Co. G, Fifth Veteran Infantry, June 2, 1864.

Moore, Thomas — Age, 19 years. Enlisted, April 18, 1861, at Brooklyn, to serve three years; mustered in as private, Co. H, May 23, 1861; deserted, November 30, 1862, from hospital, Washington, D.C.

Moran, Thomas — Age, 23 years. Enlisted, April 18, 1861, at Brooklyn, to serve three years; mustered in as private, Co. E, May 23, 1861; discharged for disability, September 24, 1861, at Arlington, Va.; also borne as Thomas J. and Thomas P. Moran.

Morgan, Edwin D. — Age, 24 years. Enlisted at Brooklyn, to serve three years; mustered in as private, Co. B, December 11, 1861; deserted, December 14, 1862, from hospital at Washington, D.C.; also borne as Edward D. Morgan.

Morgan, Wesley — Age, 35 years. Enlisted, September 25, 1862, at Brooklyn, to serve three years; mustered in as private, Co. C, September 25, 1862; transferred to Co. H, Fifth Veteran Infantry, June 2, 1864; prior service in Co. E, Seventy-First Militia.

Morley, John — Age, 24 years. Enlisted at Brooklyn, to serve three years; mustered in as private, Co. B, September 9, 1861; wounded in action, July 1, 1863, at Gettysburg, Pa; died of his wounds, September 20, 1863, at Newark, N.J.

Morong, Israel — Age, 42 years. Enlisted, September 17, 1862, at Brooklyn, to serve three years; mustered in as private; unassigned, September 19, 1862; no further record.

Morrell, Abram — Age, 23 years. Enlisted, August 21, 1862, at Brooklyn, to serve three years; mustered in as private, Co. C, August 22, 1862; transferred to Co. H, Fifth Veteran Infantry, June 2, 1864; also borne as Morrill.

Morrell, John — Age, 21 years. Enlisted, at Brooklyn, to serve three years; mustered in as private, Co. C, September 30, 1861; wounded in action, July 1, 1863, at Gettysburg Pa.; transferred to Fifth Veteran Infantry, June 2, 1864.

Morrill, Benjamin A. — Age, 43 years. Enlisted, April 18, 1861, at Brooklyn, to serve three years; mustered in as private, Co. C, May 23, 1861; discharged for disability, May 23, 1862, at Upton Hill, Va.; also borne as Benjamin J. Morrell.

Morris, Charles H. — Age, 30 years. Enrolled, April 18, 1861, at Brooklyn, to serve three years; mustered in as second lieutenant, Co. H, May 21, 1861; as captain, Co. K, July 16, 1861; discharged for disability, January 18, 1863; commissioned second lieutenant in Fourteenth Militia, May 6, 1861, with rank from April 25, 1861, not commissioned captain.

Morris, James — Age, 19 years. Enlisted at Brooklyn, to serve three years; mustered in as private, Co. K, December 5, 1863; transferred to Co. G, Fifth Veteran Infantry, June 2, 1864.

Morris, Thomas — Age, 32 years. Enlisted

at Brooklyn, to serve three years; mustered in as private, Co. K, January 12, 1864; transferred to Co. K, Fifth Veteran Infantry, June 2, 1864.

Morris, William J.—Enlisted at Brooklyn, to serve three years; mustered in as private, Co. K, October 11, 1861; deserted June 12, 1863.

Morrison, Richard—Age, 32 years. Enlisted, December 28, 1863, at Brooklyn to serve three years; mustered in as private, Co. I, December 30, 1863; discharged for disability, April 3, 1864, at Culpeper, Va.

Morrow, James 1st—Age, 18 years. Enlisted, April 18, 1861, at Brooklyn, to serve three years; mustered in as private, Co. F, May 23, 1861; deserted February 22, 1862, at Upton Hill, Va.

Morrow, James 2d—Age, 21 years. Enlisted at Brooklyn, to serve three years; mustered in as private, Co. F, September 19, 1861; discharged for disability, February 25, 1864.

Morrow, Richard—Age, 21 years. Enlisted, April 18, 1861, at Brooklyn, to serve three years; mustered in as private, Co. F, May 23, 1861; discharged, October 8, 1862, at Washington, D.C.

Morrow, Thomas—Age, 23 years. Enlisted, April 18, 1861, at Brooklyn, to serve three years; mustered in as private, Co. A, May 23, 1861; deserted March 1, 1863, from hospital.

Morton, Charles—Age, 25 years. Enlisted at Brooklyn, to serve three years; mustered in as private, Co. F, December 19, 1863; deserted, December 22, 1863, at Kelly's Ford, Va.; also borne as James Morton.

Mott, Henry G.—Age, 19 years. Enlisted, July 1, 1861, at Brooklyn, to serve three years; mustered in as private, Co. I, August 1, 1861; wounded in action on July 21, 1861, at Bull Run, Va.; deserted January 24, 1862, at Upton Hill, Va.

Mott, John—Age, 18 years. Enlisted, July 1, 1861, at Brooklyn, to serve three years; mustered in as private, Co. I, August 1, 1861; discharged for disability, February 5, 1863, at Alexandria, Va.

Mott, Wilson S.—Age, 22 years. Enlisted, December 16, 1863, at Brooklyn, to serve three years; mustered in as private, Co. K, December 23, 1863; discharged for disability July 20, 1864, at Wilets Point, New York Harbor.

Mudge, Frederick R.—Age, 30 years. Enlisted at Brooklyn, to serve three years; mustered in as private, Co. I, December 31, 1863; transferred to Co. G, Fifth Veteran Infantry, June 2, 1864; also borne as Mudger.

Muller, Willim—Age, 26 years. Enlisted, April 18, 1861, at Brooklyn, to serve three years; mustered in as private, Co. H, May 23, 1861; deserted January 26, 1862, at Upton Hill, Va.; also borne as Miller.

Mullins, William—Age, 26 years. Enlisted at Brooklyn, to serve three years; mustered in as private; unassigned, October 28, 186; no further record.

Mulvehill, William P.—Age, 25 years. Enlisted, December 15, 1863, at Brooklyn, to serve three years; mustered in as private, Co. K, December 21, 1863; discharged for disability, March 7, 1864, at Culpeper, Va., also born as Mulverhil and William B. Mulerill.

Mungerford, John—Age, 20 years. Enlisted, April, 18, 1861, at Brooklyn, to serve three years; mustered in as private, Co. G, May 23, 1861; mustered out with company on June 6, 1864, at New York City; also borne as Mungovin.

Munkenbeck, ____—Age, 19 years. Enlisted, August 19, 1862, at Brooklyn, to serve three years; mustered in as private, Co. K, August 20, 1862; discharged for disability February 14, 1863, at Convalescent Camp, Va.

Munson, Owen—Enrolled and appointed assistant surgeon November 29, 1862; discharged February 16, 1863; commissioned assistant surgeon December 5, 1862, with rank from November 29, 1862, vice D.B. Dewey, resigned.

Murphy, Michael — Age, 21 years. Enlisted, September 2, 1862, at Brooklyn, to serve three years; mustered in as private, Co. H, September 3, 1862; wounded in action, April 29, 1863, at Reynolds Crossing, Va.; died of his wounds May 8, 1863, at FitzHugh House, Va.

Murphy, Orlando — Age, 18 years. Enlisted at Brooklyn, to serve three years; mustered in as private, Co. H, November 8, 1861; deserted January 25, 1862, at Upton Hill, Va.

Murphy, Peter — Age, 22 years. Enlisted, April 18, 1861, at Brooklyn, to serve three years; mustered in as private, Co. B, May 23, 1861; captured in action, July 1, 1863, at Gettysburg, Pa.; paroled and sent to Camp Chester, Pa., July 1863; no further record.

Murray, James — Age, 26 years. Enlisted, April 18, 1861, at Brooklyn, to serve three years; mustered in as private, Co. A, May 23, 1861; killed in action, July 21, 1861, at Bull Run, Va.

Murray, John — Age, 21 years. Enlisted at Brooklyn, to serve three years; mustered in as private, Co. K, December 7, 1863; transferred to Co. B, Fifth Veteran Infantry, June 2, 1864.

Murray, William — Age, 21 years. Enlisted, May 18, 1861, at Brooklyn, to serve three years; mustered in as private, Co. B, May 23, 1861; died of disease, August 12, 1861, at Brooklyn, N.Y.

Mussehl, Charles — Age, 21 years. Enlisted, April 18, 1861, at Brooklyn to serve three years; mustered in as private, Co. F, May 23, 1861; promoted corporal, no date; killed in action, September 14, 1862, at South Mountain, Md.

Myckolsky, Alexander — Age, 27 years. Enlisted at Brooklyn, to serve three years; mustered in as private, Co. K, January 11, 1864; transferred to Co. G, Fifth Veteran Infantry, June 2, 1864; also borne as McCloskey.

Myers, Clemens J. — Age, 31 years. Enlisted, December 4, 1863, at Brooklyn to serve three years; mustered in as private, Co. G, December 8, 1863; transferred to Co. D, Fifth Veteran Infantry, June 2, 1864; also borne as Clements J. Myers.

Myers, David — Age, 29 years. Enrolled, April 18, 1861, at Brooklyn, to serve three years; mustered in as first lieutenant, Co. C, May 23, 1861; promoted captain, July 1, 1861; wounded in action September 17, 1862, at Antietam, Md.; died of his wounds, September 25, 1862; not commissioned first lieutenant; commissioned captain in Fourteenth Militia, July 8, 1861, with rank from July 1, 1861.

Myers, Evert, Jr. — Age, 27 years. Enlisted, April 18, 1861, at Brooklyn, to serve three years; mustered in as private, Co. C, May 23, 1861; promoted sergeant, October 1, 1861; discharged August 26, 1863; also borne as Everet J. Meyers.

Myers, George F. — Age, 22 years. Enlisted, April 18, 1861, at Brooklyn, to serve three years; mustered in as private, Co. D, May 23, 1861; deserted February 14, 1862, from Camp Marion, Upton Hill, Va.

Myers, James H. — Age, 25 years. Enlisted, April 18, 1861, at Brooklyn, to serve three years; mustered in as corporal, Co. F, May 23, 1861; returned to ranks, no date; discharged for disability, August 1, 1861, at Arlington, Va.

Myers, John — Age, 24 years. Enlisted, April 18, 1861, at Brooklyn, to serve three years; mustered in as private, Co. F, May 23, 1861; discharged for disability, July 29, 1861, at Arlington, Va.

Myers, John F., Jr. — Age, 19 years. Enlisted, August 8, 1862, at Brooklyn, to serve three years; mustered in as private, Co. H, August 14, 1862; missing in action, July 1, 1863, at Gettysburg, Pa.; no further record.

Nash, William A. — Age, 27 years. Enlisted, August 20, 1862, at Brooklyn, to serve three years; mustered in as private, Co. G, August 21, 1862; transferred to Co. D, Fifth Veteran Infantry, June 2, 1864.

Nellis, John — Age, 17 years. Enlisted, at Brooklyn, to serve three years; mustered in as private, Co. E, November 2, 1861; discharged, August 10, 1862; subsequent service in Co. E, Fifth Artillery; also borne as John N. Nellis.

Nelson, John — Age, 30 years. Enlisted, August 29, 1862, at Brooklyn, to serve three years mustered in as private, Co. D, August 30, 1862; transferred to Co. I, Fifth Veteran Infantry, June 2, 1864.

Nesbit, James — Age, 40 years. Enlisted, July 1, 1861, at Brooklyn, to serve three years; mustered in as private, Co. I, August 1, 1861; discharged for disability, January 30, 1863, at Alexandria, Va.

Nesbitt, James — Age, 22 years. Enlisted, April 18, 1861, at Brooklyn, to serve three years; mustered in as private, Co. D, May 23, 1861; promoted corporal November 1, 1862; wounded in action, July 1, 1863, at Gettysburg, Pa.; transferred to Veteran Reserve Corps, December 1, 1863.

Nesbitt, Thomas — Age, 17 years. Enlisted, December 5, 1863, at Brooklyn, to serve three years; mustered in as private, Co. I, December 8, 1863; deserted, January 1, 1864, at Kelly's Ford, Va.

Nestor, Patrick — Age, 30 years. Enlisted, April 18, 1861, at Brooklyn, to serve three years; mustered in as private, Co. G, May 23, 1861; killed in action, September 17, 1862, at Antietam, Md.; also borne as Nester.

Newberg, Seneca — Age, 27 years. Enlisted, December 12, 1863, at Brooklyn, to serve three years; mustered in as private, Co. K, December 23, 1863; transferred to Co. G, Fifth Veteran Infantry, June 2, 1864; also borne as Seneca Newberry.

Newkirk, William — Age, 22 years. Enlisted, April 18, 1861, at Brooklyn, to serve three years; mustered in as private, Co. F, May 23, 1861; deserted October 20, 1861, at Upton Hill, Va.

Newman, John — Age, 26 years. Enlisted, April 18, 1861, at Brooklyn, to serve three years; mustered in as private, Co. F, May 23, 1861; promoted corporal, no date; missing in action, July 1, 1863, at Gettysburg, Pa.; returned October 8, 1863; wounded in action, May 8, 1864, at Piney Branch Church, Va.; no further record.

Newman, William B. — Age, 35 years. Enlisted, April 18, 1861, at Brooklyn, to serve three years; mustered in as private, company of engineers, May 23, 1861; mustered out August 28, 1861, at Arlington, Va.

Nichols, Lewis, Jr. — Age, 26 years. Enlisted, April 1, 1861, at Brooklyn, to serve three years; mustered in as corporal, Co. B, May 23, 1861; promoted first sergeant, November 1, 1862; wounded in action, May 10, 1864, at Laurel Hill Va.; mustered out company, June 6, 1864, at New York City, as Louis Nichols.

Noack, Robert C. — Age, 26 years. Enlisted, September 12, 1862, at Brooklyn, to serve three years; mustered in as private; unassigned, September 15, 1862; no further record.

Nolan, James C. — Age, 25 years. Enlisted, May 18, 1861, at Brooklyn, to serve three years; mustered in as private, Co. B, May 23, 1861; deserted, August 11, 1861, at Arlington, Va.

Nolan, John — Age, 36 years. Enlisted at Brooklyn, to serve three years; mustered in as private, Co. C, September 28, 1861; discharged for disability, May 25, 1862, at Falmouth, Va.

Nolan, Timothy — Age, 21 years. Enlisted, August 23, 1862, at Brooklyn, to serve three years; mustered in as private, Co. D, August 25, 1862; transferred to Co. H, Fifth Veteran Infantry, June 2, 1864.

Noonan, Daniel — Age, 19 years. Enlisted at New York City to serve three years; mustered in as private; unassigned, March 8, 1864; no further record.

Norris, Charles — Age, 18 years. Enlisted, April 18, 1861, at Brooklyn to serve three years; mustered in as private, Co. H,

May 23, 1861; discharged, March 31, 1864; also borne as Charles F. and Charles T. Norris and as Charles Morris.

Norton, Cyrus B.—Age, 35 years. Enlisted at Brooklyn, to serve three years; mustered in as private, Co. I, December 26, 1863; transferred to Co. G, Fifth Veteran Infantry, June 2, 1864; also borne as Cyrus B. Naughton.

Norton, Patrick—Age, 38 years. Enlisted, April 18, 1861, at Brooklyn to serve three years; mustered in as private, Co. B, May 23, 1861; promoted corporal, February 1, 1863; mustered out with company, June 6, 1864, at New York City.

Nugent, Francis—Age, 30 years. Enlisted, December 31, 1863, at Brooklyn, to serve three years; mustered in as private, Co. K, January 5, 1864; transferred to Co. G, Fifth Veteran Infantry, June 2, 1864.

Nuthman, Theodore—Age, 26 years. Enlisted, August 21, 1862, at Brooklyn to serve three years; mustered in as private, Co. A, August 22, 1862; mustered out on May 13, 1865, at Fort Columbus, New York Harbor; also borne as Numan.

Nutt, James—Age, 18 years. Enlisted, April 18, 1861, at Brooklyn, to serve three years; mustered in as private, Co. F, May 23, 1861; deserted November 17, 1861, at Upton Hill, Va.

Nuttman, William—Age, 22 years. Enlisted, April 18, 1861, at Brooklyn, to serve three years; mustered in as private, Co. E, May 23, 1861; mustered out with company June 6, 1864, at New York City.

O'Brien, Bury J.—Age, 21 years. Enlisted, August 26, 1862, at Brooklyn, to serve three years; mustered in as private, Co. D, August 27, 1862; transferred to Co. I, Fifth Veteran Infantry, June 2, 1864; also borne as Benj. J. and Bary J. O'Brien.

O'Brien, David—Age, 23 years. Enlisted at Brooklyn, to serve three years; mustered in as private; unassigned, September 30, 1862; no further record.

O'Brien, John—Age, 40 years. Enlisted, December 8, 1863, at Brooklyn, to serve three years; mustered in as private, Co. K, December 23, 1863; transferred to Co. G, Fifth Veteran Infantry, June 2, 1864.

O'Brien, Patrick—Age, 25 years. Enlisted at Brooklyn, to serve three years; mustered in as private, Co. I, December 8, 1863; transferred to Co. G, Fifth Veteran Infantry, June 2, 1864; also borne as O'Brian.

O'Brien, Thomas—Age, 25 years. Enlisted at Brooklyn, to serve three years; mustered in as private, Co. K, December 17, 1863; transferred to. Co. G, Fifth Veteran Infantry, June 2, 1864.

O'Connell, Eugene—Age, 41 years. Enlisted at Brooklyn, to serve three years; mustered in as private, Co. K, December 8, 1863; transferred to Co. G, Fifth Veteran Infantry, June 2, 1864.

O'Connell, James C.—Age, 25 years. Enlisted, April 18, 1861, at Brooklyn, to serve three years; mustered in as private, Co. H, May 23, 1861; deserted July 31, 1861, at Arlington, Va.

O'Connor, Edward A.—Age, 23 years. Enlisted, September 5, 1862, at Brooklyn, to serve three years; mustered in as private, Co. A, September 6, 1862; wounded in action, July 1, 1863, at Gettysburg, Pa.; deserted August 5, 1863, from hospital at Germantown, Pa.

O'Connor, Francis—Age, 25 years. Enlisted, April 1, 1861, at Brooklyn, to serve three years; mustered in as private, Co. H, May 23, 1861; discharged for disability, November 30, 1862, at Philadelphia, Pa.

O'Connor, John—Age, 21 years. Enlisted, June 30, 1861, at Brooklyn, to serve three years; mustered in as private, Co. I, August 1, 1861; transferred to Veteran Reserve Corps, November 6, 1863.

O'Connor, John—Age, 27 years. Enlisted, April 18, 1861, at Brooklyn, to serve three years; mustered in as private, company of engineers, May 23, 1861; mustered out August 28, 1861, at Arlington, Va.

O'Conor, Daniel—Age, 19 years. Enlisted at Brooklyn to serve three years; mustered in as private, Co. A, November 30, 1863; transferred to Co. A, Fifth Veteran Infantry, June 2, 1864.

O'Donnell, William C.—Age, 21 years. Enlisted, April 18, 1861, at Brooklyn to serve three years; mustered in as private, Co. H, May 23, 1861; discharged for disability, June 27, 1863, at New York City.

O'Flaherty, John—Age, 23 years. Enlisted at Brooklyn, to serve three years; mustered in as private, Co. G, December 7, 1863; transferred to Co. K, Fifth Veteran Infantry, June 2, 1864.

O'Flaraty, William—Age, 18 years. Enlisted at Brooklyn, to serve three years; mustered in as private, Co. K, December 11, 1863; transferred to Co. G, Fifth Veteran Infantry, June 2, 1864; also borne as O'Flaherty.

O'Gara, John—Age, 18 years. Enlisted at Brooklyn, to serve three years; mustered in as private, Co. F, October 17, 1862; transferred to Co. K, Fifth Veteran Infantry, June 2, 1864.

Ogle, Charles—Age, 42 years. Enlisted at Brooklyn, to serve three years; mustered in as private, Co. G, December 8, 1863; discharged August 23, 1864, at New York City.

O'Hare, George—Age, 27 years. Enlisted, April 18, 1861, at Brooklyn to serve three years; mustered in as private, Co. A, May 23, 1861; deserted September 25, 1861, at Arlington, Va.; also borne as O'Hard.

O'Kaffe, Patrick—Age, 23 years. Enlisted, June 30, 1861, at Brooklyn, to serve three years; mustered in as private, Co. K, August 1, 1861; captured in action, August 29, 1862, at Bull Run, Va.; exchanged, no date; deserted, April 27, 1863; also borne as O'Keefe.

O'Keefe, Thomas—Age, 19 years. Enlisted, August 23, 1862, at Brooklyn, to serve three years; mustered in as private, Co. G, August 25, 1862; deserted December 17, 1862, at Rappahannock, Va.

Oliver, John—Age, 22 years. Enlisted, June 30, 1861, at Brooklyn, to serve three years; mustered in as sergeant, Co. K, August 1, 1861; returned to ranks, no date; transferred to Co. G, Fifth Veteran Infantry, June 2, 1864.

Oliver, John—Age, 32 years. Enlisted, April 18, 1861, at Brooklyn, to serve three years; mustered in as private, company of engineers, May 23, 1861; mustered out August 28, 1861, at Arlington, Va.

Oliver, John A.—Age, 34 years. Enlisted, September 10, 1862, at Brooklyn, to serve three years; mustered in as private, Co. D, September 11, 1862; deserted, October 25, 1863, from Convalescent Camp, Alexandria, Va.

O'Neil, Daniel—Age, 21 years. Enlisted, April 18, 1861, at Brooklyn, to serve three years; mustered in as private, Co. F, May 23, 1861; discharged for disability January 30, 1863; also borne as William O'Neil.

O'Neil, William—Age, 25 years. Enlisted, September 19, 1862, at Brooklyn, to serve three years; mustered in as private, Co. H, September 20, 1862; missing in action, July 1, 1863, at Gettysburg, Pa.; returned, December 10, 1863; transferred to Co. I, Fifth Veteran Infantry, June 2, 1864; also borne as O'Niell.

O'Niel, George—Age, 25 years. Enlisted, April 18, 1861, at Brooklyn, to serve three years; mustered in as private, Co. A, May 23, 1861; killed in action, August 29, 1862, at Bull Run, Va.; also borne as O'Neal.

O'Rielly, Francis—Age, 22 years. Enlisted, April 18, 1861, at Brooklyn, to serve three years; mustered in as private, Co. B, May 23, 1861; deserted, October 27, 1863, at Bristoe Station, Va.

O'Rielly, James—Age, 27 years. Enlisted at Brooklyn, to serve three years; mustered in as private, Co. B, April 15, 1862; discharged for disability, February 27, 1863, at Philadelphia, Pa.; also borne as O'Reilly.

Osborne, George—Age, 37 years. Enlisted,

September 5, 1862, at Brooklyn, to serve three years; mustered in as private, Co. A, September 6, 1862; transferred to Co. I, Fifth Veteran Infantry, June 2, 1864; also borne as Osborn.

Ostrande, Marcus B.—Age, 24 years. Enlisted, May 18, 1861, at Brooklyn, to serve three years; mustered in as corporal, Co. D, May 23, 1861; returned to rank, no date; killed in action, July 21, 1861, at Bull Run, Va.

Ostrander, Peter W.—Age, 31 years. Enlisted, April 18, 1861, at Brooklyn, to serve three years; mustered in as private, company of engineers, May 23, 1861; mustered out, August 28, 1861, at Arlington, Va.

O'Sullivan, Jeremiah—Age, 23 years. Enlisted, April 18, 1861, at Brooklyn, to serve three years; mustered in as private, Co. F, May 23, 1861; deserted, January 5, 1862 at Upton Hill, Va.

O'Sullivan, Timothy—Age, 27 years. Enlisted, April 18, 1861, at Brooklyn, to serve three years; mustered in as private, Co. F, May 23, 1861; wounded and captured in action, July 21, 1861, at Bull Run, Va.; paroled, January 17, 1862; discharged for wounds, April 29, 1862.

Otis, Harison—Age, 41 years. Enlisted, December 15, 1861, at Brooklyn, to serve three years; mustered in as private, Co. K, December 21, 1861; transferred to Co. G, Fifth Veteran Infantry, June 2, 1864.

Owen, Robert H.—Age, 18 years. Enlisted, April 18, 1861, at Brooklyn, to serve three years; mustered in as private, Co. E, May 23, 1861; wounded in action, July 21, 1861, at Bull Run. Va.; discharged for wounds, February 22, 1862, at Upton Hill, Va.

Owsky, Jacob H.—Age, 26 years. Enlisted, December 1, 1863, at Brooklyn, to serve three years; mustered in as private; unassigned, December 7, 1863; no further record.

Packard, Peres A.—Age, 31 years. Enlisted, August 29, 1862, at Brooklyn, to serve three years; mustered in as private, Co. C, August 30, 1862; transferred to Co. H, Fifth Veteran Infantry, on June 2, 1864.

Palmer, John—Age, 22 years. Enlisted, April 18, 1861, at Brooklyn, to serve three years; mustered in as private, Co. H, May 23, 1861; mustered out with company, June 6, 1864, at New York City.

Parcels, James M.—Age, 18 years. Enlisted at Brooklyn, to serve three years; mustered in as private, Co. C, November 8, 1861; discharged for disability, June 25, 1862, at Washington, D.C.

Parker, John—Age, 18 years. Enlisted at Brooklyn, to serve three years; mustered in as private, Co. B, February 4, 1863; transferred to Co. I, Fifth Veteran Infantry, June 2, 1864.

Parry, William H.—Age, 33 years. Enlisted, August 27, 1862, at Brooklyn, to serve three years; mustered in as private, Co. D, August 28, 1862; transferred to Co. I, Fifth Veteran Infantry, June 2, 1864.

Passano, Medora—Age, 22 years. Enlisted April 18, 1861, at Brooklyn, to serve three years; mustered in as private, Co. F, May 23, 1861; deserted July 21, 1861, at Bull Run, Va.

Passein, Alfred—Age, 18 years. Enlisted, May 4, 1861, at Brooklyn, to serve three years; mustered in as private, Co. G, May 23, 1861; transferred to Veteran Reserve Corps, January 1, 1863.

Patterson, Thomas J.—Age, 25 years. Enlisted, April 18, 1861, at Brooklyn to serve three years; mustered in as private, Co. A, May 23, 1861; deserted July 21, 1863, at Washington, D.C.; also borne as Thomas G. Patterson.

Paynton, George W.—Age, 25 years. Enlisted, August 20, 1862, at Brooklyn, to serve three years; mustered in as private, Co. A, August 21, 1862; discharged for disability, December 24, 1862; also borne as Rynton and Pynton.

Peach, Edward—Age, 35 years. Enlisted, April 18, 1861, at Brooklyn, to serve three years; mustered in as private, Co. D, May 23, 1861; discharged for disability March 26, 1862.

Pearce, Charles T.— Age, 28 years. Enlisted, April 18, 1861, at Brooklyn, to serve three years; mustered in as private, Co. C, May 23, 1861; promoted corporal, January 1, 1864; mustered out June 14, 1864, at New York City; also borne as Charles F. Pearce.

Pearce, Edward E.— Age, 36 years. Enrolled, April 18, 1861, at Brooklyn, to serve three years; mustered in as second lieutenant, Co. B, May 23, 1861; as first lieutenant, August 29, 1862; mustered out with company, June 6, 1864, at New York City; commissioned second lieutenant in Fourteenth Militia, May 4, 1861, with rank from May 2, 1861, original; first lieutenant, October 24, 1862, with rank from August 29, 1862.

Pearson, Alanson— Age, 19 years. Enlisted, April 18, 1861, at Brooklyn, to serve three years; mustered in as private, Co. C, May 23, 1861; wounded in action, September 14, 1862, at South Mountain, Md.; died of his wounds October 27, 1862, at Brooklyn, N.Y.

Peck, James— Age, 18 years. Enlisted at Brooklyn, to serve three years; mustered in as private, Co. K, December 5, 1863; discharged for disability, March 31, 1864.

Peck, William F.— Age, 22 years. Enlisted, May 4, 1861, at Brooklyn, to serve three years; mustered in as private, Co. G, May 23, 1861; discharged for disability June 17, 1861, at Camp Wood, Arlington, Va.

Peddie, Alexander— Age, 20 years. Enlisted, May 18, 1861, at Brooklyn, to serve three years; mustered in as private, Co. G, May 23, 1861; transferred to Co. D, Fifth Veteran Infantry, June 2, 1864.

Peitsch, Edmund— Age, 35 years. Enlisted, May 18, 1861, at Brooklyn, to serve three years; mustered in as private, Co. D, May 23, 1861; discharged for disability May 26, 1862, at hospital, Falls Church, Va.

Pelliginy, Louis— Age, 21 years. Enlisted at Brooklyn, to serve three years; mustered in as private, Co. I, February 23, 1864; transferred to Co. G, Fifth Veteran Infantry, June 2, 1864.

Pendergast, Joseph H.— Age, 25 years. Enlisted, April 18, 1861, at Brooklyn. To serve three years; mustered in as corporal, Co. A, May 23, 1861; promoted sergeant, no date; discharged for disability, October 14, 1862, at Philadelphia, Pa.

Pendleton, William— Age, 32 years. Enlisted, September 4, 1862, at Brooklyn, to serve three years; mustered in as private, Co. G, September 5, 1862; died of typhoid fever, January 4, 1863, at Stanton Hospital, Washington, D.C.

Pendrell, Albert— Age, 18 years. Enlisted, April 18, 1861, at Brooklyn, to serve three years; mustered in as private, Co. C, May 23, 1861; promoted corporal, November 1, 1862; wounded in action July 1, 1863, at Gettysburg, Pa.; died of his wounds, July 2, 1863; also borne as Albert M. Pendrell and Pendrill.

Pennington, John H.— Age, 21 years. Enlisted, April 18, 1861, at Brooklyn, to serve three years; mustered in as private, Co. A, May 23, 1861; discharged for disability, July 27, 1861, at Arlington, Va.

Perine, Daniel— Age, 42 years. Enlisted, August 20, 1862, at Brooklyn, to serve three years; mustered in as private, Co. E, August 21, 1862; transferred to Co. A, Fifth Veteran Infantry, June 2, 1864; also borne as Perrine.

Perpignan, Albert H.— Age, 21 years. Enlisted, May 18, 1861, at Brooklyn, to serve three years; mustered in as private, Co. D, May 23, 1861; discharged for disability, January 1, 1863, at Fairfax, Va.; also borne as Albert C. Perpegnan, Jr.

Perry, Fulgence— Age, 25 years. Enlisted, April 18, 1861, at Brooklyn, to serve three years; mustered in as private, Co. A, May 23, 1861; discharged for disability, January 10, 1863, at Providence, R.I.; again enlisted, January 20, 1864; transferred to

Co. B, Fifth Veteran Infantry, June 2, 1864; also borne as Fulgence A. Perry.

Perry, James H.—Age, 18 years. Enlisted, April 18, 1861, at Brooklyn, to serve three years; mustered in as private, Co. E, May 23, 1861; discharged on August 15, 1861, for promotion to second lieutenant, Co. I, Forty-Eighth Infantry.

Peters, Daniel—Age, 24 years. Enlisted, April 18, 1861, at Brooklyn, to serve three years; mustered in as private, Co. E, May 23, 1861; discharged for disability, October 24, 1862, at Philadelphia, Pa.

Pettiner, Joseph—Age, 20 years. Enlisted, August 18, 1862, at Brooklyn, to serve three years; mustered in as private, Co. B, August 19, 1862; transferred to Co. K, December 19, 1862; dishonorably discharged for desertion, June 26, 1863; also borne as Petner; true name Joseph Wade; subsequent service, Co. E, Seventy-Fifth Infantry.

Pettit, Clinton—Age, 22 years. Enlisted, April 18, 1861, at Brooklyn, to serve three years; mustered in as private, Co. H, May 23, 1861; transferred to Veteran Reserve Corps, July 27, 1863.

Pfeiffer, George—Age, 29 years. Enlisted, July 1, 1861, at Brooklyn, to serve three years; mustered in as private, Co. K, August 1, 1861; transferred, same date, to Co. F; discharged for disability, May 15, 1862, at Alexandria. Va.

Phelan, John—Age, 25 years. Enlisted at Brooklyn, to serve three years; mustered in as private, Co. K, February 26, 1864; transferred to Co. G, Fifth Veteran Infantry, June 2, 1864; also borne as Phalen.

Phillip, Benjamin D.—Enrolled and appointed second lieutenant, no date; wounded in action, July 21, 1861, at Manassas, Va.; discharged for disability January 2, 1862; prior service, Seventy-First Militia; not commissioned second lieutenant.

Phillip, William—Age, 29 years. Enlisted, April 18, 1861, at Brooklyn, to serve three years; mustered in as private, Co. B, May 1, 1861; mustered out with company on June 6, 1864, at New York City; also borne as Wm. H. Philips.

Pierce, Charles B.—Age, 20, years. Enlisted. May 18, 1861, at Brooklyn, to serve three years; mustered in as private, Co. D, May 23, 1861; missing in action, December 13, 1862, at Fredericksburg, Va.; no further record.

Pierce, Frederick—Age, 28 years. Enlisted, September 9, 1862, at Brooklyn, to serve three years; mustered in as private, Co. H, September 10, 1862; no further record.

Pinckney, William H.H.—Age, 19 years. Enlisted, August 26, 1862, at Brooklyn, to serve three years; mustered in as private, Co. C, August 27, 1862; promoted corporal, January 1, 1864; transferred to Co. H, Fifth Veteran Infantry, June 2, 1864.

Pine, O. Stesdmead—Age, 18 years. Enlisted at Brooklyn, to serve three years; mustered in as private, Co. H, December 28, 1863; transferred to Co. I, Fifth Veteran Infantry, June 2, 1864; also borne as Stedman O. Peni and Pine.

Pink, Samuel T.—Age, 20 years. Enlisted, April 18, 1861, at Brooklyn, to serve three years; mustered in as private, Co. A, May 23, 1861; deserted October 10, 1862.

Pittman, William H.—Age, 23 years. Enlisted, April 18, 1861, at Brooklyn, to serve three years; mustered in as private, Co. E, May 23, 1861; mustered out with company, June 2, 1864, at New York City; also borne as Pettman.

Plant, Charles—Age, 23 years. Enlisted, April 18, 1861, at Brooklyn, to serve three years; mustered in as private, Co. C, May 23, 1861; wounded in action, July 1, 1863, at Gettysburg, Pa.; mustered out, June 14, 1864, at New York City.

Plasket, George—Age, 21 years. Enlisted, April 18, 1861, at Brooklyn, to serve three years; mustered in as private, Co. E, May 23, 1861; deserted February 5, 1862, at Upton Hill, Va.; also borne as George W. Plaskitt.

Plass, Garwood — Age, 35 years. Enrolled, April 25, 1861, at Brooklyn, to serve three years; mustered in as captain, Co. G, May 23, 1861; discharged for disability October 10, 1863; commissioned captain in Fourteenth Militia, April 28, 1861, with rank from same date.

Plows, Joseph E. — Age, 27 years. Enlisted, May 18, 1861, at Brooklyn, to serve three years; mustered in as private, Co. D, May 23, 1861; promoted corporal, October 11, 1861; wounded in action, August 29, 1862, at Bull Run, Va.; promoted sergeant, November 11, 1862; discharged for disability, November 29, 1862, at Philadelphia, Pa.

Pollard, Calvin — Age, 19 years. Enlisted, April 24, 1861, at Brooklyn, to serve three years; mustered in as private, Co. G, May 23, 1861; discharged for disability, June 17, 1861; again enlisted, January 15, 1862; mustered in as private, Co. D, January 10, 1862; transferred to U.S. Army, November 6, 1862.

Pomerick, Robert — Age, 28 years. Enlisted, April 18, 1861, at Brooklyn to serve three years; mustered in as private, Co. A, May 23, 1861; killed in action on July 21, 1861, at Bull Run, Va.; also borne as Pomerich.

Poole, George — Age, 18 years. Enlisted, at Brooklyn, to serve three years; mustered in as private, Co. F, December 3, 1863; transferred to Co. K, Fifth Veteran Infantry, June 2, 1864; also borne as Pool.

Porter, George — Age, 21 years. Enlisted, August 25, 1862, at Brooklyn, to serve three years; mustered in as private, Co. B, August 26, 1862; deserted, September 3, 1862, at Keedysville, Md.

Porter, George A. — Age, 31 years. Enlisted at Brooklyn, to serve three years; mustered in as private, Co. K, January 5, 1864; transferred to Co. G, Fifth Veteran Infantry, June 2, 1864.

Porter, James — Age, 21 years. Enlisted, December 14, 1863, at Brooklyn, to serve three years; mustered in as private, Co. K, December 24, 1863; transferred to Co. G, Fifth Veteran Infantry, June 2, 1864.

Post, Andrew — Age, 18 years. Enlisted, January 18, 1864, at Brooklyn, to serve three years; mustered in as musician, Co. I, January 27, 1864; transferred to Co. G, Fifth Veteran Infantry, June 2, 1864; also borne as Poss.

Post, Stephen — Age, 23 years. Enlisted, April 18, 1861, at Brooklyn, to serve three years; mustered in as private, Co. A, May 23, 1861; transferred to Co. I, Fifth Veteran Infantry, June 2, 1864.

Potter, Charles R. — Age, 25 years. Enlisted, April 18, 1861, at Brooklyn, to serve three years; mustered in as private, Co. E, May 23, 1861; discharged for disability September 13, 1861, at Arlington, Va.

Potts, John G. — Age, 33 years. Enlisted, August 21, 1862, at Brooklyn, to serve three years; mustered in as private, Co. B, August 22, 1862; wounded in action, July 1, 1863, at Gettysburg, Pa.; discharged for wounds, October 13, 1863, at Chestnut Hill Hospital, Philadelphia, Pa.

Pouch, Alfred H. — Age, 19 years. Enlisted, May 18, 1861, at Brooklyn, to serve three years; mustered in as private, Co. D, May 23, 1861; deserted on January 10, 1862, from Camp Marion, Upton Hill, Va.

Poucher, Abram — Age, 20 years. Enlisted, April 18, 1861, at Brooklyn, to serve three years; mustered in as private, Co. A, May 23, 1861; wounded in action, August 29, 1862, at Bull Run, Va.; died of his wounds, September 6, 1862.

Powell, Elias — Age, 21 years. Enlisted, May 18, 1861, at Brooklyn, to serve three years; mustered in as private, Co. B, May 23, 1861; discharged for disease, September 17, 1861, at Arlington, Va.

Powell, George H. — Age, 27 years. Enlisted, April 18, 1861, at Brooklyn, to serve three years; mustered in as private, Co. D, May 23, 1861; discharged for disability, June 18, 1861, at New York City.

Powell, William — Age, 18 years. Enlisted, April 18, 1861, at Brooklyn, to serve three years; mustered in as private, Co. A, May 23, 1861; wounded in action, April 29, 1863, at Reynolds Crossing, Va.; mustered out with company June 6, 1864, at New York City, as William B. Powell.

Power, William — Age, 22 years. Enlisted, April 18, 1861, at Brooklyn, to serve three years; mustered in as private, Co. A, May 23, 1861; killed in action, August 23, 1862, at Rappahannock Station, Va.; also borne as Wm. Powers.

Powers, John. — Age, 19 years. Enlisted, April 18, 1861, at Brooklyn, to serve three years; mustered in as private, Co. C, May 23, 1861; discharged for disability June 16, 1861.

Prentice, Ezra P. — Age, 24 years. Enlisted at Brooklyn, to serve three years; mustered in as private, Co. G, August 23, 1862; appointed wagon and returned to company, no date; transferred to Co. K, Fifth Veteran Infantry, on June 2, 1864.

Prescott, Charles R. — Age, 26 years. Enlisted, April 18, 1861, at Brooklyn, to serve three years; mustered in as corporal, Co. F, May 23, 1861; captured in action, July 21, 1861, at Bull Run, Va.; died August 14, 1861, at Richmond, Va.

Price, James — Age, 19 years. Enlisted, April 18, 1861, at Brooklyn, to serve three years; mustered in as private, Co. C, May 23, 1861; discharged for disability, June 5, 1862, at Patent Office Hospital, Washington, D.C., as James A. Price; also borne as Pryce.

Provenzale, Michael — Age, 21 years. Enlisted, April 18, 1861, at Brooklyn, to serve three years; mustered in as private, Co. D, May 23, 1861; deserted, August 16, 1862, from camp at Culpeper, Va.; also borne as Provinzale.

Pugh, Joseph C. — Age, 21 years. Enlisted, April 18, 1861, at Brooklyn to serve three years; mustered in as private, Co. E, May 23, 1861; transferred to Veteran Reserve Corps, October 7, 1863.

Putnan, Strod S. — Age, 18 years. Enlisted at Brooklyn, to serve three years; mustered in as private, Co. H, February 15, 1864; transferred to Co. K, Fifth Veteran Infantry, June 2, 1864.

Putney, Thomas — Age, 26 years. Enlisted at New York City to serve three years; mustered in as private; unassigned, July 26, 1861; no further record.

Quigley, Thomas — Age, 20 years. Enlisted, April 18, 1861, at Brooklyn, to serve three years; mustered in as private, Co. F, May 23, 1861; discharged for disability September 17, 1861, at Arlington, Va.

Quinn, Edmond — Age, 44 years. Enlisted, December 12, 1863, at Brooklyn, to serve three years; mustered in as private, Co. E, December 21, 1863; transferred to Co. H, Fifth Veteran Infantry, June 2, 1864.

Rab, Jacob — Age, 18 years. Enlisted, November 18, 1861, at Hudson to serve three years; mustered in as private, Co. G, November 20, 1861; captured in action, July 1, 1863, at Gettysburg, Pa.; returned to company August 30, 1863; mustered out June 27, 1864, at New York City, as Jacob A. Raab.

Rae, William C. — Age, 23 years. Enrolled, April 18, 1861, at Brooklyn, to serve three years; mustered in as sergeant, Co. B, May 23, 1861; promoted first sergeant, February 15, 1862; mustered in as second lieutenant, August 29, 1862; killed in action May 10, 1864, at Spotsylvania, Va.; commissioned second lieutenant, October 24, 1862, with rank from August 29, 1862.

Raff, William — Age, 31 years. Enlisted, August 27, 1862, at Brooklyn, to serve three years; mustered in as private, Co. A, August 28, 1862; transferred to. Co. I, Fifth Veteran Infantry, June 2, 1864.

Randolph, Abel F. — Age, 39 years. Enlisted, August 27, 1862, at Brooklyn, to serve three years; mustered in as private, Co. H, August 28, 1862; transferred to Co. I, Fifth Veteran Infantry, June 2, 1864; also borne as Albert F. Randolph.

Randolph, Albert F.—Age, 34 years. Enlisted at Brooklyn, to serve three years; mustered in as private, Co. H, August 19, 1862; wounded in action, September 17, 1862, at Antietam, Md.; discharged for wounds, January 13, 1863, at New York City.

Randolph, Albert T.—Age, 35 years. Enlisted, December 9, 1863, at Brooklyn, to serve three years; mustered in as private, Co. E, December 23, 1863; transferred to Co. H, Fifth Veteran Infantry, June 2, 1864; also borne as Albert F. Randolph.

Rankin, James D.—Age, 23 years. Enlisted, April 18, 1861, at Brooklyn, to serve three years; mustered in as private, Co. H, May 23, 1861; discharged for disability, January 7, 1863, at Washington, D.C.

Rankin, William—Age, 22 years. Enlisted, April 18, 1861, at Brooklyn, to serve three years; mustered in as private, Co. H, May 23, 1861; promoted corporal, May 25, 1862; sergeant, January 1, 1863; killed in action, May 8, 1864, at Laurel Hill, Va.

Rascol, Jules—Age, 21 years. Enlisted, April 18, 1861, at Brooklyn, to serve three years; mustered in as private, Co. F, May 23, 1861; deserted, November 20, 1862, from Camp Parole, Annapolis, Md.

Raser, Warren B.—Age, 18 years. Enlisted, April 25, 1861, at Brooklyn, to serve three years; mustered in as private, Co. G, May 23, 1861; wounded in action, July 1, 1863, at Gettysburg, Pa.; promoted corporal, no date; sergeant, January 8, 1864; mustered out with company, June 6, 1864, at New York City; also borne as Rasor.

Ratchford, Michael—Age, 21 years. Enlisted, August 25, 1862, at Brooklyn, to serve three years; mustered in as private, Co. H, August 26, 1862; missing in action July 1, 1863, at Gettysburg, Pa.; returned October 8, 1863; died of disease February 4, 1864, at Brooklyn, N.Y.

Rawley, William—Age, 37 years. Enlisted, December 10, 1863, at Brooklyn to serve three years; mustered in as private, Co. I, December 13, 1863; died of disease January 27, 1864, at Alexandria, Va.; also borne as Rowley.

Raymona, Henry A.—Age, 28 years. Enlisted, April 18, 1861, at Brooklyn to serve three years; mustered in as private, Co. C, May 23, 1861; discharged for disability on August 17, 1863; also borne as Raymond.

Redding, John—Age, 24 years. Enrolled, April 18, 1861, at Brooklyn, to serve three years; mustered in as corporal, Co. A, May 23, 1861; promoted sergeant, June 18, 1861; mustered in as second lieutenant, July 1, 1861; as first lieutenant, August 4, 1861; as captain, January 7, 1863; mustered out with company, June 6, 1864, at New York City as John W. Redding; commissioned second lieutenant, Fourteenth Miliitia, July 8, 1861, with rank from July 1, 1861, vice John H. Styles, promoted; first lieutenant, August 1, 1861, with rank from August 5, 1861, vice John H. Styles, resigned; captain, March 17, with rank from December 24, 1862, vice R.B. Jordan, promoted.

Reed, John—Age, 22 years. Enlisted, April 18, 1861, at Brooklyn, to serve three years; mustered in as private, Co. A, on May 23, 1861; wounded in action July 1, 1863, at Gettysburg, Pa.; mustered out with company, June 6, 1864, at New York City; also borne as James Reed.

Rees, Louis—Age, 22 years. Enlisted, September 8, 1862, at Brooklyn, to serve three years; mustered in as private, Co. F, September 9, 1862; transferred to navy, April 19, 1864.

Rehkamp, Bernard—Age, 30 years. Enlisted, August 26, 1862, at Brooklyn to serve three years; mustered in as private, Co. B, August 27, 1862; transferred to Co. I, Fifth Veteran Infantry, June 2, 1864.

Reiley, James—Age, 26 years. Enlisted, August 27, 1862, at Brooklyn, to serve three years; mustered in as private, Co. D, August 28, 1862; transferred to Co. I, Veteran Infantry, June 2, 1864; also borne as Reilly and Riley.

Reill, Jacob — Age, 23 years. Enlisted, August 22, 1862, at Brooklyn, to serve three years; mustered in as private, Co. F, August 25, 1862; wounded in action, July 1, 1863, at Gettysburg, Pa.; transferred to Veteran Reserve Corps, no date; from which discharged, July 17, 1865, at Washington, D.C.

Reilly, Patrick — Age, 28 years. Enlisted, June 30, 1861, at Brooklyn, to serve three years; mustered in as private, Co. K, August 1, 1861; wounded in action August 29, 1862, at Manassas, Va.; discharged for disability February 25, 1863, at Point Lookout, Md.

Reinhard, Julius — Age, 22 years. Enlisted at Brooklyn, to serve three years; mustered in as private, Co. E, September 9, 1862; transferred to Co. H, Fifth Veteran Infantry, June 2, 1864.

Renouf, Charles E. — Age, 20 years. Enlisted, April 18, 1861, to serve three years; mustered in as private, Co. C, May 23, 1861; discharged for disability November 14, 1862, at Washington, D.C.

Revere, George W. — Age, 24 years. Enlisted, August 20, 1862, at Brooklyn to serve three years; mustered in as private, Co. H, August 21, 1862; deserted November 2, 1863, from hospital, New York City.

Revere, William — Age, 26 years. Enlisted, May 18, 1861, at Brooklyn. to serve three years; mustered in as private, Co. D, May 23, 1861, discharged for disability, November 5, 1862, at hospital, Washington, D.C.

Reycroft, John — Enlisted at Brooklyn, to serve three years; mustered in as private, Co. K, July 1, 1861; transferred to Co. G, August 1, 1861; no further record.

Reynolds, George B. — Age, 22 years. Enlisted, August 20, 1862, to serve three years; mustered in as private, Co. E, August 21, 1862; deserted October 25, 1862, from hospital at Frederick, Md.

Reynolds, Hobby — Age, 30 years. Enlisted, August 19, 1862, at Brooklyn to serve three years; mustered in as private, Co. E, August 20, 1862; wounded September 17, 1862, at Antietam, Md.; transferred to Co. H, Fifth Veteran Infantry, June 2, 1864.

Reynolds, James E. — Age, 19 years. Enlisted, April 18, 1861, at Brooklyn to serve three years; mustered in as private, Co. E, May 23, 1861; mustered out with company June 6, 1864, at New York City; also borne as John E. Reynolds.

Reynolds, John — Age, 35 years. Enlisted at New York City, to serve three years; mustered in as private; unassigned, March 9, 1864; no further record.

Reynolds, Stanley — Age, 18 years. Enlisted, June 30, 1861, at Brooklyn to serve three years; mustered in as private, Co. K, August 1, 1861; deserted, June 22, 1863.

Reynolds, William A. — Age, 36 years. Enlisted at New York City to serve three years; mustered in as private, Co. I, March 1, 1862; transferred to Co. G, Fifth Veteran Infantry, June 2, 1864.

Rheude, John F. — Age, 18 years. Enlisted, April 18, 1861, at Brooklyn to serve three years; mustered in as private, Co. H, May 23, 1861; transferred to Co. H, Fifth Veteran Infantry, June 2, 1864.

Rhiem, Joseph — Age, 21 years Enlisted, May 18, 1861, at Brooklyn, to serve three years; mustered in as private, Co. B, May 23, 1861; dishonorably discharged, August 2, 1862, at Falmouth, Va.; also borne as Rhein and Relvin.

Rhine, Louis — Age, 22 years. Enlisted, August 29, 1862, at Brooklyn, to serve three years; mustered in as private; unassigned, August 30, 1862; no further record.

Rhodes, James — Age, 19 years. Enlisted, April 25, 1861, at Brooklyn to serve three years; mustered in as private, Co. G, May 23, 1861; promoted sergeant, no date; discharged for disability, January 20, 1863; also borne as John J. Rhodes.

Ribot, John.—Age, 38 years. Enlisted at Brooklyn, to serve three years; mustered in as private, Co. E, December 16, 1863; discharged for disability, March 6, 1864, at Culpeper, Va.; also borne as Riebert.

Rice, George H—Age, 19 years. Enlisted April 18, 1861, at Brooklyn to serve three years; mustered in as corporal, Co. A, May 23, 1861; promoted sergeant, no date; discharged for disability December 30, 1862, at Harewood Hospital, Washington, D.C.

Rice, Robert—Age, 23 year. Enlisted, April 25, 1861, at Brooklyn, to serve 3.
years; mustered in as private, Co. G, May 23, 1861; deserted January 22, 1862, at Upton Hill, Va.

Rich, Erskine—Age, 20 years. Enlisted, September 9, 1861, at New York City to serve three years; mustered in as private, Co. H, September 13, 1861; wounded and captured while on picket, November 18, 1861, at Falls Church, Va.; paroled, February 22, 1862; discharged September 8, 1862, for promotion as second lieutenant, Thirty-First Infantry.

Rich, James B.—Age, 24 years. Enlisted at Brooklyn, to serve three years; mustered in as private, Co. B, September 15, 1862; wounded in action, July 1, 1863, at Gettysburg, Pa.; transferred to Co. H, Fifth Veteran Infantry, June 2, 1864.

Rich, Theodore F.—Age, 19 years. Enlisted, September 9, 1861, at New York City to serve three years; mustered in as private, Co. H, September 13, 1861; captured while on picket, November 18, 1861, at Falls Church, Va.; paroled, February 22, 1862; discharged April 13, 1862, at Camp Prospect, Va.

Richardson, David P.—Age, 30 years. Enlisted, April 18, 1861, at Brooklyn to serve three years; mustered in as private, Co. E, May 23, 1861; deserted on September 2, 1861, at Arlington, Va.

Richardson, Joseph—Age, 20 years. Enlisted, April 25, 1861, at Brooklyn to serve three years; mustered in as private, Co. K, May 23, 1861; discharged for disability on October 9, 1861, at Arlington, Va.; also borne as Joseph V.B. Richardson.

Richardson, Mattiah J.—Age, 28 years. Enlisted as private, Co. E, August 26, 1862; promoted corporal, no date; transferred Brooklyn, to serve three years; mustered to navy, no date; also borne as Matthias Richardson; prior service in Co. C, and Co. H, Fifty-Third Infantry.

Richardson, Simeon H.—Age, 29 years. Enlisted, July 1, 1861, at Brooklyn to serve three years; mustered in as private, Co. I, August 1, 1861; captured in action on July 21, 1861, at Bull Run, Va.; paroled, no date; discharged May 21, 1862, at Washington, D.C.

Richardson, Thomas—Age, 22 years. Enlisted, September 2, 1862, at Brooklyn to serve three years; mustered in as private, Co. C, September 3, 1862; wounded May 10, 1864, at Laurel Hill, Va.; transferred to Co. I, Fifth Veteran Infantry, on June 2, 1864.

Richardson, Thomas—Age, 20 years. Enlisted, August 26, 1862, at Brooklyn to serve three years; mustered in as private, Co. E, August 27, 1862; transferred to Fifth Veteran Infantry, June 2, 1864.

Richmond, Charles H.—Age, 21 years. Enlisted, December 16, 1863, at Brooklyn to serve three years; mustered in as private, Co. E, December 23, 1863; transferred to Co. H, Fifth Veteran Infantry, June 2, 1864.

Richmond, Frank W.—Age, 18 years. Enlisted, April 18, 1861, at Brooklyn to serve three years; mustered in as private, Co. H, May 23, 1861; transferred to Co. G on January 1, 1863; missing in action, July 1, 1863, at Gettysburg, Pa.; returned, October 10, 1863; promoted corporal, no date; mustered out with company, June 6, 1864, at New York City.

Richmond, Henry W.—Age, 19 years. Enlisted, December 16, 1863, at Brooklyn, to serve three years; mustered in as private, Co. E, December 23, 1863; transferred to Co. H, Fifth Veteran Infantry, June 2, 1864.

Richmond, John H.—Age, 16 years. Enlisted, April 18, 1861, at Brooklyn to serve three years; mustered in as musician, Co. F, May 23, 1861; discharged for disability on November 19, 1862, at New York City; also borne as John S. Richmond.

Richmond, Van D.—Age, 17 years. Enlisted, April 18, 1861, at Brooklyn to serve three years; mustered in as musician, Co. E, May 23, 1861; discharged for disability on February 12, 1863, at hospital, Washington, D.C.

Riker, Edward—Age, 18 years. Enlisted, August 30, 1862, at Brooklyn, to serve three years; mustered in as private, Co. D, September 3, 1862; transferred to Co. C, Fifth Veteran Infantry, June 2, 1864.

Riker, Joseph—Age, 18 years. Enlisted, April 18, 1861, at Brooklyn, to serve three years; mustered in as private, Co. C, May 23, 1861; mustered out June 14, 1864, at New York City, as Joseph L.D. Riker.

Riley, Hugh—Age, 18 years. Enlisted, April 25, 1861, at Brooklyn to serve years; mustered in as private, Co. D, May 23, 1861; deserted at Falmouth, Va., on August 5, 1862; also borne as Butt.

Riley, Hugh—Age, 25 years. Enlisted, April 25, 1861, at Brooklyn, to serve three years; mustered in as corporal, Co. G, on May 23, 1861; returned to ranks, no date; deserted on November 9, 1861, at Upton Hill, Va.

Riley, James—Age, 29 years. Enlisted, August 13, 1862, at Brooklyn to serve three years; mustered in as private, Co. F, August 14, 1862; promoted corporal February 1, 1863; wounded in action April 29, 1863, at Reynolds Crossing, Va., and May 12, Spotsylvania, Va.; transferred to Veteran Reserve Corps, October 3, 1864; discharged June 17, 1865, as of Fifty-First Company, Second Battalion, at Satterlee Hospital, Philadelphia, Pa.

Riley, Thomas—Age, 22 years. Enlisted at Brooklyn, to serve three years; mustered in as private; unassigned, October 2, 1862; no further record.

Riley, William H.—Enlisted, August 25, 1862, at Brooklyn, to serve three years; mustered in as private, Co. H, August 26, 1862; transferred to Veteran Reserve Corps on March 16, 1864.

Rilley, Philip—Enlisted, April 18, 1861, at Brooklyn, to serve three years; mustered in as private, Co. A, May 23, 1861; also borne as Riley; no further record.

Ringland, Joseph—Age, 30 years. Enlisted at Brooklyn, to serve three years; mustered in as private, Co. F, August 29, 1862; promoted corporal, no date; Co. G, Fifth Veteran Infantry, June 2, 1864.

Ritchie, Jacob—Age, 38 years. Enlisted, April 18, 1861, at Brooklyn to serve three years; mustered in as private, company of engineers, May 23, 1861; mustered out August 28, 1861, at Arlington, Va.

Roach, William—Age, 21 years. Enlisted at Brooklyn, to serve three years; mustered in as private; unassigned, December 21, 1863; deserted, no date, from Hart's Island, New York Harbor.

Robbins, John R.—Age, 41 years. Enlisted, August 26, 1862, at Brooklyn to serve three years; mustered in as private, Co. D, August 27, 1862; transferred to Co. C, November 13, 1862; to Co. H, Fifth Veteran Infantry, June 2, 1864; also borne John B. Robbins.

Roberts, Elias E.—Age, 26 years. Enlisted, August 25, 1862, at Brooklyn to serve three years; mustered in as private, Co. F, August 27, 1862; missing in action on July 1, 1863, at Gettysburg, Pa.; returned, October 8, 1863; promoted corporal; returned to ranks, no dates; transferred to Co. K, Fifth Veteran Infantry, June 2, 1864.

Roberts, Erastus B.—Age, 37 years. Enlisted, September 13, 1862, at Brooklyn to serve three years; mustered in as private, Co. B, September 15; wounded in action on July 1, 1863, at Gettysburg, Pa.; died of his wounds, July 4, 1863.

Roberts, John — Age, 22 years. Enlisted at Brooklyn, to serve three years; mustered in as private, Co. K, on January 19, 1864; deserted, February 20, 1864.

Roberts. Richard M. — Age, 24 years. Enlisted, June 30, 1861, at Brooklyn to serve three years; mustered in as corporal, Co. K, August 1, 1861; promoted sergeant on January 1, 1863; transferred to Co. K, Fifth Veteran Infantry, June 2, 1864.

Robertson, Nathaniel — Age, 20 years. Enlisted April 18, 1861 to serve three years; mustered in as private, Co. H, May 23, 1861; mustered out on May 13, 1865, at Fort Columbus, New York Harbor.

Robinson, Hugh — Age, 25 years Enlisted, April 18, 1861, at Brooklyn to serve three years; mustered in as private, Co. H, May 23, 1861; deserted September 27, 1861, at Arlington, Va.; also borne as Rolbrison.

Robinson, John — Age, 34 years. Enlisted, December 9, 1863, at Brooklyn to serve three years; mustered in as private, Co. G, December 23, 1863; transferred to Co. K, Fifth Veteran Infantry, June 2, 1864.

Robrecht, Charles — Age, 19 years. Enlisted. April 18, 1861, at Brooklyn to serve three years; mustered in as private, Co. A, May 23, 1861; promoted corporal, no date; sergeant, April 5, 1863; mustered out with company, June 6, 1864, at New York City.

Roche, John — Age, 21 years. Enlisted, August 28, 1862, at Brooklyn to serve three years; mustered in as private, Co. D, August 29, 1862; transferred Co. I, Fifth Veteran Infantry, June 2, 1864; also borne as Roach.

Rochefort, John F. — Age, 29 years. Enlisted, April 18, 1861, at Brooklyn to serve three years; mustered in as private, Co. F, May 23, 1861; discharged February 20, 1862, for promotion as second lieutenant, Independent Corps Light Infantry.

Rodgers, Thomas — Age, 26 years. Enlisted, December 21, 1863, at Brooklyn to serve three years; mustered in as private, Co. F, December 30, 1863; deserted on April 19, 1864, at Culpeper, Va.; also borne as Rogers.

Rogers, David D. — Age, 31 years. Enlisted, April 18, 1861, at Brooklyn to ranks, to serve three years; mustered in as sergeant, Co. B, May 23, 1861; returned to date; mustered out with company, June 6, 1864, at New York City.

Rogers, George — Age, 20 years. Enlisted, July 31, 1861, at Brooklyn to serve three years; mustered in as private, Co. I, August 4, 1861; transferred to Co. Second Battalion, Twelfth U.S. Infantry, no date; also borne as George E. Rogers.

Rogers, George H. — Age, 20 years. Enlisted, April 18, 1861, at Brooklyn, to serve three years; mustered in as private, Co. E, May 23, 1861; captured in action, July 21, 1861, at Bull Run, Va.; paroled, no date; discharged June 15, 1862.

Rogers, George L. — Age, 27 years. Enlisted, August 28, 1862, at Brooklyn to serve three years; mustered in as private; unassigned, August 29, 1862; no further record.

Rogers, Summers — Age, 23 years. Enlisted, April 18, 1861, at Brooklyn to serve three years; mustered in as private, Co. A, May 23, 1861; promoted corporal, no date; deserted September 25, 1861, at Arlington, Va.

Rogers, William H. — Age, 28 years. Enlisted, April 18, 1861, at Brooklyn to serve three years; mustered in as private, Co. A, May 23, 1861; discharged for disability on April 3, 1862, at Upton Hill, Va.

Roiker, Jacob F. — Age, 34 years. Enlisted, September 25, 1862, at Brooklyn to serve three years; mustered in as private, Co. E, September 28, 1862; wounded, no date; transferred to Co. H, Fifth Veteran Infantry, June 2, 1864; also borne as Roeck and Roceker.

Roller, George — Age, 23 years. Enlisted at

Brooklyn, to serve three years; mustered in as private, Co. H, October 1, 1861; captured and paroled, no dates; discharged April 4, 1862, at Camp Prospect, Va.

Rooney, Edward — Age, 23 years. Enlisted, April 18, 1861, at Brooklyn, to serve three years; mustered in as private, Co. F, May 23, 1861; deserted, July 5, 1861, at Arlington, Va.

Rooney, Thomas — Age, 19 years. Enlisted, April 18, 1861, at Brooklyn, to serve three years; mustered in as private, Co. A, May 23, 1861; mustered out with company on June 6, 1864, at New York City, as Roony.

Rose, Gottlief — Age, 23 years. Enlisted at Brooklyn, to serve three years; mustered in as private, Co. K, December 28, 1863; transferred to Co. I, Fifth Veteran Infantry, on June 2, 1864.

Rose, Samuel R. — Age, 32 years. Enlisted, August 20, 1862, at Brooklyn, to serve three years; mustered in as private, Co. A, August 21, 1862; killed in action, September 14, 1862, at South Mountain, Md.

Ross, William J. — Age, 30 years. Enlisted at Brooklyn, to serve three years; mustered in as private, Co. H, August 20, 1862; transferred to Co. K, Fifth Veteran Infantry, on June 2, 1864; commissioned, not mustered, second lieutenant, April 13, 1864, with rank from same date.

Rossell, Wilber F. — Age, 18 years. Enlisted, September 29, 1862, at Brooklyn to serve three years; mustered in as private, Co. D, September 30, 1862; transferred to Co. G, June 1, 1863; to Fifth Veteran Infantry, June 2, 1864; also borne as Russell.

Roswell, Horace — Age, 34 years. Enlisted, August 20, 1862, at Brooklyn, to serve three years; mustered in as private, Co. G, . August 21, 1862; deserted on January 8, 1863, at Belle. Plains, Va.

Roth, Charles — Age, 28 years. Enlisted, April 18, 1861, at Brooklyn to serve three years; mustered in as private, Co. A, May 23, 1861; discharged May 25, 1864.

Roth, Valentine — Age, 34 years. Enlisted, August 23, 1862, at Brooklyn to serve three years; mustered in as private, Co. A, August 25, 1862; transferred to Fifth Veteran Infantry, June 2, 1864.

Rough, John — Age, 24 years. Enlisted, September 11, 1862, at Brooklyn, to serve three years; mustered in as private; unassigned, September 15, 1862; no further record.

Rourke, James — Age, 21 years. Enlisted, April 18, 1861, at Brooklyn, to serve three years; mustered in as private, Co. H, May 23, 1861; transferred to Co. C, Fifth Veteran Infantry, June 2, 1864; also borne as James W. Rourke and Rouke.

Rourke, James — Age, 22 years. Enlisted, April 18, 1861, at Brooklyn, to serve three years; mustered in as private, Co. A, May 23, 1861; deserted November 10, 1862, while on the march; also borne as James M. Rourke.

Ruff, William — Age, 21 years. Enlisted at Brooklyn, to serve three years; mustered in as private; unassigned, October 21, 1862; no further record.

Rule, Henry B. — Age, 34 years. Enlisted, August 22, 1862, at Brooklyn to serve three years; mustered in as private, Co. H, August 23, 1862; discharged December 22, 1862, at Fairfax Seminary, Va.

Rushmore, Thomas B. — Age, 22 years. Enlisted, April 18, 1861, at Brooklyn to serve three years; mustered in as private, Co. C, May 23, 1861; discharged for disability on February 6, 1863, at Washington, D.C.

Russell, Alexander W. — Age, 27 years. Enlisted, April 18, 1861, at Brooklyn. To serve three years; mustered in as private, company of engineers, May 23, 1861; mustered out August 28, 1861, at Arlington, Va.

Russell, Patrick — Age, 33 years. Enlisted, August 21, 1862, at Brooklyn to serve three years; mustered in as private, Co. G, August 22, 1862; wounded in action on April 29, 1863, at Reynolds Crossing,

Va.; deserted, June 28, 1863, near Emmettsburg, Md.

Ryan, David — Age, 25 years. Enlisted, April 25, 1861, at Brooklyn, to serve three years; mustered in as sergeant, Co. G, May 23, 1861; discharged for disability on July 27, 1861, at Arlington, Va.

Ryan, John — Age, 29 years. Enlisted, April 18, 1861, at Brooklyn, to serve three years; mustered in as private, Co. E, May 23, 1861; killed in action, July 21, 1861, at Bull Run, Va.

Ryan, John — Age, 22 years. Enlisted, August 21, 1862, at Brooklyn, to serve three years; mustered in as private, Co. A, August 22, 1862; wounded in action, July 1, 1863, at Gettysburg, Pa.; transferred to Co. B, Twenty-Fourth Regiment, Veteran Reserve Corps on December 4, 1864; from which discharged, February 18, 1865, at Washington, D.C.; borne as John T. Ryan.

Ryan, John — Age, 30 years. Enlisted, August 29, 1862, at Brooklyn, to serve three years; mustered in as private; unassigned, August 30, 1862; no further record.

Ryan, Martin — Age, 29 years. Enlisted at New York City, to serve three years; mustered in as private; unassigned, July 26, 1861; no further record.

Ryan, William — Age, 18 years. Enlisted, June 30, 1861, at Brooklyn, to serve three years; mustered in as private, Co. K, August 1, 1861; promoted corporal, April 1861; wounded in action, April 1, 1863; wounded in action, May 3, 1863, at Chancellorsville, Va.; transferred to Co. K, Fifth Veteran Infantry, June 2, 1864.

Sabine, Henry C. — Age, 19 years. Enlisted, September 4, 1862, at Brooklyn to serve three years; mustered in as private, Co. E, September 5, 1862; transferred to Co. H, Fifth Veteran Infantry, on June 2, 1864.

Sage, Augustus B. — Age, 21 years. Enlisted, September 29, 1862, at Brooklyn to serve three years; mustered in as private; unassigned, September 30, 1862, no further record.

Sagendorph, John V. — Enlisted at Hudson, to serve three years; mustered in as private, Co. G, November 30, 1861; deserted, June 1, 1862, at Falmouth, Va.

St. John, George G. — Age, 38 years. Enlisted, August 20, 1862, at Brooklyn to serve three years; mustered in as private, Co. D, August 21, 1862; transferred to Co. C on November 13, 1862; to Co. H, Fifth Veteran Infantry, June 2, 1864.

St. John, Stephen A. — Age, 24 years. Enlisted, September 16, 1862, at Brooklyn to serve three years; mustered in as private, Co. H, September 17, 1862; transferred to Co. I, Fifth Veteran Infantry, June 2, 1864.

St. Legier, James — Age, 31 years. Enlisted at Brooklyn, to serve three years; mustered in as private, Co. G, December 9, 1863; transferred to Co. K, Fifth Veteran Infantry, June 2, 1864; also borne as St. Ledger and St. Leger.

Salter, Theodore R. — Age, 25 years. Enrolled, April 18, 1861, at Brooklyn to serve three years; mustered in as first lieutenant, Co. F, May 23, 1861; killed in action on July 21, 1861, at Bull Run, Va.; commissioned first lieutenant in Fourteenth Militia on May 4, 1861, with rank from May 2, 1861; original.

Sampson, Alfred M. — Age, 23 years. Enlisted, September 11, 1862, at Brooklyn to serve three years; mustered in as private; unassigned, September 12, 1862; no further record.

Sanford, Marcus B. — Age, 18 years. Enlisted, April 18, 1861, at Brooklyn to serve three years; mustered in as private, Co. H, May 23, 1861; discharged on May 23, 1864, at Washington, D.C.

Sands, Joseph — Age, 21 years. Enlisted, April 18, 1861, at Brooklyn to serve three years; mustered in as private, Co. A, May 23, 1861; transferred to Veteran Reserve Corps, July 1, 1863; also borne as Joseph H. Sands.

Sang, Frederick Age, 21 years. Enlisted, August 20, 1862, at Brooklyn to serve three years; mustered in as private, Co. A, August 21, 1862; wounded in action on July 1, 1863, at Gettysburg, Pa.; transferred to Co. H, Fifth Veteran Infantry, June 2, 1864.

Sara, Mario — Age, 27 years. Enlisted, October 1, 1861, at Brooklyn, to serve three years; mustered in as musician in band, October 24, 1861; discharged, August 17, 1862, at Camp Halstead, Va.

Satchell, George A. — Age, 19 years. Enlisted, April 18, 1861, at Brooklyn to serve three years; mustered in as private, Co. A, May 23, 1861; promoted sergeant, April 5, 1863; mustered out with company, June 6, 1864, at New York City.

Satchell, William — Age, 19 years. Enlisted, May 18, 1861, at Brooklyn to serve three years; mustered in as private, Co. B, May 23, 1861; mustered out with company on June 6, 1864, at New York City.

Saunders, Frederick N. — Age, 20 years. Enlisted, April 18, 1861, at Brooklyn to serve three years; mustered in as private, Co. B, May 23, 1861; promoted corporal no date; mustered out with company, June 6, 1864, at New York City; also borne as M. Sannders.

Savage, James W. — Age, 31 years. Enlisted at Brooklyn, to serve three years; mustered in as private, Co. C, September 3, 1861; deserted March 1, 1864, at Washington, D.C.

Savage, William — Age, 36 years. Enlisted, December 10, 1863, at Brooklyn to serve three years; mustered in as private, Co. I, December 13, 1863; transferred to Co. G, Fifth Veteran Infantry, June 2, 1864.

Schell, Charles C. — Age, 23 years. Enlisted, April 18, 1861, at Brooklyn to serve three years; mustered in as private, Co. E. May 23, 1861; killed in action on July 21, 1861, at Bull Run, Va.

Schmidt, Charles — Age, 26 years. Enlisted, December 11, 1863, at Brooklyn to serve three years; mustered in as private, Co. I, December 13, 1863; transferred to Fifth Veteran Infantry, June 2, 1864; also borne as Charles Smith.

Schmidt, Henry — Age, 29 years. Enlisted at Brooklyn, to serve three years; mustered in as private, Co. F, May 23, 1861; missing in action, July 21, 1861, at Bull Run, Va.; no further record.

Schmidt, Johann — Age, 29 years. Enlisted at Brooklyn, to serve three years; mustered in as private, Co. F, December 21, 1863; transferred to Co. B, Fifth Veteran Infantry, June 2, 1864; also borne as John Schmidt and Smith.

Schmidt, Robert — Age, 21 years. Enlisted, October 24, 1862, at Brooklyn to serve three years; mustered in as private, Co. K, October 25, 1862; transferred to Veteran Reserve Corps; no date.

Schmith, Jacob — Age, 24 years. Enlisted, April 18, 1861, at Brooklyn to serve three years; mustered in as private, Co. F, May 23, 1861; promoted corporal, January 12, 1863, mustered out with company, June 14, 1864, at New York City; also borne as Schmidt.

Schnepe, Henry — Age, 25 years. Enlisted at Brooklyn, to serve three years; mustered in as private, Co. H, August 30, 1862; wounded in action, July 1, 1863, at Gettysburg, Pa.; transferred to Co. I, Fifth Veteran Infantry, June 2, 1864; also borne as Schneph.

Scholes, Clayton — Age, 19 years. Enrolled, April 18, 1861, at Brooklyn to serve three years; mustered in as private Co. C, on May 23, 1861, promoted first lieutenant, Co. I, July 1, 1861; killed in action, July 21, 1861, at Bull Run, Va.; not commissioned first lieutenant.

Schoonmaker, Charles — Age, 31 years. Enlisted, December 12, 1863, at Brooklyn, to serve three years; mustered in as private, Co. E, December 23, 1863, transferred to Co. H, Fifth Veteran Infantry, June 2, 1864; also borne as Schoemaker.

Schryver, Alfred E. — Age, 20 years. Enlisted, April 18, 1861, at Brooklyn to serve three years; mustered in as private, Co.

H, May 23, 1861; mustered out, May 13, 1865, at Fort Columbus, New York Harbor, as Schriver.

Schultz, Herman — Age, 25 years. Enlisted at Brooklyn, to serve three years; mustered in as private, Co. F, December 18, 1863; discharged for disability, March 7, 1864, at Culpeper, Va.; prior service in Co. D, Thirty-Fifth Infantry.

Schurig, Charles — Age, 25 years. Enrolled, April 18, 1861, at Brooklyn to serve three years; mustered in as sergeant, Co. H, May 23, 1861; promoted first sergeant on March 1, 1862; captured, no date; paroled on December 6, 1862; mustered in as first lieutenant, to date from November 10, 1862; wounded in action, May 8, 1864, at Piney Church, Va.; mustered out with company June 6, 1864, at New York City; commissioned first lieutenant on October 24, 1862, with rank from September 10, 1862, vice J.M. Grumman, died of wounds received in action.

Schwebel, Francis H.— Age, 40 years. Enlisted, April 18, 1861, at Brooklyn to serve three years; mustered in as private, Co. F, May 23, 1861; discharged for disability August 5, 1861, at Arlington, Va.

Schweigert, John — Age, 19 years. Enlisted, at Brooklyn, to serve three years; mustered in as private, Co. K, July 26, 1861; deserted, January 25, 1863, at Belle Plains, Va.

Scofield, George — Age, 21 years. Enlisted, May 18, 1861, at Brooklyn to serve three years; mustered in as private, Co. B, May 23, 1861; deserted, March 30, 1862, at Alexandria, Va., as Schofield.

Scofield, George B.— Age, 22 years. Enlisted, April 18, 1861, at Brooklyn to serve three years; mustered in as private, company of engineers, May 23, 1861, mustered out August 28, 1861, at Arlington, Va.

Scofield, James T.— Age, 18 years. Enlisted, April 18, 1861, at Brooklyn to serve three years; mustered in as private, company of engineers, May 23, 1861, mustered out August 28, 1861, at Arlington, Va.; again enlisted, September 18, 1861; mustered in as private, Co. C, September 24, 1861; promoted sergeant, March 1, 1863; wounded in action on July 3, 1863, at Gettysburg, Pa.; discharged for disability March 25, 1864, at Philadelphia, Pa.

Scott, David — Drum major, Twenty-Fourth Infantry; transferred to this regiment as principal musician, May 15, 1862, reduced to musician and transferred to Co. A on April 4, 1863; re-transferred to Twenty-Fourth Infantry, May 10, 1863; prior service in Twenty-First Infantry.

Scott. George W.— Age, 22 years. Enlisted, April 25, 1861, at Brooklyn to serve three years; mustered in as private, Co. G, May 23, 1861; discharged for disability June 17, 1861.

Scott, Robert — Age, 30 years. Enlisted, April 18, 1861, at Brooklyn to serve three years; mustered in as private, Co. E, May 23, 1861; killed in action, July 21, 1861, at Bull Run, Va.

Scrimager, William B.— Age, 20 years. Enlisted, September 17, 1861, at Brooklyn, to serve three years; mustered ,in as private, Co. D, September 25, 1861, died of disease, September 10, 1862, at Leesburg, Md.

Scudder, Julius — Age, 28 years. Enlisted, August 27, 1862, at Brooklyn to serve three years; mustered in as private, Co. C, August 29, 1862; transferred to Co. I, Fifth Veteran Infantry, June 2, 1864.

Seaman, James — Age, 19 years. Enlisted, September 13, 1862, at Brooklyn to serve three years; mustered in as private, unassigned September 15, 1862; no further record.

Seaman, Walter — Age, 19 years. Enlisted, April 18, 1861, at Brooklyn to serve three years; mustered in as private, Co. E, May 23, 1861; wounded in action, July 1, 1863, at Gettysburg, Pa.; mustered out with company, June 6, 1864, at New York City.

Sears, William H.—Age, 20 years. Enlisted at Brooklyn, to serve three years; mustered in as private, Co. I, February 3, 1864; transferred to Co. G, Fifth Veteran Infantry, June 6, 1864; also borne as William A. Sears.

Seivert, John—Age, 34 years. Enlisted, December 10, 1863, to serve three years; mustered in as private, Co. I, December 13, 1863; captured December 19, 1863, at Kelly's Ford, Va.; died of disease, September 16, 1864, at Andersonville, Ga.; also borne as Sives, Sivert and Sivest.

Semmonite, William H.—Age, 20 years. Enlisted, July 26, 1861, at Brooklyn. To serve three years; mustered in as corporal, Co. K, August 1, 1861; returned to ranks no date; discharged for disability, February 14, 1863, at Washington, D.C.; also borne as Emmonite.

Semonite, Radcliffe—Age, 26 years. Enlisted, August 22, 1862, at Brooklyn to serve three years; mustered in as private, Co. D, August 28, 1862; transferred to Co. A, Fifth Veteran Infantry, June 2, 1864; also borne as Samonite.

Seri, Charles—Age, 32 years. Enlisted, April 18, 1861, at Brooklyn, to serve three years; mustered in as private, Co. F, May 23, 1861; wounded in action, August 29, 1862, at Bull Run, Va.; discharged for disability, November 12, 1862, at Washington, D.C.; also borne as Teri.

Seymour, James—Age, 24 years. Enlisted, April 18, 1861, at Brooklyn, to serve three years; mustered in as private, Co. H, May 23, 1861; killed while on picket, November 18, 1861, at Falls Church, Va.

Seymour, James C.—Age, 19 years. Enlisted, September 19, 1861, at Brooklyn to serve three years; mustered in as private, Co. E, September 24, 1861; died of disease on October 9, 1861, at Arlington, Va.

Shaffer, Thomas W.—Enlisted, April 18, 1861, at Brooklyn, to serve three years; mustered in as private, Co. H, May 23, 1861; discharged for heart disease, January 21, 1863, at Convalescent Camp, Alexandria, Va.

Shanley, John—Age, 19 years. Enlisted, May 18, 1861, at Brooklyn, to serve three years; mustered in as private, Co. G, May 23, 1861; transferred to Co. D, Fifth Veteran Infantry, June 2, 1864.

Shanley, Thomas—Age, 24 years. Enlisted, July 1, 1861, at Brooklyn, to serve three years; mustered in as private, Co. G, July 5, 1861; deserted, July 22, 1861, at Arlington, Va.

Shannon, John—Age, 21 years. Enlisted, April 18, 1861, at Brooklyn, to serve three years; mustered in as private, Co. H, May 23, 1861, promoted sergeant, January 1, 1863, wounded in action on July 1, 1863, at Gettysburg, Pa.; mustered out with company on June 6, 1864, at New York City.

Shaw, Edward F.—Age, 18 years. Enlisted at Brooklyn, to serve three years; mustered in as private, Co. E, February 24, 1862; deserted February 23, 1863, from hospital at Washington, D.C.

Shaw, John—Age, 19 years. Enlisted at Brooklyn, to serve three years; mustered in as private, Co. H, October 1, 1861; deserted January 23, 1862, at Upton Hill, Va.

Shaw, William—Age, 21 years. Enlisted, April 18, 1861, at Brooklyn, to serve three years; mustered in as private, Co. H, May 23, 1861; promoted corporal, January 1, 1863; wounded in action, April 29, 1863, at Pollock's Mills Creek, Va.; missing in action July 1, 1863, at Gettysburg, Pa.; returned to company, October 9, 1863; mustered out with company June 6, 1864, at New York City.

Shaw, William S.—Age, 42 years. Enlisted, August 27, 1862, at Brooklyn to serve three years; mustered in as private, Co. C, August 28, 1862; transferred to Co. I, Fifth Veteran Infantry, June 2, 1864.

Sheader, William—Age, 23 years. Enlisted, December 9, 1863, at Brooklyn to serve three years; mustered in as private, Co.

E, December 23, 1863; transferred to Co. H, Fifth Veteran Infantry, June 2, 1864; also borne as Schrader and Shrader.

Shelton, George N.—Age, 27 years. Enlisted, April 18, 1861, at Brooklyn to serve three years; mustered in as sergeant, Co. E, May 23, 1861; promoted first sergeant on August 4, 1861; discharged for disability, July 26, 1862, at Alexandria, Va.

Sherlock, Samuel R.—Age, 30 years. Enlisted, September 22, 1862, at Brooklyn to serve three years; mustered in as private, Co. F, September 23, 1862, on expiration of furlough, January 15, 1864.

Sherman, Charles P.—Age, 21 years. Enlisted, April 18, 1861, at Brooklyn to serve three years; mustered in as private, company of engineers, May 23, 1861; mustered out August 28, 1861, at Arlington, Va.

Sherman, William B.—Age, 34 years. Enlisted, at Brooklyn to serve three years; mustered in as private, Co. E, December 4, 1863; discharged for disability on March 9, 1864, at Culpeper, Va.

Shiel, James—Age, 20 years. Enlisted, May 18, 1861, at Brooklyn to serve three years; mustered in as private, Co. B, May 23, 1861; deserted August 30, 1861, at Arlington, Va.

Shier, Charles H—Age, 29 years. Enlisted, April 25, 1861, at Brooklyn to serve three years; mustered in as sergeant, Co. G, May 23, 1861; deserted July 5, 1861, at Arlington, Va.

Shook, Revere D.—Age, 19 years. Enlisted, April 18, 1861, at Brooklyn to serve three years; mustered in as private, Co. H, May 23, 1861; deserted, January 23, 1862, at Upton Hill, Va.

Siedel, Ernest—Age, 24 years. Enlisted at Brooklyn, to serve three years; mustered in as private, Co. F, July 1, 1861; killed in action, July 21, 1861, at Bull Run, Va.

Silva, John N.—Age, 19 years. Enlisted, September 16, 1862, at Brooklyn to serve three years; mustered in as private, Co. E, September 17, 1862; captured in action on July 1, 1863, at Gettysburg, Pa.; paroled, no date; transferred to Co. H, Fifth Veteran Infantry, on June 2, 1864.

Simmons, Charles—Age, 21 years. Enlisted, April 25, 1861, at Brooklyn to serve three years; mustered in as private, Co. G, May 23, 1861; promoted corporal, no date; killed in action, August 29, 1862, at Bull Run, Va.

Simmons, Robert—Age, 30 years. Enlisted, April 18, 1861, at Brooklyn to serve three years; mustered in as private, Co. A, May 23, 1861; killed in action on July 21, 1861, at Bull Run, Va.

Simon, Jacob—Age, 35 years. Enlisted at Brooklyn, to serve three years; mustered in as private, Co. F, December 4, 1863; transferred to Co. K. Fifth Veteran Infantry, on June 2, 1864; also borne as Symon.

Singer, Edmund—Age, 25 years. Enlisted, July 1, 1861, at Brooklyn to serve three years; mustered in as private, Co. I, August 1, 1861; deserted, December 26, 1861, at Upton Hill, Va.; also borne as Senger.

Sissen, Bordon—Age, 26 years. Enlisted at Brooklyn, to serve three years; mustered in as private, Co. C, September 30, 1861; wounded in action, August 29, 1862, at Bull Run, Va.; died of his wounds, September 18, 1862, at Georgetown, D.C.; also borne as Pardon Sesson.

Sisty, Benjamin F.—Age, 30 years. Enlisted, September 9, 1862, at Brooklyn to serve three years; mustered in as private, Co. H, September 10, 1862; wounded in action on August 29, 1863, at Pollock's Mills Creek, Va.; discharged September 25, 1863.

Skarren, John H.—Age, 25 years. Enlisted, April 18, 1861, at Brooklyn to serve three years; mustered in as corporal, Co. F, May 23, 1861; promoted sergeant, August 5, 1861; first sergeant, February 1, 1863; wounded in action, July 1, 1863, at Gettysburg, Pa.; mustered out May 23, 1864, at New York City.

Skelton, Alonzo — Age, 24 years. Enlisted at Brooklyn, to serve three years; mustered in as private, Co. H, August 14, 1862; promoted corporal, July 1, 1863; transferred to Co. G, Fifth Veteran Infantry, June 2, 1864.

Skelton, Thaddeus — Age, 25 years. Enlisted April 18, 1861, at Brooklyn to serve three years; mustered in as private, Co. H, May 23, 1861; discharged for disease on September 24, 1861, at Arlington, Va.

Slattery, Cornelius — Age, 21 years. Enlisted, August 25, 1862, at Brooklyn to serve three years; mustered in as private, Co. H, August 26, 1862; transferred to Co. I, Fifth Veteran Infantry, June 2, 1864.

Slocum, Charles — Age, 19 years. Enlisted at Brooklyn, to serve three years; mustered in as private, Co. F, November 30, 1863, transferred to Co. K, Fifth Veteran Infantry, June 2, 1864.

Smith, ASA B. — Age, 27 years. Enlisted, June 30, 1861, at Brooklyn, to serve three years; mustered in as private, Co. I, August 1, 1861; transferred to Veteran Reserve Corps on July 1, 1863.

Smith, George W. — Age, 19 years. Enlisted, October 21, 1861, at Brooklyn to serve three years; mustered in as private, Co. C, October 26, 1861; discharged for disability on June 14, 1862, at Washington, D.C.

Smith, George W. — Age, 15 years. Enlisted, September 13, 1861, at Brooklyn to serve three years; mustered in as musician, Co. C, September 18, 1861; deserted November 2, 1861, at Upton Hill, Va.

Smith, George W. — Age, 18 years. Enlisted, January 16, 1864, at Brooklyn to serve three years; mustered in as private, Co. K, January 27, 1864; transferred to Co. G, Fifth Veteran Infantry, June 2, 1864.

Smith, Henry — Age, 15 years. Enlisted, April 18, 1861, at Brooklyn, to serve three years; mustered in as musician, Co. H, May 23, 1861; deserted August 1, 1861, at Arlington Va., as Henry S. Smith.

Smith, Henry — Age, 28 years. Enlisted. September 13, 1862, at Brooklyn to serve three years; mustered in as private; unassigned, September 15, 1862; no further record.

Smith. Henry C. — Age, 18 years. Enlisted, December 1, 1861, at Hudson, to serve three years; mustered in as private, Co. G, December 10, 1861; discharged for disability July 12, 1862, at Carver Hospital, Washington, D.C.

Smith, Isaac C. — Age, 24 years. Enlisted, April 18, 1861, at Brooklyn, to serve three years; mustered in as sergeant, Co. G, May 23, 1861; discharged for disability on September 12, 1862, at Washington, D.C.; also borne as John Smith.

Smith, James — Age, 15 years. Enlisted, April 18, 1861, at Brooklyn, to serve three years; mustered in as musician, Co. D, May 23, 1861; deserted August 2, 1861, at Camp Wood, Arlington, Va.

Smith, John — Age, 25 years. Enlisted, April 18, 1861, at Brooklyn, to serve three years; mustered in as private, Co. H, May 23, 1861; mustered out with company, June 6, 1864, at New York City.

Smith, John H. — Age, 39 years. Enlisted on May 18, 1861, at Brooklyn to serve three years; mustered in as private, Co. D, May 23, 1861; deserted, November 23, 1861, at Camp Marion, Upton Hill, Va; also borne as John W. Smith.

Smith, Jonathan A. — Age, 23 years. Enrolled, April 18, 1861, at Brooklyn to serve three years; mustered in as corporal, Co. C, May 23, 1861; promoted sergeant major on August 3, 1861; mustered in as second lieutenant, Co. K, February 19, 1863; mustered out with company, June 6, 1864, at New York City; commissioned second lieutenant on February 10, 1863, with rank from January 18, 1863.

Smith, Joseph — Age, 27 years. Enlisted, May 18, 1861, at Brooklyn to serve three years; mustered in as private, Co. D, May 23, 1861; discharged for disability on January 21, 1863, at Washington, D.C.

Smith, Lawrence — Age, 23 years. Enlisted, December 11, 1861, at Brooklyn to serve three years; mustered in as private, Co. G, December 13, 1861; wounded in action on August 29, 1862, at Bull Run, Va.; transferred to Co. C, Fifth Veteran Infantry, on June 2, 1864.

Smith, Michael — Age, 17 years. Enlisted at Brooklyn, to serve three years; mustered in as private, Co. C, June 30, 1861; appointed musician, no date; deserted January 22, 1862, at Upton Hill, Va.

Smith, Mitchell T. — Age, 25 years. Enlisted, April 18, 1861, at Brooklyn to serve three years; mustered in as private, Co. A, May 23, 1861; deserted on July 21, 1863, at Washington, D.C.; also borne as Mitchell F. Smith.

Smith, Orsamus — Age, 28 years. Enrolled at Culpeper, Va., to serve three years; mustered in as surgeon, April 23, 1864; mustered out with regiment, June 6, 1864, at New York City; commissioned surgeon, April 7, 1864, with rank from March 26, 1864.

Smith, Rudolph — Age, 20 years. Enlisted, April 18, 1861, at Brooklyn to serve three years; mustered in as private, Co. C, May 23, 1861; transferred to Co. G, Twenty-Fourth Regiment, Veteran Reserve Corps, on February 12, 1864; also borne as Rudolph H. Smith.

Smith Samuel — Age, 17 years. Enlisted, May 18, 1861, at Brooklyn to serve three years; mustered in as musician, Co. D, May 2, 1861; deserted, October 8, 1861, from Camp Marion, Upton Hill, Va.

Smith, Smith — Age, 41 years. Enlisted, August 26, 1862, at Brooklyn to serve three years; mustered in as private, Co. E, August 27, 1862; transferred to Veteran Reserve Corps on November 15, 1863.

Smith, Theodore — Age, 18 years. Enlisted, April 18, 1861, at Brooklyn to serve three years; mustered in as private, Co. E, May 23, 1861; discharged August 8, 1861.

Smith, Walter M.C. — Age, 24 years Enlisted, April 18, 1861, at Brooklyn to serve three years; mustered in as private, Co. F, May 23, 1861; discharged for disability on September 10, 1862, at Washington, D.C.

Smith, William — Age, 21 years. Enlisted, April 18, 1861, at Brooklyn to serve three years; mustered in as private, Co. D, May 23, 1861; deserted September 16, 1862, from camp near South Mountain, Md.; apprehended October 23, 1863; no further record.

Smith, William — Age, 39 years. Enlisted, September 19, 1862, to serve three years; mustered in as private, Co. F, September 20, 1862; transferred to Veteran Reserve Corps, no date; from which discharged, July 10, 1865, as of Co. G, Third Regiment, Burlington, Vt.

Smith, William — Age, 30 years. Enlisted at Brooklyn, to serve three years; mustered in as private, Co. K, December 5, 1863; transferred to Co. G, Fifth Veteran Infantry, on June 2, 1864; also borne as William H. Smith.

Smith, William E. — Age, 22 years. Enlisted, December 4, 1863, at Brooklyn to serve three years; mustered in as private, Co. E, December 8, 1863; transferred to Co. H, Fifth Veteran Infantry, June 2, 1864.

Smith, William H. — Age, 16 years. Enlisted, April 18, 1861, at Brooklyn to serve three years; mustered in as private, Co. E, May 23, 1861; discharged August 8, 1861.

Smith, William H. — Age, 22 years. Enlisted at Brooklyn, to serve three years; mustered in as private, Co. F, December 17, 1863; transferred to Co. K, Fifth Veteran Infantry, June 2, 1864.

Smith, William J. — Age, 24 years. Enlisted, April 18, 1861, at Brooklyn, to serve three years; mustered in as private, Co. C, May 23, 1861; wounded in action, July 1, 1863, at Gettysburg, Pa.; transferred to Co. B, Twenty-Fourth Regiment, Veteran Reserve Corps, on December 4, 1863.

Smith, William S.—Age, 25 years. Enlisted, April 18, 1861, at Brooklyn, to serve three years; mustered in as private, Co. D, May 23, 1861; re-enlisted as a veteran on March 1, 1864; wounded in action, May 12, 1864, at Spotsylvania, Va.; transferred to Co. I, Fifth Veteran Infantry, June 2, 1864.

Smith, William Z.—Age, 18 years. Enlisted, January 29, 1862, at Brooklyn to serve three years; mustered in as private, Co. D, January 30, 1862; transferred to Co. G, November 1, 1863; to Co. K, Fifth Veteran Infantry, June 2, 1864.

Smithson, Edward H.—Age, 22 years. Enlisted, July 1, 1861, at Brooklyn to serve three years; mustered in as private, Co. D, August 4, 1861; wounded in action on August 29, 1862, at Bull Run, Va.; discharged for disability February 25, 1863, at David's Island, New York Harbor.

Smock, George W.—Age, 20 years. Enlisted, April 18, 1861, at Brooklyn, to serve three years; mustered in as private, Co. A, May 23, 1861; promoted corporal, no date; wounded in action, April 29, 1863, at Fredericksburg, Va.; discharged for wounds, September 9, 1863, at Annapolis, Md.

Snedeker, Alonzo—Age, 21 years. Enlisted, April 18, 1861, at Brooklyn, to serve three years; mustered in as private, Co. H, May 23, 1861; deserted January 23, 1862, at Upton Hill, Va., as Alonzo V.B. Snedeker.

Snedeker, Rudolph—Age, 19 years. Enlisted at Brooklyn, to serve three years; mustered in as private, Co. I, January 4, 1864; transferred to Co. G, Fifth Veteran Infantry, June 2, 1864.

Snow, George—Age, 19 years. Enlisted, April 18, 1861, at Brooklyn, to serve three years; mustered in as private, Co. A, May 23, 1861; discharged for disease of lungs, July 18, 1861; also borne as George W. Snow.

Snyder, Iaace—Age, 35 years. Enlisted, April 18, 1861, at Brooklyn, to serve three years; mustered in as private, Co. C, May 23, 1861; transferred to Veteran Reserve Corps, July 16, 1863.

Snyder, William—Age, 32 years. Enlisted, April 18, 1861, at Brooklyn, to serve three years; mustered in as sergeant, no date; mustered out, August 28, 1861, at Arlington, Va.

Solomons, William—Age, 25 years. Enlisted, September 24, 1862, at Brooklyn to serve three years; mustered in as private; unassigned, September 25, 1862; no further record.

Spaulding, Alonzo N.—Age, 30 years. Enlisted, April 18, 1861, at Brooklyn to serve three years; mustered in as private, Co. D, May 23, 1861; mustered out with company on June 6, 1864, at New York City.

Spaulding, William—Age, 20 years. Enlisted, April 18, 1861, at Brooklyn to serve three years; mustered in as private, Co. A, May 23, 1861, deserted September 16, 1862.

Spear, Leopold—Age, 20 years. Enlisted, April 18, 1861, at Brooklyn to serve three years; mustered in as private, Co. E, May 23, 1861; discharged for disability, January 2, 1863, at Alexandria, Va., as Leopold Spear; also borne as Spiet.

Spear, William H.—Age, 26 years. Enlisted at Brooklyn, to serve three years; mustered in as private, Co. D, September 9, 1862; transferred to Co. I, Fifth Veteran Infantry, on June 2, 1864.

Spelcy, Samuel C.—Age, 19 years. Enlisted, April 19, 1861, at Brooklyn, to serve three years; mustered in as private, Co. E, May 23, 1861; wounded in action on August 30, 1862, at Bull Run, Va.; discharged for disability, April 25, 1864, at Annapolis, Md.; also borne as Spellcey.

Spencer, Robert—Age, 20 years. Enlisted, June 30, 1861, at Brooklyn to serve three years; mustered in as private, Co. I, August 1, 1861; appointed wagoner and returned to company as private, no dates; re-enlisted as a veteran, December 31,

1863; transferred to Co. G, Fifth Veteran Infantry, June 2, 1864; also borne as Robert B. Spencer.

Spowers, John J.—Age, 22 years. Enlisted at Brooklyn, to serve three years; mustered in as private, Co. E, August 25, 1862; missing in action, July 1, 1863, at Gettysburg, Pa.; returned to company, November 5, 1863; transferred to Co. H, Fifth Veteran Infantry, June 2, 1864.

Squires, Frank—Age, 20 years. Enlisted, April 18, 1861, at Brooklyn to serve three years; mustered in as private, Co. E, May 23, 1861; discharged for disability on September 14, 1861.

Stack, James—Age, 21 years. Enlisted, May 18, 1861, at Brooklyn to serve three years; mustered in as private, Co. B, May 23, 1861; deserted, August 11, 1861, at Arlington, Va.

Stackmeyer, John G.—Age, 37 years. Enlisted, December 31, 1863, at Brooklyn, to serve three years; mustered in as private, Co. I, January 4, 1864; transferred to Co. G, Fifth Veteran Infantry, June 2, 1864.

Stackpole, Michel—Age, 26 years. Enlisted, May 18, 1861, at Brooklyn to serve three years; mustered in as private, Co. B, May 23, 1861; re-enlisted as a veteran on March 1, 1864; deserted on expiration of veteran furlough, April 17, 1864.

Stafford, James P.—Age, 19 years. Enlisted, April 18, 1861, at Brooklyn to serve three years; mustered in as private, Co. D, May 23, 1861; transferred to Veteran Reserve Corps, February 15, 1864.

Stahn, Christopher H.—Age, 19 years. Enlisted, August 18, 1862, at Brooklyn to serve three years; mustered in as private, Co. D, August 19, 1862, deserted October 31, 1862, from camp at Smoketown, Md.

Stanton, Edward H.—Age, 30 years. Enlisted, April 18, 1861, at Brooklyn to serve three years; mustered in as private, Co. H, May 23, 1861; deserted on July 17, 1861, at Arlington, Va.

Stapleton, William—Age, 24 years. Enlisted, April 25, 1861, at Brooklyn to serve three years; mustered in as private, Co. G, May 23, 1861; killed in action on July 21, 1861, at Bull Run, Va.

Staunton, Lawrence—Age, 24 years. Enlisted, April 18, 1861, at Brooklyn to serve three years; mustered in as private, Co. B, May 23, 1861; promoted corporal on January 1, 1864; wounded in action, May 10, 1864, at Laurel Hill, Va.; mustered out with company June 6, 1864, at New York City, as Laurence Stanton.

Stears, William L.B.—Age, 34 years. Enrolled at Brooklyn, to serve three years; mustered in as captain, Co. E, April 18, 1861; discharged, December 11, 1861; also borne as Stearns; commissioned captain in Fourteenth Militia, February 17, 1860, with rank from April 10, 1859.

Steele, John—Age, 21 years. Enlisted, September 29, 1862, at Brooklyn to serve three years; mustered in as private; unassigned, September 30, 1862; no further record.

Steen, Benjamin—Age, 20 years. Enlisted, April 18, 1861, at Brooklyn to serve three years; mustered in as corporal, Co. C, May 23, 1861; wounded in action on August 28, 1862, at Groveton, Va.; discharged for disability, December 1, 1862, at Alexandria, Va., borne as Benjamin S. Steend.

Stephens, Enoch—Age, 30 years. Enlisted, June 30, 1861, at Brooklyn to serve three years; mustered in as first sergeant, August 1, 1861; returned to ranks, no date; transferred to Co. I, Fifth Veteran Infantry, June 2, 1864.

Stephens, John—Age, 23 years. Enlisted, July 26, 1861, at Brooklyn to serve three years; mustered in as private, Co. K, August 1, 1861; transferred to Co. I, Fifth Veteran Infantry, June 2, 1864.

Stevens, Charles—Age, 21 years. Enlisted, July 30, 1861, at Brooklyn to serve three years; mustered in as private, Co. I, August 4, 1861; deserted, June 1, 1863; also borne as Charles D. Stevens and Steven.

Stevens, Edwin — Age, 25 years. Enlisted, May 18, 1861, at Brooklyn, to serve three years; mustered in as private, Co. D, May 23, 1861; discharged for disability, November 11, 1861.

Stevens, George W. — Age, 22 years. Enlisted, May 18, 1861, at Brooklyn, to serve three years; mustered in as private, Co. D, May 23, 1861; promoted corporal, October 11, 1861; discharged for disability, October 10, 1862, at Washington, D.C.

Steward, Henry N. — Age, 27 years. Enlisted, April 18, 1861, at Brooklyn to serve three years; mustered in as sergeant, Co. C, May 23, 1861; discharged for disease on February 3, 1863, at Annapolis, Md.

Stewart, Edward — Age, 27 years. Enlisted at New York City, to serve three years; mustered in as private; unassigned, March 10, 1864; no further record.

Stewart, John — Age, 22 years. Enlisted, April 18, 1861, at Brooklyn, to serve three years; mustered in as private; company of engineers, May 23, 1861; mustered out on August 28, 1861, at Arlington, Va.

Stewart, William — Age, 29 years. Enlisted, April 25, 1861, at Brooklyn to serve three years; mustered in as corporal, Co. G, May 23, 1861; promoted sergeant, March 1, 1862; discharged, May 10, 1862, at Falmouth, Va.; also borne as Stuart.

Stewart, William — Age, 33 years. Enlisted, October 18, 1862, at Brooklyn to serve three years; mustered in as private, Co. B, October 20, 1862; no further record.

Stewart, William H. — Age, 26 years. Enlisted at Brooklyn, to serve three years; mustered in as private, Co. H, August 20, 1862; wounded in action, July 1, 1863, at Gettysburg, Pa.; discharged for wounds, December 22, 1863, at New York City; also borne as Steward.

Stillwell, George — Age, 24 years. Enlisted, April 19, 1861, at Brooklyn to serve three years; mustered in as private, Co. B, May 23, 1861; mustered out with company on June 6, 1864, at New York City.

Stohr, Christopher C. — Age, 19 years. Enlisted, August 18, 1861, at Brooklyn to serve three years; mustered in as private; unassigned, August 19, 1861; no further record.

Stone, Malcom — Age, 22 years. Enlisted, April 18, 1861, at Brooklyn, to serve three years; mustered in as private, Co. E, May 23, 1861; wounded in action, July 21, 1861, at Bull Run, Va.; discharged for wounds, December 3, 1862.

Stone, Matthew — Age, 27 years. Enlisted at Brooklyn, to serve three years; mustered in as private, Co. E, December 29, 1863; transferred to Co. H, Fifth Veteran Infantry, June 2, 1864.

Storms, Abram — Age, 28 years. Enlisted, October 1, 1861, at Brooklyn, to serve three years; mustered in as musician in band, October 24, 1861; discharged, August 17, 1862, at Camp Halstead, Va.

Storms, William H. — Age, 26 years. Enlisted at Brooklyn to serve three years; mustered in as private, Co. B, September 12, 1862; transferred to Veteran Reserve Corps, no date; from which discharged, July 6, 1865, as of Co. G, Twentieth Regiment, at Wilmington, DE.

Storrer, Aaron A. — Age, 30 years. Enlisted, April 18, 1861, at Brooklyn, to serve three years; mustered in as private, Co. E, May 23, 1861; missing in action, July 1, 1863, at Gettysburg, Pa.; returned to company, no date; mustered out with company, June 6, 1864, at New York City.

Storz, Adolph — Age, 20 years. Enlisted at Brooklyn, to serve three years; mustered in as private; unassigned, May 17, 1864; mustered out, May 8, 1865, at Hart's Island, New York Harbor.

Stout, George M. — Age, 18 years. Enlisted, September 5, 1861, at Brooklyn to serve three years; mustered in as private, Co. D, September 17, 1861; wounded in action on July 1, 1863, at Gettysburg Pa.; transferred to Co. I, Fifth Veteran Infantry, on June 2, 1864.

Straffel, Edward — Age, 22 years. Enlisted, April 18, 1861, at Brooklyn to serve three years; mustered in as private, Co. F, May 23, 1861; deserted, May 20, 1862.

Stauss, Louis — Age, 22 years. Enlisted, April 25, 1861, at Brooklyn to serve three years; mustered in as private, Co. G, May 23, 1861; promoted corporal, no date; mustered out with company, June 6, 1864, at New York City; also borne as Strouse and Strouss.

Stryker, William H. — Age, 19 years. Enlisted, April 18, 1861, at Brooklyn to serve three years; mustered in as private, Co. H, May 23, 1861; wounded while on picket November 18, 1861, at Falls Church, Va.; discharged for wounds, January 15, 1862.

Stuart, Charles — Age, 21 years. Enrolled, April 25, 1861, at Brooklyn to serve three years; mustered in as first sergeant, Co. G, May 23, 1861; as first lieutenant on March 5, 1862; dismissed, September 15, 1862; not commissioned first lieutenant.

Stuart, James D. — Age, 23 years. Enlisted, August 20, 1862, at Brooklyn to serve three years; mustered in as private, Co. H, August 21, 1862; wounded in action on April 29, 1863, at Fredericksburg, Va.; discharged for wounds, November 19, 1863, at New York City; also borne as Stuard.

Stubbs, Michael — Age, 22 years. Enlisted. April 18, 1861, at Brooklyn to serve three years; mustered in as private, Co. E, May 23, 1861; wounded in action on July 1, 1863, at Gettysburg, Pa.; promoted sergeant, December 1, 1863; mustered out with company on June 6, 1864, at New York City.

Sullivan, Michael — Age, 21 years. Enlisted, April 18, 1861, at Brooklyn to serve three years; mustered in as private, Co. E, May 23, 1861; died of disease on August 31, 1861, in hospital, Arlington, Va.

Styles, John H. — Age, 36 years. Enrolled, April 18, 1861, at Brooklyn to serve three years; mustered in as first lieutenant, Co. A, May 23, 1861; discharged for disability on August 2, 1861; commissioned first lieutenant in Fourteenth Militia, July 8, 1861, with rank from July 1, 1861.

Summer, Matthias — Age, 34 years. Enlisted at Brooklyn, to serve three years; mustered in as private, Co. K, December 7, 1863; transferred to Co. I, Fifth Veteran Infantry, June 2, 1864.

Summers, William — Age, 24 years. Enlisted, April 18, 1861, at Brooklyn to serve three years; mustered in as private, Co. H, May 23, 1861; discharged for promotion, September 3, 1861, at Arlington, Va.

Supper, William — Age, 22 years. Enlisted, April 18, 1861, at Brooklyn to serve three years; mustered in as private, Co. F, May 23, 1861; discharged for disability on March 31, 1862.

Sutherland, Alexander — Age, 23 years. Enlisted, April 18, 1861, at Brooklyn to serve three years; mustered in as private, Co. G, May 23, 1861; transferred to Reserve Corps, July 1, 1863; also borne as Southerland.

Sutton, John A. — Age, 24 years. Enlisted, July 26, 1861, at Brooklyn to serve three years; mustered in as private, Co. K, August 1, 1861; discharged for disability on September 15, 1862, at Washington, D.C.

Swalm, William F. — Age, 24 years. Enrolled, April 18, 1861, at Brooklyn to serve three years; mustered in as assistant surgeon, May 23, 1861; discharged on November 15, 1862; not commissioned in 1861; not mustered, assistant surgeon, February 23, 1864, with rank from January 18, 1864.

Swan, James — Age, 24 years. Enlisted, April 18, 1861, at Brooklyn, to serve three years; mustered in as private, Co. C, May 23, 1861; missing in action on August 29, 1861, at Bull Run, Va.; no further record; also borne as Sworm.

Sweeney, Daniel — Age, 23 years. Enlisted, January 19, 1864, at Brooklyn to serve three years; mustered in as private, Co. H, January 27, 1864; transferred to Co. I, Fifth Veteran Infantry, June 2, 1864; also borne as Sweny.

Sweeney, Hugh S.—Age, 18 years. Enlisted, August 25, 1862, at Brooklyn to serve three years; mustered in as private, Co. F, August 26, 1862; transferred to Co. K, Fifth Veteran Infantry, June 2, 1864.

Switzer, John M.—Age, 21 years. Enlisted, April 18, 1861, at Brooklyn, to serve three years; mustered in as private, Co. D, May 23, 1861; mustered out with company on June 6, 1864, at New York City; also borne as John H. Switzer.

Syke, Rudolph—Age, 44 years. Enlisted, December 12, 1863, at Brooklyn, to serve three years; mustered in as private, Co. E, December 21, 1863; transferred to Co. H, Fifth Veteran Infantry, June 2, 1864; also borne as Seick.

Talford, Charles R.—Age, 23 years. Enlisted, April 18, 1861, at Brooklyn to serve three years; mustered in as private, Co. C, May 23, 1861; discharged for disability on August 19, 1861, at Arlington, Va.

Tassie, Thomas—Age, 21 years. Enlisted, August 29, 1862, at Brooklyn, to Co. K, serve three years; mustered in as private, Co. F, August 30, 1862; transferred to Fifth Veteran Infantry, June 2, 1864.

Taylor, George—Age, 21 years. Enlisted, April 18, 1861, at Brooklyn, to serve three years; mustered in as private, Co. C, May 23, 1861; deserted January 31, 1862.

Taylor, James W.—Age, 25 years. Enlisted, September 22, 1862, at Brooklyn to serve three years; mustered in as private, Co. E, September 23, 1862; transferred to Veteran Reserve Corps, July 1, 1863.

Taylor, John T.—Age, 21 years. Enlisted, July 31, 1861, at Brooklyn, to serve three years; mustered in as private, Co. I, August 4, 1861; re-enlisted as a veteran, March 24, 1864; transferred to Co. D, Fifth Veteran Infantry, June 2, 1864.

Taylor, Robert S.—Age, 22 years. Enlisted, April 18, 1861, at Brooklyn, to serve three years, mustered in as private, Co. E, May 23, 1861; captured in action, August 28, 1862, at Gainesville, Va.; paroled, no date; mustered out with company, June 6, 1864, at New York City.

Taylor, Robert—Age, 32 years. Enlisted, April 18, 1861, at Brooklyn, to serve three years; mustered in as private, Co. H, May 23, 1861; transferred to Veteran Reserve Corps, August 5, 1863; mustered out, April 18, 1864, as of Co. E, Fourteenth Regiment, Veteran Reserve Corps.

Taylor, Walter—Age, 22 years. Enlisted, April 18, 1861, at Brooklyn, to serve three years; mustered in as private, Co. H, May 23, 1861; killed while on picket, November 18, 1861, at Falls Church, Va.

Taylor, William—Age, 30 years. Enlisted, April 18, 1861, at Brooklyn, to serve three years; mustered in as private, Co. A, May 23, 1861; deserted on November 6, 1862.

Teasdale, Charles—Age, 31 years. Enlisted, April 18, 1861, at Brooklyn to serve three years; mustered in as private, Co. E, May 23, 1861; promoted corporal, no date; sergeant, December 1, 1863; mustered out with company, June 6, 1864, at New York City.

Tehan, Thomas F.—Age, 22 years. Enlisted, June 30, 1861, at Brooklyn, to serve three years; mustered in as private, Co. I, August 1, 1861; promoted first sergeant, no date; mustered out July 20, 1864, at Washington, D.C., as Teahan.

Ten Eyck, Conrad A.—Age, 21 years. Enlisted, April 18, 1861, at Brooklyn to serve three years; mustered in as private, Co. C, May 23, 1861; deserted October 10, 1862, at Alexandria, Va.

Ten Eyck, David—Age, 21 years. Enlisted, September 13, 1862, at Brooklyn to serve three years; mustered in as private, Co. B, September 15, 1862; killed in action on July 1, 1863, at Gettysburg, Pa.

Ten Eyck, Martin—Age, 19 years. Enlisted, April 18, 1861, at Brooklyn, to serve three years; mustered in as private, Co. E, May 23, 1861; deserted on expiration of furlough, January 31, 1862, at Brooklyn, N.Y.

Thatford, Joseph—Age, 21 years. Enlisted

at Brooklyn, to serve three years; mustered in as private, Co. D, December 4, 1861; promoted corporal, no date; captured and paroled, no dates; deserted, September 10, 1863, from parole camp at Westchester, Pa.

Thatford, Stephen H.—Age, 22 years. Enlisted, May 18, 1861, at Brooklyn, to serve three years; mustered in as private, Co. D, May 23, 1861; wounded in action, August 29, 1862, at Bull Run, Va.; died of his wounds September 20, 1862, at Washington, D.C.

Thetford, Charles E.—Age, 19 years. Enlisted at Brooklyn, to serve three years; mustered in as private, Co. E, October 17, 1861; discharged for disability, October 17, 1862, at Washington, D.C.

Thetford, William—Age, 21 years. Enlisted at Brooklyn, to serve three years; mustered in as private, Co. C, October 12, 1861; deserted February 2, 1862; also borne as William R. Thetford.

Thiery, Augustus—Age, 26 years. Enlisted, April 18, 1861, at Brooklyn, to serve three years; mustered in as private, Co. F, May 23, 1861; promoted corporal, no date; sergeant, February 1, 1863; mustered out, June 14, 1864, at New York City.

Thomas, Andrew—Age, 40 years. Enlisted at Brooklyn, to serve three years; mustered in as private, Co. K, December 28, 1863; discharged for disability, March 7, 1864, at Culpeper, Va.; also borne as Ansel Thomas.

Thomas, John—Age, 36 years. Enlisted, April 18, 1861, at Brooklyn, to serve three years; mustered in as private, Co. C, May 23, 1861; discharged for disability June 12, 1862, at Washington, D.C.

Thomas, Jonathan—Age, 20 years. Enlisted, September 18, 1861, at Brooklyn, to serve three years; mustered in as private, Co. C, September 24, 1861; wounded in action, September 17, 1862, at Antietam, Md.; died of his wounds October 10, 1862, at Snaketown, Md.

Thompson, Alonzo F.—Age, 23 years. Enlisted, August 20, 1862, at Brooklyn, to serve three years; mustered in as private, Co. C, August 23, 1862; discharged for disability, March 10, 1863, at Washington, D.C.

Thompson, Charles S.—Age, 24 years. Enlisted, July 1, 1861, at Brooklyn, to serve three years; mustered in as private, Co. I, August 1, 1861; discharged for disability, December 6, 1862, at Washington, D.C.

Thompson, Edward G.—Age, 27 years. Enlisted, August 28, 1862, at Brooklyn, to serve three years; mustered in as private, Co. D, August 29, 1862; transferred to Co. I, Fifth Veteran Infantry, June 2, 1864.

Thompson, John—Age, 23 years. Enlisted at Brooklyn, to serve three years; mustered in as private; unassigned, October 10, 1862; no further record.

Thompson, William A.—Age, 24 years. Enlisted, August 22, 1862, at Brooklyn, to serve three years; mustered in as private, Co. H, August 26, 1862; deserted, December 16, 1862; subsequent service in Co. D, First Engineers.

Thorp, James E.—Age, 38 years. Enlisted at Brooklyn, to serve three years; mustered in as private; unassigned, September 12, 1862; no further record.

Thurston, Robert P.—Age, 32 years. Enlisted, August 28, 1862, at Brooklyn, to serve three years; mustered in as private, Co. E, August 29, 1862; wounded in action July 1, 1863, at Gettysburg, Pa.; died of his wounds July 28, 1863.

Thurston, William P.—Age, 37 years. Enlisted at Brooklyn, to serve three years; mustered in as private, Co. E, December 3, 1863; transferred to Co. H, Fifth Veteran Infantry, on June 2, 1864.

Tibbals, Albert C.—Age, 21 years. Enlisted, April 18, 1861, at Brooklyn, to serve three years; mustered in as private, Co. H, May 23, 1861; mustered out with company, June 6, 1864, at New York City, as Tibballs.

Tickner, Alfred P.—Age, 24 years. Enlisted,

August 21, 1862, at Brooklyn, to serve three years; mustered in as private, Co. E, August 23, 1862; wounded in action, December 13, 1862, at Fredericksburg, Va.; transferred to Co. H, Fifth Veteran Infantry, on June 2, 1864.

Tickner, Augustus B.—Age, 22 years. Enlisted, May 18, 1861, at Brooklyn to serve three years; mustered in as private, Co. D, May 23, 1861; captured in action July 21, 1861, at Manassas, Va.; paroled, no date; mustered out May 21, 1862, at Washington, D.C.

Tickner, Edward A.—Age, 21 years. Enlisted. May 18, 1861, at Brooklyn to serve three years; mustered in as private, Co. D, May 23, 1861; deserted September 20, 1861, from Camp Wood, Arlington, Va.

Tigney, William, H.—Age, 21 years. Enrolled, April 18, 1861, at Brooklyn to serve three years; mustered in as commissary sergeant, May 23, 1861; first lieutenant, Co. F, September 29, 1862; as quartermaster, March 23, 1863; mustered out with regiment on June 6, 1864, at New York City; commissioned first lieutenant, October 24, 1862, with rank from September 29, 1862, vice James H. Jordan, promoted; quartermaster, August 18, 1863, with rank from March 2, 1863, vice A.S. Cassidy, resigned.

Tinker, J. Fred—Age, 21 years. Enrolled, July 1, 1861, at Brooklyn, to serve three years; mustered in as private, Co. K, August 1, 1861; promoted sergeant, March 10, 1862; mustered in as first lieutenant, January 8, 1863; mustered out with company, June 6, 1864, at New York City; commissioned first lieutenant, October 24, 1862, with rank from September 17, 1862, vice J.B. Howard, promoted captain and assistant quartermaster, U.S. Volunteers.

Tinker, Richard M.—Age, 20 years. Enlisted, June 30, 1861, at Brooklyn to serve three years; mustered in as private, Co. K, August 1, 1861; transferred to Co. G, Fifth Veteran Infantry, June 2, 1864.

Titus, Charles—Age, 23 years. Enlisted, April 18, 1861, at Brooklyn, to serve three years; mustered in as private, Co. E, May 18, 1861; discharged for disability April 13, 1862, at Upton Hill, Va.

Tobey, Charles B.—Age, 33 years. Enrolled, April 18, 1861, at Brooklyn to serve three years; mustered in as first sergeant, Co. C, May 23, 1861; as first lieutenant August 1, 1861; as captain October 24, 1862; discharged February 1, 1863; commissioned first lieutenant in Fourteenth Militia August 12, 1861, with rank from August 5, 1861; vice Wm. H. Burnett, resigned; captain, October 24, 1862, with rank from September 21, 1862, vice D. Myers, died of wounds received in action.

Tobey, George W.—Age, 18 years. Enlisted, April 18, 1861, at Brooklyn, to serve three years; mustered in as private, Co. C, May 23, 1861; wounded in action August 29, 1862, at Groveton, Va.; died of his wounds, November 25, 1862, at Georgetown, D.C.

Tompkin, William H.—Age, 21 years. Enlisted, April 18, 1861, at Brooklyn to serve three years; mustered in as corporal, Co. D, May 23, 1861; promoted sergeant October 11, 1861; wounded in action, August 29, 1862, at Bull Run, Va.; mustered out with company, June 6, 1864, at New York City.

Tompkins, Robert B.—Age, 24 years. Enlisted, May 18, 1861, at Brooklyn to serve three years; mustered in as private, Co. D, May 23, 1861; wounded in action on August 30, 1862, at Bull Run, Va.; discharged for disability, December 19, 1863, at Convalescent Camp, Alexandria, Va.

Tomsey, B.—Age, 17 years. Enlisted, April 18, 1861, at Brooklyn, to serve three years; mustered in as private, Co. E, May 23, 1861; promoted corporal, no date; sergeant December 1, 1863; wounded June 10, 1864; absent in hospital, Washington, D.C., at muster out of company; also borne as James B. Tomsey.

Toppins, John — Age, 25 years. Enlisted, June 30, 1861, at Brooklyn, to serve three years; mustered in as private, Co. K, August 1, 1861; deserted April 27, 1863, from hospital.

Travis, George W. — Age, 20 years. Enlisted, April 18, 1861, at Brooklyn, to serve three years; mustered in as private, Co. H, May 23, 1861; deserted, February 10, 1862, Upton Hill, Va.

Trippett, John B. — Age, 24 years. Enlisted April 18, 1861, at Brooklyn, to serve three years; mustered in as private, Co. C, May 23, 1861; discharged March 28, 1862, borne as Trippeth.

Trotter, William — Age, 25 years. Enlisted at Brooklyn, to serve three years; mustered in as private, unassigned, September 19, 1862; no further record.

Trull, George — Age, 34 years. Enlisted, December 16, 1863, at Brooklyn, to serve three years; mustered in as private, Co. F, December 21, 1863; discharged for disability, March 7, 1864, at Culpeper, Va.; also borne as Truce.

Tucker, Adonirane J. — Age, 44 years. Enlisted at Brooklyn, to serve three years; mustered in as private, Co. G, December 8, 1863; transferred to Co. K, Fifth Veteran Infantry, June 2, 1864.

Tucker, Francis — Age, 25 years. Enlisted, April 18, 1861, at Brooklyn, to serve three years; mustered in as corporal, Co. F, May 23, 1861; wounded in action, September 17, 1862, at Amtietam, Md.; died of his wounds October 12, 1862.

Tucker, John — Age, 23 years. Enlisted, September 5, 1862, at Brooklyn, to serve three years; mustered in as private; unassigned, September 8, 1862; no further record.

Turley, Andrew — Age, 22 years. Enlisted, April 18, 1861, at Brooklyn, to serve three years; mustered in as private, Co. A, May 23, 1861; transferred to Co. C, Sixteenth Regiment, Veteran Reserve Corps, September 30, 1863; re-transferred to this company on April 5, 1864; no further record.

Turnbull, David H. — Age, 26 years. Enlisted, May 18, 1861, at Brooklyn, to serve three years; mustered in as private, Co. D, May 23, 1861; discharged for disability, February 17, 1863, at Convalescent Camp, Va.; again enlisted, January 14, 1864; transferred Co. I, Fifth Veteran Infantry, June 2, 1864.

Turner. Charles D. — Age, 22 years. Enlisted at Brooklyn, to serve three years; mustered in as private; unassigned, February 15, 1864; no further record.

Twaits. James B. — age, 23 years. Enlisted, April 15, 1861, at Brooklyn, to serve three years; mustered in as private, Co. H, May 23, 1861; promoted sergeant, no date; wounded in action, August 29, 1862, at Bull Run, Va.; discharged for wounds, February 9, 1863, at Washington, D.C.; also borne as Tuaits.

Tyler, H.P. — Age, 26 years. Enlisted, April 18, 1861, at Brooklyn. to serve three years; mustered in as private, Co. C, May 23, 1861; discharged for disability, September 7, 1861, at Arlington, Va.; also borne as Henry D. Tyler.

Twibill, William F. — Age, 25 years. Enrolled, April 18, 1861, at Brooklyn, to serve three years; mustered in as private, Co. H, May 23, 1861; promoted sergeant, Co. K, August 1861; mustered in as second lieutenant, June 18, 1862; as captain February 26, 1863; mustered out with company, June 6, 1864, at New York City; also borne as Twibelle; not commissioned second lieutenant; commissioned captain February 10, 1863, with rank from January 18, 1863, vice C.H. Morris, resigned.

Uffendill, Isaiah — Age, 34 years. Enrolled, April 18, 1861, at Brooklyn, to serve three years; mustered in as first lieutenant, Co. B, May 18, 1861, as captain, August 29, 1862; mustered out with company, June 6, 1864, at New York City; commissioned first lieutenant in Fourteenth Militia, May 4, 1861, with rank from May 2, 1861, original; captain, October 24, 1862, with rank from August 29, 1862, vice G. Mallory, killed in action.

Uffendill, John — Age, 19 years. Enlisted, September 22, 1861, at Brooklyn, to serve three years; mustered in as private, Co. D, September 25, 1861; discharged for disability, January 26, 1863, at Convalescent Camp, Va.

Unckels, David S. — Age, 22 years. Enrolled, April 18, 1861, at Brooklyn, to serve three years; mustered in as private, Co. A, May 23, 1861; promoted second lieutenant, August 5, 1861; discharged for disability, December 22, 1862; commissioned second lieutenant in Fourteenth Militia, August 12, 1861, with rank from August 5, 1861, vice John W. Redding, promoted.

Unckels, Frank — Age, 22 years. Enlisted, September 8, 1862, at Brooklyn, to serve three years; mustered in as private, Co. A, September 9, 1862; missing in action, July 1, 1863, at Gettysburg, Pa.; returned, October 8, 1863; transferred to navy April 18, 1864; also borne as Francis Unkles.

Underhill, William P. — Age, 25 years. Enlisted at Brooklyn, to serve three years; mustered in as private; unassigned, December 15, 1863; no further record.

Urie, William — Enlisted at New York, to serve three years; mustered in as private Co. I, March 1, 1862; promoted corporal, no date; transferred to Co. B, Fifth Veteran Infantry, June 2, 1864.

Uzzell, James D. — Enlisted at Falmouth, Va., to serve three years; mustered in as private, Co. A, August 3, 1862; dishonorably discharged, December 20, 1862; also borne as Charles D. Uzzell.

Valentine, Henry — Age, 19 years. Enlisted, April 25, 1861, at Brooklyn to serve three years; mustered in as private, Co. G, May 23, 1861; deserted, January 1, 1863, at Manassas, Va.; also borne as Henry C. Valentine.

Van Bell, John — Age, 22 years. Enlisted, April 18, 1861, at Brooklyn, to serve three years; mustered in as private, Co. E, May 23, 1861; promoted sergeant, no date; wounded in action, July 1, 1863, at Gettysburg, Pa.; promoted first sergeant December 26, 1863; mustered out with company June 6, 1864; also borne as Van Belle.

Van Brunt, Henry — Age, 24 years. Enlisted at Brooklyn, to serve three years; mustered in as private, Co. A, August 20, 1862; killed in action, September 17, 1862, at Antietam, Md.

Van Brunt, Martin — Age, 23 years. Enlisted at Brooklyn. to serve three years; mustered in as private, Co. K, December 7, 1863; wounded in action, no date, at the Wilderness, Va.; died of his wounds, May 27, 1864, at Washington, D.C.

Van Duyne, Charles H. — Age, 19 years. Enlisted at Brooklyn, to serve three years; mustered in as private, Co. H, August 14, 1862; discharged for disability, December 12, 1862, at headquarters, New York Harbor.

Van Horn, William H. — Age, 24 years. Enlisted, May 18, 1861, at Brooklyn to serve three years; mustered in as private, Co. D, May 23, 1861; discharged for disability on January 30, 1863, at Belle Plains, Va.

Van Ingen, Peter D. — Age, 26 years. Enlisted August 20, 1862, at Brooklyn to serve three years; mustered in as private, Co. K, August 22, 1862; wounded in action on April 29, 1863, at Reynold's Crossing, Va.; transferred to Veteran Reserve Corps, September 30, 1863.

Van Keuren, Isaac — Age, 40 years. Enlisted, April 18, 1861, at Brooklyn to serve three years; mustered in as private, Co. C, May 23, 1861; discharged, June 6, 1864, at New York City.

Van Pelt, Walter — Age, 22 years. Enlisted, May 18, 1861, at Brooklyn, to serve three years; mustered in as private, Co. D, May 23, 1861; promoted corporal, no date; killed in action, August 30, 1862, at Bull Run, Va.

Van Voorhies, George E. — Age, 18 years.

Enlisted, May 18, 1861, at Brooklyn to serve three years; mustered in as private, Co. B, May 23, 1861; discharged August 22, 1861, at Washington, D.C.

Van Winkle, Peter—Age, 24 years. Enlisted at New York City, to serve three years; mustered in as private, unassigned, July 26, 1861; no further record.

Van Wycklen, Abraham—Age, 20 years. Enlisted, April 25, 1861, at Brooklyn to serve three years; mustered in as private, Co. H, May 23, 1861; discharged for disability on June 6, 1861, at Washington, D.C.

Verzi, Liberal—Age, 26 years. Enlisted, April 18, 1861, at Brooklyn, to serve three years; mustered in as private, Co. F, May 23, 1861; discharged for disability on February 6, 1862, at Upton Hill, Va.

Victory, John P.—Age, 26 years. Enlisted, April 18, 1861, at Brooklyn, to serve three years; mustered in as private, company of engineers, May 23, 1861; mustered out on August 28, 1861, at Arlington, Va.

Vizors, Thomas—Age, 23 years. Enlisted at Brooklyn, to serve three years; mustered in as private, Co. G, December 19, 1863; deserted March 29, 1864, at Culpeper, Va.; also borne as Vigors.

Vliet, John—Age, 26 years. Enrolled, April 18, 1861, at Brooklyn, to serve three years; mustered in as first sergeant Co. D, May 23, 1861; as second lieutenant October 11, 1861; as first lieutenant October 1, 1862; as adjutant July 15, 1863; mustered out with regiment, June 6, 1864, at New York City; not commissioned second lieutenant; commissioned first lieutenant October 24, 1862; with rank from October 1, 1862.

Volkner, Edward—Age, 22 years. Enlisted, April 18, 1861, at Brooklyn, to serve three years; mustered in as private, Co. C, May 23, 1861; mustered out, May 30, 1864, as John Valkner; also borne as Voelkmer.

Von Gessner, Carl—Age, 24 years. Enlisted, August 21, 1862, at Brooklyn, to serve three years; mustered in as private, unassigned, August 22, 1862; no further record.

Von Rielfe, Hector—Age, 39 years. Enlisted, December 7, 1863, at Brooklyn, to serve three years; mustered in as private, Co. K, December 8, 1863; transferred to Co. K, Fifth Veteran Infantry, June 2, 1864; also borne as Von Rifle.

Von Schellenberg, Anton—Age, 38 years. Enlisted at Brooklyn, to serve three years; mustered in as private; Co. E, December 15, 1863; transferred to Fifth Veteran Infantry, June 2, 1864. also borne as Antony Schellenburg and Schilenburg.

Voorheis, Clark G.—Age, 24 years. Enlisted. July1, 1861, at Brooklyn, to serve three years; mustered in as sergeant, Co. K, August 1, 1861; promoted first sergeant, March 10, 1862; missing in action, July 1, 1863, at Gettysburg, Pa.; returned October 8, 1863; transferred to Co. K, Fifth Veteran Infantry, June 2, 1864.

Wacke, O'Hagen E.G.—Age, 24 years. Enlisted, April 18, 1861, at Brooklyn, to serve three years; mustered in as private, Co. C, May 23, 1861; deserted October 11, 1861, at Arlington Heights, Va.; also borne as Edward Wackerhagen.

Wade, William P.—Age, 23 years. Enlisted, April 18, 1861, at Brooklyn, to serve three years; mustered in as private, Co. E, May 23, 1861; killed in action July 21, 1861, at Bull Run, Va.

Wagner, Adam—Age, 25 years. Enlisted at Brooklyn, to serve three years; mustered in as private, Co. B, September 30, 1862; transferred to Co. C, Fifth Veteran Infantry, on June 2, 1864.

Wagner, Frederick—Age, 28 years. Enlisted, April 19, 1861, at Brooklyn, to serve three years; mustered in as private, Co. B, May 23, 1861; discharged for disability July 23, 1863, at Convalescent Camp, Va.

Wagner, John—Age, 28 years. Enlisted, October 9, 1862, at Brooklyn, to serve three years; mustered in as private, Co. B, October 10, 1862; wounded in action

May 10, 1864, at Laurel Hill, Va.; died of his wounds May 16, 1864.

Wakefield, Charles E.—Age, 22 years. Enlisted, April 18, 1861, at Brooklyn, to serve three years; mustered in as private, Co. E, May 23, 1861; mustered out with company, June 6, 1864, at New York City.

Waldron, Hampdon—Age, 21 years. Enrolled at Albany, to serve three years; mustered in as second lieutenant, Co. I, April 2, 1862; as first lieutenant, Co. D, December 9, 1863; mustered out June 3, 1864, at New York City; commissioned second lieutenant, April 2, 1862, with rank from same date.

Walker, Louis—Age, 20 years. Enlisted, April 18, 1861, at Brooklyn. to serve three years; mustered in as private, Co. E, May 23, 1861; transferred to Sixty-Seventh Infantry, December 2, 1861; also borne as Louis A. Walker.

Wallace, William—Age, 19 years. Enlisted, September 10, 1862, at Brooklyn, to serve three years; mustered in as musician, Co. H, September 11, 1862; missing in action July 1, 1863, at Gettysburg, Pa.; returned March 17, 1864; transferred to Co. K, Fifth Veteran Infantry, June 2, 1864.

Wallace, William—Age, 24 years. Enlisted, April 25, 1861, at Brooklyn, to serve three years; mustered in as private, Co. G, May 23, 1861; discharged for disability on August 6, 1862, at Washington, D.C.

Walshaw, John—Age, 43 years. Enlisted, April 18, 1861, at Brooklyn, to serve three years; mustered in as private, Co. C; discharged for disability, July 30, 1861, at Arlington, Va.

Walter, George W.—Age, 22 years. Enlisted, April 18, 1861, at Brooklyn to serve three years; mustered in as private, Co. E, May 23, 1861; discharged for disability on December 2, 1862, at Philadelphia, Pa.; also borne as Walters.

Walters, Henry—Age, 23 years. Enlisted, August 26, 1862, at Brooklyn, to serve three years; mustered in as private, Co. C, August 30, 1862; wounded in action on July 1, 1863, at Gettysburg, Pa.; transferred to Co. I, Fifth Veteran Infantry, June 2, 1864.

Walters, Isaac H.—Age, 19 years. Enlisted, May 18, 1861, at Brooklyn, to serve three years; mustered in as private, Co. B, May 23, 1861; discharged, November 26, 1861, at Brooklyn, N.Y.

Walters, James H.—Age, 30 years. Enlisted, September 18, 1861, at Brooklyn to serve three years; mustered in as private, Co. K. September 24, 1861; died of disease on September 12, 1862, at Washington, D.C.

Walton, John—Age, 22 years. Enlisted, September 2, 1862, at Brooklyn, to serve three years; mustered in as private, Co. H, September 4, 1862; captured in action, July 1, 1863, at Gettysburg, Pa.; paroled, no date; transferred to Co. K, Fifth Veteran Infantry, on June 2, 1864.

Walton, Joseph—Age, 22 years. Enlisted, September 3, 1862, at Brooklyn to serve three years; mustered in as private, Co. H. September 5, 1862; wounded in action on July 1, 1863, at Gettysburg, Pa.; died of his wounds, July 3, 1863.

Walton, William—Age, 19 years. Enlisted, December 26, 1863, at Brooklyn to serve three years; mustered in as private, Co. K, December 30, 1863; transferred to Co. I, Fifth Veteran Infantry, June 2, 1864.

Walz, John—Age, 34 years. Enlisted at Brooklyn, to serve three years; mustered in as private, Co. K, December 9, 1863; transferred to Co. H, Fifth Veteran Infantry, on June 2, 1864; also borne as Waltz.

Warburton, Samuel—Age, 20 years. Enlisted, August 25, 1862, at Brooklyn to serve three years; mustered in as private, Co. D, August 30, 1862; wounded in action May 10, 1864, at Laurel Hill, Va.; transferred to Co. I, Fifth Veteran Infantry, June 2, 1864; also borne as Warberton.

Ward, James — Age, 21 years. Enlisted, August 27, 1862, at Brooklyn, to serve three years; mustered in as private, Co. C, August 29, 1862; wounded in action, July 1, 1863, at Gettysburg, Pa.; transferred to Veteran Reserve Corps, no date.

Ward, Joseph P. — Age, 23 years. Enlisted, April 18, 1861, at Brooklyn, to serve three years; mustered in as private, Co. E, May 23, 1861; deserted June 24, 1861, at Washington, D.C.

Ward, Michael — Age, 28 years. Enlisted at Brooklyn, to serve three years; mustered in as private, Co. B, October 6, 1862; wounded in action, May 10, 1864, at Spotsylvania Court House, Va.; discharged for wounds, July 18, 1864, at New York City.

Ward, Thomas H. — Age, 20 years. Enlisted, April 18, 1861, at Brooklyn, to serve three years; mustered in as private, Co. D, May 23, 1861; transferred to Veteran Reserve Corps on January 31, 1864.

Ward, William H. — Age, 19 years. Enlisted. April 18, 1861, at Brooklyn, to serve three years; mustered in as sergeant, Co. F, May 23, 1861; discharged for disability, August 17, 1861, at Arlington, Va.

Waring, Fred A. — Age, 18 years. Enlisted. June 30, 1861, at Brooklyn, to serve three years; mustered in as private, Co. K, August 1, 1861; transferred to Co. K, Fifth Veteran Infantry, June 2, 1864.

Warner, Benjamin — Age, 20 years. Enlisted. April 18, 1861, at Brooklyn, to serve three years; mustered in as private, Co. F, May 23, 1861; deserted September 22, 1861, at Arlington, Va.

Warner, John F. — Age, 21 years. Enlisted, April 18, 1861, at Brooklyn, to serve three years; mustered in as private, Co. D, May 23, 1861; captured in action July 21, 1861, at Bull Run, Va.; paroled, no date; deserted June 5, 1862, from Camp Parole, Annapolis, Md.; apprehended on September 10, 1863; no further record.

Warren, Frank M. — Age, 19 years. Enlisted, April 18, 1861, at Brooklyn, to serve three years; mustered in as private, Co. E, May 23, 1861; transferred to Veteran Reserve Corps on August 1, 1863; also borne as Francis M. Warren.

Warren, Henry — Age, 40 years. Enlisted, May 18, 1861, at Brooklyn, to serve three years; mustered in as private, Co. B, May 23, 1861; discharged for heart disease, June 16, 1861, at Washington, D.C.

Warren, James — Age, 39 years. Enlisted, August 25, 1862, at Brooklyn, to serve three years; mustered in as private, Co. D, August 26, 1862; discharged for disability, December 23, 1862, at Baltimore, Md.

Warren, Thomas R. — Age, 24 years. Enlisted, April 18, 1861, at Brooklyn, to serve three years; mustered in as private, Co. E, May 23, 1861; deserted, July 24, 1861, at Arlington, Va.

Warren, William B. — Age, 26 years. Enlisted, August 25, 1862, at Brooklyn, to serve three years; mustered in as private, Co. D, August 26, 1862; transferred to Co. C, November 14, 1862; to Co. H, Fifth Veteran Infantry, June 2, 1864.

Warren, William F. — Age, 28 years. Enlisted, August 22, 1862, at Brooklyn, to serve three years; mustered in as private, Co. G, Fifth Veteran Infantry, June 2, 1864.

Warthmann, Henry — Age, 34 years. Enlisted, April 18, 1861, at Brooklyn, to serve three years; mustered in as private, Co. F, May 23, 1861; deserted October 23, 1861, at Upton Hill, Va.

Waterbury, Zeno C. — Age, 26 years. Enlisted, August 20, 1862, at Brooklyn, to serve three years; mustered in as private, Co. H, August 25, 1862; mustered out, May 31, 1865, at Washington, D.C.

Waters, Lewis — Age, 23 years. Enlisted, April 18, 1861, at Brooklyn, to serve three years; mustered in as principal musician in band; reduced to musician, and transferred to Co. F, June 1, 1861; to Co. G, November 1, 1861; deserted November 10, 1861, at Upton Hill, Va.; also borne as Wasser, Ludwig Waser and Louis Watel.

Watts, James — Age, 27 years. Enlisted at Brooklyn, to serve three years; mustered in as private, Co. D, September 18, 1862; transferred to Co. I, Fifth Veteran Infantry, on June 2, 1864.

Webb, Robert W. — Age, 35 years. Enlisted, April 18, 1861, at Brooklyn, to serve three years; mustered in as private, company of engineers, May 23, 1861; mustered out August 28, 1861, at Arlington, Va.

Webb, Thomas — Age, 19 years. Enlisted, September 15, 1862, at Brooklyn, to serve three years; mustered in as private, Co. G, September 17, 1862; deserted, no date; absent in arrest at Fort Columbus, New York City, October 31, 1863; no further record.

Webber, Charles F. — Age, 35 years. Enlisted, April 18, 1861, at Brooklyn, to serve three years; mustered in as private, Co. A, May 23, 1861; wounded in action, July 1, 1863, at Gettysburg, Pa.; died of his wounds, July 19, 1863.

Webster, Robert — Age, 23 years. Enlisted, June 30, 1861, at Brooklyn, to serve three years; mustered in as private, Co. I, August 1, 1861; transferred to Co. G, Fifth Veteran Infantry, June 2, 1864.

Weeks, Andrew — Age, 19 years. Enlisted, May 18, 1861, at Brooklyn, to serve three years; mustered in as private, Co. D, May 23, 1861; deserted November 11, 1861, from Camp Marion, Upton Hill, Va.

Weeks, George D. — Age, 27 years. Enlisted, April 18, 1861, at Brooklyn, to serve three years; mustered in as private, company of engineers, May 23, 1861; mustered out August 28, 1861, at Arlington, Va.; also borne as George W. Weeks.

Weeks, Thomas — Age, 28 years. Enlisted, October 1, 1861, at Brooklyn, to serve three years; mustered in as musician in band, October 24, 1861; discharged, August 17, 1862, at Camp Halstead, Va.

Weinberg, John — Age, 44 years. Enlisted at New York City, to serve three years; mustered in as private; unassigned, March 12, 1864; no further record.

Welch, Edward — Age, 20 years. Enlisted at New York City, to serve three years; mustered in as private; unassigned, March 5, 1864; no further record.

Weisser, Arthur F. — Age, 19 years. Enlisted, April 18, 1861, at Brooklyn to serve three years; mustered in as private, Co. H, May 23, 1861; discharged for disability on February 16, 1863, at Buffalo, N.Y.

Welch, Robert — Age, 28 years. Enlisted, August 27, 1862, at Brooklyn, to serve three years; mustered in as private, Co. F, August 29, 1862; wounded in action on July 1, 1863, at Gettysburg, Pa.; transferred to Co. K, Fifth Veteran Infantry, June 2, 1864.

Welch, William H. — Age, 21 years. Enlisted at Brooklyn, to serve three years; mustered in as private; unassigned, October 25, 1862; no further record.

Wells, John A. — Age, 32 years. Enlisted, July 1, 1861, at Brooklyn, to serve three years; mustered in as corporal, Co. I, August 1, 1861; deserted, January 22, 1862, at Upton Hill, Va.

Welsh, Edward — Age, 18 years. Enlisted at Brooklyn, to serve three years; mustered in as private, Co. A, December 16, 1863; appointed musician and returned to company as private, no dates; transferred to Co. A, Fifth Veteran Infantry, June 2, 1864.

Welsh, James — Age, 22 years. Enlisted at Brooklyn. to serve three years; mustered in as private, Co. F, December 15, 1863; discharged for disability March 7, 1864, at Culpeper, Va.

Welsh, Oscar — Age, 18 years. Enlisted, April 18, l861, at Brooklyn, to serve three years; mustered in as private, Co. A, May 23, 1861; promoted corporal, January 1, 1863; mustered out with company June 6, 1864, at New York City.

Welsh, William — Age, 22 years. Enlisted at Brooklyn, to serve three years; mustered in as private, Co. E, March 4, 1862; discharged for disability February 3, 1863, at Washington. D.C.; also borne as Walsh.

Werner, Francis — Age, 23 years. Enlisted at Brooklyn, to serve three years; mustered in as private, Co. K, December 8, 1863; transferred to Co. G, Fifth Veteran Infantry, June 2, 1864; also borne as Wolner and Frank Werner.

Werrman, Ludwig — Age, 27 years. Enlisted, December 8, 1863, at Brooklyn to serve three years; mustered in as private, Co. K, December 23, 1863; transferred to Co. H, Fifth Veteran Infantry, June 2, 1864; also borne as Warnmer, Weinmer and Weimer.

Wescott, George E. — Age, 21 years. Enlisted, April 18, 1861, at Brooklyn to serve three years; mustered in as sergeant, Co. E, May 23, 1861; promoted first sergeant, no date; returned to ranks December 26, 1863; transferred to Veteran Reserve Corps February 15, 1864; also borne as Westcott.

West, James — Age, 23 years. Enlisted, April 18, 1861, at Brooklyn, to serve three years; mustered in as private, Co. H, May 23, 1861; mustered out with company on June 6, 1864, at New York City.

West, John D. — Age, 22 years. Enlisted, April 18, 1861, at Brooklyn to serve three years; mustered in as private, Co. E, May 23, 1861; discharged for disability September 13, 1861, at Arlington, Va.

West, Rowland R. — Age, 30 years. Enlisted, April 18, 1861, at Brooklyn, to serve three years; mustered in as private, Co. C, May 23, 1861; discharged, October 28, 1861, for promotion.

Westcole, James E. — Age, 28 years. Enlisted, April 18, 1861, at Brooklyn, to serve three years; mustered in as private, Co. C, May 23, 1861; deserted March 8, 1863, at Washington, D.C. also borne as Westcott.

Westlake, David B. — Age, 27 years. Enlisted at Brooklyn, to serve three years; mustered in as private, Co. K, December 30, 1863; transferred to Co. H, Fifth Veteran Infantry, June 2, 1864.

Weston, John D. — Age, 23 years. Enlisted, June 30, 1861, at Brooklyn. to serve three years; mustered in as private, Co. I, August 1, 1861; wounded in action, July 1, 1863, at Gettysburg, Pa.; discharged for disability, October 26, 1863, at New York City.

Weston, Joseph M. — Age, 20 years. Enlisted, April 18, 1861, at Brooklyn, to serve three years; mustered in as private, Co. A, May 23, 1861; mustered out with company, June 6, 1864, at New York City; also borne as J.W. Weston.

Whaley, Charles — Age, 19 years. Enlisted, April 20, 1861, at Brooklyn. to serve three years; mustered in as private, Co. G, May 23, 1861; wounded in action August 29, 1862, at Bull Run, Va.; died of his wounds September 6, 1862, at Washington, D.C.; also borne as Charles M. Whaley.

Whaley, William P. — Age, 41 years. Enlisted at Brooklyn, to serve three years; mustered in as private, Co. A, December 3, 1861; wounded in action, July 1, 1863, at Gettysburg, Pa.; transferred to Co. A, Fifth Veteran Infantry, June 2, 1864.

White, Edward — Age, 21 years. Enlisted at New York City, to serve three years; mustered in as private; unassigned, March 12, 1864; no further record.

White, George W. — Age, 19 years. Enlisted, September 1, 1862, at Brooklyn, to serve three years; mustered in as private, Co. E, September 3, 1862; transferred to Co. H, Fifth Veteran Infantry, June 2, 1864.

White, Henry — Age, 21 years. Enlisted, August 27, 1862, at Brooklyn, to serve three years; mustered in as private, Co. G, August 28, 1862; transferred to Co. K, Fifth Veteran Infantry, June 2, 1864.

White, James — Age, 30 years. Enlisted, July 1, 1861, at Brooklyn, to serve three years; mustered in as private, Co. K, August 1, 1861; discharged for disability, December 26, 1862, at Alexandria, Va.

White, John — Age, 21 years. Enlisted. August 29, 1862, at Brooklyn, to serve three years; mustered in as private, Co. G, August 30, 1862; died of gangrene June 21, 1864, at Third Division Hospital, Alexandria, Va.

White, John — Age, 35 years. Enlisted at Brooklyn, to serve three years; mustered in as private, Co. D, September 8, 1862; transferred to Co. E, November 13, 1862; killed in action, May 10, 1864, at Laurel Hill, Va.

Whitlock, James — Age, 20 years. Enlisted, August 20, 1862, at Brooklyn, to serve three years; mustered in as private, Co. I, Fifth Veteran Infantry, June 2, 1864.

Whitman, Philip — Age, 25 years. Enlisted, May 18, 1861, at Brooklyn to serve three years; mustered in as private, Co. D, May 23, 1861; discharged for disability January 10, 1863, at Providence, R.I.

Whitmore, Francis S.— Age, 19 years. Enlisted, April 18, 1861, at Brooklyn, to serve three years; mustered in as private, Co. H, May 23, 1861; transferred to Co. K, 121st Infantry, no date.

Whitney, Stewart — Age, 20 years. Enlisted, August 28, 1862, at Brooklyn, to serve three years; mustered in as private, Co. E, August 30, 1862; transferred to Co. H., Fifth Veteran Infantry, June 2, 1864.

Whittall, George — Age, 18 years. Enlisted. August 26, 1862, at Brooklyn, to serve three years; mustered in as private, Co. E, August 27, 1862; transferred to Co. H, Fifth Veteran Infantry, June 2, 1864.

Wier, Daniel — Age, 19 years. Enlisted, July 1, 1861, at Brooklyn, to serve three years; mustered in as private, Co. I, August 1861; deserted, October 28, 1862, at Alexandria, Va.

Wier, Donald M.— Age, 40 years. Enlisted, July 1, 1861, at Brooklyn, to serve three years; mustered in as private, Co. I, no date; died of disease, July 28, 1861, at Arlington, Va.

Wiggins, Lester T.— Age, 18 years. Enlisted, April 18, 1861, at Brooklyn to serve three years; mustered in as private, Co. E, May 23, 1861; captured in action, July 21, 1861, at Bull Run, Va.; paroled, no date; discharged for disability, March 30, 1863, at Camp Parole, Annapolis, Md.

Wiggins, William — Age, 18 years. Enlisted, April 18, 1861, at Brooklyn to serve three years; mustered in as private, Co. D, May 23, 1861; deserted, October 18, 1861, from Camp Marion, Upton Hill, Va.

Willcox, George W.— Age, 25 years. Enlisted, August 10, 1862, at Brooklyn to serve three years; mustered in as private, Co. A, August 20, 1862; died of pneumonia on November 8, 1862, at Mount Pleasant Hospital, Washington, D.C.

Wilkins, Lemuel — Age, 18 years. Enlisted, September 25, 1862, at Brooklyn to serve three years; mustered in as private, Co. D, September 26, 1862; transferred to Co. G, June 1, 1863; to Co. K, Fifth Veteran Infantry, June 2, 1864; prior service Thirteenth Militia.

Wilkinson, David A.— Age, 19 years. Enlisted, April 18, 1861, at Brooklyn to serve three years; mustered in as private, Co. H, May 23, 1861; captured in action on August 29, 1862, at Bull Run, Va.; exchanged and deserted, October 1862.

Wilkinson, Edward — Age, 29 years. Enlisted, October 1, 1861, at Brooklyn to serve three years; mustered in as musician in band, October 24, 1861; mustered out August 17, 1862, at Camp Halstead, Va.

Wilkinson, James — Age, 37 years. Enlisted, January 2, 1864, at Brooklyn to serve three years; mustered in as private, Co. K, January 4, 1864; discharged for disability on March 7, 1864, at Culpeper, Va.; also borne as John Wilkinson.

Wilkinson, William A.— Age, 25 years. Enlisted at Brooklyn, to serve three years; mustered in as private, Co. K, September 3, 1862; missing in action, July 1, 1863, at Gettysburg, Pa.; returned to company October 8, 1863; transferred to Co. K, Fifth Veteran Infantry, June 2, 1864.

Williams, Charles — Age, 21 years. Enlisted, September 3, 1862, at Brooklyn to serve three years; mustered in as private, Co. B, September 4, 1862; transferred to Co. I, Fifth Veteran Infantry, June 2, 1864.

Williams, George — Age, 18 years. Enlisted at Brooklyn, to serve three years; mustered in as private, Co. A, December 17, 1863; transferred to Co. B, Fifth Veteran Infantry, June 2, 1864.

Williams, Henry R.—Age, 22 years. Enrolled, April 18, 1861, at Brooklyn to serve three years; mustered in as private, Co. D, May 23, 1861; promoted corporal on October 11, 1861; mustered in as second lieutenant, October 1, 1862; as first lieutenant on August 18, 1863; wounded September, 1863; discharged for wounds April 25, 1864; commissioned second lieutenant October 24, 1862, with rank from October 1, 1862.

Williams, John—Age, 20 years. Enlisted, April 18, 1861, at Brooklyn, to serve three years; mustered in as private, Co. F, May 23, 1861; appointed wagoner, no date; mustered out, June 14, 1864, at New York City.

Williams, Thomas—Age, 39 years. Enlisted, December 14, 1863, at Brooklyn to serve three years; mustered in as private; unassigned, December 15, 1863; no further record.

Williams, William—Age, 38 years. Enlisted, September 11, 1862, at Brooklyn to serve three years; mustered in as private, Co. B, September 12, 1862; killed in action on May 10, 1864, at Laurel Hill, Va.

Williamson, William T.—Age, 40 years. Enlisted, May 18, 1861, at Brooklyn to serve three years; mustered in as private, Co. D, May 23, 1861; discharged for disability on May 25, 1862, at Falmouth, Va.

Wills, Thomas—Age, 30 years. Enlisted at Brooklyn, to serve three years; mustered in as private, Co. F, December 14, 1863; deserted February 15, 1865, from Summit Hospital, Philadelphia, Pa.

Wilmarth, Frederick D.—Age, 34 years. Enlisted at Brooklyn, to serve three years; mustered in as private; unassigned, February 16, 1864; transferred to Co. I, Fifth Veteran Infantry, June 2, 1864.

Wilson, David C.—Age, 19 years. Enlisted, April 18, 1861, at Brooklyn, to serve three years; mustered in as private, Co. C, May 23, 1861; discharged for disability, June 16, 1861.

Wilson, David L.—Age, 19 years. Enlisted at Brooklyn, to serve three years; mustered in as private, Co. D, September 9, 1862; transferred to Co. I, Fifth Veteran Infantry, June 2, 1864.

Wilson, Joseph—Age, 18 years. Enlisted, July 1, 1861, at Brooklyn, to serve three years; mustered in as private, Co. C, August 4, 1861; promoted corporal, no date; discharged, January 1, 1864, for promotion to second lieutenant, Co. F, Thirty-Ninth Infantry; also borne as Joseph Wilson, Jr.

Wilson, Rivers S.—Age, 19 years. Enlisted, July 28, 1861, at Brooklyn, to serve three years; mustered in as private, Co. E, August 1, 1861; deserted November 11, 1861, at Arlington, Va.

Wilson, William—Age, 27 years. Enlisted, April 18, 1861, at Brooklyn, to serve three years; mustered in as private, Co. F, May 23, 1861; mustered out June 14, 1864, at New York City.

Winn, John—Age, 18 years. Enlisted at Brooklyn, to serve three years; mustered in as private, Co. F, December 15, 1863; appointed musician, no date; transferred to Co. G, Fifth Veteran Infantry, June 2, 1864.

Winn, Michael—Age, 20 years. Enlisted, May 18, 1861, at Brooklyn, to serve three years; mustered in as private, Co. G, May 23, 1861; wounded in action, August 30, 1862, at Bull Run, Va.; died of his wounds, October 1, 1862, at Alexandria, Va.

Winstanley, Henry H.—Age, 19 years. Enlisted, June 30, 1861, at Brooklyn, to serve three years; mustered in as private, Co. I, August 1, 1861; promoted sergeant, no date; re-enlisted as a veteran, March 23, 1864; transferred to Co. G, Fifth Veteran Infantry, June 2, 1864; also borne as Henry W. Winstanley.

Winters, Hugh J.—Age, 24 years. Enlisted,

September 3, 1862, at Brooklyn, to serve three years; mustered in as private, Co. K, September 5, 1862; discharged for disability, June 12, 1863, at Convalescent Camp, Va.

Wise, John H.—Age, 25 years. Enlisted, April 18, 1861, at Brooklyn, to serve three years; mustered in as private, Co. C, May 23, 1861; promoted corporal, no date; sergeant, January 1, 1864; mustered out June 14, 1864, at New York City; also borne as Weise.

Wolcott, Henry—Age, 19 years. Enlisted at Brooklyn, to serve three years; mustered in as private, Co. K, October 14, 1861; re-enlisted as a veteran, March 8, 1864; transferred to Co. G, Fifth Veteran Infantry, on June 2, 1864.

Wollan, Charles—Age, 23 years. Enlisted, December 12, 1863, at Brooklyn, to serve three years; mustered in as private, Co. F, December 21, 1863; transferred to Co. K, Fifth Veteran Infantry, on June 2, 1864; also borne as Wallan.

Wolstencroft, Thomas—Age, 37 years. Enlisted at Brooklyn, to serve three years; mustered in as private, Co. G, August 20, 1862; deserted June 28, 1863, while on the march near Emmetsburg, Md.; also borne as Wilsoncroft, Wilstencroft, Wolstencroff and Woolstencroft.

Wood, Alfred M.—Age, 33 years. Enrolled, April 4, 1861, at Brooklyn, to serve three years; mustered in as colonel May 23, 1861; discharged for disability October 18, 1862; commissioned colonel, Fourteenth Militia, April 13, 1858, with rank from March 30, 1858.

Wood, John—Age, 23 years. Enlisted at Brooklyn, to serve three years; mustered in as private, Co. B, September 9, 1861; wounded in action, August 29, 1862, at Bull Run, Va.; discharged for wounds February 24, 1863, at Baltimore, Md.

Wood, Lorenzo D.—Age, 22 years. Enlisted, April 18, 1861, at Brooklyn, to serve three years; mustered in as private, Co. H, May 23, 1861; mustered out with company, June 6, 1864, at New York City, as Lorenzo D.C. Wood.

Wood, Michael—Age, 21 years. Enlisted. May 18, 1861, at Brooklyn, to serve three years; mustered in as private, Co. B, May 23, 1861; deserted, October 23, 1861, at Upton Hill, Va.

Woodhead, James—Age, 22 years. Enlisted, August 29, 1862, at Brooklyn to serve three years; mustered in as private, Co. C, August 30, 1862; wounded in action on July 1, 1863, at Gettysburg, Pa.; discharged for disability, February 26, 1864.

Woods, Curtis H.—Age, 36 years. Enlisted, September 15, 1862, at Brooklyn to serve three years; mustered in as private, Co. B, September 16, 1862; killed in action on July 1, 1863, at Gettysburg, Pa.

Woodward, Charles D.—Age, 22 years. Enlisted at Brooklyn, to serve three years; mustered in as private; unassigned, January 9, 1864; no further record.

Woodward, George H.—Age, 20 years, Enlisted, August 25, 1862, at Brooklyn to serve three years; mustered in as private, Co. D, August 26, 1862; transferred to Co. I, Fifth Veteran Infantry, June 2, 1864.

Woolen, Charles—Age, 23 years. Enlisted, December 12, 1863, at Brooklyn to serve three years; mustered in as private; unassigned, December 23, 1863; no further record.

Woolstencroft, Alfred—Age, 24 years. Enlisted, April 18, 1861, at Brooklyn to serve three years; mustered in as private., Co. C, May 23, 1861; captured in action on July 21, 1861, at Bull Run, Va.; paroled, June 2, 1862, at Washington, D.C.; no further record.

Wooostencroft, Richard—Age, 20 years, Enlisted, April 18, 1861, at Brooklyn to serve three years; mustered in as private, Co. C, May 23, 1861; discharged for disability on March 27, 1863, at Alexandria, Va.

Worts, Charles—Age, 24 years. Enlisted, April 18, 1861, at Brooklyn to serve three years; mustered in as private, Co. A, May 2, 1861; discharged for disability, August 2, 1861, at Arlington, Va.

Wreford, William J.—Age, 18 years. Enlisted, August 20, 1862, at Brooklyn to serve three years; mustered in as private, Co. K, August 1, 1862; wounded in action on July 1, 1863, at Gettysburg, Pa.; promoted corporal, no date; transferred to Fifth Veteran Infantry, June 2, 1864.

Wright, Frederick E.—Age, 19 years. Enlisted, September 6, 1862, at Brooklyn to serve three years; mustered in as private, Co. B, September 8, 1862; wounded in action on July 1, 1863, at Gettysburg, Pa.; died of his wounds July 27, 1863.

Wriglet, Squire—Age, 19 years. Enlisted, July 1, 1861, at Brooklyn to serve three years; mustered in as private, Co. I, August 1, 1861; missing in action, August 29, 1862, at Bull Run, Va.; no further record.

Wyman, William—Age, 44 years. Enlisted, October 1, 1861, at Brooklyn to serve three years; mustered in as musician in band, October 24, 1861; discharged on August 17, 1862, at Camp Halstead, Va.

Yates, Benjamin P.—Age, 22 years. Enlisted, April 18, 1861, at Brooklyn to serve three years; mustered in as private, Co. C, May 23, 1861; discharged for disability on January 10, 1863, at Washington, D.C.

Yeaman, Robert, Jr.—Age, 19 years. Enlisted, August 20, 1862, at Brooklyn to serve three years; mustered in as private, Co. H, August 21, 1862; transferred to Co. I, Fifth Veteran Infantry, June 2, 1864.

York, John F.—Age, 19 years. Enlisted, April 18, 1861, at Brooklyn to serve three years; mustered in as private, Co. E, May 23, 1861; promoted sergeant, December 1, 1862; re-enlisted as a veteran, March 23, 1864; transferred to Co. H, Fifth Veteran Infantry, on June 2, 1864.

Young, Ferdinand—Age, 18 years. Enlisted, July 1, 1861, at Brooklyn to serve three years; mustered in as private, Co. K, August 1, 1861; deserted, January 20, 1863, Belle Plains, Va.

Young, John F.—Age, 18 years. Enlisted, July 1, 1861, at Brooklyn, to serve three years; mustered in as corporal, Co. I, August 1, 1861; promoted sergeant, no date; discharged for disability December 15, 1862.

Young, John H.—Age, 21 years. Enlisted, April 18, 1861, at Brooklyn, to serve three years; mustered in as private, Co. D, May 23, 1861; promoted corporal on November 1, 1862; wounded in action July 1, 1863, at Gettysburg, Pa.; mustered out with company June 6, 1864, at New York City; also borne as John Y. Young.

Young, John S.—Age, 22 years. Enlisted, July 31, 1861, at Brooklyn, to serve three years; mustered in as private, Co. I, August 4, 1861; transferred to Fifth Veteran Infantry, June 2, 1864.

Zellinsky, Ferdinand—Age, 23 years. Enlisted, April 18, 1861, at Brooklyn, to serve three years; mustered in as private, Co. A, May 23, 1861; promoted corporal, no date; discharged for disability February 13, 1863, at Harewood Hospital, Washington, D.C.; also born as Zellerisky and Zyelinsky.

Chapter Notes

Introduction
1. C.V. Trevis, and Don Marquis, *History of the the Fighting Fourteenth*, Baltimore MD: Butternut & Blue, 1994; originally published by Brooklyn Eagle Press in 1911.

Chapter 1
1. Cory David. "Brooklyn and the Civil War," *Journal of Long Island History*, vol. 2 (Spring 1862): 1–2.
2. Laws of the State of New York, 70th Session, May 13, 1847, 355.
3. C. Tevis and Marquand. *Fighting Fourteenth*, Brooklyn Eagle Press, 1922, 7–10.
4. *New York Daily Times*, May 9, 1854.
5. *Boston Atlas*, May 13, 1854; Reported in *New York Times*, May 15, 1854.
6. *New York Daily Times*, May 29, 1854.
7. *Brooklyn Daily Eagle*, June 5, 1854.
8. Edward A Lambert, *Brooklyn Daily Eagle*, June 7, 1854. Written on June 6.
9. *Brooklyn Daily Eagle*, June 10, 1854.
10. *Ibid.*, June 12, 1854.
11. *Ibid.*
12. Elen Snyder-Greenier, *Brooklyn* (Philadelphia: Temple University Press, 1996), 39.
13. H.S. Commanger, ed., *The Civil War Archive* (New York: Black Dog and Leventhal, 2000), 45.
14. *New York Times*, December 12, 1860. Edward Spann, *Gotham at War* (Wilmington: DE: Scholarly Resources, 2002), 6.
15. *Brooklyn Daily Eagle*, Editorial, April 10, 1861.
16. Henry Stiles, *A History of the City of Brooklyn*, vol. II (Bowie, MD: Heritage Books, 1993), 439.
17. *Ibid.*, 241.
18. *Brooklyn Daily Times*, April 15, 1861; *Brooklyn Daily Times*, April 27, 1861.

Chapter 2
1. Henry Hazelton, *Boroughs of Brooklyn, Queens, Counties of Nassau and Suffolk* (New York: Lewis Historical Pub. Co., 1925), 279.
2. State of New York, Annual Report of the Adjutant General. Submitted to the Legislature Jan. 31, 1869. Hereafter referred to as Adjutant General's Report.
3. *Brooklyn Daily Eagle*, May 17, 1861.
4. Stiles, 455.
5. *Brooklyn Daily Eagle*, May 17, 1861.
6. *Brooklyn Daily Eagle*, May 16, 1861.
7. *Brooklyn Daily Eagle* May 18, 1861.
8. Col. Fowler's own story printed in *Tevis*. Hereafter referred to as Fowler Papers.
9. Adjutant General's Report, Fowler Papers.
10. *Brooklyn Daily Eagle* , May 20, 1861.
11. Robin Smith and Ron Field, *Uniforms of the Civil War* (London: Brassey's Press, 2001), 95; Fowler Papers; Philip Haythornthwaite, *Uniforms of the Civil War* (New York: Macmillan, 1976), 154–55.
12. Fowler papers.
13. *Brooklyn Daily Eagle*, May 20, 1861.
14. *Brooklyn Daily Eagle*, May 21, 1861.
15. *Brooklyn Daily Eagle*, letter to editor from Headquarters Co. C. 14th Regiment, Washington, May 21, 1861.
16. Adjutant General's Report.
17. *The War of the Rebellion, A Compilation of the Official Records of the Union & Confederate Armies*, series 1, vol. 2 (Washington DC: Government Printing Office, 1890–1901), 7. Hereafter referred to as *OR*.
18. Adjutant General's Report.
19. Fowler Papers.
20. Adjutant General's Report.
21. Fowler Papers.
22. Fowler Papers.
23. Letter to the editor of the *Brooklyn Daily Eagle* from W.M., dated May 24, 1861, and printed May 27, 1861.
24. Letter from Lieut. William H. Burnett dated May 23, 1861; letter from T.J. Conaut to his mother dated May 23, 1861, and printed in the *Brooklyn Daily Eagle* on May 27, 1861.
25. Letter from J.B. published in *Brooklyn Daily Eagle*, May 31, 1861.
26. Fowler Papers, Adjutant General's Report, *Brooklyn Daily Eagle*; letter from J.B. published on May 31, 1861.

27. Letter by J.M.H. in *Brooklyn Daily Eagle*, June 4, 1861.
28. Muster roll of the 14th Brooklyn printed in Tevis.
29. Letter by W.A.C. in *Brooklyn Daily Eagle*, June 7, 1861.
30. Letter from Co. D to *Brooklyn Daily Eagle*, June 7, 1861, written June 1, 1861.
31. Fowler Papers.
32. *Brooklyn Daily Eagle*, June 22, 1861; Fowler Papers.
33. Letters to *Brooklyn Daily Eagle* published June 26, 1861, and written on June 18 and June 17, 1861, by Sgt. G.B. Jones, 14th Regiment.
34. *New York Times*, June 24, 1861; speech by H.W. Beecher.
35. *Brooklyn Daily Eagle*, June 29, 1861.
36. *Ibid*.
37. *Brooklyn Daily Eagle*, June 29, 1861.
38. Robin Kelley and Earl Lewis, eds., *To Make Our World Anew* (New York: Oxford University Press, 2000), 229.
39. Frank Morris, ed., *Rebellion Record, a Diary of American Events*, June 25, 1861 (New York: Arno Press, 1977), 7.
40. Adjutant General's Report; Fowler Papers.
41. *OR*, series 1, vol. 51, part 1, 408–409.
42. Fowler Papers.
43. *OR*, series 1, vol. 51, part 1, 413–414.
44. *Brooklyn Daily Eagle*, July 18, 1861. From a letter written July 13, 1861.
45. *Brooklyn Daily Eagle*, July 16, 1861. Letter from W.A. Ludden, written July 14, 1861.
46. *Brooklyn Daily Eagle*, July 17, 1861. Written on July 14, 1861.

Chapter 3

1. Alfred Roman, *The Military Operations of Gen. Beauregard*, vol. 1 (New York: DaCapo Press, 1994), 77–78.
2. Ezra Warner, *Generals in Gray* (Baton Rouge: Louisiana State University Press, 1959), 22.
3. *Confederate Military History*, vol. 4 (Wilmington, NC: Broadfoot, 1987), 95.
4. Ezra Warner, *Generals in Blue* (Baton Rouge: Louisiana State University Press, 1964), 298.
5. *Confederate Military History*, 95–96.
6. Fowler Papers.
7. *OR*, series 1, vol. 2, part 1, 312.
8. *Ibid.*, 326, General Order #22.
9. *Ibid.*, 383.
10. *OR*, series 1, vol. 2, 474; E.P. Alexander, *Military Memoirs of a Confederate* (New York: Scribner, 1907), 31.
11. *Ibid.*, 384.

12. John Imboden, "Incidents of the First Bull Run," in *Battles and Leaders of the Civil War*, vol. 1, eds. Robert Johnson and Clarence Buel. Reprint (New York: Castle Books, 1991), 325.
13. *New York Times*, July 23, 1861.
14. John Casler, *Four Years in the Stonewall Brigade* (Guthrie, OK: State Capital Printing Co., 1893), 36. This version of what Bee said is quoted as often as, "There stands Jackson. Like a stone wall." For an excellent treatment of what was said by Bee, see James Robertson Jr., *Stonewall Jackson: The Man, the Soldier, the Legend*, 835.
15. *OR*, series 1, vol. 2, 492–94; *Confederate Veteran*, vol. 8, 367.
16. Joanna McDonald, *We Shall Meet Again* (Shippensburg, PA: White Mane Books, 1999), 80; John Hennessy, *The First Battle of Manassas* (Lynchburg, VA: H.E. Howard, 1989), 67.
17. *OR*, series 1, vol. 2, part 1, 383–384.
18. McDonald, 109; *OR*, series 1, vol. 2, 385.
19. Burke Davis, *They Called Him Stonewall* (New York: Holt Reinhardt and Winston, 1954).
20. U.S. Congress, Joint Committee On the Conduct of the War, vol. 2, 1863, 145. Hereafter referred to as JCCW.
21. James Robertson, *Stonewall Jackson: The Man, the Soldier, the Legend* (New York: Macmillan, 1997), 265.
22. McDonald, 109.
23. William C. Davis, *Battle at Bull Run* (Garden City, NY: Doubleday, 1977), 207; Casler, 27.
24. Davis, *Battle at Bull Run*, 206.
25. Casler, 37.
26. Fowler Papers; McDonald, 117.
27. C. Fonderden, *A Brief History of Military Career of Carpenter's Battery* (New Market, VA: Hinkel, 1911), 13; McDonald, 121.
28. JCCW, Testimony of Capt. W. Averell, 217.
29. *New York Times*, July 23, 1861.
30. Massachusetts Historical Society, Beal Papers, letter to his parents dated July 23, 1861.
31. Fowler Papers.
32. Charles Coffin, *The Boys of '61* (Boston: Estes and Lauriat, 1884), 24.
33. *Richmond Dispatch*, July 23, 1861.
34. Coffin, 25.
35. William C. Davis, *The Deep Waters of the Proud* (Garden City, NY: Doubleday, 1982), 77.
36. William C. Davis, *First Blood* (Alexandria, VA: Time Life Books, 1983), 149, 150.
37. *New York Times*, July 24, 1861; Andrew Coopersmith, *Fighting Works* (New York: New Press, 2004), 79.
38. Shelby Foote, *The Civil War: A Narrative* (New York: Vintage Books, 1958), 82.
39. Jefferson Davis, *The Rise and Fall of the Confederate Government*, vol. 1 (New York: D. Appleton, 1912), 354–356; Roman, 114–116.
40. Letter from John Vliet to his mother, July

23, 1861. Vliet Papers, Brooklyn Historical Society.
41. Manassas Battlefield National Park, Reference Library, Wells File Wells incorrectly refers to the 1st New York Fire Zouaves when in reality it was the 11th New York Fire Zouaves.
42. Letter written by John Jenkins to the *Sunday Mercury* published August 25, 1861.
43. Letter written by Joseph Sands on July 23,1861, and printed in the *Brooklyn Daily Eagle* on July 26, 1861.
44. John Hennessy, *The First Battle of Manassas*, 2nd edition (Lynchburg, VA: H.E. Howard, 1989), 124–26.
45. JCCW testimony of Gen. Patterson and Gen. Scott, 7.
46. Mary Anna Jackson, *Life and Letters of Stonewall Jackson* (New York: Harper & Bros., 1892), 178.
47. Frederick Phisterer, *New York in the War of the Rebellion*, vol. 4 (Albany, NY: J.B. Lyon, 1912).

Chapter 4

1. Bernard Nadal, *The Christian Boy Soldier* (New York: Steam Printing House, 1862), 14, 16, 17, 20.
2. Letter by A. McCue to the *Brooklyn Daily Eagle*, dated July 23, 1861, printed on July 25, 1861.
3. Letter by John P. Victory, written on July 25, 1861, and printed in the *Brooklyn Daily Eagle* on July 31, 1861.
4. Stiles, 456.
5. *Brooklyn Daily Eagle*, July 24, 1861.
6. *OR*, series 2, vol. 3, 724.
7. *Ibid.*, 728.
8. *Ibid.*
9. *Ibid.*, 739.
10. *Ibid.*
11. Letter from Col. A.M. Wood to Congressman Odell, published in the *Brooklyn Daily Eagle*, Nov. 19, 1861.
12. *OR*, series 2, vol. 2, 1,115
13. *OR*, series 2, vol. 4, 788; *Congressional Globe*, 37th Congress, 2nd Session, 5–6.
14. *OR*, series 2, vol. 3, 321
15. *Brooklyn Daily Eagle*, March 4, 1862.
16. H.E. Howard, ed., *The Eagle and Brooklyn*; *Brooklyn Daily Eagle*, 148, 386.

Chapter 5

1. Fowler Papers.
2. *Brooklyn Daily Eagle*, July 31, 1861, signed Ed.
3. Letter from William Collins, to his parents, dated July 23, 1861, printed in the *Brooklyn Daily Times*, July 26, 1861.

4. *New York Tribune*, July 23, 1861.
5. Letter from J.C., in *Brooklyn Daily Times*, dated July 31, 1861.
6. *Brooklyn Daily Eagle*, August 3, 1861.
7. Tevis, 153.
8. *Rebellion Record*, 523
9. *Brooklyn Daily Eagle*, August 30, 1861.
10. Letter written by John Jenkins, published in the *Sunday Mercury* on August 25, 1861.
11. *Brooklyn Eagle*, Sept. 9, 1861.
12. *Brooklyn Eagle*, Sept. 3, 1861.
13. *Brooklyn Eagle*, July 30, 1861.
14. JCCW, "Barbarities of the Rebels at Manassas," 37th Congress 2nd Session, House of Representatives, #10, vol. 2, 1863, 1–2. Testimony of Dr. J.M. Homiston.
15. JCCW, 3. Testimony of Gen. James Ricketts.
16. JCCW, 4. Testimony of Pvt. Louis Francis.
17. Letter by George Macy, Co. K, 14th Regiment, dated Sept. 26, 1861, from Arlington, VA (New York Historical Society).
18. William Swinton, *Army of the Potomac* (New York: Konecky & Konecky, 1995), 75.
19. Adjutant General's Report; Fowler Papers.
20. Letter by John Jenkins, published in the *Sunday Mercury* on Oct. 6, 1861.
21. *OR*, series 3, vol. 3, 262
22. Fowler Papers.
23. *Ibid.*
24. Letter by John Jenkins, published in the *Sunday Mercury*, September 29, 1861.
25. *OR*, series 1, vol. 5, 442.
26. *Ibid.*, 443.
27. *Ibid.*
28. Fowler Papers.
29. Diary of Josiah Grumman in the Brooklyn Historic Society, hereafter referred to as BHS.
30. Tevis, 347.
31. Special Order 544, Department of Military and Naval Affairs, Albany, NY.
32. *Brooklyn Daily Eagle*, January 9, 1862.
33. *Brooklyn Daily Eagle*, January 13, 1862, from One of the Boys.
34. *Brooklyn Daily Eagle*, Commentary February 13, 1862.
35. *OR*, series 3, vol. 1, 953.
36. Fowler Papers.
37. Fowler Papers; Tevis, 253.
38. Tevis, 187.

Chapter 6

1. Warner, *Generals in Blue*, 12.
2. Adjutant General's Report; Tevis, 30; Fowler Papers.
3. JCCW, 5. Testimony of Frederick Scholes.
4. *Brooklyn Daily Eagle*, March 21, 1862.
5. Adjutant General's Report.

6. Letter from John Brown to his sister, dated March 24, 1862 (Manassas Battlefield National Park Library).
7. Rufus Dawes, *Service with the 6th Wisconsin* (Madison: State Historical Society of Wisconsin, 1890), 38.
8. *OR*, supplement part 2, vol. 45, 235.
9. Adjutant General's Report; Fowler Papers.
10. Tevis, 162.
11. *Brooklyn Daily Eagle*, February, 22, 1901.
12. W. Fox, *Regimental Losses in the American Civil War 1861–1865* (Albany, NY: Albany Publishing Co., 1893), 117.
13. *Ibid.*
14. Fowler Papers.
15. Adjutant General's Report.
16. *OR*, supplement, part 2, vol. 45, 235.
17. Tevis, 34.
18. Fowler Papers.
19. *OR*, supplement, part 2, vol. 45, 235; Tevis, 34.
20. *OR*, series 1, vol. 12, part 2, 301.
21. Adjutant General's Report.
22. *OR*, series 2, vol. 4, 274.
23. *OR*, series 1, vol. 12, 102–103.
24. *Ibid.*, 102.
25. Adjutant General's Report.

Chapter 7

1. Warner, *Generals in Blue*, 376.
2. Warner, *Generals in Gray*, 180–183.
3. *War Sketches from Cedar Mt. to Bull Run, Written by a Staff Officer* (Buffalo, NY: Young, Lockwood and Co.'s Steam Press, 1882), 7; Harnickell Papers, Brooklyn Historical Society.
4. James Longstreet, *From Manassas to Appomattox* (Secaucus, NJ: Blue and Gray Press, 1984), 157.
5. Adjutant General's Report.
6. Curt Anders, *Hearts in Conflict* (New York: Carol Publishing, 1994), 193.
7. John Hennessy, *Return to Bull Run* (New York: Simon and Shuster, 1993), 60.
8. Adjutant General's Report lists 2 men killed and 6 wounded during this artillery duel while the *OR* supplement part 2, vol. 45, 231, lists 1 man killed and 6 wounded. Phisterer lists 1 man killed.
9. Letter written on September 15, 1862, from a soldier of the Fourteenth, who identified himself as "Brooklyn."
10. Letter from Lieut. Col Samuel R. Beardsley, 24th NY Infantry, to his wife, written August 27, 1862 (Manassas National Battlefield Park Library).
11. *OR*, series 1, vol. 12, part 2I, 603.
12. S.E. Chanler, "In the Thick of It: What the Iron Brigade Experienced," *National Tribune*, October 17, 1895.
13. Adjutant General's Report.
14. *OR*, supplement, part 2, vol. 45, 231; Adjutant General's Report.
15. Longstreet, *From Manassas to Appomattox*, 167.
16. John Gibbons, *Personal Recollection of the Civil War* (New York: G.P. Putnam & Son, 1928), 49.
17. *OR*, series 1, vol. 12, part 1, 215.
18. "The Virginia Campaign of Gen. Pope," *Papers Read Before the Military Historical Society of Mass, 1876*, 77, 80, vol. II (Boston: Ticknor, 1886), 62–65.
19. *OR*, series 1, vol. 12, part 2, 74.
20. Theron Haight, "Gainesville, Groveton and Bull Run," *War Papers Read Before the Commanding of the State of Wisconsin, Military Order of the Loyal Legion of the U.S.*, vol. II (Milwaukee, 1896), 358, 359.
21. John Hennessy, *Return to Bull Run*, 164, 165.
22. Alan Nolan, *The Iron Brigade* (Bloomington: University of Indiana Press, 1998), 204.
23. Dawes, 59–60.
24. Hennessy, *Return to Bull Run*, 166; John Hennessy, *Historical Report on the Troop Movements for the Second Battle of Manassas* (Denver, CO: National Park Service, 1985), map no. 1.
25. William Blackford, *War Years with Jeb Stuart* (New York: Charles Scribner Sons, 1945), 116, 117.
26. Hennessy, *Return to Bull Run*, 167.
27. Blackford, 120, 121.
28. Theron Haight, "King's Division: Fredricksburg to Manassas," *War Papers Read Before the Commandery of the State of Wisconsin, Military Order of the Loyal Legion of the U.S.*, vol. II (Milwaukee, 1896), 344.
29. William Allen, *The Army of Northern Virginia in 1862* (New York: Houghton Mifflin, 1892), 233.
30. Theron Haight, "Gainesville, Groveton, and Bull Run," 362.
31. Hennessy, *Troop Movements*, 46.
32. John Bryson, *History of the Thirtieth New York Volunteers* (Albany, NY: New York State Library), 52.
33. *Ibid.*, 53.
34. Gibbons, *Personal Recollections*, 57.
35. Edward Nichols, *Toward Gettysburg* (University Park: Pennsylvania State University Press, 1958), 107.
36. Hennessy, *Return to Bull Run*, 198, 99.
37. Bryon, 55.
38. Adjutant General's Report.
39. J.A Judson to Porter, May 9, 1878, *Porter Papers*, Library of Congress. Reported in Hennessy, *Troop Movements*, 167, Map #6.
40. Hennessy, *Return to Bull Run*, 291.
41. Bryson, 57.

42. *OR*, series 1, vol. 12, part 2, 367.
43. Haight, "Gainesville, Groveton and Bull Run," 364–65.
44. Hennessy, *Return to Bull Run*, 296.
45. Haight, "Gainesville, Groveton and Bull Run," 365.
46. *Brooklyn Daily Eagle*, letter dated August 31, 1862, and printed on September 2, 1862.
47. Adjutant General's Report.
48. *OR*, series 1, vol. 12, part 3, 748.
49. Edie James, letter to his wife Eliza, September 14, 1910, National Park Service Library.
50. Adjutant General's Report.
51. Edie James, letter dated September 14, 1910.
52. Tevis, 241, 294.
53. Letter from John C. Cox to Charles Baldwin, dated April 1, 1896, quoted in Tevis.
54. Swinton, 188.
55. Bryson, 60; David Hamer, "*One Man's War*," Manuscript at Manassas National Battlefield Park Library, 24.
56. *OR*, series 1, vol. 12, part 3, 756; Hennessy, *Return to Bull Run*, 325.
57. Hennessy, *Return to Bull Run*, 327, 28.
58. *OR*, series 1, vol. 12, part 2, 368.
59. Hennessy, *Troop Movements*, 306; Hennessy, *Return to Bull Run*, 336.
60. Haight, "Gainesville, Groveton & Bull Run," 368, 369.
61. *Ibid.*, 369; Gates Report, *OR*, series 1, vol. 12, part 2, 375–376.
62. Longstreet, *From Manassas to Appomattox*, 187.
63. Haight, "Gainesville, Groveton & Bull Run," 369; Hennessy, *Return to Bull Run*, 353.
64. E.D. Willets, "Gallant Louisiana Troops," *Philadelphia Weekly Times*, December 24, 1881, quoted in Hennessy, *Troop Movements*, 355.
65. *OR*, series 1, vol. 12, part 2, 668, 669.
66. Hennessy, *Troop Movements*, map #12.
67. *Ibid.*, map #16; Swinton, 191; Bryson, 64.
68. E.M. Woodward, *Our Campaign*, 182, quoted in Hennessy, *Second Bull Run*.
69. Adjutant General's Repot.

Chapter 8

1. *OR*, series 1, vol. 12, part 2, Page 344; *OR*, supplement, part 2, vol. 45, 237 Adjutant General's Report.
2. *OR*, series 1, vol. 19, part 2, 169.
3. Warner, *Generals in Blue*, 290, 291.
4. Stephen Sears, ed., *The Civil War Papers of George B. McClellan* (New York: Tichnor and Fields, 1989), 400–404.
5. William Allan, "Strategy of the Campaign of Sharpsburg, or Antietam, September 1862," *Papers of the Military Historical Society of Massachusetts* 3 (1888), 76.
6. *OR*, series 1, vol. 19, part 1, 145.
7. Swinton, 200; Anders, 231.
8. *OR*, supplement, part 2, vol. 45, 237; Adjutant General's Report.
9. *OR*, series 1, vol. 19, part 1, 146.
10. Stephen Sears, *Landscape Turned Red* (New Haven, CT: Ticknor and Fields, 1983), 129.
11. Curtis Older, *The Land Tracts of the Battlefield of South Mountain* (Westminster, MD: Willow Bend Books, 1999), 45; James Murfin, *The Gleam of Bayonets* (Baton Rouge: Louisiana State University Press, 1965), 167.
12. Adjutant General's Report.
13. *OR*, series 1, vol. 19, part 1, 144, 145.
14. *OR*, series 1, vol. 19, part 1, 941.
15. D.H. Hill, "The Battle of South Mountain, or Boonesboro," in *Battles and Leaders of the Civil War*, vol. 2, 564–565.
16. John Bloss, *Antietam and the Lost Dispatch: A Paper Prepared and Read Before the Kansas Commandery of the M.O.L.L.U.S.*, January 6th, 1892 (Wilmington, NC: Broadfoot, 1992).
17. Ezra Ayers Carman Collection, New York Public Library; Adjutant General's Report.
18. *OR*, series 1, vol. 19, part 1, 221.
19. D.H. Hill, 573.
20. *Ibid.*, 574.
21. *Ibid.*
22. *OR*, series 1, vol. 19, part 1, 221–222.
23. *OR*, series 1, vol. 19, part 1 231–232; Michael Priest, *Before Antietam: The Battle for South Mountain* (Shippensburg, PA: White Mane, 1992), 253–256.
24. Ezra Ayers Carman Collection.
25. Bryson, 70.
26. Priest, 256.
27. Some experiences of Capt. Cardona in Tevis, 149–150.
28. Murfin, 181.
29. Harry Mitchell, "The Fighting Fourteenth. The Battle of South Mountain," *Brooklyn Advance*, vol. 11 (February 1885), 253–256.
30. *OR*, series 1, vol. 19, part 1, 232; Priest, 259.
31. Priest, 263.
32. Ezra Ayers Carman Collection.
33. Letter by Joseph Pettiner, September 20, 1862, in Fourteenth Brooklyn File in Antietam Battlefield National Park. Joseph Pettiner, whose real name was Joseph Wade, was discharged for desertion on June 26, 1863.
34. *OR*, series 1, vol. 19, part 1, 232.
35. *OR*, series 1, vol. 19, part 11, 289.
36. Priest, 313–14.
37. Swinton, 207.
38. *Ibid.*, 221.

39. *Ibid.*, 221.
40. *Ibid.*, 232.
41. Thomas Clemens, ed., "A Brigade Commander's First Fight: The Letters of Colonel Walter Phelps, Jr. During the Maryland Campaign," in *Antietam: The Maryland Campaign of 1862*, ed. Mark A. Snell (Mechanicsburg, PA: Stackpole, 1997).
42. Phisterer, 2,930.

Chapter 9

1. Joseph Harsh, *Taken at the Flood* (Kent, OH: Kent State University Press), 1999, 299.
2. Ezra Ayers Carman Collection.
3. Sears, *Landscape Turned Red*, 168.
4. Ezra Ayers Carman Collection.
5. Sears, *Landscape Turned Red*, 169.
6. *Ibid.*, 175.
7. Murfin, 200; *OR*, series 1, vol. 19, part 1, 147–149.
8. *OR*, series 1, vol. 19, 29–30.
9. Harry Mitchell, "The Battle of Antietam, *Brooklyn Advance*, vol. 12 (May–Dec. 1885), 16–21.
10. *OR*, series 1, vol. 19 part 1, 29–30; *OR*, series 1, vol. 19, part 1, 217
11. Ezra Warner, *Generals in Blue*, 129–130.
12. Ezra Ayers Carman Collection.
13. Sears, *Landscape Turned Red*, 181, map 183.
14. Harsh, 370.
15. *OR*, series 1, vol. 19, part 1, 955–6; *OR*, series 1, vol. 19, part 1, 967–69; Sears, *Landscape Turned Red*, 116.
16. Murfin, 212.
17. *OR*, series 1, vol. 19 part 1, 218.
18. Sears, *Landscape Turned Red*, 192.
19. Dawes, *Service with the Sixth Wisconsin*, 90.
20. Ronald Baily, *The Bloodiest Day* (Alexandria, VA: Time Life Books, 1984), 74–75; Sears, *Landscape Turned Red*, 197.
21. Bailey, 75.
22. Dawes, 91
23. *Ibid.*
24. George Otott, "Clash in the Cornfield: The 1st Texas Volunteer Infantry in the Maryland Campaign," in *Antietam: The Maryland Campaign of 1862*, ed. Mark A. Snell (Mechanicsburg, PA: Stackpole, 1997).
25. Sears, *Landscape Turned Red*, 197–98.
26. W.D. Pritchard, "Civil War Remembrances," unpublished manuscript (1898), Antietam National Battlefield Library.
27. James McPherson, *Crossroads of Freedom* (New York: Oxford University Press, 2002), 118–119.
28. *OR*, series 1, vol. 19, part 1, 234; *OR*, series 1, vol. 19, part 1, 225.
29. Letter by Joseph Pettiner, September 20, 1862 in Fourteenth Brooklyn File at Antietam Battlefield National Park Library.
30. Bevin Alexander, *Lost Victories* (New York: Holt, 1992), 236.
31. *OR*, series 1, vol. 19, part 1, 218.
32. *Ibid.*, 923.
33. Perry Jamieson, *Death in September* (Fort Worth, TX: Ryan Price, 1995), 65.
34. Eicher, 352–61.
35. Murfin, 298; Eicher, 363.
36. Sears, *Landscape Turned Red*, 202; Murfin, 221.
37. Clemens, 66.
38. *OR*, series 1, vol. 19, part 1, 239.
39. Longstreet, 263; Eicher, 363.
40. *OR*, series 1, vol. 19, part 2, 627.
41. Swinton, 222; *OR*, series 1, vol. 19, part 1, 211.
42. *OR*, series 1, vol. 19, part 1, 70–71.
43. Adjutant General's Report.
44. Phisterer, 2930.

Chapter 10

1. *Brooklyn Daily Eagle*, September 4, 1862, report sent September 2, 1862.
2. *Brooklyn Daily Eagle*, September 18, 1862, report sent on September 16, 1862.
3. *Ibid.*
4. *Brooklyn Daily Eagle*, written September 7, 1862, printed September 9, 1862.
5. Adjutant General's Report.
6. *Brooklyn Daily Eagle*, September 29, 1862.
7. *Brooklyn Daily Eagle*, written September 2, 1862, printed on September 4, 1862.
8. Adjutant General's Report.
9. Dawes, 102–103.
10. *Brooklyn Daily Eagle*, September 24, 1862.
11. *Brooklyn Daily Eagle*, September 29, 1862.
12. Webb Garrison, *Civil War Stories* (New York: Promontory Press, 1997), 22, 411–12.
13. *Brooklyn Daily Eagle*, September 29, 1862.
14. *Brooklyn Daily Eagle*, September 27, 1862.
15. *Brooklyn Daily Eagle*, September 29, 1862.
16. *Brooklyn Daily Eagle*, September 30, 1982.
17. *Brooklyn Daily Eagle*, October 23, 1862.

Chapter 11

1. *OR*, series 1, vol. 21, part 1, 48, 57
2. *OR*, series 1, vol. 129, part 1, 72
3. Allan Nevins, *War for the Union*, vol. 2 (New York: Konecky and Konecky, 1960), 328.
4. *OR*, supplement, part 2, vol. 45, 238–39; Adjutant General's Report.
5. *OR*, series 1, vol. 19, part 2, 545.
6. Warner, Ezra, Generals in Blue, 57.
7. Report on the Conduct of the War, vol. 1, 650.

8. *OR*, series 1, vol. 19, part 2, 583.
9. George Rable, *Fredericksburg! Fredericksburg!* (Chapel Hill: University of North Carolina Press, 2002), 57.
10. Vorin Whan, *Fiasco at Fredericksburg* (Philadelphia: University of Pennsylvania Press, 1961), 24; Rable, 57, Map, 67; *OR*, supplement, part 2, vol. 45, 239.
11. Whan, 30-32, 39, 43; *OR*, series 1, vol. 21, 87-89; Adjutant General's Report.
12. E.P. Alexander, 171.
13. J.G. Hutchinson, J.G., "Fredericksburg," in War Sketches and Incidents, vol. 2 (Des Moines: Iowa Commandery, M.O.L.L.U.S, 1893), 261-262; Whan, 49; Longstreet, 297-298.
14. Foote, 30-31; Longstreet, 307.
15. Swinton, 240-241; *OR*, series 1, vol. 21, part 1, 469; *OR*, supplement, vol. 45, part 2, 239; Adjutant General's Report.
16. *OR*, series 1, vol. 21, part 1, 87-89.
17. William F. Smith, "Franklin's 'Left Grand Division,'" in *Battles and Leaders of the Civil War*, vol. 3, 133-134 (Smith commanded the Sixth Corp. of Franklin's Grand Division); Committee on the Conduct of the War, Report of the Joint Committee on the Conduct of the War (Washington, 1863) vol. 1, 701.
18. James Longstreet, "The Battle of Fredericksburg," in *Battles and Leaders of the Civil War*, vol. 3, 76.
19. Warner, Ezra, *Generals in Blue*, 396-397.
20. Whan, 62-63; *OR*, series 1, vol. 21, part 1, 469.
21. Whan, 63-64; *OR* series 1, vol. 21, part 1, 643.
22. *OR*, series 1, vol. 21, part 1, 468-470; Adjutant General's Report.
23. J.H. Stein, *History of the Army of the Potomac* (Philadelphia: J.B. Rogers Printing Co., 1892), 278-279.
24. *OR*, series 1, vol. 21, part 1, 470.
25. Daniel Sutherland, *Fredericksburg and Chancellorsville: The Dare Mark Campaign* (Lincoln: University of Nebraska Press, 1998), 64; Adjutant General's Report. The report indicates that the Fourteenth marched for nine miles over difficult and circuitous roads before going into bivouac, while Phelps's report in *OR*, series 1, vol. 21, part 1, 470, indicates that the entire brigade went into bivouac a mile from the Rappahannock on the same ground they had occupied on the night of Tuesday, December 11.
26. *OR*, series 1, vol. 21, 67.
27. Phisterer, 2,930.

Chapter 12

1. *OR*, series 1, vol. 25, part 1, 1566-1576.
2. Earnest B. Furguson, *Chancellorsville,*
1863 (New York: Alfred H. Knopf), 1992, 7, 10-11; Adjutant General's Report.
3. Stephen Sears, *Chancellorsville* (New York: Houghton Mifflin Co., 1996), 1920; Adjutant General's Report.
4. Furguson, 17.
5. *Ibid.*, 18-19.
6. *OR*, series 1, vol. 25, part 2, 5.
7. Warner, *Generals in Blue*, 233-34.
8. Sears, *Chancellorsville*, 64-65.
9. *Ibid.*, 66.
10. Warner, *Generals in Blue*, 532-33.
11. John Bigelow Jr., *Chancellorsville* (New York: Smithmark, 1995), 36.
12. JCCW, 112.
13. Bigelow, 492.
14. Adjutant General's Report.
15. *OR*, supplement, part 2, vol. 45, 240.
16. Letter to the Sunday Mercury, from "C," April 6, 1863.
17. *OR*, series 1, vol. 25, part 2, 255-256, 262.
18. *Ibid.*, 266-267.
19. *Ibid.*, 268.
20. Alan T. Nolan, *The Iron Brigade* (Bloomington: Indiana University Press, 1998), 204-205; Abner Doubleday, *Chancellorsville and Gettysburg* (New York: Da Capo Press, 1994), 5.
21. Letter from Hooker to Lincoln, in Bigelow, 161
22. Nolan, 205; *OR*, supplement, part 2, vol. 45, 241; Adjutant General's Report.
23. Adjutant General's Report.
24. Donald Smith, *The Twenty-Fourth Michigan* (Harrisburg, PA: Stackpole, 1962), 88. The Term "Zouave" is incorrectly used here. The uniform of the Fourteenth was that of a "Chasseaura-pede."
25. Nolan, 205.
26. Letter by John Vliet, May 12, 1863, Vliet Papers.
27. O.B. Curtis, *History of the Twenty-Fourth Michigan* (Detroit: Winn Hammond, 1891), 121-122; Smith, 87-89; *OR*, supplement, part 2, vol. 45, 231.
28. Doubleday, 5.
29. Cullen, Joseph, "The Battle of Chancellorsville," *Civil War Times* 7 (May 1968): 7.
30. *OR*, series 1, vol. 51, part 1, 1009-1010.
31. Letter by John Vliet, May 12, 2963, Vliet Papers.
32. Swinton, 270-273.
33. Adjutant General's Report.
34. Noel Harrison, *Chancellorsville Battlefield Sites* (Lynchburg, VA: H.E. Howard, 1990), 4.
35. James B. Rich, "Quaker Soldier: Letters of James B. Rich to Sue J. Sheppard (1862-1864)," *Bulletin of the Historical Society of Montgomery Co.* ed. James B. Rich, vol. 25 (Spring 1987): 283.

36. Letter by George C. Gordon, 24th Michigan, May 1, 1862, Geocities.com.
37. Gary W. Gallagher, "East of Chancellorsville," in *Chancellorsville: The Battle and Its Aftermath*, ed. Gary W. Gallagher (Chapel Hill: University of North Carolina Press, 1996), 39.
38. Sears, 159; Furguson, 103.
39. Swinton, 274; Bigelow, 178; Furguson, 98.
40. *OR*, series 1, vol. 25, part 1, 262–263; Davis, 136–137; Furguson, 99.
41. *OR*, series 1, vol. 25 part 1, 263; Adjutant General's Report.
42. *OR*, series 1, vol. 25, 796–797; Gallagher, *Chancellorsville*, 40.
43. Gallagher, *Chancellorsville*, 43; *OR*, series 1, vol. 25, part 1, 262.
44. Sears, *Chancellorsville*, 423.
45. *Ibid.*, 358.
46. *Ibid.*, 372.
47. Adjutant General's Report.
48. Sears, *Chancellorsville*, 422; Bigelow, 419.
49. *OR*, supplement, part 11, vol. 45, 241; Tevis, 73.
50. Swinton, 303–307.
51. E.P. Alexander, 195.
52. James Robertson, *Stonewall Jackson* (New York: Macmillan, 1997), 729.
53. *Ibid.*, 753.
54. *Brooklyn Daily Eagle*, June 11, 1863.
55. Phisterer, 2930.

Chapter 13

1. Edwin Coddington, *The Gettysburg Campaign* (New York: Scribner's Sons, 1984), 4–5.
2. Shelby Foote, *Stars in Their Courses* (New York: The Modern Library, 1994), 17.
3. Longstreet, 235–40.
4. *OR*, series 1, vol. 27, part 1, 31–32; Letter from Halleck to Hooker, JCCW, vol. 1, 154.
5. J.H. Stein, *History of the Army of the Potomac* (Philadelphia: J.B. Rogers Printing Co., 1892), 443–444; *OR*, series 1, vol. 27, part 1, 58–61.
6. *OR*, series 1, vol. 27, part 1, 60.
7. *Ibid.*, 59–60.
8. *OR*, vol. 27, part 3, 369.
9. *OR*, vol. 27, part 1, 61; *OR*, vol. 27, part 3, 374.
10. Warner, *Generals in Blue*, 315–316.
11. *OR*, supplement, vol. 45, part 2, 242; Adjutant General's Report.
12. Warner, *Generals in Blue*, 110.
13. Letter by John Vliet, June 6, 1863, Vliet Papers.
14. Coddington, 29.
15. *OR*, supplement, vol. 45, part 2, 242; Adjutant General's Report; Tevis, 76.
16. Orville Thomson, *Narrative of the Service of the Seventh Indiana Infantry in the War for the Union* (Baltimore, MD: Butternut and Blue, 1993), 160.
17. Letter written by J.J. to the *Sunday Mercury*, June 23, 1863.
18. Tevis, 77–78.
19. Letter from "J.J." to the *Sunday Mercury*, June 23, 1863.
20. Swinton, 317; Adjutant General's Report, Tevis, 77–78.
21. Letter from James Rich to Sue Sheppard, in "Quaker Soldier," 284–285.
22. Letter from "J.J." to the *Sunday Mercury*, June 23, 1863.
23. *OR*, series 1, vol. 27, part 1, 142–144; *OR*, series 1, vol. 27, part 1, 114, 144; Adjutant General's Report.
24. Harry W. Pfanz, *Gettysburg: Culps Hill and Cemetery Hill* (Chapel Hill: University of North Carolina Press, 1993), 13–14; Adjutant General's Report.
25. James L. McLean, *Cutler's Brigade at Gettysburg* (Baltimore, MD: Butternut and Blue, 1994), 28.
26. Harry W. Pfanz, *Gettysburg: The First Day* (Chapel Hill: University of North Carolina Press, 2001).
27. Letter from John Vliet to C. Collins, July 2, 1863, in *Journal of Long Island History*.
28. Longstreet, 352.
29. Southern Historical Society Papers, vol. 4, 157. Hereafter referred to as SHSP.

Chapter 14

1. *OR*, series 1, vol. 27, part 3, 416; David Martin, *Gettysburg, July 1* (Conshohocken: PA: Combined Books, 1995), 53.
2. *OR*, series 1, vol. 27, part 1, 934; *OR*, series 1, vol. 27, part 2, 637–38.
3. Pfanz, *Gettysburg, the First Day*, 70.
4. Coddington, 267.
5. Martin, 93.
6. Noah Andre Trudeau, *Gettysburg: A Testing of Courage* (New York: Harper Collins, 2002), 175–176; Martin, 100.
7. Martin, 202; James Hall to John Bachelder, December 29, 1869, in *The Bachelder Papers*, eds. David and Audrey Ladd (Dayton, OH: Morningside House, 1994), 386.
8. *OR*, series 1, vol. 27, part 1, 286.
9. For an interesting analysis of this question, see Coddington, *Gettysburg Campaign*, note #46, Chapter 11, 686.
10. Coddington, 269; Trudeau, 184.
11. E.T. Boland, "Death of Gen. Reynolds: An Ex-Confederate Who Was a Witness Describes the Event," *National Tribune* (May 1915).

12. Hopkins, T.S. "Death of Gen. Reynolds, It Came from a Volley Not from a Sharpshooter," *National Tribune* (April 1910).
13. NY Monuments Commission for the Battlefield of Gettysburg. *New York at Gettysburg*, vol. 1 (Albany, NY: Lyons Co.), 1900. Hereafter referred to as *NY at G*.
14. *OR*, series 1, vol. 27, part 2, 649.
15. James L. McLean, *Cutler's Brigade at Gettysburg* (Baltimore: Butternut and Blue, 1994), 66, 70.
16. *NY at G*, vol. 3, 992.
17. *OR*, series 1, vol. 27, part 1, 281–282, 266.
18. *NY at G*, 736; Col. Fowler's Recollections of Gettysburg in Tevis, 132–133.
19. Pfanz, *Gettysburg: The First Day*, 90.
20. McLean, 100; Martin, 162.
21. Report of John Jenkins to the *Sunday Mercury*, written on Aug 6, 1863, published on Aug. 9, 1863; Burke Davis, *The Civil War: Strange and Interesting Facts* (New York: Wings Books, 1969), 154–56.
22. Warren Hassler, *Commanders of the Army of the Potomac* (Baton Rouge: Louisiana State University Press, 1962), 45.
23. McLean, 100; Martin, 120–121.
24. *NY at G*, 1,006.
25. McLean, 107.
26. Fowler, *Recollections*, 133; Tevis, 83–84.
27. Tucker, 115; *OR* series 1, vol. 27, part 2, 649.
28. *OR*, series 1, vol. 27, part 1, 286–287.
29. *OR*, series 1, vol. 27, part 1, 266; *OR*, series 1, vol. 27, part 1, 286–287; *OR*, series 1, vol. 27, part 2, 649.
30. John Jenkins letter to the *Sunday Mercury*, August 9, 1863, written August 6, 1863.
31. Tevis, 148–149.
32. This dispute is treated affectively by McLean, in *Cutlers Brigade at Gettysburg*, 106–115 and in Lance Herdegen and William Beaudot, *In the Bloody Railroad Cut at Gettysburg* (Dayton, OH: Morningside House, 1996), 287–299.
33. Pfanz, *Gettysburg: The First Day*, 123.
34. McLean, 129.
35. Tevis, 84–85.
36. *OR*, series 1, vol. 27, part 1, 282.
37. *OR*, series 1, vol. 27, part 1, 282; Cutler, 132.
38. McLean, 51, 134–140.
39. Martin, 209.
40. *OR*, series 1, vol. 27, part 1, 282–283.
41. McLean, 140.
42. *OR* series 1, vol. 27, part 1, 704, 286–287.
43. McLean, 141.
44. *NY at G*, 25.
45. Letter from John Jenkins to the *Sunday Mercury*, written August 6, 1863 and published August 9, 1863.
46. Tevis, 136.
47. Coe, A.S. "The Fourteenth New York Zouaves." *National Tribune*, August 13, 1885; McLean, 214–215.
48. Report of two paroled prisoners published in the *Brooklyn Daily Eagle*, July 7, 1863.
49. Tevis, 37; *OR*, series 1, vol. 27, part 1, 286–287.
50. *NY at G*, 26.
51. Letter from "J.J." to the *Sunday Mercury*, July 12, 1863.
52. James McPherson, *Hollowed Ground* (New York: Crown Publishers, 2003), 51–52.
53. Letter by John Vliet, May 28, 1863, Vliet Papers.
54. Coddington, 297.
55. McPherson, *Hollowed Ground*, 51.
56. McLean, 144.
57. Charles Stevenson, "Red-legged Devils at Gettysburg." *National Guardsman* (July, 1958): 12.
58. Letter from John Vliet to Charles Collins, July 2, 1863, in *Journal of Long Island History*.

Chapter 15

1. Longstreet, 363.
2. Sears, *Gettysburg* (New York: Houghton Mifflin, 2003), 229.
3. John Cox, *Culp's Hill* (Boston: Da Capo Press, 2003), 44.
4. *Ibid.*, 44–46.
5. Swinton, 342; Longstreet, 363–364.
6. Swinton, 342.
7. Doubleday, 157.
8. Coddington, 377–378.
9. Coddington, 383; *OR*, series, I, vol. 27, part 2, 319.
10. Lafayette McLaws, "Gettysburg," in *Southern Historical Society Papers*, vol. 7, 64–90, 69–70.
11. *OR*, series 1, vol. 27, part 2, 367–368.
12. Tucker, 300.
13. Pfanz, *Culp's Hill and Cemetery Hill*, 86; McLean, 149.
14. McLean, 150.
15. Cox, 57–58; *OR*, series 1, vol. 27, part 1, 826–827.
16. Warner, *Generals in Blue*, 196–97.
17. *Ibid.*, 58, 63–64.
18. *OR*, series 1, vol. 27, part 1, 858–859.
19. Sears, *Gettysburg*, 326.
20. Coddington, 430–431.
21. McLean, 152.
22. *OR*, series 1, vol. 27, part 2, 533.
23. McLean, 152,154.
24. *Ibid.*, 156.
25. Letter from Col. E.B. Fowler to John Bachelder, October 2, 1889, *Bachelder Papers*, 1,638; Pfanz, *Culp's Hill and Cemetery Hill*, 222.

26. Cox, 131.
27. Terrance Murphy, *10th Virginia Infantry* (Lynchburg, VA: H.E. Howard, 1989), 78. In the files of Gettysburg National Military Park.
28. *Ibid.*, 79.
29. McLean, 161; Adjutant General's Report.
30. McLean, 161.
31. A. Wilson Greene, "Henry Slocum and the Twelfth Corps" in *The Second Day at Gettysburg*, ed. Gary Gallagher (Kent, OH: Kent State University Press, 1993), 114, 127, 195.
32. Cox, 149, 151; *OR*, series 1, vol. 27, part 2, 536.
33. George Thayer, "Gettysburg: As We Men on the Right Saw It." Read Before the Ohio Commandery M.O.L.L.U.S. Cincinnati: Sherock Co., May 5, 1886.

Chapter 16

1. *OR*, series 1, vol. 27, part 2, 308.
2. Longstreet, 385–386.
3. William G. Piston, "Cross Purposes: Longstreet, Lee, and Confederate Attack Plans for July 3 at Gettysburg," in *The Third Day at Gettysburg and Beyond*, ed. Gary Gallagher. (Chapel Hill: University of North Carolina Press, 1998), 35.
4. *OR*, series 1, vol. 27, part 2, 320.
5. Jeffrey Wert, *Gettysburg: Day Three* (New York: Simon and Shuster, 2001), 59–60; Pfanz, *Gettysburg: Culp Hill and Cemetery Hill*, 287.
6. Sears, *Gettysburg*, 361.
7. Pfanz, *Gettysburg, Culp Hill and Cemetery Hill*, 287.
8. Pfanz, *Gettysburg, Culp Hill and Cemetery Hill*, 288; *OR*, series 1, vol. 27, part 2, 510–512, 513, 518–519.
9. Pfanz, *Gettysburg, Culp Hill and Cemetery Hill*, 288–289.
10. Fowler, *Recollections*, 136–139.
11. George Collins, *Memories of the 149th Regiment, New York Volunteer Infantry*. Published by the author, 1891, 144.
12. Tevis, 150.
13. Pfanz, *Gettysburg: Culp's Hill and Cemetery Hill*, 306.
14. Tevis, 98.
15. Collins, 145.
16. *OR*, series 1, vol. 27, part 2, 504–505.
17. *OR*, series 1, vol. 27, part 1, 858.
18. Sears, *Gettysburg*, 371.
19. *OR*, series 1, vol. 27 , part 2, 511.
20. Adjutant General's Report.
21. Tucker, 325.
22. Gettysburg National Military Park Library, Verticle File V-29 PC 90510 and V8-29 PC 90520.
23. Adjutant General's Report.
24. John Busey and David Martin, *Regimental Strengths and Losses at Gettysburg*. Hightstown, NJ: Longstreet House, 1994, 262; Fox, 215.

Chapter 17

1. *OR*, series 1, vol. 27, part 2, 322, 360, 448, 471.
2. Pfanz, *Gettysburg: Culp's Hill and Cemetery Hill*, 365.
3. Swinton, 367; Adjutant General's Report
4. Letter from Lieut. Wm. C. Rae, to his sister Carrie, August 13, 1863, in the collection of Mr. and Mrs. Charles W. Luzier at the Gettysburg National Military Park Library.
5. Adjutant General's Report.
6. *Ibid.*
7. Swinton, 383; Tevis, 107.
8. National Archives, Box 531, Ct-Mart. LL-975, Robert Jordan.
9. Dawes, 218.
10. National Archives, Box 531, Ct-Mart. LL-975, Robert Jordan.
11. Swinton, 280–290; Adjutant General's Report.
12. Swinton, 390–393; Adjutant General's Report.
13. Swinton, 394–395.
14. *OR*, series 1, vol. 29, part 1, 690–692.
15. Warner, *Generals in Blue*, 400–401.
16. *OR*, series 1, vol. 29, part 2, 520.
17. *OR*, series 1, vol. 29, part 1, 692.
18. *OR*, series 1, vol. 29, part 11, 521–522.
19. *OR*, series 1, vol. 29, part 1, 521.
20. *Ibid.*
21. Swinton, 395.
22. Letter from J. Jenkins to the *Sunday Mercury*, December 8, 1863.
23. Adjutant General's Report.
24. Phisterer, vol. 4, 2,930.

Chapter 18

1. Adjutant General's Report; Tevis 109–111.
2. Letter from John Jenkins to the *Sunday Mercury* dated February 9, 1864 and printed February 14, 1863.
3. Letter from John Jenkins to the *Sunday Mercury*, April 4, 1864.
4. *OR*, series 1, vol. 33, 717.
5. Brooks Simpson, *Ulysses S. Grant* (New York: Houghton Mifflin, 2002), 246.
6. Geoffrey Perret, *Ulysses S. Grant* (New York: Random House, 1997), 287.
7. Jean Edward Smith, *Grant* (New York: Simon & Schuster, 2001), 286.
8. Bruce Catton, *Grant Takes Command, 1863–1865* (Boston: Little, Brown, 1969), 127.
9. *OR*, series, 1, vol. 33, 669, General Order #98.

10. Ulysses S. Grant, *Personal Memoirs of U.S. Grant*, vol. 2 (New York: Charles Webster, 1885), 127–129; Warren Hassler, *Commanders of the Army of the Potomac* (Baton Rouge: Louisiana State University Press, 1962), 206.
11. Gordon Rhea, *The Battle for Spotsylvania Court House and the Road to Yellow Tavern* (Baton Rouge: Louisiana State University Press, 1997), 22.
12. J.F. Fuller, *The Generalship of Ulysses S. Grant* (London: John Murray, 1929), 225.
13. Edward Steere, *The Wilderness Campaign* (Harrisburg, PA: Stackpole Books, 2001), 26–27.
14. Morris Schaff, *Battle of the Wilderness* (New York: Houghton Mifflin, 1910), 58–59.
15. Steere, 26–27.
16. *OR*, series 1, vol. 36, part 2, 331.
17. *Ibid.*, 332.
18. *OR*, series 1, vol. 36, part 1, 622. Adjutant General's Report.
19. Rhea, 27–28.
20. Adjutant General's Report.
21. Rhea, 157–160; Robert Garth Scott, *Into the Wilderness with the Army of the Potomac* (Bloomington: Indiana University Press, 1985), 36.
22. *OR*, series 1, vol. 36, part 2, 415; Rhea, 231, *OR*, series 1, vol. 36, part 2, 952.
23. Rhea, 365.
24. Noah Trudeau, *The Bloody Road South* (Boston: Little Brown, 1989), 29.
25. Adjutant General's Report Tevis, 115.
26. Phisterer, 2,930.

13. Rhea, 147; *OR*, series 1, vol. 36, part 1, 625.
14. Tevis, 121.
15. *Ibid.*, 122.
16. Rhea, 238; Tevis, 128.
17. *OR*, series 1, vol. 36, part 11, 637–638.
18. Rhea, 283.
19. *Ibid.*, 285–289.
20. *OR*, series 1, vol. 36, part 2, 654.
21. Matters, 233.
22. Horace Porter, *Campaigning with Grant* (New York: Century, 1897), 108.
23. *OR*, series 1, vol. 36, part 2, 656.
24. Rhea, 303.
25. Rhea, 304, Tevis, 124.
26. Tevis, 124.
27. Rhea, 327; *OR*, series 1, vol. 36, part 2, 700; Tevis, 124.
28. *OR*, series 1, vol. 36, part 2, 700.
29. *OR*, series 1, vol. 36, part 2, 757; Tevis, 124.
30. Matters, 297; Tevis, 125.
31. *OR*, series 1, vol. 36, part 1, 72; *OR*, series 1, vol. 36, part 2, 845–850; Tevis, 125.
32. *OR*, series 1, vol. 36, part 1, 232–233; *OR*, series 1, vol. 36, part 2, 864–872.
33. Tevis, 125.
34. *OR*, series 1, vol. 40, part 1, 474–474.
35. *OR*, series 1, vol. 36, part 3, 55, 64; Matters, 334; Tevis, 1125.
36. Letter from William C. Rae to his sister, November 18, 1863, Fredericksburg, National Military Park Library.
37. Fox, 215.

Chapter 19

1. Swinton, 442; Adjutant General's Report
2. Swinton, 444.
3. William Matters, *If It Takes All Summer* (Chapel Hill: University of North Carolina Press, 1988), 65.
4. *Ibid.*, 67.
5. *OR*, series 1, vol. 36, part 1, 625, 634
6. Rhea, 62.
7. *OR*, series 1, vol. 36, part 1, 625.
8. Tevis, 119.
9. Rhea, 147
10. *Ibid.*
11. Matters, 150; Tevis, 121.
12. *OR*, series 1, vol. 36, part 1, 625.

Chapter 20

1. Tevis, 126.
2. *OR*, series 1, vol. 36, part 3, 453.
3. Tevis, 126–127.
4. *Brooklyn Daily Union*, May 25, 1864.
5. *Brooklyn Daily Union*, May 25, 1864; *Brooklyn Times*, May 25, 1864.
6. *Brooklyn Daily Union*, May 25, 1864.
7. *Brooklyn Daily Eagle*, May 26, 1864; *Brooklyn Daily Union*, May 25, 1864.
8. Tevis, 127–128.
9. *Brooklyn Daily Eagle*, May 26, 1864.
10. *Brooklyn Daily Times*, May 26, 1864.
11. *Ibid.*
12. Busey and Martin, 262; Tevis, 142–144.

Bibliography

Historical Societies

Brooklyn Historical Society
  Diary of Josiah Grumman.
  Harnickell Papers: War sketches from Cedar Mt. to Bull Run.
  Vliet Papers.
Historical Society of Montgomery County
  Bulletin of the Historical Society of Montgomery County Pennsylvania.
Long Island Historical Society
  Journal of Long Island History.
Massachusetts Historical Society
  "Caleb Beal to My Parents." July 23, 1861, Caleb H. Beal Papers.
Military Historical Society of Massachusetts
  William Allan, "Strategy of the Campaign of Sharpsburg, or Antietam." *Papers of the Military Historical Society of Massachusetts.* Vol. 3, 1888.
New York Historical Society
  George Macy letter, September 26, 1861.
  War of 1861–1865 Letters.
Southern Historical Society
  Southern Historical Society Papers. Vol. 4.

Libraries

Antietam National Battlefield Park Library
  Joseph Pettiner. Letter. September, 20, 1862.
  W.D. Pritchard. "Civil War Remembrances." Unpublished manuscript, 1893.
Fredericksburg National Battlefield Park Library
  Lt. William C. Rae. Letter to his sister. November 1863.
Gettysburg National Battlefield Park Library
  Lt. William C. Rae. Letter to Carrie. August 13, 1865.
  Verticle Files V-29 PC90510 and V8-29 PC90520.
Manassas National Battlefield Park Library
  Corp. John A. Wells file.

David Hamer. "One Man's War." Unpublished manuscript.
James Edie. Letter to his wife, Eliza. September 14, 1910.
John Brown. Letter to his sister. March 24, 1862.
Lt. Col. Samuel R. Bardsley, 24th New York Infantry. Letter to his wife. August 27, 1862.
New York Public Library
  Ezra Ayers Carman Collection.

New York State Documents

"Annual Report of the Adjutant General, January 31, 1869." Albany, NY: Department of Military & Naval Affairs.
Laws of the State of New York. 70th Session, May 13, 1847.
NY Monuments Commission for the Battlefield of Gettysburg. *New York at Gettysburg.* Vol. 1. Albany, NY: Lyons Co., 1900.

Newpapers

Boston Atlas
Brooklyn Advance
Brooklyn Daily Eagle
Brooklyn Daily Times
Brooklyn Daily Union
New York Daily Times
Philadelphia Weekly Times
Richmond Dispatch
Sunday Mercury (New York)

Federal Documents

Committee on the Conduct of the War. *Report of the Joint Committee on the Conduct of the War.* Vol. 1, Washington, D.C.: Government Printing Office, 1863.
Congressional Globe. 37th Congress, 2nd Session.

The War of the Rebellion, A Compilation of the Official Records of the Union and Confederate Armies. Washington, D.C.: Government Printing Office, 1890–1901.

Books and Articles

Addison, Edward, ed. "Quaker Soldier: Letters of James B. Rich to Sue J. Sheppard (1862–1864)," *Bulletin of the Historical Society of Montgomery Co.* vol. 25 (Spring 1987).

Allen, William. *The Army of Northern Virginia in 1862.* New York: Houghton Mifflin, 1892.

Alexander, Bevin. *Lost Victories.* New York: Holt, 1992.

Alexander, E.P. *Fighting For the Confederacy: Personal Recollections of Gen. Edward Porter Alexander.* Edited by Gary Gallagher. Chapel Hill: University of North Carolina Press, 1989.

———. *Military Memoirs of a Confederate.* New York: Scribner, 1907.

Anders, Curt. *Hearts in Conflict.* New York: Carol Publishing, 1994.

Atkinson, Charles F. *Grant's Campaigns of 1864 and 1865: The Wilderness and Cold Harbor, May 3–June 3, 1864.* London: H. Rees, 1908.

Baily, Ronald. *The Bloodiest Day.* Alexandria, VA: Time Life Books, 1984.

Belo, A.H., and William Robbins. "The Battle of Gettysburg," *Confederate Veteran Magazine* 8, no. 4 (1900), 165–68.

Biddle, Chapman. *The First Day of the Battle of Gettysburg.* Philadelphia: J.B. Lippincott, 1880.

Bigelow Jr., John. *Chancellorsville.* New York: Smithmark Publishers, 1995.

Blackford, William. *War Years with Jeb Stuart.* New York: Charles Scribner Sons, 1945.

Bloss, John. *Antietam and the Lost Dispatch: A Paper Prepared and Read Before the Kansas Commandery of the M.O.L.L.U.S.,* January 6th, 1892. Wilmington, NC: Broadfoot, 1992.

Boland, E.T. "Beginning of the Battle of Gettysburg." *Confederate Veteran Magazine* 14, no. 7 (1906), 301.

———. "Death of Gen. Reynolds: An Ex-Confederate Who Was a Witness Describes the Event." *National Tribune,* May 1915.

Bryson, John. *History of the 30th New York State Volunteers.* Unpublished manuscript. New York State Library, Albany, NY.

Busey, John, and David Martin. *Regimental Strengths and Losses at Gettysburg.* Hightstown, NJ: Longstreet House, 1994.

Busey, John W. *These Honored Dead: The Union Casualties at Gettysburg.* Hightstown, NJ: Longstreet House, 1988.

Casler, John. *Four Years in the Stonewall Brigade.* Guthrie, OK: State Capital Printing Co., 1893.

Catton, Bruce. *Grant Takes Command, 1863–1865.* Boston: Little, Brown, 1969.

Chandler, S.E. "In the Thick of It: What the Iron Brigade Experienced." *National Tribune,* October 17, 1895.

Clemens, Thomas, ed. "A Brigade Commander's First Fight: The Letters of Colonel Walter Phelps, Jr. During the Maryland Campaign." In *Antietam: The Maryland Campaign of 1862,* edited by Mark A. Snell. Mechanicsburg, PA: Stackpole, 1997.

Coddington, Edwin. *The Gettysburg Campaign.* New York: Scribner's Sons, 1984.

Coe, A.S. "The Fourteenth New York Zouaves." *National Tribune,* August 13, 1885.

Coffin, Charles. *The Boys of '61.* Boston: Estes and Lauriat, 1884.

Collins, George K. Memoirs of the 149th Regt. N.Y. Vol. Infty., 3rd Brig., 2d. Div., 12th and 20th A.C., by Capt. Geo. K. Collins. Syracuse, NY: Published by the author, 1891.

Commager, H.S., ed. *The Civil War Archive.* New York: Bobbs-Merrill Co., 1950.

Confederate Military History. Wilmington, NC: Broadfoot, 1987.

Coopersmith, Andrew. *Fighting Words.* New York: New Press, 2004.

Cory, David. "Brooklyn and the Civil War." *Journal of Long Island History* 2 (Spring, 1862), 1–15.

Cox, John. *Culp's Hill.* Boston: Da Capo Press, 2003.

Cullen, Joseph. "The Battle of Chancellorsville." *Civil War Times* 7 (May 1968).

Curtis, O.B. *History of The Twenty Fourth Michigan.* Detroit: Winn Hammond, 1891.

Davis, Burke. *The Civil War: Strange and Interesting Facts.* New York: Wings Books, 1969.

———. *They Called Him Stonewall.* New York: Holt, Reinhardt and Winston, 1954.

Davis, Jefferson. *Rise and Fall of the Confederate Government.* Vol. 1. New York: D. Appleton, 1912.

Davis, William C. *Battle at Bull Run.* Garden City, NY: Doubleday, 1977.

———. *First Blood.* Alexandria, VA: Time Life Books, 1983.
———. *The Deep Waters of the Proud.* Garden City, NY: Doubleday, 1982.
Dawes, Rufus. *Service with the 6th Wisconsin.* Madison: State Historical Society of Wisconsin, 1890.
Doubleday, Abner. *Chancellorsville and Gettysburg.* New York: Da Capo Press, 1994.
———. *Gettysburg Made Plain.* New York: DeVinnes Press, 1887.
Douglas, Henry K. *I Rode with Stonewall.* Chapel Hill: University of North Carolina Press, 1940.
Dyer, Frederick H. *A Compendium of the War of the Rebellion.* New York: Thomas Yoseloff, 1959.
Eicher, David. *The Longest Night.* New York: Simon and Schuster, 2001.
Fonderden, C. *A Brief History of the Military Career of Carpenter's Battery.* New Market, VA: Hinkel, 1911.
Foote, Shelby. *Stars in Their Courses.* New York: The Modern Library, 1994.
———. *The Civil War: A Narrative.* New York: Vintage Books, 1958.
Fox, W. *Regimental Losses in the American Civil War, 1861–1865.* Albany, NY: Albany Pub. Co., 1893.
Freeman, Douglas Southall. *Lee's Lieutenants: A Study in Command.* 3 Vols. New York: Charles Scribner's Sons, 1942–49.
Fuller, J.F. *The Generalship of Ulysses S. Grant.* London: John Murray, 1929.
Furguson, Earnest B. *Chancellorsville, 1863.* New York: Alfred H. Knopf, 1992.
Gaff, Alan D. *Brave Men's Tears: The Iron Brigade at Brawner Farm.* Dayton, OH: Morningside House, 1996.
Gallagher, Gary W. "East of Chancellorsville." In *Chancellorsville: The Battle and Its Aftermath.* Edited by Gary W. Gallagher. Chapel Hill: University of North Carolina Press, 1996.
———, ed. *The First Day at Gettysburg: Essays on Confederate and Union Leadership.* Kent, OH: Kent State University Press, 1992.
———, ed. *The Second Day at Gettysburg: Essays on Confederate and Union Leadership.* Kent, OH: Kent State University Press, 1993.
———, ed. *The Spotsylvania Campaign.* Chapel Hill: University of North Carolina Press, 1998.
Garrison, Webb. *Civil War Stories.* New York: Promontory Press, 1997.

Gettysburg Magazine. Dayton, OH: Morningside House.
Gibbons, John. *Personal Recollection of the Civil War.* New York: G.P. Putnam and Son, 1928.
Grant, Ulysses S. *Personal Memoirs of U.S. Grant.* Vol. 2. New York: Charles Webster, 1885.
Greene, A. Wilson. "Henry Slocum and the Twelfth Corps." In *The Second Day at Gettysburg.* Edited by Gary Gallagher. Kent, OH: Kent State University Press, 1993.
Haight, Theron. "Gainesville, Groveton and Bull Run." *War Papers Read Before the Commandery of the State of Wisconsin, Military Order of the Loyal Legion of the United States.* Vol. 2. Milwaukee: Burdick, Armitage & Allen, 1896.
———. "King's Divison: Fredericksburg to Manassas." *War Papers Read Before the Commandery of the State of Wisconsin, Military Order of the Loyal Legion of the United States.* Vol. 2. Milwaukee: Burdick, Armitage & Allen, 1896.
Harrison, Noel. *Chancellorsville Battlefield Sites.* Lynchburg, VA: H.E. Howard, 1990.
Harsh, Joseph. *Taken at the Flood.* Kent, OH: Kent State University Press, 1999.
Hassler, Warren. *Commanders of the Army of the Potomac.* Baton Rouge: Louisiana State University Press, 1962.
———. *Crisis at the Crossroads.* Tuscaloosa: University of Alabama Press, 1970.
———. "The First Day's Battle of Gettysburg." *Civil War History* 6 (Sept., 1960), 259–276.
Haythornthwaite, Philip. *Uniforms of the Civil War.* New York: Macmillan, 1976.
Hazelton, Henry. *The Boroughs of Brooklyn and Queens, Counties of Nassau and Suffolk, Long Island, New York, 1609–1924.* New York: Lewis Historical Publishing Co., 1925.
Hennessy, John. *Historical Report on the Troop Movements for the Second Battle of Manassas.* Denver: National Park Service, 1985.
———. *Return to Bull Run.* New York: Simon and Shuster, 1993.
Herdegen, Lance, and William Beaudot. *In the Bloody Railroad Cut at Gettysburg.* Dayton, OH: Morningside House, 1996.
Hill, D.H. "The Battle of South Mountain, or Boonesboro." In *Battles and Leaders of the Civil War.* Vol. 2. Edited by Robert Johnson and Clarence Buel. Reprint. New York: Castle Books, 1991.

Holzer, Harold. *A Guide to Civil War Records in New York State Archives*. New York: Fordham University Press, 1999.

Hopkins, T.S. "Death of Gen. Reynolds, It Came from a Volley Not from a Sharpshooter." *National Tribune* (April 1910).

Hutchinson, J.G. "Fredericksburg." In War Sketches and Incidents. Vol. 2, Des Moines: Iowa Commandery, M.O.L.L.U.S, 1893.

Imboden, John. "Incidents of the First Bull Run." In *Battles and Leaders of the Civil War*. Vol. 2. New York: Castle Books, 1991.

Jackson, Mary Anna. *Life and Letters of Stonewall Jackson*. New York: Harper and Bros. 1892.

Jamieson, Perry. *Death in September*. Fort Worth, TX: Ryan Price Publishers, 1995.

Kelley, Robin, and Earl Lewis, eds. *To Make the World Anew*. New York: Oxford University Press, 2000.

Ladd, David, and Audrey Ladd, eds. *The Bachelder Papers*. Dayton, OH: Morningside House, 1994.

Lambert, Edward. "Proclamation by Edward Lambert — Mayor of the City of Brooklyn." *Brooklyn Eagle*, June 6, 1854.

Lockwood, John. *Our Campaign around Gettysburg*. New York: A.H. Rome & Brothers, 1864.

Longstreet, James. *From Manassas to Appomattox*. Secaucus, NJ: Blue and Gray Press, 1984.

_____. "The Battle of Fredericksburg." In *Battles and Leaders of the Civil War*. Vol. 3. Edited by Robert Johnson and Clarence Buel. Reprint. New York: Castle Books, 1991.

Martin, David G. *Gettysburg, July 1*. Conshohocken: PA: Combined Books, 1995.

_____. *The Second Bull Run Campaign. July–August 1862*. Conshohocken, PA: Combined Books, 1997.

Marvel, William. *Mr. Lincoln Goes to War*. New York: Houghton Mifflin, 2006.

Matters, William. *If It Takes All Summer*. Chapel Hill: University of North Carolina Press, 1988.

McDonald, Joanna. *We Shall Meet Again*. Shippensburg, PA: White Mane Books, 1999.

McLaws, Lafayette. "Gettysburg." In Southern Historical Society Papers. Vol. 7, 64–90.

McLean, James L. *Cutler's Brigade at Gettysburg*. Baltimore: Butternut and Blue, 1994.

McPherson, James. *Crossroads of Freedom*. New York: Oxford University Press, 2002.

Mitchell, Harry. "The Battle of Antietam." *Brooklyn Advance*. Vol. 12, May–Dec. 1885.

_____. "The Fighting Fourteenth. The Battle of South Mountain." *Brooklyn Advance*. Vol. 11, February 1885.

Montgomery, James S. *The Shaping of a Battle: Gettysburg*. Philadelphia: Chilton Co., Book Division, 1959.

Morris, Frank, ed. *The Rebellion Record: A Diary of American Events*. New York: Arno Press, 1977.

Murfin, James. *The Gleam of Bayonets*. Baton Rouge: Louisiana State University Press, 1965.

Murphy, Terrance. *10th Virginia Infantry*. Lynchburg, VA: H.E. Howard, 1989.

Nadal, Bernard. *The Christian Boy Soldier*. New York: Steam Printing House, 1862.

Nevins, Allan. *War for the Union*. Vol. 2. New York: Konecky and Konecky, 1960.

Nichols, Edward. *Toward Gettysburg*. University Park: Pennsylvania State University Press, 1958.

Nolan, Alan. *The Iron Brigade*. Bloomington: Indiana University Press, 1998.

Older, Curtis. *The Land Tracts of the Battlefield of South Mountain*. Westminster, MD: Willow Bend Books, 1999.

Otott, George. "Clash in the Cornfield: The 1st Texas Volunteer Infantry in the Maryland Campaign." In *Antietam: The Maryland Campaign of 1862*, edited by Mark A. Snell. Mechanicsburg, PA: Stackpole, 1997.

Perret, Geoffrey. *Ulysses S. Grant*. New York: Random House, 1997.

Pfanz, Harry W. *Gettysburg: Culps Hill and Cemetery Hill*. Chapel Hill: University of North Carolina Press, 1993.

_____. *Gettysburg: The First Day*. Chapel Hill: University of North Carolina Press, 2001.

Phisterer, Frederick. *New York in the War of the Rebellion*. Vol. 4. Albany, NY: J.B. Lyon, 1912.

"The Communities of New York and the Civil War: The Recruiting Areas of the New York Civil War Regiments." In Phisterer's New York in the War of the Rebellion 1861–1865, edited by C.E. Dornbusch. New York: New York Public Library, 1962.

Piston, William. "Cross Purposes: Longstreet, Lee, and Confederate Attack Plans for July 3 at Gettysburg." In *The Third Day at Gettysburg and Beyond*, edited by Gary Gallagher. Chapel Hill: University of North Carolina Press, 1998.

Pollard, Edward A. *The Second Battle of Manassas*. Richmond, VA: West & Johnston, 1862.

Porter, Horace. *Campaigning with Grant*. New York: Century Publishing, 1897.

Priest, Michael. *Before Antietam: The Battle for South Mountain*. Shippensburg, PA: White Mane, 1992.

Rable, George. *Fredericksburg! Fredericksburg!* Chapel Hill: University of North Carolina Press, 2002.

Rhea, Gordon. *The Battle for Spotsylvania Court House and the Road to Yellow Tavern*. Baton Rouge: Louisiana State University Press, 1997.

_____. *The Battle of the Wilderness, May 5 and 6, 1864*. Baton Rouge: Louisiana State University Press, 1994.

Robertson, James. *Stonewall Jackson: The Man the Soldier, the Legend*. New York: Macmillan, 1997.

Roman, Alfred. *The Military Operations of General Beauregard*. Vol. 1. New York: Da Capo Press, 1994.

Schaff, Morris. *Battle of the Wilderness*. New York: Houghton Mifflin, 1910.

Schroth, Raymond. *The Eagle and Brooklyn*. Westport, CN: Greenwood Press, 1974.

Scott, Robert Garth. *Into the Wilderness with the Army of the Potomac*. Bloomington: Indiana University Press, 1985.

Sears, Stephen W. *Chancellorsville*. New York: Houghton Mifflin, 1996.

_____. *Gettysburg*. New York: Houghton Mifflin, 2003.

_____. *Landscape Turned Red: The Battle of Antietam*. New York: Houghton Mifflin, 1983.

_____, ed. *The Civil War Papers of George B. McClellan: Selected Correspondence, 1860–1865*. New York: Ticknor & Fields, 1989.

Simpson, Brooks. *Ulysses S. Grant*. New York: Houghton Mifflin, 2002.

Smith, Donald. *The Twenty-Fourth Michigan*. Harrisburg, PA: Stackpole, 1962.

Smith, Jean. *Edward Grant*. New York: Simon and Schuster, 2001.

Smith, Robin, and Ron Field. *Uniforms of the Civil War*. London: Brassey's, 2001.

Smith, William F. "Franklin's 'Left Grand Division.'" In *Battles and Leaders of the Civil War*. Vol. 3. Edited by Robert Johnson and Clarence Buel. Reprint. New York: Castle Books, 1991.

Snyder-Greenier, Elen. *Brooklyn*. Philadelphia: Temple University Press, 1996.

Spann, Edward. *Gotham at War*. Wilmington, DE: Scholarly Resources, 2002.

Stackpole, Edward J. *They Met at Gettysburg*. Harrisburg, PA: Stackpole Books, 1957.

Steere, Edward. *The Wilderness Campaign*. Harrisburg, PA: Stackpole Books, 2001.

Stein, J.H. *History of the Army of the Potomac*. Philadelphia: J.B. Rogers Printing Co., 1892.

Stevenson, Charles. "Red-legged Devils at Gettysburg." *National Guardsman* (July, 1958): 12.

Stiles, Henry. *A History of the City of Brooklyn*. Vol. 11. Bowie, MD: Heritage Books, 1993.

Styple, William. *Writing and Fighting the Civil War*. Kearny, NJ: Belle Grove, 2000.

Sutherland, Daniel. *Fredericksburg and Chancellorsville: The Dare Mark Campaign*. Lincoln: University of Nebraska Press, 1998.

Swinton, William. *Army of the Potomac*. New York: Konecky and Konecky, 1895.

Tevis, C., and Marquand. *The Fighting Fourteenth, The Fowler Papers*. New York: Brooklyn, Eagle Press, 1911. Reprint. Baltimore, MD: Butternut & Blue, 1993.

Thayer, George. "Gettysburg: As We Men on the Right Saw It." Read Before The Ohio Commandery M.O.L.L.U.S. Cincinnati: Sherock Co., May 5, 1886.

Thomson, Orville. *Narrative of the Service of the Seventh Indiana Infantry in the War for the Union*. Baltimore: Butternut and Blue, 1993.

Trudeau, Noah Andre. *Gettysburg: A Testing of Courage*. New York: Harper Collins, 2002.

Tucker, Glenn. *High Tide at Gettysburg: The Campaign in Pennsylvania*. New York: Smithmark, 1995.

Warner, Ezra. *Generals in Blue*. Baton Rouge, Louisiana State University Press, 1964.

_____. *Generals in Gray*. Baton Rouge: Louisiana University Press, 1959.

Wert, Jeffrey. *Gettysburg: Day Three*. New York: Simon and Shuster, 2001.

Whittier, Edward. "The Left Attack (Ewell's), Gettysburg." In *Campaigns in Virginia, Maryland and Pennsylvania*. Vol. 3. Boston: Military Historical Society of Mass., 1903.

Index

Alabama Regiments: (5th) 140; (8th) 178; (13th) 140
Alexander, E.P. 26, 105, 124
Alexandria line 23
Anderson's Division 80, 124
Angel Gabriel (John Orr) 6, 7, 9
Annandale, Va. 25, 41
Antietam 1, 34, 79, 84, 86, 87, 88, 89, 90, 91, 93, 94, 95, 96, 98, 101
Aquia Creek 187
Archer, Gen. James 106, 134, 137, 138, 140, 141, 142, 143, 151
Auger, C.C. 52, 53, 54, 58
Averell, William 27, 28, 38

Baldwin, Charles 6, 8, 41, 74
Baltimore, Md. 14, 15, 80, 128, 132
Baltimore Turnpike 133, 152, 155, 158, 159, 161, 168
Bank's Ford 111
Barksdale, William 106, 122
Beauregard, Brig. Gen. P.G.T 23, 26, 27, 31, 32, 44
Bee, Bernard 126, 127
Beecher, Henry Ward 19, 97, 98
Belle Plain 111, 115, 116
Blackburn's Ford 56, 129
Bleeding Kansas 98
Blue Ridge Mountains 66, 80, 81, 101, 127
Boonesboro Turnpike 80, 81, 82, 87
Brawner, John 69
Brawner Farm 58, 69, 70, 71
Brooklyn 1, 2, 3, 5–20, 23, 27, 29, 30, 33–37, 40, 41, 42, 43, 44, 45, 47, 48, 49, 50, 51, 54, 56, 60, 66, 73, 74, 76, 77, 95, 96, 97, 99, 117, 186, 188, 189, 190
Brooklyn Daily Eagle 11, 13, 14, 16, 37, 41, 124
Brooklyn Navy Yard 11, 45
Buford, Gen. John 132, 133, 137, 138, 139
Burleigh, William 98
Burnside, Ambrose 26, 28, 94, 101, 103, 104, 106, 107, 108, 109, 110, 11, 175, 178, 179, 185
Butterfield, Col. Daniel 18

Cabell, J.L. 37, 38, 39
Calef's Artillery 145, 151
Camp Marion 50, 53, 55, 78, 80
Camp Misery 56

Camp Odell 13, 16
Camp Prospect 59, 60
Candy's Brigade 158, 161
Cardoner, Ramon 52, 84, 117, 161
Carman, Ezra 83, 85
Casler, John 29
Catlett Station 56, 60, 68, 70, 129
Catoctin Mountains 165
Cedar Run 66
Cemetery Hill 133, 148 149 152 153, 154, 155, 156, 159, 160, 163, 164
Centreville 25, 26, 31, 32, 37, 49, 53, 56, 69, 70, 75, 77, 78, 167
Chambersburg 127
Chambersburg Road 2, 133, 137, 139, 140, 141, 142, 143
Chancellorsville, Va. 1, 111, 122, 124, 125, 126, 129, 149, 150, 156, 169, 170, 190
Chasseur-a-pied 3, 14, 148
Codori Farm 139
Coe, A.S. 147
Collins, William 41, 42
Cox, John 74, 75
Crampton's Gap 81, 102
Cub Run 26, 31, 37
Culp, Wesley 163, 164
Culpeper, Va. 62, 66, 67, 68, 101, 104, 126, 127, 166, 168, 172, 175, 176
Culp's Hill 133, 148, 150, 152–164
Cummings, A.C. 29
Cutler, Lysander 128, 139, 140, 143, 145, 146, 150, 155, 161, 169, 170, 174, 177, 184, 185, 186
Cutler's Brigade 128, 139, 140, 145, 150, 156, 161, 177, 182, 184

Dailey, James 29
Darrow, Joseph 36, 37
Davis, Jefferson 23, 31, 32, 66, 95
Davis, Gen. Joseph 2, 134, 137, 140, 143, 144, 151
Dawes, Rufus 1, 2, 70, 91, 92, 97, 144, 167
DeBevoise, William 51, 81, 86, 89, 94, 128
Deep Run 104, 106, 120, 128
Democrats 10, 12
Devil's Den 133, 160
Doubleday, Abner 2, 69, 70, 76, 84, 85, 86, 90, 91, 92, 103, 108, 109, 118, 132, 138, 140, 143, 150, 151

316 Index

Doubleday's Brigade 70, 71, 72, 83, 85
Doubleday's Division 85, 90, 91, 97, 103, 108, 109, 114, 153
Dougherty, Edward 37, 44
Dunkard Church 88, 89, 90, 91, 92, 94
Duryea, Hermenus 9, 14
Dutch 5

Earley's Brigade 90
Early, Jubal 120, 122
Emmitsburg Road 133
Ewell, Richard 70, 71, 126, 127, 145, 150, 154, 155, 156, 160, 168, 175

Fairfax Court House 22, 25, 26, 47, 48, 56
Fall's Church 46, 48, 53, 74
Falmouth, Va. 59, 60, 67, 105, 111, 124
Fifth New York Veteran Regiment 187
First Battle of Bull Run 23, 24, 25
Fitzhugh Crossing 119, 120, 125
Fort Greene Park 12, 188, 189
Fort Sumter 10, 11, 23, 90
Fourteeh Regiment Opera Group 17, 21, 73, 174
Fowler, Col. E.B. 5, 18, 30, 41, 43, 44, 46, 47, 48, 51, 52, 58, 59, 72, 73, 74, 81, 113, 123, 128, 132, 139, 140, 141, 142, 143, 144, 146, 148, 150, 151, 157, 161, 167, 169, 178, 179, 182, 183, 184, 185, 187
Fox's Gap 181
Francis, Louis 45
Franklin, Gen. William B. 103, 104, 106, 107, 109, 119, 121
Franklin Crossing 116, 121
Frederick City 81, 82
Fredericksburg, Va. 1, 34, 58, 59, 60, 61, 66, 103, 104, 105, 106, 107, 110, 111, 113, 114, 116, 117, 118, 119, 120, 121, 122, 124, 125, 126, 127, 187, 190
Fry, James 21
Fulton Avenue 100, 188
Fulton Ferry 13, 14, 188, 189

Gainesville, Va. 1, 58, 68, 69, 71, 73, 86, 106, 125, 167
Garnett, Richard 83, 85, 87
Garnett's Brigade 83, 85, 87
General Order No. 9 113
General Order No. 13 121
General Order No. 182 92
Georgia Regiments 21; (8th) 44; (13th) 121; (18th) 92
Gibbon, John 71, 91, 92, 93, 94, 109
Gibbon's Brigade 57, 58, 69, 70, 71, 76, 91
Grand Division 103, 104, 105, 106, 107; Center 103, 107; Left 103, 104, 105, 106, 107, 109, 119; Right 103, 107
Greene, George 155, 156, 157, 158, 161, 162
Greene's Brigade 155, 156, 157, 158, 161, 162, 163, 164
Griffin's Battery 21, 26, 28

Groveton, Va. 1, 69, 71, 72, 74, 75, 77
Grumman, Josiah 49, 74
Guilford Station 130, 131

Hagerstown, Md. 80, 81, 82, 87, 127
Hagerstown Turnpike 87, 88, 89, 90, 91, 92, 93, 133
Haight, Theron 76
Halleck, Henry 62, 68, 78, 80, 85, 103, 110, 127, 174, 175
Hall's Artillery 139, 140, 142
Hamilton Crossing 106, 120
Hampton, Wade 28, 192
Hampton's Legion 61, 132, 133, 134
Hanover, Va. 23, 66, 80, 81, 82, 87, 94, 101, 127, 163
Harpers Ferry 28, 92
Harris Light Cavalry 58, 60, 67
Hartwood Church 129
Hatch, John 57, 62, 66, 72, 75, 78, 81, 82, 83, 84, 85, 86, 87
Hatch's Brigade 57, 66, 69, 70, 71, 83, 85,
Heintzalman, Col. S.P. 25
Henry House Hill 27, 28, 30, 34, 190
Heth, Henry 126, 133, 134, 137
Hill, Gen. A.P. 70, 94, 120, 126, 127, 133, 148, 154, 160, 170
Hill, Gen. D.H. 80, 81, 82, 83, 86, 87, 90, 94, 106, 109
Homistan, Joseph 44, 45
Hood, Gen. John Bell 77, 90, 92, 94, 126, 154, 160
Hood's Division 92, 93, 94, 106
Hooker, Joseph 81, 82, 89, 90, 91, 92, 93, 94, 103, 107, 113, 114, 115, 116, 119, 121, 122, 123, 124, 126, 127, 128, 129, 131
Hooker's Corp. 81, 89, 92
Howard, O.O. 106, 122, 123, 132, 146
Hunter, Col. D.M. 21, 25
Hunter's Division 25, 26
Hyer, Joseph 18, 19

Imboden, John 26, 27
Indiana Regiments: (3rd Cavalry) 60; (7th) 128, 134, 150, 154, 155; (19th) 57, 71, 121, 129, 140, 142

Jackson, Thomas 27, 29, 34, 50, 60, 66, 68, 69, 70, 71, 72, 73, 80, 81, 82, 92, 93, 104, 106, 107, 109, 118, 120, 123, 124, 126, 149, 190
Jenkins, John 33, 144, 170, 172
Johnston, Gen. Joseph E. 23, 27, 31, 32, 34, 66
Joint Committee on the Conduct of the War 28
Jones, Col. Edward 15
Jordan, Robert 41, 98, 166, 167, 168, 183
Jourdan, Maj. James 30, 48, 51

Kane's Brigade 158, 161
Keedysville 87, 89
Kelly's Ford 116, 167

Kemper, Delaware 31
Kemper, James 83
Kilpatrick, Judson 60, 61
King, Rufus 60, 61, 69, 71, 82
King's Division 66, 68, 70, 71, 72

Lambert, Edward 7, 8
Lawton's Brigade 92
Lee, Fitzhugh 2, 48, 74
Lee, Gen. Robert E. 48, 62, 66, 67, 68, 80, 81, 82, 85, 87, 89, 92, 94, 95, 101, 104–107, 116, 118, 119, 122, 124, 126, 127, 129, 130, 152, 153, 154, 160, 165, 168, 175, 177, 179, 184, 185, 190
Lee, S.D. 76, 90
Lewis, Elijah 12
Lincoln, Abraham 10, 12, 18, 43, 62, 66, 79, 101, 102, 103, 113, 12, 129, 174
Little Round Top 133, 152, 154, 169
Long Bridge 17, 20
Longstreet, James 73, 76, 82, 83, 86, 104, 106, 107, 126, 127, 154, 156, 158, 160, 175, 178
Louisiana Regiments: (1st) 77, 157; (2nd) 157; (6th) 121; (10th) 157; (14th) 57; (15th) 157; (Tigers) 54
Low, A. A. 12
Lowe, T.S.C. 46

Mallory, George 5, 41, 54, 59, 73
Manassas 24, 26, 38, 44, 45, 48, 69, 70, 77, 98, 108, 113, 114, 125, 129, 130, 190
Manassas Junction 23, 34, 56, 68, 69, 71, 175
Mansfield's Corp 92
Marsh Creek 132, 134, 139
Marye's Hill 105, 107, 109
Maryland 20, 78, 80, 81, 96, 101, 102, 108, 127, 131, 132, 157
Massachusetts Regiments: (6th) 15; (19th) 106; (20th) 106, 177
Massaponax Creek 59, 109
Matthews Hill 26, 27
McCarty, Michael 8, 43
McClellan, George 43, 46, 55, 59, 60, 78, 79, 80, 81, 82, 85, 89, 92, 94, 95, 97, 101, 102, 103, 104, 108, 126, 163
McDowell, Gen Irvin 2, 16, 21, 22, 23, 25, 26, 28, 29, 30, 31, 34, 40, 43, 44, 46, 47, 50, 52, 55, 58, 59, 60, 66, 68, 69, 71, 72, 75, 78, 108, 114, 186
McLaws, Lafayette 80, 106, 122, 124, 126
McLaws Division 80, 106, 122, 124
McNeill, John 48
McPherson's Farm 140
McPherson's Ridge 133, 138, 142, 151
McPherson's Woods 140, 141, 142, 151
Meade, Gen. George 77, 78, 92, 108, 109, 123, 127, 131, 132, 134, 151, 152, 153, 154, 156, 164, 165, 168, 169, 170, 175, 184, 185
Michigan Regiments: (1st) 29; (7th) 106; (24th) 57, 117, 118, 120, 121, 142

Military Road 106, 107
Miller Cornfield 90, 91
Mississippi Regiment: (2nd) 140, 141, 143, 144; (11th) 140; (13th) 106; (17th) 106; (21st) 107; (42nd) 140, 141, 143, 144
Mud March 113, 114
Munson's Hill 45, 46, 47

Nadal, B.H. 36
Napoleon, Louis 44
National Turnpike 81
New Market, Va. 61, 81
New York City 7, 9, 10, 191
New York Regiment: (5th) 187; (8th) 21, 26, 27; (11th) 17, 28; (12th) 18; (15th) 104; (22th) 53, 62, 69, 76, 81, 83, 86, 128; (24th) 53, 62, 69, 71, 76, 81, 83, 97, 128; (26th) 85; (27th) 23, 26, 28; (30th) 53, 57, 62, 69, 71, 76, 81, 83, 128; (55th) 49; (56th) 51; (69th) 33; (76th) 139, 141, 142, 145, 146, 170, 179; (79th) 49; (80th) 49; (82nd) 49; (83rd) 49; (84th) 49, 50, 52, 158; (95th) 139, 140, 141, 142, 143, 145, 167, 169, 182; (137th) 157, 158; (147th) 139, 141, 147, 157, 162, 182; (149th) 161
Newton, John 153, 167, 170, 174
Ni River 185, 186
Nicodemus Hill 90, 91
North Carolina Regiment: (1st) 157; (3rd) 157; (5th) 56, 145; (12th) 145; (23rd) 145; (55th) 140

Odell, Moses 13, 14, 39, 44, 99, 100
Orange Court House 66, 176
Orange Plank Road 169, 170
Orr, John 6, 7, 9

Patrick, Marsena 69, 71, 76, 83
Patton, George 40
Peach Orchard 160
Pelham, John 27, 108
Peninsula Campaign 55, 59, 79, 108, 119
Pennsylvania Regiments: (56th) 128, 134, 139, 140, 141, 142, 145, 155, 177, 182; (87th) 163; (150th) 142; (157th) 156
USS *Perry* 11
Pettigrew, Gen J. Johnston 133, 134, 137
Pettiner, Joseph 85, 93
Phelps, Walter 62, 81, 82, 83, 85, 86, 91, 92, 93, 94, 108, 109, 115, 121
Pickett, George 106, 126, 160
Pollocks Mill Creek Crossing 116, 119
Pope, John 62, 67, 68, 69, 72, 75, 77, 80, 126
Port Royal 104, 117, 118, 119, 120
Porter, Andrew 21, 25, 26, 27, 28, 31
Porter, Fitzjohn 44, 46, 48, 71, 72, 73, 75
Potomac River 1, 16, 20, 22, 24, 46, 48, 55, 78, 80, 87, 89, 95, 101, 102, 103, 111, 120, 126, 127, 131, 132, 166
Price, G.H. 27

Index

Proclamation 8, 9
Prospect Hill 105, 109

Quaker Cannons 53, 110

Rae, William 165, 186
Rapidan River 66, 67, 116, 119, 123, 168
Rappahannock River 58, 59, 66, 67, 104, 105, 107, 111, 117, 119, 122, 123
Rappahannock Station 67, 68, 166, 175
Reorganization of State Militia 49
Reynolds, Gen. John 21, 26, 71, 75, 77, 101, 107, 108, 111, 114, 116, 117, 121, 122, 123, 132, 138–141, 151, 153
Rice, James 167, 169, 172, 174, 177, 179, 182, 183, 184
Rich, James 119, 130
Richmond Dispatch 30
Ricketts, James 28, 45, 85
Ricketts Battery 28
Ricketts Division 66, 75, 91
Rodes, Robert 90, 120, 126, 145
Rodes Division 120, 126, 145, 160
Round Top 133, 152, 154, 159
Ruffin, Edmund 31

Sandford, Maj. Gen. Charles 18, 19
USS *Savannah* 11
Schimmelfennig, Alexander 150
Scott, Maj. Gen. Winfield 18, 23, 34, 42, 63, 66, 78, 113, 174
Second Battle of Bull Run 65, 77, 96
Sedgwick, John 179, 184
Seminary Ridge 133, 139, 141, 153, 154
Sharpsburg, Md. 81, 86, 87, 88, 89, 94, 95, 96, 101, 127
Shenandoah Valley 25, 34, 60, 80, 90, 127, 129,
Shepherdstown, Md. 87, 95, 127
Sickles, Gen. Daniel 116, 123, 153, 154, 156
Skelly, Jack 163, 164
Skinkers Creek
Slidell, John 39, 40
Sloan, Samuel 12
Smith, Jesse 7
Smith, Kirby 31
South Mountain 1, 78, 80, 81, 82, 84, 85, 86, 87, 96, 113, 125, 127, 190
Spangler, John 152; farm 152, 161; lane 161; meadow 152; spring 152
Spotsylvania Court House 173, 178, 179, 180, 181
Stafford Heights 105, 106
Stanton, Edwin 51
Stark's Division 91, 92
Steuart, Gen. George 156, 157, 158, 162, 184
Steuart's Brigade 157, 160, 161

Stuart, J.E.B. 28, 48, 49, 68, 90, 106, 107, 108, 109
Sudley Springs 26
Sudley Springs Road 71, 72
Sullivan, Timothy 62, 71, 72, 76
Sullivan's Brigade 72, 75, 76, 77
Sulphur Springs 102
Sumner, Edwin 75, 94, 103, 107, 109,
Sunken Road 90, 94
Swain, William 45

Taliaferro, William 70, 71, 91, 106
Taneytown, Md. 132, 133, 134
Taylor, Zachary 42, 48, 113
Thoroughfare Gap 68, 73
Trent Affair 39
Turner's Gap 81, 82
Tyler, Gen. Daniel 25, 26

Union Defense Committee 12
United States Ford 119, 121, 123
Upton's Hill 46, 47, 55, 56, 78

Victory, John 37
Virginia Regiments: (1st) 83; (1st Cavalry) 48; (2nd) 27, 163; (4th) 27; (5th) 27; (7th) 83rd; (10th) 157, 158; (11th) 83; (17th) 83; (18th) 37, 83, 85; (19th) 83, 85; (24th) 83; (27th) 27, 30, 157; (28th) 83, 85; (33rd) 27, 28, 29; (42nd) 185; (44th) 156; (48th) 156; (50th) 156; (56th) 83
Vliet, John 32, 128, 132

USS *Wabash* 11
Wade, Virginia (Jenny) 163, 164
Wadsworth, Gen. James 30, 33, 34, 114, 116, 121, 122, 123, 134, 139, 141, 142, 144, 145, 146, 150, 153, 154, 161, 174, 177, 178
Waldron, Hampton 52
Warren, Gen. Gouverneur 123, 170, 172, 174, 175, 176, 177, 178, 179, 184, 185, 186
Warren's Corp 179, 184, 185, 186
Warrenton, Va. 26, 60, 61, 68, 101, 102, 129, 166
Warrenton Turnpike 28, 69, 70, 72, 75, 77, 129
Washburne, Elihu 174
West Point 23, 25, 33, 53, 62, 63, 78, 103, 108, 127, 155
West Woods 88, 89, 90, 91
Williamsport, Pa. 127
Winder, John 39, 91
Wisconsin Regiments: (2nd) 57, 71, 121, 140, 142; (6th) 1, 2, 57, 70, 71, 91, 97, 120, 121, 128, 140, 142, 143, 144, 145, 146, 157, 167; (7th) 57, 71, 121, 140, 142
Wood, A.M. 12, 13, 30, 37, 38, 189
Wood, Pvt. 129
Wood, Fernando 10

www.ingramcontent.com/pod-product-compliance
Ingram Content Group UK Ltd.
Pitfield, Milton Keynes, MK11 3LW, UK
UKHW041923140426
5217IPUK00014B/290